Iran and the Gulf

IRAN AND THE GULF:
A Search for Stability

EDITED BY
JAMAL S. AL-SUWAIDI

THE EMIRATES CENTER FOR STRATEGIC
STUDIES AND RESEARCH

3-19-02

Published in 1996 by
The Emirates Center for Strategic Studies and Research
PO Box 4567, Abu Dhabi, United Arab Emirates

Copyright © 1996 by The Emirates Center for Strategic Studies
and Research

Distributed by British Academic Press
an imprint of I.B.Tauris, Victoria House
Bloomsbury Square, London WC1 4DZ
175 Fifth Avenue, New York NY10010

A full CIP record for this book is available from the British
Library

A full CIP record for this book is available from the Library
of Congress

Library of Congress catalog card number: available

ISBN 1 86064 143 1 hardback
ISBN 1 86064 144 X paperback

The Emirates Center for Strategic Studies and Research

The Emirates Center for Strategic Studies and Research (ECSSR), established on 14 March 1994 in Abu Dhabi, United Arab Emirates, is an independent research institution dedicated to the promotion of professional research and educational excellence in the UAE and the Gulf area. ECSSR serves as a focal point for scholarship on political, economic, and social issues pertinent to the UAE, the Gulf, and the Middle East regions through the sponsorship of empirical research and scientific studies conducted by scholars from around the globe.

The Center seeks to provide a forum for the scholarly exchange of ideas on these subjects by hosting conferences and symposia, organizing workshops, sponsoring a lecture series featuring prominent scholars and international dignitaries, and publishing original and translated books, research papers, translated studies, and two occasional paper series. ECSSR also sponsors an active program which provides research fellowships as well as grants for the writing of scholarly books and for the translation, into Arabic, of works relevant to the Center's mission. To support its research activities, ECSSR has acquired specialized holdings for its UAE Federation Library and has created a state-of-the-art Information Center. Utilizing current Internet capabilities and on-line services, ECSSR is establishing an electronic database which will be a unique and comprehensive source for information on Gulf topics.

Through these and other activities, ECSSR aspires to engage in mutually beneficial professional endeavors with comparable institutions worldwide, and to significantly contribute the general educational and scientific development of the UAE.

Contents

Figures and Tables

Figures

Tables

Abbreviations

ACDA	Arms Control and Disarmament Agency [US]
ASW	antisubmarine work
ATA	Aviation Technology Affairs [Iran]
AWACS	airborne warning and control system
BVR	beyond-visual-range [targets]
CIA	Central Intelligence Agency
CASCO	Caspian Sea Cooperation Organization
CIS	Commonwealth of Independent States [former Soviet republics]
CRS	Congressional Research Service [US]
ECO	Economic Cooperation Organization
FAC	fast attack craft
GCC	Gulf Cooperation Council
GPS	global positioning system
IAEA	International Atomic Energy Agency
ICJ	International Court of Justice
IDB	Islamic Development Bank
IISS	International Institute for Strategic Studies
IMF	International Monetary Fund
INS	inertial navigation systems
IR	Iranian rial
IRGC	Islamic Revolutionary Guards Corps
IRP	Islamic Republic Party
LMI	Liberation Movement of Iran [Nehzat-e Azadi-e Iran]
MEK	Mojahedin-e Khalq
NAFTA	North American Free Trade Agreement
NIOC	National Iranian Oil Company
NPT	Non-Proliferation Treaty
OECD	Organization for Economic Cooperation and Development
OIC	Organization of the Islamic Conference
OIRAP	Organization of the Islamic Revolution in the Arabian Peninsula
OPEC	Organization of Petroleum Exporting Countries
PRC	People's Republic of China

R&D	research and development
RPV	remotely piloted vehicle
SHORAD	short-range air defense system
SNSC	Supreme National Security Council
UAE	United Arab Emirates
WMD	weapons of mass destruction

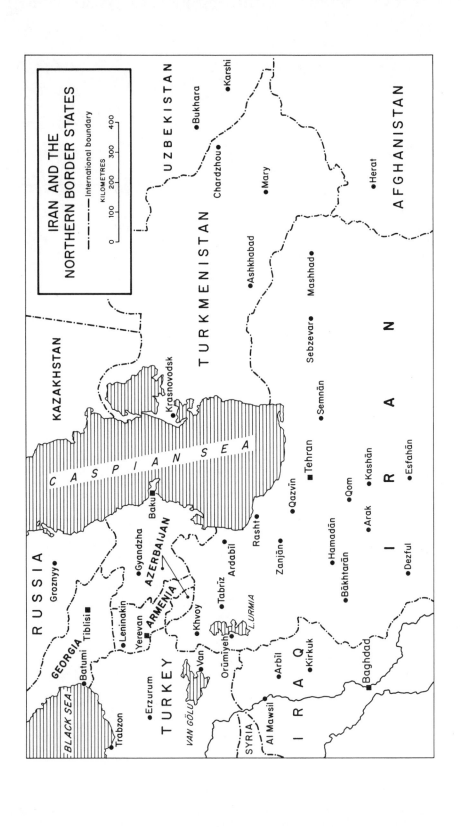

IRAN AND THE
NORTHERN BORDER STATES

——·——·—— International boundary

KILOMETRES
0   100   200   300   400

KAZAKHSTAN

UZBEKISTAN

•Karshi

•Bukhara

•Chardzhou

•Mary

AFGHANISTAN

•Herat

TURKMENISTAN

•Ashkhabad

Mashhad•

CASPIAN SEA

•Krasnovodsk

Sebzevar•

•Semnān

RUSSIA

•Groznyy

GEORGIA
Batumi■ Tiblisi■

BLACK SEA

•Trabzon

•Leninakin

Yerevan■ ARMENIA

•Gyandzha

AZERBAIJAN

Baku■

Ardabil•

Rasht•

Zanjān•

•Qazvin

■Tehran

•Kashān

•Qom

I   R   A   N

•Arak

•Esfahān

•Khvoy

•Tabriz

L. URMIA

Orūmiyeh•

•Van

VAN GÖLÜ

TURKEY

•Erzurum

•Hamadān

•Bākhtarān

•Dezful

SYRIA

Al Mawsil•

•Arbil

•Kirkuk

I   R   A   Q

Baghdad■

Introduction

Jamal S. al-Suwaidi

Uncertainties associated with the transition from the Cold War era to a yet elusive New World Order abound and are, perhaps, nowhere more compellingly exemplified than in the mosaic of factors that affect Iranian politics and determine both the country's internal economic well-being and its dealings with the outside world. Tenuous relations with the Arab Gulf states in particular have given rise to concerns over regional stability, and beg the question as to what measures – whether political, economic, or social in nature – are likely to promote enduring peace and prosperity in the Gulf. In an attempt to find answers, this work presents the views of foremost scholars on Iran and the Gulf in order to render a comprehensive and balanced account of the key issues confronting the area at the dawn of the twenty-first century.

Arguably the most volatile region in the world, where global economic interests intersect with regional political pressures, the Gulf, by virtue of its immense hydrocarbon deposits and the contrasting policies of its constituent states, will continue to figure prominently in the annals of strategic studies and international security analyses. Equally, Iran, considered the linchpin of Western strategy during much of the Cold War, will continue to play a pivotal role in Gulf affairs by virtue of its geography, population size, ideology, and regional leadership ambitions. Regional and external concerns over Iran's bid to appear a paragon of sociopolitical development to neighboring countries, in particular the Arab states bordering the Gulf, frequently define the analytical prism through which Iranian foreign policy is interpreted. Yet the complexity of Iranian political socialization, Tehran's recalcitrant position towards Arab neighbors and the West, and its oscillating policies and enigmatic power structure together complicate the formulation of simple explanations. Instead, scholarly inquiry into Iran's decision-making apparatus, its policy formulation process, the gravity of its policies past and present, and what they may portend for the future, must proceed carefully and with tempered ambition.

Mindful of this analytical challenge, the following collection of views represents a concerted effort to pay due deference to those aspects and issues of Iranian politics without which an assessment of Gulf stability and security is scarcely possible, and which are of paramount interest to Arab Gulf neighbors. Because these topics are often difficult to separate from the contextual backdrop that links domestic with foreign policy, or regional with international affairs, the chapter sequence follows, as far as possible, a delineation of subject matter according to four sections. The first, entitled "The Theocratic Challenge," introduces the Iranian polity with a look at the role of religion in shaping contemporary political ideology and the evolution of political institutions before and after the revolution. Contrasting internal with external policy determinants, the second section on "Foreign Policy in a Changing Region" turns to the variables that govern Iranian policy *vis-à-vis* its neighbors, including those driven by domestic considerations and those in response to both regional and extra-regional actors. The latter encompasses an examination of the emerging ties between the Islamic Republic and the newly independent states of Central Asia.

Perhaps the most heated debate in the discourse on Iran today is addressed in the book's third section, namely the country's seemingly startling military ambitions and its economic future. Avoiding the simplicity and self-serving logic that permeates much of the literature on this topic, the combination of two thoughtfully argued chapters on Iranian military programs and capabilities (with one focusing on the vexing problems that trouble Iran's economic development) offers a sobering insight into the trade-offs that confront the leadership in establishing national policy priorities. The book's final section examines the relationship between Iran, on the one hand, and the United States and the Gulf Cooperation Council (GCC) states on the other, focusing on the domestic factors contributing to Iranian foreign policy and the various security dynamics active in the Gulf region.

In keeping with this outline, Chapter 1, by Mehdi Noorbaksh, examines the precepts that underpin the symbiotic relationship between religion and politics in post-revolutionary Iran. What role Islam should assume in shaping political institutions and governance of the state emerged as a central issue in the wake of the 1979 revolution. Several orientations prevailed under the rubric of Islamic revivalism that capture reformist, puritanical, and populist elements. Noorbaksh illuminates how the forces of reformist Islam and puritanical Islam, supported by populism in their struggle for power, entered the debate over religion and politics. He traces the arguments on both sides and demonstrates how various factors contributed to the intensification of the debate over democracy and democratic institutions in Iranian society. His examination of Mehdi Bazargan's concept of "Islamic democratic government" is particularly refreshing, as it brings out the nuances in philosophical dispositions on the issue among the protagonists who define that debate. Noorbaksh's thoroughly informed conclusion – judging whether Puritanism has run its course or not – is timely reading and deserving of careful scrutiny, considering tensions in modern-day Iran over the wisdom of adhering to ideological tenets inspired by the revolution to cope with the influx of Western values.

Moving from the revolution's formative influences on ideology to its impact on political institutions, Chapter 2, by Bahman Baktiari, assesses the performance of key post-revolutionary institutions to determine the degree to which the ruling elite has tolerated, if not actively encouraged, limited popular participation in government. Having eliminated the vestiges of the monarchical regime, how did Ayatollah Khomeini proceed in concurrently consolidating his power and establishing the requisite institutions that to this day account for the continuation of the Islamic regime? Similarly, how did he manage to stay above the fray of domestic conflict and factionalism – adjudicating or inserting himself only when the political order was deemed to be under serious threat – and how did successors for the position of *faqih* affect the stability of the regime, particularly in the post-Khomeini period? Examining these questions at length, the author provides an instructive insight into the most salient determinants of Iran's leadership direction since the revolution.

The third chapter, by Roy Mottahedeh, elaborates on a dimension alluded to in Chapter 2, namely the evolution of the dual concept of the "source of emulation," or *marja-e taqlid,* and the "guardianship of the jurist," or *velayat-e faqih*. This duality started to assume central importance with the accession of Khomeini in 1979, when the acknowledgment of the Shi'ite leadership and the endorsement of the Iranian government were no longer independent of one another due to the constitutional adoption of the leadership of a single supreme *marja'*. The recent deaths of senior members of the Shi'ite religious establishment, including Ayatollahs Khomeini, Kho'i, Golpaygani, and Araki, have drawn further attention to the reinterpretation of the guardianship of the jurist. Mottahedeh's detailed survey of this cardinal concept underpinning Iranian politics is therefore a timely contribution that sheds light on the capacity of a revolution to endure without adhering to the tenet of its architect.

Part Two, centering on Iran's external relations with neighboring and extra-regional countries, opens with Mohsen Milani's study of Iran's Gulf Policy. Challenging the belief that the leadership in Tehran is intractably ideological and/or implacably nationalistic, Milani offers a decidedly more optimistic view of Iran's foreign policy since the death of Khomeini. He examines the factors that imbue policy decisions with moderation, dominated no longer by ideological considerations but by pragmatically inspired national interests. Caught up in "revolutionary romanticism" at first, the Islamic Republic, Milani argues, was under the stewardship of the fundamentalists who, by way of the war with Iraq, galvanized the public toward greater radicalism in the name of Islamic revivalism. Nationalists, who drew their support mostly from technocrats and the modern-oriented middle class, were marginalized in the process, while the country's foreign policy became a single-minded quest to assert an international position unencumbered by alignments with the outside. Conversely, the post-Khomeini era is marked by an attempt to turn around an anemic, war-ravaged economy under the guidance of the more pragmatic Hashemi Rafsanjani, who ascended to the presidency after a constitutional change that no longer requires the office to be occupied by a leading *marja'*. The gradual shift away from state ownership of industries, price regulation, and government subsidies, as well as the promotion of free-trade zones, illustrate Tehran's sincerity in economic reconstruction. To this end, Milani maintains, Iran has embarked on a foreign policy *vis-à-vis* the Gulf states that is informed by the acceptance of the political status quo, by accommodation to a US-orchestrated regional balance-of-power, by a rapprochement with Saudi Arabia, and by an effort to enhance the country's influence over the region's oil policy. Iran's abstention from actively interfering in Iraq's civil war, despite atrocities against Shi'ites in the South, and its swift condemnation of its neighbor's invasion of Kuwait, both signal a proclivity to engage in regional affairs with a measure of pragmatism in mind. The author concludes on a heuristic note, positing the primacy of regional fora over international mechanisms to resolve differences among Gulf states. In the post-industrial age, where the global distribution of wealth is increasingly determined by newly formed powerful trading blocks, economic integration among regional states is imperative lest they should find themselves sidelined in the evolving world order. Worse, without cultivation of mutual economic stakes, Milani states, the sought-after political common ground that sustains enduring regional stability may never materialize.

In Chapter 5 James Bill proposes an analytical framework that concentrates on the interactions among Iran, Iraq, the United States, and the GCC member states as a collective. Within this framework, suggestive of a game-theoretic approach, Bill examines the domestic and international constraints that impinge on these four political actors in their pursuit judiciously to balance conflicting interests. Questions over the political legitimacy and social identity of Gulf states intersect with vital interests of the West (and increasingly the East) in ways that precipitate the maelstrom of instability that gives rise to interstate war. The combination of a regional hegemon (Iran), a military aggressor (Iraq), a fragile coalition (GCC), and a global hegemon (the US), all converging at arguably the world's most geostrategic area, makes for a charged atmosphere governed by intolerance rather than deference, by self-indulgence rather than mutuality, and by an overriding sense of zero-sum games associated with political maneuvering. Bill provides a profile of the four pillars sustaining the rectangle of tensions, highlighting their respective strengths and weaknesses, in order to identify the potential for a lessening of these tensions. He further speculates about the need for local rulers to yield to pressures for democratic pluralism and for the United States to assume a less visible position on Gulf affairs, both actions that may help introduce the lasting stability that for so long has eluded the area.

Clearly, regional stability is unlikely to flourish without an appreciable improvement in relations between the two major protagonists, Iran and Iraq – a point emphasized in Chapter 6 by Geoffrey Kemp, who sketches an overview of the most salient issues that define Iran's foreign policy and reactions to it by the international community. In particular, Kemp reflects on Iran's effort to shore up its image in the face of negatively disposed Western media, US-led economic embargoes and push for political isolation, and GCC members increasingly tied to formal defense agreements with Washington and several European capitals. Although the break-up of the Soviet Union has left a political vacuum in Central Asia, Iran's capacity to influence events in that area is circumscribed by a moribund economy which, if not put on life-support (i.e., massive foreign aid/investment and fundamental restructuring), may rapidly disintegrate. Equally incisive is Kemp's assessment of Iran's military capability. Charges of military threats emanating from Iran are tempered with observations of a fragile hardware supplier base, reports of limited defense expenditures, and alternative explanations painting a more innocuous picture. Conversely, the author's section on terrorism and subversion – covering Iran's involvement in the Maghreb, Sudan, and Turkey – is decidedly more supportive of the prevailing view expounded by the media. Similarly, it is difficult to dissociate Iran from others attempting to derail the peace process. However, Iran is a long way from being the unfettered spoiler in the Gulf, Kemp adds. Lingering unrest and turmoil along its periphery (including Georgia, Azerbaijan, Afghanistan, and Iraq), as well as an on-going dispute with the UAE over Iran's occupation of the Gulf islands of Abu Musa and the Tunbs, present Tehran with a set of vexing problems. Moreover, relations with Syria and Iraq may be affected significantly by events over which Tehran has increasingly little or no control (namely an Israel–Syria rapprochement and Iraq's re-entry into the oil market).

In view of the rising importance of the GCC alliance in the formation of security arrangements in the Gulf, Chapters 7 and 8 are largely devoted to the dyadic relationship between Iran and two key members of that grouping. In Chapter 7 Anwar Gargash looks at a range of issues that over time have defined relations between Iran and its Gulf neighbors. His extended treatment of the bilateral ties between the UAE and Iran exemplifies the complex multidimensionality of Gulf politics that often bedevils local decision-makers in their search for tension-reducing measures. While Iran may indeed be chasing after its past glory to regain influence lost since the fall of the Shah, the Tehran leadership is burdened with formidable challenges, both at home and abroad, that significantly constrain its ability to pursue ambitious foreign policy objectives. Gargash's chronicling of the historical evolution of Iran's relations with its Arab neighbors, and his stressing of the major turning points over time, help one gain an appreciation of the centrality of perceptions in the formulation of policy on both sides of the Gulf. The inextricable link between oil, economic prosperity, political stability, and extra-regional interference generates a web of national interests that complicates the precise identification of ideological differences separating the Gulf littoral states. In turn, perception, rather than reality, may govern inter-state relations. This crucial problem is addressed by the author in his coverage of the numerous obstacles to a regionally sponsored security arrangement encompassing all Gulf countries. On the other hand, there are identifiable domestic reasons for the sometimes erratic shifts in Iran's foreign policy; these are frequently tied to the ebb and flow of moderates versus radicals that inform policy. The duality in position *vis-à-vis* the West, especially the United States, is a case in point: Strident rhetoric often alternates with tempered signals of accommodation. The post-Khomeini period, in particular, has seen a rise in calls urging more amicable economic pragmatism in contrast to those that continue to be inspired by inimical political idealism. Like Iran's foreign policy in general, the dispute over the Gulf islands of Abu Musa and the Tunbs has been affected by Tehran's shifting position over time. Having traced the dispute back to its inception, Gargash examines how it turned into a nagging contest that continues to cloud UAE–Iran relations. While there are irrefutable facts "on the ground" that are difficult to overlook, there is a "wall of suspicion" dividing Iran and its Gulf neighbors that must also be tackled to establish a climate conducive to peaceful resolution of contentious issues. An integral part of that process is the establishment of institutional mechanisms for confidence-building measures, the author concludes.

Tensions between Iran and Saudi Arabia are potentially the most taxing on the Gulf region. Hence Chapter 8, by Saleh al-Mani', is central to the book's theme. His discussion of the historical events that marked the evolution of ties between these two countries and the role of competing *ulama* in shaping their direction is followed by an assessment of how each country's outlook on religion has influenced, if not determined, government policy *vis-à-vis* one another. Al-Mani' contrasts the historical process of nation-building in Saudi Arabia with that in Iran to illustrate the distinct theocratic features of political alliances that emerged in each society. He highlights the major turning points over time, such as the ascendancy of the Pahlavi dynasty and Iran's religious revivalism of the 1980s, in order to compare the role of the *ulama* in each country. The strikingly different approaches to the conduct of foreign policy are further magnified by the author's analysis of the utility of supra-national organizations during policy implementation. This point is exemplified in the case of support to the Mujahedin in Afghanistan and the Hizbollah in Lebanon. The ideological rift produced by the 1979 revolution introduced a period marked by a leadership contest between Saudi Arabia and Iran over the hearts and minds of the Muslim world that goes beyond sectarian differences. Riyadh's difficulty in effectively responding to the challenge is compounded by the post-Khomeini bifurcation, which introduced a competition between moderates and more radical elements within Iranian politics. Vying for coveted seats in a fairly cumbersome policy-making apparatus, these groups visibly complicate a reading of what motivates Iranian foreign policy. The record to date seemingly indicates parallel inputs as Riyadh is able to engage Tehran in functional cooperation to support a common energy and environmental policy and jointly fight drug trafficking, while at the same time Saudi leaders are forced to counter Tehran's attempts to disturb the *hajj* (pilgrimage to Mecca) and to share in the custody of the two holy mosques. Similarly, they may coordinate their position on the issue of Iraqi opposition groups and renew ambassadorial ties, even though a simmering territorial dispute (as happened over Abu Musa in 1992) may offset such gains. The author shares the view that political moderation in Iran is driven by economic necessity and suggests that to establish lasting stability, Saudi Arabia and Iran must commence a dialogue that addresses the religious element in their relationship.

Considering Iran's geostrategic location, on the fault line separating the old Soviet empire from the Arab world, the question arises as to the impact of the Soviet collapse on the stability of the Gulf region. Chapter 9, by W. Nathaniel Howell, offers a lucid treatment of this increasingly important issue. Specifically, what are the effects of Soviet-generated "anomalies, discontinuities, and grievances" as the newly independent republics of Northwest Asia, an area encompassing Central Asia and the Transcaucasus, look south to Iran? Howell, in his review of Iran's policy on Northwest Asia since the disintegration of the Soviet Union, concentrates on several important aspects: namely, the capacity of Iran to influence events in Northwest Asia, including the potential for religious radicalism to affect the evolving political thinking; the principal goals that govern Iran's foreign policy *vis-à-vis* the newly independent states; and the probable diplomatic trade-offs associated with policies that encourage competition with Russia, Turkey, or Saudi Arabia for hegemony over Iran's northern neighbors. Clearly, the opening of Northwest Asia poses both opportunities and challenges for Tehran. A policy of declared non-interference during the Soviet era may give way to a decidedly more activist role that seeks to maximize Iranian gains from the continuing strife in the Caucasian republics and Tadjikistan. However, the attendant risks of such a policy may outweigh any payoff. Turmoil along Iran's northern frontier could linger for many years as Russia and its near neighbors gradually settle into a new continental order. A prolonged period of adjustment may spell incalculable dangers for Tehran, with equally unforeseeable consequences for stability to the south. Indeed, as the author suggests, the opening of Northwest Asia is likely to magnify the importance of the Gulf because of greater access to trade routes connecting Iran's northern neighbors with the open seas and Middle East markets. The former Soviet republics may also welcome tighter infrastructural integration with Iran to reduce their exposure to and dependence on a still shaky Russian economy. Thus instabilities in the north or south could seriously reverberate in both directions, the prospect of which may gradually render Iran a status quo power keenly aware of the necessity for constructive engagement to safeguard mounting regional economic stakes.

Part Three begins with Kenneth Katzman's study of the influence of Iran's radical factions over military institutions. Knowing the extent to which the revolutionary vanguard controls military policy may explain the occasional belligerent tone in government pronouncements and the intensity with which political objectives are pursued by military means. Whether Iran is intent on redressing a perceived power imbalance – whereby the Tehran leadership seeks to recapture the lost glory of regional hegemon, only now without the US strings the Shah had to tolerate – is something upon which experts disagree. However, there is little doubt that the US dual-containment policy, stipulating more severe trade sanctions against Iraq as opposed to Iran, enables Tehran to attain more easily a level of regional preponderance. Again, deciphering Iran's real intentions is an exercise that is not straightforward. The synergism that derives from approaching the problem from various angles is likely to yield the greatest insight. Katzman's focus on the Revolutionary Guard to examine how political objectives intersect with those of the military offers an added dimension to arguably the most vexing issue occupying analysts on Iran. Although much surrounding the Guard is shrouded in secrecy and disinformation, the author's treatment of the organizational set-up and the delineation between regular and Guard forces is instructive: It helps explain patterns in military hardware acquisition, modes of operational engagement, and the frequency and location of military exercises. Assuming that the Revolutionary Guard is essentially a political establishment with arms, how must one view its propensity for irrational action? What is its role in setting policy and in determining when, and which, military means are employed in support of it? Tied to the political fortunes of the Ayatollahs, the Revolutionary Guard's input would appear to correlate inversely with that of the moderates. Similarly, ideological objectives may override practical considerations in guiding procurement decisions and operational concepts. Answers are found in Katzman's tracing of the professional development of Revolutionary Guard leaders, their ascendancy to key positions in decision-making bodies (e.g. the Supreme Defense Council), and the Guard's wide functions, encompassing both domestic and international tasks. Furthermore, the author addresses the degree to which the Guard supports radical groups around the Middle East and influences the selection and posting of ideological brethren entering Iran's foreign service. Whether the Revolutionary Guard is bound to accumulate more power over the military depends on a host of factors that are probably still unfolding, given Iran's currently tumultuous economy and volatile political climate.

Gauging the Iranian military threat is a daunting task and, as shown in the previous chapter, one fraught with methodological and interpretative problems. Hence Anthony Cordesman, in Chapter 11, prefaces his analysis with caveats that alert the reader to the difficulty in extracting conclusive impressions, even if based on a plethora of painstakingly detailed data covering the range of elements that go into sound threat assessment. Asking the right questions is crucial: For example, does Iran's recent military buildup constitute a shift toward a more aggressive posture, or is it merely an attempt to recover from the ruins of the prolonged war with Iraq? While concentrating on capabilities, rather than intentions, may be more fruitful, how does one manage the perennial conundrum of separating offensive from defensive capabilities or, worse, military from civilian applications? The functional versatility of today's technology and the ever greater infusion of dual-use items into the development of military equipment very much define the capabilities of modern armed forces. Sustaining them has become ever more costly, however. Cordesman's examination of Iran's military expenditures and the computational pitfalls that complicate the calculation of accurate figures illustrates the difficulty in measuring Tehran's real military effort. His comparative assessment of arms suppliers and arms transfers to Iran and its Gulf neighbors is revealing, perhaps dispelling some of the distortions that dominate discourse on this subject. Iran, Cordesman argues, faces severe economic, social, and management constraints in its bid to revitalize its armed forces. Demographic pressures, infrastructural demands, and costly inefficiencies in industry are but a few of the factors behind difficult trade-offs in resource allocation. Supplied by economically troubled countries, Iran must also cope with a set of planning uncertainties that render logistics support highly fragile, and deep ethnic divisions hamper the formation of effective combat units. Still, the author's assessment of Iran's military services shows that Tehran has a number of contingency capabilities at its disposal that should not be dismissed. His detailed accounting of equipment acquisition, operating conditions, and the state of personnel and training highlights the strengths and weaknesses Iran could bring to bear, or would suffer from, in a confrontation with its neighbors. Having profiled Iran's paramilitary forces, Cordesman's final section addresses the problem of weapons of mass destruction (WMD). Again, a mixed picture emerges due to the multidimensionality of this issue. Iran's search for a nuclear capability is handicapped by international efforts to prevent it from acquiring fissile material, by technical short-comings in the area of missile guidance and intelligence, and by limited competence to design and operate the requisite technology. In comparison, Iran encounters negligible obstacles in the chemical weapons sphere, where international restrictions are virtually non-existent and the technical de-mands for accurate delivery against a target are minimal. While the author outlines the range of most likely scenarios that could be precipitated by Iranian military forays, and explores the type of responses to counter such moves, he reserves judgment on Tehran's nuclear intentions in view of the paucity of facts on the size and nature of the Iranian program. Conversely, he expresses little doubt as to the criticality of a functioning alliance system – based on both regional participation and alignment with key outside powers capable of projecting force from afar – in order to safeguard the stability of the region. He hastens to add, though, that however solid the military preparations, they alone rarely make for a peaceful neighborhood.

The road to a stable environment in the Gulf may very much hinge on Tehran's ability to revive Iran's seemingly faltering, if not comatose, economy. The spate of stories reaching the news media on the economic hardship that is gripping Iranian society is put in perspective by Hooshang Amirahmadi in Chapter 12. He makes a forceful argument about the link between Iran's economic condition and regional stability. Convinced that equitable relations among Gulf neighbors based on mutuality of interest flow from a realization that economic prosperity is at the heart of long-term stability, Amirahmadi examines the two five-year plans put together by the Iranian government to guide the country's economic development since 1989. His discussion of the factors that led to the design of the first plan, the ensuing modifications, and the pros and cons of the revised plan capture the tenuous balance decision-makers had to strike in their attempt to get the economy moving after the costly war with Iraq. Between mutually exclusive and difficult-to-reconcile planning goals, the first blueprint for Iran's postwar economic revival offered little hope for tangible material progress. Efforts concurrently to pursue infrastructural improvement, control inflation and unemployment, stem the budget deficit, promote exports, and optimize resource extraction could hardly proceed without setting strict priorities to avoid a situation where too many projects chase too few rials. Though too ambitious from the outset, the first five-year plan was hampered by a host of other factors, according to Amirahmadi. The combination of erroneous assumptions, hasty modi-fications, managerial incompetence, and an ill-conceived exchange-rate

policy, to name a few, greatly limited the chances for a successful implementation of the plan. While the first plan did register some positive
signs, the author cautions that they were due to other factors. In that
regard, his sectoral analysis of Iran's economy and his evaluation of
government policy on subsidies, privatization, and unemployment provides
a welcome insight. Equally informative is his comparison of the first
with the second five-year plan. Having contrasted the main features of
each, Amirahmadi identifies several shifts in planning priorities and
elaborates on the challenges that are likely to befall implementation of
the second plan. His policy recommendations suggest a redefinition of
the role of the people in national affairs, whereby accountability between
ruler and ruled as well as economic diversification away from hydrocarbon-
based industries govern strategic planning for the future. Cognizant of
the international pressures levied against Iran, the author comments on
the merits of economic embargoes and alternative ways to encourage
cooperative engagement.

In Part Four, Jamal S. al-Suwaidi adopts the perspective that the Islamic
Republic of Iran is generally viewed today by the international community
as a major threat to the stability of the Gulf region, and undertakes a
four-part examination of the Islamic Republic's role in the Gulf security
debate. The chapter begins by focusing on the domestic factors that
contribute to the Iranian foreign policy process. Following an overview
of the history of US–Iranian relations, the post-Cold War relationship
between the United States and Iran is examined. The third and final
sections discuss the relationship between the GCC states and Iran and
examine the security dynamics that attend that strained relationship,
including the economic factors that influence Gulf security.

PART ONE

The Theocratic Challenge

CHAPTER I

Religion, Politics, and Ideological Trends in Contemporary Iran

Mehdi Noorbaksh

The three factors of Islam as a mobilizing faith and ideology in the Iranian revolution – the participation of the clergy and the leadership of Ayatollah Khomeini in the revolutionary process, the role of Muslim intellectuals in Islamic resurgence prior to the revolution, and their involvement in laying out revolutionary strategy – were crucial in installing a symbiotic relationship between religion and politics in post-revolutionary Iran. This relationship, which brought a new idiosyncratic flavor into Iranian politics, paved the way for a clash between different interpretations of religion and its role in the politics and government of the country. In this regard, no other questions have created such fervor in Iranian society today as have the questions of what interpretation of Islam should have what impact on government and its institutions, and how Islam can best promote participatory politics and pluralism in government and society. Who should represent this government and who should rule in an Islamic government?

Although during the last century religion had played a monumental role in the politics of this nation, especially in the Tobacco Uprising of 1890, the Constitutional Revolution of 1905–11 and the nationalization of oil under Musaddiq (1950–53), the Iranian revolution alone directly involved the clergy in the politics of government. The clergy, who in the past had not been directly involved in the politics of government and had maintained the autonomy of their religious institutions, were given the opportunity, for the first time in Iranian history, to face the challenges of governance. The outcome raised fundamental questions in the realm of religion and politics in the country. Three issues – 1) the Shah's severe suppression, which had not allowed open debate on institutions of government and politics in the society in the past; 2) the rapid revolutionary upheavals of 1978–79; and 3) the concealed nature of the clerics' conception of government, religion, and politics – led to a confusion in the domain of the interaction of religion and politics and the role that the clerical establishment had to play in the post-revolutionary government in Iran. As the clergy imposed its political will on politics and government, a substantial portion of the Iranian society, including some of the Muslim intellectuals who were an integral part of the revolution, were alienated from government. Consequently, a clash of differing points of view over religion and government in post-revolutionary Iran came to the fore between those who dominated power and those who were alienated from the politics of government in the country.

In this chapter, an attempt is made to address the two questions at the core of this clash and the continuing debate over the nature of government and its institutions in post-revolutionary Iran. The first question concerns the definition of "Islamic government" or "Muslim government" by each group. The second dwells on how ideological interpretations of each group set the guidelines for the debate over government and its institutions.

Introduction

The Iranian revolution of 1979 marked the end of monarchy and paved the way for the establishment of a new political entity based upon emerging values that were fundamental in delegitimizing the old regime. These new values, which had been nourished for several decades on the axioms of religion, nationalism, and expectation of legal and political settings, were reflected in the Iranian revolution's slogan of "Independence, Freedom, and Islamic Republic." For those who advocated freedom and republican government in the Iranian revolution, monarchism was rejected as a source of tyranny and arbitrary rule (istibdad). In objecting to the dictatorship and tyranny of the Pahlavi regime, Mehdi Bazargan argued in his 1964 military trial: "Dictatorship is the biggest enemy of the human race … It generates identity crisis in the society … It annuls the ethics and moral fabric of the society."[1] In 1978 Ayatollah Khomeini objected to the Shah's rule, stating: "Now the regime of the Shah is ruling tyrannical over our oppressed people. He continues to rule in defiance of the law and wishes of the people …"[2] These assessments, which were shared by a majority in various strata of Iranian society, helped in forging an alliance among secular nationalists, Muslim intellectuals, and clergy in opposing the Pahlavi regime in a process toward revolution.

The opposition was aware of the nature of the government under the Pahlavi monarchy and was well acquainted with its foe. At the same time, opposition groups were quite sure of their own demands in terms of their desire to establish a government based on democratic values and pluralism in society. This demand was reflected in the slogan of the Iranian revolution, which was conceived in Paris and repeated by the leadership and Ayatollah Khomeini in Najaf and Paris. In a message to the people of Azerbaijan, Khomeini wrote in February 1978, one year before the Iranian revolution, "Let the noble, cherished, and beloved people of Azerbaijan know that they are not alone in their struggle for justice, independence and freedom."[3] Defiance of dictatorship, tyranny, and arbitrary rule, and advocacy for the rule of law, freedom, and democracy in the framework of the Islamic republic constituted the core of understanding among all who participated in the revolution. That understanding between the leadership and intellectuals led to the writing of the first Iranian constitution in Paris, which accommodated democratic institutions in government and society.

Among the Muslims, the four Islamic orientations which, more than any other ideological inclination, molded the revolutionary course of action were puritanical Islam, populist Islam, modernist Islam, and reformist Islam. The puritanists were those who belonged to higher echelons of the seminaries and the clerical establishment, and some among the educated classes who supported Khomeini and his bid for political power within the country. The populists were the lay clerics and their supporters, who were not necessarily in favor of fundamental change and revolution within the country. In the past, this orientation was best represented by Fada'iyan-e Islam, led by Navvab Safavi, who demanded that the Shah rule as a monarch respecting and implementing religious values.[4] During the Iranian revolution, populist Islam was immensely politicized; its leaders followed Khomeini and joined forces with the puritanists in opposing the regime of the Shah. Puritanists and populists were both supporters of *Islam-e fiqahati*, a terminology created after the Iranian revolution to denote the relationship between the source of imitation (Marja'e Taqlid) and his followers (Muqallidin). The later concept of *Islam-e Nab-e Muhammadi* (the pure Muhammadan Islam) was further developed to emphasize the significance of that relationship between the leader and the followers, to promote the notion of a perceived "Islamic obligation" of following the source of authority in religion, in this case Khomeini, and to deny others who questioned that relationship any role in the power politics of the country.

Modernist Islam was best represented by the Mujahedin-e-Khalq, whose ideology was a blend of Islam and Marxism. As the puritanists and the populists denied any role for the Mujahedin in the post-revolutionary government, and as the Mujahedin themselves were very concerned about participating in power, the latter soon became isolated from politics and found no other alternative than to retreat and to oppose the leadership, the government, and later the revolution.

The last group, the supporters of reformist Islam, who were very fundamental in the course of the Iranian revolution, joined forces with Khomeini and were responsible not only for religious awakening prior to the Iranian revolution and ideological training of the younger generation within the universities, but also for designing revolutionary strategy during the course of revolutionary upheaval. Before the Iranian revolution, the most important figures of this orientation were Mehdi Bazargan, Ayatollah Mutahhari, Ayatollah Taliqani, and Dr. Ali Shari'ati inside the country, and Ibrahim Yazdi, Mustafa Chamran, and a few others on the outside.

As Khomeini and the supporters of puritanical Islam dominated power within the country and the forces of populist Islam became fundamental in supporting puritanism in its bid for power, the clash of ideologies on government and its institutions between puritanical Islam and reformist Islam came to the political fore. Currently, with one group, the puritanists, in absolute control of the political machinery of the country, and the other, the reformists, stripped of power and of the right formally to establish their own political organizations, the debate over religion, politics, and government between the two has attracted the most attention, especially among the educated and middle class in Iran. The inclination among the supporters of puritanical Islam is toward authoritarianism led by an established hierarchy of clerics. The supporters of reformist Islam advocate a pluralistic democracy which generates its legitimacy from the people, and works within the framework of the dominant values in the society. These inclinations inside and outside of the government, as well as the values that the revolution has imposed on the society in terms of molding new demands in the domain of politics and government, helped form a government in post-revolutionary Iran colored by authoritarianism, theocracy, and democracy.

Puritanism, Politics, and Government

Ayatollah Khomeini's views on government were first known in the 1970s through lectures he delivered to seminary students in Najaf. Before these lectures his views on politics and government were reflected for the first time in his book *Kashf-e Asrar,* which was published in Iran in 1943. Although *Kashf-e Asrar* was intended to answer other questions, part of it can be considered an introduction to Khomeini's theory of *velayat-e faqih* (Governorship of the Jurist). This book shows very clearly that Khomeini had developed his special orientation toward government in the 1940s when he was in Iran. He had developed this theory under the influence of Mullah Ahmad Naraqi (1771–1829), who, for the first time in the history of Shi'ite jurisprudence, attempted to justify the government of Faqih in his book *Awa'id al-Ayyam.*[5] The reason why, in *Kashf-e Asrar,* Khomeini did not emphasize the leading role of the *ulama* in government and argued in favor of a temporal ruler permitted by them to rule was the impracticality at the time for the clerical establishment to rule themselves. A majority of the clergy were apolitical. The reformer Ayatollah Abdulkarim Ha'iri Yazdi had depoliticized the Islamic seminary in Qum in the 1940s. Later the leadership of Ayatollah Borujerdi in Qum had further depoliticized the clergy and created a boundary between religion and politics. Because of this the Shah had created a close relationship with Ayatollah Borujerdi, a relationship based upon mutual respect for each others' domain of power and influence in the country.

When *velayat-e faqih* was conceived and presented by Khomeini as a theory of government, the majority of the clergy were apolitical. Khomeini's primary in presenting this framework of government was to encourage the clergy to become active in politics. In a few of his speeches in 1977 and 1978, especially when Muslim intellectuals such as Bazargan and others repeatedly denounced the regime of the Shah and its oppressive measures against the people, Khomeini objected to non-political clergy and asked for their participation in opposition. When the revolution came, many were skeptical of Khomeini's enthusiasm and conviction regarding the implementation of the theory of *velayat-e faqih* in the post-revolutionary government in Iran. There was still doubt on the part of Khomeini at the time of the Iranian revolution that the theory could be implemented in a revolution that embraced all strata of Iranian society from secular nationalists to Muslim intellectuals and to the most conservative sectors. Some argue that Khomeini was totally convinced of the possibility of implementing his theory of government after the victory of the Iranian revolution. There is ample evidence questioning the credibility of this argument. The first constitution, the initial draft of which was completed in Paris, did not contain any reference to the institution of *velayat-e faqih.* It was accepted by Khomeini with only minor changes, and he supported a referendum on this constitution immediately after the Iranian revolution. His close associates in Paris also confirm the sincerity of his desire to establish a government in Iran after the revolution in line with the first written constitution, which did not make any specific reference to the role of the clergy in government and most certainly defined a pluralistic society and representational government.[6] Since this constitution was not very specific in some areas, and left enough loopholes for some to influence the power-politics of the country, the majority in the Revolutionary Council supported the drafting of a more detailed constitution, based upon the first draft, by the people's representatives to be elected to the Majlis Khobregan (Assembly of Experts).

At the onset of the Iranian revolution Khomeini was very sensitive to the consensus of the people. On his first day in Tehran he announced in the Behesht-e Zahra cemetery that, "With the support of the people I ask for the establishment of a government. Because the people trusted me, I establish this government."[7] Later, when he asked Mehdi Bazargan to establish his provisional government, he indicated, "As the people showed support through demonstrations in the country for the leadership and its decisions and according to my Islamic and legal duty ... I ask you to establish a provisional government."[8] He was sincere in his conviction of a need for the people's support for and society's consensus on the institution of government in line with democratic values and representational government.

The theory of *velayat-e faqih* had proponents in Iran among the puritanists and the populists who filled the first Assembly of Experts to draft revolutionary Iran's first constitution. Among these were personalities like Ayatollah Beheshti, who was devoted to this theory and was fundamental in leading a collective endeavor and a majority in the Assembly of Experts to secure a position for *vali-e faqih* in the constitution, and a dominant role for the clergy in the power-politics of the nation.[9] In response to those who advocated democratic government and criticized Article 5 of the constitution, which was under debate in the Assembly of Experts and was intended to guarantee the position of the *faqih* in the constitution, Beheshti argued:

> The Islamic government is based on an ideology, different from a democratic republic. What ... others have suggested is indeed appropriate for a democratic republic, but it fails to meet the requirements of Islam ... Since our nation throughout the revolution and in the plebiscite voted for an Islamic republic, then, under this foundation which they selected, in this article and the others of this constitution, we will, under the rules and the foundation

of Islam, delegate the leadership to a knowledgeable Faqih, a leader acquainted with Islam.[10]

The leadership of Beheshti, the collective action of the supporters of the theory of *velayat-e faqih*, and the consent of Khomeini were all fundamental in establishing the government of the *faqih* in postrevolutionary Iran.

In *Kashf-e Asrar*, Khomeini's views on politics are stated very clearly. Contrary to the view that in this book he carefully defends monarchy[11] he follows a consistent argument in harmony with the theory of *velayat-e faqih* that he later presented as a framework of government. In response to those who criticized the *ulama* for opposing any government in the time of occulation of the Shi'ite Twelfth Imam, Khomeini, in *Kashf-e Asrar*, attempted to defend the *ulama*'s support for government, and occasionally unjust governments, on the grounds that they had preferred these governments over not having government at all.[12] As far as the *ulama*'s support for monarchy is concerned, he contended:

> they [the *ulama*] did not oppose the government institution and if they have opposed a monarch in the past it was because they had thought he was against the interest [salah] of the nation. Otherwise they have not yet opposed the principal foundation of monarchy, and many of the Ulama cooperated in the past with monarchs in their government including Khajeh Nasir Tusi, Allameh Helli, Muhaqqeq Thani, Sheikh Baha'i, Muhaqqeq Damad, Majlisi, and others.[13]

In defense of the government or *velayat-e faqih* at the time of occulation of the Twelfth Imam, he resorted to similar traditions (*ahadith*) in *Kashf-e Asrar* that he used three decades later to defend his argument for the theory of *velayat-e faqih* in the book *Islamic Government* (Hukumat-e Islami).[14] He contends in this book that:

> Some people argue that it is not necessary that the government be under the control of Faqih. The government can remain under the control of anyone, but he has to have the permission of Fuqaha to dispense his authority. In the past some of the monarchs had obtained that permission.[15]

In response to this argument he states:

> This is right that a Faqih can give this permission ... But they do not argue that not everyone can offer this permission to everyone he wishes. Not only do the Mujtahids [religious scholars] not have this permission, but the messenger of God also did not have this permission. They [the *mujtahids*] can only offer this permission to those who do not defy the laws of God,

which are based upon justice and wisdom. Only those who desire to establish the law of the land after the law of God can obtain this permission.[16]

In this argument, Khomeini has attempted to define clearly the source of authority in a government under the control of the religious establishment. The sources of authority in this case and according to Ayatollah Khomeini are the *fuqaha*, who can offer this permission and at the same time deny the temporal ruler from having this authority.

In *Islamic Government*, Khomeini followed a similar argument with one major difference. In it, he was adamant in favoring his true source of authority, the *faqih*, to rule directly and establish his prescribed framework for an Islamic government. To accomplish this, he had to overcome two major tasks: first, to declare that monarchy is illegitimate Islamically and must be replaced by another form of government, and second, to dismantle erected barriers between religion and politics and denounce those – especially among the clergy – who were apolitical or opposed the clergy's involvement in politics. In defiance of monarchy he argues, "Islam proclaims monarchy and hereditary succession wrong and invalid."[17]

In so far as the second task of dismantling the barrier between religion and politics is concerned, he describes the responsibility of the clergy in Najaf as:

Present Islam to the people in its true form, so that our youth do not picture the akhunds [clergy] sitting in some corner in Najaf or Qum, studying the questions of menstruation and parturition instead of concerning themselves with politics, and draw the conclusion that religion must be separate from politics. This slogan of separation of religion and politics and the demand that Islamic scholars not intervene in social and political affairs have been formulated and propagated by the imperialists; it is only the irreligious who repeat them.[18]

In order to justify the establishment of an Islamic government Khomeini contends:

A body of laws alone is not sufficient for a society to be reformed. In order for law to ensure the reform and happiness of man, there must be an executive power and an executor. For this reason, God Almighty, in addition to revealing a body of law [i.e., the ordinances of the Shari'a], has laid down a particular form of government together with executive and administrative institutions. The Most Noble Messenger (peace and blessings be upon him) headed the executive and administrative institutions of Muslim society. In addition to conveying the revelation and expounding and interpreting the articles of faith and the ordinances and the institutions of Islam, he under-took the implementation of law into being the Islamic state.[19]

He further argues, "The Sunna and the Path of the Prophet constitute a proof of the necessity for establishing government. First, he himself established a government, as history testifies."[20]

Among many qualities of a functioning government and a viable political system, the one that attracted Khomeini the most was the power of the government to implement the law. This was a natural inclination, since the main expectation from a *marja'* in the seminaries was to know the Islamic laws and develop expertise in these laws. *Maraj'i* in Shi'ism were recognized mostly by their books of law, *Tuzih al-Masa'il.* Considering this confined area of expertise among the *mujtahids* and the desire that they play a role in leading an Islamic government, Khomeini chose to define the needs of government to fit the capabilities of the clergy, stating, "Islamic government is a government of law." He then proceeds to rationalize as to why those who run this government must possess the knowledge of Islamic law. He explains:

> Since Islamic government is a government of law, knowledge of the laws is necessary for the ruler, as has been laid down in tradition. Indeed, such knowledge is necessary not only for the ruler, but also for anyone holding a post or exercising some government functions. The ruler, however, must surpass all others in knowledge ... Knowledge of the law and justice, then, constitute fundamental qualifications in the view of the Muslims. Other matters have no importance or relevance in this connection.[21]

In answering the question of who possessed the knowledge of the Islamic law and had the quality of being just, Khomeini argues:

> The two qualities of knowledge of the law and justice are present in countless Fuqaha of the present age. If they would come together, they could establish a government of universal justice in the world. If a worthy individual possessing these two qualities arises and establishes a government, he will possess the same authority as the Most Noble Messenger (upon whom be peace and blessings) in the administration of society, and it will be the duty of all people to obey him.[22]

As the experts of law, then, the clergy are given the responsibility to interpret and implement the law.

This theoretical foundation for *velayat-e faqih* was laid down by Khomeini in the late 1960s, when he was in Najaf. The theory was supported by a majority in the Assembly of Experts, which was chaired by Ayatollah Beheshti and filled by those who were mostly in his line of thinking on government and politics. In Article 5 of the newly drafted constitution it was written:

During the Occulation of the Lord of the Age (may God hasten his renewed manifestation), the governance and leadership of the nation devolve upon the just and pious Faqih who is acquainted with the circumstances of his age; courageous, resourceful, and possessed of the administrative ability; and recognized and accepted as leader by the majority of the people.[23]

The responsibilities of this leader was defined by the Article 110 as:

1. Appointment of the *fuqaha* to the Council of Guardians;
2. Appointment of the supreme judicial authority of the country;
3. Appointment of the supreme command of the country;
4. Appointment of the supreme commanders of the three branches of the armed forces; and,
5. Declaration of war and peace.[24]

These responsibilities were all debated in the Assembly of Experts at the beginning of the Iranian revolution.

But several factors contributed significantly to Khomeini's surpassing his limitations within the legal framework of the Iranian constitution. The first was his charisma and leadership in the revolution, which naturally paved the way for his unrestrained influence in society and its institutions, including the government. The second related to a tendency among the advocates of *velayat-e faqih* within the clergy to involve him step-by-step in every facet of decision-making in the country. The third was, of course, the role that he had to play as a mediator between various factions within the country's politics. The first of these conflicts arose between the provisional government of Bazargan and the clergy-dominated institutions of power within the society, including the power bases established by Ayatollah Beheshti and his colleagues within the Islamic Republic Party (IRP) and its surrounding institutions.[25] A very specific philosophy of government was advocated by Beheshti and his colleagues, in that they believed the intellectuals running government should pursue agendas sanctioned by clergy associated with the IRP and other institutions of power in post-revolutionary Iran. This orientation was completely in line with Khomeini's argument in *Kashf-e Asrar* in which the claim was made that whoever controls the government machinery must have the permission of the *fuqaha* and recognize their prerogatives. Although Ayatollah Khomeini hesitated at the outset to influence government policies directly, and wished to avoid the clergy's direct involvement in government institutions – for example, forbidding Ayatollah Beheshti to run for the presidency in the first elections – the clergy themselves supported and advocated a stronger role for themselves in national politics, leading inevitably to Khomeini's involvement in both internal and foreign policies. His hesitation regarding the clergy's involvement was clearly spelled out by one of his closest confidants, Ayatollah Mutahhari. In defense of the clergy's separation from government, Mutahhari argues:

> Because of its independence from government, the Shi'ite clergy has been successful in the last century in leading several movements and revolutions. Now that there is an Islamic government, he [Khomeini] believes that ruhaniyyat [clergy] must remain independent from the government, remaining with the masses and not mixing with government. He vehemently opposes the clergy's total involvement with government, albeit an Islamic one, as exists in Sunni Islam. He disagrees with clergy becoming part of the government or occupying official positions.[26]

Indeed, this was the position of Khomeini at the beginning of the revolution, and not the position of the clergy in favor of direct involvement. The need for advocacy for such direct involvement was clear in that they had to convince Khomeini himself to influence government policies directly in order to pave the way for their own direct occupation of governing positions.

Khomeini extended his influence over the domestic policies of the country and became directly involved in foreign policy, including later policies regarding the war with Iraq. Besides paving the way for the direct involvement of the clergy in the politics of government and domination of every facet of decision-making in the country, he amended his theory of *velayat-e faqih* in 1987 to give more power to the government, which by now was his government, run by the clergy. In the new amendment in which he called for the "Absolute Authority of the Faqih," the *faqih* was authorized to delegate unlimited power to his government in any way that the leader of government perceived was necessary, and in the interest of the government and not necessarily of the people. The question was what can facilitate the task of governing, especially in the area of domestic politics. The issue here was the creation of a mechanism in which the government could guard its own interests against the interests of the governed. This new *fatwa* by Khomeini was a response to the crises of government and an emerging friction between the more conservative clergy in the Guardian Council and those who were running the government and having to be more practical in matters perceived to be critical for effective government. Khomeini responded positively to the question raised by the minister of labor, who asked:

> Is it possible [for the government] to impose necessary conditions [*shurut-e elzami*] on the institutions which had used and are using the services and facilities of the government including electricity, water, raw materials, roads, ports ...[27]

A positive answer by Khomeini to this question gave the government the authority to abrogate unilaterally all contracts with other private institutions and citizens of the country if this was perceived to be necessary and in the interests of the government.

This was a new concept, not easily understood by all clergy supporting the *velayat-e faqih*. Some were very suspicious of the consequences of this new *fatwa*, especially in regard to its unconstitutionality. Three days after its announcement Ayatollah Khamene'i, as the president of the country, attempted to create a balance between this *fatwa* and the implied principles in the constitution of the country. He made a speech in which he attempted to return emphasis to the constitution in order to prevent potential illegalities arising where government institutions used the *fatwa* to justify government interests.[28] The Guardian Council (Showray-e Negahban) wrote a letter to Khomeini conveying its concern about future government policies, justified by the precepts of this *fatwa*, imposing regulations which would possibly be against the "original law of Islam."[29] Khomeini's response to this letter indicated that the authority of government went beyond what the minister of labor asked. He reiterated that the government had absolute authority in imposing its rule in ways that it perceived necessary, without any condition.[30]

The new *fatwa* was seen as backing for the speaker of the Majlis, Hashemi Rafsanjani, and the nation's more pragmatic politicians, and as a boost for the government of Hossein Musavi. Ayatollah Khamene'i, who was more skeptical about the consequences of this *fatwa*, especially with regard to his own position as president, attempted through public speeches to limit the effect of this decree on the country's politics. He argued in a Friday Prayer speech that:

> This step in the Islamic system of government did not intend to overlook the Islamically accepted rules of the country. It is obvious that some wished to understand this *fatwa* differently ... Ayatollah Khomeini's [new *fatwa* and its content] ... sets conditions within the framework of the accepted Islamic regulations and not beyond that.[31]

As the controversy over the content and intent of Khomeini's *fatwa* escalated among the clergy and friction between the more conservative and the more pragmatic clergy reached its height, the leader of the Iranian revolution made clear his position for the last time. In a new statement responding to Ayatollah Khamene'i, he announced:

> You do not consider rightful what God has conferred on Nabi Akram [the prophet] as the absolute authority [over the people]. This is one of the most important regulations of God and has preference over other minor regulations. The interpretation that government has authority within the regulation of God is contrary to my statement ... The government can repeal unilaterally all contracts agreed upon with the people.[32]

This announcement ended the debate in favor of the more pragmatic clergy and weakened the position of the president, Ali Khamene'i, and the more conservative among the Guardian Council who were in search of loopholes to maintain their influence over the Majlis and other institutions of government.

After Ayatollah Khomeini's latest dictum, the conservatives retreated and the theory of Absolute Authority of Faqih (*velayat-e mutlaqeh-e faqih*) was imposed. The previous advocates of *velayat-e faqih* accepted the precepts of this theory, having no other choice. The more conservative clergy joined the more pragmatic in defending the legitimacy of the new theory according to their understanding of the Islamic law, the precepts of the theory of *velayat-e faqih* and what was presented by Khomeini in his new argument defining the boundaries, role, and function of government. In defense of this theory, Ayatollah Jannati, one of the conservative members of the clergy, argued in the Friday Prayer:

> For example, if it were necessary for the people to go to war and they did not agree, the leader could order them to go ... The Islamic leader looks at the Islamic law, relies on his justice, recognizes the interests involved and consults, if necessary, and orders. The people must obey, whether they like it or not. When the leader recognized something has to be done, it must be done although the people do not agree.[33]

Another clergy from the conservative rank, Ayatollah Mishkini, argued, "What is wrong with what a Faqih can do in abrogating the rights of ownership of some people, or saying that Iraq (for example) must be like this or Iran like that. We can consider these [decrees] as secondary regulations [*ahkam-e thanaviyyeh*]."[34] The leader of the Friday Prayer of Yazd argued, "The best condition in an Islamic government is the agreement of the people to submit themselves fully to the will of their *vali-e faqih* and commit themselves to accepting his authority."[35]

The new authority for the *faqih* raised a host of questions in the domain of the responsibility of the Guardian Council with regard to its possible disagreement with the bills passed in the Majlis. In reality, the Absolute Authority of the Faqih was proposed to resolve the impasse that existed between the Guardian Council, with a more conservative outlook, and the pragmatic orientation in the government and Majlis led by Hashemi Rafsanjani. In an editorial in 1987, *Keyhan International* questioned what should be done if there were a conflict between the Majlis and the Guardian Council. The solution, according to *Keyhan,* was reliance on the leader as the final arbitrator and on his leadership in line with the precepts of the Absolute Authority of the Faqih.[36] In response to the same question raised by reporters, Ayatollah Musavi Ardebili, the head of Iran's judiciary system, had responded, "In the light of the new *fatwa* [absolute authority of the *faqih*], if we look at the laws passed by the Majlis, we find that they must be revised. Thus, 90 percent of our problems will be solved." Here Musavi Ardabili was referring to the conflict between the pragmatic Majlis and the conservative Guardian Council, which prevented many bills passed in the Majlis from being enacted as they were considered un-Islamic by the Council. In response to another question in the same line, Ardebili said that in the future if the views of the Guardian Council differed from those of the imam (Ayatollah Khomeini) then, "It has been agreed that they have to accept the Imam's views."[37]

Thus the new theory of Absolute Authority of the Faqih gave credence to advocates of *velayat-e faqih* to argue further for extension of the power of the *faqih* into other areas in which his leadership could make a difference in terms of settling disputes and ending friction. With total neglect for the defined constitutional responsibilities of the leader, the advocates of this theory perceived no limits to the power of the *faqih*. In 1989 Ayatollah Azari Qumi, one of the conservative supporters of the theory wrote, "The Vali-e Faqih does not have any other responsibility other than establishing the Islamic system [of government], even though he [the *faqih*] might have to stop temporarily the performance of Prayer, Fasting, Pilgrimage ... even belief of Tawhid [the concept of the unity of God]." He further argued, "The Vali-e Faqih can choose someone to replace him after his death. This person can be a Marja', Mujtahid or anyone else."[38] This new prescription for the authority of the *faqih* and the exaggeration of his power by a conservative clergy was intended to further the power of the *faqih* to domains not heretofore conceived by many, even among the clerical establishment. Assigning to a *faqih* the power to stop the Muslim community from performing its obligatory religious rituals was a far cry from previous discussions of politics and leadership and had no precedent in the history of Shi'ite jurisprudence.

This orientation toward government and its institutions gradually dominated the power in post-revolutionary Iran. The supporters of *velayat-e faqih* went so far as to argue that the legitimacy of the entire political system was generated not from the legal contract between the leader and the nation or the consensus of the people, but from the leader himself. Ayatollah Musavi Ardebili contended, "We have to say that in reality the government, Majlis, the government officials ... are under the authority of Vali-e Faqih. They obtain their legitimacy from him and they cannot do anything contrary to his views."[39] Muhammad Javad Larijani, another advocate of the theory of *velayat-e faqih*, argued that the people can influence the government and the political system by questioning the legitimacy of the government and its performance. In democratic societies the people's opinion constitutes the basis of government legitimacy. But in an Islamic government disapproval of the people for the government manifests itself only in the absence of their cooperation with the government in its policy implementation and performance. He then raises the question of whether the people's opinion in an Islamic government ruled by *vali-e faqih* carries any significance. In answering this question, he argues that "this opinion is legitimate only when it is accepted by a legitimate ruler and not independently."[40] He further explains that in an Islamic government the origin of all forms of legitimacy are traced to *vali-e faqih* and that "the opinion of the people does not have anything to do with the legitimacy [of the government]." He then questions the rationale of those who argue that in an Islamic government the people are free to choose the head of the government. Responding to this question he explains that:

> The statement of those who argue that, in an Islamic Government God has given the people the right to choose the leader for running their affairs, is an accurate statement in the logic of the liberals and not the theory of Velayat-e Faqih. [In this system] Vali-e [*faqih*] is the symbol of legitimacy, and submission to his will is binding not because of the legal expediency, but because that is a duty.[41]

A similar line of argument has been followed by other supporters of *velayat-e faqih*. Ayatollah Mesbah Yazdi argues that the government of the *vali-e faqih* is a manifestation of the government of God (Shu'a'i az Hakemiyyat-e Khuday-e Mutta'al) on earth.[42] After a lengthy argument that the "government of God" on earth can only be represented by the *vali-e faqih*, he explains, "The laws passed by the specialists in the legislative, judiciary, and executive [branches of the government] can gain their legitimacy from the head of the government, the Vali-e Faqih, without whose confirmation these laws lack legitimacy."[43] In addition, in his view acceptance of the government and its regulation under the *vali-e faqih* is not only legally binding, but is an Islamic responsibility and a duty.[44]

The theory of *velayat-e faqih* and its advocacy of a hierarchical power structure became a dominant norm in government after the Iranian revolution. Since November 1979, subsequent to the first nine months of the provisional government of Mehdi Bazargan, the country has been governed by different administrations, all with a high degree of dedication to this theory of government. As the theory began to dominate politics and the governing institutions inside the country, the more democratic tendencies became isolated from the power-politics of the country. Supporters of the theory, especially those among the clergy, held expectations of the *faqih* leading this government that went beyond the legal limitations in the Iranian constitution. As the influence of the leader extended to every facet of policy-making and government, and the barriers of constitutionality and legality were torn down, more restrictions were placed on democratic rights as defined in the Iranian constitution. The leadership demanded curbs on freedom of expression, freedom of assembly, and freedom of participation in national politics, all rights secured in the country's constitution. When Bazargan decided to run for the presidency in the 1980s, his credentials were not approved by Ayatollah Khomeini and he was dismissed.

Two reactions to this development were observed. One of these, which was political, was from the secular sector and the leftist tendencies in Iranian society. They were mostly of the opinion that religion and politics must be separated entirely. Some of the advocates of secularism as well as those of leftist orientations argued that there is a paradox between Islam and democracy, and that Islam as a religion is not compatible with democratic institutions in government.[45] But a different reaction to this development in the nation's power-politics was seen from the advocates of Islamic reformism. This group argued in opposition to the theory of *velayat-e faqih* and in favor of the compatibility of Islam and democracy, and the establishment of democratic institutions in the country within the framework of the accepted norms and values of the society.

Reformist Islam and the Role of Islam in Democratic Government

The first group among the Muslim intellectuals to react to this new development in Iranian post-revolutionary politics was Nehzat-e Azadi-e Iran (Liberation Movement of Iran – LMI), under the leadership of Mehdi Bazargan, the prime minister of the provisional government after the Iranian revolution. Contrary to the reaction of the secular and leftist groups, the supporters of reformist Islam, mainly from among the Muslim intellectuals, reacted to this new development by resorting to ideological counter-arguments, generated from the tenets of Islam, defending democratic values in government and society. In support of the argument that Islam is fully compatible with democracy, in defense of the people's right to participation in the political and social affairs of the society, and in defiance of the concentration of power in the hands of a few or an individual, the Islamic reformers resorted to Islamic precepts such as *shura* (consultation) and *amr be al-Ma'ruf va nahy an al-munkar* (commanding right and prohibiting wrong) to defend the concept of an Islamic government with democratic institutions. *Shura* was one of the critical conceptual tools to which Ayatollah Na'ini resorted at the beginning of this century, at the time of the Constitutional Revolution in Iran, in order to reject *istibdad* (dictatorship) and defend his argument in support of constitutionalism and a parliamentary system of government. In his pioneering treaty, *Tanbih al-Ummah va Tanzih al-Millah,* Na'ini defended the parliamentary system as a legitimate form of government, fulfilling the conditions of *shura* and the people's participation in the affairs of the nation. Na'ini argues in this book that:

> The authority of the Islamic government and its leader are very limited. The leader [of this government] cannot influence [any course of policy] and proceed for any action without taking into account the opinion and consultation of the people. Because all the people cannot be assembled for their opinions and not all are capable to offer right judgments, the pious and wise people should be assembled, consulted, and their opinions should be obtained ... The true authority of Islamic government is in the politics and affairs of the nation and is based on the participation of all people and upon consultation with these wise individuals elected through national public consultative assemblies.[46]

Two years after the coup against the democratic government of Muhammad Musaddiq, Na'ini's book was rediscovered and annotated in 1955 by Ayatollah Mahmud Taliqani, one of the leading voices of reformist Islam in Iran. In the introduction to this treaty, Taliqani referred to *shura* as a cornerstone of Na'ini's argument for a legitimate government, and emphasized further the role of consultation and participation in the politics of a legitimate, constitutional, and legal government. Contrary to Ayatollah Khomeini, who, in *Kashf-e Asrar* in the 1940s, attempted to secure a power base for the clergy in his desired type of government, Ayatollah Taliqani, in the reissued *Tanbih al-Ummah va Tanzih al-Millah* in the 1950s, attempted to secure the people's right of direct participation in politics and to introduce his ideal of government based upon the Islamic notion of *shura*. After the Iranian revolution, Taliqani was identified as a staunch supporter of *shura*, a legitimate base for Islamic democratic government, and on occasion showed his dismay over the views of those among the advocates of puritanical Islam who defended a special hierarchy of power led by the clergy. Critical of the arguments of the supporters of puritanism in the Assembly of Experts, which diminish the notion of *shura*, Taliqani argued a few months after the Iranian revolution:

> I stated hundreds of times that the notion of Shura is one of the most significant concepts in Islam. God said to the prophet [Muhammad], with his greatness, consult the people, consider them important so that they understand they have responsibility and they should not rely on the leader ... Still in the Assembly of Experts they argue about this Qur'anic concept and the way it has to be implemented in the society ... This is an important concept in Islam. It means the people must participate in consultation in their families and units of the society.[47]

The focal point in the arguments of Na'ini and Taliqani, the *shura*, denoting the necessity of participatory politics, was reiterated by supporters of reformist Islam after the Iranian revolution, not only to re-emphasize the Islamic basis of political participation, but also to stress the significance of this concept in the process of generating support and legitimacy for the government. This legitimacy was attainable, according to some of these arguments, only when the people participate in politics through *shura*, learning about issues, their responsibilities, and political processes. In other words, these writers used the concept of *shura* to explain how the process or processes of socialization must take place in a Muslim society. Ezzatullah Radmanesh, one of these writers, contends, "Through Shura, every individual is involved in learning about democracy and the ways through which guarding democratic institutions become possible."[48]

Reza Ustadi describes how the concept of *shura* was introduced by Islam to re-emphasize the right of and responsibility for political participation. According to him, Muhammad adopted this concept and consulted with the people for the following reasons. He wanted the people to learn about political processes and political issues, to offer their opinions so that he could learn of other views on political issues, to gain people's support for his government through generation of legitimacy, and finally for the people to understand that his government was not a dictatorship.[49]

A few months after the Iranian revolution, the puritanists defended *velayat-e faqih* against *shura* and against the people's direct participation in national power-politics. The Islamic Republic Party (IRP) published its first booklet, *Shi'ite va Shura*, in which it defended *velayat-e faqih* as a framework for an ideal form of government and criticized *shura* as a deficient concept incapable of offering solutions for governmental stability and efficiency. In this booklet, the IRP resorted to three incidents in Islamic history in order to prove both the inefficiencies of the concept and the fact that *shura* and consultation can have disastrous consequences. The first of these episodes involved the *shura* in Saqifeh Bani Sa'ideh which was held for the purpose of choosing a leader for the government after the death of Muhammad in 632; the second was the *shura* held after the death of Caliph Umar in 644 to choose his successor; and the third involved the *shura* in the battle of Siffin in 658. The IRP claimed in this booklet that, as the result of these three, *shura* were not satisfactory for Shi'ites, [thus] Shi'ism during its history has "followed unconditionally the [twelve Shi'ite] Imams and viewed Shura contemptuously." The booklet further resorted to a host of arguments including one that the first Shi'ite Imam, Ali, disapproved of the concept of *shura* and emphasized *velayat* (the imamate leadership) as the viable form of leadership and government.[50]

By resorting to these refutations of *shura*, the IRP was not interested in perceiving how historical facts proved or disproved its argument, but in generating skepticism about the counter-argument of *shura* as a viable form of participatory politics, discussed widely among Muslim intellectuals during and after the Iranian revolution. Abdul Ali Bazargan, the son of Mehdi Bazargan and an active member of the Liberation Movement of Iran inside the country, rebuffed the IRP's argument and defended the concept of *shura* and the direct participation of the people in the affairs of the country. In his book *Shura va Bey'at: Hakemiyyat-e Khuda dar Hukumat-e Mardum*, he defined *shura* as "the government of the people under the absolute authority of God." Bazargan argued that, "An Islamic government without Shura is not different from a dictatorship."[51] Mehdi Bazargan himself believed likewise, saying, "An Islamic government cannot be other than a democratic government relying on the nation and run by Shura."[52]

In his description of *shura*, Abdul Ali Bazargan resorted to Na'ini's book, Taliqani's arguments, historical facts, and especially the Qur'an and the tradition (*hadith*) of Muhammad. At the beginning of his book he quoted his mentor, Ayatollah Taliqani, defending the concept of *shura* by saying, "Oh Muslims, those who hear my voice inside and outside the country, this [*shura*] is the only way for reform [*islah*], movement, and revolutionary evolution of a country [toward progress]."[53] Bazargan further argues:

> If by Imam [leader], the spiritual leadership of the nation is in mind, then the people recognize such leader or leaders. But if by Imam, all leadership in the government and affairs of the country is considered, then this leader must be chosen by the people and gains legitimacy [*mashru'iyyat*] and accept-ability [*maqbuliyyat*] through Shura. In a system governed by Shura, the capable individuals can choose or nominate a leader who is wise and ... for the government. Then if the people agree, they can vote [*bey'at*] for him and impose their influence in the selection process. This is a system of majority which obtains legitimacy and acceptability through two steps ... Thus Islamic government is the realization of the absolute authority of God by the government of the majority ... In this government, the leader cannot be imposed on the people, but he has to be chosen by the people's free will and independence of opinion.[54]

Concerning the argument of some of the traditional Islamic scholars and the advocates of *velayat-e faqih* in puritanical Islam that the decisions of *shura* are not binding on the leader, the supporters of *shura* among the reformists argue:

> The leader must implement the decision of the people [in *shura*]. He should not influence arbitrarily this decision, which could lead to a lack of support of the people [for his government]. The leader should not be indecisive after the final conclusion is reached in the Shura, and should trust in God and implement decisions with authority and confidence.[55]

Throughout this argument, the attempt is made to invalidate the notion of *velayat-e faqih*, which, according to its advocates, negates the precept of *shura* and binding decisions of the people in this institution.

Among the clergy, there were many who opposed the theory of *velayat-e faqih*, some of whom wrote in defense of *shura*, participatory politics, and the election of governmental leadership by the people. Ayatollah

Mutahhari was one of those clergy who rejected the concept of guardianship (*velayat*) and argued in favor of representation (*vekalat*) in government. After arguing that any ruling government must be legitimate in the opinion of the people, he argues that there are two kinds of legitimacy, according to the Islamic interpretation of *ulama*, for the leader in a political system. In jurisprudence, Mutahhari contends, there is an argument supporting a kind of legitimacy stemming from *velayat*. Mutahhari was in favor not of this kind of leader and legitimacy as defined by the jurisconsults in Islam, but of a government representative of the people. He not only contends that the people should elect the government authorities, but also emphasizes the point that it is their right according to Islam to participate in this electoral process.[56]

A similar argument has been presented by Salehi Najaf Abadi, a well-known *alim* whose writings gained him a reputation for innovation and for a new interpretation of the Islamic tenets. For Najaf Abadi, the leader of an Islamic government is called *vali-e faqih*. But *faqih* for him does not necessarily mean someone who has graduated from the Islamic seminaries and met the requirement of traditional Islamic education; for Najaf Abadi and later for Ayatollah Muntazeri, he is someone who is knowledgeable about the affairs of the government and can be characterized as a pious and just individual. He contends, "The Vali-e Faqih [political leader] comes to existence through a contract between the people and the leader. Both sides must be satisfied with the terms of this contract ... If he [the leader] violates the terms of the contract, he can be dismissed by the experts [chosen by the people]."[57] He further argues, "Thus, Velayat-e Faqih means political representation of the people by the Faqih in the affairs of the people. And this is the government of the people by the people and for the people."[58]

Another leading religious scholar, Ayatollah Muntazeri, argues in favor of representational government and participatory politics in line with Najaf Abadi's discussion. He contends, "Assigning the responsibility of government to one person is based on a contract between the leader and the people, and voting [*bey'at*] for such a leader legitimizes his authority."[59] Ayatollah Muntazeri, in contrast to Ayatollah Khomeini, states that the argument that the *faqih* or *fuqaha* (plural of *faqih*) are responsible for the establishment and running of the government at the time of occulation does not have a strong base in Islamic sources and cannot withstand a vigorous examination.[60] For Muntazeri, the difference between a secular democracy and an Islamic government is that in the latter the leader must be pious and wise and the laws must be Islamic.[61] In his argument,

Muntazeri not only attempts to emphasize participatory politics and the basis of legitimacy of a government which is generated from the people, but also tries to repudiate the precepts of the theory of *velayat-e faqih*.

But as freedom of expression was considered a necessary condition for the establishment of *shura* and democratic institutions in a viable participatory government and society, the advocates of reformist Islam began, in their writings, to defend the freedoms which were severely restricted under the government of *velayat-e faqih*. The reformists legitimized and defended freedom of expression under the Islamic notion of *amr-e be al-ma'ruf va nahy an al-munkar*. One of the leading figures in the forefront of this battle was Mehdi Bazargan and the political party he was leading, the Liberation Movement of Iran (LMI). In one of his articles, "Religion and Freedom", Bazargan raised this question, "How can an individual dispense his religious responsibility in regard to Amr-e Be al-Ma'ruf va Nahy-e An al-Munkar without enjoying the freedom of opinion and expression and without judicial and political security?"[62]

In a book published by the LMI, on the topic that lack of freedom can harm a country's independence, it is written:

> One of the components of freedom is that the people of this country can observe, under the magnifying glass, the performances of the government and the actions of its office holders and criticize them when necessary with no fear. The people should have the freedom to rise up against any deviations witnessed and to write and speak of them according to their responsibility under the Islamic notion of Amr-e Be Ma'ruf va Nahy An al-Munkar.[63]

The discussion further proceeds to delineate characteristics of a "closed society" and an "open society." According to the LMI, the open societies of the developing nations are more stable:

> In contrast to closed societies in which governments are constantly in a state of accelerating instability and resorting to greater pressure and suppression, in open societies governments firmly establish their roots, expanding and affirming personal freedoms and increasing citizen participation in the politics and support for the government.[64]

During the Iran–Iraq war, the LMI resorted to the concept of *amr be al-ma'ruf* to secure the Islamic right of freedom of speech in order to criticize government war policies. However, the leadership in power rationalized their own monopoly, limiting discussions of this issue to a few individuals by giving final authority to the *vali-e faqih* to authorize the government in any action. Yet, the LMI consistently argued that the people and their representatives in the Majlis must be given that authority to oversee and criticize the government's war policy.[65] Critics of this type of monopolization of decision-making later concluded that the Iran–Iraq war reaffirmed the crucial need for consultation and the necessity for the people's participation in influencing policy.

Mehdi Bazargan addressed the issue of freedom in a society under the rule of Islam differently. Bazargan and his son, Abdul Ali Bazargan, substantiated their arguments in defense of freedom by resorting to the Qur'an and Islamic tradition. For Bazargan and other advocates of reformist Islam, Islamic tenets have secured individual rights and freedoms for the members of an Islamic society. Besides the argument that an Islamic government is democratic in nature and is run by the institution of *shura*, Bazargan states that:

> In an Islamic government, the people participate in running the affairs of the society, and there is a mutual commitment between the government and the people. In terms of expressing an opinion or criticism, not only is it allowed to be expressed with total freedom, but such criticism becomes obligatory [*vajib*] according to the principle of Amr-e Be al-Ma'ruf va Nahy-e An al-Munkar, especially when right [*haq*] must be defended and oppression and wrong must be confronted.[66]

Critical of the way the clergy and Ayatollah Khomeini dispensed power under the gloom of *velayat-e faqih* and the demand by the clergy for an unconditional following of its leadership by the people, Bazargan began to question the essence of the relationship between the *marja'* (Shi'ite source of imitation), in this case the political leader, and the followers. He asked:

> Does the territory of Ijtihad [self-reasoning in different issues by the *marja'* and declaration of *fatwa*] and Taqlid [following] extend to the point at which the followers must blindly do so even in their understanding of the issues? Is it the case that the people should not understand beyond his understanding, should not ask questions and should not have any demand from the leadership? This Ijtihad is a constraint on freedom of thought and expression.[67]

Bazargan refers to the history of Islam and especially how the Prophet Muhammad conducted the affairs of the early Islamic community to prove that *velayat-e faqih* lacks historical support and that the Muslim government must function within a democratic framework. He even goes so far as to argue in favor of non-Muslim rights of criticism of the Muslim government in an Islamic society. He criticizes the *fuqaha* for their insensitivity toward issues concerning freedom of expression for Muslims and non-Muslims in an Islamic society. He contends that because the *fuqaha* have not been directly involved in the past in issues concerning government, they have not developed viable frameworks for the working of an Islamic government.[68] His son, Abdul Ali Bazargan, follows a similar line of argument in his books, *Freedom in the Qur'an* and *Freedom in the Nahjulbalaqa*, in defense of freedom and individual rights in an Islamic society.[69]

In response to Khomeini's theory of the absolute authority of the *faqih* (*velayat-e mutlaqeh-e faqih*), Bazargan and the Liberation Movement of Iran produced a text entitled *Tafsil va Tahlil-e Velayat-e Mutlaqeh-e Faqih*, in which the theory and its precepts are questioned and rejected. The book holds a unique position among those critical of the theory, since it was the only book published by a group of non-clergy with scholarly methods challenging the precepts of *velayat-e faqih* while Khomeini was still alive. In the book, the LMI goes into detail in order to reject the theories of *velayat-e faqih* and *velayat-e mutlaqeh-e faqih* by resorting to an ideological and not a political argument. The contention of the book is that, contrary to the argument of the advocates of *velayat-e faqih*, there is no basis for this theory of government in Islam. Under one heading, "Velayat-e Mutlaqeh-e Faqih does not have any basis in Islam and it is a polytheism [*shirk*]," the LMI argues:

> The advocates of the theory of Velayat-e Faqih, including Mullah Ahmad Naraqi and Ayatollah Khomeini, did not substantiate any of their arguments with reference to the Qur'an. Some individuals defending this theory in the past have resorted to a few verses in the Qur'an. However, not only are there no references to support the concept of Velayat-e Faqih, monarchy, political leadership, Fuqaha, spiritual personalities, or clergy in any Qur'anic verses, but the Qur'an has condemned, at the same time, any claims by anyone to partnership with God in having absolute authority over the people.[70]

The merit of this argument was in its strong wording and Qur'anically substantiated position, one which has never been offered elsewhere in refutation of this theory since the Iranian revolution.

In the last few years, several factors have contributed to the intensification of the debate over democracy and democratic institutions in Iranian society. These include the death of Ayatollah Khomeini in 1988, the disillusionment of a substantial portion of Iranian society with governmental policies, especially in areas of liberty and individual rights, the imposition of more restrictions over freedom and authoritarian infringements of people's constitutional rights, and finally people's observation of a strong inclination among authorities running the government toward a full sway of authoritarianism. The advocates of reformist Islam have launched afresh a campaign to promote democratic values in government and society. The word "democratic", characterizing the nature of the Islamic government, was suggested by Mehdi Bazargan to Khomeini for the first time in Paris at the end of 1978. He proposed to Ayatollah Khomeini that the government after the Iranian revolution be termed the "Democratic Government of the Islamic Republic of Iran" instead of "Islamic Republic of Iran." This suggestion was rejected by Khomeini, who contested that Islamic government was democratic in nature. The discussion of a concept of "Islamic democratic government" by Bazargan has generated fervor and gained momentum within the last few years. One of the leading figures to join forces in defense of religious democratic government (*hukumat-e democratic-e dini*) is Abdul Karim-e Soroush. In the tradition of philosophers and social thinkers, yet with his own innovative approach, Soroush has attempted to address new issues in the realm of religion, government, and democratic values.

The first question for Soroush is how an individual's perception of religious concepts can change and evolve and how this perception can influence various choices anyone can make concerning different issues, including politics, in the realm of human society. In his well-known book, *Qabz va Bast-e Theorik-e Shari'at,* Soroush argues that human understanding of religious concepts is always in an evolutionary process and is subject to change even though specific concepts remain unchanged. He further argues that any understanding of a religious concept can stand only as long as a better argument or understanding is not able to replace it.[71] In other words, no one can have a monopoly over the absolute understanding of a religious concept as long as there is freedom of expression and debate in a given society. When it comes to politics, the implication of this argument is that no one can claim the absolute truth about any theory he or she offers about the way an ideal government should be structured. Only through debate and experience can one understand why one kind of government is better than the other and why some forms can generate more legitimacy than others.

As Islam has been understood or explained in a variety of ways to justify the necessity of adopting a course of action or policy, and rights have been violated by resorting to specific interpretations of religion and reasoning under the authority of the *faqih,* Soroush has attempted to go beyond religion and resorts to issues possessing extra-religious values to define the qualities of an ideal government. In his arguments he invests heavily in the intellectual and universal values generated by various societies throughout history. He initiates this endeavor by drawing the boundaries of his expectations of how an acceptable religion can fulfill the requirements of universal values such as justice and freedom. According to Soroush:

> A religion must be humane, and this respect for humanity by a religion is a reason to prove that it is a true religion. If the religion is humane, then its government [religious government] is also legitimate. Thus, respect for human rights, including justice and freedom, not only confirms the democratic nature of a government, but also the religious nature of it ... Respect for justice and humanity is a condition for accepting a religion. This means that a religion which does not respect and consider human rights and human needs of justice and freedom cannot be accepted. A religion must be rightful, rationally and ethically.[72]

This criterion for a true religion sets the stage for other arguments by Soroush in which he attempts to convince his audience that concepts such as justice and freedom which are advocated by democratic societies are at the same time at the core of Islam as a faith. The conclusion, then, is that an Islamic government cannot be anything else but democratic. This notion is shared by other reformers, including Bazargan, who also believe that Islamic government is either democratic or it is not an Islamic government.

In terms of democratic values and how they should be addressed, Soroush goes beyond religious arguments and attempts to create a separate framework for analysis. The reason for this is obvious: Soroush is well aware that if he discusses what Islam has to offer in any specific area, especially in the domain of politics and society, those clergy who perceive themselves as being experts of religion will impose their conceptual limitations on his argument. Soroush contends:

> The natural rights of humans cannot be defined in any other way except to agree that their protection can usher in a rational and humane life. It can also bring prosperity, security and progress to human society. These rational ideals, such as justice, prosperity and freedom from discrimination, dogmatism, conflict, ignorance, oppression ... are the fruit of the history of human experimentation. These ideals are accepted by all rational and reasonable thinking individuals and cannot be easily rejected because of religious dogmatism.[73]

Concerning this the willingness among the clergy to impose their religious dogma on society, Soroush argues:

History gives testimony to the fact that religious regulations by and religious thoughts among clergy and religious leaders have changed and evolved dramatically. There once was a time in which the church would burn those who opposed its dominant doctrines, and Muslims could not imagine that one day women might participate in the legislative process. The essence of these views has changed. Thus, no one can consider such constantly changing and evolving views as the precepts of God and human rights and invite or compel the people to accept them.[74]

Mehdi Bazargan addresses this question differently. He argues:

We should not think that all those who broke barriers of human values and violated freedoms were necessarily bad people. We should not think that in the Middle Ages, the church was imposing its will on the people with bad intentions. Many of the leaders of the church at that time were pious fathers full of mercy and without self interest and aggrandizement. Every religion or religious leader that takes responsibility for the imposition of the government of God on the people, once limited within the dogmatism of a belief system and disregarding the realities of this world and the rights of its individuals, must perceive the natural consequences including ignorance, oppression and compulsion.[75]

The basic argument of both is that religious dogmatism inevitably leads toward the violation of rights and the imposition of a specific doctrine on society. A similar argument was proffered by Ayatollah Na'ini in the Iranian constitutional movement at the beginning of this century. Na'ini described and condemned two types of dictatorships: religious and political.[76]

Soroush is also sensitive about conditions under which an Islamic democratic government can be established. Such a government, he says, can be established only in a religious and not in a secular society. In response to those who are ambivalent about or oppose the democratic nature of Islamic government, Soroush contends:

If they argue that we cannot have a religious democratic government in a non-religious society, and this government cannot satisfy the people in this society, they are right and their argument is indisputable. In that society [non-religious] the best government is a non-religious democratic government. But if they argue that we cannot ever have a religious democratic government even in a religious society, it is a dubious argument. It is appropriate to say that religious democratic governments are for religious societies and in these societies it is not democratic to have non-religious democratic governments.[77]

Here Soroush, like Bazargan, emphasizes society's willingness to accept

Islamic rule without compulsion. In a similar vein Mutahhari argues, "Did Islam come only to establish a society in which the people follow its rule? No ... Islam came to create love and faith ... in the heart of the people. Faith cannot be imposed on the people."[78]

But how can one establish a sturdy relationship between a religion and democratic values? This relationship can be firmly established, according to Soroush, only when a stable relationship can be maintained between religion (*shar'*) and intellect (*aql*). He contends:

> The religious governments can be democratic or non-democratic. To see if they are democratic or not, one should look first at the amount of their reliance on collective intellect [*aql Jam'i*], and second on the degree of their respect for human rights. The union of democracy and religion represents the success in reconciling intellect and religion ... In order to democratize a religious government, flexibility in the understanding of religion and preference for intellect are needed. This intellect is of course collective intellect, which is based on the participation of all and relys on human experience. Obtaining this collective intellect is not possible except through a democratic process ... The democratic governments rely on collective intellect to mediate conflicts and resolve problems. In religious governments this judgment is biased toward the religion, and in dictatorships the judgment is in the hands of an individual and imposed by force. But we know that religion itself does not participate in the process of this judgment. There are different kinds of understanding and interpretation of religion which play that role in the process of this judgment. This process is a rational process.[79]

Soroush, like Bazargan and other reformers, is critical of the current state of jurisprudence (*fiqh*) in Iran.[80] He is very much in favor of a dynamic jurisprudence which preoccupies itself with issues in the realm of ideals, and not a dogmatic *fiqh* with limited scope and preoccupied with religious regulations. He argues:

> The forced following for jurists' opinions should not be the characteristics and criteria of a religious society. As al-Ghazali described, the science of Fiqh has roots in this world. When Fiqh stripped itself from a free and brave faith, it became more worldly. With this worldly science, one cannot build an ideal and righteous society.[81]

But Soroush is not only criticizing dogmatic *fiqh*, he is also critical of the relationship between the *faqih* and the followers and the prescription for blind following in *Islam-e fiqahati* (Islam based on the judgment of the *fuqaha*). This blind following has more than anything else helped dogmatic *fiqh* to establish its domination over society and the politics of the country. Soroush contends:

The faith of the [blind] followers like their conceptions and like their actions are similar and exposed to influence. But is the faith of those who question and search the same [as the blind followers]? Is blind following [taqlid] worthy of anything? As a religious society becomes more religious, it becomes more free and more in quest of freedom and it replaces dogmatic faith with a faith based upon inquiry.[82]

Concerning the nature of the Islamic democratic government and its laws, Soroush argues:

[In an Islamic government] the people recognize the authority of God in the laws, and this is the right of the faithful ... But the rights to understand these laws, their interpretation according to the interest of the society and justice, are secured for the people. Consequently, the people's encounter with these laws is similar to their encounter with nature. Although the people are constrained within nature, they are creative.[83]

At the end of his second long article, "Mudara Va Mudiriyyat-e Mu'menan," and in defense of an Islamic democratic government, Soroush refers again to Na'ini, who was a major influence on all advocates of reformist Islam, especially in the domain of participatory politics and Islamic democracy. He concludes:

The religious dictatorship which Ayatollah Na'ini objected to cannot be dismantled except through a democratic intellect. The religious dictatorship is the worst of dictatorships because the religious leader who is a dictator believes that [ruling in a dictatorial manner] is not only his right but also his responsibility. Only by a democratic religion and protection of a true faith can one guard himself against those [dictators' perceived] rights and responsibility.[84]

But the reformists were also engaged on a different front, challenging the domination of power and restriction of liberties by the puritanists. As part of the Iranian constitution reflected the idealism of the revolution in securing rights and freedom, the reformists blamed the puritanists for negating these rights and infringing the basic principles of the contract in the Iranian constitution. The argument surrounds Article 9 of the constitution and similar precepts in this document. In Article 9 it is written:

In the Islamic Republic of Iran, the freedom, independence, unity, and territorial integrity of the country are inseparable from each other, and their preservation is the duty of the government and of all individual citizens. No individual, group or authority has the right to infringe in the slightest way the political, cultural, economic, and military independence or the territorial integrity of Iran under the pretext of exercising freedom. Similarly, no authority has the right to withdraw legitimate freedoms, even by establishing laws and regulations for that purpose, under the pretext of preserving the independence and territorial integrity of the country.[85]

On numerous occasions, Bazargan and the Liberation Movement of Iran referred to this and other Articles, including 23, 24, 25, 26, 28, 32, 34, and 108, to reprimand the government for its violation of the rights guaranteed in the constitution of the country. In one such statement they contend:

> The foundations for freedoms of opinion and profession, lack of censorship of the press and means of communication, and other freedoms have been secured in the constitution of the country. The realization of these freedoms, which is a necessary condition for the progress of this nation in different fields, is one of the great ideals of our nation. The realization of other ideals is not possible without total freedom for this nation.[86]

As radicalism was taking root in the society and puritanists and populists were directly and indirectly supporting this new wave in the Iranian society, violation of constitutional principles in the areas of freedom and rights was a matter of serious concern for many among the reformers. In an interview, two weeks before his assassination, Ayatollah Mutahhari said, "If this revolution intends to restrict freedoms, it will create its own plague. And if it is not sensitive to social justice, it will be exposed to danger."[87] This concern was shared by many who later witnessed the rise of radicalism with the taking of the American Embassy in Tehran in 1980 and the support of the leadership, puritanists, and populists for this action.

The debate over the form of government and society in post-revolutionary Iran continues as the supporters of reformist Islam and puritanical Islam resort to arguments generated from their distinct interpretations. Although political domination and the search for power have primarily a strong political component, in the case of Iran they have also a religious flavor, if not a religious justification. Those puritanists advocating *velayat-e mutlaqeh-e faqih* rely mostly on an interpretation of Islam in government and politics which is authority-oriented, has a totalitarian outlook, and disregards the human rights and democratic essence of participatory politics. At the core of this orientation lies a belief system relying on a specific orientation in traditional *fiqh* that considers humans to be "minors" (*saqir*), "forlorn" (*mahjur*), "incompetent" (*naqes*), and in need of guardianship (*qayyem*). This "guardian" concept, which was used mostly in Shi'ite jurisprudence to regulate the affairs and secure the rights of minors at the time of their parents' death, was extended by some to the social and political affairs of the community. The foundation of Ayatollah Khomeini's argument in defense of *velayat-e faqih* is based on the precepts of this traditional jurisprudence. In his arguments defending *velayat-e faqih*, Khomeini contends, "The people are incompetent [*naqes*], imperfect [*nakamel*], and are in need of perfection [*kamal*]."[88] To complete this journey toward perfection, he argues, the people are in need of a "head of government [*hakem*] who is a trustworthy [*amin*] and pious [*saleh*] guardian."[89] Ayatollah Beheshti regarded guardians differently, as he spoke in favor of *dictatory-e sulaha* (the dictatorship of the pious individuals) equivalent to benevolent dictatorship.

On the other side of the spectrum are the advocates of reformist Islam, whose interpretation of Islam as regards politics and government has roots in the contentions of the Islamic political philosophers, and not necessarily political jurisprudence, and in individuals like al-Farabi (870–950) who wrote in *Al-Madinah al-Fadilah* (Ideal State), *Siyasah Madaniyyah* (On the Government of City-State) and *Tahsil al-Sa'adah* (Book on Attaining Happiness) about the ideal government and the differences between despotic and democratic states.[90] In contrast to those of the puritanists, the political views of the reformists have been shaped in favor of pluralism and human rights, especially in areas of freedom of expression and participation in politics, and against the consolidation of power in favor of any group within the society.

These two views, one by the advocates of puritanical Islam and the other by reformist Islam, continue to influence not only the debate over the government and society in Iran, but also the direction of politics. The puritanists supporting the theory of *velayat-e faqih* insist on the *faqih* as a true source of authority generating legitimacy for political institutions and decisions. They trust the wisdom of one person, the *faqih*, to plan the destiny of a nation. They continue to believe that the *faqih* is qualified to make decisions that ordinary people cannot. In an interview, Muhammad Kazem Anwar Luhi, the chief editor of *Resalat Newspaper*, and a member of a division of the puritanists, argued that when Ayatollah Khomeini decided to end the war with Iraq in 1988, he knew something that no one else in the country could know. In an attempt to justify Khomeini's decision, Anwar Luhi further argued that it was only after this decision that the Iraqi forces were demolished by the second Gulf War.[91]

Currently, the ardent supporters of the theory of *velayat-e faqih* are pushing hard to designate a *marja'*, following the death of Ayatollah Araki, who will also be supportive of the theory. With such a *marja'* and a new president supporting the theory and Ayatollah Khamene'i in the next election, this orientation would be successful in dominating even more institutions of power within the country. The role of the Majlis may be crucial in this new development, depending on who sits in the next parliament.

On the other side of the spectrum, Ebrahim Yazdi, a former foreign minister and a leading figure in the Liberation Movement of Iran and among the reformists, believes that the time for the establishment of democratic institutions is approaching in Iran. He argues that the Iranian revolution ended *saltanat* (monarchy) in Iran and that the experience of post-revolutionary Iran discredited the historical reputation of the clergy.[92] According to him, the time has come for the gradual transformation of the political system into an Islamic democratic government. The new developments in Iran, which are reflected in open debate over democracy within Iranian society, the publication of several magazines by the supporters of democratic institutions in the country, and the debate and discussion over the national economy and politics in different publications within Iran, are all signs encouraging optimism about the democratization of the government and society. Some individuals feel the need to prepare the society for this transformation. Bazargan argues that:

> All the cultural and informational institutions of the country must teach the people and explain to them that a country cannot live without freedom, government of the people, and democratic institutions ... We have to understand freedom, we have to believe in it and implement it with truthfulness, trust, and love.[93]

The unfinished revolution makes any prediction about what course Iranian politics may take in the near future very difficult. What is obvious is that puritanism was not successful in establishing a viable political system in Iran. Does it mean that the conditions are ripe for the transformation of the political system inside Iran or that the reformists are able to expedite this process as they did in the revolution? We shall have to wait and see.

CHAPTER 2

The Governing Institutions of the Islamic Republic of Iran: The Supreme Leader, the Presidency, and the Majlis

Bahman Baktiari

Theda Skocpol's *States and Social Revolutions* compared three great transformations of the past: the French revolution of the late 1700s, the
Russian revolution of 1917 through the 1930s, and the Chinese revolution
of 1911 through the 1960s. She defined all of these as "social revolutions"
that embodied rapid, basic transformations of a society's state and class
structures accompanied by and in part accomplished through popular
revolts from below.[1] The Iranian revolution of 1979 was not that different
from these great revolutions. It was a significant socio-political movement
that through a long process culminated in the uprisings of 1978–79. It
shocked the world and set in motion a process that continues to baffle
many observers.

At the time of this writing, sixteen years have passed since the Islamic
revolution. During these years, the ruling elite has managed to withstand
challenges and threats ranging from internal armed opposition to eight
years of devastating war started by Saddam Hussein of Iraq. Most
important of all, the ruling elite sustained the stability of the Islamic
Republic after the death of Ayatollah Khomeini in June 1989, and the
war between a United Nations Coalition and Iraq in 1991.

In the context of the enormous attention given to internal rivalries
and factionalism, few observers have linked the regime's survival to the
institutionalization process and the creation of a unique political system
in a country that has had a long history of monarchical structure. Therefore, the following discussion will evaluate the performances of post-
revolutionary institutions of the supreme leader, the presidency, and the
Majlis (parliament). The evaluation will explain the role of these institutions in the policy-making process, as well as the ruling elite's success

47

in sustaining their stability. In contrast to the regimes who prefer stability through the consolidation of central control and a development program that would enhance their position and the security of their state, the ruling elite in revolutionary Iran has opted for popular participation within certain parameters, decentralization of state power, an ideological/cultural strategy to adapt and revise the ideals of the Islamic revolution of 1979, and conflict management through informal procedures. This makes the Iranian system, at least in formal terms, more "democratic" than many other governments.

The Post of Supreme Leader

From supreme jurisconsult to supreme leader   As long as Ayatollah Khomeini headed an opposition movement, he envisioned a "new Iran" modeled on early Islam. Once in power, Khomeini and his disciples knew that they could not rule by means of revolutionary slogans. They were called upon to take over the affairs of the state rather than discuss them. The revolutionaries wasted no time in eliminating the vestiges of the mon-archical regime. Before coming to power, Khomeini had set up a Revolutionary Council to implement this task by organizing elections for an Assembly of Experts to write a new constitution.

The framework of the Islamic Republic's political system was deter-mined by an 83-member Assembly of Experts, which met in 1979. The clerical faction led by the late Ayatollah Beheshti successfully defeated the secular nationalists' attempts to draft a document that did not include a significant role for Ayatollah Khomeini.[2] The role envisioned for Khomeini was that of *faqih*, the supreme jurisconsult, to lead the nation in the absence of Imam Mahdi (the hidden Twelfth Imam who is expected to return as the Messiah). The concept was derived from Khomeini's lectures in the late 1960s and early 1970s, when he was in exile in Iraq waging a relentless campaign against the Shah's regime. His endeavor to bring about an Islamic state ruled by the *faqih* was tied to his successful strategy of overthrowing the monarchy.[3]

The initiative for making Khomeini the *faqih* was originally advocated by middle-ranking clerics and provincial clerics during the elections for the Assembly of Experts in the summer of 1979. It is suggested that this initiative emerged as a defensive reaction to the opposition from secular intellectuals, and out of the fear that the clerics may be pushed out of the political process.[4] During the debates in the Assembly of Experts only three members felt secure enough to cast an abstention vote, whereas

57 voted for Article 107, creating a position that exceeded the powers granted to the king in the 1906 constitution.

Articles 107 to 112 define the powers of the *faqih*. He controls the armed forces, declares war, and selects four of the seven members of the Supreme National Defense Council, the highest military decision-making body in the country. He has unlimited powers with regard to civil administration, and determining the suitability of presidential candidates. He also has the power of appointing six members of the Council of Guardians in the Majlis, whose responsibility is to ensure that legislation is compatible with Islam.

Overall, the supreme jurisconsult is the highest authority in the Islamic Republic and possesses extensive powers. As stated by a member of the Assembly of Experts, Makerem Shirazi, "these articles are crucial to the future of the Islamic Republic, and even though I support this principle, I feel that it will endanger the constitution, the future of the Islamic revolution, and for this reason I must speak up and ask that we modify these articles." During Shirazi's statement, another member repeatedly interrupted him and accused him of disloyalty.[5] The late Ayatollah Beheshti, who wrote the articles in the constitution, argued that: "Khomeini has been accepted and recognized by the majority of the people and therefore his leadership is not an imposition on the people."[6]

As *faqih*, Ayatollah Khomeini expanded his power and institutionalized the office by establishing three personal interrelated networks. First, he established his authority over important state bureaucracies by appointing his personal representatives (known as the imam's representatives) in all major government agencies. In appointing these people, he instructed them to be vigilant and involved in all affairs. An "imam's representative" was directly above the minister and other functionaries and received his instructions not from the prime minister, but from Khomeini's office. They were valuable in the first years of the Islamic revolution when the revolutionaries initiated a campaign of purging the bureaucracies of individuals deemed not to be ideologically committed. The representatives were Khomeini's "eyes and ears" and were accountable only to him.

Second, shortly after arriving in Iran, Khomeini issued a decree setting up an Islamic Revolutionary Guards Corps, as well as a network of revolutionary committees, whose goals were to neutralize any threat to the state. The Revolutionary Guards checked the powers of the regular armed forces, and the committees controlled the masses and the streets. By controlling these important security forces, Khomeini not only facilitated the victory of his supporters in the post-revolutionary power struggle, but also institutionalized the authority of his office by creating a mini-state within the state.

The third area of institutionalization involved Khomeini's consolidation of the teacher–student relationship in clerical circles such as the Faizeyeh Seminary in Qum. The roots of this relationship went back to the 1960s, when Khomeini directed several anti-Shah demonstrations, and his students were instrumental in these activities. Leaders of this group were President Rafsanjani, Mahmoud Doa'i (current editor of *Ettela'ate,* the largest daily in Tehran), Hojjati-Kermani, and Khosrowshahi (former ambassador to the Vatican). Rafsanjani explained the impact of Khomeini's revolutionary stance against the Shah in the 1960s: "Mr. Khomeini was the vanguard, and struggled more firmly than many others in the cause. I, who was with him, was his student and found his approach to my liking, drew closer to him. That year [1962], for the first time, I began political activity."[7] After the revolution, he placed them in powerful positions, as leaders of Friday prayer services, religious organizations, and thousands of mosques.

Throughout his decade of rule, Khomeini effectively used these networks to consolidate the Islamic Republic. His charisma and *marja'iat* made him all the more influential in elevating his office. On religious matters, Khomeini was asked to issue judgments on pilgrimage, private property in Islam, inheritance laws, nationalization of trade and land reform, and banking. His decrees were law, and all government agencies were mandated to implement them. On political matters, Khomeini used his authority to determine the fate of the American hostages, the war with Iraq, and the controversial book written by Salman Rushdie.

His power was also crucial in domestic conflict management and factionalism in the Islamic Republic. He stood above the factions, determined what is tolerable in the Islamic Republic, and interfered only when the political order was threatened. In one case of factional conflict in 1988, Prime Minister Musavi, Speaker of the Majlis Rafsanjani, and President Khamene'i asked Khomeini "to delineate our duties for reconstruction and allow Ahmad Khomeini [the Ayatollah's son], to join us in a group to supervise the effort." In rejecting this, Khomeini warned them about projecting the appearance of disunity and admonished them for not having solved their differences.[8] Perhaps the most important step toward institutionalizing the position of the *faqih* was the decision to seek a successor to Khomeini as early as 1982. With his approval, the Assembly of Experts designated Ayatollah Hossein Ali Montazeri as the successor. The latter was born in a peasant family in the city of Najafabad in 1921.

He studied under Khomeini and in the early 1960s became a teacher in the Faizeyeh seminary in Qum. Khomeini's closeness to Montazeri was well illustrated by the fact that Montazeri lived for several months in the house owned and occupied by Khomeini before the latter's expulsion in late 1964. His revolutionary background and relationship to Khomeini were the main reasons for his selection as successor. Once the Assembly of Experts formally announced its decision, Montazeri's portraits were displayed alongside those of Khomeini, and the media followed suit by singing Montazeri's praises. A new title was given to him: *faqih-e aliqadr.*

Protecting the institution of faqih: removing Montazeri The decision to select Montazeri as the next *faqih* was problematic from the beginning. Despite good revolutionary credentials and a long history of opposition to the Shah's regime, Montazeri could never replace Khomeini. The latter's claim to the titles of "imam" and "guardian of the revolution" rested on spirituality, charisma, and respect from the religious hierarchy in Qum. In comparison, Montazeri lagged far behind. He lacked his mentor's theological scholarship, despite the title of grand ayatollah, which was given to him by the media after his selection. One report soon after his selection accurately predicted his future: "Unlike Ayatollah Khomeini, he will not be able to stand above the battle. He may have to engage in a succession struggle against powerful, ambitious, and clever leaders like Khamene'i and Rafsanjani."[9]

Montazeri's political fate was determined in October 1986 when he failed to prevent the arrest of a number of his dependents who had opposed the secret contacts with the United States. He never let go of this defeat. In a detailed letter addressed to Montazeri, Ahmad Khomeini expressed "profound regrets" that Montazeri failed to "heed the Imam's calls." The letter, dated 29 April 1989, was published in full in all the dailies in Tehran on 17 May 1989, covering more than three pages. Ahmad Khomeini wrote: "On 4 October 1986, the Imam wrote to Montazeri stressing that the Ayatollah's reputation was being seriously questioned in light of murder and other charges brought against Mehdi Hashemi" (brother of Montazeri's son-in-law). Montazeri wrote back in a defiant tone, defending Mehdi Hashemi, and stating that he would "stay away from politics," meaning that he would no longer support the official policies of the Islamic Republic.

From the summer of 1988 on, Montazeri went on the offensive against all the senior officials of the Islamic Republic. In a letter dated 1 October 1988, Montazeri, in a very pointed manner, told Prime Minister Musavi:

We will get no results with frequent arrests, harshness, punishments, detentions, and killings. Besides, we will cause discontent among the people who are the country's and the revolution's capital assets. We will cause irreparable injustice to many people because of the narrow-minded, draconian and uncaring officials in charge of the ministry of security and information.[10]

Montazeri continued his offensive during the celebrations of the tenth anniversary of the revolution. In his speech, he decried the "shouting of slogans that shut us off from the rest of the world." Signs of Rafsanjani's discomfort with Montazeri was revealed in an editorial in a pro-Rafsanjani daily:

It is a fact, a bitter one though, that in the past decade, we busied ourselves with sloganeering, rather than taking action ... A more critical problem, however, is the absence of an approach based on principles, to Ayatollah Montazeri's viewpoints. This failure stems from yet another problem of apprehending dimension, i.e., the multiplicity of decision-making centers in the country.[11]

It was a matter of days before Khomeini lost his patience. In a stern response, he sent a warning to Montazeri: "I declare explicitly to those who have access to radio, television, and the press, that as long as I am around I shall not allow the government to fall into the hands of the (*liberalha*)."[12] In their last meeting at the end of February 1989, it seemed certain that the political relationship between "tutor" and "student" had come to an end. According to Ahmad Khomeini, Montazeri spoke "for more than half and hour. The Imam kept silent." When he stood up to leave, the imam said, "Most of what you have said was untrue. May God forgive me and bring about my death."

With Ayatollah Montazeri's resignation, the vacancy for Khomeini's successor was officially opened. The Western media speculated that this was a blow to the "moderate" camp, i.e., Rafsanjani.[13] However, the events discussed show that this conclusion is incorrect. The process of Montazeri's demise went back to the 1986 events associated with the Iran–Contra affair. He was dealt a blow by those who had been involved in that relationship. According to one source, Ahmad Khomeini himself had been pushing for Montazeri's dismissal as early as late 1986.[14]

The new faqih: *Ayatollah Ali Khamene'i*   On 3 June 1989, shortly before midnight, Ahmad Khomeini informed the Islamic world that "the lofty spirit of the Leader of Muslims and free men everywhere, His Excellency Imam Khomeini, has gone to heaven." The Khomeini decade ended without a designated successor. Less than 24 hours after his death, the 83-member Assembly of Experts began debating the issue of post-Khomeini leadership. Even in his political testament, Khomeini did not mention anyone as a qualified successor. The Islamic Republic faced a serious leadership crisis: There was no one who had the *combined* qualities of religious and political stature similar to Ayatollah Khomeini. The manner in which the crisis was solved sustained the continuity of the institutions of the *faqih*.

Ayatollah Ali Meshkini, president of the Assembly, stated that in a letter he had written to Imam Khomeini in April 1989, the imam "had said that he prefers a man to succeed him rather than a council." The reason was that "all three to five members of the Leadership Council had to be qualified, and to find such individuals in a short time was difficult."[15] According to a member of the Assembly, the proposal to have a council was defeated by 44 to 32. It is important to note the large number of those who desired a council, which reflected that, for many, the option before them, Khamene'i, was not acceptable. Nevertheless, the Assembly finally voted for Khamene'i, with 60 votes in favor and 14 against.[16]

Khamene'i did not have the religious credentials, and a major concern was that many of Khomeini's followers might switch allegiance to other senior *ulama* who had not been completely supportive of the Islamic Republic's policies. The question is why Khamene'i was selected, when in Qum there were three prominent religious leaders: Golpaygani, Mar'ashi, and Qumi. The Assembly announced that Ayatollah Araki was to be the religious leader. He was a hundred years old at the time of this announcement, and died on 1 December 1994. Thus, in the past two years, Ayatollahs Kho'i, Golpaygani, and Mar'ashi have died, and this has plunged the Iranians into a serious dilemma for there are no more senior Iranian *marja'* acceptable on a large scale. In summary, the Assembly of Experts' selection of Khamene'i was not based on the principle that the *faqih* must be a *marja'*. Rather, the Assembly revised the constitution in order to fit the selection. Ayatollah E. Amini stated that Khamene'i's selection was "according to the condition of the day, and it is unlikely that in the future a qualified supreme religious leader would reach this position." In a letter from Montazeri, the latter told Khamene'i that, "God willing, you will consult with their eminences, the Ayatollahs, while dealing with important and epoch-making issues."[17]

An overview of Khamene'i's style and ideology: 1989–94 Ayatollah Khamene'i is five years younger than Rafsanjani (Khamene'i was born in 1939, Rafsanjani in 1934), and certainly without Rafsanjani's support his selection would not have been possible. They had known each other since the 1960s, and their close collaboration in the post-revolutionary period was common knowledge. But Khamene'i was not a senior theologian, he was a *hojjatoleslam*. It was not expected that he would become another Ayatollah Khomeini.

During the first few months of his rule, Khamene'i maintained a low profile and sought to sustain the continuity of the institution by establishing his "fairness" in dealing with competing factions. He did not change the vast personal network put in place by Ayatollah Khomeini, and made very few appointments. He talked more in terms of carrying the torch left by Ayatollah Khomeini, like refusing to rescind the *fatwa* against Salman Rushdie, and continued to denounce the United States in the same language, calling it "the Great Satan." Moreover, Rafsanjani's election as president in August 1989 raised the expectation that a new pragmatic alliance was emerging.

This expectation was fueled by frequent public statements made by the two. Khamene'i endorsed Rafsanjani's First Five-Year Plan, and during the Kuwaiti crisis, he allowed Rafsanjani to formulate Iran's neutrality position while he engaged in public criticism of the United States, effectively denying the radical faction the opportunity of accusing the government of being complacent.[18] Finally, during the Majlis elections in April 1992, which were the first important post-Khomeini elections in the country, Khamene'i effectively deprived the radical faction of ideological support by refusing to address their contention that the government was limiting their participation by confining the process of candidacy (see the section on the Majlis, below).

Since 1992, Khamene'i has gradually transformed the institution of *faqih* by increasing his political staff and advisers. He has appointed representatives who report to him on issues such as the progress of the Iran–Iraq peace process and prisoner of war exchange. It is reported that many of his former cabinet officials (Khamene'i was president from 1981 to 1989) who are in Rafsanjani's government still maintain strong links to his office (e.g., Foreign Minister Ali Velayati and Petroleum Minister Aqazadeh). Furthermore, Khamene'i has identified himself more with the conservative faction in the Majlis led by Nateq Nuri. In 1993, the director-general of radio and television, Muhammad Hashemi (brother of Rafsanjani), had come under intense criticism from this faction for allowing the broadcasting of too many "non-Islamic" programs. After the leadership of the Majlis consulted with Khamene'i, the latter used his authority to remove Hashemi.

On the religious front Khamene'i has not been able to establish strong ties with the *ulama* in Qum. When the senior Ayatollah Mohammad Ali Araki died on 29 November 1994, the head of the judiciary, Ayatollah Yazdi, called Khamene'i "the logical successor." He advanced two arguments on behalf of Khamene'i. First, Yazdi stated that Khamene'i "is fully qualified on the basis of traditional criteria to be recognized both as a jurist and as a *marja'* and is on par with other senior clerics in this domain." Second, Yazdi claimed that at a time "when a true Islamic government is in power, something more is needed from the most senior religious authority than the traditional qualifications of piety, justice, knowledge of religious and ritual matters, and of Islamic law." He stated that "knowledge of current affairs, international relations and high government policy are also needed. In this domain, it is Khamene'i," Yazdi argued, "who possesses the highest qualification."[19]

What Ayatollah Yazdi overlooked was the fact that the constitution was amended in 1989 to enable Khamene'i's succession. As discussed earlier, the requirement that the supreme leader be a source of emulation was dropped, meaning that the spiritual and political leadership of the community would be separated in the post-Khomeini period. Even as a "supreme leader," Khamene'i's political rulings do not carry the weight and authority of Ayatollah Khomeini, and he has been less able to resolve differences between Iran's senior clerics, and government and revolutionary institutions on major policy issues. Moreover, he has undermined his legitimacy by allowing his close associates to refer to him as the "logical replacement" to be the senior *marja'*.

In response to this pro-Khamene'i campaign, the Qum establishment quietly let it be known that if such action were taken, the establishment would not support it. They did this by declaring several times that the Shi'as could still follow the instructions of the *marja's* who had passed away. Faced with this opposition, Khamene'i declared that his current responsibilities did not permit him to take an additional role, meaning that after three weeks Ayatollah Yazdi's bid to claim the office of senior spiritual leader exclusively for Khamene'i did not succeed.

The death of the senior Shi'a Ulama has created a vacuum, and the ruling elite in the Islamic Republic are concerned about the outcome. Khamene'i should be careful not to interfere in this process since this may lead to dissension in the Shi'a world, as well as greater opposition to his leadership position from high-ranking *ulama*. Besides, one Majlis deputy has already publicly called for a constitutional revision to eliminate this institution. "The international relations of states," he declared, "are not compatible with the decision-making system in Iran ... All of them speak with one voice, only in Iran we have a system that has multiple centers."[20] Furthermore, the longer-term emergence of Khamene'i as the supreme religious authority is far from assured.

The Presidency

The changing role of the presidency   Originally, the constitution of 1979 designed a weak and bifurcated executive branch headed by a president with more ceremonial role than actual power. The head executive in charge of policy was the prime minister, who formed his preferred cabinet, subject to a vote of confidence from the parliament. The president was elected by universal suffrage for a term of four years and, as in the United States, could be re-elected for a final four-year term. However, the political inadequacies of two chief executives – prime minister and president – exacerbated factional conflict.[21]

Several times during his tenure, Khamene'i and the prime minister engaged in open ideological disputes over the extent of presidential powers. When Khamene'i was re-elected for his second term in 1985, he wanted to use his new mandate to remove the radical prime minister, Mir Hossein Musavi. As early as 1984, Khamene'i had hinted at the fact that he wanted constitutional changes to increase his authority. The prime minister had responded that the post of president was ceremonial in nature to ensure that Iran would not be ruled by a dictator. Defenders of Khamene'i pointed to the fact that the "political conditions" of 1979–80 had persuaded the Assembly of Experts to limit the powers of the president.[22]

Clearly, the prime minister was not in the position to challenge a newly elected president, particularly a cleric who was close to Ayatollah Khomeini. In a speech before a crowd in Qum, Musavi stated: "I consider myself a drop in the ocean of this self-sacrificing nation and deem every step forward as the result of this great nation's selflessness and co-operation."[23] However, Khamene'i kept up the pressure by repeating his point that "the duty to choose a government, to present a prime minister, and to present the ministers to the Majlis is, in fact, the most important task of the president."[24]

Both protagonists referred to the "views of Imam Khomeini" in substantiating their arguments. This led to the drafting of a letter by 135 members of the Majlis to Khomeini asking him to provide "guidelines" in connection with the next government. In the letter, the deputies paid tribute to "the achievements of Musavi in running the affairs of the state despite serious economic difficulties and war-related problems." Typical of Ayatollah Khomeini's political style, an equivocal reply came from him:

> I find Engineer Musavi to be a religious and committed individual, and that, considering the existing conditions in the country, I consider his government a successful one. Therefore, I do not believe a change of government to be advisable at present. Furthermore, the right to choose belongs to the president and to the Majlis, and this right must be respected.[25]

In the end, the radical faction won the political battle because Khomeini did not want to initiate an institutional change of this magnitude during the war with Iraq. However, when the war ended on 18 July 1988, the political situation was different and the structural weaknesses of the Islamic Republic's institutions had to be addressed.

On 24 April 1989, Ayatollah Khomeini issued a decree creating the Council for the Reappraisal of the Constitution. He appointed 20 individuals, and the Majlis appointed another 5, bringing the total membership to 25. Khomeini instructed the Council to finish its work in two months.[26] In a general statement, Khomeini ordered the Council to consider ways to better manage the executive affairs and did not specify any set guidelines for their deliberations. The latter operationalized its duties into four committees: leadership, centralization in the executive branch, legislative, and judiciary.

After six sessions, the Committee on Centralization in the Executive Branch produced a draft proposal for the Council in late May 1989. The chairman of the Committee was Khamene'i. The report recommended the following:

1. The president will be the head of the executive branch.
2. The president has all the authority of the executive branch.
3. The president presents the ministers to the Majlis for a vote of confidence.
4. The president has the right to remove any of the ministers, and if half of the cabinet is changed, he should receive a fresh vote of confidence for the new cabinet.

In sum, the post of prime minister was abolished. Rafsanjani, who favored these changes, had already declared his candidacy and pleaded with the deputies that Iran's economic and social problems will be easier to manage:

We need to think about getting more powerful. And please do not think I am paving the way for myself as president. The Majlis deputies used to call me Vakil od-Douleh (defender of the government) because ... I consistently supported the executive branch.[27]

The new version of the Iranian presidency is similar to that of the United States. The Iranian president chooses the first vice-president, who is accountable to the president. The latter selects and dismisses ministers who must be confirmed by the Majlis. His power is to conduct economic and foreign policies has been substantially increased, as he chairs the newly created Supreme National Security Council. In the event of a presidential vacancy, an election to refill the office must be held within 50 days. However, as summed up by one scholar, the Iranian presidency:

is the only system in the world in which the elected president must be approved by an unelected Faqih; it is the only system in which the removal of the president is ultimately dependent on a decision of the Faqih; it is the only system in which the president, indeed the entire executive, is subordinated to a religious authority; and perhaps, it is the only system in the world in which the executive branch exercised no control over the armed forces.[28]

Rafsanjani's presidency: from 1989 to the present   On 30 July 1989, Rafsanjani received 15,551,783 votes out of the total 16,454,641 votes cast. At the same time, 95 percent of those who voted approved the 45 amendments to the constitution. Elected at the age of 55, he took over the newly strengthened presidency. In his inaugural speech, he warned the hardliners to forgo their "extremism" and allow for a new economic recovery. He hinted that his long friendship with Khamene'i would be an important asset:

My cooperation with the great leader in the past 30 years has been with honesty, sincerity, harmony and unanimity ... Until this day, we have been together in the most difficult situations, and not even once have we allowed doubts to creep into our hearts in carrying out our divine duties.[29]

During the same ceremony, Khamene'i stressed that the "new chapter" that started with this election did not mean that Iran was turning to new policies: "A new era, if it means turning against the main line drawn by our dear Imam, will never come in our revolution."[30] Hence, a Khamene'i–Rafsanjani alliance seemed to be emerging with the perception that Rafsanjani was the man in charge.

We can identify three features of Rafsanjani's presidential style. He involves his cabinet more intimately in policy development and implementation. This tendency is clearly evident in economic policies, such as the adoption of a single exchange rate for Iranian currency and the privatization process. He has been very protective of his cabinet ministers when they have been challenged by the Majlis. Every time the Majlis has forced the resignation of a cabinet minister, Rafsanjani has responded by re-appointing that minister as "special vice-president." In August 1993, the Majlis refused to give a vote of confidence to Mohsen Nourbakhsh, minister of finance. Rafsanjani responded by appointing Nourbakhsh as his "special adviser on economic planning." His cabinet-style presidency is best demonstrated by the fact that he has maintained a continuity in the ministers he selected in 1989, and when re-elected in 1993, out of 23 ministers, only 6 were new, and one was reshuffled.

A second prominent feature of Rafsanjani's presidency is its technocratic make-up. In his cabinet, many did not have "revolutionary" credentials. The educational background of the ministers indicates that seven of them possess doctoral degrees, nine are engineers, and only two (security and justice), are clerics. More importantly, the religious rankings of the clerics did not exceed the level *hojjatoleslam*, which is the same as the president's ranking.[31] Only one (Minister of Labor Hossein Kamali) lacks a university education. (See Figure 2.1.)

Finally, President Rafsanjani's management style fits into what scholars call the collegial model.[32] In this model, the emphasis on group problem-solving and teamwork is paramount. President Rafsanjani operates like the hub of a wheel with spokes connecting to individual advisers, ministry heads, as well as the supreme leader. He gives overlapping assignments and occasionally reaches down to communicate directly with subordinates of cabinet heads in order to get more information. In a political system that has a supreme leader with its own circle of advisers, the collegial presidential model requires close contact and continuing interaction between the president and the supreme leader. (See Figure 2.2.)

For the collegial model to be effective, a shared interest in all major policy problems is expected, and an understanding must be developed to regulate initiative, consultation, the articulation of disagreements, and collective judgment. Rafsanjani's approach presupposes the fact that he and Khamene'i are close enough to make this collegial approach work. However, in the complicated post-Khomeini factional environment, more than cordiality is needed for effective policy-making.

By adopting the collegial model, Rafsanjani has taken certain risks, and

Foreign Affairs

Ali Akbar Velayati

Born 1324 (1945–46),Tehran
MD Pediatrics
(Tehran and US)

Sciences and Higher Education

Seyyed Hashemi-Golpaygani

Born 1325 (1946–47), Najaf
Ph.D. Electrical and medical
engineering (US)

Defenses

Muhammad Farzandeh

Born 1332 (1953–54), Abadan
MA Industrial management
(US)

Agriculture

'Esa Kalantari

Born 1331 (1952–53)
Ph.D. Agriculture (US)

Industries

Muhammad Ne'matzadeh

Born 1324 (1945–46), Tabriz
MA Industrial management
(US)

Minister of the Reconstruction Crusade

Gholamreza Foruzesh

Born 1334 (1955–56)
Engineering degree
(Tehran)

Energy

Bijan Namdar-Zanganeh

Born 1331 (1952–53),
Kermanshah
MA Engineering

Petroleum

Gholamraza Aqazadeh

Born 1327 (1948–49), Kho'ei
BA Mathematics and
computers (Tehran)

Post, Telegraph, and Telephone

Seyyed Muhammad Gharazi

Born 1327 (1948–49),
Esfahan
MA Electronics (Tehran)

Health Care Treatment

'Ali Reza Marandi

Born 1318 (1929–30),
Esfahan
Ph.D. Pediatrics (US)

Education and Training

Muhammad 'Ali Najafi

Born 1330 (1951–52), Tehran
MA Mathematics (US)

Minister of the Interior

'Ali Muhammad Besharati-Jahromi

Born 1323 (1944–45), Jahrom
BA Education

Justice

Muhammad Esma'il Shushtari

Born 1328 (1949–50),
Shushtari
Theology studies
(Qum and Najaf)

Commerce

Yahya Al-e Eshaq

Born 1328 (1949–50), Tehran
BA Commercial management

Housing

'Abbas Ahmad Akhundi

Born 1336 (1957–58)
MA Engineering

Labor

Hoseyn Kemali

Born 1331 (1952–53), Borujerd
Technical diploma in
metalwork

Roads and Transportation

Akbar Torkan

Born 1331 (1952–53), Tehran
Mechanical engineering

Intelligence (Security)

'Ali Fallahian

Born 1328 (1949–50), Njafabad
Theology and principles of
theology

Heavy Industries

Seyyed Muhammad Hadi Nezhad-Hoseynian

Born 1325 (1946–47), Tehran
MA (US)

Cooperatives

Gholamreza Shafe'i

Born 1330 (1951–52), Marand
Mechanical engineering

Culture and Islamic Guidance

Mostafa Mirsalim

(Nominated the week of
14 February 1994)

Figure 2.1 Rafsanjani's cabinet ministers

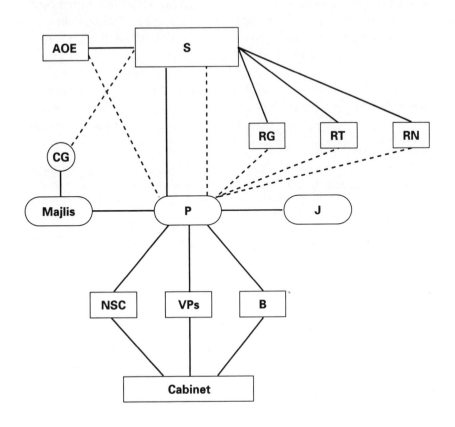

—————— Institutional Structure

- - - - -   Personal Network

S	Supreme Leader (Khamene'i)	**B**	Budget Office
AOE	Assembly of Experts	**RG**	Revolutionary Guards /
CG	Council of Guardians		Armed Forces / Militias
P	President (Rafsanjani)	**RT**	Radio and television
NSC	National Security Council	**RN**	Religious networks
VPs	Vice-Presidents	**J**	Judiciary

Figure 2.2 The political system of the Islamic Republic of Iran

its preservation continues to exact a price on his popularity. In the context of his relationship with Khamene'i, Rafsanjani repeatedly finds himself on the defensive because Khamene'i has the habit of suddenly taking the initiative or intervening in an important policy matter. Rafsanjani and Khamene'i have important tactical, not substantive, disagreements, on matters such as assessment of US intentions, and the best strategy and tactics for dealing with the United States. Khamene'i has been more vocal in condemning American policies – particularly the peace process – whereas Rafsanjani has been careful and calculating in expressing his views.

> We do not regard what is taking place as real peace. We believe it is one-sided ... However, as regards practical interference, executive action, or the physical prevention of development ... as far as these are concerned, we have not done and we will not do so.[33]

Part of the explanation for the problems of policy-making in Rafsanjani's presidency centers on his personality. He is a man of moderation and sincere commitments. He has excellent interpersonal skills in dealing with advisers, mediating differences, and maintaining teamwork among them. He refined these skills when he was the speaker of the Majlis from 1980 to 1988. During the first years of his presidency, one major attribute of Rafsanjani's personality seemed to be "active-positive": self-confident, flexible, enjoys the exercise of his presidential power, optimistic, and emphasizes the "rational mastery" of his environment.

However, the lack of tangible rewards from the promised economic reforms, as well as repeated challenges from the Majlis and hardliners to his proposals, have transformed his "active-positive" personality into a "passive-positive" one, defined as a personality that is "involved in politics out of a sense of duty and not because he enjoys it, responds rather than initiates, avoids making difficult choices, is reluctant to act decisively, and is superficially optimistic."[34] Rafsanjani's re-election in 1993 with 63 percent of the votes reflected the erosion of public confidence in his presidency and the perception that his style of leadership is not effective.

In judging the Iranian presidency under Rafsanjani, it may be argued that more than the nature of the factional politics by which a president is politically constrained must be taken into consideration. Moreover, Rafsanjani is challenged by a parliament that asserts an increasingly influential role in the day-to-day micro-management of policies. Whatever the argument, it is evident that public perception of the president is strongly linked to the prevailing economic situation, and this is the catalyst giving rise to a more assertive parliament.

The Majlis

The structure and role of the Majlis   The constitution of the Islamic Republic allocates extensive powers to a unicameral, 270-member Majlis. Forty-eight articles (out of 177) expand on these powers. They range from important national security issues (declaring war, emergency, ratification of treaties, and granting military basing rights) to economic issues (borrowing, credits, and hiring of foreign experts) to the accountability of the executive (cabinet confirmation, impeachment, investigations of "any affairs deemed important").

Perhaps one would not expect to read arguments in favor of parliament by fundamentalist religious thinkers like Ayatollah Khomeini. However, without his sanction, the Islamic Republic of Iran would not have had an Islamic Consultative Assembly or the Majlis. He saw parliament as an important part of the Islamic Republic's body politic: "Consultation, debates, criticism, and responsibility is what an Islamic Majlis is all about … It is the organ that enacts laws to benefit the poor and the disinherited … It is an organ that imparts a sense of participation to the people." In a speech in 1984, Khomeini stated that the Majlis stood "at the head of the institutions of the Islamic Republic and is Islamic and national."[35]

As of 1992, 24 provinces have been divided into 196 electoral districts, with one separate category for the religious minorities defined as the Zoroastrians, Jews, Assyrians, and Armenians. A population census is conducted every ten years to determine whether a district should be given additional seats. A seat will be added for every 150,000 people. Currently, the capital, Tehran, has the largest number of seats, at 37, while the province of Ilam holds the smallest, consisting of two deputies. Similar to other parliamentary institutions, the Iranian Majlis functions through committees. But unlike other parliaments, the Iranian Majlis has a Governing Board which is an all powerful body made up of twelve members: the speaker, two deputy-speakers, three commissioners, and six secretaries. The members are elected by the deputies on an annual basis, and the powers of this board range from enforcing the by-laws of the Majlis to receiving and introducing proposals forwarded by the deputies. The board exercises control over whether a given proposal is placed on the agenda, and depending on what faction controls the Governing Board the process of legislative debate can be affected significantly. The composition of the board reflects the existing factional alignment in the Majlis.

Another unique feature of the Iranian Majlis is the Council of Guardians. It is composed of six senior theologians and six Islamic lawyers. The six theologians are appointed by the *faqih* for a period of three years, and the six lawyers are appointed by the Majlis. Their function is to oversee the enactment of laws and reject any that are "in contravention of the principles and precepts of the official religion of the country,"[36] i.e., Shi'a Islam.

The electoral process   The elections of the Majlis are direct, with a system of double-balloting (similar to the French system). Eligible candidates must have Iranian citizenship, be between the ages of 25 and 85, have no record of "moral corruption," believe in the Islamic Revolution, and be able to read and write. Candidates must receive absolute majority (over 50 percent of the votes). In the absence of an absolute majority, the candidates with the highest number of votes compete in the second round of elections. The law grants considerable power to the Council of Guardians "to ensure that elections are not to be a threat to the system and the revolution." According to the law, the Council of Guardians appoints a five-member Central Committee to operate within the Ministry of the Interior. The Central Committee has total authority from the Guardianship Council to appoint other bodies to supervise the electoral process. In this capacity, the Central Committee is structured into 25 Provincial Committees (one for each province), and a three-member District Committee (one for each district). This vertical structure keeps the Council of Guardians abreast of all the developments, irregularities, violations, etc. The Council has authority to annul, or temporarily halt any elections, or recommend legal action against a candidate.[37] (See Figure 2.3.)

In the past decade, there have been four uninterrupted elections, with a turnover ratio of over 60 percent, higher than that of most parliamentary elections in the developed countries. In the First Period (1980–84), Rafsanjani's faction was in the majority. In the Second Period (1984–88), it lost its majority, and no clear faction had the upper hand. In the Third Period (1988–92), opponents of Rafsanjani, the radical faction, controlled the Majlis. Finally, in the Fourth Period (1992–present), a socially conservative faction defeated the radicals, and now has a majority in the Majlis. Their numbers range from 150 to 180 votes. The radical faction in the Fourth Majlis has fewer than forty members.

Following the death of Ayatollah Khomeini, supporters of Rafsanjani mounted a concerted effort to limit the chances of re-election for the radicals in the Majlis. In determining a candidate's eligibility, Khamene'i and Rafsanjani pressured the Council of Guardians to give more emphasis

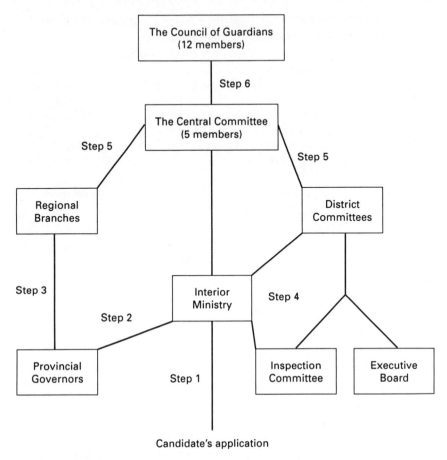

Figure 2.3 The approval process for candidacy: the Majlis

to ideological criteria, arguing that this had always been the norm. After all, they stated, "did the Council not reject the candidacy of those who were members of the Communist Party in 1983?" On 10 March 1992, Khamene'i met with the members of the Central Committee of the Guardianship Council. He stated that the

> durability of our Islamic system depends on conformity to its laws and regulations. No corrupt person should be allowed to enter an institution that has the function of legislating ... The criteria for judging the eligibility of candidates must include practices of moral, economic, and political corruption.[38]

With this statement, Khamene'i clearly exposed his anti-radical preference in the factional in-fighting.

The radicals led by Mohtashami and Khoiniha criticized the campaign against them. Mohtashami was the most vocal:

> In the past, our factions were ostracized for their unquestioned commitment to the revolutionary philosophy of the Faqih; now, the same people are attacking us for our infidelity to the Faqih and his chosen successor. These people who call for absolute fidelity to the Supreme Leader [Khamene'i] are the same people that were and continue to be opposed to the concept of a Faqih ... It is as clear as daylight to me that these people are doing what the wicked strategies of America and its European allies want.[39]

By the end of March 1992, 3,150 candidates had filed applications for candidacy, among them 55 women. In Tehran alone, 168 candidates competed for 37 seats. The elections date was set for 10 April 1992. Not surprisingly, 35 percent of the candidates (1,060) were rejected by the Council of Guardians, among them the incumbent deputy speaker, Sadig Khalkhali, and Ebrahim Asqarzadeh, the leader of the students who took over the American Embassy in 1979. Two other incumbents who were involved in the seizure of the embassy, Hedayat Aqa'i and Muhammad Behzadian, were also rejected. Overall, 40 incumbents, including six radical clergymen, did not "qualify." Prominent radicals like Mohtashami and Karrubi were allowed to run, but lost the elections. Opponents of the radicals ran under the platform of "Loyalty to the Imam's Line, Fidelity to the Leader, support for Rafsanjani," and the radicals ran under the "Grand Coalition" (E'telafe Bozorg).[40]

The 1992 parliamentary election results surprised even Rafsanjani's supporters, whose exaggerated concerns had led them to manipulate the electoral process. It is reasonable to assume that even without those "unfair" restrictions placed on the radicals, they may not have won. The dismal showing of prominent radicals like Mohtashemi and Karrubi showed that the voters did not approve of the platform of the radicals which called for the state to maintain its revolutionary vigor. In spite of the euphoria created by the radicals' defeat, Rafsanjani's expectation that the new majority in the Majlis would be supportive of his government's proposals was short-lived.

The fourth Majlis: 1992–94 The victors in the parliamentary elections were those who had been sponsored by the Society for Combatant Clergy. Despite the name, the members of this organization are anything but "combatant." Composed of conservative clergy and laymen, the society has its origins in 1977, when "a group of disciples of Imam Khomeini" began meeting weekly to discuss and exchange information. The first participants were Ayatollah Mottahari (assassinated in 1979), Ayatollah Beheshti (assassinated in 1981), Hojjatoleslam Javad Bahonar (assassinated in 1981), Rafsanjani, Khamene'i, and Mahdavi-Kani, currently executive secretary of the society. What members of this society have in common is political-social conservatism and links to the powerful merchant class in the Bazaar. The platform of the society calls for measures to open up the economy and encourage privatization and foreign investments. Socially, they are conservative and watchful of "Western" values, which they see as incompatible with Islamization.[41]

In the opening session of the Majlis, Speaker Nateq Nuri stated:

> I do not believe in the division known as the left and the right. We must try to solve our problems free of such ideological labeling. We have a leader, and our guidelines should be, and are based on instructions by the leader. Of course, our tastes might differ, but this should not mean clashes and rudeness.[42]

Rafsanjani told the new deputies of the Majlis to be more supportive of his economic reforms as outlined in the forthcoming budget proposal: "They should not question it 10, 15, 20 times every morning, saying do this for that project, do that for this province."

However, the new Majlis did not go along with Rafsanjani. First, they attacked the policies of the Ministry of Islamic Guidance for not taking the threat of "Western cultural onslaught" seriously. Khamene'i also abandoned Rafsanjani on this issue when a group of Majlis deputies met with him and discussed their dissatisfaction with Minister Mohammad Khatemi. Khamene'i supported them and made a harsh speech calling "the Western cultural onslaught more than attack; it is cultural night raid."[43] Immediately after Khamene'i's speech, Khatemi resigned his post.

Another anti-government initiative by the Majlis came on 1 September 1992. The Majlis undermined the central authority of the government by passing a comprehensive bill on the governing of the country, which stripped the Ministry of Interior of its power to run the nation's cities. The bill called for the creation of eleven-member city councils to supervise and approve mayoral selections, an important power that had belonged to the Ministry of Interior. The fact that under this law the deputies have the power to select seven out of eleven councilmen in their localities was a major gain for the power of the Majlis.[44]

The Fourth Majlis also came down hard on state-controlled radio and television in 1993. This powerful body had been under the control of

Muhammad Hashemi (Rafsanjani's brother) for over a decade. In a resolution, the Majlis condemned him for allowing the television to broadcast *Billy Budd*, a 1962 film based on Herman Melville's novel about an eighteenth-century seaman who is court-martialled for killing a sadistic master-at-arms. The criticism was based on the characterization of Budd as highly moral, even though he was implicitly illegitimate. On 13 February 1994, Khamene'i exercised his authority by replacing Hashemi. Officially the latter "resigned," but it was well known that the new Majlis had undermined him. Khamene'i again followed the wishes of the conservative majority. On 15 February 170 members signed the following letter to Khamene'i:

> The enlightened message of Your Excellency regarding the appointment of a new director [Ali Larijani] for radio and television has revitalized our revolutionary commitment to fight Western cultural onslaught, and your instructions have established the line between what is acceptable in Islam. We are grateful to your wisdom and commitment to strengthen the legacy of Imam Khomeini.[45]

Overall, the Fourth Majlis has remained consistently vocal on a variety of socio-economic issues. Nevertheless, one notable weakness has been in the area of national security and foreign policy. Since its inception in 1980, the Majlis in Iran has had two prominent foreign policy actions: release of the American hostages and the severing of diplomatic relations with Britain in 1989 over Salman Rushdie's *Satanic Verses*. This institutional weakness is not peculiar to Iran. Parliaments in most developing countries experience the same problem. Nevertheless, the current Majlis is an assertive body, and its determination to maintain its independence from the executive will continue.

Conclusion

Since the revolution of 1979, the institutionalization of the Islamic Republic's body politic has continued to evolve into distinct structures of authority. The clerics have been successful so far in sustaining the institutions of the Islamic Republic. In contrast to the Shah's period, the institution of the Majlis today enjoys a far more autonomous role. However, a major challenge to the Islamic Republic's institutions of governance may come from having too many institutions that serve parallel purposes: the Assembly of Experts and the Majlis, the Supreme Leader and the President, the revolutionary Baseej forces and the regular armed forces, the imam's representatives in the ministries and the appointed cabinet ministers, and many other examples. The fundamental question is how long these institutions will survive without coming into conflict with each other. Such an eventuality is realistic indeed, not just speculative.

CHAPTER 3

Shi'ite Political Thought and the Destiny of the Iranian Revolution

Roy P. Mottahedeh

Even those who have little sympathy with Hegel have been drawn to his stunningly evocative phrase, "the cunning of reason," for we have no more concise way of saying that unintended consequences appear as an idea enters the arena of events, some following from the logic of the idea itself and some from the interaction of the idea with its surroundings. This chapter examines the evolution – in which reason's cunning is dramatically at work – of two key ideas in the making of the Iranian revolution, the ideas of the "source of imitation" or *marja'iyah* and "the guardianship of the jurist" or *velayat-e faqih*. It then describes some recent understandings of those ideas. Necessarily, in a discussion of this length, the treatment of these themes has been selective and much has been omitted.

Considerable scholarly literature now exists on both *marja'iyah* and the guardianship of the jurist.[1] Quite properly, discussions of the origin of hierarchy among Twelver Shi'ite *ulama* go back to the birth of the Usuli school in the time of Vahid Behbahani, who died in the 1790s, or the early years of the thirteenth Hijri century. The Usuli school is usually held to have reached full development with Murtada Ansari (d. 1281 AH/ 1864 AD), who was most likely the first *mujtahid* to receive international recognition by the majority of Twelver Shi'ites as the religious "leader" of the community. This leadership, it is claimed, showed its real power when, in December 1891, the great majority of the Iranian Shi'ite community obeyed a *fatwa* of a subsequent leader of the Shi'ite community, Hajj Mizra Hasan Shirazi, to abstain from the sale and use of tobacco. In this case the Shah had granted a humiliating concession on the production, sale, and export of all Iranian tobacco to a British subject, and the *fatwa* was so effective that it caused the Shah to revoke the concession. According to this standard account, the prestige gained by Shirazi's success was consolidated in the period between 1947 and 1961 when Ayatollah Borujerdi led the Shi'ite community. In fact, some historians claim that he was the first supreme leader of the Twelver Shi'ites to use his power to organize the clergy properly.

The intellectual underpinning of this evolution was the assertion by the Usuli school that law could be interpreted only by *mujtahids*, whose warrants to do so were believed to be handed down in a chain of discipleship that had its origins among the inner circle of the infallible Imams of Twelver Shi'ism. According to the precepts of the Usuli school, the believers who were not *mujtahids* were to choose from among these *mujtahids* (who, in this century, have seldom if ever exceeded two hundred individuals) a single jurist whom they believe to be "most learned," *a'lam*. This *mujtahid* is their "source" or *marja'* , to follow on issues affected by Islamic law. Among the *mujtahids*, only a few of the most prominent issued manuals for the believers who seek to imitate them; most *mujtahids* would be embarrassed to claim *a'lamiyah*.

One reading of the logical consequences of this view would point to a political conclusion: if this office of *marj'iyah* in some sense represented the authority of the absent Twelfth Imam, then did this not mean that the most learned *marja'* also had the worldly authority of the Twelfth Imam? In 1970 Khomeini drew this conclusion in his celebrated book, *The Guardianship of the Jurist*. The theory was enshrined in the Iranian Constitution of 1979, which treats the leadership of a single supreme *marja'* as the norm. Subsequently, the "logic" of political events led to the 1989 revision of the Constitution that requires the "guide" or "leader" (*rahbar*) of the nation be a *mujtahid* but not necessarily a *marja'*.

Thus far the accepted interpretation among scholars of modern Iran has been given. This interpretation is wrong, not in what it includes, but in what it leaves out. The concept of Islamic government has been present in Islamic thought in many forms for a long time; and "the guardianship of the jurist" is by no means the only context in which it exists in Shi'ite sources.[2] The idea of a leadership among the *ulama* is strongly advocated by many great Sunni thinkers. Al-Ghazali (d. 505 AH/1111 AD), for instance, says that a layman should follow the opinion of the jurist who is most learned in the law (*afqah*) over the most pious (*awra'*). Al-Khatib al-Baghdadi (d. 463 AH/1071 AD), in *al Faqih wa'l-Mutafaqqih*, assumes that it is popular knowledge in any community as to who is the most learned jurist (*a'lamuhum bi ahkam ad-din*), hence the one to whom the believers should turn. 'Abd al-Wahhab al-Sha'rani in his *al-Tabaqat al-Sughra*, says of one of his contemporaries in tenth/sixteenth century Egypt: "He is now the *marja'* for the people of Egypt in the writing of legal opinions (*fa'innahu 'l-ana marja' ahli Misra fi tahriri l'fatawa*)".[3] It is interesting to note that Sha'rani lived at the dawn of the period in which the Ottoman empire would force the *ulama* under its sway into a hierarchy unmatched in the rigor of its organization by any Twelver Shi'ite government past or present.

Another omission in the traditional scholarly account of the *velayat-e faqih* is the pre-Khomeini history of the "guardianship of the jurist." The idea had existed not only in the very early nineteenth century in the thought of Hajj Mullah Ahmad Naraqi, who is cited by Khomeini, but had been accepted in limited ways by other jurists. Khomeini's book is, in fact, an extract from his commentary on *al-Makasib*, the masterwork of Murtada Ansari. In its first formulation, when Khomeini in his lectures in Najaf discussed Ansari's rejection of "the guardianship of the jurist," he restated the traditional view of the *usulis* that every *mujtahid* must follow his own judgment, which implies that no *mujtahid* need defer to another in matters of government. These lectures were published in installments the morning after they were delivered. But when the fasciculi were gathered into a book, Khomeini stated that if one *faqih* (i.e., a *mujtahid* who is a *marja'*) possessing knowledge and justice undertakes the task of government, "he will possess the same authority as the Most Noble Messenger in the administration of society and it will be the duty of all people to obey him."[4] Presumably "all people" includes other *mujtahids*; and it is here that Khomeini may break with tradition, a point to which we will return.

As for the period since the Iranian revolution, the standard interpretation omits key events leading up to the amendment of the constitution. It was, most importantly, the political success of the *ulama* who were not *marja's*, principally Rafsanjani, that led to the amendment. But ideologically the concept of *marja'iyah* had been undergoing change through the course of events. On 20 April 1982, after Ayatollah Shari'atmadari was associated with Sadiq Qubtzadeh's plot against the government, the Association of Combatant Clerics of Tehran, and then, in rapid succession, the Association of Teachers of Qum and the Council of Guardians announced him stripped of his *marja'iyah*. It was not clear how, in traditional Usuli terms, a Shi'ite could be considered "the most learned" jurist by a large segment of the Shi'ite world one day, and on political grounds lose his authority on the next when, to all appearances, only his loyalty to the government and not his learning had decreased.

Political considerations again appeared to have forced a reinterpretation of the guardianship of the jurist when, on 28 March 1989, Ayatollah Husain Ali Montazeri resigned under pressure. At the end of 1985, Montazeri had been declared "the deputy of the Leader" by the Council of Experts, the group empowered to choose the *marja'* who should be the "leader." From that time on Montazeri was seen as the heir apparent to Khomeini, which implied that when Khomeini remained silent on any issue, Montazeri could speak with high authority. Montazeri exercised the right to intervene in the judiciary and to assume control of the traditional educational system of *madrasahs* and of the universities and other aspects of public life. Although he was (and perhaps still is) an advocate of an aggressive foreign policy, he proved to be a force for moderation in domestic politics. For example, he argued for the transfer of ownership of uncultivated land (*mawat*) to a new cultivator even if the land had known a previous owner, thus placing himself between the conservative views of Ayatollah Golpaygani, who held that land must be certifiably abandoned before its ownership can be transferred, and the radical view of Ayatollah Meshkini-Ardabili, who holds that even a hired laborer cultivating land is performing *ihya'al-mawat*, and thereby becomes – at least for the period of the crop – a partner of the owner.[5]

Montazeri's views proved unpalatable. In a sermon delivered on 11 February 1989, the tenth anniversary of the revolution, he indulged in self-criticism, as well as in criticism of the government's record over the preceding decade. The slogans of the past ten years, he claimed, had made Iran "isolated in the world and caused the people to view us with pessimism … The people of the world thought our only task here in Iran was to kill … Prisons must be emptied and forces mobilized for reconstruction." Iranians should repent their "social and political mistakes." In addition, he criticized restrictions on free expression and said that he himself was sometimes censored.[6]

Those who disliked Montazeri, or regarded criticism of the regime as betrayal, jumped to the defense of the government's record. Khamene'i told a large crowd in Azadi Square that Iran had diplomatic relations with all but a few nations that were illegitimate and had a history of plotting against Iran. On 13 February Musavi said that the principal intention of those who cast aspersions on the revolution was "to make use of weak-spirited people" and "to sow seeds of doubt about the revolution."[7]

On 28 March following a meeting of the Council of Experts, Khomeini, accepting Montazeri's forced resignation, wrote:

As you have written, the position of leadership of the Islamic Republic is
a difficult task and a heavy responsibility that requires endurance greater
than you possess ... I see your interest and that of the Islamic Republic in
your being a jurist so that the people and the regime may benefit from your
views.

Again, one might ask: If Montazeri was chosen heir-presumptive primarily
for his learning, why had he lost his position so abruptly?[8]

A complicating factor in understanding the significance of this event
was Khomeini's celebrated declaration issued in January of 1988, in which
he spelled out the meaning of the statement, already found in his book,
that the jurist-leader inherited the authority of the Prophet. It is not
clear, given the strong abstract claims already advanced in his book, that
this declaration represented an innovation in Khomeini's thinking. But
for him to say openly that an Islamic government could suspend fasting,
prayer, and pilgrimage to Mecca was electrifying. It provoked some soul-
searching and a debate which is outside the scope of this chapter, except
to say that the book-length rebuttal of Khomeini's declaration by the
former prime minister Mehdi Bazargan offered yet another fully articulated
and very different position on the guardianship of the jurist. It is important for this chapter, however, to note that Khomeini based these
powers of the state in part on "the wider interests of the community,"
here clearly invoking a well-known principle in Shi'ite law, *hifz an-nizam* or
"the preservation of order," a commonweal principle for the suspension
of law similar to *istislah*, *maslahah*, and other commonweal principles used
in the Sunni schools of law. Those out of sympathy with the government
felt that the increasingly frequent use of the principle of "the preservation
of order" was turning it into a principle of "reason of state."[9]

With Khomeini's death and the subsequent completion and ratification
of the 1989 amendment of the constitution, the government was free to
choose as "leader" a *mujtahid* who was not a *marja'*. The former Speaker
of the Parliament, Rafsanjani, who had emerged as the most popular
elected official after the revolution, became president – an office that had
been largely ceremonial but under the revised constitution received increased power, including control of the budget. Khamene'i, holder of
the formerly ceremonial presidency, received Khomeini's position as
spiritual "leader," although he could not inherit Khomeini's charismatic
authority. Khamene'i had studied for five years in Qum at the "graduate"
level, called *kharij*, "beyond the texts," in which students learn to debate
and discuss without a text in front of them, a process which – after a
considerable period of study – prepares the most talented students to

receive the title *mujtahid*. Khamene'i, who was in his fifties, received this title only when Khomeini, on his death bed in the presence of two witnesses, reportedly recognized Khamene'i as a *mujtahid*. Khamene'i, who by and large had been a cooperative player with Rafsanjani, was quickly approved by the significant bodies of the clergy, including the Association of Teachers in Qum, which represents the collective opinion of the most learned ulama. At this point Iranians followed Ayatollah Kho'i, Ayatollah Mar'ashi-Najafi, or Ayatollah Golpaygani as their *marja's*; there was now a more purely religious leadership outside the government and a more politically religious leadership inside the government.

Khamene'i turned out to have a mind and aspirations of his own. He adopted with gusto the role of guardian of pristine revolutionary values, which he had foreshadowed in his speech on the tenth anniversary of the revolution. He worried about slipshod standards of dress and public morality. He kept the issue of Salman Rushdie in the foreground, when Rafsanjani, who had seemed to be his patron, wanted it to slip into the background; more recently he has sided with those who have economic entitlements acquired through the revolution, while Rafsanjani has been trying to restore a free-market system.[10]

The cunning of reason was at work in yet another area. It was "reasonable" to expect the spiritual "leader" to find his own voice (and, not coincidentally, his own constituency, since he seemed to strike the populist note that many had felt to be absent since Khomeini had died). It was also both "reasonable" that Khamene'i should aspire to reunite true spiritual authority, the *marja'iyah*, with the uncertain authority he had gained as "leader," and reasonable that the leading men of the *ulama* establishment, older and – by most conventional measures – more learned than Khamene'i, should reject such aspirations.

The drama unfolded accordingly. On Thursday 9 December 1993, Ayatollah Golpaygani died; he had been predeceased by Ayatollah Kho'i and was at the time of his death recognized by the overwhelming majority of Iranian Shi'ites as their *marja'*. Already at Golpayegani's funeral a split was evident; some of the *ulama* prevented Khamene'i from saying the "prayer for the dead," a task reserved for the most respected associate of the deceased and performed by Golpaygani at Khomeini's funeral. The Association of Teachers abandoned its usual meeting place, the library of the prestigious Faiziyeh Madrasah, and did not invite observers from the Shi'ite communities abroad, such as Shams al-Din and Fadl Allah from Lebanon. Instead they met clandestinely so that the followers of Khamene'i could not interrupt their deliberations.[11]

The actual vote within the Association of Teachers is an interesting reflection of the different strategies the leading *ulama* thought appropriate at this juncture. Many favored the election of Ayatollah Sistani, who lived in Najaf in Iraq. In his early seventies, Sistani is comparatively young by ayatollah standards, but he has great learning, is the *marja'* for the Shi'ites of Iraq, and – most importantly – he believes that the clergy should shun political office completely. A fair number secretly supported Montazeri, believing him to be the most learned; but Khomeini's rejection of him made it impossible to refer to him except obliquely. In the end, the majority of the fifty or so *mujtahids* present persuaded all members to endorse the declaration that "the office of marja' is exclusively established in the Grand Ayatollah Hajj Sheikh Muhammad 'Ali Araki."[12]

The choice was not unexpected. Araki had unquestionably acquired the rank of *mujtahid* and had long been famous for his piety, although not for his learning. Now, at the age of ninety-nine, he no longer closely followed what was going on around him and was a candidate whose mere presence as *marja'* would block the ambitions of Khamene'i and who could be counted on to take a fairly passive role. Moreover, the choice of Araki coincided with the wishes of the circle around Rafsanjani, the president, which were that Khamene'i had interfered too often in matters of policy. Nevertheless, there were members of the *ulama* who supported Khamene'i's ambitions. On 12 December, in a memorial service in Tehran, the head of the Majlis, Nateq Nuri, said, referring to the many mourners present there and at the funeral: "This is a sign of the deep religious faith in and following for his excellency Ayatollah Khamene'i, the Leader of the Islamic revolution." Another issue that remained unresolved was in the interpretation of the Association's statement appointing Araki: if the office was "exclusively established" (*muta'ayyan*) in one person as *marja'* this surely meant that there was exclusive establishment only in the collective public view of the *ulama*, who continued to believe individually that there were other legitimate *marja's* such as Sistani. Had a second semi-official office been created to give the Association of Teachers a united face *vis-à-vis* the state?[13]

Ayatollah Araki died at the age of one hundred on 29 November 1994, having given only one year's respite from struggles over clerical leadership. This time Khamene'i was better prepared, in part because Araki had been at death's door for three weeks. Already in the second week of November, Ayatollah Ahmad Jannati, well known for quixotic statements such as his appeal to the Muslims of Europe to take over the governments of that continent, announced that it was precisely the "enemies" of the Islamic Republic who favored the appointment of a non-political *marja'*. But at first his strategy seemed unclear. Only days before Araki's death the ever-busy Jannati announced that Khamene'i, "the Leader of the Islamic Republic, did not accept the position of marja'iyah which had been offered to him repeatedly."[14]

Khamene'i's modesty, genuine or strategic, had not left his supporters idle. At Araki's funeral a portion of the crowd shouted: "Khamene'i is the Imam; he is the marja' of the Shi'ites." Then, the Association of Teachers in Qum endorsed a list of seven candidates, including Khamene'i, only a few days after warning the government not to interfere in the choice of the *marja'*. One hundred fifty of the 270 members of the parliament endorsed the list and, in their statement, declared Khamene'i to be "the most informed person concerning Islam and the Islamic world and the most qualified authority for the leadership of the Muslim society." On 9 December the head of the judiciary, Ayatollah Yazdi, declared Khamene'i as Iran's sole *marja'* and warned the senior clergy not to disobey him. Khamene'i was increasingly called "the highest marja'."[15]

No one who paused to think could believe that this man of fifty-five years, who in Qum had never been permitted to teach a really advanced text, was in the same league of learning as the other six candidates on the list. But some obviously did not consider this, and those who did, and yet endorsed Khamene'i, clearly believed that political experience and ideological orientation counted for as much as – or more than – learning. Almost as striking was the comment that the Association of Teachers added to their list: they declared it a positive aspect of Shi'ism that the believer could choose his or her *marja'*. The majority of the top clergy were trying to diffuse authority, however much the theory of the guardianship of the jurist might favor uniting political authority with *marja'iyah*, while at the same time the government was trying to keep clerical leadership ensconced in its midst. Yet, as the Qur'an so eloquently says:

$$\text{ومَكَرُوا ومَكَرَ ٱللهُ وٱللهُ خَيرُ ٱلماكِرِينَ}$$

(III:54). Five days after Yazdi's declaration, Khamene'i declined the *marja'iyah* inside Iran but said he was willing to be the *marja'* for Shi'ites outside of Iran, most of whom in any case are followers of Ayatollah Sistani in Iraq. Iranians now jokingly asked each other whether they should obtain copies of Khamene'is manual on proper behavior to keep in their suitcases for their trips abroad. The cunning of reason – which included both reasons of state and the logical entailment of the political theory behind the Iranian constitution – had left *marja'iyah* everywhere and nowhere at the same time. Ironically, the many seemingly essential compromises appeared to have left no one, at least for the time being, with the religious legitimacy the leading *mujtahid*s had enjoyed on the eve of the revolution.

No survey of the evolution of ideas on the guardianship of the jurist would be complete without reference to the fate and ideas of Ayatollah Montazeri. Barred from consideration, harassed, and confined to Qum, he has gained support to be the highest *marja'* because of his very refusal to compromise, a position that Shi'ites have always respected in a clergyman. He has the most popular class at Qum, with about one thousand students, and his reinterpretation of the guardianship of the jurist is the boldest step so far taken by clergymen in favor of this theory. Basically, he says that the heart of the theory is elective government, because – among other reasons – God gave man disposal over his personal resources, and therefore a voice (as well as an inner predilection to have a voice) in the government that taxes him. The guardian-jurist is a representative of all society, which needs to entrust its collective interests to a central authority who, however, remains answerable to society. If this strikes an American reader as somewhere between Tom Paine and Thomas Jefferson, it is buttressed with careful argument from the traditional sources of Islamic law.[16]

Even this survey of one aspect of political thought and its transformation shows how multi-centered political life in Iran has become. Most importantly, there is a three-way stand-off between a pragmatic administration, represented by the presidency, a socially and economically conservative parliament, and the economic radicals, who want more state intervention in everything. From Khomeini's time to the present, much of the argument over the legitimacy and scope of authority of the office of *marja'* has been closely tied to the struggle over conflicting economic and social policies, although it should be remembered that "factions" united on any issue will very seldom completely overlap with factions formed over another issue. Struggles over these conflicts are complicated by the degree to which the present Iranian constitution reflects the French Constitution of the Fifth Republic, which assumed that the president (namely, de Gaulle) and the majority in the legislature would agree, a condition often not realized in either system. Moreover, from a religious point of view, there is a tension in Islam as in so many other religions between individual responsibility and leadership. As Khomeini acknowledged in his first draft of *The Guardianship of the Jurist*, a *mujtahid* cannot submit himself before the fact to the forthcoming opinions of another *mujtahids*. Iranian public life has reached something of a stalemate not only because of the stand-off between the parliament, presidency, and radicals, but also because it was impossible to build a true hierarchy of subordination in the sense of the Catholic Church. Twelver Shi'ism is a system in which the leader can lead, but his most important potential "subordinates" (*mujtahids* who do not claim to be *marja's*) are obliged by a religious precept *not* to follow. One can seek the political logic of creating a "papacy," as the ever inventive Ayatollah Jannati has suggested, but such an institution would run against the logic of Twelver Shi'ism's millennium-long construction of the behavior of the believer in the absence of infallible advice.[17]

Nevertheless, this millennium-long discussion has dramatically changed in the past two centuries. The change reflects the increase in communication and travel, which has made it physically possible for the highest *marja'* to be in touch with the faithful throughout the world. The "manuals" for the ordinary believer that are issued by the *marja'* seem to have become common only in the nineteenth century. Organization has developed in the granting of the degree of *ijtihad*, increasingly a formal matter. And, in post-revolutionary Iran, a system of informal deference has given way to a system of election through balloting, whether in the Council of Experts set up by the constitution or in the self-generated Association of Teachers in Qum.[18]

Yet, the greatest influence on the transformation of the clergy has been its interface with the emerging modern state. Already during the Safavid dynasty a bureaucratic government had created hierarchy in the clergy. Al-Karaki, for example, as the government-installed head of the religious establishment, was called "the *mujtahid*" of his time, a title that seems to imply that any potential *mujtahids* were not encouraged to offer opinions while al-Karaki was in power.[19] The modern state, however, is a much more powerful affair. As the modern state emerged, the *ulama* saw the need for more centralized clerical leadership to stand up to the state, although rivalry and the lack of a real hierarchical principle meant that Shi'ites, who theoretically favored a central religious authority, have managed to produce such widely recognized leaders for only limited periods in the past two centuries. The idea of deferential leadership based upon consensus among fairly limited communities of *ulama*, found in Egypt, Iran, and other parts of the Islamic world, is fairly old, as we have seen. But an activist leadership is new and still, for many of the *ulama*, goes against the grain.

Machiavelli is often seen as the origin of modern Western political thought because he identified a public realm that had its own interests and named this realm the "state." The name has stuck, and many believe that the morality of government cannot be guaranteed by the personal morality of the ruler, as seemed true when we had "governments" but not yet "states." With the birth of the state, a question opened which has never been closed: Can any individual, by his or her virtue, "irradiate" the state with goodness? With the Iranian revolution a religious clergy, which was only loosely hierarchical, attempted to create a "republic of virtue," in part by creating an individual "source" of virtue, a tradition that goes back at least as far as Plato's *Republic*. Fifteen years after this experiment began, with revolutionary fervor very much diminished and serious economic and social problems on every side, it remains an open question as to whether the Iranian state and Iranians as individuals can agree on the same single source as a highest arbiter of morality for the state and for the individual. Has the "cunning of reason" irreversibly created a *de facto* independent statist sphere that will last, or is this sphere only a temporary outcome of the reversible cunning of men?

PART TWO

Foreign Policy in a Changing Region

CHAPTER 4

Iran's Gulf Policy: From Idealism and Confrontation to Pragmatism and Moderation

Mohsen M. Milani

With the end of the Cold War, the West lost its conspicuous and powerful nemesis, the Soviet Union. An obvious replacement has not been found. This confuses the Western policy-makers, who for decades viewed the world through a Manichaean framework. It is also generating competing paradigms that explain the dynamics of the emerging new world order. In one of these evolving paradigms, militant Islam, with Iran as its heart and soul, is portrayed as a menace to the West.[1] Today, alarmists talk about the inevitable "clash of civilizations" between Christianity and an alliance of Islam and Confucianism.[2] The men of the turban in Tehran have been directly or indirectly linked to nearly every tragic incident of terrorism, from Lebanon to Buenos Aries, and have been accused of supporting or inspiring the burgeoning Islamic movements that haunt the Islamic world from Egypt to Algeria to Gaza. Given this mindset, it is hardly surprising that Iran's current Gulf policy is labeled as messianically imperialistic, and that its overtures of moderation are disregarded as clever diplomatic initiatives to disguise its dual conspiracy: to impose hegemony and export revolution.[3] Many of these are highly exaggerated assertions.

This writer maintains that Iran's Gulf policy is no longer confrontationalist and based on idealistic principles, as it was during the Iran–Iraq war. That posture was necessary to consolidate the Islamic revolution and the rule by the fundamentalists as the new elites. Today, Iran's policy, moderate and pragmatic in tenor, is dedicated to regional stability and to a peaceful resolution of the regional conflicts, including the Abu Musa conflict. Three factors have led to this change. First, Iran is in transition to the reconstruction phase of the revolution. Since the death of Ayatollah Ruhollah Mussavi Khomeini (1902–89), Iran's Gulf policy has been based more on national interests than on ideological considerations. Tehran has recognized that it does not have the ability to alter radically the region's political map or to export its revolution. Second, the Islamic Republic has begun to rebuild Iran's shattered economy. Toward this goal, it seeks to contribute to regional stability, to improve political relations, and to expand commercial activities with its Arab neighbors, particularly with the members of the Gulf Cooperation Council (GCC). By contributing to stability on its southern border, Iran pursues two objectives: to persuade the Arab oil producers to lower production levels and increase oil prices, and to concentrate on the Muslim republics of Central Asia, where the 1991 collapse of the Soviet Union created alluring political and economic opportunities. Finally, the United States' military presence in the region and its determination to protect its interests and allies have convinced Tehran that the most prudent policy is to accept the status quo.

Revolutionary Romanticism and its Limits

When more than two centuries ago the French revolutionaries celebrated the world's first modern revolution, they were intoxicated with the dream of creating a new France and a new European order. So optimistic were they about this mission that they replaced the Gregorian calendar with a revolutionary calendar that started at zero and renamed every month of the year.[4] Those who opposed them were decapitated by the guillotine, the instrument of death the revolutionaries left as a legacy. Gradually, the revolutionaries recognized the difficulty of changing France's well-entrenched institutions and traditions and the dominant European order. Many revolutionaries were themselves guillotined, and the revolution, under some pressure from Great Britain and its allies, acquired a more moderate temperament.

Using the experience of the French and other revolutions, Crane Brinton hypothesized that revolutions usually begin with moderation, move toward extremism, and finally return to sanity in the Thermidorian reaction.[5] He coined this phrase in reference to the month of Thermidor, when Maximilien Robespierre, the chief architect of the Reign of Terror, was guillotined. Some aspects of his analysis can be applied to the evolution of Iran's Gulf policy.

Like the French revolutionaries, Iran's revolutionaries started their rule in 1979 by pursuing a utopian agenda, believing in the inevitable triumph of Islam and their ability to create a new man. Examples abound: Ayatollah Khomeini declared in 1979 that the revolutionary government was obligated to provide free electricity and water for the poor, and the Islamic constitution stipulates that the Islamic Republic must support the meek and the disinherited in every part of the globe.[6] Also revealing is V. S. Naipaul's discussion of the mindset of some Iranian revolutionaries in the book *Among the Believers*, which illustrates how deeply revolutionary romanticism was embedded in the minds of the Islamic radicals and how dangerously inflated their estimates of Iran's capabilities were.[7]

It was this revolutionary romanticism and the desire to Islamicize Iran that quickly and divisively polarized the country. This polarization proceeded rather slowly during Mehdi Bazargan's rule (February–November 1979). Bazargan was a Persian first, a Muslim second. A devout Muslim but a passionate nationalist, he believed that the protection of Iran's territorial integrity and economic interests must form the basis of Iran's foreign relations. Consequently, his Gulf policy was not radically different from that of the Shah's. Although he rejected Iran's role as the "policeman of the Gulf," Bazargan was unprepared either to dismantle the Shah's military establishment, or to terminate Iran's major military treaties with the United States.[8] He developed congenial relations with Washington and with Iran's Arab neighbors, based on mutual respect, reciprocity, and non-interference in each other's affairs. Iraq, however, was alone among the Gulf countries in not responding positively to this conciliatory policy. The tense bilateral relations deteriorated further when, in opposition to the occupation of the American Embassy in Tehran in November 1979, Bazargan resigned.

The hostage crisis was a turning point in the history of the Islamic Revolution. Marking the triumph of the fundamentalists and the demise of the nationalists, it drove the revolution toward radicalism and facilitated a power shift from the nationalists, who received much of their support from the modern middle class, to the fundamentalists, whose core support were the *ulama*, the lower classes, and the traditional middle class.[9] Although the fundamentalists, who lacked the skills needed to manage the country's international affairs, failed to formulate a coherent policy with clear objectives and strategy, they nevertheless changed the direction of the country's foreign relations. In theory, the principle of "Neither East nor West," which rejected any alignment with either of the two superpowers and emphasized an independent foreign policy, became the cornerstone of their policy.[10] In practice, however, vehement opposition to the United States was the primary concern of the new rulers. With this critical departure from the Western/American camp, Iran became increasingly entangled in the politics of the Islamic world.

The desire to revive Islam became the essence of this entanglement.

Given its proximity to Iran and its sizable Shi'a population, the Gulf was naturally the first area where the Islamic Republic could flex its ideological muscle. This is why the possibility of the spread of the Islamic Revolution generated a justifiable fear among the Arab nations. Ayatollah Khomeini's declaration that Islam was incompatible with the institution of the monarchy – the dominant form of government in the region – coupled with the inflammatory rhetoric from Iranian officials who denounced all the Gulf states as stooges of "American imperialism," intensified this fear. Iraq, with its considerable Shi'a population, felt vulnerable, too. Taking advantage of Iran's internal chaos and its debilitating international isolation brought about by the hostage crisis, Iraq invaded Iran in September 1980. President Saddam Hussein hoped, among other things, to replace the Shah as the hegemon of the region and to destroy the Islamic revolution.[11] But he failed to understand that wars have historically helped consolidate revolutions and strengthen the radical elements. The invasion of France by the armies of Austria and Prussia in April 1792, for instance, made it possible for the radical Jacobins to defeat the moderate Girondists and impose the Reign of Terror.

In Iran, the war consolidated the Islamic revolution, undermined the moderates, accelerated the drive toward radicalism, and unified the whole country behind Ayatollah Khomeini. But Khomeini, unlike Bazargan, was a Muslim first, a Persian second. His ultimate allegiance was to Islam. A pan-Islamist, he was obsessed with Islam.[12] It was his love for Islamic revival that guided his Gulf policy, which was totally subordinated to his war policy.

At first, Iran's objective was to expel Iraq from Iranian soil; hence, the popular and intensely nationalistic support for the war. By 1982, Iran had retaken Khoramshahr and had begun its offensive on Iraqi soil. At that time, the Arab League, supported by the GCC, called for an immediate ceasefire and offered Iran a sizable compensation. Defiantly, Tehran rejected this and other peace proposals. In fact, Iran's war objectives expanded: Khomeini was now determined to topple Saddam Hussein, to spread his revolution to the region and beyond, and to become the region's ideological hegemon. This confrontationalist and highly ideological policy crystallized itself in the slogan of "War, War, until Victory." Some believed that they would defeat Iraq and establish an Islamic government there. There seemed to be no limits to revolutionary fantasy, as some zealots believed that "Karbala is only the first stop on the road to Jerusalem." There were domestic considerations for this change and for the continuation of the war. In reality, the Islamic Republic was simultaneously fighting two interrelated wars: externally against Iraqi aggression and internally against those who opposed Iran's Islamicization. Stalemate was the result of the first war, victory of the second.

The war with Iraq was a blessing in disguise for the fundamentalists. During the war, the legal and educational systems were Islamicized and a comprehensive cultural revolution was launched. The war made it easier for the fundamentalists to consolidate the revolution and defeat their enemies: President Abul Hasan Bani Sadr, whose ideology they abhorred, was removed from office and forced into exile; the People's Mujahedin-e Khalq organization, an Islamic-socialist group that enjoyed considerable support among the youth, was seriously weakened and was compelled to move its operations out of Iran; the National Front, that last bastion of Iranian nationalism, was neutered and its publication offices shut down; the Moscow-backed Tudeh Party, the agenda-setter of the left, was humiliated and then dismantled; and, the small but vocal Marxist and Maoist groups were treated no better than the Tudeh.[13]

The war had other benefits. First, because the armed forces were preoccupied with the war, the chances of a military coup against the fundamentalists were substantially diminished. Second, the war diverted public attention away from internal difficulties. Third, because of the war, the US economic sanctions, and the flawed trade policy, the government was forced to ration essential goods. Often, local mosques became the distribution centers for ration cards, thus placing the *ulama* at the helm of a massive distribution network. This system not only created a large black market, it also turned the mosques into a powerful economic force at the community level. Finally, the merchants and the new class of entrepreneurs benefited immensely from the war and increased their political power.

Thus, the drive toward Islamicizing Iran and the hardening of Tehran's position in the war were intimately linked.[14] Its uncompromising demand for Iraqi capitulation, its goal of spreading its revolution, and its face-to-face confrontation with the United States all isolated Iran in the region. Viewing the war as an ideological conflict between Islam and its enemies, Tehran could not take advantage of the major differences between Iraq and the littoral Arab states. Many of these countries feared Iraqi expansionism as much as they feared Iran's revolution. But Iran did little to befriend the GCC members, not all of whom wanted to support Iraq.[15] Although they all supported Iraq, it was mainly Saudi Arabia and Kuwait that lubricated the Iraqi war machine with their magnanimous financial contributions, estimated at over $35 billion.[16] In a sense, Iran was becoming a prisoner of its own ideology: Having proclaimed the Arab countries of the Gulf as stooges of the United States, Tehran could not form an alliance of convenience with any of them, or even keep them neutral, and thus became even more isolated.[17]

At first, it appeared that nothing could weaken Khomeini's resolve to win the war. In fact, for a moment in 1987 it looked like Iran could win: US House Joint Resolution 216 warned that the continuation of the war could result in an "Iranian breakthrough" which would damage US "strategic interests."[18] Consequently, a campaign was begun to prevent an Iranian victory. Under the guise of protecting Kuwaiti ships, the United States increased its military involvement. Internationally isolated, unable to gather much support to condemn the USS *Vincennes* downing of a civilian aircraft, which killed all 290 passengers, faced with waning popular support for the war, and militarily under pressure from the US and Iraq, Iran at last accepted a UN ceasefire resolution in July 1988.[19]

Both Iran and Iraq failed to decode the messages the world was sending. Saddam Hussein could not digest the fact that although the West was supporting him lavishly, it was not in order to make him the region's hegemon, but merely to contain Iran, and no more. Blinded by idealism, Khomeini could not see, or perhaps refused to accept, that the two superpowers, especially the United States, would have never allowed Iran to win. Such a victory would have been detrimental to their interests and would have resulted in a major realignment in the Middle East. In the end, Saddam Hussein did not succeed in becoming the hegemon of the region or destroying the Islamic Revolution, nor did Khomeini succeed in exporting his revolution or overthrowing Saddam Hussein. Sadly, the war, whose staggering cost is estimated to exceed both nations' total oil revenues in this century, devastated their economies, killed thousands of people, and made millions more homeless.[20] It is lamentable that Henry Kissinger's hope of having two losers in that war was realized.

Domestic Bases of Iran's Gulf Policy prior to the Invasion of Kuwait

In June 1989, Ayatollah Khomeini died. With the exception of Mozaffar ad-din Shah Qajar, Khomeini was the first Iranian ruler of the past 150 years to die in office. All other rulers, save for Naser ad-din Shah Qajar who was assassinated, were forced into exile, where they eventfully died. This fact helps confirm that the revolution was consolidated before Khomeini's death.

But the Iran he left to his successors was far different from the one he took over from the Shah. It was an internationally isolated country with a tarnished image. It was an Iran exhausted from the tumultuous consequences of experiencing both revolution and devastating war in one decade. During his rule, the population grew rapidly, while the country's oil revenues diminished significantly, and Iran lost its leadership role in the Organization of Petroleum Exporting Countries (OPEC). Without resorting to foreign borrowing, the government spent much of its scare resources to finance a costly war and to compensate the war victims. Thus, the government did little to improve the economy, and by the end of the war, Iranians had experienced a 50 percent reduction in their real per capita income.[21] For this reason, the people began to demand the "peace dividend." Because he was a unique product of unique historical circumstances, Khomeini could ignore the public outcry about deteriorating economic conditions, declaring that the "Iranian people did not make the revolution to own watermelon," a symbolic reference that underscored his rejection of materialism as the *sine qua non* of the revolution. His successors, however, could not ignore the economic situation; they had to improve, or at least promise to improve, the economy. And this is exactly what his successors promised.

After Khomeini's death, Seyyed Ali Khamene'i was elected as the *faqih* and Ali Akbar Hashemi Rafsanjani was popularly elected Iran's fourth president. They ascended to power only after the Islamic constitution was revised: the *faqih* no longer had to be a leading *marja'-e taqlid* (source of emulation), and the president's powers were substantially augmented.[22] The president is now in charge of the Supreme Council of National Security, which coordinates the activities related to defense, intelligence, and foreign policy. These constitutional changes reflected the transition from the consolidation to the reconstruction phase of the Islamic revolution and the re-emergence of the state as a central force of authority.[23]

Rafsanjani's election brought to power the pragmatic faction of the fundamentalist camp and made economic reconstruction the top priority.[24] His first five-year development plan (1988–93) was based on attracting foreign capital, importing modern technologies, increasing oil revenues, and borrowing on the international market. Operating under inhospitable conditions, Rafsanjani has been able to invigorate the oil industry. Some of the major refineries and oil platforms have been repaired and oil production has increased. There has been a small shift away from state ownership of the major industries, price regulation, expensive subsidies, and the closing of Iranian markets to foreign products, to a more market-regulated economy, privatization of a few strategic industries, reduced subsidies, and the opening of Iranian markets to foreign products and investments. The two free-trade zones in the Qeshm and Kish islands and the operation in Iran of a few American-based companies, like Coca-Cola and R. J. Reynolds, are only a few examples of this new economic policy. But perhaps the most symbolic manifestation of the new economic climate is that the revolutionary graffiti on city walls are being gradually replaced by billboards advertising European and Japanese products. Rafsanjani recognized that without some major changes in Iran's foreign policy his economic program would fail. This is why he proceeded with a cautious *rapprochement* with the West and changed the essence of Iran's Gulf policy, a policy in which Iranian nationalism plays a much larger role than before.

Besides the factors alluded to above, Rafsanjani's own world view was an important impetus behind this critical transition. Among his many books and articles, including the translation from Arabic to Persian of a book about Palestine, *Amir Kabir* is his most serious scholarship. This book, written in the 1960s when the young Rafsanjani was intensely engaged in anti-Shah activities, is about the strong and reform-minded prime minister in the mid-nineteenth century who is appropriately regarded as the father of Iranian nationalism.[25] Rafsanjani's selection of Amir Kabir as the focus of his research reveals much about him. He wrote the book because of his admiration for the reformist prime minister and also because "from an Islamic perspective, Amir Kabir seemed interesting to me [Rafsanjani] and because as a nationalist he initiated moves and rendered services that were compatible with my own Islamic views."[26] This subtle recognition that Iranian nationalism and Islam can be rendered compatible distinguishes Rafsanjani from many other figures in the Islamic Republic – he is simultaneously a dedicated Muslim and a Persian nationalist.

If we define pragmatism as a philosophy based on "accepting the world pretty much as it is and working with compromise and caution to move it in incremental steps along a preferred path," then Rafsanjani's new Gulf policy was remarkably pragmatic and moderate in temperament.[27] The new policy was based on three considerations. First, Iran cannot change the region's political map, a fact recognized by some young elements in the foreign policy establishment even before Rafsanjani was inaugurated, and now more widely accepted.[28] Second, Iran tried to adjust itself to a new balance of power in the region. The United States played a major role in creating this new balance of power. During and immediately after the end of the Iran–Iraq war, the objectives of the United States were to keep the Soviet Union out of the region, to contain Iran, and to protect its enormous oil investments.[29] Thus, it pursued a strategy that strengthened Saudi Arabia militarily as a deterrent against both Iran and Iraq, helped form the Gulf Cooperation Council to prevent the spread of the war, and improved relations with Iraq.[30] After the end of the war, both Iraq and Saudi Arabia, which had emerged with the best-equipped armed forces in the region, hoped to impose their hegemony. And the GCC had become a power to be reckoned with.

Facing these realities, the Rafsanjani administration hoped to achieve three objectives. The first was to contain Iraq. Iran tried to convince the regional countries that Iraq was expansionist and posed the greatest threat to their rule. As Washington was at the time cuddling up to Saddam Hussein, Iran's warnings about Iraq landed on deaf ears. The second objective was to improve relations with the GCC, which required a commitment to regional stability. Rafsanjani said that, "Iran must stop making enemies" and refrain from intervening in the internal affairs of others, an unambiguous signal that the export of revolution was no longer a policy objective.[31] He in effect recognized the legitimacy of the region's states.

Recognizing Saudi Arabia's growing power and its leadership role within the GCC, Iran began a dialogue with Saudi Arabia. However, relations could not be improved quickly. The hardliners strongly opposed any rapprochement: the memory of the Mecca tragedy, in which some four hundred pilgrims were killed, was still fresh in Iran. Moreover, the two nations' disagreements over the number of Iranian pilgrims allowed at Mecca, their rivalry in Central Asia and Afghanistan, their diametrically opposed oil policies, and their leadership claims over the Islamic world were and still are serious obstacles to improving bilateral relations.

Improving relations with the other littoral countries proved to be much easier for Tehran. This was possible partly because of the sizable Persian population in these countries. Moreover, with the notable exception of Kuwait, these countries were not following an overtly anti-Iran policy during the Iran–Iraq war. In fact, Tehran maintained relatively good relations with the United Arab Emirates and Oman during the war. After the war, the volume of trade between Iran and its smaller Gulf neighbors substantially increased. Moreover, these states were encouraged to invest in Iran; and, in turn, Iran created two free-trade zones in Qeshm and Kish to solidify its ties with them and to attract foreign capital.

Iran's third objective was to increase its influence on the region's oil policy, pushing for lower production levels and higher prices. This proved to be the least successful aspect of Rafsanjani's policy. With the notable exception of Iraq, the Gulf nations opposed his policy. The factors that determined the price of oil were simply beyond Tehran's reach and power.[32] In short, Iran, the champion of radical change for much of the 1980s, became an advocate of regional stability and cooperation. Soon after Iran formulated this policy, however, Iraq invaded Kuwait, the United States stationed its troops in the region, and the Soviet Union collapsed, forcing Tehran to rethink its strategy.

Iran's Policy Following the End of the Cold War

Iraq ended its war with Iran with an impressive arsenal of weapons of mass destruction, a large and battle-hardened army, and about $80 billion in foreign debt.[33] By invading Kuwait, Iraq made itself another victim of the policy of containing the Islamic revolution: to contain the revolution, Iraq invaded Iran; to prevent losing the war, Iraq armed itself heavily; and this militarization effort led to borrowing, which created Iraq's financial crisis, which in turn led to conquest.

Iran was the first Gulf country to condemn Iraq and to demand its total and unconditional withdrawal from Kuwait.[34] The introduction of thousands of US troops into the region, coupled with Saddam Hussein's attempt to entangle Iran in the conflict, placed Rafsanjani in a delicate position, however. To appease Tehran, Saddam Hussein even accepted the 1975 Algiers Agreement, writing to Rafsanjani, "Now that you have gotten everything you have asked for, we must work together to expel the foreign troops."[35] Rafsanjani accepted the peace offer but rejected any collaboration with Iraq. Neither did he follow the advice of some hardliners. Arguing that the United States was planning to establish a military base in the region, which would then make it a much more dangerous threat than Iraq, they proposed the options of either siding with Iraq or opposing both Baghdad and Washington. Rejecting such suicidal policies, Rafsanjani opted for what this author calls "active neutrality": to maximize Iran's national interests by standing on the sidelines without antagonizing either Baghdad or Washington.

Active neutrality and Tehran's implementation of the UN-imposed sanctions against Iraq were proof that Iran's new Gulf policy was not tactical. But even more revealing was Tehran's inaction during the Iraqi civil war. After Iraq's violent expulsion from Kuwait, there were popular uprisings by the Kurds in the North and the Shi'ites in the South. While the Kurds were at least allowed to establish a token government, the Shi'ites met a tragic end. Fearful that a Shi'ite victory could lead to the Balkanization of Iraq and to increased Iranian influence, the allies preferred a wounded Saddam Hussein to a Shi'ite or even a democratic government.[36] Consequently, the Iraqi army was allowed to crush the Shi'ites brutally while the world watched in cynical silence. Although the Islamic Republic sympathized with the Shi'ites and called for Saddam Hussein's resignation, and although some Iran-based Iraqis were permitted to go to Iraq to fight with the rebels, Iran remained remarkably passive during the bloody civil war. Tehran did not want to spoil what it had gained through active neutrality. Bluntly stated, national interests rather than Islamic solidarity dictated Iran's policy.

Iraq's defeat was welcomed by Tehran, for its rival was now relegated to "a preindustrial age." However, Iraq's defeat, auspicious as it was for Iran, was hardly as significant as the military presence of the United States in the region and the dissolution of the Soviet Union. Despite these momentous changes, which had rendered the policy of "Neither East nor West" obsolete, the goals of Tehran's Gulf policy have remained intact, although Tehran has modified some of its diplomatic tactics.

The collapse of the Soviet Union has meant that Tehran can no longer rely on Moscow to neutralize Washington.[37] This has diminished Iran's bargaining position with the West and has created instability on its northern borders, specifically in the republics of Armenia, Azerbaijan, and Turkmenistan. But in this chaos, Tehran saw unprecedented opportunities to expand its influence in these Muslim republics with whom it shares deep cultural, linguistic, and religious ties. The close economic cooperation between Iran and these republics and the signing of various protocols in the past few years confirm Iran's commitment to regional stability.

In the Gulf, too, Iran has remained committed to regional stability and economic cooperation, both of which are intimately linked to its prosperity. Virtually all of its petroleum exports, which constitute more than 90 percent of the government's revenues, and a sizable portion of its imports, pass through the Gulf. In conducting its policy, however, Iran has to deal with the United States, whose military presence has exponentially increased in the post-Gulf War period.

Despite occasional fiery rhetoric by some *ulama*, Iran has reluctantly accepted the US military presence as a *fait accompli*. Historically, however, Iran has always opposed the presence of foreign troops in the area, believing that regional issues and conflicts must be resolved by regional players. Even the overtly pro-American Muhammad Reza Shah opposed having the US military replace that of Great Britain. In the 1960s, after Britain decided to withdraw its forces from the Gulf, the Shah told Asadollah Alam, his close confidante, that "the Americans should realize our opposition to foreign intervention in the ... Gulf is serious."[38] Thus, the US desire to establish military bases and replace Britain dates back to the late 1960s, and Iran's opposition to the US military presence predates the Islamic Republic of Iran. The Islamic Republic's opposition to the stationing of American troops, therefore, has nothing to do with extremism or with Islam. It reflects a conflict between two nations with different national interests. But Tehran has accepted the status quo not only because it logically has no better choice at this time, but also because it benefits from the US presence. Washington's policy of containing Iraq, monitoring its military activities, and preventing its rearmament – identical to Iran's Iraq policy – has allowed Tehran to focus on reconstruction and on rapprochement with the GCC.

Much more damaging to Iran than the US military presence is Washington's current policy of "dual containment."[39] Whereas the Bush administration used a "carrot and stick" approach, based on the notion of "good will begets good will," the Clinton administration has pursued a multifaceted campaign to isolate, if not to destabilize, Iran. The United States has also opposed Iran's active participation in any regional security arrangement. Not only has Washington sold huge quantities of modern armaments to the members of the GCC, especially Saudi Arabia, but it has also signed defense treaties with Kuwait and other GCC members that would allow for frequent US and joint military training exercises in their waters.[40] The sad fact is that the Gulf has become the world's most militarized region. Excluding the expenditures for Qatar and the expenditures for Iran and Iraq in 1992 (on which information is not available), the countries of this region have spent a staggering $157 billion on military expenditures from 1989 to 1992.[41]

Iran has tried, albeit unsuccessfully, various non-military means to minimize the impact of the US presence and its policy of "dual containment." The Rafsanjani administration has tried to reduce regional tension, avoid direct confrontation with Washington, and persuade GCC members that what is good for America is not necessarily good for them. Tehran has urged the GCC members to distance themselves from the United States by pursuing a non-aligned foreign policy, arguing that by collaborating with the United States they will deprive themselves of popular and Islamic legitimacy and will probably meet a fate no happier than that of the Shah. Iran has repeatedly pointed out that because of its desire to control the region and keep the price of oil low, the West has historically tried to divide the nations of the region by accentuating their differences, pitting one country against another, and preventing their unity. The present US policy, Tehran believes, is in total harmony with this traditional strategy. Although the Iraqi invasions of Iran and Kuwait in less than one decade have convinced most GCC members that Iraq, not Iran, poses the greatest threat to their survival, Iran has failed to convince the GCC members to distance themselves from Washington.

Nevertheless, neither has the United States been able to create a new collective security arrangement, nor has the GCC become any stronger in the post-Cold War era. After the liberation of Kuwait, there was much enthusiasm about creating a viable regional security arrangement. President Bush even hinted that Iran could participate in such an arrangement. But Iran was never invited, and President Clinton is adamantly against any Iranian participation. At first, the GCC considered entering into a military alliance with the poorer Arab countries of Syria and Egypt. But recognizing the inherent dangers of inviting these countries into this region, they quickly and wisely abandoned the idea.[42] The fact that no security arrangement has yet been constructed is not due to Iran's policy: Saudi Arabia, the driving force behind the GCC, and the United States recognize that a viable security apparatus must include Iran, something neither power is prepared to accept at this juncture.

Having failed by diplomatic means to persuade the countries of the GCC to distance themselves from Washington, Tehran has focused on those issues that can solidify its ties with them, such as containment of Iraq and increased trade. Ironically, the current and mutual policy of Iran and the GCC to contain Iraq has remarkable similarities to policies pursued by the Shah in the 1970s. The mutuality of interests has created a favorable climate for both sides to proceed with a much-needed rapprochement. But the potentially explosive Abu Musa conflict may reverse this positive trend.

A New Approach or the Failed Policies of the Past

The world is rapidly moving in a new direction: regional integration and cooperation. While it is impossible to conceptualize the exact configuration of the post-Cold War era, one thing is clear: regional trading blocks and economic integration are the dominant and arguably the irresistible trend of the future. The evidence is overwhelming. Western Europe, with its diverse peoples, soon will be unified, most likely with a unified currency. In 1994, Mexico, Canada, and the United States signed the North American Free Trade Agreement (NAFTA), which is designed to open up the markets of these large economies, to increase regional integration and trade, and to eliminate or reduce tariffs. In the same year, all North American nations with the exception of Cuba, which was not allowed to participate, signed an agreement that will increase economic cooperation and trade among them. For the past few years, the prosperous and productive nations of Southeast Asia have already been moving in that direction.

With much of the world already moving toward regional integration, the countries of the Gulf seem to belong to a different age and a different path. Unless they reverse their present course, every single one of them, large and small, powerful and weak, risk becoming marginalized in a new global economy. The Gulf nations have a great deal in common: besides being Muslim, they are all rich in oil reserves and therefore do not suffer from scarcity of capital, a factor debilitating for so many developing countries. Only economic integration and greater political unity can bring long-term stability, prevent the marginalization of the region in the evolving world order, and allow the region's nations to become the largest importers not of weapons, as is the case today, but of goods and technologies that can raise the living standards of their people.

After two devastating wars that have depleted many of the Gulf region's precious resources, the region needs to be viewed using a different paradigm. The oil-rich region must be conceptualized as one unit, not as isolated entities. Instability in one component of that unit will inevitably lead to instability in others. Imposing one's hegemony on others may bring short-term stability, but it is a recipe for long-term chaos. The best guarantor of stability is economic integration, as the incentives for military confrontation would be reduced if each country in the region were to have sufficient investments in the others' economies. Unrealistic as this may sound, it is the only remaining alternative. If the region is to move in that direction, the regional powers must try to resolve their differences peacefully. They must move forward and form regional banks; regional cultural, educational, and charitable centers, and regional court systems where regional conflicts are addressed and, it is to be hoped, resolved. The manner in which Iran and the United Arab Emirates decide to resolve their contention over the sovereignty of the Abu Musa and the Tunb islands will reveal much about the future direction of the Gulf.

The Abu Musa dispute has once again fueled Arab suspicions about

Iran's hegemonic intentions. It began in August 1992, when Iran expelled some migrant workers who lacked proper documentation from a Sharjah ferry. Tehran justified its action, which it called an internal security matter, by claiming that the 1971 Iran–Sharjah Memorandum of Understanding granted Iran control over security matters.[43] At first, the United Arab Emirates demanded direct negotiations with Iran. Tehran accepted. Quickly, Egypt and some other Arab states announced that they were ready to defend the smaller Arab state against "Persian expansionism." Encouraged by this support, the UAE suddenly demanded negotiations, not only about Abu Musa but also about the two Tunb islands that Iran controls. Tehran rejected the proposal. Today, emboldened by its close ties with Washington and London, and encouraged by the generous support it receives from the other GCC members and the Arab League, the UAE insists on arbitration by the International Court of Justice. Rejecting that court's right to render judgment on what Tehran considers an internal conflict, Iran continues to call for direct, bilateral negotiations. If this conflict is to be resolved peacefully, then both sides must be exceptionally sensitive to the domestic constraints under which they operate. Clearly, both have conflicting claims over the disputed islands. Given the scope of this chapter, only Iran's position and dilemma will be addressed.

The Abu Musa dispute is potentially explosive because it reopens a bitter chapter of the colonial legacy. In 1887, the British took over these three disputed islands, which Iran claims were under Iranian jurisdiction.[44] Iran protested the British occupation and ever since has claimed sovereignty over them. In 1971, when the British left the region, the governments of Iran and Britain reached an agreement: Iran was to share the sovereignty of Abu Musa with Sharjah, while controlling the other two islands. In return, Iran opposed neither the formation of the United Arab Emirates nor the May 1970 independence of Bahrain.[45] "By the time that Iran accepted the finding of the United Nations mission and relinquished her claim to Bahrain," wrote one expert, "it was widely believed that in return, Iran had been promised the possession of the three islands."[46] At the time, the Shah felt so strongly about regaining the islands that he publicly declared that Iran would use every conceivable method, including force, to do so.[47] Rejecting a British proposal to lease the islands, the Shah argued that "what is yours cannot be leased to you."

Current Iranian policy toward the islands is no different from that of the Shah. Ayatollah Khamene'i, President Rafsanjani, and many other leaders have repeatedly reiterated that they will not abandon or compromise Iran's sovereignty over the islands. It must be mentioned that the majority of Iranians support the status quo in the three islands. The Islamic Republic simply cannot relinquish Iran's historical claim over the islands; to do so would be nothing short of a political suicide.

The leaders of the UAE, too, are under pressure from nationalists, Pan-Arabists, and outside agitators not to succumb to the Iranian demands. Their national pride and honor are also at stake. And it is precisely because both sides are under such tremendous pressure that they need to negotiate directly and reach some kind of consensus. If they cannot reach an understanding through direct negotiations, how can an international court, without enforcement power, resolve their conflict?

So far, both sides have demonstrated much civility in conducting their affairs. The two countries have lucrative economic ties, and even during the Iran–Iraq war they maintained cordial relations. There is no reason why the two sides cannot continue moving in the same direction of cooperation and dialogue.

Today, most GCC members, including Saudi Arabia, have territorial claims on each other: Iraq has its territorial claim over Kuwait, and Iran can also raise the issue of Bahrain's sovereignty. It serves everyone's interests in the region to help Iran and the UAE resolve their conflict peacefully. Should Iran and the United Arab Emirates resolve their conflict peacefully and through direct bilateral negotiations, they could establish a new and a much-needed framework for resolving regional conflicts. Indeed, they could become trend-setters in the region.

Two wars and much death and destruction in the past fifteen years demand a new approach toward the resolution of regional problems. Peace, not war and preparation for war (militarization); economic integration and increased regional trade, not economic isolation and protectionism; and political dialogue and unity, not political mistrust and suspicion. These are the essential ingredients of a paradigm that may save the region from future calamities.

CHAPTER 5

The Geometry of Instability in the Gulf: The Rectangle of Tension

James A. Bill

The Gulf is a critical global political and economic chokepoint. Here, huge hydrocarbon resources exist in an environment of endemic social and political instability. The eight Gulf states possess approximately 600 billion of the world's 900 billion barrels of proven reserves of petroleum. Despite the collapse of the Soviet Union, the region also remains geo-strategically important due to the belt of instability that exists in the Central Asian republics. This rim of uncertainty is connected to the Gulf through the large buffer state of Iran, which links the Gulf directly to Central Asia. Furthermore, as the Gulf war of 1990–91 graphically indicated, the United States, the world's superpower, views the Gulf as an area vital to its own national interests. Its political and military presence there is deeply apparent to all the littoral nations.

The oil-rich Gulf region is the locus of two major forms of instability, exogenous and indigenous. The exogenously generated instability involves interstate conflict such as that which occurred in the seven-year Iran–Iraq war and in the subsequent struggle between Iraq and the coalition of countries that came to the defense of Kuwait. Other forms of inter-state Gulf conflict include numerous border disputes and contentious debates about the control of large oil and gas fields.

The indigenous roots of instability are even more important than the dramatic instances of interstate conflict. These roots of potential upheaval are numerous and deeply embedded in the sands of the Gulf. They, in turn, can be divided into two categories: social problems of identity and political problems of legitimacy. The identity crisis is a fundamental issue exacerbated by the numerous divisions in Gulf societies. These divisions include tensions between Persians and Arabs, Shi'ites and Sunnis, expatriate workers and the small citizen workforces, and the wealthy economic elites and the poorer classes of the population.

These primary social classifications are further divided within themselves. The Shi'a–Sunni distinction, for example, can be broken down into Persian (*Ajam*) Shi'ites and Arab Shi'ites. The Arab Shi'ites are themselves divided into two other categories, those who originate from Bahrain (*Baharna*) and those whose ancestral roots are located in eastern Saudi Arabia (*Hassawi*). Furthermore, cutting across the Shi'a–Sunni divide are various iterations of Islam. Both Shi'a and Sunni communities are fragmented by the struggle between a populist Islamic ideology and an establishment (official) Islamic belief system. This particular confrontation between populist Islam (*al-Islam al-sha'bi*) and establishment Islam (*al-Islam al-rasmi*) could become a serious divisive issue within the Gulf states.[1] In situations where the issue of identity is uncertain and confused, the populist Islamic message carries a special resonance.

The legitimacy crisis concerns issues such as personal freedoms and human rights, the emphasis on rule by law, and effective political participation. The peoples of the Gulf states must feel that they have a stake in their particular political systems; they must know that they are, in some degree, serious partners in the political decision-making that affects their lives. These states must work to build "civil society," a society in which there is a tolerance for diverse opinions and an openness to new and different ideas.[2] The existence of civil society promotes legitimacy which in turn builds a shared solidarity that strengthens the state against internal upheaval and external aggression.

Traditionally, legitimacy was built upon participatory networks consisting of *majlises* and *diwaniyyehs*, personalistic free-floating assemblies organized around specific influential leaders. The *majlis* system provided access and enabled members of the populace to present their petitions and demands. With expanding modernization and sharply increasing populations, this traditional, localized system is less effective than it once was. As a result, Gulf states have begun to establish other participatory bodies such as country-wide consultative assemblies and parliaments.

The drive to build legitimacy through effective national participation has begun in the Gulf. Kuwait has led the way in this important process of political institutionalization. The October 1992 Kuwaiti elections resulted in the establishment of a national assembly in which 30 opposition members hold seats. The discussions and debate in the assembly have been vigorous. Moves in the direction of serious political participation have also occurred in the other Gulf states. In Saudi Arabia, for example, the ruling family has put in place a *majlis al-shura*. Although carefully handpicked and neither seriously representative nor autonomous, the very existence of some kind of national *majlis* in Saudi Arabia indicates the direction that the political winds are blowing in the Gulf.

Although there is a clear recognition that problems of identity and legitimacy must be confronted by the political leaders of the Gulf states and although steps have been taken to address these issues, these two core problems still loom large in the region. As such, they will remain as underlying causes of uncertainty and instability in the Gulf.

The Political Rectangle in the Gulf

The four corners of the Gulf rectangle of tension include Iran, the GCC (Gulf Cooperation Council), Iraq, and the United States. The complex relationships that link these four actors include patterns of collaboration and conflict, continuity, and change. By identifying and isolating these relationships, one may develop a better sense of the political future of the Gulf. In order to do this most expeditiously, one must first systematically describe each of the corner actors in the system. Figure 5.1 provides a diagrammatic representation of this system.

Iran: the revolutionary regional hegemon   With a population twice that of all the other Gulf states combined, Iran stands as the demographic giant in the region. By the year 2025, the Islamic Republic is projected to have a population of 160 million, considerably more than any other Middle Eastern country, including Egypt and Turkey.[3] Iran has rich oil deposits, the second largest natural gas reserve in the world, a sizable educated middle class, a battle-tested military, and an institutionalized political system.

Iran has done relatively well in addressing the problems of identity and legitimacy. There is a constitutional system in place that includes an elected president, an elected 270-person parliament (Islamic Majlis), a cabinet nominated by the president but approved by the Majlis, a predominant "leader" (*faqih*), and a series of intermediate councils whose members are either appointed or elected. The Islamic Republic's elections, conducted every four years since 1980, provide the franchise to every Iranian, male and female, age 16 and over. The *Economist* magazine includes Iran as one of only seven Muslim countries out of a total of 39 that can "hesitantly be called democracies."[4] In the words of the article's author, "Surprised respect is due to the Islamic revolutionaries of Iran for holding freeish elections that have produced a parliament happy to argue with the government."[5] Despite these strengths, Iran has been the scene of

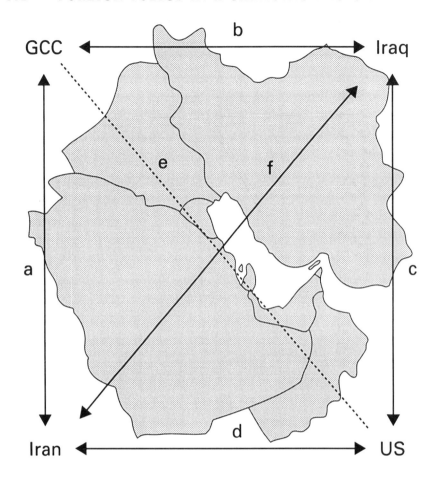

Figure 5.1 The Gulf rectangle of tension, 1995

considerable electoral manipulation. More seriously, Iran's human rights record has been abysmal.

Iran's power position in the Gulf rectangle is further strengthened by its close association with Shi'a Islam. Since 1501, Shi'ism has been the state religion of Iran, and the Islamic Republic stands as the major nation-state promoting the Shi'a faith system. Since there are Shi'ites residing in each of the other seven Gulf states, Iran shares a common ideological mindset with many of the citizens of the other Gulf countries.

The Islamic Republic of Iran, on the other hand, is beset by a number of crippling problems. Its economy is in shambles; the scale of corruption is unprecedented; its swollen administrative system is staffed by un-productive and incompetent bureaucrats; its industrial establishment is paralyzed and inefficient; and, in part because of American policy, it remains isolated from much of the international community. Iran's prob-lems can best be summarized as follows: At the time of the revolution, when Iran's population was 38 million, it had an economic infrastructure that was barely adequate to meet the needs of that population. Today, Iran's population is 62 million people yet the infrastructure is still one built to sustain and support 38 million people. Furthermore, Iran is the home to more refugees than any other country in the world. The Islamic Republic must feed, clothe, and shelter approximately 3,500,000 refugees, most of whom are Afghans. Despite its many problems, Iran is the regional hegemon.[6] Regardless of the complexion of the political system, huge numbers of Iranians will populate the shores of the Gulf.

The Gulf Cooperation Council: the fragile regional coalition   Formed in May 1981, the GCC consists of six countries: Saudi Arabia, Kuwait, Oman, Qatar, Bahrain, and the United Arab Emirates (UAE). The GCC is a loose confederation of conservative states designed to protect the political status quo in the Gulf. The GCC's principal purpose has been to enhance the security of its member states; it is not accidental, therefore, that the organization was founded in the wake of the Iranian revolution.

The power position of the GCC rests almost entirely upon the con-siderable economic resources of its members. The oil reserves of the GCC countries, for example, outstrip those of Iran by a factor of five to one and those of Iraq by four to one. In an attempt to bolster their respective military positions in the Gulf, the member states of the GCC have spent huge sums of money, purchasing some of the most sophis-ticated airplanes, tanks, and missile systems in the world.

Nonetheless, their small populations and armed forces, and divergent interests have left the GCC states exposed before regional powers such as Iran and Iraq. In 1995, the population of the GCC countries is estimated to be slightly more than 20 million people, only a third of the population of Iran.[7] The demographic vulnerability of these states is further evident in the fact that one country, Saudi Arabia, accounts for 70 percent of the GCC's total population.

A further detrimental factor influencing the GCC corner of the Gulf rectangle involves the sharp divisions that cut through the coalition. The economic power and political influence of Saudi Arabia is dominant. The Saudi voice, within the councils of the GCC, is the loudest. Also, because each of the six members of the organization is a sovereign state in its own right, perceptions and interests vary widely. Divisions within each of the GCC countries further complicates the system. The UAE, for example, is composed of seven distinct emirates.

The system of political interaction between the GCC states has acted both as a source of stability and as a cause of instability. The structure's very looseness and the fact that the cleavages crisscross the system result in a certain flexibility and balance.[8] On the other hand, the incessant rivalry and competition present the constant specter of conflict and violence. One leading scholar of the Gulf, therefore, writes about the "uneasiness of the equilibrium which persists between competing forces in the area".[9] He goes on to explain that "these forces, whether in the form of territorial rivalries ... of dynastic rivalries among their respective ruling families, or of rivalries among them on national and economic grounds, give the Gulf a unique character in regional and international affairs."[10]

Besides these interstate GCC rivalries, each Gulf country confronts the internal problems of identity and legitimacy referred to above. The political systems of these small states have managed to survive for two major reasons. First, their leaders have generally been astute and sensitive to the needs of their people. Sheikh Zayed Bin Sultan Al-Nahyan of Abu Dhabi is a major case in point. Second, the leaders of the GCC countries have had access to extraordinary financial resources that they have shrewdly used to buttress their rule and to placate the potential opposition.

In sum, the GCC is challenged by many levels and types of division. Nonetheless, many of the cleavages are cross-cutting and tend to balance one another in a system of numerous fractionating and fluctuating forces.

Iraq: the military aggressor state The Iraqi actor in the Gulf rectangle of tension is both powerful and aggressive. Iraq's offensive military activity against its neighbors was most recently seen in its initiation of both Gulf wars of the 1980s and early 1990s. Its invasions of Iran on 22 September 1980, and of Kuwait on 2 August 1990, stand as striking evidence of the Iraqi government's political intentions. In both cases, the regional aggressor state sought to take territory from its neighbors through the use of force. Despite its costly defeat in the second Gulf war, Iraq continues to cast covetous eyes in the direction of Kuwait, and most Iraqis, regardless of their positions concerning Saddam Hussein, share a deep belief that Kuwait should rightfully be an integral part of Iraqi territory. Iraq reminded the world of its position in this regard in October

1994, when Saddam Hussein unexpectedly moved significant numbers of troops to the Kuwaiti border. This action not only alarmed Kuwait, but it caused the United States to respond with a significant military deployment to the Gulf region.

After Saudi Arabia, Iraq has the largest petroleum reserves in the Middle East. It has a large, educated middle class, and its professionals are among the most talented in the Arab world. Despite the dictatorial rule of Saddam Hussein, a relatively effective process of political institutionalization has taken root in Iraq. The Ba'ath party has been the instrument for this institutionalization as its branches extend widely throughout the country. Despite the devastation of two wars, the Iraqi military remains a relatively formidable force. Iraq has more advanced aircraft, tanks, and missiles than Iran, and its standing army is over three times as large as that of all the GCC countries combined.

Like the other actors in the Gulf rectangle, however, Iraq suffers from a number of weaknesses. These weaknesses are social and political in nature. Socially, Iraq is a country with especially deep internal divisions. The major divisions involve the Kurds in the North and the Shi'ites in the South. Iraqi governments have sought for many years to contain and control these groups. Since the Iraqi defeat in the second Gulf war, the United States has taken the lead in a policy that has created externally protected zones of autonomy in the Kurdish area of the North and, to a lesser extent, in the Shi'a-populated South. Furthermore, a punishing economic embargo has sharply curtailed Iraq's capacity to market its petroleum.

Politically, the continuing existence of the Saddam Hussein dictatorship has greatly compromised the important principle of legitimacy. Under Saddam Hussein, Iraq has the dubious record of being a particularly oppressive police state. As long as he remains in power, Iraq will be a society with a huge gap between the political leadership and the general population.

Viewed dynamically, however, Iraq will be a force to be reckoned with in the Gulf for many years to come. Its rich oil reserves, competent technocracy, and relatively large population (second to Iran in the Gulf) are indicators of Iraq's long-term importance. Today, however, Iraq remains weakened and contained in the aftermath of the 1990–91 war. The continuing fallout from the war has compromised Iraq's territorial integrity, diminished its economic and political power, and dulled its national image.

The United States: the intrusive global hegemon   Throughout recent history, the Gulf has witnessed the presence of a global great power that has profoundly influenced the social, political, and economic dynamics of the region. The Dutch and then the British exerted enormous influence in the region from the seventeenth to the twentieth centuries. The British, in particular, dominated Gulf affairs for over two hundred years. Through a wide array of instruments such as the ubiquitous East India Company, the Royal Navy, and the Trucial Oman Scouts, Great Britain oversaw Gulf affairs until the early 1970s. From the early nineteenth century, the "Gulf was fitted into Britain's worldwide system of informal empire."[11]

In 1968, Great Britain announced its intention to withdraw its forces east of Suez, and in 1971, it implemented this dramatic decision. In the past quarter-century, the United States has slowly moved into the region, taking over more and more responsibility as time has passed. The deepening American presence in the Gulf has been accelerated by US economic interests that depend upon favored access to the rich oil deposits of the region.

Heavily lubricated by oil, US–GCC relations are tightened by commerce and trade. Table 5.1 provides data that demonstrate the strength of this commercial connection. Between the end of the Gulf war in 1991 and the end of 1994, the United States exported $41 billion in goods to the GCC countries. In return, US imports from the GCC coalition totaled $46 billion. Crude petroleum accounted for over 90 percent of US imports from Saudi Arabia and Kuwait. When refined and derivative products are included, oil-related products accounted for over 95 percent of American imports from these two Gulf countries. Table 5.1 also indicates the overwhelming economic presence of Saudi Arabia, which accounts for nearly 75 percent of the GCC's commercial activity with the United States.

Between 1987 and 1993, total Saudi trade with the United States doubled. During these years, Saudi Arabia was America's largest supplier of crude oil, providing nearly double that sold by any other country. By 1995, Saudi Arabia had become one of America's top 15 international trading partners. Today, Saudi Arabia transacts more trade with the US than do countries such as Australia, Switzerland, Israel, India, Spain, Indonesia, or Brazil.[12]

The disruptive instability occasioned by the Iranian revolution of 1978–79, the Iran–Iraq war of 1980–88, and the Iraqi invasion of Kuwait in 1990 have effectively drawn the United States into a direct and unprecedented presence in the Gulf. Besides its considerable commercial

Table 5.1 US trade with GCC countries, 1991–94 (millions of dollars)

		1991	1992	1993	1994*	Totals
Saudi Arabia	Exports	6,572.0	7,163.3	6,665.6	5,719.8	26,120.7
	Imports	10,978.3	11,285.7	8,431.5	7,009.8	37,705.3
Kuwait	Exports	1,228.3	1,326.9	1,009.0	997.0	4,561.2
	Imports	35.9	310.0	2,003.4	1,644.8	3,994.1
UAE	Exports	1,455.7	1,552.4	1,811.4	1,497.2	6,316.7
	Imports	713.9	871.9	744.5	462.2	2,822.5
Bahrain	Exports	501.0	488.7	653.1	620.4	2,263.2
	Imports	86.8	71.2	109.4	140.0	407.4
Oman	Exports	203.5	257.4	265.3	268.8	994.8
	Imports	115.0	207.3	305.0	347.0	974.3
Qatar	Exports	147.4	189.1	166.3	155.6	658.4
	Imports	29.7	76.0	72.3	88.6	266.6
US export total		40,915,000				
US import total		46,170,200				

Note: * Estimate based upon projection from January–June 1994 statistics.
Source: US Department of Commerce.

and military presence in Saudi Arabia, the United States has approximately ten thousand troops both on the water and in port in the Gulf region. Following the October 1994 incident in which Saddam ominously moved his troops toward the Kuwaiti border, the United States increased the number of its aircraft stationed in the Gulf for long-term duty from 70 to 130. The United States also prepositioned equipment for armored brigades in Kuwait and Qatar and began negotiations with other Gulf states to accept a third brigade.[13]

In his State of the Union address on 23 January 1980, President Jimmy Carter stated that "an attempt by any outside force to gain control of the … Gulf region will be regarded as an assault on the vital interests of the United States of America, and such an assault will be repelled by any means necessary, including military force."[14] Every American president since Carter has affirmed this extraordinary commitment, and US forces have subsequently been involved in numerous military engagements in the region. The principal example, of course, was the movement of nearly half a million American troops to the Gulf in the war against Iraq in 1990–91.

In analyzing the power position of the US corner of the Gulf rectangle of tension, it is an uncontestable fact that American economic, technological, and military capacity is overwhelmingly superior to that of any of the littoral Gulf states. With the collapse of the Soviet Union, the United States stands as the sole global superpower. The devastating nature of US technological and military might was witnessed in the Gulf during the campaign against Iraq in 1990–91.

Despite the overwhelming might of American power, the global hegemon is circumscribed in its capacity to bring its power to bear in the Gulf. Geographically, the Gulf is 8,000 miles away from the American homeland. This fact alone imposes limits and costs on the external actor. Even though the United States has "prepositioned" weapons, facilities, and troops in the region, it must still maintain a long and expensive lifeline to the Gulf theater.

A related and more serious obstacle to the American position involves internal political constraints. As sole global superpower, the United States is increasingly pressured to intervene in a number of explosive trouble spots around the world. In recent years, the challenges have emanated from places like Somalia, Rwanda, Bosnia, North Korea, Cuba, and Haiti. There has been pressure of various degrees for American intervention in each of these cases. Moreover, in a world of great incoherence, the number of conflicts and serious crises is sure to increase. In such a situation, even a global hegemon has limitations – economic, political, and military.

At home, the United States is confronted by internal problems that encompass everything from health care and education to crime, drugs, and environmental deterioration. Political capital, social energy, and financial resources are required to address such issues. Many Americans, both in government and outside of government, consider these domestic priorities to be most urgent. As a result, the American people are increasingly reluctant to approve and fund overseas interventions.

Observers sometimes overlook the heavy financial costs of military intervention in the Gulf. Estimates indicate, for example, that it costs over $150 million to move one aircraft-carrier battle group from the Pacific to the Gulf.[15] While most official estimates of the cost of the October 1994 military movement into the Gulf suggested between several hundred million and one billion dollars, the actual cost was closer to $5 billion. Although its allies in the GCC reimburse the United States for most of these costs, the expenditures represent a heavy burden for even these oil-rich states, which desperately require funds for their own expanding developmental and security needs.

With the passage of time, it appears that the United States will intervene internationally only under exceptional circumstances. Future interventions will occur if there is an immediate and direct threat to US basic interests and if the costs of such interventions (whether financial or human) are modest and reasonable. The case of Somalia demonstrated that the American public has a low level of tolerance for activities that take American lives in faraway places.

Despite the costs and trauma of the 1990–91 Gulf war, the US has demonstrated that it will intervene in the region when its perceived vital interests are threatened. The movement of Iraqi troops towards the Kuwaiti border in October 1994 brought a dramatic American military response. Nonetheless, in comparison to the 1990–91 conflict, this response was limited. It is doubtful that the global hegemon can respond indefinitely with hundreds of thousands of troops whenever a crisis develops in the Gulf. Certainly, Iraq, and possibly Iran, will continue to probe and test American resolve and capacity to project power in the Gulf.

In sum, although the global hegemon may possess overwhelming power in comparison to the other actors, does the American superpower have the will and capacity to bring that power to bear on situations of crises as they proliferate across the world? Although it is impressively superior to local actors in most indices of power, even the US faces limitations.

The Dynamics of System-Instability in the Gulf

The Gulf system can be best described as a rectangle of system-challenging tension in which each of the actors exists in a tenuous state of balanced conflict with each of the other actors. There is one important exception to this delicately balanced rectangle of tension. The global hegemon (the US) has entered the system in a collaborative arrangement with the fragile coalition actor (the GCC). This sole line of cooperation represents a case where the weakest of the three regional actors has its position reinforced by an external actor. In the case of the Gulf region, the US–GCC line of alliance represents the dominant force dedicated to preserving the regional status quo. Figure 5.1 provides a diagrammatic representation of this geometric model.

Because the global hegemon strongly backs the weaker status quo-oriented actor, it finds itself inevitably in conflict with the two change-oriented regional powers, i.e., Iran and Iraq. Iran and Iraq, in turn, are locked in conflict with each other. The revolutionary regional hegemon and the militaristic aggressor state are natural adversaries, each seeking regional dominance. In this situation, it seems to be in the interest of the status quo coalition actor (GCC) and its backer, the global hegemon (US), to reinforce and encourage the natural tension that exists between the two more powerful regional actors.

The Iran–Iraq War of the 1980s, therefore, was supported in varying degrees by the GCC coalition and its external patron, the United States. Both the coalition and the global hegemon provided substantial amounts of assistance to the Iraqi aggressor state during the war. They did so based upon their own calculations that Iraq was less of a threat to the Gulf system than Iran. With its large and somewhat alien (Persian, Shi'ite) population and with its expansive revolutionary mindset born of the revolution of 1978–79, Iran was viewed as a serious threat by both regional and global status quo powers. In this case, the global hegemon not only perceived its regional friends to be threatened, but it also found itself, in the larger international context, to be the direct object of much of the animosity of the revolutionary Gulf hegemon. Given its extensive support for the Shah's regime and its active opposition to the revolution, the United States inevitably entered into a conflictual relationship with post-revolutionary Iran.

The Gulf system is highly unstable in nature. Misperceptions and miscalculations by any actor or combination of actors can lead directly to violence and to the system's collapse. This, in fact, occurred when the militaristic aggressor state, Iraq, turned on its weaker neighbor, indeed on its recent ally, the GCC coalition, and launched a military attack on Kuwait in August of 1990. Only the massive intervention of the international community in defense of the coalition thwarted the Iraqi aggression. In intervening, the coalition succeeded in defending the existence of both Kuwait and the viability of the GCC itself. The loss of Kuwait would have splintered and significantly weakened the GCC. Also, the military intervention of the global hegemon protected the general political status quo in the Gulf, at least for the time being.

The numerous lines of conflict (e.g., Iran–Iraq, Iraq–GCC, GCC–Iran, Iran–US, US–Iraq) are shown in Figure 5.1. The lone line of cooperation is the GCC–US relationship. Violent conflict can break out any time along the five major lines of tension. Furthermore, the intensity of the tension between actors is deepened over time in the Gulf system.

When confronted with serious internal problems, the actors in this system of balanced tension are likely to engage in more aggressive external political activities. Since both Iran and Iraq in particular face numerous domestic crises, one can expect continuing trouble along the current lines of conflict. There are many examples of this principle of the relationship of internal–external crises in the Gulf region. Saddam Hussein invaded Iran at a time when revolutionary messages emanating from Iran were stirring internal unrest in parts of Iraq and across the Gulf. Ayatollah Khomeini kept the revolution from faltering in Iran by continuing the war beyond the time when his country could have achieved a favorable ceasefire. Saddam attacked Kuwait at a time when both his political and economic systems were faltering after the long war with Iran. Iran continues to rally its population by stressing adversarial actions taken by the United States. The US government in turn has used Iranian actions to rally its people in support of its own policies in the Middle East.

A second observation concerning increasing instability in the Gulf relates to the widening impact of any conflict. In the Gulf, where the system has been interlocking and overlapping in character and where chains of rivalry have existed over time, one conflict tends to exacerbate another. The reverberating Iranian revolution of the late 1970s led into the Iran–Iraq war of the 1980s, which in turn fed into the Kuwait-coalition war against an Iraqi invader in the early 1990s. It is unlikely that the cycle of conflict is yet complete.

In such a volatile system, it is very difficult for any actor to remain aloof from regional conflict. This tendency to conflict-proliferation is heightened by the existence of a rich natural resource in the region. Petroleum is a conflict accelerator. In both recent Gulf wars, therefore, all the Gulf states were involved on one side or the other. In the long Iran–Iraq conflict, the GCC states generally took the side of Iraq. In the subsequent war, they opposed Iraq.

Because of its extraordinary oil wealth and its geostrategic position, the Gulf region is closely linked into the international system. During the Cold War years when there were two global hegemons, both the Soviet Union and the United States were bound closely into the Gulf network, the Soviet Union through ties with Iraq and the US through relationships with Iran and Saudi Arabia. With the end of the Cold War and the collapse of the Shah's regime in Iran, the United States has been forced to maintain one link into the Gulf, Saudi Arabia and, more generally, the GCC. The twin-pillar policy has given way to a single-pillar policy. This principal linkage, therefore, has been strengthened and reinforced by the global hegemon. On the other hand, in the process of maintaining and strengthening its presence in the Gulf through close ties with the GCC, the United States has frontally confronted the Islamic Republic of Iran, i.e., the global hegemon and the regional hegemon stand in fundamental confrontation with one another. This encounter is the most important line of tension diagrammed in Figure 5.1 (see path d).

Regional and Global Hegemons: Collaboration or Conflict?

The two revolutionary Gulf states, Iraq and Iran, are also the most populous and militarily powerful states in the region. According to reputable demographic projections, these two countries will account for over 80 percent of the population of the Gulf by the year 2025.[16] Iran and Iraq, therefore, seem certain to be especially influential in the region in coming years. In the short term, Iraq, a military predator state currently governed by Saddam Hussein, requires special attention. Viewed strategically, however, Iran is most important.

With a population over three times that of Iraq and barring any major economic or political catastrophe, Iran's position as regional hegemon seems assured. Even today, it is difficult to discuss seriously any regional agreement or security pact without the active participation of the Islamic Republic.

Although the GCC and its individual members, as well as Iraq, undoubtedly play important roles in determining the Gulf's political future, the fate of the region may very well be decided primarily by the relationship that develops between the regional hegemon, Iran, and the global hegemon, the United States. If this strained, contentious, and outright hostile relationship continues to deteriorate, today's uneasy political balance could easily explode into violent conflict tomorrow. If this relationship moderates and improves, however, the situation in the Gulf is likely to be brighter for all who inhabit the region.

Since the 1978–79 revolution, Iran's relations with the United States have been poor. American indignation with Iranian behavior was most vigorous when Iranian extremists held 52 US diplomats hostage for 444 days in 1979–80. Iran, on the other hand, remembers the strong American opposition to its revolution and the US tilt to Iraq during the long and costly Iran–Iraq war.

Both the regional and global hegemons have a long list of grievances against one another. The United States decries Iranian support for political violence abroad (especially its backing of the Hizbollah and Hamas groups), Iran's blemished human rights record at home, and Iranian independent foreign policy which includes vociferous official opposition to the Palestinian–Israeli peace talks. Iranians, on the other hand, remember July 1988, when a sophisticated Aegis-class cruiser, the USS *Vincennes*, shot down a civilian Iranian Airbus, killing all 290 passengers. Iranians were outraged when US government spokesmen lied about the incident and when the American naval officer who had ordered the attack was awarded a medal of commendation.[17] Furthermore, Iran opposes the heavy American military presence in the Gulf (a body of water 8,000 miles from the United States but bordered for 1,500 miles by Iran) and resents the numerous acts of US punishment such as the continuing economic embargo against the importation of most Iranian goods into America.

There are two mutually reinforcing general reasons for the US government's active opposition to the Islamic Republic. First, Washington has been pursuing a crudely fashioned foreign policy whereby it has generally opposed the rise of regional hegemons. This has, of course, been especially the case with respect to those regional great powers that have developed stubbornly independent foreign policies. Examples include North Korea and China in East Asia, North Vietnam in Southeast Asia, Nicaragua and Cuba in Latin America, Sudan and Libya in North Africa, and Iran and Syria in the Middle East.[18] With the collapse of the Soviet system, the United States stands alone as world superpower. In this position, it seeks to discourage the formation of pockets of power over which it has little or no control.

The US government also is sharply opposed to the Islamic Republic of Iran because it stands as a special threat to American economic interests. Iran's starkly independent (often viewed as recalcitrant) political behavior – in a region where Western economic interests float on a sea of oil – is a matter of considerable concern in Washington. Iran's critical geostrategic position is also seen to the north where international (including American) companies are scrambling to sign concessions in the Caspian Sea basin.[19] The United States remains strongly committed to protecting its economic interests in the Gulf – hence the massive mobilization of force it brought to bear against Iraq in the second Gulf war. Although not often admitted at the time, the fundamental reason for the intervention was the need to protect America's access to Middle Eastern oil. The continuing nature of the American commitment is evidenced by the sharp political reaction and military mobilization in response to

Saddam Hussein's troop movements in the direction of the Kuwaiti border in October 1994.

The anti-Iran campaign that persists in the United States today is encouraged and supported by political actors that are determinably pursuing their own agendas. Two actors are especially influential. The first, a radical Iranian opposition group named the Mujahedin-e Khalq, has managed to build an international propaganda machine that is extremely effective, especially in Washington. In Iran itself, however, the Mujahedin has disgraced and discredited itself by establishing its headquarters in Iraq, where it receives support and encouragement from the regime of Saddam Hussein. Despite its obvious failure in Iran, however, the Mujahedin has managed to enjoy a popular image among a group of stalwart if uninformed supporters in the US Congress.[20]

The second voice loudly condemning the Islamic Republic is the government of the state of Israel. Israeli leaders are quite clear about this. Iran is now presented as Israel's "Enemy No. 1" and "the whole Israeli political and intellectual establishment, in fact, has been galvanized to put across this message."[21] With the collapse of the Soviet Union, Israel has sought to maintain its privileged position *vis-à-vis* the United States by calling attention to a new world threat, i.e., Islamic "fundamentalism" in general and Iran in particular.

For these reasons and others, the line of conflict (see conflict path d in Figure 5.1) between Iran and the United States is especially tense. The strength of this line of contention overrides that of all the other lines of rivalry inherent in the Gulf system. Furthermore, the unprecedented heavy US presence throughout the Gulf places the two countries in dangerously close proximity to one another. As long as the regional and global hegemons confront one another, political stability in the Gulf remains extremely precarious.

As the global hegemon maneuvers to squeeze, isolate, and weaken the Islamic Republic, it in fact strengthens the forces of extremism that continue to smoulder in Iran. Such policy risks crippling and humiliating the regional hegemon, and could cause it to pursue increasingly desperate and aggressive political activities. The greater the tension between the United States and Iran, the closer the system approaches violent explosion.

Furthermore, the unpredictable political and military actions of Iraq, the military aggressor state in the region, will also directly and violently challenge Gulf stability. The majority of Iraqis, for example, are committed to the conquest of Kuwait, which they believe belongs to them. Since Iran is the only littoral Gulf state that can confront Iraq, the

Islamic Republic carries special significance to the GCC countries. An alienated Iran, under fierce pressure from the global hegemon, could conceivably ally itself in many different degrees and ways with Iraq. Such an alliance could be disastrous for the GCC coalition, which would then require a total and long-term commitment of support from the global hegemon.

In this situation, it might be in the interests of the GCC states to work to ameliorate the tension and to lessen the confrontation between Iran and the United States. Since the GCC actor is the sole regional force in alliance with the global hegemon, it is only the members of this coalition that can reasonably expect to influence the behavior of the American superpower.

In the early years of the revolution, Iran adopted an unfriendly, hostile attitude towards the GCC countries. By radio and television, the Islamic Republic spread its *tablighat* (sacred propaganda) across the Gulf and at times pro-Iranian groups engaged in violent, disruptive activities in various Gulf states. This policy began to change in the late 1980s, when Khomeini died and the war with Iraq ended. In November 1989, Iran convened a major international conference in Tehran entitled "The Persian Gulf." Iran used this conference as the vehicle to announce a new foreign policy towards the Gulf, one of solidarity (*hambastegi*) and peaceful coexistence with its immediate neighbors. Since that time, the regional hegemon has taken some acts to lessen the tension and distrust between itself and the GCC bloc. Despite Iran's sporadic gestures of friendship towards its immediate neighbors (Iraq excluded), the line of tension (see line a in Figure 5.1) between the Islamic Republic and its Arab GCC neighbors will continue to exist. Incidents such as the recent differences concerning the Gulf islands of Abu Musa and the Tunbs, the quarrels over Iranian attendance and behavior during the *hajj*, and fundamental foreign policy differences concerning the Arab–Israeli issue are cases in point. Iran has acted in an extremely clumsy and heavy-handed manner with respect to the Abu Musa controversy. This has been particularly troubling to the United Arab Emirates. The underlying tension between Iran and the GCC states persists also due to the inconsistent and strident rhetoric that emanates from the Islamic Republic.

As long as there is distrust and animosity between the regional and global hegemons, there will be distrust and animosity between the regional hegemon and the local allies of the global hegemon. Iranian leaders are well aware of this, and in their speeches they repeatedly attempt to warn the Gulf states about this linkage with the United States. In the process,

Iranian leaders are of course seeking to draw the GCC countries closer to the Iranian axis.

Iranian leader (*faqih*) Ali Khamene'i, therefore, defiantly proclaims that Iran is "neither scared nor afraid of anyone, nor do we need anyone." He goes on to say that "colonialism's old policy is to divide and rule ... to create discord." Khamene'i then invites the GCC states to unite, collaborate, and cooperate with the Islamic Republic against Europe and America, who "want cheap oil." President Rafsanjani reinforces this message in a direct appeal to the Gulf Arabs: "My dear fellows, let us sit together and be friends. Iran is next to you. We can support each other and create a regional security organization so that we will not have to pay blackmail to American soldiers or sell our oil cheaply."[22]

Traditionally, the states that compose the GCC coalition have managed to survive politically through diplomatic skill and astuteness. The leaders of these political entities have shrewdly maintained their systems of rule through the application of a mixture of traditional political participation and the recruitment of timely intervention by external actors. As humankind approaches the twenty-first century, however, the GCC countries may wish to consider adopting new domestic and foreign policies.

At home, the GCC states are challenged by the core problems of identity and legitimacy. Success in addressing these issues will build solidarity and credibility. The traditional leadership might consider sharing decision-making power with skilled and talented groups committed to building new and stronger political systems and states. A transformed leadership would mean a transformed consciousness that would in turn provide new regional policy.

Such policy might consider, among other things, a carefully planned withdrawal from total reliance on an external, intrusive global force and a growing cooperative relationship with the regional states, especially with the regional hegemon. The increasing American presence, which risks converting the GCC countries into military outposts or territorial aircraft-carriers for the global hegemon, is guaranteed to provoke and alienate the local forces of nationalism and Islamic populism. Such unleashed forces would in turn intensify the confrontation between the global and regional hegemons.

The alternative to future violence and conflict in this explosive rectangle of tension is for a lower US profile in the region and some kind of rapprochement between the global hegemon and the Islamic Republic. If this were to occur, the lines of conflict that now mark the Gulf rectangle of tension could slowly give way to relations of cooperation and collaboration. The geometry of the Gulf system today reflects short-term, enforced, artificial stability that masks an underlying axis of instability. The new Gulf system would be characterized by occasional ripples of unrest at the surface while the strategic political foundation would be solid and enduring.

CHAPTER 6

The Impact of Iranian Foreign Policy on Regional Security: An External Perspective

Geoffrey Kemp

The purpose of this chapter is to examine the impact of current Iranian policy on regional security, with special reference to the security of the Gulf. By virtue of its population size, history, geography, and natural resources Iran is destined to be a major player in the security of the Gulf, no matter who rules in Tehran. A strong, vibrant and self-confident Iran with reconstituted military forces would clearly pose problems for weaker neighbors and give voice to those who claim that Iran seeks to exercise hegemony over the region. On the other hand, a weak, suspicious, and divided Iran – such as exists today – poses different, but significant threats to regional security. Even if a counter-revolution turned Iran into a pro-Western democracy, quarrels would likely persist with its Arab neighbors and the West over such issues as oil production and pricing, as was the case when the Shah ruled Iran.[1]

The Iranian regime has a highly negative image in the Western media and in many Gulf countries. It is accused of promoting terrorism in Europe, the Americas, and throughout the Middle East; undermining the Middle East peace process; killing and torturing its own citizens; persecuting religious minorities and especially the Baha'is; calling publicly for the murder of Salman Rushdie; and making territorial claims against its Gulf neighbors. In addition, Iran is accused of undertaking a major arms buildup including sophisticated submarines, missiles, advanced combat aircraft, and perhaps nuclear weapons.

Those who disagree with this characterization of Iranian behavior argue instead that it is Iran that is threatened and militarily insecure. Isolated internationally, Iran faces trouble on all its borders. To its west, north, and east are dangerous or unstable regimes whose violent activities may spill over and undermine its own internal cohesion. To the south lies a suspicious group of rich Arab countries, well armed and protected by the world's remaining superpower. It is not difficult, in other words, to see why *any* regime in Tehran would feel insecure in this particular neighborhood. To demonize Iran, further isolate its leaders, and hurt its economy ensures future dangers and chaos throughout the region.

The Iranian regime has made efforts to improve its image with the world community, including the international financial institutions, but these have met with only muted success. America's preeminent political and military position in the Middle East poses a key threat to the Iranian regime. Iran's leaders were awed not only by the speed and effectiveness with which American and other military forces destroyed Saddam Hussein's war machine (in contrast to their own humiliating and costly defeat by these same forces), but also by the fact that in the *aftermath* of Desert Storm the US presence remains very visible. The key Arab Gulf states now have more formal bilateral military relations with the United States and are expanding military cooperation with each other, as well as building up their own arsenals. The rapid and forceful US response to Iraqi military moves in October 1994 only reinforced this Iranian perception of a US–GCC alliance.

Similarly, the redrawing of the Middle East map as a result of the Gulf War and the break-up of the Soviet Union has created new and fluid frontier zones to Iran's west, north, and east that pose challenges as well as create opportunities. The defeat of Iraq during Desert Storm left the central Iraqi government at odds with Iraqi Kurds and Shi'ites. While the breakup of Iraq is unlikely, the overall instability of the region could undermine any Iranian advantages gained from a weaker Iraqi government and military. The conflict between Armenia and Azerbaijan and the links between independent Azerbaijan and Iranian Azerbaijan are just two of the many regional issues that have direct consequences for Iran. As for Central Asia, Iran's influence in the new republics will depend upon economic relations, including infrastructure, more than ideological ties. A host of countries, especially Russia, have opportunities that will likely prevent Iran from assuming a dominant position among foreign players.

Iran's difficulties with the international community, especially the West and the Gulf Arabs, come at a time when the country is experiencing profound political and economic distress. The power struggle between President Rafsanjani and his conservative opponents, led by Supreme Religious Leader Ayatollah Khamene'i, continues against a backdrop of growing domestic discontent, economic weakness, and volatile international relations. In the last two years, the pragmatic and moderate policies that President Rafsanjani began to enact in 1990 have been weakened or dismissed.

In 1994 Iran again experienced urban riots. For the general populace, low wages, rampant inflation, rising prices, insufficient housing, idle factories, and unemployment are daily reminders of Iran's economic disarray. The government postponed the second five-year plan and the GDP per capita is projected to shrink 2 percent this year for the first time in five years. Nostalgia is widespread for the old days when the Shah reigned, the mullahs were quiescent, and America was a friend rather than the Great Satan. Short of an unexpected increase in foreign exchange earnings, economic problems will persist and pressures for the mullahs to step down from day-to-day government will grow.

In recent months there have been a number of smaller challenges to the existing government. The key question is whether these are early signs of the impending collapse of the regime or merely insignificant acts that will do little to alter Iran's general direction. Prominent military figures have issued open letters calling on the government to step aside. Writers and lawyers have called on the government to protect free speech rights, and a more coordinated opposition is emerging to challenge the regime at the parliamentary election in two years' time. Many observers believe that the government itself is facing a crisis of national confidence and is circling the wagons.

Against this backdrop of weakness and dissent, Iran nevertheless poses a number of threats to regional interests which must be carefully examined. These include direct military challenges to the security of the GCC states; possible nuclear, chemical, and biological weapons programs; subversion of friendly regimes such as Saudi Arabia and Egypt; acts of terrorism against the regime's opponents and secularists in other Muslim countries; and opposition to the Middle East peace process. It is useful to distinguish between overt military threats, on the one hand, and those that relate more to subversion and terrorism, on the other. In a time of limited resources, Iran has been more selective in its support for Islamic militancy abroad. In an effort to maximize the effectiveness of its funding, it has kept up support for militant movements and violence that make headlines while withdrawing support from more mainstream Islamic movements.

Military Threats

Iran's professional military leaders now believe that superior military power is decisive in shaping the strategic environment in the Middle East. They learned this lesson the hard way – through their defeat in the Iran–Iraq war and the vivid images of Desert Storm. As a consequence they believe that military preparedness must be granted a high priority. Iran cannot rely on a "people's war" fought with inferior equipment for its defense – a belief its leaders trumpeted in the early idealistic days of the Iran–Iraq war. Instead, Iran needs large stockpiles of modern weapons and a professional force-in-being. The problem is that Iran has neither the trained manpower nor the money to match the conventional capabilities of the United States and its allies. It may therefore be tempted to focus its strategy on subversion and terrorism while exploring short-cut routes to obtain weapons of mass destruction, including a small number of nuclear weapons.

Conventional rearmament   Iran is trying to rebuild, restructure, and modern-ize its armed forces. Although it currently has some money to buy advanced arms on the international market, and most weapons are not difficult to find, the problem of supplier reliability and total costs remains. Russia, for example, may have an ample supply of arms, but it has yet to demonstrate an ability to provide long-term support to its customers. Service is believed to be unreliable and erratic, and spare parts are often unavailable. The issue of Russian weaponry was further complicated for Iran by President Yeltsin's pledge to President Clinton in late September 1994 that Russia would not sign any new defense contracts with Iran. However, Russia agreed to continue to fulfill existing contracts.

The lessons of international sanctions imposed on Iran during the Iran–Iraq war suggest that self-reliance must be one of Iran's long-term goals, if only to avoid future humiliations. This would entail increased domestic production of arms and support items and a decrease in its dependency on foreign supplies. However, the undeveloped state of Iran's domestic armaments industry ensures that weapons produced locally will be inferior to those purchased on the international arms market.

To mitigate the impact of US and West European sanctions, Iran has developed supply relationships with Russia and some of the remaining communist states to buy new aircraft, submarines, tanks, and missiles. While their service leaves much to be desired, Russia, North Korea, and China manage to provide some advanced conventional weaponry. Iran's modernization program should benefit from the arms glut; the problem remains, however, that while arms supplies from multiple sources may tend to reduce the hardships of future sanctions, the inefficiencies of operating different weapons from different suppliers tend to increase.

Iran's exact expenditures for arms purchases have been difficult to pinpoint. In 1992, the Central Intelligence Agency (CIA) estimated that Iran was spending $2 billion on arms purchases. The Iranian minister of defense, Akbar Torkan, claimed that Iran's entire defense budget in 1993 was only $850 million.[2] There was a significant decrease in Iranian purchases in 1992–93. The Stockholm International Peace Research Institute (SIPRI) reported that Iran spent $867 million on the import of major conventional weapons in 1993. Several defense analysts put the 1993 figure around $800 million.

A better indicator than the actual numbers, however, is the general trend of an across-the-board buildup. Iran is rebuilding its military forces, modernizing its equipment, and seeking the most advanced arms where possible. These developments do not necessarily imply aggressive intent. This is still a reasonable program, given Iranian needs and comparisons with past Iranian force levels and those of neighboring states; Iran still has a long way to go to be militarily effective.[3]

If these trends continue and anticipated purchases materialize, Iran could eventually develop a much enhanced naval capability. Its acquisition plans include Russian Kilo-class diesel submarines, Russian SU-24 Fencer attack aircraft, Chinese Silkworm anti-ship missiles and, possibly, the Russian TU-22M Backfire bomber armed with the Kitchen stand-off air-to-surface missile. With a coastline far longer than that of Iraq and more widely dispersed naval assets, Iran could slow the access of major ships through the Gulf and cause trouble for US forces.

All evaluations of Iran's capabilities are dogged by the paucity of concrete facts about the Iranian buying spree. This creates uneasiness as to the accuracy of available estimates. A modernization program is under way, but there is no sense of its parameters. Observers have difficulty assessing the buildup, especially without an end point in sight. Moreover, Iran has yet to decide on an appropriate force structure and doctrine, assure continuity of arms suppliers, standardize its hybrid equipment, replenish stocks, and upgrade existing equipment. These are not easy tasks.

There are, of course, more benign explanations as to what is happening. A comparison of the current inventory against Iran's forces at the peak of the Shah's buildup in 1978–79 reveals that Iran has only one-third to one-half of the major weaponry it had then. It has less than half as many tanks as at the time of the Shah's fall, and most of these are outdated and improperly equipped for night warfare. Iran has a good amount of tube artillery, but is unable to use it properly since it lacks the fire control and target acquisition systems. Iran's approximately one hundred attack helicopters date back to the 1970s. Compared with its well-armed neighbors, Iraq and Saudi Arabia, Iran's potential military threat diminishes. And unlike Iraq and Saudi Arabia, Iran has not been a profligate spender on arms. In fact, if one accepts the 1979 baseline year, trends in military capability and balance have shifted against Iran.

Weapons of mass destruction   There is widespread belief in Western intelligence circles that Iran has embarked on a covert nuclear weapons program. If true, it would represent a new, dangerous threat to the Middle East and would eclipse all other points of contention. There is concern over the security of nuclear weapons and their associated technologies in the former Soviet Union. The specter of an oil-rich Middle East country which harbors nuclear ambitions, finding it much easier to circumvent control regimes in pursuit of covert nuclear options, is very well substantiated. The August 1994 seizures of smuggled radioactive goods in Germany suggest that such a scenario is quite plausible. Some individuals within the Islamic Republic's hierarchy see a utility in Iran pursuing a nuclear weapons program. There is strong evidence that the Iranians are engaged in a modest nuclear research program with possible military implications.

However, confusion abounds regarding the evidence that the Iranians are physically assembling the infrastructure and the teams necessary for a full-fledged nuclear weapons program. In 1992 Iran permitted the International Atomic Energy Agency (IAEA) to inspect its listed nuclear facilities and other installations alleged to contain nuclear activity. On this occasion, the IAEA found no evidence of illegal actions, though some doubt exists within the intelligence community as to whether the IAEA team looked in the right places. According to the open literature, there is no known secret facility in Iran that is physically engaged in the process of building components for nuclear weapons at this time. CIA Director James Woolsey said on 23 September 1994, that "Iran is 8–10 years away from building such weapons, and that help from the outside will be critical in reaching that timetable." He also noted Iranian efforts to purchase nuclear technology and weapons, especially in Russia. The announcement in early January 1995 that Russia had finally agreed to begin work on the unfinished nuclear reactors at Bushehr further confirmed suspicions about Iran's nuclear intentions. Few Western economists accept Iran's argument that it needs nuclear power stations to help redress long-term energy needs.

While Iran has very demanding domestic needs, its hard currency revenues are sufficiently large in aggregate terms that if a small percentage were siphoned off to support nuclear activity, it would amount to a sizable sum. It might be enough to tempt countries or individuals hard-pressed for money to sell Iran the necessary knowledge or technology. Furthermore, Iran has a significant number of well-educated scientists and engineers. The experiences of the Soviet Union, China, and North Korea – poor countries in macroeconomic terms – further illustrate how advanced national security projects can be developed if major resources are allocated to such ends on a priority basis.

The uncertainty about the nuclear program poses a policy dilemma for the United States. Elevating concerns about an Iranian bomb to the top of the list of priorities may weaken US credibility on a whole array of technology-transfer issues and undermine nonproliferation strategies elsewhere. Furthermore, strident American rhetoric that includes discussion of preemptive or covert operations against Iran to stop its nuclear weapons program could have precisely the reverse effect.

On the other hand, taking a relaxed approach and dismissing nuclear rumblings as Mujahedin and Zionist propaganda is more irresponsible. It is essential to focus intelligence efforts on Iran. If Iran is progressing, the West must heighten controls on exports, enact sanctions against those countries or individuals who are party to proliferation, and compel the IAEA to conduct more spot inspections of suspicious Iranian facilities. However, even under safeguards Iran may develop the infrastructure and specialist training in nuclear engineering that could at some point in the future be turned to weapons use, if Iran were prepared to withdraw from the Non-Proliferation Treaty (NPT) or embark on a covert program as both Iraq and North Korea have done.

In September 1994, at the third session of the NPT extension preparatory committee, Iran attacked the Western position on a number of issues. A key Iranian criticism dealt with Article IV of the NPT, which includes the right of non-nuclear states to peaceful nuclear technology. Iran contends that despite this article, the United States and others have repeatedly blocked Iranian attempts to acquire technology for nuclear energy. It was reported that Iran was considering withdrawing from the NPT over this issue.[4] The issue is especially sensitive for Iran, given the US concessions made to North Korea in this very area.

Iran's nuclear ambitions are bound to be influenced by how credible the international community is in persuading Iran that Iraqi nuclear weapons are under permanent international control. Iran must be convinced that an Iraqi program will not reemerge once new leadership comes to power in Baghdad. This will not be an easy task. In the long run it is important to include Iran in any arms control regime in the Middle East. Israel will never agree to Middle East arms control regimes involving nuclear weapons unless Iran, and probably Pakistan, are subject to strict verification standards.

In addition to a possible nuclear weapons program, some analysts express concern about Iran's nascent biological weapons programs. Once developed, biological agents could, in theory, be used for both terrorist and regular military operations. Iran also has the capability to produce chemical weapons, though it signed the Chemical Weapons Convention.

Assessing the military threats   Iran currently poses no significant land threat to any of its Gulf neighbors, including Iraq. Iran's army and air forces would face more severe logistical problems in projecting power into the Arab Gulf states than Iraq encountered. A land invasion of the Arabian peninsula would require initial confrontation with Iraq, which still has the largest ground forces in the region. Any attack across the Gulf waters would require major amphibious and air-lift capabilities, which are presently beyond Iran's capabilities.

Nevertheless, Iran is a maritime power with a long coastline. Beyond simple acts of intimidation against its weaker neighbors, Iran could pose dangers for US and GCC maritime operations if its sea-denial capabilities continue to improve. US aircraft carriers would probably not risk entering the Gulf in the event of likely hostilities with Iran, at least in the early days of confrontation. Hence, they would be limited to air operations from positions in the Arabian Sea and the Gulf of Oman. This, in turn, would limit the range and intensity of naval air operations over Iranian targets, especially those north of Isfahan. The most serious naval challenge to the American fleet would be posed by a combination of submarines, mines, surface-to-air missiles, and long-range strike aircraft with stand-off missiles. While US carriers based outside the Gulf could conduct isolated bombing raids deep into Iran, this could not be done on a sustained basis without land-based air-refueling facilities. According to Western naval intelligence sources, Iranian submariners have struggled to rectify the poor performance of the batteries in their two new Russian-built Kilo-class submarines; Iran has made approaches to Kilo-class sub veterans in "an Indian naval establishment" for help in overcoming the battery challenge since the Indian navy has eight Kilo-class submarines.[5]

To conclude, there is little likelihood that Iran can pose much of a conventional threat to the Gulf as long as the United States maintains a strong forward military presence, expands defense cooperation with the GCC countries, continues to be effective in limiting technology and Western arms suppliers to Iran, maintains cooperative relations with Russia, and commands wide-ranging political support throughout the Middle East. If, however, some of these conditions were to change, Iran's military challenges would be more difficult to counter. The United States cannot assume that the next major crisis in the Gulf will be a repeat of Desert Shield and Desert Storm.

Terrorism and Subversion

While Iran's military potential poses a long-term threat to the Gulf, there are other causes for more immediate concern, namely, Iran's subversion of friendly regimes and support for terrorism, and its rejection of the Arab–Israeli peace process. If Iran and its rejectionist allies succeed in promoting radical regimes in the Middle East, American military strength, no matter how powerful, may not be sufficient to prevent the erosion of stability and increasing threat to the Gulf itself.

Iran's activities in Sudan and North Africa   On 18 August 1993 the US government announced that Sudan would be added to the State Department's list of countries supporting terrorism; they had evidence that Sudan harbors such terrorist groups as Hizbollah and the Palestinian Islamic Jihad. The action underlined Sudan's ever-growing link to Iran, which is a major supporter of these organizations. Tehran supplies Sudan with arms and ammunition and uses it as a training ground for Islamic and Palestinian paramilitary groups. The extent of Iranian influence over Sudan remains unclear.

In addition to US government concerns, officials in Tunisia, Saudi Arabia, Egypt, and Algeria contend that Sudan is a launching pad for Iranian-style militancy and the supplier of significant logistical support for terrorist organizations across the region. Egyptian officials and media spokesmen have initiated a large-scale campaign to assign blame to Iran and Sudan for the surge of violence within Egypt. Arab officials also allege that Iran is supporting Tunisia's banned al-Nahda fundamentalist movement and the Islamic Salvation Front in Algeria. Sources at the Iranian Foreign Ministry stated in November 1992 that Tehran is committed to supporting "the legitimate Algerian revolution against tyranny and arrogance".[6] On 27 March 1993, Algeria announced that after "analyzing the international situation and particularly the interference of certain countries in Algeria's internal affairs, as well as their declared support for terrorism, the High Committee of State has decided to break diplomatic relations with Iran and recall our ambassador to Sudan."[7]

To many Iranian officials, the willingness of Western and Arab countries to publicize Iran's complicity appears hypocritical and self-serving. These countries falsely blame Iran for indigenous opposition movements that harbor legitimate grievances.

Iran has also been implicated in attacks on Jewish and Israeli targets. Approximately one hundred people were killed on 18 July 1994, in a bombing of Jewish organizations in Buenos Aires. Coupled with two bombings in London on 26–27 July, and a 20 July bomb explosion on a Panamanian plane, the disaster in Argentina led a resurgence in international terrorism. Israel has charged that Hamas and the Lebanese-based Hizbollah are responsible for the blasts; Israeli and US officials have also singled out Iran. Iranian operatives have been linked to the 17 March 1992 bombing of the Israeli embassy in Buenos Aires in which nearly thirty people were killed. The Iranian government has repeatedly denied any connection. On 8 May 1992, the US Department of State alleged Iranian involvement in the attack.[8]

Iranian involvement in terrorist attacks in Turkey has also been alleged. Following the 24 January 1993 death of prominent Turkish journalist Ugur Mumcu, segments of the Turkish press accused Iran of having orchestrated the fatal car-bombing. In early February, Turkish Interior Minister Ismet Sezgin announced the arrest of nineteen members of a group called Islamic Action that he claimed had been trained in Iran. They were charged with the murder of two pro-secular journalists, including Mumcu, and an Iranian dissident, Ali Akbar Ghorbani. Ghorbani had been a member of the People's Mujahedin.[9]

Iran supports several organizations that have well-established records of committing acts of terrorism. According to the US State Department and other sources, Iran offers financial, political, and/or logistical support to Hizbollah, Hamas, the Popular Liberation Front, and possibly the Islamic Jihad.

Iran's rejection of Israel and the peace process   The Iranian government severed relations with Israel in February 1979, soon after the overthrow of the Shah. The Islamic Republic has always rejected Israel's right to exist and supported the more rejectionist elements of the Palestinian movement.

Support for Hizbollah and other militant groups is another manifestation of Iranian opposition to the peace process. Hizbollah, Hamas, or other militant groups aligned with Iran can be used to disrupt the process and rattle participants.

In the wake of the Israeli–Palestinian agreement, Iranian rejectionism carries greater risks for Iran's foreign and economic relations, especially the potential for friction with Europe and Japan. Both have been far more willing to deal with Iran than the United States has been. With their strong support for the peace agreements, Europe and Japan may be more likely to heed US calls for diminished ties with Iran and support rejection of Iranian requests for debt relief from the international financial institutions. Iran strongly denounced the Israeli–Jordanian treaty signed on 26 October 1994. Khameine'i called the Arab–Israeli agreements "an unjust compromise." In addition to criticism of King Hassan and King Hussein, he referred to Israel as "the Zionist knife-wielders who are alien to human sentiments."[10]

Relations between Iran and its Neighbors

Iran's relations with Syria   Syria remains the key Middle East country with which Iran continues to maintain good relations. However, the end of the Cold War and Syria's dramatic reappraisal of its role in the Arab–Israeli peace process has cast a shadow over the enduring qualities of the Tehran–Damascus axis. Both countries continue to collaborate in supporting Hizbollah, and Syria continues to allow weapons to be shipped from Iran to Lebanon. However, if Israel and Syria reach an accord leading to peaceful relations, an end to all violent activity by Hizbollah and Iran's role as arms supplier will surely be part of the agreement. Syria would also be under great pressure to refrain from further cooperation with Iran on weapons developments and arms transfers. The result would be to weaken Iran significantly and force its leaders to rethink their strategy towards the Arab world and Iran's role as leader of the rejectionist front. On the other hand, if Israel and Syria fail to reach an agreement, Syria and Iran are capable of strengthening the power of the rejectionists. This, in turn, could exacerbate strategic relations with Israel and intensify the overall regional arms race.

Russia: cooperating with Tehran?   Iran's relations with Russia are multifaceted and lack the zero-sum quality of the US–Iranian confrontation. Russian leaders hope that by promoting and expanding political and economic ties with the Islamic Republic, they will help to maintain stability in Central Asia, avoid the spread of radical Islam, and stimulate trade and commercial cooperation.

Russia is threatened by unrest around its periphery. Conflict and turmoil in Georgia, Armenia, Azerbaijan, Tadjikistan, and Afghanistan contribute to regional instability and undermine Russian efforts to secure its new borders, protect Russian minorities in the former republics, and promote economic ties. Russia believes that stability is also in Iran's basic interest. Tehran fears that the crisis in Azerbaijan may engulf the approximately twenty million Azeris living in Iran. Both sides hope Russian–Iranian cooperation will help contain the crisis. Meanwhile, Iran needs arms and seeks inclusion in Central Asian and Gulf politics. Both Russia and Iran believe they can benefit from strong and stable bilateral relations.

Yet, even as some Russians advocate a closer relationship with Iran, Russian fears of Islamic fundamentalism are genuine and, under certain circumstances, could weaken the Iranian connection. If confrontation intensifies between Iran and the Gulf Arabs – with whom Russia has good relations – Russia may be forced to side with Iran on the one hand or the United States and Arab Gulf states on the other. Considering the importance of its relations with the United States and the financial pull of the Gulf states, Iran would likely come in a distant second.

The Russian dilemma on arms sales and the peace process raises another set of issues. Russian–Iranian cooperation in the military arena has led to several major arms sales, particularly since 1989.[11] Russia holds that the weapons will only be sold for self-defense. These arms exports are so important to the Russian economy that even the most pro-Western Russian leader would have a hard time turning down this opportunity. On the other hand, Russia takes its co-sponsorship of the Arab–Israeli peace process seriously and would like a greater role in the future. This will inevitably lead to further friction with Iran, given Iran's vehement opposition to the multilateral peace process. As mentioned above, US–Russian talks could curtail Russian–Iranian arms transactions. The war in Chechnya further complicates the Russian–Iranian equation.

One of the key strategic issues to be decided in the near future concerns the routing for oil egress from Central Asia to the world markets. One reason Russia is so desperate to retain control of Chechnya concerns that region's key geographic position along the oil pipeline routes from the Caspian Sea, Turkmenistan, and Uzbekistan to the Black Sea. In theory, oil from these Central Asian countries could be exported through either

Turkey or Iran. If Iran completes its rail line from Meshed to Turkmenistan, it could provide a very lucrative alternative that could undermine Russian dominance of several of its important neighbors.

The Gulf Arab states and Iran   Iran's relations with the Arab Gulf countries operate on two tracks: on the one hand is a decided need to cultivate friends, escape regional isolation, and continue important trade relations; on the other hand, Iran nurtures a desire to assert an independent and forceful foreign policy. In view of recent Iranian behavior towards the GCC countries, it can be questioned whether Iran's leaders have the skill and acumen needed to balance these two often contradictory goals. Indeed, relations between Iran and its Arab neighbors have been strained for decades, especially since the revolution. Fearful of Islamic revivalism, most Arab states supported Iraq during the Iran–Iraq war and paid huge sums of money to sustain Saddam Hussein's war effort. The shock and trauma of Iraq's invasion of Kuwait in 1990 put all of the GCC countries on notice that they could quite literally be obliterated by aggressive neighbors. Given the vast asymmetries in population and wealth between the GCC and neighboring countries such as Iran, Iraq, and Yemen, it is not surprising that security is of paramount concern.

While the security umbrella of the United States provides a strong deterrent against major aggression of the kind that occurred in 1990, the American presence may be less effective against political threats and subversion. Given the complicated sociology of most GCC countries – large foreign populations of diverse ethnic and religious backgrounds – internal security issues are an increasingly important factor in regional stability. It is in this context that the Iran threat looms large.

The Gulf states have grown increasingly apprehensive that Iran is determined to become the regional hegemon. Moreover, whatever conciliatory moves Iran may have been willing to make have been obscured by its bullying tactics over control and sovereignty of the islands of Abu Musa and the Tunbs. Iran's claim to the islands has generated widespread apprehension. What began as a dispute between Sharjah and Iran has escalated to a dispute first with the UAE, then with the GCC, and now with the Arab League. The issue is one of principle, but there are also strong strategic overtones. If Iran were to gain sovereignty over the islands it could extend its territorial waters into large areas that contain much oil. The UAE has proposed submitting the dispute to the International Court of Justice for resolution. However, to date, Iran has refused to accept this avenue of reconciliation. So long as the dispute remains unresolved and Iran continues to occupy and reinforce Abu Musa, tensions between Iran and the GCC will continue.

Since the Iraqi invasion of Kuwait in August 1990, Kuwait, Bahrain, Qatar, and Oman have all signed defense cooperation agreements with the United States. The UAE also signed an agreement on 25 July 1994. A less formalized arrangement with Saudi Arabia is also in place.[12] A similar array of actions were involved in the various military agreements. The agreement with Bahrain "expanded a previous agreement to include a joint exercise program, access to ports and airfields, and prepositioning of equipment." The United States and Kuwait "signed a 10-year agreement allowing US access to ports and facilities, prepositioning of military equipment, and joint training."[13] With Oman, American officials renewed an existing facilities-access agreement. As a result of Saddam Hussein's moves in October 1994, Kuwait agreed to allow a squadron of US planes to be based in Kuwait and to expand the number of US tanks stored in the Gulf state. Qatar agreed to store a brigade's worth of armor. Since the end of the Gulf War, allied aircraft have been based in Saudi Arabia to enforce the no-fly zone.[14]

Iran–Iraq relations: does Saddam Hussein serve Iranian interests?   Iraq's internal security is threatened by the hostility of both Kurds and Shi'ites to Saddam Hussein's rule after the Gulf War. Despite their failure, the Kurdish and Shi'ite revolts in the spring of 1991 raised doubts about the future of Iraq as a unified state, and the possibility of independent provinces, if not states, in the north and south. In addition, Saddam Hussein's ruthless suppression of dissent before, during, and after the Gulf War has led to speculation that even if he is ousted, civil strife may follow, as there are no trained political cadres to replace him or his regime. The unity of Iraq is further complicated by Kurdish in-fighting and Iraq's scheme to drain and clear the marshes in the south.

Iraq is now a pariah with an economy in shambles, its vast oil resources underutilized as international ostracism continues. Although Iraq is not permanently sidelined, the coming years do not bode well for Saddam Hussein's regime unless he can persuade the United Nations to lift the sanctions on Iraqi oil sales. While Russia, Turkey, and France have economic incentives to lift sanctions against Iraq, none of these countries has so far shown any interest in a direct confrontation with the United States over Iraq as long as Saddam Hussein remains in power. This does not bar Iraq from courting other potential patrons like China or buying weapons on the well-stocked open market. Yet these approaches will take time. Without a great power rivalry, the replenishment of Iraqi weaponry is a more difficult task, although once it resumes major oil exports, its market could become very attractive to a host of arms suppliers, including Russia, China, and Eastern Europe.

A weak Iraq leaves Iran in a stronger military and economic position. However, the fact that the Islamic regime has chosen to antagonize its Arab Gulf neighbors, who themselves are fearful of Iraq, is a sure sign that the regime has a divided, inconsistent foreign policy. Iran is unable to exploit fully its natural geopolitical advantages and the plight of its most dangerous regional rival. However, if its leaders can agree on a single foreign policy and overcome the country's severe economic crisis, Iran is capable, by dint of geography, population, and ambition, of exercising considerable power and influence over the Gulf region. Whether this represents a "hegemonic aspiration" is a matter for debate, but much will depend on how politically secure the conservative Arab states of the Gulf are and the extent to which the American presence in the region deters or spurs Iranian ambitions.

Could Iran and Iraq ever patch up their differences to the point of cooperating with each other against the American-led coalition? While there are undoubtedly some areas where both countries work together, especially in sales of limited quantities of smuggled Iraqi oil, Iran has much to lose if it connives in the rehabilitation of Saddam Hussein. If he is rehabilitated, sanctions will be lifted and Iraq will once more be able to use its money to buy weapons and intimidate its neighbors. Given its smaller population and huge untapped oil reserves, Iraq would be able to devote a greater percentage of its revenues to military expenditure than could Iran. This would not only pose a major threat to the region, but since Saddam Hussein is likely to be in a hurry to seek revenge for his Gulf War humiliations, Iraqi oil would flood the market, further depressing oil prices, which, in turn, would have a profoundly negative impact on the Iranian economy.

On the other hand, if Saddam Hussein were replaced by a less tainted but nevertheless nationalist and anti-Western leader, a rapprochement with Tehran might be conceivable. If the new Iraqi leadership were able quickly to persuade the international community to lift sanctions, Iran might calculate that it would be to its advantage to establish good relations rather than be seen as the enemy. In turn, the Iraqis might find it useful to satisfy Iranian demands on issues such as the status of the Iranian opposition forces currently stationed in Iraq. Both countries might find common ground in efforts to deny the Kurds greater autonomy, and certainly both sides would want to challenge American military domination and the international efforts to deny both countries advanced armaments.

In the summer of 1994, Saddam Hussein appeared to be closer to getting sanctions lifted. The Iraqis had complied in nearly every area of UNSCOM's work. The next stage, monitoring of Iraqi weapons sites, was set to begin as early as September. Even Rolf Ekeus, head of the UN inspection team, admitted that after six months of Iraqi monitoring compliance, sanctions could be lifted. France, Russia, and Turkey were already pushing for lifting sanctions in the near term. According to some reports, major economic deals were under negotiation with Iraqis; many businesses are poised to return to the Iraqi market.

Baghdad's threatening military moves in early October undermined the Iraqi campaign to get sanctions lifted. A rapid and forceful US response helped bring about an end to the crisis. Iraq seemed to regain momentum on 10 November when it officially recognized the newly demarcated border and Kuwaiti sovereignty. A few days later at the United Nations Security Council, only Britain sided with the US effort to minimize the significance of the Iraqi move.

Conclusions

Over the next ten years Iran and Iraq could pose serious challenges to their neighbors. The need to deter these countries will continue. This deterrent will have to involve an American military commitment to the security of the Gulf. Yet, although Iran and Iraq are the source of such concern, *both* countries, in different ways, also feel threatened and their own insecurities may contribute to the dynamics of mutual threat escalation. The leaders in both Baghdad and Tehran presently feel beleaguered, paranoid, and intimidated by the changes occurring in the neighborhood and the international environment.

But each country has very different institutions and power structures. The removal of one man, Saddam Hussein, could bring about a dramatic change in Iraq, and Iraq might be able to restore its credibility in the Arab world and the West if a new, more acceptable leadership assumed power. Iran's mullahs, on the other hand, are fighting a rear-guard action to save a revolution, and the removal of one or two leaders will make little difference to the governance of the country. There seems little doubt that the unpopularity of the Iranian regime is second only to the impotence of the opposition both inside and outside the country. Most Iranians would probably rejoice if the mullahs were removed from power.

The moment of truth for Iran will come if and when Syria's leader Hafez Al-Asad finally agrees to peace with Israel. At that time Iran will have to sever its ties with Hizbollah in Lebanon and decide if it wants to be the last country in the region to reject Israel's right to exist. If it continues to advocate the violent overthrow of the Jewish state, it will find itself increasingly isolated and shunned in the international community and find it more difficult to solve its economic problems, which in turn will further erode support for the regime.

Iranian rejection of the Arab–Israeli peace process and support for regimes and groups intent on using force to overthrow legitimate governments ensure continued conflict with moderate states in the Middle East and with outside powers, especially the United States. Indeed, Iran's leaders have rejected American calls for an official dialogue to discuss major points of contention. While there are significant voices in Tehran who favor such a dialogue, the radical factions headed by Khameine'i have effectively torpedoed any prospects for talks in the near future. Many American observers of Iranian politics believe that what the radicals fear is not so much American military power but rather America itself as the leader of Western secularism and the generator of a global culture that threatens the very essence of the revolution. Iran's ability to influence political events in the Middle East is clearly linked to other factors over which it has only marginal, if any, control. A revolution in Algeria leading to the establishment of an Islamic regime could have profound implications for the stability of the Mediterranean, including Egypt. A collapse of the Arab–Israeli peace process, aided and abetted by Iranian interference, could also have a profound and negative domino effect on the region. The resurgence of Saddam Hussein or an equally ruthless successor in Iraq could likewise spell danger.

Reduced to its most simple logic, what we now have in the Middle East and the Gulf are two competing trends: the pro-West, pro-peace movements that foresee a region more integrated with the economies of Europe, North America, and Asia, and the more theocratic, conservative movements that stress separateness from the West and a determination to establish independent ideologies even if this leads to confrontation. From an American perspective, the search for an optimum policy toward Iran and the Gulf remains illusive and fraught with dangers. At one level, military cooperation with the GCC has gone from strength to strength, and the deployments of American forces to Kuwait during October 1994 demonstrated that it will be a long time before either Iran or Iraq will be able directly to challenge the United States and the GCC with military force. However, the political and sociological dimensions of Gulf security pose more complicated problems. Without GCC cooperation the US cannot protect the Gulf from major threats. Yet pushing such cooperation too far and too fast runs the risk of overloading the delicate political system and could play into the hands of those who bitterly oppose the GCC governments, including opposition groups within these nations.

CHAPTER 7

Iran, the GCC States, and the UAE: Prospects and Challenges in the Coming Decade

Anwar Gargash

With the end of the second Gulf war Iran commenced its attempts to consolidate its regional role in the Gulf. Following a decade of internal instability and external confrontations, the Iranian leadership felt that the moment was favorable to regain what it viewed as its rightful place in the region. Its aim was to recover influence lost since the late 1970s, when imperial Iran was the dominant power on Gulf shores.

The changing regional environment is certainly more conducive to an increasing Iranian role in the Gulf. These changes include the defeat of Iraq and the marginalization of its regional role in the coming years, and the dramatic collapse of the Soviet Union, traditionally the major threat to Iran's territorial integrity. The latter has furthermore created a less threatening environment for Iran on its northern borders, which will allow Tehran to devote more energy and resources to its southern arena. Iranian ambitions, however, face a series of formidable challenges in the coming period. These challenges include the political and military presence of the West in the Gulf, the distrust of Iranian intentions by the countries of the area, difficult economic conditions, and an unstable internal political climate.

Iran's relations with the United Arab Emirates demonstrate the complexity and multidimensional aspects of Arab–Persian interregional relationships. On the one hand, the connection includes established cultural and social ties as well as active and substantial trading links. On the other hand, the relationship faces mutual mistrust and misperception. In the case of Iran and the UAE, the islands issue constitutes the major obstacle to a complete normalization of relations.

Perception and Reality: Iran's Role in the Gulf

The Gulf is extremely important to Iran. The long Iranian coastline (1,200 km) occupies all of its northern boundary and is Iran's main window onto the outside world. Iran and the Sultanate of Oman control the strategic Strait of Hormuz, through which Iran exports all of its oil production. Most of Iran's oil industry – with oil income accounting for 65 percent of Iran's 1994 budget[1] – is situated in or near the Gulf, and most of its oil production is exported from ports on the Gulf. There is no denying that Iran is a major Gulf power with legitimate interests and concerns.

The psychological environment plays a major role in determining Iranian policy toward the Gulf region. Many in Iranian circles believe that the natural state of affairs in the Gulf is one where Tehran is the principal power. As a result, Iranians feel that the lengthy British presence in the area denied them their rightful place for a long period of time.[2] These perceptions, which are influenced by historical interaction, continue to affect Tehran's foreign policy towards its Arab neighbors.

Psychological considerations have also played an important role in reinforcing these perceptions. An Iranian academic points out that because of the meager information available to the Iranian decision-maker, he depends to a large degree on psychological inputs and symbols. Most important among these are historical cases and experiences.[3] The major indication here is the belief that Iran must continue to play the role of the primary Gulf power. Yet historically, Iran was never the dominant naval power except for brief periods of time, such as during the reign of Nadir Shah in the eighteenth century and the height of the Pahlavi dynasty. J. B. Kelly, a prominent British historian of the Gulf, remarked on the late Shah's naval buildup in the following terms:

> While the Shah plainly regarded his fledgling navies a glittering instrument of his will, the reality was somewhat different. The sea has never been the Persians' natural element. Persia has no indigenous naval or maritime tradition, and seamen cannot be conjured from the waves by royal command.[4]

Yet the Pahlavi rulers were immensely successful in building a regional force, and as a result were able to transform "the reach of the Iranian geostrategic dream into some kind of reality."[5] That this goal was accomplished was due to favorable regional and international conditions. Foremost among these was the American backing of the Shah, a support that was augmented as a result of Washington's experience in Vietnam.

The United States intended to depend on its regional allies, and a principal ally was Iran. Certainly, the Iranian political leadership did not lack ambition. At the height of his power, the late Shah felt that hegemony over the Gulf was only a step towards a greater regional role, extending to the Arabian sea and to the Indian ocean.[6]

In addition to external support and internal ambition, the increasing revenue from oil contributed to the transformation of Iran into a major Middle Eastern power. Under the late Shah, Iran became the major pillar in the American security policy for the Gulf, known as the twin-pillar policy. In the meantime, the Shah did not hesitate to flex his muscles and use his substantial force. This was amply demonstrated in the occupation of the Tunb islands in 1971, by the military interference in Dhofar to subdue the Marxist rebellion, and in the clashes with Iraq prior to the signing of the 1975 Algiers Accord, an agreement that was considered an important political victory for the Shah. In this context, Shahram Chubin and Charles Tripp argue that the major motivator of modern Iranian nationalism is not territorial expansion, but rather an attempt to increase Iran's influence and stature in the region.[7]

Influenced by these episodes of recent history as well as by its deeper, yet selective, historical recollection, Iran considers the reversals of the 1980s – which commenced with the events of the Iranian revolution and continued with the Iran–Iraq war – as temporary setbacks that need to be corrected. While this perception is historically inaccurate, an under-standing of it is essential in order to recognize Iranian policy in the coming period. This is especially important since foreign policy does not necessarily depend on a complete and accurate reading of events, but is influenced by subjective considerations. One must note that despite the great shift from a monarchic to a revolutionary republican system, Iran's goals in the area have neither shifted nor changed. Clearly the state's national interests were far more important than revolutionary or ideo-logical polemics. The Islamic Republic's foreign policy, which was transformed drastically toward various issues, remained static in the Gulf.

To reiterate, Iran, which played the role of the major regional power for a long period of time, does not seek to abandon that role. Its size, location, and population of over 60 million adds credence to its ambitions. A recent editorial in the *Tehran Times* stresses this point. Following the Victory-4 maneuvers in the Gulf waters, the paper commented:

> The Islamic Republic decided to demonstrate its military might in the ...
> Gulf not because the country is pursuing an expansionist policy, but because

it was felt necessary to demonstrate Iran's ability to maintain security in this sensitive part of the world.[8]

The Development of Iranian Relations with the Arab States of the Gulf

Iran is the only non-Arab state in the Gulf. This distinction, on numerous occasions, has not been a very happy one, especially with the development of modern nationalism in the area. Painful episodes such as the Iran–Iraq war have increased distrust between Iran and its Arab neighbors.

In the Gulf three powers with regional ambitions emerge: Iran, Iraq, and Saudi Arabia are the main competitors. The other states, as a result of their smaller size, cannot seek an ambitious political role. Iraq is by far Iran's major regional concern. The two countries have undergone years of competition, mutual interference, and, in the Iran–Iraq war, one of the most devastating wars in the area. While Iraq is the most densely populated Gulf Arab state, its population is relatively small compared to that of Iran. Furthermore, its limited access to the Gulf forms a major hinderance to Baghdad's attempts to play the leading regional role. Although Iraq came out of its eight-year war with Iran with considerable status, much of this prestige was lost as a result of the second Gulf war and the international isolation of the Iraqi regime. These factors have contributed to the declining role of Baghdad on the regional scene and have consequently increased Iran's standing in the area.

Another Gulf state with regional ambitions is Saudi Arabia. Tehran views Riyadh with suspicion. A large part of this is due to the long-standing theological differences between Iranian Shi'ism and Saudi Arabia's Sunni Hanbali school. It is, at the same time, a complex relationship between one regime seeking to change the status quo and another seeking to defend it. Moreover, Saudi–Iranian relations have been competitive even at the height of cooperation, when the two countries were led by King Faisal and the Shah.[9] This period witnessed a great degree of strategic and security cooperation as well as a common fear of leftist infiltration in the area.

Despite this cooperation, which was reinforced by regional and international changes, relations were not always smooth. Saudi Arabia led the moderate camp in OPEC, while Iran sought ever higher oil prices. The decreasing demand for OPEC oil in the mid-1980s naturally increased the tension between the two states. Riyadh, through its huge production capacity and influence in OPEC, was able to consolidate its regional role, especially with Iran and Iraq locked in a prolonged war. The influence amassed by the Saudis was not viewed with pleasure in Tehran. Revolutionary Iran remains critical of what it calls "unilateral Saudi decisions" within OPEC and of Riyadh's subordination of the organization's interests to those of the West.[10] Iran has continued to view with suspicion the close Saudi–American relationship, attacking this relationship frequently.

Iran also considers the creation of the GCC in 1981 as an extension of Saudi influence over the other Gulf states. Perhaps the lowest point in the relationship between the two countries came about in 1987, following violent clashes between the Saudi authorities and Iranian pilgrims during the annual *hajj* pilgrimage to the Holy Places within the Kingdom of Saudi Arabia. Despite repeated attempts to patch up their differences, these efforts soon failed for one reason or another.

Judging from Iranian–Saudi dynamics, one must point out that ideological considerations are not the primary force behind Iranian foreign policy, especially if these considerations conflict with Iran's national interests. The reality is that in the majority of instances Iranian foreign policy has been pragmatic, if not Machiavellian, and has sought, above all, to serve Iranian national interests. For instance, Iran has maintained, throughout fourteen years of revolution, very tight connections with Pakistan in spite of Islamabad's close association with Washington. This pragmatic streak was further evident when Iran secretly purchased Israeli weapons during its war with Iraq, while simultaneously publicly denouncing the Jewish state.[11]

As the Iran–Iraq War progressed, the differences between Iran and the GCC states became more pronounced. Although political reasons were responsible to a large extent, economic considerations contributed to the friction. The fact that the sparsely populated GCC states control huge oil reserves will create an even less amicable atmosphere in the future. In this context, Chubin, who has written that Iran has no territorial ambitions in the region, does not rule out a future scenario that includes an Iranian "resource grab."[12] Such a scenario emphasizes the economic "imbalance" and envisions an Iranian occupation of an offshore oil field, regardless of any historical claims.

Factors Affecting Iranian Policy in the Gulf

Future Iranian policy toward the Gulf will be determined by or at least influenced by various internal and regional factors. Three of these factors will be addressed below: the collapse of the Soviet Union and the new conditions in Central Asia, security arrangements in the Gulf, and the internal politics of Iran.

The collapse of the Soviet Union and the new conditions in Central Asia   The collapse and breakup of the Soviet Union, following the unsuccessful coup of August 1991, caused a major strategic change in Iran's regional outlook. Following centuries of fear from its northern neighbor, Iran now finds that it no longer has any border with an expansionist state. Instead, its northern borders are now shared with weak new states: Turkmenistan, Azerbaijan, and Armenia. As a result, Iran not only feels more secure, but also believes that its diplomacy can influence the northern region in a way that was not possible before. By virtue of its revolutionary ideology, Iran is tempted to try to increase its influence in this area. Yet Iranian influence faces an uphill struggle, considering the ethnic and religious differences in the area. A long tradition of secularism and Iran's failed economic model have formed additional obstacles to Iran's influence. Yet the changes are not completely positive, and Iran is naturally worried about the fluid situation in this region. It does not cherish the prospects of civil strife close to its border. In the meantime, Tehran has been fighting a three-way struggle for influence with Turkey and Russia.

Iran is also worried about Azeri–Turkish nationalism spreading into its northwestern region. This is a potentially serious problem for the republican regime. There are approximately ten to twelve million Iranian citizens of Azeri ethnicity, which is double the number residing in the Republic of Azerbaijan.[13] The sensitivity of this issue is evident in Iran's lack of support for the Baku regime in the Armenia–Azerbaijan conflict over the Nagorno-Karabakh enclave.[14] Iran describes itself as an honest broker in this dispute. This position, however, puts the regime in an awkward spot, as it cannot easily explain its support for the Christian state rather than for the Shi'ite one.

Yet as far as Iran's Gulf policy is concerned, the improving conditions in the Central Asian region will liberate many of Iran's diplomatic and material resources. As a result, Tehran will be able to direct increasingly more of its attention to its southern region. The Russian decision not to sign any new arms agreements with Iran will slow down Tehran's plans and somewhat "liberate" Iran's policy in the area, which, in the past, took careful note of its dependence on Moscow in this vital arena.

Iran and security arrangements in the Gulf   As a result of the second Gulf crisis Iran achieved several strategic goals. The most important of these objectives were the Iraqi concessions contained in Saddam Hussain's letter to President Rafsanjani on 14 August 1990. In this letter, Baghdad reaffirmed its acceptance of the Algiers Agreement, and, as a result, the two countries returned to the 1980 status quo. Morally, the events confirmed Iran's repeated assertions that the Ba'athist regime in Baghdad was the aggressor in their eight-year war. Furthermore, Iran's neutral position in the second Gulf war helped ease its international isolation, while on the regional front, Iraq's military defeat augmented Iran's relative power.

With the end of the Iraqi occupation of Kuwait, the GCC states renewed their search for a security formula that would be both effective and politically sensitive to their requirements. It was clear that the Gulf states do not possess the necessary capability to defend themselves. At the same time, they could not depend on the large network of Arab contacts built over the past three decades. Evidently an Arab solution to the security dilemma was not forthcoming.

The Iraqi invasion of Kuwait, while the most dramatic, was only one episode of instability in the region. Throughout the 1980s the Gulf witnessed an incessant period of tension. The need for Western assistance in formulating an effective security arrangement was very clear. The Gulf states sought to purchase sophisticated weapons systems, and at the same time planned to organize and increase the size of their military. This included the Saudi plan to expand its forces to 200,000 men in the next five to seven years.[15] The previous rejection of a Western presence in the area was substituted by a realization that only such a presence could guarantee the Gulf's security – a position that had evolved slowly with Kuwait's request for American protection of its oil tankers in 1987. An Iranian academic writes that this significant event represents a watershed in the policies of the GCC states towards Tehran from one of conciliation to one of confrontation.[16]

The transformation of the attitude of the Gulf states affected inter-Arab relations. The idea of an Arab security arrangement suffered from the notorious instability of Arab–Arab relations. The "Damascus Declaration," which represented the Arab solution to the Gulf security predicament, lacked credibility. It was not taken seriously from the outset, despite the fact that many of the Western states viewed the declaration as a possible nucleus for an effective security strategy for the area and one that ultimately would be backed by Western guarantees. This was not to be the case, especially following Egypt's withdrawal of its 38,000-man army in May 1992, and Syria's withdrawal of its troops one month later. The Damascus Declaration, as a solution, did not comfort the Gulf states.[17] In this context, various officials in the Gulf voiced their apprehensions towards the declaration. The speaker of the Kuwaiti assembly, Ahmad Al-Sadoon, commented that the declaration was a "rash" reaction to the security vacuum following the immediate liberation of Kuwait.[18] The Omani minister of state for foreign affairs was even harsher and commented sarcastically that the effectiveness of the declaration would not be felt for five centuries.[19]

The search for a collective solution by the Gulf states was clearly unsuccessful. The small population of the GCC states and their different priorities meant that an indigenous solution was not a realistic prospect. In addition, the various Arab states of the Gulf did not fully agree on a common threat. As a result each state initiated a unilateral search for security, resulting in the emergence of a series of agreements with Washington. In September 1991 Kuwait was the first to sign a mutual defense agreement, which is to endure for ten years. These agreements were mostly sensitive to the Arab political environment and to internal American considerations. This was evident in their "beyond the horizon" approach and the absence of permanent American bases.[20]

At the height of this significant debate over future security arrangements in the Gulf, Iran was on the periphery. This was a very uncomfortable position for the Iranian regime to be in, and the clerical leadership was anxious to influence the course of the debate. Yet the West and the GCC states did not trust Iranian intentions in spite of its neutral stance in the war. In the immediate aftermath of the war, Iran sought to play a responsible role. It demonstrated its concern for stability in the area and opposed, together with Syria and Turkey, the partition of Iraq for fear of the Kurdish problem.[21] Furthermore, Iran did not effectively interfere to support the Shi'a uprising in southern Iraq.[22]

However, the list of Iran's previous adventures was too long for the GCC states to ignore. For over a decade Iranian activity seriously undermined the stability of many of the GCC states. This included the 1981 aborted coup attempt in Bahrain; a series of bombings in Kuwait in the early 1980s, along with the attempted assassination of the Amir in 1985; and the ongoing problems during the *hajj* seasons. As the US secretary of state commented, the GCC states continue to mistrust Iran deeply.[23]

These fears are reinforced by Arab allies of the GCC states who frequently point to Iran's ambitions in the area. This is amply clear in the public statements of President Hosni Mubarak of Egypt.[24] During his visit to the Gulf in May 1993, Iran was the major topic of his discussions, and it was rumored that Oman was attempting to mediate between Cairo and Tehran.[25]

Iran, meanwhile, continued to preach its traditional strategy of excluding foreign presence from the Gulf, insisting that Gulf security is the responsibility of the littoral powers. Iran realized that although a Western presence will not threaten the position of the region's smaller states, it will challenge its role as the major regional power by virtue of its size and population. The exclusion of superpower presence is not a purely Iranian reaction to surrounding events, but is similar to the response of other regional powers, such as India or Indonesia, to their security environment.[26] In Iran's case these considerations are magnified as a result of the state's virulent anti-Western rhetoric and deep-rooted fear of the West, in particular of the United States. These feelings are further reinforced by a collective historical memory, both on the popular and the elite level, of the old colonial powers attempting to control Iranian decision-making. In this context, the Shah's policy of alliance with the West represents a departure from traditional Iranian strategic thinking. Current Iranian apprehension of an American role and fears of encirclement are in line with the traditional Iranian mindset.[27]

Naturally, the Iranian leadership began to voice objections to its being excluded from the security debate. Iran was especially upset with the Damascus Declaration, particularly with the Egyptian role, and many angry statements emerged from Tehran. The Iranian press pointed out that Syria and Egypt should concentrate on "defending the rights of Muslims against Zionism" and not interfere in the geographically distant Gulf.[28] During the initial period, these criticisms were far harsher than the condemnation of the American role. In fact, the Iranian foreign minister stated on 31 December 1990 that the presence of foreign troops in the area was understandable since no other solution that guarantees security and stability in the region was available.[29] Iran during this period realized that only Western interference would nullify Iraqi gains in Kuwait. Its ideological orientation and its internal politics, however, made it impossible for Iran to support the "Great Satan."

These positions soon changed to the predictable Iranian rejection of foreign presence. Foreign Minister Velayati recently stated that "the presence of aliens in the region, especially their military forces, would not contribute to safeguarding the regional security. They are after their own interests and benefits."[30] President Rafsanjani also criticized the agreements signed by the various GCC states with Washington, stating:

"we are opposed to these pacts and believe that any military presence of the Westerners in the region is a factor disturbing peace and stability."[31] Furthermore, Iran was afraid that in the emerging world order, the United States would attempt to isolate it. These fears were augmented by various statements from Washington describing Iran as a dangerous outlaw state.[32] Similar opinions spread within influential American circles following the Gulf War.[33] The revolutionary regime was soon on the defensive regarding its human rights record, its assistance to radical organizations in countries such as the Sudan, and its opposition to the Middle East peace process.

Following the liberation of Kuwait, Iranian and Arab attempts to start afresh commenced. This was especially true with reference to Saudi Arabia and Kuwait, since previous relations had been extremely tense. Iranian relations with Riyadh, which had been severed in 1988, were resumed in March 1991. Furthermore, agreement was reached on the extremely emotional and contentious issue of the number of Iranian pilgrims allowed to perform the annual *hajj*. This rapprochement was followed by high-level contacts. In April 1991, President Hashemi Rafsanjani met King Fahd in Riyadh. This meeting was followed by a visit of Saudi Foreign Minister Prince Saud Al-Faisal to Tehran in June 1991, the first visit of a senior Saudi official since the fall of the Shah.

Iranian–Kuwaiti relations experienced considerable improvement following the end of the Iran–Iraq war. Iranian Foreign Minister Ali Akbar Velayati visited Kuwait weeks before the invasion, and during Iraq's occupation of his country, Sheikh Sabah Al-Ahmed, the Kuwaiti foreign minister, visited Iran and offered his apologies for past Kuwaiti support for the Ba'athist regime. Hopes were high during this phase of a GCC–Iranian rapprochement. The general optimism in the area was echoed by the foreign minister of Qatar, Mubarak Al-Khatir, who stated during the GCC foreign ministers' meeting in May 1991 that Iran was a friendly state and a neighbor and had to play a role in the area's security.[34]

Needless to say, Iranian strategic interests were closely associated with the GCC states during this period. Iran realized that any changes benefitting Iraq might have long-term repercussions on the regional balance of power. The congruence of interests, however, was short-lived, and Iranian foreign policy returned to its previous pattern. Iranian diplomacy did not use wisely the moral credit accumulated in the aftermath of the Gulf war. The regime's anti-Western polemics and interpretation of its national interests soon undermined its relations with many of its neighbors. The unfolding Iranian policy towards the three occupied islands was indicative of these changes on the regional front.

On the other hand, the policies of the GCC states towards Iran has not been unified. While some of these states have viewed Iranian policy with suspicion, others have enjoyed a more amicable relationship. The divergence of views is largely the result of geostrategic considerations, slightly different security priorities, and the state of bilateral relations. For example, while a shared concern over the Strait of Hormuz brings Oman and Iran closer, the dispute over the islands pushes the UAE and Iran apart.

Internal conditions and Iranian foreign policy in the Gulf   As in the case of many revolutions, the Iranian revolution experienced bitter and violent internal confrontations. In the initial stage, the conflict involved liberal and nationalist forces on one side and religious forces on the other. With the republic's rapid transformation into a theocratic state, however, the nature of the disputes shifted, and internal conflicts involved different wings within the religious establishment. The suspension of the Islamic Republican Party, representing the ruling clergy, did not stop the internal disputes, which became polarized along factional lines.

The connection between the internal and external spheres is an intimate one in Iran's case. This was amply demonstrated from the early days of the republic, when radical students forced the fall of the provisional government of Prime Minister Mehdi Bazargan. Radical elements used the meeting of Bazargan and his foreign minister, Ibrahim Yazdi, with the American national security advisor, Zbigniew Brzezinski, as a pretext to occupy the American embassy and derail the normalization process with Washington.[35] In the course of these events, the radical elements forced a reorientation of Iran's foreign policy. The occupation of the American embassy in 1979 was the beginning of a radical foreign policy that helped undermine many of the non-religious elements, including President Abul Hasan Bani Sadr and Foreign Minister Sadiq Qutbzadeh.

A significant development internally was Ayatollah Khomeini's acceptance in November 1984 of the need for economic and diplomatic relations that would end the international isolation of the regime. The decision was an important factor in rationalizing the country's foreign policy. Another important step at normalizing the internal situation was the decision to accept the ceasefire with Iraq in 1988. This decision was followed by the overthrow of Ayatollah Montazeri as heir to Ayatollah Khomeini in 1989, an ouster that allowed the emergence of the twin leadership of Khamene'i and Rafsanjani. Following the death of Khomeini, this twin leadership was able to score an important political victory, marginalizing the radical elements within the regime. These steps included increasing the powers of the president and ousting two important "radicals," Prime Minister Hussein Musavi and Interior Minister Ali Akbar Mohtashemi. In the meantime, the "moderates" scored a big victory in the parliamentary elections and were able to take a neutral stand in the second Gulf war.[36]

The primary goal of the twin leadership was the economic revival of the country following the protracted war with Iraq. The leadership's pragmatism revealed itself in various speeches and comments, such as the statement by President Rafsanjani, upon taking office, that Iran cannot build dams with slogans alone.[37] To give top priority to the economy came as no surprise, for it was clear that the Islamic Republic was facing a major economic crisis. Foreign debt had increased drastically, and the dollar, valued at 700 riyals at the beginning of the revolution, was now valued at 3,000 riyals. These financial constraints caused serious problems for Iranian industry, which could not afford to buy necessary raw materials.

Attempts to breathe life into the Iranian economy proved to be more difficult despite serious attempts by President Rafsanjani to raise the standard of living, which included devaluing the Iranian riyal.[38] In the spring of 1994, an Iranian paper supportive of the president reported, "almost six years after Iraq's military aggression ended we can at best say the situation has been deteriorating."[39] In fact, Rafsanjani's political prospects were clearly connected with the success of his economic program. His plans faced stiff resistance from many influential circles, including "radical" elements within the system. Many of these groups wanted the state to continue to play the major part in running the economy. They opposed the privatization plans and the improvement of economic relations with the West.

The failure of Rafsanjani's reforms thus far has hurt his standing. Early indicators of his diminishing influence were provided by the fall of his electoral popularity. In the last presidential election, Rafsanjani received 63.2 percent of the popular vote, down from 94.5 percent of the popular vote in 1989. In addition, the government was unhappy with the 57.6 percent participation figures.[40] These results were undoubtedly a worrysome sign, indicating widespread political apathy among the population.

Furthermore, the Khamene'i–Rafsanjani partnership has not been as smooth as expected. The difference in perspective between the posts of leader and president has been amplified by the economic situation. The two positions have an inherent contradiction: the presidency seeks to augment Iran's political and economic interests, while the leadership is concerned with ideological and theological matters. The lines are not clearly drawn, and neither leader enjoys the clout of the late Ayatollah Khomeini. This has created constant tension between the two posts, which has been aggravated by Rafsanjani's economic failure. Khamene'i has sought to distance himself from certain unpopular economic measures, such as the abolition of some subsidies which have contributed to greater inflation. In addition, the two differed on the urgency of restoring relations with the West, and certainly anti-Western statements made by Khamene'i were much more extreme than those of Rafsanjani.

The differences between the "moderates" and "radicals" are largely responsible for the contradiction in Iran's foreign policy. This is evident in the inconsistent statements that have been made concerning the Gulf. Furthermore, Rafsanjani is not always in control as far as foreign policy is concerned. His emphasis on the economy, and his realization that his political future is connected with achieving these economic goals has meant that he would allow tactical concessions in the foreign policy sphere to be made to the radical factions. This is evident in the independent nature of many of Iran's security organizations, an autonomy that was demonstrated in the foreign campaign to liquidate the enemies of the republic, especially members of the Mujahedin-e Khalq and the Kurdish opposition groups.[41] Furthermore, Rafsanjani was unable to reverse the religious *fatwa* in the Salman Rushdie affair. This failure has been detrimental to the improvement of relations with the West, complicating the cooperation his economic reforms acutely need. These and other considerations have led many observers to point out the duality of Iranian foreign policy. Chubin sees the duality in the presence of moderates and radicals, as well as in realists and revolutionaries at the same time. He also sees it in Tehran's attempts to simultaneously seek economic co-operation with the West and to attack it verbally.[42] Others see the duality in Iran's uncompromising regional policy towards some countries and its accommodating policy towards others.[43]

This apparent duality and the contradicting statements, while high-lighting internal differences, are also indicative of the regime's lack of confidence in its stability. What is clear is that Iranian decision-making is far from the rational model of foreign policy-making since it involves sharp competition between institutions and personalities. In view of these considerations, the internal environment will continue to affect Iran's Gulf policy negatively. The contradictions and the lack of clarity will only add to the suspicion of Iran's intentions among the GCC states and generally cloud the future outlook in the Gulf.

Iran and the United Arab Emirates

Iranian relations with the UAE began on a sour note. First, the dispute over the three islands, Abu Musa, Greater Tunb, and Lesser Tunb, intensified with Britain's decision to withdraw from the Gulf. The dispute was not settled successfully, and Iranian forces occupied the Tunbs, and imposed a *fait accompli* on the new state. Despite this violent episode, the UAE wished to maintain good relations with Iran. This was largely due to regional considerations, particularly the continuing border dispute between Abu Dhabi, the largest of the Emirates, and Saudi Arabia. Riyadh had refused to extend diplomatic recognition to the new federation as a form of pressure on Abu Dhabi, which meant that Iran would play a balancing role in this critical period.

Another reason for the strained relations was that the UAE, following Britain's withdrawal from the Gulf, felt extremely vulnerable. The security vacuum gave cause for alarm. The rebellion in Dhofar was undermining stability in the region, and the Marxist government in Aden worried the conservative regimes. These factors emphasized the Shah's role as a defender of the conservative status quo, and his military, while at times overbearing, was an essential tool in defeating leftist radicalism.

Despite the political tensions, trade and cultural links between the UAE and Iran remain significant. An important trading partner of Iran has been and continues to be Dubai. It is a commercial link that has its roots in the late nineteenth century with Dubai's replacement of Lingah as the main port in the southern Gulf. Most of the trade between the two nations is conducted through Dubai, which acts as a major re-export center for Iran. In spite of the problems plaguing the Iranian economy, these trading links continued to grow. Dubai's total non-oil foreign trade with Iran has increased from $571 million in 1989 to $1.13 billion in 1993, representing 6.46 percent of the total foreign trade of Dubai. These figures are more substantial in the re-export sphere: Iran ranks first with re-exports worth approximately $900 million, representing a 32 percent share of Dubai's total re-exports.[44]

On the cultural and social spheres, the Gulf waters – rather than being an obstacle to cultural interaction – provided contact between the northern and southern shores. In fact, it was faster and safer to travel from Sharjah or Ras al-Khaimah to Lingah and Bandar Abbas than to travel by road to Muscat and the interior. Many Arab tribes and families lived on both shores of the Gulf, and Arabic was widely spoken in southern Persia. One can even notice the interaction in the architecture of Arab and Persian towns on the shores of the Gulf. Yet relations were strained at times, and suffered during periods of nationalistic fervor, such as the period coinciding with the rise of Reza Shah Pahlavi and during Gamal Abdul Nasser's assertion of Arab nationalism.

Notwithstanding the dispute over the islands, the two states achieved an acceptable *modus vivendi* after the declaration of the federation. Iran recognized the UAE 48 hours after its declaration. Diplomatic relations, however, had to be delayed for another eleven months.[45] Naturally, the UAE, still sensitive to the occupation of the islands and to criticism in the Arab world, did not seek to normalize relations immediately.

In the initial phase the relationship between the two states was somewhat cool. Yet Iran maintained good contacts with members of the federation, notably Dubai and Sharjah. Improvements came about with continued bilateral contacts. There was a strong and obvious need to balance Saudi influence, especially in view of the continuing border dispute. Bilateral contacts culminated in the 1975 visit to Iran by Sheikh Zayed Bin Sultan Al-Nahyan, the president of the UAE. This visit consolidated the process of normalizing relations between the two states. However, the UAE was wary of the Shah's ambitions. With increasing oil revenues at his disposal, the Shah was especially interested in addressing the issue of Gulf security, seeking to play a pivotal role in any arrangement. Iran was becoming the major pillar of Western security designs for the Gulf, and the Shah, with his active role in Dhofar, was being described as the policeman of the Gulf.

As far as the UAE was concerned, the 1974 agreement settling the Abu Dhabi–Riyadh border dispute brought a certain amount of balance to regional relations. This improvement negated the need to balance Saudi Arabia with Iran, and the UAE could play a more neutral regional role. This new equation was apparent in the UAE's lukewarm response to Iranian plans for Gulf security.[46]

The fall of the Shah in early 1979 was viewed with serious concern in the UAE. The conservative status quo had received a serious blow, and the prospects of instability in the area and the images of civil strife in Iran were not comforting. The success of the revolution, however, brought some hope that the protracted islands issue would be resolved. This was a naïve notion on the part of some circles in the UAE, and it was based on various declarations by Iranian officials calling for a review of all agreements from the Shah's period. Certainly, the chaotic situation in Iran could not, and did not, produce a coherent Gulf policy. While certain voices in the Iranian leadership emphasized the need for neighborly relations with the Gulf states, others criticized the Western links of these states.

With the outbreak of the Iran–Iraq war in September 1980, the UAE tried to maintain a tenuous neutrality, especially since it was becoming clear that it would be a protracted war. The UAE, concerned with the effects of the war on its stability, joined the newly formed GCC. Nevertheless, at many junctures it took a neutral position differing from its Saudi and Kuwaiti partners. This prudent independence was mainly dictated by geostrategic considerations. Nonetheless, these policies were sharply criticized by Baghdad, which sought to portray the war as an Arab–Persian confrontation. *Keyhan International* commented on the UAE's stand during the war in the following terms:

> The UAE under the pragmatic leadership of Sheikh Zayed Bin Sultan al Nahyan never abstained from condemning the conflict as a curse to the region, and with the good offices of Oman did its best to defuse the crisis that was bringing the area to the verge of bankruptcy.[47]

Iran–UAE relations largely follow the pattern of relations between a large regional power and a smaller neighbor. The larger power is frequently insensitive to the fears and aspirations of the smaller state and seeks to impose its views and outlook on many of the bilateral and regional issues. In the highly charged atmosphere of Gulf politics these tendencies take on an exaggerated dimension. On the other hand, the smaller state is wary and suspicious of the intentions of the larger regional power and is extremely sensitive to issues of sovereignty and territorial integrity.

The Islands Dispute

The main impediment to normalizing Iranian relations with the UAE remains the issue of the three islands, Abu Musa and the two Tunbs. Furthermore, this dispute complicates Iranian relations with other Gulf states. A press assessment of Iran's foreign policy reiterated this view, stating that the islands issue "prevented Iran's relations with its southern neighbors from going deeper than the surface."[48]

As previously mentioned, the Shah's demands for the islands delayed the declaration of the federation. Following the withdrawal of his claims over Bahrain he was adamant that Iran would not concede its demands over the three islands. Yet the Shah was anxious to reach a deal with the Emirate of Sharjah over Abu Musa and with the Emirate of Ras Al-Khaimah over the Tunbs. After all, his main concern was stability in the

Gulf. He also sought to show that Iran's dispute was not with the new state, but with the departing colonial power.

A Memorandum of Understanding was reached with the Emirate of Sharjah which stipulated that neither party would relinquish its claims of sovereignty or recognize the other party's claims. It divided jurisdiction between the two parties, with Iran controlling the north of the Island and Sharjah controlling the southern part, including the village of Abu Musa. The memorandum had no time limit and designated that both flags fly on the respective parts and that oil production be equally shared.[49] In the case of Ras Al-Khaimah, no aggreement was concluded since the Shah insisted on full Iranian sovereignty because of the islands' strategic location and their proximity to the Iranian mainland. As a result, Iranian troops invaded the Tunbs and occupied them by force on 29 November 1971.

The UAE was not in a position to confront the Shah. The newly formed state had to deal with the more immediate concerns connected with nation-building. As a result, the federal government's response was restrained. Arab declarations of support, especially by Libya and Iraq, were received with skepticism. Furthermore, the UAE realized that the conservative Arab regimes, including Saudi Arabia and Egypt, did not seek to confront Iran over this issue. Security Council deliberations concerning the dispute also favored allowing time for the workings of quiet diplomacy.[50]

At first, Iran adhered to the Abu Musa Agreement, but with the revolution and the escalating Iran–Iraq war Tehran began to violate the various clauses. This was especially true during the tanker war in 1987–88. The UAE, on the other hand, was concerned with stability and felt that it was not a time to pursue its demands aggressively. It raised the issue at its annual UN speech to the General Assembly. This posture shifted dramatically following the end of Iraq's occupation of Kuwait and Iranian attempts to create new realities on Abu Musa. Furthermore, the UAE emphasized the link between the agreement on Abu Musa and the military occupation of the Tunbs. These issues increased in priority on the federation's agenda of bilateral relations with Iran. Internally, the responsibility for managing the issue was transferred from the Emirate of Sharjah to the federal foreign ministry. The Iranians, on the other hand, argue that the UAE's recent escalation of the crisis is connected to American policy and presence in the area.[51] This position reflects the insensitivity of Iranian foreign policy to the issues concerning its neighbors, and an attempt to classify these concerns as part of the Western encirclement of the Islamic Republic.

The UAE position emphasized the need for a comprehensive solution that would address the Abu Musa dispute and the occupation of the Tunbs. This stand was developed further into the need to submit the contending claims to the International Court of Justice (ICJ), and to accept the body's decision, whatever that may be. Undoubtedly, it is a sophisticated position with a great deal of appeal in a world concerned with the peaceful settlement of regional disputes.

The Iranian response was rigid. Iran criticized the UAE's decision to seek an ICJ ruling as being premature, arguing that not all possibilities were exhausted. The Iranians kept insisting on continuing bilateral discussions.[52] Yet it was not apparent how these deliberations could succeed when Iran refused to discuss the occupation of the Tunbs, arguing that they are sovereign Iranian territories.

Tehran tried to direct the negotiations to concentrate solely on the Abu Musa Agreement. This willingness, however, contradicted actions on the ground. Iran, in a clear violation of the memorandum, compelled the island's residents to enter and exit through an Iranian point of entry. In addition, it began to restrict the presence of foreigners on the island, including the teachers, technicians, and other foreign workers employed on the UAE part of the island.[53] This stance was graphically demonstrated when Iran refused to allow Arab teachers, who were travelling on the ferry *Al-Khatir*, to disembark.[54] The UAE felt that these acts were meant to harass the Arab population of the island, estimated at seven hundred, pressuring them to leave. Furthermore, Iran began insisting that all non-inhabitants be required to obtain Iranian permits to visit the island. Recent accounts indicate a substantial decline of Abu Musa residents living on the Island; an estimated one hundred and eighty-five islanders remain and their village is cordoned with barbed wire, allowing only a single road to the port.[55]

President Rafsanjani spoke of the need to control security on the island, pointing to armed foreigners captured by Iran in the vicinity of Abu Musa.[56] Yet Iran did not produce evidence verifying such claims. Foreign Minister Velayati stated erroneously that the 1971 agreement did not allow foreigners on the island.[57] These claims were not accurate, however, as the agreement gave neither party an exclusive right on security. Nor did it address the presence of foreigners on the island. Iran was clearly attempting to reinterpret the memorandum, in a manner which would provide more leverage to Iran than the original text. Of particular importance was Iran's desire to control the security of the island and its territorial waters. In fact, Iran's Supreme National Security Council (SNSC), headed by President Rafsanjani, stated that the security of Abu Musa was part of Iran's responsibility.[58]

Bilateral negotiations held in Abu Dhabi in September 1992 failed due to Iran's refusal to discuss its occupation of the Tunb Islands or refer the issue to the ICJ.[59] Significantly, the Iranian Foreign Ministry statement on the breakdown of the talks did not mention Tehran's refusal to discuss the occupation, which led to the unsuccessful outcome of the negotiations.[60] Following the failure of these talks, Iran's SNSC stated that it had no territorial ambitions in the Gulf, yet asserted its position on the islands. Furthermore, the eruption of the border dispute between Qatar and Saudi Arabia enabled Iran to characterize the dispute with the UAE as yet another border entanglement in the region.[61]

The UAE, on the other hand, expressed its intention to pursue aggressively a peaceful diplomatic offensive through regional and international bodies such as the Arab League and the UN. Iran was extremely alarmed with this strategy for several reasons, three of which are discussed below.

First, Iran felt that it was being targeted by the United States, and that the escalation of this issue was part of containing its influence. Iranian perceptions and historical experiences reinforced this belief. This was expressed by an editorial in *Keyhan International*, which viewed the development as "the old story of foreign hands trying to disturb the peace in the area."[62] Meanwhile, Ayatollah Khamene'i stated that "the propaganda surrounding the Iranian island of Abu Musa is part of a conspiracy by the enemies of the Ummah to divide Iran from its neighbors."[63] He added that the West was behind the dispute, especially the United States and Britain.[64] This position was repeated later, with more clarity, in an editorial by the hardline and influential paper, the *Tehran Times*, stating:

> In the wake of the second ... Gulf war and the arrival of armed forces from the U.S. and other Western countries, the UAE suddenly put forward, no doubt after consultation with Western governments, the ridiculous claim of sovereignty over the three islands of the Lesser and the Greater Tunb and Abu Musa ... The UAE government seems to be interested only in creating a publicity uproar and exerting pressure on Iran in international circles.[65]

A second reason for Iran's reaction is that a protracted diplomatic duel would increase the influence in the Gulf of other Arab powers, notably Egypt. Iranian foreign policy has always attempted to limit such influence. This was evident in Iran's condemnation of Arab League statements supporting the UAE. It accused the League of taking an "irresponsible position," disturbing the security of the Gulf.[66] In addition, the Iranian press was critical of President Mubarak's visit to the Gulf in May 1993, charging that it was an attempt to deflect attention from his domestic problems.[67]

A third reason is that the dispute could tarnish Iran's revolutionary image in various Muslim and Third World circles. Iran was suddenly playing the role of Goliath against the UAE's David. Preferring the role of righteous underdog, the revolutionary regime is uncomfortable with this position from a public relations perspective. The UAE's insistence on referring the dispute to the ICJ is a powerful tool in this contest. This sensitivity is evident in early Iranian denials of reports describing violations of the memorandum on Abu Musa.[68]

Various attempts at mediation have proved futile, and an early settlement is not envisaged. In November of 1994, the Omani minister for foreign affairs expressed his skepticism regarding the success of a mediation effort at the present time.[69] Meanwhile, the UAE has reiterated its demands for an ICJ hearing and its willingness to adhere to the outcome. In this attempt, it was supported by the GCC partners who called on Iran to agree to refer the issue to the ICJ.[70]

Latest developments include the potential of an escalation of the dispute. The UAE fears that Iranian plans to build a desalination plant and start a regular air service to Abu Musa from Bandar Abbas are a prelude to the settlement of Iranian citizens on the island, thereby changing its demographic composition.[71] The fear is a genuine one, and is based on various eyewitness and news reports indicating the presence of three thousand to four thousand soldiers on Abu Musa compared with just over one hundred men in 1992.[72] Local accounts report an extensive construction effort, including barracks and entrenched heavy tanks and artillary.[73] These accounts coincide with news reports of Iranian missiles in various islands in the Gulf. Clearly the situation is not based on misperceptions of Iran's intentions and is connected to facts on the ground.

Iranian–Arab Relations in the Gulf: Towards the Year 2000

The future course of Iranian–Arab relations in the Gulf represents a major conundrum. The manner in which many of the states of the region will deal with Tehran will be largely influenced by Iran's dealings with these regimes.[74] The Islamic Republic is the largest of the Gulf states.

Resultingly, it is a significant factor in the future direction of inter-Gulf relations.

Prospects for improving relations, however, do not seem very bright in view of Iran's fluid politics and search for a regional role. Tehran, through its shifting positions and contradictory official statements, has not been able to alleviate suspicion in the area. Historical experiences, including the Shah's imperial policies, such as the occupation of the Tunb Islands, and attempts to control the island of Abu Musa, consolidate the fear of an Iranian hegemonic role.

Persistent internal instability and factional fighting in Iran will continue to alarm Tehran's neighbors. In their dealings with the Islamic Republic, the Arab states of the Gulf are often uncertain of who the real decision-makers are. Radical elements within the revolution remain powerful, having won several significant victories against President Rafsanjani. These groups continue to preach their revolutionary ideology and remain extremely critical of the Gulf Arab states. They believe in the universality and exportability of their model. Moreover, as indicated by R. K. Ramazani, they do not worry about Iran's international isolation. In fact, they subscribe to Khomeini's dictum that Iran must be isolated to be independent.[75]

The continuing influence of these groups and the probability of their control of the political system cast a strong shadow of instability on the area. At the very least their presence will ensure the continued duality and lack of clarity of Iran's foreign policy. This will mean that the confidence gap in the Gulf will not be bridged. A careful examination of Iranian press reports demonstrates this important point. In May 1993, these reports spoke of an improving relationship with Kuwait following the visit by Foreign Minister Velayati, yet only five months later the same paper harshly criticized Kuwait and its ruling family because of Kuwaiti support for the UAE. The emotive language used on both occasions was exaggerated.[76] Furthermore, the persistence of Iran's economic difficulties and the failure of the current economic policy coupled with the great population expansion will only add to the tension in the area. A widening economic gap that might place Iran in the "have not" camp may open up the area to a number of dangerous possibilities.

Internally, the regime faces serious challenges in the coming years. These challenges will undoubtedly undermine Iran's ability to conduct a rational and effective foreign policy. Wide sectors of Iranian society, including the large middle class, are suffering economically and can no longer be subdued by ideological fervor. Commenting on present conditions, a prominent Iranian historian stated, "When an ossified state sits atop an energetic society, it can seldom maintain stability for very long."[77] This might be a premature judgment, but a simple reading of Iran's modern history demonstrates that it is not one of gradual evolution. On the contrary, the modern history of Iran is one characterized by sharp turns and radical changes. This, needless to say, further mystifies future prospects in the area. It also calls for great caution in dealing with events and personalities on the Iranian scene.

The wall of suspicion between Iran and its Gulf neighbors can be overcome only through new foundations, taking into account past experiences and mistakes. Foremost is non-interference in each others' internal affairs and the peaceful resolution of regional disputes. These hopes, however, are long-term in nature and, unfortunately, there are no indications that the search has begun. Confidence-building measures are needed, and such measures need to be employed over a long period of time. For these to be effective, they must go beyond the political sphere toward creating the institutions and mechanisms of economic cooperation and cultural understanding in the region.

In the aftermath of the second Gulf war and in view of the important Western role in the security of the GCC states, the American connection is an essential one in GCC security arrangements. In the turbulent Gulf of the 1990s, this role will continue to be essential. Iran's acceptance of these links will be an indispensable factor influencing the course of relations in the area.

CHAPTER 8

The Ideological Dimension in Saudi–Iranian Relations

Saleh al-Mani'

Over the past fifteen years since the revolution in Iran, many Western political analysts have been preoccupied with the Iran–Iraq war or the Iraqi invasion of Kuwait and mostly addressed Iranian–Saudi relations as a by-product of regional wars. Others have studied the rivalry between the two countries as a reflection of a clash between Arab and Iranian nationalism.[1] The immediate urgency of the first Gulf war, with its two protagonists representing diametrically opposed forms of government, the territorial and border disputes, and historical interference in each other's minority affairs, all provided a justifiable ground to consider other regional differences as merely secondary in importance to the bloody and costly wars. The memories of these conflicts overshadowed other potentially volatile regional and ideological issues that have led in the past decade to ideological competition between Iran and Saudi Arabia. The following analysis attempts to address the development of foreign policy within the context of parallel and competing religious institutions staffed by two competing groups of *ulama*, appealing to universal Islamic values, yet, at times, being prisoners of antagonistic suspicions and beliefs, and affecting the respective foreign policy of each state.

Background

Iran has historically interacted politically and economically with the western, Arab shores of the Gulf. Like a small and shallow lake, the Gulf has always reflected the ebb and flow of military fortunes of the Arab and the Iranian powers. In the seventeenth century, the Omani rulers extended their domain to a small stretch of the Iranian territories overlooking the Gulf and established satellite colonies as far east as the Sind province

158

(Pakistan). Nadir Shah, during his reign, occupied Muscat between 1738 and 1741.[2] In the 1970s, the Shah of Iran sent 35,000 men to fight the Marxist insurgents in Oman. The Gulf region has also been important commercially to the Islamic Republic since 1980, as the UAE ports of Dubai and Sharjah provided a major backdoor through which embargoed Western goods could reach Iran. With the success of the Islamic revolution in Iran in 1979, a new type of relationship and policy toward Saudi Arabia and the Gulf states emerged in Tehran, reflecting not merely revolutionary fervor, but also the form and character of a particular, and sometimes messianic, view that attempts to use the mechanism of state edifice to advance an ideological stance, both at home and in the immediate region adjoining Iran.

The Genesis of the Islamic Republic

Most Islamic and "traditional revolutions" in the Middle East which succeed in building a state tend to be based on a religious/military contract between *ahl al-saif* (people of the sword), and *ahl-qalam* (people of the pen), or *ulama*. This alliance between a military-cum-political leader and a religious sheikh tends to lend political legitimacy to the state, and to put ideology into a dynamic form or agitation that not only spreads the *madhhab* (school of religion) into a larger area, but fortifies and expands state structures and institutions into a larger political domain.

The sealing of the religious—political alliance in 1744 between Muhammad Ibn Saud, the paternal founder of Al-Saud's second dynasty, and Muhammad Ibn Abdul-Wahhab succeeded in establishing a flourishing state in Nejd in the eighteenth century. Saudi Arabia is today an extension of that state, applying the same rules and ideology and abiding by the same contract that bound Al-Saud to Al-Sheikh, or the descendants of Sheikh Ibn Abdul-Wahhab. A similar process of nation-building based on a successful alliance between the Shi'a clergy of the Turkoman tribes and the Safavid dynasty took place in the latter part of the fifteenth century. This alliance succeeded in 1501 in establishing one of the first Shi'a states in the Muslim East. This collaboration resulted in the conversion of most of the Iranian plateau and parts of Iraq to the Jaafari *madhhab* and in the process expanded Safavid rule to as far east as Northern India and Turkistan. By the early decades of the Qajari rule in Iran (1785–1925) the Shi'a "hierarchy" had become so powerful and wealthy that they had freed themselves from the political tutelage characteristic of the Safavid era (1501–1722) to the point of achieving their own autonomy.[3]

The next logical possibility was to assert the superiority of the "hier-acracy" over the state by extending clerical authority to the political sphere. In the Islamic Republic, Khomeini succeeded in the millennial drive not merely to create a state for Shi'ism, but to create a theocratic Shi'a state in which the clerics hold all strings of power and dictate the laws of the state, and direct most of its institutions.[4] In neighboring Saudi Arabia, the *ulama*, having had full religious and ideological authority over the civil society and a share of the economic gains from the oil wealth, satisfied themselves in playing second fiddle to the political leaders of the country. The *ulama* provided legitimacy to the state and learned religious opinion (*fatwa*) in periods of massive change or crisis. *Shariah* became the govern-ing theory, and its laws acted as the basic law of the land. There have been periods of competition between established religious figures and marginal young Islamic revivalist groups that sought to challenge the subordinate rule of the *ulama* in the political structure; but given the pragmatic nature of the community of *ulama*, those groups remained marginal. Their demands, however, found their way to and were systemic-ally absorbed within existing laws without necessarily giving such elements significant political representation. This alienated them and may have driven some of them away from the main political and religious domain. In Pahlavi Iran, on the other hand, the Shah failed to heed many calls for religious reform and sought instead to coerce the religious establishment along with other social strata. The religious establishment in Saudi Arabia, which is less organized and has a small cadre, continued through the period of state-building to enjoy privileged status, both economically and ideologically.

In Saudi Arabia the size of most mobilized political groups was small. Tribal leaders and Islamic *ulama* have historically had deep roots in society. The new state sought to incorporate the traditional elites of clerics and tribal leaders into the political system through a process of urbanization. City centers brought tribal population into direct contact with religious authority. Even when aspiring young educated elites made themselves available, they were easily incorporated into the burgeoning bureaucracy. A sense of indirect participation by function was extended to the new elites and by ideology to the mobilized tribal population. The religiously educated middle class was also absorbed into the civil service, to the point that over the past ten years roughly one-third of the Saudi bureau-cracy was staffed by graduates of religious schools and universities.[5] Thus, participation by function and ideology encompassed a multidimensional strata of traditional and new elites. The guiding role of the *ulama* was further emphasized when the new educated elites were touched by the winds of religious revivalism. Shared ideology became the equivalent of passive political participation as society grew more complex, and as the role of bureaucracy grew to incorporate larger domains of society, functional participation became, *inter alia*, a substitute for political participation. This enlarged role of bureaucracy was very important in the distribution of the goods and benefits of a rich state. Yet the development of bureaucracy was colored by the dominant ideology and the role of the religious establishment, which became the guardian of public morals and presided over many important functions in society, such as educational policies for females at all levels, from grade school through university.

The Islamic revivalist movement that touched most of the Arab world and Iran in the 1980s left its imprint on the new and professional elites who began to follow the popular mood. In the process, they adopted a quasi-religious ideology which made them more acceptable to the traditional segments of society and blurred the differences between the new groups and the old students of theology. Yet the competition between the new and the old elites was not won without skirmishes, one of which was the labeling of advocates of the neo-modernist school of literature (*al-madrasah al-tahdiethieh*) as heretical. There were also skirmishes over women's rights.

The parallel between post-revolutionary Iran and Saudi Arabia is most striking. Both political systems provide a particular model of an Islamic state; both states appeal to the universal values of Islam; both consider *shariah* as the basic law of the land; and the clerics in both states play a major role in organizing and governing their respective societies. "The society for upholding high virtues and elimination of evil" plays in both countries the role of a religious police that ensures strict adherence to the edict and letter of *shariah*. In both countries education, particularly of women, is directed by the religious establishment; and in the organization and staffing of diplomatic missions the religious elites play an important, albeit secondary role.[6] Yet, in Iran the *ayaat* seem today to be in total control of most government institutions and ministries, while in Saudi Arabia the *ulama* provide the norms of society and some of the governing regulations of the state, but retain a veto power on any regulation perceived to contradict the *shariah*. In sum, the power structures of the *ulama* in Iran have historically paralleled those of the state, while in Saudi Arabia they have historically been part of it.

The Impact of Religion on Foreign Policy

The all-encompassing role of religion in Iran and Saudi Arabia has not only affected the quasi-theocratic nature of the political system, it has also colored and affected its foreign policy. Having the two holiest mosques of Islam within its boundaries, Saudi Arabia has prided itself as the leader of the Islamic commonwealth of nations. It has strived to coordinate the foreign policies of many Islamic states and to mobilize the public opinion in those states to support Arab causes, such as lending support to the Palestinian national movement, calling for the return of Jerusalem to Palestinian authority, supporting the Mujahedin in Afghanistan, and most recently providing humanitarian and political support to the Muslims in Bosnia.

Saudi foreign policy employed two vehicles for conducting this Islamic policy: one formal, under the aegis of the Organization of the Islamic Conference (OIC), the other informal through the auspices of non-governmental organizations such as Rabitah Al-Alam Al-Islami, which provides basic relief work to destitute Islamic communities in Afghanistan and Africa and engages in *dawah* (religious vocation) activities. A third, perhaps more important, organization is the Fiqh Muslim Congress, which is a non-governmental organization that convenes its annual meetings in Mecca prior to the *hajj* season to discuss and debate major religious issues facing the Muslim world. The Fiqh Congress provides a platform for *ulama*, *fuqaha*, and learned elders throughout the world to give a consensus view, or *fatwa*, on important issues facing the *ummah* (the Islamic community). This triad of Islamic organizations, both governmental and non-governmental, has enabled Saudi Arabia to build stature for itself in the community of Islamic states and to carry its policies into the Islamic world, which has reinforced its regional role and policies.

Against this backdrop and aware of the doctrinal and philosophic differences that separate the two states, Iran, since the revolution, has attempted to challenge the predominant position of leadership enjoyed by Saudi Arabia. While still a full member of the OIC, Iran chose to boycott most of its meetings. Only selectively, and when such meetings affected its security concerns, did it choose to participate. This was the case when the Islamic states gathered in 1980 for the Lahore meeting of the OIC foreign ministers to discuss the OIC strategy for dealing with the Soviet invasion of Afghanistan. When Iraq was winning segments of official Islamic opinion in 1982 to its view of the hostilities with Iran, the latter decided to end its boycott of OIC meetings temporarily and to participate in the twelfth meeting of the foreign ministers in Niamey, Niger, in November of 1982.[7] When Soviet withdrawal from Afghanistan was imminent in December of 1988, Iran chose to reactivate its independent role in order to help the interests of some guerrilla groups in the Mujahedin, sometimes on purely sectarian grounds, which almost broke the fragile unity of the Mujahedin provisional government.

In lieu of formal governmental organizations at its disposal, Iran under Khomeini strove to grasp the mantle of leadership of some revivalist groups that appeal to Islamic unity but largely restrict membership to Jaafari elements.[8] This was the case with Iran's support for Hizbollah in Lebanon, for Hizb Al-Dawah in Iraq, and for the Imam-line group in Kuwait. Threatening the status quo in neighboring Gulf states became an ethos and a *modus operandi* for the Islamic Republic. Such calls for Islamic unity were therefore suspect as the regime in Tehran sought to coerce and sometimes cajole neighboring states in order to distance these countries from Iraq during the war. The ideological character and message of the revolution was therefore used effectively during the Khomeini period to serve the larger security interests of the state.

In post-Khomeini Iran there appears to be emerging a double-track foreign policy for Iran, with each track harboring often incompatible views. The one favored by the old Khomeini guards centers on a traditionalist-revolutionary thesis; the other is based on the traditional diplomatic approach of state-to-state relations. Revolutionary logic will still find an outlet on the regional level, which may at times impede traditional state policies. As the revolution ages such methods might gain subtlety.

Doctrinal Impediments

The historical rift that existed in the Muslim world between the four schools of Sunna jurisprudence and the three major schools of Shi'a left a dark shadow in the heart of every Muslim. In his book *Islamic Government*, Ayatollah Khomeini attempted to strike a note of conciliation between the two sects of Islam. While whitewashing and neglecting the doctrinal differences, he attempted to placate the majority of Muslims through his recognition of the important contributions of the Ottoman Empire to the Muslim Ummah. He nonetheless elevated the status of Imams to those of heavenly bodies, surpassing the status of God's prophets.[9] His particularism was evident in the use of symbols and citations of the prophet Muhammad, Caliph Ali, and the Twelve Imams.[10] Once in power, however, Ayatollah Khomeini seemed to have neglected his own call for Islamic unity. The Iranian constitution of 1979 and the amendments to the constitution in August of 1989 failed to address the religious and political rights of non-Jaafaris in Iran, particularly those of the Hanafi Kurds, the Turkomans, and the Maliki Baluchis. This calculated neglect, argued many in the Gulf region, was not helpful to the cause of Islamic unity.

Over the past decade many books were written in the Islamic world which challenged Khomeini's legitimacy to speak on behalf of the nation of Islam. Some were purely rhetorical. Others questioned the theoretical underpinnings of the Shi'a schools of thought; they attacked Al-Keleini's work *Al-Kafi* as being the embodiment of *glou*, or mystification of imams, and considered such books as deviations from the letter of the Holy Qur'an, and therefore heretical. Those writers may have been motivated by a religious purpose, but the paucity of the number of books (21 since 1979) suggests that some of those writers may have been politically motivated as well.[11]

In the meantime a small group of writers in Egypt began to call for a dialogue between the Shi'a and the Sunna *ulama*. One such writer was Ali Abd-l-Wahid Wafi who, in 1983, authored a book, *Bain Al-Shiah Wal-Sunnah* (Between the Shi'a and the Sunna), which called for a historic compromise between the *ulama* of the two sects. Such a call was not new. Nadir Shah (1688–1747) worked for a similar compromise, when in 1743 he gathered the *ulama* of Sunna and Shi'a in Najaf. At that time, he presided over a new religious contract between the two groups according to which the Shi'a *ulama* were to refrain from *sabb* (blasphemy against Abu-Bakr and Umar), and from *glou*. Nadir Shah's historic attempt was motivated by his imperial design, since two factions of his military command were divided on sectarian lines. This historic compromise seems to have ended with the assassination of Nadir Shah four years later.[12]

Another attempt at compromise was advanced by Jamal Al-Din Al-Afghani and his disciples in Egypt, who sought at the end of the last century to create a united Islamic state that went beyond particular and sectarian loyalties. In 1959, a third attempt was promulgated by the Sheikh Al-Azhar, Mahmoud Shaltout, who, at the instigation of Jamal Abdul-Nasser, issued a *fatwa* considering the Shi'a Al-Ithnie Ashariah (the Twelvers) as a fifth school of Islamic jurisprudence and allowed the *ulama* of Al-Azhar to base their *fatwa* on Jaafari books of *fiqh*.

A group of Sunni scholars took issue with Shaltout's *fatwa*. One such critic of the Sheikh was the Syrian Islamic scholar, Muhib Al-Din Al-

Khatib. Al-Khatib based his criticism on the thesis that the four most eminent works of *fiqh* in the Shi'a sect, namely al-Keleini's *Al-Kafi* (The Copious), Al-Hilley's *Al-Sirair* (The Concealment), Ibn Al-Numan's *Al-Irshad* (The Guidance), and Al-Seid Al-Murtada's work, *Al Masaail Al-Nassiriyah* (The Nassiriyah Issues), were all blasphemous of the two Caliphs, Abu Bakr and Omar. He postulated that some of these texts (particularly *Al-Kafi*), cannot be considered part of the Islamic *fiqh* because they elevate the status of the Imams to those of prophets. Al-Khatib went even further and considered Al-Tussi's assertion that the Qur'an had omitted "Surat Al-Wilayah," in which Imam Ali's "right of 'wilayah'" is supposedly indicated in the Holy Book as absolute *Kufr*, or unbelief in religion.[13]

The line of criticism adopted by Muhib Al-Din Al-Khatib against the attempt to find congruence among "two diverse belief systems," which was published for the first time in 1960, reappeared in the last ten years in the writings of Ibrahim Al-Jabhan in Saudi Arabia, Ihsan Ilahi Zahir in Pakistan, and Muhammad Mal-Ullah in Egypt. All of these writers followed the same line, rejecting a dialogue with the Shi'a clerics until those *ulama* begin to purify their education and writings from all profanity accorded to Sahabah (Muhammad's Companions).[14] Unfortunately, Ilahi Zahir lost his life in Pakistan for addressing these issues.

Shi'a clerical attempts to find a compromise between their traditional approach and the *ulama* of Sunna seem to have impelled a great Iraqi Ayatollah, Muhammad Baqr Al-Sudr, to reassess the traditional Shi'a animosity expressed towards Muawiah. While Al-Sudr was still critical of Muawiah's policies and political orientation, he nonetheless credited Mu-awiah with saving the Islamic state during a period of uncertainty. This fresh reinterpretation of history (by Al-Sudr) may according to Chibli Mallat have served a political objective of the Iraqi opposition for an approach towards the Sunni population in Iraq.[15]

Another independent Iranian scholar wrote a critical review of books concerning traditional Shi'a *fiqh* (jurisprudence). In his book, *Al-Shiah Wal-Tashieh* (Shi'a and Rectification), Abul-Hasan Al-Mawsawi Al-Asbahani called on Shi'a *ulama* to clear their reference books of all profanities accorded to Muhammad's Companions and to remove from the *madhhab* all myths and practices unrelated to the true teachings of Islam.[16] And finally, Ayatollah Ali Khamene'i, Iran's spiritual leader, issued a religious *fatwa* on 14 June 1994, banning the lashing of one's body as a form of repentance during the Ashura memorial of Imam Hussein. He considered such practices as irreligious and unfit for a good Muslim.

The Impact of the Ideological Rift on
Foreign Policy

Henry Kissinger wrote in 1961 that ideologically motivated states tend to pursue a positive foreign policy of grand design, which not only is difficult to fulfill but tends to destabilize the existing international system.[17] Iran as a revolutionary state has pursued a foreign policy of grand design since 1979. Aside from challenging the existing distribution of power and wealth in the international system, it sought to appeal to the Islamic masses through symbolic gestures, like the *fatwa* against Salman Rushdie, and through challengimg the legitimacy of the Islamic state system.

The diadic view of the world that governs the thoughts of Ayatollah Khomeini tended to divide the world into two halves: Al-Mustadhafoun (the wretched), and Al-Mustakbiroun (the refomonic). This world view is also cast upon the world of Islam and seeks to distinguish between popular Islam and the so-called official Islam. The implication of such a world view upon the historical rift between the Sunna and Imamiyah (a major Shi'a school) is something that Ayatollah Khomeini was not necessarily interested in examining. What is clear was Khomeini's view of the Gulf states as allied to the forces of Mustakbiroun, hence part of his diadic framework.

One of the most salient factors in Khomeini's attempt to challenge the Islamic legitimacy of the Gulf states was his drive to use religion as a factor in his foreign policy towards those states. The response of those same states has also been cast in a similar vein. Al-Khomeini had called for a shared Islamic sovereignty over the Islamic Holy cities of Mecca and Madinah. His prime minister, Musavi, was quoted in 1984 as advocating the sending of "forces belonging to all Muslim nations" to Mecca and Madinah. However, Hashemi Rafsanjani, then speaker of the Majlis, retracted the prime minister's statement by the end of that year.[18] The Iranian government nonetheless organized a conference in London in January 1988, calling for abdication of Saudi sovereignty over Al-Haramain Al-Sharifen (The Two Holy Mosques).[19] Due to an outcry against this interference in the internal affairs of Saudi Arabia, Iranian spokesmen altered their propaganda. After the 1994 *hajj* season Hujjat al-Islam Hassan Rohani, vice-speaker of the Iranian Majlis, issued a statement on 31 May 1994, calling for "the administration of the Hajj ceremonies by the Islamic countries" and added that "Iran was willing to send volunteers to Mecca to administer the Hajj."[20] The people of Saudi Arabia rejected such a stand by the Iranian government and looked with suspicion to its designs and propaganda. The Saudi government, by virtue of the 1926 Islamic Congress held in Mecca, and through the long and tedious historical task of building a unified state, viewed such suggestions by the Iranian leaders as a threat to the sovereignty and unity of the country.

In order to shake the positive image of Saudi Arabia in the Islamic world, the Iranian leadership did embark on a systematic policy of creating disturbances during the *hajj*. These disturbances are caused in part by differences in the symbolic meaning of *al-hajj* in the two states. However, such activities were not limited to peaceful marches and sometimes included violent clashes with police in which human life was lost. At times, such behavior led Khomeini to offer his apology on the part of some Iranian pilgrims. But the campaign did not cease during his lifetime. At other instances Iran was accused, as in 1987, of smuggling a sizable number of explosives during the *hajj* season. In addition, during the *hajj* of 1987, clashes between pilgrims from Iran and other Islamic countries led to the death of 402 people in Mecca: 275 from Iran, 42 from other countries, and 85 Saudi policemen. As a result Iran boycotted the *hajj* season for two years and severed its diplomatic ties with Saudi Arabia. In 1989, actual bombs were detonated by Iranian agents in Mecca. If one combines such acts with other violent measures directed at Saudi diplomats during the 1980s, one cannot escape the conclusion that Iran was seeking to intimidate the Saudi leadership and to challenge the Saudi Islamic authority and administration of the *hajj* rites.

The Saudi Response

Saudi Arabia, like Iran, has sought refuge in religion for its policies toward other Islamic states. In the case of Iran, it has sought to limit the total number of pilgrims, Iranian pilgrims in particular, to 55,000 per annum after their actual number increased from 74,963 in 1979 to 157,395 in 1987.[21] Some of Iran's pilgrims had already become troublesome for the Saudi security authorities and a nuisance to pilgrims from other parts of the Islamic world. Saudi Arabia sought and received the support of the Seventeenth Islamic Foreign Ministers Meeting in Amman in 1987, which adopted a specific formula limiting the number of pilgrims visiting the Holy Land every year to perform the *hajj* to one per thousand of the total number of the population of the given Muslim country. The Islamic states, members of the OIC, enthusiastically supported this formula, since it saved their countries valuable foreign currency reserves. For Saudi Arabia, the new formula helped to lessen the pressure on existing housing services that are provided to the pilgrims free of charge by the state. It also improved enforcement of law and order during the *hajj*.

By marshalling the support of other members of the OIC, Saudi Arabia has succeeded in emphasizing its authority as the Guardian of the Islamic Holy Cities and in increasing its privileged status in the community of Muslim nations. This apparent diplomatic success, in addition to the 1987 incident in Mecca, may have pushed the Iranian government to take the radical decision to boycott the *hajj* season in 1988 and 1989. Iranian agents, however, continue to instigate acts of defiance in Mecca. Such acts may reflect an alienation on the part of the Iranian regime or an attempt to force the Gulf states to extend financial aid to Iran to help in the postwar reconstruction program.

Saudi Arabia has further sought to obtain the political backing of traditional Islamic institutions in the Muslim world, such as Al-Azhar in Egypt, and Jamaat Islamiah in India. This competition for the hearts and minds of Muslim opinion, particularly of the Islamic *ulama*, continues. While both sides can offer financial aid to Muslim benevolent societies and schools throughout the developing and developed world, only Saudi Arabia can entice the pious Muslims of every *madhhab* to visit the Holy Cities of Mecca and Madinah.

Such competition has nonetheless been tempered with occasional goodwill gestures by the Saudi leadership towards Iran. In opening remarks to the Ninth Islamic Conference of Muslim Information Ministers held in Jeddah in October of 1988, the Saudi monarch expressed hopes that "our brothers from Iran would participate fully in the workings of the conference in the near future." Less than two months later, agents of a Lebanese guerrilla group allied to Iran, the Soldiers of Justice, assassinated two Saudi diplomats, Saleh Al-Malki and Ahmed Al-Amri, in Bangkok and in Karachi, respectively.[22] The Saudis have also attempted since 1985 to engage Tehran in a diplomatic dialogue at the level of foreign ministers.

Iran, for its part, has cooperated with Saudi Arabia in oil production quota negotiations at OPEC meetings and in combatting drug traffic. The two countries, even in the dark days of the Iran–Iraq war, have worked very closely with each other to save the Gulf flora and fauna from the ecological dangers of oil spills. Yet despite this functional cooperation, ideological and doctrinal differences remain a significant impediment to the conduct of normal relations between these two Islamic states.

The Iraqi Invasion of Kuwait and its Impact on the Ideological Competition

The relationship between Saudi Arabia and Iran changed considerably in the aftermath of the Iraqi invasion of Kuwait. Iran's neutrality in the conflict helped to lessen the tensions in Saudi—Iranian relations. In fact, the relationship between the two countries may have begun to show amicable signs in the postwar period. Crown Prince Abdullah met President Rafsanjani in Dakkar, Senegal, in December 1990, for the first time in a decade. The two countries agreed to reopen their respective embassies in each other's capitals and elevated their diplomatic representation to an ambassadorial level on 2 March 1992. Riyadh and Tehran were discussing the future of Iraq after the presumed withering away of the present government. Hostile media exchanges abated and droves of Muslim pilgrims from Iran were demonstrating peacefully in 1991 in Mecca and Madinah, something they had not done since 1980.

Like Egypt, and to a certain extent Turkey, Iran became a chief beneficiary of the second Gulf war. Its armaments were tremendously increased by the arrival and confiscation of 150 Iraqi warplanes during the course of the war. President Rafsanjani resumed his country's participation in Islamic international forums such as the OIC. Iran's institutions and universities were receiving grants and loans from the Islamic Development Bank (IDB). It seemed that what revolutionary Iran was unable to achieve by supporting various splinter groups and organizations, the Islamic Republic was able to accomplish through the diplomatic councils of the Islamic Conference.

Indeed, during the Dakkar Sixth Islamic Summit held in December 1990, Iran was able to claim the prestige of representing the Asian Islamic group. At the conference, Rafsanjani sought to increase the tension between Saudi Arabia and its former friends, Yemen and the Sudan. After the conference he visited both countries and engaged in two parallel initiatives towards the two countries: one, a state-to-state relationship, the other, informal contacts with sympathetic political parties and mass organizations.

Sectarian differences with the Sudan did not impede this approach. Both Yemen and the Sudan were in dire need of oil, weapons, and an external ally. For the short run, Iran could fulfill some of these needs; however, over the long haul, it could not come close to the level of former aid provided by Saudi Arabia. Yemen soon became aware of this, and began to reapproach its neighbor to the north.

The aggressive approach of Rafsanjani to the rest of the Gulf states did not set well with Saudi Arabia. Iran, in 1992, was flexing its muscles against the United Arab Emirates, particularly in its forceful occupation of the island of Abu Musa in the summer of 1992. This aggressive stand was coupled with other signs of militarization, as was evidenced by a significant purchase of advanced weapons from Russia including combat aircraft, three submarines, and hardware to relaunch its nuclear program.[23]

Despite the build up of military arsenals in Iran, the relationship with Saudi Arabia remained intact, albeit at a more fragile level. In the spring of 1992, the two countries seemed to be coordinating their policies toward the Iraqi opposition groups. Saudi Arabia invited the head of the Hizb Al-Dawah party in Iraq, Sheikh Muhammad Baqir Al-Hakim, who makes Tehran his headquarters, to participate in the February meeting of the Iraqi opposition groups. The meeting in Riyadh did not succeed in announcing a government in exile; however, it unified various groups, organizations, and personalities in a front against the regime of Saddam Hussein. More importantly, Al-Hakim's visit reinforced a new pragmatic approach on the part of Saudi Arabia, as it accepted the concept of a future regime in Baghdad with major participation by the Shi'a clergy. Interviews given by Al-Hakim during his visit to Riyadh successfuly reduced fears that Iran sought to create an Iranian satellite state in a post-Saddam Iraq.[24]

Developments since 1990

The honeymoon in relations between Saudi Arabia and Iran, which began in August 1990, allowed the two competing states to examine issues of mutual concern more closely in order to identify areas of potential cooperation. This approach was fruitful to both countries insofar as ideological factors could no longer derail the policy of accommodation.

Saudi Arabia was eager to normalize its relations with its neighbor to the east. Such a relationship would not be as good as the one that existed during the regime of the Shah, but from a Saudi perspective the Gulf has already experienced too many wars, and it desperately needed a stable environment.[25] Iran, on its part, was eager to build a *modus vivendi* with its Arab neighbors of the Gulf. As with any other state, foreign policy planning and conduct did not always follow neat lines. Two powerful groups within Iran were also exerting some pressures on Rafsanjani and his regime. One group was the "nationalists," who reversed the Khomeini policy of neglecting military readiness and dreamed of building a powerful

Iranian state. The nationalists not only sought to modernize the Iranian fleet and land-based forces, but also engaged in attempts to intimidate the United Arab Emirates and Oman. The enlargement of the occupation of Abu Musa island in 1992, and subsequent annexation of the two Tunbs by the Iranian Parliament in April 1993, produced great concerns throughout the region.[26]

The balance of power within Iran, oscillating since the death of Imam Khomeini, seemed to have stabilized by 1993 in favor of President Ali Khamene'i and his conservative allies at the expense of President Rafsanjani and his pragmatist group. While Khamene'i and his group may have reigned supreme, Rafsanjani was committed to showing the conservative elements that better relations with Saudi Arabia would improve the Iranian economy. In September 1993, he made strong overtures to the Saudi leadership to help Iran increase its production quota in OPEC. He contacted the Saudi monarch on 27 September by telephone, and the two countries engaged for a short time in a flurry of diplomatic exchanges.

The consultations contributed to the Saudi endorsement within OPEC of increases in Kuwaiti and Iranian levels of production and a freeze on the Saudi and UAE production quotas.[27] As a result, the daily production quota for Iran increased by 260,000 barrels a day.[28] In return, it was understood in Abu Dhabi and Riyadh that Iran was finally willing to settle the islands dispute with the UAE in a peaceful way through bilateral negotiations. Iranian Foreign Minister Ali Willayati visited Saudi Arabia and announced in Qatar on 7 October 1993 that he had carried an official invitation to King Fahad to visit Iran and that the king had accepted.[29] This seemed to be the zenith of the honeymoon and the two countries were almost on the verge of an historic compromise that would settle almost all major issues of contention.

This did not occur, however. The news did not sit well with some segments of the Iranian public, particularly the hardliners. One hundred Iranian students at Tehran University demonstrated against the extension of the invitation.[30] Some religious personalities began to attack Saudi Arabia and its leaders in the Iranian press.[31] This media campaign, coming within weeks of Saudi concessions in Vienna, was an affront to Saudi Arabia. A Saudi communiqué on 16 March 1994 aptly exclaimed that Saudi Arabia could not understand the contradictory policies of Iran.[32]

The abrupt decision of the Iranian government not to discuss the "islands" issue in the planned round of negotiations in Tehran in early October between the UAE and Iran soured relations further.[33] Thus negotiations were damaged on the eve of the proposed meeting. Saudi

Arabia felt that its conciliatory policies towards Iran had been misread as a sign of weakness; it therefore changed course and adopted a tougher stance.

This approach was evident during the 1994 pilgrimage season, as Saudi Arabia decreased the number of Iranian pilgrims permitted to attend the *hajj*. Iran's pilgrimage quota according to the OIC-adopted formula was 55,000. Since 1990, Saudi Arabia has permitted twice this number. Given the shortages of housing and the construction works in the mosques of Mecca and Madinah, however, Saudi Arabia chose to discontinue this practice and it adopted a new policy in the *hajj* season of May 1994, limiting the number to 55,000, in line with the quota. The interior minister of Saudi Arabia also vowed to prohibit any political marches and distribution of leaflets and political propaganda during the *hajj* in the two holy cities.[34]

The Iranian leadership did not accept this limitation and sought an expansion of the number of pilgrims allowed into the country. The Iranians claimed that they had more than 170,000 would-be pilgrims on the waiting roster; that other Islamic states are not filling their OIC quotas; and, that Iran, in the words of Ayatollah Khamene'i, should be allowed more privileges in this regard.[35] The Saudis on their part increased the number of visas issued to Iranian pilgrims to 65,000, but stuck to their earlier decision not to allow the head of the Iranian Pilgrimage Mission in Mecca to hold mass rallies and marches. Any such gathering of 65,000 pilgrims or a portion thereof in the narrow streets of Mecca, the Saudis argued, would disrupt transport and services in the Holy City, particularly on the eve of the pious Muslim movement from Mecca to the the other towns of Mina and Arafat. Other segments of the Saudi population, a large part of it the conservative Hanbalis (followers of Imam Ahmad Bin Hanbal), were alarmed by Ayatollah Khamen'i's plans to build a memorial shrine for Imam Khomeini in Madinah, an act which is counter to the teachings of the Hanbalis.[36] Thus the latest Saudi policies *vis-à-vis* Iran may have had some popular support.

On a practical level, the Iranian response to the Saudis' new approach may have produced some positive results. Despite continuing bad press, Iran's spiritual leader Ayatollah Ali Khamene'i ordered the cancellation of the proposed pilgrimage marches and began to moderate his stance toward Saudi Arabia. In his Aid Al-Adha speech to the Iranian nation, on 23 May 1994, he called for a new round of negotiations with Saudi Arabia to bring the question of the *hajj* quota to a mutually acceptable level.[37] The same call was voiced by another hardliner, Ayatollah Yazdi, head of the Supreme Court. This change of a stance on the part of Khamen'i and Yazdi brought about sharp criticism from their followers, particularly in *Keyhan* and other newspapers.[38] And for some time it appeared that the policy toward Saudi Arabia had become an internal political issue. Additionally, economic pressures were inducing Ali Akbar Nateq Nuri, speaker of the Majlis and former interior minister, to call for normalization of relations with Saudi Arabia and other Gulf states.[39]

Building a Lasting Peace in the Gulf

Relations between Saudi Arabia and Iran should not be channeled through traditional diplomatic interactions or limited to periodic functional cooperation. The buildup of tensions at the ideological and policy levels between the two states has already taken its toll. Social scientists have previously suggested that functional cooperation would, over time, have an effect on the foreign policy of states. The case of Saudi–Iranian relations has shown two competing and parallel policies at work. It is interesting that ideological competition did not run roughshod over the oil policies of the two countries. Neither has cooperation within OPEC engendered similar cooperation in other areas or issues of foreign policy. The foreign policy of each state continues to exhibit some ideological particularism of their respective societies. Only in a few instances has their foreign policies escaped the ideological paradigm and become accommodative, particularly when state interests were so vital.

On other socio-religious issues, like *hajj*, the competition remains, but perhaps at a lower level today than a decade earlier; and there is a deep sense in Tehran and in Riyadh that the *hajj* issue must be brought to a mutually acceptable solution. Within political cultures that relegate foreign policy as a function of the ideological imperative, the foreign policy of each state will continue to exhibit binary tensions, and perhaps even temporary deterioration. However, the ideological rift between the two states is not necessarily unbridged. Requirements for building a stable structure of peace in the Gulf necessitate bold initiatives in the ideological domain.

There have been earlier attempts to find common universal denominations between Islam and Christianity in the famed Islamic–Christian dialogue, conducted in the early 1970s with the active participation of some of the *ulama* in Saudi Arabia. Other successful attempts at a dialogue between the Shaafi *ulama* and the Ziedi *ulama* in Yemen in the 1950s succeeded in bringing the Ziedieh closer to the four schools of Sunna.

The success of the dialogue in Yemen was such that the books of some imminent Ziedi scholars, like Imam Al-Shokani, Imam Al-Sunaani, and Ibn Al-Wazir are now considered major *fiqh* refrences by Sunni *ulama*.

Today, Al-Azhar and the *ulama* of Al-Hawzah Al-Deinieh (Shi'a circle of scholars and students) in Najaf and Qum can begin a historic task of closing the ranks of Muslims, regardless of the *madhhab*. The visionary work that has already gained some precedent must examine all the under-pinnings that run counter to the original text of the Qur'an and *hadith* (sayings of the prophet). Both sides must accept the cultural diversity and the historical burden of the rift and work to bring the adherents of the two Islamic schools closer to each other. Other intellectuals and writers on both sides of the Gulf must work assiduously to lead and inspire this dialogue. The *ulama* of Sunna and Shi'a are not necessarily encouraged to compromise the basis of their *madhhabs*, but must amend non-religious and non-Islamic practices that degrade the common heritage of Muslims.

While continuous tension may describe the relationship between the Iranian and Saudi *ulama*, there are signs of small and incremental changes occurring in both countries. Those changes could be helpful in providing a similar methodology for arriving at common grounds for religious legislation, or *fatwa*. While Shi'a clergy have historically relied on informed judgment of a living *faqih* (personified *ijtihad*), and Sunna *ulama* have historically relied on *ijmaa* (consensus of religious opinion), a new genera-tion of Sunna *ulama* in Saudi Arabia have begun to rely on *ijtihad* as a basis of legislation, or *fatwa*, since it is a legitimate method of dealing with new and novel conditions facing the state and society (*al-masaleh al-mursalah*), or public welfare codes.[40]

In the final analysis, ideology, or a particular interpretation of a single event, tend to create an historic cultural and ideological divide that in the long run may endanger interstate relations and complicate and politicize regional rivalries. In ideologically motivated cultures, the division between state policies and existing belief systems is not clearly drawn or easily ascertained. Ideological competition tends to void state policies in the external domain of the needed internal support, even in semi-authoritarian states. The need is therefore urgent to re-engage in an inter-*madhhab* dialogue, which is likely to be long and tedious and will not necessarily produce immediate results. The mere existence of such a dialogue will help to ascertain the universal dimension of the brotherhood of Islam and diminish particularism. It will not only allow policy-makers in the two states to pursue fruitful diplomatic negotiations, but it will also provide the building blocks for a peaceful, developing Gulf region.

CHAPTER 9

Iran's Policy in Northwest Asia:
Opportunities, Challenges, and Implications

W. Nathaniel Howell

The Setting: History Resumed

The sudden implosion of the Soviet Union in 1991 presented Iran with a northern vista that is, at once, hauntingly familiar and surprisingly alien. With minimal warning, the empire Moscow inherited from Tsarist Russia and assiduously consolidated over the seven decades of Soviet rule disintegrated, bequeathing independence to a series of fragile new entities within borders drawn primarily to perpetuate Soviet control. Like a massive movement of tectonic plates, the geopolitical fault line between Russo-Soviet culture and Persian, Turkic, and Islamic cultures shifted. For most of the period of Soviet control, the indigenous peoples of Northwest Asia – the region stretching from Central Asia to the Transcaucuses – were carefully insulated from natural historic linkages with Iran, Turkey, and the Muslim world beyond.[1] In a sense, the flow of history, suspended during that period, resumed, but with a difference.[2] At the end of the twentieth century, both Iran and Northwest Asia had been affected by their separate and distinct experiences during this interval of enforced separation. The context for a resumption of interaction had changed in ways that were neither immediately clear nor predictable.

The collapse of empires is invariably a destabilizing phenomenon. Imperial systems inevitably distort or suspend the natural evolution of subordinate ethnic groups and societies, even when their intent is benign. By channeling political, economic, and social development in directions that serve the vision and interests of the metropole, they set up anomalies, discontinuities, and grievances that encourage future instability and conflict. One has merely to review areas of crisis and instability in today's headlines to identify sociopolitical aftershocks of failed imperial schemes.[3] The new states of Northwest Asia, viewed from Tehran or elsewhere, possess a particularly tenuous identity, even when compared to other former parts of the Soviet periphery. Although the region possesses a rich cultural heritage, its political shape has almost no basis in pre-Soviet history and seems to be essentially the product of Stalinist policies designed to forestall the evolution of viable independent entities.[4] They may succeed despite these handicaps, but the task of nation-building facing them is a daunting one and confronts policy-makers in Tehran, in Ankara, and elsewhere with multiple imponderables and uncertainties.

The disappearance of the Soviet state on the northern frontiers of the Middle East was so abrupt and unanticipated that neither the newly independent peoples of Northwest Asia nor neighboring states like Iran were afforded an opportunity to adjust to or prepare for the new constellation of relationships. Unlike the Ottoman Empire, whose decline was evident for decades before its fall, or the European empires, which made accommodation with varying degrees of success for a transition to independence, the Soviet Union imploded, ironically, at a moment when its military power along its southern periphery appeared to be at its zenith. In the decade before 1991, Moscow not only pursued a substantial military campaign in Afghanistan but significantly enhanced its power projection capabilities in the region. During the mid-1980s, the military structure based in Baku was upgraded from a secondary, defensive front to an offensively-oriented *Teatr Voennykh Dyeistviy* (theater of war operations), commanded by one of the most capable Soviet generals, the former commander of the elite Group of Soviet Forces in East Germany. While the motivations behind these changes remain obscure, Iran and Turkey no doubt were cognizant of the fact that the concentration of military capability stationed opposite them was probably the most powerful the Soviet Union (or the Russian Empire) had ever deployed in the region. There was little reason for Iran to anticipate that the massive concentration of power on its frontiers was on the verge of collapsing inward.

Northwest Asia played almost no part in the momentous events that sealed the fate of the Soviet Union. Unlike the Baltic and other republics of the USSR, predominately Muslim republics in Central Asia and Transcaucasia achieved independence without producing meaningful independence movements. As a consequence, they were denied even the most rudimentary opportunity to define elements of a distinctive and shared identity, articulate their aspirations, or shape their institutions before the problems and responsibilities of independence were thrust upon them. And, because the regimes and peoples there played no significant part in their ultimate "liberation," there was neither a basis nor an occasion for them to reach out for support to neighboring states, such as Iran or

Turkey. Paradoxically, when their natural links with the Muslim world were restored, the societies of Northwest Asia possessed no "living" legacy of contact with even their closest neighbors.

Iran was also a passive spectator of the momentous political earthquake that restored ethnic and cultural connections severed by decades of Russian and Soviet control. There are some indications that Tehran nurtured a low-priority aspiration to restore communication with indigenous populations in Northwest Asia and periodically sought, for example, Moscow's agreement to the establishment of Iranian consulates there.[5] As a general proposition, however, Northwest Asia does not appear to have figured importantly in the formulation of Iranian foreign policy. Maintaining a workable, non-threatening relationship with its powerful Soviet neighbor had to be Tehran's overriding concern for reasons of national security. One suspects that even if there had been viable movements among the indigenous peoples of Northwest Asia agitating for independence from Soviet control, Iran would still have deemed it prudent to avoid antagonizing Moscow on the issue. In their absence, Iran found it easier to follow a conservative course, eschewing positions that would have challenged Soviet policies, including official criticism of the neglect or suppression of Islam in territories governed from Moscow. When Soviet controls were unexpectedly swept away, therefore, Iran found itself without either the ideological underpinnings or the diplomatic record on which to base a forward strategy to its north.

For the first time in almost two centuries, the Iranians do not share a frontier with a more powerful Russian-based state. Relations between Tehran and Moscow were stabilized following the Second World War, but the dominant motif of the relationship was one of Russian expansion and pressure at the expense of Persian control and influence.[6] Although Iran was able ultimately to accommodate itself to the disparity of power with its northern neighbor, the initiative was essentially with Moscow; power and influence could be projected south of the common border but not in the opposite direction.

The collapse of the Soviet state and the emergence of fragile independent states along Iran's 1,600-mile frontier east and west of the Caspian Sea theoretically reversed the power polarity. Iran is arguably stronger and more stable than its new neighbors and is no longer vulnerable to conventional threat or intimidation from that direction. It is doubtful, however, that Iran has been entirely comfortable and confident with this sudden reversal of fortunes. One Iranian ambassador has provided a glimpse of Tehran's ambivalence:

We used to look north at our border and we saw a giant hostile power there, and although it was hostile, we had the impression that it was stable. We knew what it was going to do, and we learned to do business with it. Now we look to the north and we see as many as seven different countries in that area, all of them unstable, and [this] changes the strategic equation.[7]

A similarly cautious note was sounded openly by President Hashemi Rafsanjani as Moscow's control of the Soviet periphery teetered on the edge of collapse. Speaking in the uncertain interval between the failed coup attempt against Gorbachev and the final dissolution of the empire, the Iranian president warned that "it is not in our interest that there should be unrest, clashes, and quarrels along our long border."[8]

These sober assessments contrast sharply with concerns expressed by some commentators that Iran would regard the reopening of Northwest Asia as an unmitigated opportunity to pursue radical and destabilizing objectives there.[9] A brief review of Iranian policies and behavior in the intervening three years is, therefore, essential in assessing Iran's goals in the fledgling states of Transcaucasia and Central Asia.

The Record: Iran Returns to Northwest Asia

During a routine official visit to Turkmenistan in October 1994, the Iranian deputy foreign minister, Manuchechr Mottaki, was given a tour of the town of Turkmenbashi by the town's mayor.[10] Reporting the event, the Ashgabat newspaper, *Turkmenskaya Iskra* (Turkman Spark), makes a particular point of noting that Mr. Mottaki was shown "the former Iranian representation building," unoccupied by Iran for most of the last one hundred years.[11] According to the account, discussions included preparations for the opening of an Iranian Consulate in Turkmenbashi.

Four aspects of this otherwise mundane news item are worth highlighting for the insights they reveal into the Iranian position in the region. First, exchanges of visits and delegations between Tehran and regional capitals have become a routine feature of the diplomatic scene, reflecting a web of state-to-state relationships created since 1991. Second, ancient, dimly remembered links with Iran and Persian culture constitute a potential asset for Iran in states and societies struggling to reconstitute a distinctive identity after an extended period of Soviet indoctrination and neglect or manipulation of cultural symbols. Third, despite these historical ties, there is no question of Iran and the regional cultures and societies simply picking up where they were when Russian and Soviet control severed contacts; Iran and the peoples of Transcaucasia and Central Asia have experienced decades of separate development that will influence the values and attitudes they bring to the present relationship. Finally, the irony that the Ashgabat report was published in the Russian language underlies divergent lines of development and serves as a symbolic reminder of external interests and influences that will continue to modulate their relationships with Tehran.

Whatever expectations Iran's "revolutionary idealists" may have entertained that the new states of Northwest Asia would prove a bland slate on which to superimpose their world view, Tehran has, in practice, pursued a relatively conservative course in the region.[12] Despite the artificiality of the new republics and their built-in ethnic, linguistic, and religious diversity, Iran has consistently opposed territorial rectifications on the grounds that "any alteration in the present border lines at any point in the region will aggravate tension in the whole of the region."[13] To the extent that Iran's geostrategic view may be divined from available evidence, Tehran is acting on the assumption that its national security interests and its aspirations for long-term influence in Northwest Asia can best be served by contributing to regional stability and the active cultivation of a network of bilateral and multilateral ties. The unfolding of this strategy may usefully be analyzed under four broad headings.

Maintenance of stability   Tehran has been particularly sensitive to outbreaks of ethnic conflict on or near its northern frontiers. Aside from the potential for such conflicts to expand in unpredictable ways or provide a basis for increased involvement of the Russian Federation in neighboring parts of the "near abroad," Iranian policy-makers must take into consideration the ethnic minorities within their own borders. Approximately 20 percent of Iran's population is Azerbaijani, while Turkman and Armenian minorities constitute 1 percent or less. The presence since 1991 in Northwest Asia of independent republics corresponding to these significant Iranian minorities provides an additional reason for Iran to use its influence to tamp down tensions that might spill over to affect its own citizens.

Tehran's official response to developments in the Azerbaijani Republic, beginning even before the collapse of Soviet control, illustrates the care and restraint that have characterized the Iranian approach to instability. When the Soviet authorities decided in January 1990, for example, to crack down on ethnic disorder and agitation in Baku, the action provoked outrage among Azerbaijanis and others within Iran. In stark contrast, the Iranian government, apparently concerned about potential domestic ramifications as well as its relationship with Moscow, confined itself to closing its borders with the Azerbaijan Republic and expressing concern and regret.[14] Far from encouraging Azerbaijan and other Muslim peoples within the Soviet Union to envisage independence from Moscow, Iran couched its official commentary in terms of non-interference in the internal affairs of the Soviet Union and respect for the decisions of the Soviet people. As the disintegration of the Soviet state progressed, Iran clearly accorded priority to avoiding actions that could draw the wrath of the wounded giant toward Iran. Foreign Minister Ali Akbar Velayati, commenting in late 1991 on Iranian contacts with the leadership in the republics of Northwest Asia, found it necessary to clarify, almost apologetically: "Our position is clear, we went to these republics through Moscow ... We are seriously and strong [sic] in favor of maintaining our good neighborly ties with the Soviet Union."[15]

Iran's overriding concern for the maintenance of stability on its borders has also been manifested in its policy toward the war between the republics of Azerbaijan and Armenia over the disputed enclave of Nagorno-Karabakh. Common borders with both of these new republics, historic ties with both peoples, and the presence of kindred minorities inside Iran accord particular importance to the handling of the conflict. Sensing that its relationships with the belligerents might also offer Iran an opportunity for enhancing its prestige and influence in the region, Iran engaged in sustained diplomatic efforts to broker a ceasefire.[16] In May 1992, for example, Iran invited Armenian President Ter-Petrosyan and Azerbaijani Acting President Mamedov to Tehran, where they signed a ceasefire.[17] The agreement that President Hashemi Rafsanjani had sponsored between the belligerents was dealt a fatal blow by a simultaneous Armenian offensive to capture Azerbaijan's last stronghold in the Nagorno-Karabakh enclave and open a corridor to the Armenian republic. Stung by this turn of events, Tehran condemned the "flagrant aggression" by the Armenian forces.[18] Within a month, Azerbaijani President Elchibey also antagonized Iran, claiming that Armenian territorial gains coincided with Iranian mediation, and questioning the status of Iran's Azerbaijani minority.[19] Despite public and press outcries, the Iranian government maintained its composure and, with the passing of the Elchibey regime, the rift with Azerbaijan has been repaired. Nevertheless, the episode must have driven home to Iran both the limits of its influence in resolving ethnic conflict and the thanklessness of the mediator role.

The chronic strife in Tadjikistan, the only Persian-speaking state in Northwest Asia, has presented Iran with dilemmas of a different sort. Without a common border, the state interests of Iran are less directly affected by the conflict. At the same time, the character of the power struggle in Tadjikistan is such that it can excite strong passions among both the supporters of Islamic causes[20] and the devotees of "Iranianness" within Iran.[21]

Within two years of declaring its independence, Tadjikistan was beset by a bitter and destructive civil conflict pitting the regime, composed largely of former Soviet functionaries, against a loose coalition of intellectual "democrats", the Islamic Republic Party (IRP), and several smaller groupings.[22] Whatever its emotional reaction to developments there, including the reinforcement of Russian troops to support the government and control the frontiers with Afghanistan, the Iranian authorities labored to sustain a calculated, hands-off policy. During the brief period of May–November 1992, when "opposition" elements were part of the coalition government, Iranian activity, particularly in the economic and cultural spheres, expanded significantly. Following the collapse of the coalition and the expansion of armed conflict, opportunities for Iranian–Tadjik cooperation shrank considerably, but the Iranian foreign policy establishment stubbornly refused to be drawn into a confrontational posture despite popular anger and consternation at home. On 28 January 1993, for example, the Tehran daily, *Hamshahri*, published a statement from Foreign Minister Velayati proclaiming that "developments in Tadjikistan must be regarded as internal events which have placed two groups against each other."[23] Far from taking sides or challenging the reimposition of Russian influence, Tehran seems to have played for time, salvaging as much of its relationship with the government of Tadjikistan as circumstances permitted.[24] Almost a year after the palace coup in Dushanbe, for example, the Iranian ambassador in Tadjikistan described in some detail economic and cultural activities in the Tadjik republic, although he made no reference to the civil conflict and was vague about whether the activities took place before or after the expulsion of opposition elements from the government there.[25]

In Tadjikistan, as in the Azerbaijani–Armenian conflict, Iran apparently considers that it has little to gain, and much to lose, from the persistence of tension and instability. A resolution of the power struggle in Tadjikistan would ease considerably the strain between Iran's head and heart, between cool calculations of national interest and the emotional appeal of Persian and/or Islamic solidarity. By holding itself aloof from involvement in such conflicts, Tehran can, indeed, preserve the possibilities for substantial economic and psychic benefits of acceptance and recognition as a "responsible" player in Northwest Asia.[26]

Establishment of economic and infrastructural relations   The dominant thrust of Iranian activism in the new states of Northwest Asia has been directed toward the creation of a web of economic and infrastructural relationships. The rapid collapse of the Soviet Union and Tehran's inclination to hedge its bets during the period of uncertainty for fear of offending Moscow limited the opportunity for elaborating a comprehensive diplomatic strategy.[27] By late in 1991, nonetheless, Iran had clearly begun to reach out to the emerging republics, signing a series of memoranda of understanding for bilateral cooperation in a number of fields. Construction of a railway link between Mashad and Serakhs in Turkmenistan was announced publicly as early as December of that year, providing an early indication of Tehran's determination to play to its greatest strength – Iran's geographic location. An article attributed to Foreign Minister Velayati and published on 8 August 1994 in *Turkmenskaya Iskra* contains a lucid expression of Iran's underlying policy rationale:

> The Islamic Republic of Iran is in a particularly favorable situation as regards the new independent states of Central Asia and Transcaucasia. Iran has acquired new neighbors to the north with which it shares a mutual desire to develop cooperation on a bilateral as well as a multilateral regional basis.[28]

Iran's pursuit of concrete links with the Northwest Asian hinterlands has, for reasons of geography, pivoted on its relationship with Turkmenistan, Iran's gateway to Central Asia. By late 1994, Foreign Minister Velayati was able to summarize an impressive array of projects either under way or in the planning stages: eleven border crossings opened with highway repair, and reconstruction work reportedly at least 70 percent complete;[29] work on the railway link from Mashad to Serakhs and Tedzhen scheduled for completion by the end of 1994;[30] establishment of air routes to Baku, Almty (Alma Ata), and Ashgabat, with additional flights to Tashkent and Dushanbe planned; and development of existing and new Iranian ports on the Caspian Sea to connect with Baku and Turkmenbashi.[31] Serious efforts are also under way to finalize plans for a gas pipeline with a capacity of 15 to 30 billion cubic meters from Turkmenistan to Turkey through Iran.[32] Although statistics on trade resulting from these efforts to tie Northwest Asian economies with that of Iran are scarce and some of the more ambitious projects still face serious problems of financing,[33] the direction of Iranian policy has been firmly established and at least some early economic benefits seem assured.[34]

Iran's expectation is that growing transport and communications links with Turkmenistan will give it greater access to the republics with which it enjoys no direct land border. Regimes as far away as Kazakhstan have, in fact, shown interest in Iran as an alternative route for their exports to the rest of the world as they seek to develop their independent economic relationships.[35] A key element of Tehran's overall strategy has been to strengthen regional economic cooperation through the existing Economic Cooperation Organization (ECO).[36] Iran was instrumental in expanding the ECO in 1992, to include Azerbaijan, Turkmenistan, Uzbekistan, Kyrgyzstan, Tadjikistan, Kazakhstan, and Afghanistan.[37] The Caspian Sea Cooperation Organization (CASCO), linking Iran with Azerbaijan, Russia, Kazakhstan, and Turkmenistan, resulted in 1992 from another Iranian initiative.[38] The clear objective of such multilateral measures is not only to bolster Iran's relations with the governments and economies of Northwest Asia, but to establish Iran as the linchpin, geographically and organizationally, of a series of interlocking fora. Thus Russia, one regional rival, is included in CASCO and Turkey, another competitor, belongs to the ECO, but only Iran is a member of both. Whether either is as effective as Tehran might hope may, therefore, be less important than the fact that Iran is established as the pivotal actor.

Extension of cultural influence The barriers that came down in 1991–92 restored natural lines of communication and cultural interchange between newly independent peoples in Northwest Asia and kindred civilizations in Iran and Turkey. As a result of decades of Soviet-enforced isolation from their roots and the conscious promotion of Marxist secularism, however, the new societies were essentially unknown quantities, even to observers in Tehran and Ankara.[39] "Revolutionary idealists" may have dreamed of finding beyond their frontiers a cultural vacuum ripe for proselytization, but Iranian decision-makers recognized the limits of their understanding of the new circumstances and proceeded cautiously in promoting Iranian cultural influence.[40]

Although only Tadjikistan is Persian-speaking,[41] aspects of Persian culture are widely shared among the ethnically Turkic peoples of Northwest Asia. It is not surprising, therefore, that Iran has taken advantage of this shared tradition in developing its relations with the states of Northwest Asia or that the new republics, struggling to redefine and differentiate their identities, have been receptive, in varying degrees, to its appeal. It is perhaps instructive that one of the first cultural objectives pursued by Iran was the adoption of the Zoroastrian/Iranian New Year, *Nowruz* (21 March) as a national holiday by the republics of Central Asia.[42] Much of the Iranian effort in the area appears to emphasize facets of Persian culture without overt political content that might excite the suspicion or hostility of local regimes, frequently controlled by holdovers from the Soviet era, or of nearby powers, like Russia. While Tehran undoubtedly expects its conventional cultural program – conferences and delegations; exhibitions and publications; broadcasting, educational, and training programs for students and officials, etc. – to enhance Iran's prestige and influence, it has demonstrated little readiness to risk its priority objectives by pursuing controversial or provocative cultural initiatives.

Promotion of revolutionary Islam   Unquestionably, the most striking feature of Iranian policy since the Soviet collapse is the relative absence of efforts to promote its vision of Islam in Northwest Asia. A review of the available evidence of Iranian behavior there to date fails to substantiate widespread expectations in Russia,[43] the West, and the Middle East that Tehran would seize upon the fragility of the new states and emerging societies to destabilize the region and proselytize its inhabitants.

Iranian spokesmen are generally obscure when addressing the issue, possibly for domestic consumption,[44] but more commonly stress Tehran's willingness to accept any political system adopted by the states of the region. In practice, Iran has demonstrated a readiness to further its national security and economic interests with regional governments irrespective of their domestic orientation or attitude toward Islamic activism. Nor has the Iranian government been deterred from following an essentially non-ideological approach by criticism in Iran. The inclusion of Tashkent among the capitals visited by Foreign Minister Velayati in the summer of 1994 is a case in point. In an editorial entitled, "Why Go to Tashkent?" the *Tehran Times* wrote:

> Uzbekistan's president, Islam Karimov, has been actively suppressing the intellectual communities of Samarkand and Bukhara, while openly instigating and interfering in Tadjikistan's bloody coup d'état. These Karimov policies and actions, together with his recent anti-Iran stance, should be enough reason for Dr. Velayati not to go to Tashkent.[45]

Although ideological differences with a particular regime may color the warmth of the relationship, at least temporarily, no case may be found in the record to date where Tehran has permitted such differences within the region to be a permanent impediment. When the government of Kyrgyzstan unexpectedly recognized Jerusalem as the capital of the state of Israel in January 1993, for example, a planned visit by the Iranian foreign minister was canceled,[46] but a few months later Iran hosted the Kyrgyz president for a state visit during which bilateral agreements on communications, banking, exchange of embassies, education, tourism, and transport were concluded.[47]

The empirical evidence tells us little about the internal disagreements within the Iranian power structure that must have attended the formulation of a pragmatic strategy in Northwest Asia. It is far from clear, however, that an aggressive campaign to export the tenets of the Iranian revolution could enjoy the success expected by the "idealists" or feared by those most worried by the prospect of Iranian influence in that region. Without question, societies in the new republics are experiencing a rebirth of interest in and observance of Islam as they attempt to overcome the effects of Soviet rule and reconnect with their past and heritage. The Soviet authorities were able, according to Martha Brill Olcott, virtually to destroy "an entire Islamic Hierarchy,"[48] but were less successful in eliminating observance of informal rituals that were often infused with indigenous, pre-Islamic content.[49] Islam, as locally understood, also apparently came to be a crucial factor in ethnic or national identity as societies strove to differentiate themselves even before the Soviet collapse. Given the nature of this evolution, it is highly doubtful that the Northwest Asian interest in reconnecting with the Islamic mainstream translates into receptivity toward a particularist doctrine exported by Iran or any other external center, particularly one close or powerful enough to pose a potential threat to recently acquired independence.

An Iranian policy heavily colored by ideological content also carries the risk of exciting active counteractions that would menace Tehran's other objectives in Northwest Asia. Of the Muslim cultures in the region, only Azerbaijan's is Shi'a and there, as in all these societies, significant secular elements contend for influence. An Iranian Islamic offensive, therefore, would encounter not only indigenous resistance, but the competition of contending interests. Turkey, for example, provides an essentially secular model, while Saudi Arabia and other Sunni countries offer an alternative to Iran's Islamic revolution. Again, according to Olcott:

> Saudi Arabia is openly funding official Muslim groups throughout Central Asia, including those in Kazakhstan, and is generally assumed to be indirectly funding the vigorous missionary work by Islamic activists from Bangladesh and the Gulf states in the Fergana Valley, which traverses Kyrgyzstan and Uzbekistan. Saudis also run a scholarship program for the religious education of Central Asians in Saudi Arabia; and are said to be the source of funding for scholarships offered by fundamentalist groups in Turkey.[50]

The prospects for a successful ideological offensive in Northwest Asia therefore probably seem more problematic from Tehran's viewpoint than many outside observers commonly assume. And, in a broader context, Iranian policies and activities that are perceived as destabilizing the region or menacing continuing Russian interests there risk provoking reactions inimical to the economic and infrastructural positions Tehran has carefully staked out along its northern border.

The Challenge: Northwest Asia from Iran's Perspective

Realistically, Tehran has no option but to deal with the new and unsettled conditions in Northwest Asia.[51] Historic tides over which it had no influence have reconfigured the landscape in ways that require Iranian responses. There is no convincing evidence that Iranian analysts were notably more prescient regarding the collapse of the Soviet Union than their Western counterparts. They manifestly did not foresee the rapidity and the finality of its fall. Well into the process, Tehran was still hedging its bets, combining exploratory contacts with the emerging republics with elaborate deference to Moscow. Whether this reaction reflected simple prudence or ambivalence about the drama unfolding before them, we cannot know. In the context of Iran's overall geostrategic situation, however, the "opening" of Northwest Asia probably posed at least as many dilemmas as opportunities.

Iran's "revolutionary" rhetoric and actions have, understandably, made it an unlikely candidate for sympathetic understanding. As Professor Ramazani points out, the distinction between "revolutionary idealists" and "revolutionary realists" is not teleological:

> Whatever the label, the important cautionary point is that the fluidity of Iranian revolutionary politics is such that today's idealists may be tomorrow's realists and vice versa, and idealists on one set of issues may be realists on another. This is why the nature of Iran's foreign policy is neither linear, nor dialectical, but *kaleidoscopic*.[52]

Such permutations, however, surely must be more than random. To understand the fluidity of Iranian politics and resulting policy decisions, consideration must be given not only to Iran's ambitions but to its fears; not merely to the regime's desire to dominate its environment but to its dread of being dominated.

Iran does not, of course, look at Northwest Asia in isolation from its other foreign policy concerns. Whether or not Iran's elites acknowledge an Iranian role in creating conditions of instability in the region, the fact remains that Iran does confront genuine security concerns on a number of fronts. Given a hostile Iraq to the west,[53] with which it waged a ruinous war, and a fragmented Afghanistan to the east, the immediate environment probably looks quite threatening from Tehran. In the Gulf, where Iran grapples with a vision of itself as the regional hegemon that predates the 1979 revolution, Tehran sees its "destiny" thwarted by neighboring states with their own sense of identity and the US policy of opposing the domination of the region by Iran or any other single power. Far from recognizing its own part, along with Iraq, in activating the American commitment and presence, Iranian revolutionaries of both the "idealist" and "realist" stripes see the position of other actors in the region, through the lens of their particularist ideology, as confirmation of hostility to Iran and its legitimate national interests.

Viewed in this light, both Iran's initial reserve regarding the collapse of the Soviet Union and its subsequent actions among the new republics of Northwest Asia are easier to comprehend. However distasteful the USSR may have been for Iran from both a Persian and an Islamic standpoint, whether under the Shah or the Ayatollah, it at least had the virtue of maintaining stability on a lengthy portion of Iran's frontiers with the outside world. Over the period since the reluctant withdrawal of Soviet forces from northern Iran at the end of the Second World War and the collapse of Soviet-sponsored "republics" in Tabriz and Mehabad, Iran and Moscow settled into an unequal, but increasingly comfortable, *modus vivendi* that supported "correct" state-to-state relations and even supported the conduct of mutually profitable economic relations. For the first time since the expanding Tsarist empire came into contact with Persian territories, Iran was relieved of the necessity of devoting military and diplomatic resources to the effort to counter direct Russian and Soviet pressures on Iran's integrity as a state. Without question, the Soviet Union possessed the power to resume the march southward and Iran knew that it could not resist a Soviet assault alone. In an ideal world, Iran would have preferred not to have to contend with a stronger rival to the north. Nevertheless, as the relationship with Moscow took on a complex but familiar shape, Tehran felt confident enough to redeploy its energies in other directions. The Soviet implosion was a challenge to Iranian assumptions, raising the specter of yet further "threats" to Iran's stability and national interests, a specter all the more frightening because of the imponderables it posed.

The restrained, conservative course that Iran has pursued in Northwest Asia provides important clues to the policy judgments reached in Tehran – policies designed to prevent the new republics from becoming a further "threat" and to reap the economic advantages of Iran's location between the former Soviet republics and the Gulf. Iranian objectives may be divided into four dimensions: 1) to prevent, or minimize the possibilities for, a recrudescence of Russian–Iran power struggle;[54] 2) to contribute to controlling ethnic, ideological, or national conflicts that might spill over into the Iranian homeland or generate the flow of additional refugees into Iran;[55] 3) to tie the new economies of the region to Iran's in order to supplement national income, stimulate domestic development, and create alternatives to dependence upon petroleum; and, 4) to advance Iran's influence in ways that will not excite the active opposition of either the regimes in the republics or the Russians.

The path that Iran has chosen to pursue in Northwest Asia is a delicate one, requiring continuous attention in order to balance competing goals, some of which are potentially inconsistent. Thus far, Tehran has achieved some success in exploiting the inherent opportunities without provoking hostile reactions, but it has done this only at the expense of eschewing the promotion of a "revolutionary" message. This is probably an acceptable compromise for the "revolutionary realists" to make in exchange for avoiding the exacerbation of confrontations or instability on another of its frontiers. Yet Iran has to be concerned that factors beyond its immediate control – particularly a humiliated and increasingly assertive Russia – could bring it into direct contact with another "hostile" force.

Both internal developments in the Northwest Asian republics and Russia's ongoing effort to redefine itself are likely to keep the region in transition and, conceivably, turmoil for some time to come. Russia, as it comes to grips with the loss of empire, has increasingly reasserted a vital interest and special role in the political, economic, and social affairs of the former republics. In the words of one commentator:

> Russia has intervened not just to support Russians abroad, but for other reasons as well. Russian troops, for example, have intervened in Tadjikistan to restore an old-line Communist regime that had been ousted by a coalition of democratic and Islamic forces in 1992. Yet despite Russia's purported concern about the spread of "Islamic fundamentalism" in Tadjikistan, Russian forces assisted a Muslim minority in driving Orthodox Christian Georgian forces from Abkhazia.[56]

While the more nationalistic elements of the Russian political spectrum have made no secret of their conviction that Russia should reestablish its control of broad regions of the former Soviet Union, statements of the government have been more nuanced. Still, a review of official policy declarations reveals a pattern of claims that Moscow has "special interests" in the "near abroad" that imply insistence on "interstate relations different from normal bilateral relations."[57]

Neither the present government in Russia nor that in Iran, however, has exhibited to date an inclination to push their bilateral rivalry to the point of confrontation, even in the contentious case of Tadjikistan. Although Russia has intervened militarily in that conflict under a Commonwealth of Independent States (CIS) mandate, it is probably haunted by the memory of the Soviet misadventure in Afghanistan.[58] Throughout 1994, Russia and Iran, with a Pakistani and United Nations presence, participated in a diplomatic process designed to bring the contending Tadjik factions into negotiations. Following an initial round of talks in Moscow in April, the process continued in Tehran in June, without palpable results. Nevertheless, apparently as a result of continuing pressures being exerted on them, the Dushanbe regime and the Tadjik opposition signed a "temporary" ceasefire in the Iranian capital. At a fourth meeting of the parties in Islamabad in November, the ceasefire was extended for a further three months. None of these efforts, as important as they are, suggests that a resolution of the brutal conflict in Tadjikistan is near at hand. Ironically, it may prove that the "influence" that both Moscow and Tehran strive to cultivate in the region is insufficient to overcome the passions and self-interests that fire local conflicts that, in turn, threaten their more central policy objectives.[59]

A renewed clash between Russian and Iranian interests in Northwest Asia is not inevitable. However, the more successful either, or both, is in consolidating its relationships and influence with the new republics, the greater the likelihood of intensified political and economic competition. Aside from the neo-imperialist strain manifest in the Russian body politic, there are a number of concrete issues and interests which have the potential to inflame the situation, even if Moscow remains firmly in the control of "moderate," reformist elements. Significant ethnic Russian communities in each of the new republics constitute a potential timebomb; direct or incidental threats to or discrimination against such minorities could quickly mobilize Russian public opinion. A widespread perception, justified or not, that Iran is engaged in promoting radical Islamic ideology or other "subversive" activities is another such explosive issue. Despite the pragmatic behavior of the Russian government to date, extreme concern about and hostility to Islamic influence are very much alive, even among moderate elements who believe, for example, that the United States is "naïve" about the Muslim "threat" in Bosnia-Herzegovina.[60] Even if Moscow and Tehran can avoid confrontation over such emotional issues, however, Russia is likely to respond negatively should it judge that Iran is successfully undercutting its self-defined economic interests in the former Soviet hinterlands. Russia has demonstrated a willingness to press the republics quite hard to acquire a share of their potentially profitable projects and to use its control of infrastructure and vestigial Soviet trading patterns to impose its will. Iran's major advantage and attraction for many of the regimes in the area is its ability to offer alternatives that will lessen their vulnerability to Moscow's writ.

Despite Iran's prudent policies, Tehran must be aware that it risks striking a raw nerve.[61] Scrupulous attention, skilled diplomacy, and considerable restraint will be required from Iran to realize the benefits of an active involvement in Northwest Asia without provoking the very instability it seeks to avoid.

Implications for Gulf Stability

In light of Iran's engagement to date in the Central Asian and Trans-caucasian republics, what are the potential implications for stability and cooperation in the Gulf? Unquestionably, the necessity for increased activism in Northwest Asia will impact Tehran's appreciation of its strategic situation and its relationships in other areas on its exceptionally long periphery. While the period of experience since the collapse of the Soviet superpower hardly constitutes an irreversible pattern, the internal logic of Iranian strategy is so compelling – and the negative consequences of alternative policies so self-destructive – that, barring a complete repudiation of the "revolutionary realists," it is reasonably safe to project current Iranian policies there into the foreseeable future.

Whatever happens in Northwest Asia, the Gulf will remain the major priority for Iran. Even the possible future reestablishment of the historic "Silk Route," linking the Mediterranean with the Far East, will not alter the reality that Iran's major source of national wealth and its primary access routes to markets are concentrated in the Gulf. Should Iran succeed in its clear drive to consolidate a role as a major *entrepôt* for the land-locked republics of Northwest Asia, the achievement will be essentially meaningless without a reasonable assurance of stability and security in and through the Gulf.[62] Paradoxically, Iran's engagement in areas to the north is likely to reinforce, rather than diminish, the central importance of the Gulf.

The choices of the new republics regarding pipelines, rail connections, roads, and other infrastructural links reflect an interest in diversifying their access to the outside world and lessening their dependence upon "imperial" patterns established during the period of Russian and Soviet domination. To meet these expectations, Iran will need to convince them not only that it harbors no intention of using its control of routes capriciously or of asserting dominance over their decisions, but also that it offers convenient and *reliable* transit. Similar considerations will motivate those countries and institutions required to underwrite the enormous costs of associated projects, requirements that are far beyond the capacity of local capital. Doubts on any of these counts will impede or prevent realization of the ambitious plans currently on the drawing boards. Intentionally or not, Iran's chosen course in Northwest Asia would seem to be nudging that country in the direction of a status quo power, as substantial investments of energy and resources create assets, benefits, and relationships it will have an escalating interest in preserving.[63] Interestingly, President Hashemi Rafsanjani has at least given thought to the dynamics of Iran's evolution. Buried in a recent television interview is an intriguing observation:

> Our guiding light has been the revolution. We are what we are because of our revolutionary *thoughts* [emphasis added]. If we lose this, we will become something else; we will become an ordinary country.[64]

Could it be that the Iranian president recognizes, as neither revolutionary zealots inside Iran nor those alarmed by Iranian rhetoric and ideology seem to, that history records no instance of a regime in a permanent state of revolutionary fervor? Given the magnitude of Iran's domestic and financial problems, there are compelling reasons for the restrained posture Tehran has adopted in Northwest Asia. In pursuit of the economic and security benefits of constructive engagement there, Iran has muted its revisionist ideology, foregoing the active promotion of its Islamic "revolution." In a region where large areas were once part of the Persian empire, Tehran has similarly failed to assert territorial claims in the name of Persian nationalism in favor of cooperation with successor states. If this careful policy is to pay off in the long term, however, Iran will need to convince its neighbors in the Gulf, and in Northwest Asia as well, that its aspirations, both north and south, are equally benign.

PART THREE

The Military–Economic Reconstruction

CHAPTER 10

The Politico-Military Threat from Iran

Kenneth Katzman

The Clinton administration has announced a policy of "dual containment" of Iran and Iraq, designed to weaken both states rather than balance them by tilting toward one or the other. According to the Clinton administration, the new strategy does not ignore balance of power considerations, but rather seeks to establish a rough parity between Iran and Iraq at lower levels of capability.[1] Since Iraq's defeat in the 1991 Gulf war, the containment of Iraq's military power has been implemented through a comprehensive package of international sanctions. These sanctions prevent Iraq from earning revenue through sales of oil and other exports and deny Iraq access to arms and other non-humanitarian imports. In spite of the US dual containment strategy, Iran is under no such restrictions. The United States (the world's number one arms supplier) and its allies do not sell arms to Iran, but there are other willing suppliers, especially Russia, China, and North Korea. Although the United States forbids its oil companies from importing Iranian crude oil (with some exceptions), Iranian oil is freely sold on the world market, generating sufficient revenues to maintain at least a modest level of military modernization. The net result, therefore, is that a military imbalance between Iran and Iraq may be developing, and this is in Iran's favor. Such an imbalance is contrary to the intent of the dual containment policy, though restoring a balance would require either 1) lifting most of the sanctions in place against Iraq, or 2) persuading the international community to apply the same sanctions to Iran as are in place against Iraq. Both of these options are politically difficult at this time.

What are the ramifications of an Iran–Iraq military imbalance favoring Iran? Most important is the possibility that Iran might behave as Iraq did just after the Iran–Iraq war ended, when a military imbalance in Iraq's favor existed. Iraq sought hegemony in the Gulf – the ability to intimidate Iran and the Gulf states into adopting policies favorable to it. Iraq's invasion of Kuwait was a manifestation of that quest for hegemony, even though it tried to justify the invasion by claiming that Kuwait was conducting "economic war on the Iraqi people," i.e., driving down the price of oil through overproduction. Similarly, with Iraq's military capabilities severely constrained by international sanctions, there are signs that Iran is now attempting to step into the power vacuum left by Iraq's defeat in the 1991 Gulf war. An early sign of this trend is Iran's virtual takeover of Abu Musa island in 1992. The former US naval commander in the Gulf, Vice-Admiral Douglas Katz, said that Iran has built military fortifications on the island, thought it has not placed heavy military equipment there yet.[2] Iran also has begun a commercial air service to the island. Iran hopes to regain what it sees as its entitlement to play the leading role in Gulf security. In contrast to the Shah's era, however, the clerical regime in Iran is hoping that its growing military power will embolden radical Islamic forces in the Gulf states, and throughout the Islamic world, to step up opposition activities against the incumbent regimes.

This view of Iran's goals in the Gulf – intimidation and promotion of Islamic revolution – is not universally shared among analysts of Gulf affairs. Some see Iranian policy as essentially defensive, i.e., to prevent US-sponsored strategic encirclement and strangulation of the clerical regime and the Islamic revolution. Some analysts who take this view contend that Iran's highly touted "military buildup" is actually quite modest, considering the extensive and expensive acquisition programs of Iran's Gulf neighbors and the extent of Iran's equipment losses at the end of the Iran–Iraq war. An extension of this argument is that Iran, as the most populous state in the Gulf, has a legitimate right to a major role in the region.

There are cogent arguments on both sides as to whether or not Iran constitutes a growing conventional military threat to the Gulf states and their ally, the United States. A rigorous analysis of Iran's politico-military intentions and capabilities must include an objective assessment of Iran's arms acquisition programs. However, the analysis must also look at organizational and political dynamics within the Iranian military structure, as well as the effect of factional politics on the overall context within which the Iranian military is operating. Some discussion of Iran's effort to export its Islamic revolution also belongs in any discussion of the Iranian threat, though these are not strictly military operations. The inclusion of revolutionary export activities in the discussion is necessitated by the fact that these activities are spearheaded by the Revolutionary Guard, which is an integral part – and even the politically most powerful part – of Iran's military structure.[3] In the view of the Guard's leadership, military and political action are coterminous, not separate and compartmentalized activities. The goal of both is to realize the late Ayatollah Khomeini's vision of an Islamic republic extending from Morocco to Bangladesh. Iran's regular military, on the other hand, does not engage in the export of revolution operations and its doctrine and tactics more closely approximate those of other conventional military forces. Any discussion of Iran's political and military intentions and capabilities, must, therefore, include assessments of the interactions between these two major components of the Iranian military structure.

Elements of Iran's Military Modernization

Although analysts differ on the implications, there is widespread agreement that Iran has been upgrading its armaments since the end of the Iran–Iraq war. It is not only adding to its arms inventory, but it is qualitatively improving its arsenal. It is doing so primarily with the help of Russia, China, and North Korea. All three of these suppliers need the hard currency that can be gained through such sales, and they have, for the most part, resisted US pressure not to arm Iran.[4] The military modernization program has thus far concentrated on advanced aircraft and naval systems, with somewhat less emphasis on ground force equipment. This trend may indicate that Iran, for now, does not consider Iraq as its most likely, or even its most important, potential military adversary. Iraqi armor and artillery played a major role in Iraq's victory in the Iran–Iraq war, and it was Iran's ground equipment that suffered the heaviest losses and capture in the last series of Iraqi offensives against Iran in 1988. Iraq's military capability – both in manpower and in major equipment inventory – stands at about 40 percent of its pre-1991 Gulf war level, sufficient to defend itself against Iran but not enough to go on the offensive against the Islamic regime.[5] The US intelligence community may feel somewhat differently; in a speech to the Washington Institute for Near East Policy on 23 September 1994, Director of Central Intelligence (DCI) R. James Woolsey listed Iran's desire to defend against Iraq as a goal equal to its desire to intimidate the Gulf states.[6]

Many Western military analysts believe that Iran is trying to attain a capability to control the Gulf or, at the very least, to deny the Gulf to hostile forces. Iran's objectives presumably include the capability to attack and cripple commercial shipping (bound for an adversary's ports) more effectively than it did during the Iran–Iraq war. The major elements of Iran's military modernization program appear to correspond to its political and military objectives.

Naval systems   Iran has focused heavily on new naval systems. The corner-stone of its naval upgrade is its purchase from Russia of three Kilo-class diesel submarines, two of which have been delivered (the first in November 1992, the second in August 1993). These submarines are reported to have cost Iran about $450 million each, and Russian personnel reportedly are training Iranian sub crews. The shallow Gulf is not an optimal environment in which to operate these submarines, and US navy officials have said that they can counter the Iranian subs, which are noisy, slow, and costly to maintain. However, the Gulf Cooperation Council (GCC) states, by themselves, cannot easily deal with Iran's submarines and the Kilos do introduce into the Gulf a threat not previously present. The US navy and the GCC states are worried about the ability of the submarines to lay mines undetected, and anti-submarine warfare is difficult in the Gulf, given its shallowness and poor acoustic properties. These concerns are compounded by reports that Iran is buying sophisticated mines, including rising mines, from China, Russia, North Korea, and Italy.[7] Some analysts believe that Iran could use these mines to try to block the Strait of Hormuz.[8] Paradoxically, therefore, rather than achieve intimidation and Iranian domination of the Gulf, the Iranian Kilos might lead to a heavier US naval presence there – the exact opposite of Iran's oft-stated objective of expelling the United States from the Gulf. Iran's minisubmarine arsenal poses an additional problem for naval forces in the Gulf because it is difficult to detect them. In 1991, prior to Iran's receipt of its first Kilo submarine, North Korea reportedly sold Iran two minisubs.[9] Iran is also said to possess one minisubmarine of German origin, and possibly an indigenous version as well.

Iran also is trying to rebuild its surface fleet, badly damaged during skirmishes with the United States during the Iran–Iraq war. It lost 20 percent of its largest ships (destroyers, frigates, and coastal combatants) in an engagement with the US Navy on 18 April 1988, although Iran later repaired and returned to service at least one of its ships. Vice-Admiral Katz reported in September 1994 that Iran had already received five Chinese-made Houdong patrol boats out of an order for ten of the vessels,[10] though they were delivered without the surface-to-surface missiles they are capable of carrying. Iran wants the C-802 missiles, while China has thus far offered only the less capable C-801; talks continue on the missiles.[11] The attack craft will reportedly be operated by the Guard navy, rather than the regular navy.[12] The new boats give Iran substantial additional capability against the Gulf state navies and, perhaps more importantly, could prove to be more effective against international shipping than did the Guard's small boat fleet during the height of the "tanker war" of 1986–88.

Advanced aircraft   The acquisition of sophisticated aircraft is the second pillar of Iran's military modernization program. The Iran–Iraq war and Iran's unsuccessful naval engagements against the United States proved to Iran the costs of its severe deficiency of operational, sophisticated aircraft. Its new aircraft will give it an increased ability to attack commercial shipping or adversarial warships. The main elements of Iran's recent aircraft purchases include MiG-29s (about thirty delivered so far) and Su-24s (about twenty delivered thus far) from Russia, as well as less capable F-7s from China. A senior official said on 27 September 1994, that Russia had also given Iran sophisticated aircraft missiles.[13] Some military analysts consider the acquisition of the Su-24 to be the greatest source of concern for the United States and its Gulf allies, in that the Su-24, which can carry heavy ordnance payloads, provides Iran with a long-range maritime strike capability.[14] The MiG-29 is intended to help Iran control the skies above any theater of operations, though it is doubtful that Iran could accomplish that objective against the US air force. Gulf state air forces might hesitate to engage the Iranians, however, if they were uncertain of US backing.

Iran also is expected to benefit from the still unexplained flight to Iran of 115 combat aircraft from Iraq at the start of Desert Storm. The windfall included 4 MiG-29s, 24 Mirage F-1s, 24 Su-24s, 44 Su-20/22s, 12 MiG-23s, and 7 Su-25s. The gradual improvement in Iranian–Iraqi relations over the past two years, however, suggests that Iran might eventually return the jets. For now, Iran can use them to train its pilots on the same aircraft Iran is buying from Russia, with less concern over the financial costs of aircraft crashes during training. Pilots capable of flying Mig-29s and Su-24s – as well as an Iranian Su-24 instructor – graduated at a ceremony in Tehran in August 1994, improving Iran's ability to integrate the new planes into its force structure.[15] Iran can also use the Iraqi planes to prop up its clients throughout the Middle East; it is reported, for instance, that Iran may have given some of the Iraqi aircraft to Sudan. It is not unreasonable to assume that, somewhere in the Middle East, possibly in Iran itself, Iran is helping train members of the Hizbollah militia of Lebanon to fly aircraft, though it is doubtful that Syria would ever allow Hizbollah to operate combat aircraft in Lebanon.

Iran was shaken by Iraq's ability to penetrate Iranian airspace during the Iran–Iraq war. To address this weakness in its air defenses, Iran reportedly has purchased Russian-made SA-5 long-range surface-to-air missiles (SAMs), SA-6s, and mobile air defense systems, including the SA-11 and SA-13. Iran also has reportedly ordered six SA-10 batteries from Russia.[16] Iran reportedly has received some Chinese SAMs as well. The Guard and the regular military reportedly have achieved a high degree of coordination on air defense, with some of the air defense network now jointly run by the Guard and regular military.[17]

Ground equipment   As noted above, Iran has been relatively slow to upgrade its ground forces. This would appear to indicate that it does not believe that Iraq's military, as currently constituted, poses an immediate threat to Iranian security. Heavy ground equipment would be of little use against the largely sea-based US Gulf presence or the Gulf states themselves, which do not share a land border with Iran. On the other hand, the slow pace of deliveries thus far may have been due to US pressure on Iran's suppliers, thought it is not clear why US pressure would have succeeded in slowing tank deliveries but failed to impede shipments of advanced aircraft and submarines. Calculating that, over the longer term, Iraq will ultimately emerge from under international sanctions and reconstitute its former military capability, Iran has placed orders that would improve its arsenal of ground armor. It has ordered at least five hundred T-72 tanks from Russia as well as at least five hundred T-55s from Czechoslovakia.[18] DCI Woolsey said in September 1994 that Iran had received some T-72s, though he did not elaborate on how many had been delivered.[19] Some reports suggest Iran may now have as many as one thousand two hundred tanks, up from about eight hundred two years ago, a possible indication that a large wave of tank deliveries has taken place within the past two years. Iran is also reported to have taken delivery of some Chinese-made artillery.

The most significant drawback to the effectiveness of Iran's ground forces is undoubtedly the continued rivalries between the Guard and the regular military. The Guard, although it has developed armored units, is still predominantly a light force of about one hundred and fifty thousand. Additional Guards serve in internal security units within Iran, and could be sent to the front on short notice. In addition, about a half million Basij volunteers can be mobilized in a crisis. The regular military has about three hundred thousand men, almost all of whom are based along the border with Iraq. During the Iran–Iraq war, the two ground forces demonstrated some ability to coordinate an amphibious operation, particularly in the successful 1986 seizure of Al Faw. However, Iran does not yet have the logistical capability to cross the Gulf successfully or to press an invasion much beyond southern Iraq. The two forces, however, along with their naval and air units, have practiced amphibious landings, and it is believed that they want to develop this capability.[20]

Ballistic missiles   Iran's interest in acquiring ballistic missiles would appear to support those analysts who see Iran attempting to develop an ability to intimidate its adversaries in the Gulf, including the United States. Iran used Chinese-supplied Silkworm missiles against Kuwaiti installations and shipping during the Iran–Iraq war and North Korean-supplied Scud B missiles against Iraqi population centers. The Silkworms are largely controlled by the Guard navy, and the Scuds are controlled, in large part, by the Guard Air Force. Since the Iran–Iraq war, Iran has purchased from North Korea a reported 150 Scud C missiles (range approximately 300–375 miles). North Korea reportedly provided Iran with technical assistance for a Scud C production plant in Iran. Currently, international concerns focus on North Korea's new medium-range missile, the Nodong 1, which is not yet operational. Published reports, quoting US officials, suggest that Iran wants to buy 150 Nodong 1s as part of an agreement whereby North Korea will also help Iran build Nodong 1 production facilities.[21] Some reports indicate that Iran has also purchased short range M-9 and M-11 missiles from China, but no deliveries of these missiles have been confirmed.

In general, all of these missiles are too inaccurate to be of direct military value. The weapons might have some politico-military impact, however, as Iraqi missiles demonstrated in traumatizing the Israeli population during the 1991 Gulf war. DCI Woolsey has said that Iran's missiles could be effective terror weapons, and that those who discount them as militarily ineffective "miss the point."[22]

Other weapons of mass destruction   The remainder of Iran's weapons of mass destruction programs do not appear to constitute an immediate threat to the Gulf states, with the possible exception of Iran's chemical weapons capability. DCI Woolsey said in September 1994 that Iran was stockpiling chemical warfare agents, but its capability to manufacture and deliver chemical weapons is believed to be less advanced than that of

Iraq prior to the invasion of Kuwait. Iran's chemical weapons program could constitute a more immediate threat to the GCC states and to US forces in the Gulf if Iran develops the ability to mount chemical warheads on its ballistic missiles. North Korea reportedly helped Syria do just that in the late 1980s,[23] and it may do so for Iran, if it has not already. Woolsey has said that the intelligence community suspects Iran of hiding a biological weapons program, but an actual biological weapons capability has not been confirmed. Iran is widely believed by the US intelligence community to be trying to develop a nuclear weapon; Woolsey said in September 1994 that Iran is still eight to ten years away from producing such a weapon. Analysts are concerned that Iran's close relationship with North Korea in the field of ballistic missiles might expand into nuclear cooperation as well, although the eight- to ten-year timetable estimate assumes some foreign help. Nonetheless, the International Atomic Energy Agency (IAEA), after visits to Iranian nuclear sites in February 1992 and November 1993, has not turned up evidence that Iran is trying to develop a nuclear weapon. Some high-ranking State Department officials have said that Iran is abiding by its obligations under the Nuclear Non-Proliferation Treaty (NPT).

Assessing Iran's Politico-Military Intentions

Assuming Iran's military modernization and weapons of mass destruction programs are as Western intelligence reports have described, how does one judge Iran's intentions? It is certainly possible, as some analysts believe, that Iran's acquisitions are motivated by a defensive fear of encirclement by hostile forces. It might see its weapons of mass destruction programs primarily as a deterrent against attacks rather than as instruments of intimidation. Other interpretations, however, can be derived from an analysis of the organizational and political dynamics attached to Iran's military acquisitions.

Politically, Iran's military structure is not evenly weighted between the regular military and the Revolutionary Guard. The Guard is a far more politically potent element within the overall Iranian military establishment. It is true that there is still some lingering mistrust between the regime and the regular military, but that does not adequately explain the regular military's political weakness *vis-à-vis* the Guard. The Guard's strength comes primarily from its deep roots in the revolution and its links to the hardliners who still dominate the revolutionary institutions and much of the Iranian power structure. Because of the Guard's political strength, the post-

Khomeini leadership (especially Rafsanjani) has expended considerable time and energy trying to control the radical impulses of the Guard and has found the regular military more pliable. The Guard still sees itself as a revolutionary political force and not as a professional military organization. As recently as late September 1994, Guard Commander-in-Chief Mohsen Reza'i again acknowledged that the Guard's role in preserving the gains of the revolution gave the Guard "a political bias," though according to Reza'i, the Guard would steer clear of infighting among clerical factions.[24]

Examples of the Guard's political power are plentiful. In 1989, the regime decided to merge the Guard ministry with the regular Ministry of Defense, hoping thereby to reduce the Guard's independence and achieve efficiencies by combining the two forces' separate military industries. In an attempt to reduce acrimony over the merger, the leadership appointed Akbar Torkan, a civilian technocrat linked neither to the Guard nor to the regular military, as the first minister of defense and armed forces logistics. The Guard, unsupportive of the ministerial combination, subtly undermined it by continuing to maintain its separate military production infrastructure, drawing partly on the engineering expertise of the Ministry of Construction Jihad. In January 1994, the Guard defense industry, headed by Reza Irankhah, claimed to have manufactured its own helicopter.[25] On 14 April 1994, the Construction Jihad revealed a locally produced tank, the Zulfiqar, which appears to be modeled on US armor sold to the Shah.[26] The Guard has used some of its engineering expertise on civilian projects; in September 1994, for example, it received a $700 million government contract to build a dam on the Karkheh River in southwestern Iran.[27]

By 1993, with Rafsanjani's popularity falling (as measured by the results of the June 1993 presidential election), the Guard succeeded in ousting Torkan from the new Cabinet. Taking over the Defense Ministry was Muhammad Foruzandeh, formerly the Guard's chief of staff, and the appointment put the ministry clearly in the hands of the Guard. Foruzandeh previously had worked in the oil industry in southern Iran. During his presidency, Rafsanjani also has been unable to dilute the Guard's authority by replacing the Supreme Defense Council with the Supreme Council for National Security as the country's highest military/ security decision-making body. The National Security Council has greater representation by Rafsanjani allies than does the SDC. Moreover, Rafsanjani's attempts to merge the command structure of the two forces have not succeeded in limiting the Guard's strength. He set up a combined headquarters in 1988, ostensibly to improve Iran's battlefield performance but really to wind down the war, and strengthened that body in 1992. However, the combined headquarters is headed by Hasan Firuzabadi, who is clearly identified with the Guard and the Basijj, rather than with the regular military, and he has not even attempted to promote a true merger between the Guard and the regular military.

The Guard is also emerging as the principal executor of Iran's military-to-military relations with other countries, especially key arms suppliers such as North Korea and China. Reza'i was treated virtually as a head of state when he visited North Korea in January 1993. He visited China on that same trip. Because of his relationships with Iran's major arms suppliers, Reza'i has become, at least *de facto*, the chief purchaser of big-ticket military items for the entire Iranian military. His central role in the procurement process ensures that much of the new acquisitions go to the Guard. Reza'i also has public links to the Pakistani, Sudanese, and Syrian armed forces, with which the Guard has extensive relationships.[28] Pakistan reportedly trains Guard ground forces; a Guard contingent is present in Sudan; and Syria allows the Guard to resupply its contingent and allied Hizbollah forces in Lebanon.

An appropriate example of the Guard's dominance can be found in Iran's naval forces. Like all components of the Iranian military, Iran's naval forces are still divided between the Revolutionary Guard, which controls Iran's minisubmarines, small boats, and new Chinese-made fast-attack craft; and the regular navy, which controls the larger ships that have been in Iran's arsenal since the Shah's reign. It appears that elements of both forces are operating the new Kilo-class submarines from Russia. Some military analysts saw cause for optimism when Ali Shamkhani, appointed to head the regular navy in 1989, took command of the Guard navy, as well, in 1990. Such a move appeared to represent a *de facto* merger of the regular and the Guard navies.

However, more important than the fact that Shamkhani heads both navies concurrently is his background and ideological outlook. He was named a rear-admiral when given command of the regular navy, but most Iranians know him as the deputy commander of the Revolutionary Guard during the Iran–Iraq war. Along with Mohsen Reza'i, Shamkhani helped build the Guard virtually from scratch, and he is still closer to Reza'i and the other Guard leaders than he is to anyone in the regular military leadership. Though he has an engineering background, Shamkhani is not, nor was he ever, a professional naval officer. Prior to the Islamic revolution, he was an urban guerrilla in southern Iran (some believe he is of Arab origin) and helped organize the Guard there when the revolution triumphed in 1979.[29] According to the Iranian press, Shamkhani had the distinction of being the last Iranian commander to evacuate Al Faw (he was then serving concurrently as Guard ground forces commander) when Iraq recaptured that peninsula in April 1988. Shamkhani is considered less impulsive than Hosein Ala'i, who preceded him as head of the Guard navy, but he is nonetheless an integral part of Iran's radical faction. It is a justifiable source of concern to the United States and the GCC states that Iran's naval forces, including the Russian-made Kilo submarines, are now under his command. Shamkhani is, at least in part, responsible for the increasingly aggressive tone of Iranian naval exercises in the Gulf over the past two years.

The potential use of Iran's naval forces is all the more a source of concern when it is noted that the deputy commander of the regular navy is Abbas Mohtaj. Like Shamkhani, Mohtaj was a senior Guard leader who had no formal naval training before entering the naval command structure. He had risen to prominence as commander of Revolutionary Guard Region Seven, consisting of most of northwestern Iran. In that position, he was responsible for suppressing insurgencies by the Kurds and other groups that flared up after the revolution.[30] He subsequently became chief of Guard headquarters and then deputy commander of Guard ground forces.

Leadership changes in the Guard air force have been cited by some analysts as a counterpoint to the developments in Iran's naval forces. The air force changes demonstrated that the Guard acknowledges that it sometimes needs to place technical competence over ideology. Its efforts to maximize its use of technology do not, however, mean that the Guard has abandoned its goals, only that, in the wake of the Iran–Iraq war, it realizes that it needs technology to better accomplish those goals. The first leader of the Guard Air Force (constituted in 1986, although it had been forming for several years previous) was Musa Refan. By all accounts, Refan was a radical ideologue who was not up to the challenge of transforming the Guard air force into a major service to rival the regular air force. Other than its missile units, which fired Scud missiles at Iraqi cities and helped defend Iran's air space, the Guard air force played little role in the Iran–Iraq war, although, in fairness, the regular air force did not distinguish itself either. Refan resigned in 1990 amid reports that he believed the Guard leadership was insufficiently supportive of him or of the Guard air force.

In 1990, the Guard promoted to commander one of its "heavyweights"

– Hosein Dehqan – to prepare it to receive some of the new, more sophisticated equipment that Iran had contracted to purchase from the Soviet Union in 1988. Up to that point, the Guard air force had been limited to using converted civilian or light training aircraft and some helicopters.[31] Dehqan had served in the mid-1980s as Guard commander in Lebanon, one of the most prestigious posts for any Guard leader and a position held only by the most radical Guard commanders. As such, and as deputy commander and then commander of the Guard air force, Dehqan was close to Reza'i and to the other Guard leaders and was able to obtain for the fledgling Guard air force greater resources than it had previously. However, Dehqan was not able to match his political clout with an understanding of the technicalities of running a more modern and sophisticated air force capable of effectively fielding Russian-made advanced aircraft.

In early 1992, Dehqan was replaced as Guard air force commander by Hosein Jalali, a regular air force officer who had served during the mid-to-late 1980s as defense minister. He was appointed defense minister in 1985 during a major cabinet reshuffle that had brought many hardliners into the cabinet, and he was perceived as sympathetic to – or at least not opposed to – the Guard's insistence on aggressive prosecution of war with Iraq until victory. In essence, the Guard itself recognized that it needed technical competence at the top of its most technology-dependent service if the Guard air force were successfully to integrate sophisticated aircraft into its arsenal. The alternatives – integrating into the regular air force led by Mansur Sattari, or forfeiting control of any of the new Russian jets – was unacceptable to the Guard. Rather than foreshadow a merger with the regular air force, the appointment of Jalali represented a step toward building up the Guard air force as a rival to the regular air force. It is entirely possible that, once the Guard air force has successfully integrated its new Russian (and Chinese) aircraft, one of the Guard leadership's inner circle will – formally or informally – take over the service.

Implications of the Guard's Political Power

Some might question whether or not it is worthwhile to analyze the Iranian military threat in terms of the backgrounds of those who drive that military. The importance of this line of analysis is to demonstrate that Iran's military – or at least its most politically important component – is not a professional military force and cannot necessarily be expected to behave like one. A professional force can be expected to predicate military decisions or advice on objective criteria and rational calculation of outcomes. An unprofessional force may often base its considerations on irrational or politically motivated impulse. This is why, in large part, the Gulf states cannot be certain that Iran's modernized arsenal will not be used against them, even if support from the United States places the balance of power in their favor. Whereas the Iranian regular military would hesitate to undertake military action that is certain to fail, the Guard has often been known to ignore such criteria, for example during a major naval attack on the US navy on 18 April 1988, in which several of Iran's largest ships were sunk or badly damaged. (The Guard was reportedly the driving force behind that attack, even though regular navy ships were actually used in the battle.) In a more recent example, US navy officials in the Gulf report that it is the Guard that has built military fortifications on Abu Musa island, even though doing so was sure to alarm the UAE, the GCC in general, and the United States.[32] Moreover, Reza'i and other Guard leaders have made clear on several occasions that the Guard is an Islamic army and that one of its objectives is to promote Islamic revolution.[33] It is difficult to believe that the Guard openly admits that it is an agent of radical revolution throughout the Islamic world and can be expected to act as a professional armed force when it comes to military affairs in the Gulf.

The Guard is also likely to connect military and revolutionary export events to internal political infighting. A professional force can be expected to demonstrate unquestioned loyalty to the existing political leadership, even if that be a new regime. The Iranian military swore fealty to the clerical regime once the Shah was overthrown. An unprofessional force, on the other hand, often becomes caught up in the political struggles within and outside a particular regime; often that force is disbanded or purged severely when its political patrons lose power. No one can imagine the Revolutionary Guard serving under a restored monarchy or a government administered by the Guard's arch enemy, the Mojahedin-e Khalq Organization (MEK). Neither is it possible to imagine either of these regimes retaining the services of the Guard were they to achieve power. To this extent, defending its political patrons internally may be more important to the Guard than defending the country from an external threat. It is likely, therefore, that if the clerical leadership were overthrown, Iran would descend into a period of violent instability, and the Guard could potentially lash out at the Gulf states as part of the internal power struggle within Iran. It is also likely that the Guard will become more aggressive if the radical faction with which it identifies loses political power to more moderate elements; it may undertake military or political actions designed to embarrass the moderates and set them back politically. This is a pattern that recurred several times during the Iran–Iraq war.[34]

Other Politico-Military Threats

Iran's military structure is very unlike that of other countries. Other nations, including Saudi Arabia, have divided militaries, but the Revolutionary Guard makes Iran unique because of the many functions it performs. The Guard is a military and an internal security force but, as noted above, it is also an exporter of the revolution force. Not only does its involvement in the export of the revolution suggest unprofessionalism in its military arm, but the Guard's subversive capabilities, in and of themselves, pose an additional direct threat to the Gulf states. For example, the Islamic Front for the Liberation of Bahrain (IFLB), a radical Islamic group backed by the Guard, organized an abortive coup attempt against the Al-Khalifa regime in Bahrain in 1981. Abd al-Hadi Mudarassi, who continues to head remnants of the group from his base in Iran, is still allowed access to Iranian broadcast facilities. Although the IFLB has been inactive for several years, it is not unreasonable to believe that the Guard and its radical allies could try to rebuild the organization into a major opposition force in Bahrain. Such an action could come in conjunction with a decision to revive Iran's claim to Bahrain, as some radical Iranian newspapers have suggested.

In Kuwait, Iran's revolutionary surrogates came closer to success than they did in Bahrain. In December 1983, members of the Kuwaiti branch of the Da'wa (Islamic Call) Party – several of whom were from Lebanese families – bombed Kuwaiti installations as well as the US and French embassies in Kuwait City. Seventeen Da'wa Party members were imprisoned and their release became a consistent demand of the Hizbollah holders of Western hostages in Lebanon. Hizbollah grew out of a branch of the Da'wa Party in Lebanon, and there were connections between the Da'wa in Lebanon and the Da'wa in the Gulf. The clerical leaders of the Da'wa were disciples of Ayatollah Khomeini and Ayatollah Muhammad Baqr al Sadr, both of whom taught in Najaf, Iraq, during the 1960s and 1970s. Both the Da'wa and Hizbollah received help from their natural allies, the Revolutionary Guard, which also was inspired by Khomeini and his Islamic revolutionary concepts. In May 1985 Da'wa activists nearly succeeded in killing the Amir of Kuwait by detonating a bomb on his motorcade route; the Amir was injured in that attack.

Iran retains some influence among opposition Shi'ite Islamic groups in the eastern province of Saudi Arabia, although these groups do not appear strong enough to be of major concern. In October 1992 Hasan Saffar, the leader of the Saudi Shi'ite opposition Organization of the Islamic Revolution in the Arabian Peninsula (OIRAP), gave an interview to an Iranian newspaper in which he was sympathetic to Iranian foreign policy and to Iran as a model of Islamic society. Saffar also acknowledged cooperation between his organization and Hizbollah, Iran's chief ally in Lebanon.[35] The Guard has used the vehicle of the annual *hajj* to try to hurt the Saudi regime directly. Ahmad Khomeini admitted in 1989 that the Guard had tried to smuggle explosives into Saudi Arabia during the 1986 *hajj*.[36] The Guard reportedly was also involved in the rioting in Mecca the following year, which led to the breaking of relations between Iran and Saudi Arabia.

It is noteworthy that, of the Gulf states, Iran's export of the revolution apparatus has been relatively inactive in the United Arab Emirates. This might be counter-intuitive, given Iran's actions on Abu Musa island and the presence of a large Iranian community in the UAE, particularly in Dubai. It is possible, however, that Iran fears a backlash against families of Iranian origin in the UAE if Iran were to try unsuccessfully to subvert any of the Emirates' regimes. Another possible explanation is that the ruling families in the UAE, realizing the subversive threat, maintain tight surveillance over families of Iranian origin. It is possible, if not likely, that Iran might turn to attempted subversion of the UAE if the UAE refuses to yield sovereignty over Abu Musa and the Tunb islands.

Currently, Iran is making significant inroads into the radical Sunni Islamic community throughout the Middle East. As a consequence, Iran's prospects for patronizing some of the Sunni Islamic opposition groups now gaining strength in the Gulf (particularly in Saudi Arabia) may be improving. Iran's most significant recent accomplishment in the Sunni Muslim world is its alliance with Sudan, which has been ruled by an Islamic-military regime since 1989. There are numerous reports that there are Revolutionary Guards in Sudan who are helping defend the regime against internal opponents and reportedly training Islamic militants involved in opposition movements in Algeria, Tunisia, Libya, Egypt, and Jordan. Sudanese diplomats acknowledge that Hizbollah elements have also been allowed into Sudan, reportedly to help the Guards train other militants. Many of the militants training under the Guard and Hizbollah in Sudan are veterans of the war in Afghanistan. For example, Cherif Gousmi, a pro-Iranian activist who fought with the Afghan Mujahedin, headed Algeria's Armed Islamic Group from April 1994 until he was killed by Algerian security forces in late September 1994.[37] Iran gained access to the Arab volunteers in Afghanistan in 1991, as the United States and Saudi Arabia – the previous patrons of the volunteers – disengaged from the Afghan conflict. The US State Department estimates that several thousand non-Afghan Muslims volunteered in Afghanistan and that, of those, "some" have become active in Islamic movements in their countries of origin.[38]

Iran is aided in its revolutionary export activities by radical Iranian diplomats, some of whom are former Guards or radical "students" who took over the US embassy in Tehran in 1979.[39] Iran has consistently posted such diplomats to its embassies in Lebanon and Syria, through which Iran assists its Guard contingent in Lebanon and its Lebanese ally, Hizbollah. In 1993, Iran posted one of its former diplomats in Beirut, Ahmad Dastmalchian, to Iran's embassy in Amman, possibly to assist pro-Iranian elements in Jordan and radical Islamic Palestinians in the West Bank. Iran's appointment of any such diplomats to the Gulf states could serve as an indication that Iran intends to step up subversive activities in those states.

Although it has taken on the trappings of a conventional military force, Iran's Revolutionary Guard has melded Iranian nationalism with the radical Islamic ideals of the revolution that created that military organization. Its leaders remain active, powerful, and radical, and the Guard was the leading force in the Iranian buildup on the islands in the Gulf during October 1994–June 1995. The recent promotion of General Headquarters Chief Hasan Firuzabadi, who is close to the Guard and the Basijj, again demonstrates the Guard's ability to prevail in military re-organizations. The Guard can be expected to resist any efforts by the regime to distance Iran from Lebanese and Palestinian groups opposing the Arab–Israeli peace process. Its allies in Iran will likely continue to look for opportunities to export the Islamic revolution. The unrest in Bahrain during December 1994–April 1995 might give Iran's radicals reason to believe they might succeed, and eventually implement Khomeini's expansive vision of region-wide Islamic revolution.

CHAPTER II

Threats and Non-Threats from Iran

Anthony H. Cordesman

Threats and Non-Threats from Iran

Analyzing Iranian military forces presents problems in estimating both intentions and capabilities.[1] In the case of intentions, Iran can be seen as a radical Islamic state with broad ambitions regionally and throughout the Islamic world, whose "moderation" – to the extent that it exists – is a product of necessity forced upon it by military and economic weakness. Iran can also, however, be seen as a state that is moving away from the ideological extremism of a charismatic religious leader towards pragmatism and an acceptance of the need for more stable relations with its neighbors and trading partners. Alternatively, it can be seen as a state that is still in the middle of an uncertain process of revolution whose future political and strategic character may not stabilize for a decade or more.

In the case of capabilities, Iran can be seen as a militarily weak state recovering from the devastating equipment losses of the Iran–Iraq war, as a state which is still heavily dependent on obsolete and partially operational military equipment bought from the West fifteen to twenty-five years ago, and as a state which is unable either to fund the new equipment it needs or to find a reliable supplier of high-technology weapons. Alternatively, it can be seen as a power re-arming to achieve hegemonic and ideological ambitions, with the near-term goal of intimidating its neighbors and the longer-term goal of dominating the region.

Iran can be viewed either as a power that emphasizes unconventional and revolutionary warfare to compensate for its other military weaknesses, or as a power that seeks to use such means to achieve its ideological goals through extremism and terrorism. It can be viewed as a power that is seeking long-range missiles and weapons of mass destruction in response to attacks by nations like Iraq, which is seeking them to compensate for its conventional weaknesses, or as a state which is seeking such weapons to achieve ideological and hegemonic ambitions.

The key problem with these different interpretations of Iran's intentions and capabilities is that all, or none, may prove to be correct. Each interpretation is a reflection of real trends within Iranian politics and can be supported by some of Iran's actions. None, however, can be said to provide a reliable explanation of Iran's present or future.[2] The fact is that Iran cannot be labeled in such simple ways.

Iran's leadership is divided, and its composition is highly unpredictable when viewed in the strategic context of what it may be in three years or three decades. For example, President Rafsanjani announced in late 1994 that he would not seek to amend Iran's constitution so that he could run for a third term. This means that Rafsanjani will leave office in August 1997. He could easily be replaced by a relative extremist like Ali Akbar Nateq Nuri, while a harder-line and more radical Khamene'i has succeeded in promoting himself into the position of supreme religious leader (*marja' ala*) of the Shi'ite faith.

Major revolutions rarely have neat endings or predictable ones, and Iran is a politically and culturally divided society. This mix of instability and uncertainties presents serious problems for Iran's neighbors and the states with strategic interests in the Gulf. Further, one does not have to point to Iran's revolutionary character to find a rationale for caution about any attempt to predict Iran's behavior and future. One could just as easily point to France or Russia during the first quarter of a century after their revolutions for examples of instability and the prolonged threat post-revolutionary states can pose to their neighbors. One can even point to the United States during its first quarter of a century of existence, and to its conduct in initiating the war of 1812, as an example of a war a democracy fought against democracy with the annexation of Canada as its primary goal.

Unfortunately, this leaves Iran's neighbors with little choice other than to focus on Iran's existing and potential military capabilities, rather than its political intentions – however "pragmatic" Iran's current leadership may or may not be. Regardless of the very different merits of political and economic containment, these uncertainties also provide a strong motive to "contain" the growth of Iranian military capability and arms transfers to Iran, and to prevent the transfer of critical dual-use technologies. Regardless of what Iran is or is not today, or may or may not be tomorrow, it must be treated as a major regional strategic risk, and no Arab proverb is less applicable in the Gulf than, "the enemy of my enemy is my friend." No states with strategic interests in the region can afford to chose between Iran and Iraq: Both nations must be seen as potential regional threats until years of good conduct prove them otherwise.

Yet military capabilities are also difficult to analyze, Iran is militarily and economically weak in many ways, but so are its neighbors. Western power projection in the Gulf is difficult, costly, and time consuming. Even today, Iran has military strengths that have considerable offensive capability. It is virtually impossible to predict the exact rate at which Iran will arm in the future. It is equally impossible to predict whether some element of the Iranian leadership will support "terrorist" or revolutionary action even if a consensus cannot be reached within the leadership as a whole, and Iran's search for weapons of mass destruction can suddenly shift the balance of power in the Gulf, regardless of whether it is defensive or aggressive in origin.

Iranian Military Expenditures

Iran's military capabilities can be measured in a number of ways: in terms of total defense effort, expenditures on arms transfers, current force size and trends, current force quality and trends, contingency capabilities, force goals and future plans, and progress in acquiring and deploying weapons of mass destruction. Unfortunately, it is far easier to be dramatic in assessing each of these aspects of Iranian military capability than it is to be accurate. Far too often, sweeping statements are made about the size of Iran's defense effort and arms transfers that cannot be sustained on the basis of the available evidence, or hostile exile groups are reported as if they were a reliable source of information on Iran's future plans.

Iranian military expenditures are a good example of the problems involved in examining Iran's capabilities. In January 1994 Iran's president, Ali Akbar Rafsanjani, gave a speech during prayers at Tehran University in which he stated that the United States had "lost the game" in trying to contain Iran's military buildup. He stated: "We are out of danger ... We're in need of practically nothing with regard to defense and we can stand on our own two feet. Iran has reached a state of stability and they can no longer do us harm."[3]

Like Rafsanjani's statement in the same speech that Iran's economy no longer had to rely on oil exports, such rhetoric had little to do with Iran's political, economic, and military realities. The speech came days before several bombs were set off in Tehran and only weeks before an assassination attempt was made on Rafsanjani's life. Iran celebrated the fifteenth anniversary of the revolution amid new reports of divisions in Iran's leadership. It was desperate for added oil revenue, and was anything but self-sufficient in defense.[4]

While some Iranian leaders have attempted to take a more pragmatic approach to managing the Iranian economy since Khomeini's death, low oil revenues, resistance from the clergy and advocates of "Islamic social-ism," and the massive corruption and inefficiency of the Islamic state have deprived these reforms of much of their effect. Near-term economic growth is only likely to reach a maximum of 25 percent of the population growth rate, even if that rate stays as low as 2.7 percent.[5]

Iran currently produces between 2.5 and 3.7 million barrels per day – usually at the lower end of this range. This oil production has given Iran annual oil revenues of $7.4 billion to $22.0 billion during the last decade, with an estimated annual income of $15.9 billion in 1992, $14.9 billion in 1993, and $12–$13 billion in 1994.[6] These revenues amount to nearly 90 percent of the value of Iran's exports, and finance about 65 percent of Iran's five-year plan.[7]

Iran, however, must rely on oil revenues to pay for both guns and butter.[8] The rest of its economy is developing at a low rate, and Iran has less wealth per capita than it did under the Shah.[9] Its real growth in GNP lagged behind its growth in population during much of the Iran–Iraq war and in 1993 and 1994. Iran's foreign debt has risen from nearly zero in 1989 to $18.8 billion in 1992, $28–$32 billion in 1993, and over $33 billion in 1994. It has managed to reschedule some of its debt payments, but this has increased interest rates. The Islamic Republic had rescheduled only $10 billion of its debt by the end of 1994, and debt repayment costs are now on a track where they will reach a peak of $4 billion a year. Iran no longer has easy access to foreign credit. Inflation is serious and exceeded 30 percent during 1993 and 40 percent during 1994.[10]

Much of Iran's agriculture and light industry is still disrupted by the combined impact of revolution, the Iran–Iraq war, and mismanagement by Iran's religious leadership. Its infrastructure and educational system are still in considerable disarray and Iran has major problems with unemployment and under-utilization of labor. Its combined rate of un-employment and disguised unemployed has almost certainly exceeded 30 percent since 1989.[11] Iran is now heavily dependent on imports of food, although it has about 45.4 cubic kilometers of internal renewable water resources – which is relatively high for a Middle Eastern country.[12] Its post-Iran–Iraq war oil revenues have not been sufficient to cover its needs for arms imports, food imports, and imports for its civil economy. These economic problems severely limit what Iran can spend on defense.

It is impossible to provide a true estimate of Iran's military spending in recent years. Iranian official economic statistics have limited reliability. The International Institute for Strategic Studies (IISS) indicates that Iran reported total military expenditures of only $1.8 billion in 1992, $2.0 billion in 1993, and $2.3 billion in 1994. The CIA reports that Iran reported military expenditures of 1,785 billion riyals in 1992 (including $808 million in hard currency) and 2,507 billion riyals in 1993 (including $850 million in hard currency).[13] These estimates are so low that it is clear they cannot cover the full current operating costs of Iran's military forces, much less all arms imports and spending on weapons of mass destruction.[14] Such figures are interesting, but they demonstrate that even the best non-governmental organizations lack both a credible data collection capability and a credible methodology for estimating military expenditures and arms sales.

The only such organization capable of making highly detailed independent estimates of Iranian defense spending is the US intelligence community, but it is slow to declassify such estimates and some of the figures it issues are inconsistent. The key unclassified source of such declassified estimates is the US Arms Control and Disarmament Agency (ACDA). ACDA's latest estimate of the trends in Iranian defense spending is shown in Table 11.1. It should be noted, however, that the ACDA spending figures are calculated in dollar equivalents and do not include civil expenditures on military industries and weapons of mass destruction (a substantial figure). They also do not price manpower or services in equivalent cost terms. As a result, the ACDA estimates of defense spending for Iran are far too low to be compared with those ACDA issues for countries in the Southern Gulf.

The ACDA totals do not reflect the fact that Iran pays its full-time active manpower much less than its neighbors do and pays almost nothing for conscripts and mobilized manpower, nor do they reflect the fact that Iran pays only a small fraction of the price the Gulf Arab states pay for operations and maintenance, services, and construction. The ACDA data include only part of Iran's total arms imports, and the ACDA data on the total personnel in armed forces only include regular forces during the period from 1981 and 1987. Even after 1987, they reflect a count of regular forces and full-time Revolutionary Guards that ignores the Basijj. The ACDA figures do seem broadly correct, however, in reflecting some important internal trends in Iranian military spending. First, it is clear from the manpower data that the Khomeini government did an extraordinarily poor job of mobilizing the nation for the Iran–Iraq war. It was

Table 11.1 Iranian military spending ($ millions) and arms transfers, 1981–91

	Military expenditures		Military expenditures as			Armed forces	
	Current	Constant (1991)	% of GNP	% of CGE	Per capita 1991	(1,000s)	(per 1,000 people)
1981	3,285	4,904	6.8	20.7	122	260*	6.5
1982	3,731	5,245	6.4	21.7	125	240*	5.7
1983	3,990	5,390	6.1	22.2	125	240*	5.5
1984	5,036	6,512	7.1	29.9	145	335*	7.5
1985	5,631	7,026	7.3	34.1	152	345*	7.5
1986	7,410	9,002	10.3	55.2	183	345*	7.0
1987	6,352	7,479	8.7	47.2	146	350*	6.8
1988	5,854	6,637	8.3	42.4	125	654	12.0
1989	4,890	5,305	6.4	36.4	96	604	11.0
1990	5,313	5,422	5.9	29.4	95	440	7.7
1991	5,647	5,647	5.7	24.9	96	465	7.9

	Arms imports		Arms exports		Arms imports as % of total imports
	Current	Constant (1991)	Current	Constant (1991)	
1981	925	1,381	0	0	6.3
1982	1,600	2,249	0	0	13.4
1983	825	1,114	0	0	4.5
1984	2,700	3,491	0	0	17.6
1985	1,900	2,370	0	0	16.3
1986	2,600	3,159	0	0	24.7
1987	2,000	2,355	0	0	20.9
1988	2,500	2,835	0	0	26.4
1989	1,300	1,410	0	0	12.4
1990	1,400	1,456	0	0	9.8
1991	1,600	1,600	30	30	8.3

* Regular forces only. Does not include Revolutionary Guards.
Source: Adapted from US Arms Control and Disarmament Agency, *World Military Expenditures and Arms Transfers, 1991–1992*, Washington, ACDA, 1994, pp. 67 and 109.

not until 1984, three years into the war, that Iran really began to develop a war economy. Even then, it at best achieved manpower parity with Iraq, although Iran had at least 2.5 times Iraq's total population.

Even allowing for the restrictions in the ACDA definition of Iranian defense spending, Iran did a poor job of mobilizing its economy. The

United States, for example, devoted up to 48 percent of its GNP to military spending during the Second World War, and Iraq spent more than 40 percent of its GNP on military expenditures during 1980–88, reaching a peak of 47.2 percent during 1986. Iraq spent even more of its GNP on military forces during the Gulf war. It spent 48 percent of its GNP on military expenditures during 1990, and 74.9 percent during 1991.[15]

At the same time, Table 11.1 shows that Iran was forced to spend a high portion of its total hard currency and import capacity on arms during the Iran–Iraq war. The figures for military expenditures and arms transfers shown in the table for the post-Iran–Iraq war period are also interesting because they show that total Iranian expenditures remained high after the ceasefire in the war, although arms imports dropped to about half their wartime level. This trend reflects a number of factors. The Iranian armed forces had to be rebuilt after major defeats in 1988, which cost the Iranian army about 40–60 percent of its total pool of major combat equipment. Iran, however, either did not or could not spend the money on arms imports needed to rebuild modern armed forces. While arms imports of $1.3 to $1.6 billion may seem high by some standards, they were scarcely enough to compensate for Iran's wartime losses.

The US Central Intelligence Agency (CIA) has issued occasional estimates of Iranian military spending which attempt to include all Iranian military expenditures, including arms imports. The CIA's latest estimates indicate that Iran spent $13.0 billion in 1991 (14–15 percent of GDP), and it is probably accurate in estimating that Iran has spent an average of 10–15 percent of its GNP on military forces and equipment since the ceasefire in the Iran–Iraq war in 1988, versus 20 percent or more of its GDP on defense during much of the Iran–Iraq war.[16] At the same time, US government experts felt that Iran might only have spent some $6 to $7 billion in 1992, $5 to $6 billion in 1993, and less than $5 billion in 1994.[17]

The IISS cannot devote the same resources to estimating military expenditures as the US intelligence community, but its estimates are still interesting. IISS data indicate that Iran spent $9,900 million in 1987–88 in the last year of the Iran–Iraq war, but that Iranian spending dropped to $5,770 million in 1989–90, $3,180 million in 1990, and $5,790 million in 1991.[18] These estimates, however, do not seem to include some key procurement expenses and many of Iran's expenditures on weapons of mass destruction, but they are probably correct in reflecting a significant postwar drop in Iran's defense spending.

If these different estimates of military spending sometimes seem more confusing than enlightening, this uncertainty is an important factor to remember in evaluating all of the data available on Iran's military efforts. It is far easier to issue an estimate – or make vague claims about a massive military buildup or defensive Iranian actions – than it is to validate such claims. Even institutions with the resources of the US intelligence community have serious problems in producing figures that are even comparable enough from year to year to reflect meaningful trends.

What all of the previous estimates do have in common, however, is that they indicate that Iran currently is not making large defense expenditures by the standards of its military spending during the Iran–Iraq war or in comparison with the standards set by its neighbors. Iraq, for example, spent $40.8 billion on military forces in 1990. It spent $24.5 billion in 1991 and $20 billion in 1992 in spite of its defeat in the Gulf war and its crippled economy. Saudi Arabia spent over $35 billion in 1993, and Kuwait spent $13.6 billion.[19]

At the same time, it must be stressed that such estimates of military expenditures are not directly comparable in definition, and it is clear from the size of its forces that Iran's military expenditures are large enough to sustain one of the two largest force structures in the Gulf and a major effort to acquire weapons of mass destruction. Iran's recent military expenditures are also far more likely to have been constrained by its low oil revenues and inability freely to obtain the arms imports it wants than by its plans and intentions.

In fact, the search for added oil revenue may well create strategic pressures on the Iranian economy and government that make Iran more aggressive in its military efforts. Iran talked in 1992 about raising production capacity from 4.2 million barrels per day in 1993 (3.6–3.8 million on-shore and 400,000 off-shore), to 4.5 million barrels per day by 1994, and 5 million barrels per day by 1995. It also discussed plans for investing $5 billion in on-shore and off-shore oil drilling, exploration, and development over the five years beginning on 20 March 1994.[20] Two years later, Iran was discussing much higher levels of investment to reach the same goal. In 1994, the National Iranian Oil Company issued plans calling for $16.6 billion in domestic financing and $9 billion in foreign financing to fund both sustained long-term production at existing levels of output and to raise production to 5 MBD. It also discussed plans to find $3.8 billion to invest in revitalizing its gas production.

It is highly uncertain that Iran can find such levels of investment capital or acquire the capability to produce at 5 MBD. Even if it does, it could easily find that it would not obtain higher real gross oil export revenues. Other states might raise their production, and Iraq may well be exporting in large amounts before it can do anything to increase its oil production. If this happens, oil prices may drop and Iran may simply end up having to sell more oil to get the same annual revenues.

Few experts believe that world oil demand will rise quickly enough to allow Iran to meet its targets for oil revenues unless other states cut production – particularly if Iraq should be allowed to resume its oil exports. This means that Iran will find it harder and harder to fund both economic development and military ambitions, and this may lead it to try to intimidate its neighbors, and to use the threat of force or unconventional warfare to put pressure on the states of the southern Gulf to adjust oil quotas and prices.

Population is another strategic pressure on Iran's economy and political structure that could make it more aggressive. Its population has nearly doubled since the revolution from 32 million to over 62 million. Oil wealth is always relative, and this is particularly true when real oil revenues drop and such a sharp increase takes place in population. Not only is Iran's current population in excess of 62 million, until recently its population growth has averaged an extremely high rate of 3.5 percent.[21] Roughly 60 to 70 percent of its population is now under the age of 25, and 40 to 50 percent is under the age of 15. The total number of students in primary schools has almost tripled from 7 million to 19 million, and the number of university students has increased from fewer than 100,000 to over one million.[22]

As a result of the mismanagement of Iranian agriculture and industry since the late 1970s, and the economic impact of the Iran–Iraq war, Iran is also now structurally dependent on a high degree of imports, which have averaged well in excess of $14 billion during the 1990s and reached $27 billion in 1992.[23] This import dependence has considerable political importance at a time when the Iranian economy is unable to fund either "butter" or "guns." Iran estimated that at least 40 percent of its population lived in poverty in 1994, and Iran needed some $12 billion in imports just to meet civil needs. This sum virtually equaled Iran's total oil export revenues and left little surplus hard currency earnings to pay for either debt servicing or arms imports. Further, it paid over $10 billion annually for various economic subsidies, and its subsidy on oil and petrochemical products was sharply increasing its domestic oil consumption and reducing the volume of what it can export.[24]

Iranian Conventional Arms Transfers

Iran's ability to import arms is another key test of its present and future capability to pose a threat to other nations in the Gulf. It is also an area where better data are available on the size and trends of Iran's efforts than on its total military expenditures – although it should again be noted that only the US intelligence community has the resources to make meaningful estimates of Iran's capabilities and that these estimates do not include dual-use civil imports that go to the military and most imports to develop weapons of mass destruction, and do not include the impact of Iran's military industries on its force strength.

Table 11.1 has already shown the ACDA estimate of Iran's arms imports through 1991, and that its total arms imports dropped sharply after the Iran–Iraq war. More current data are available through the work of Richard F. Grimmett of the US Congressional Research Service (CRS), which contains unclassified estimates corrected by US intelligence experts. These figures are summarized in Table 11.2, and they show a number of patterns that are often ignored in discussions of Iran's arms imports:

—The data showing total expenditures by source during 1986–89 and 1990–93 (part A of Table 11.2) show that Iran fell substantially short of Iraq's total arms imports during the period 1986–90, although Iraq ceased to have access to major imports in 1990.

—Iran's arms imports fell substantially after the Iran–Iraq war, although Iran lost some 40 to 60 percent of its major army equipment during its defeats in 1988 alone, and much of its other equipment holdings as of 1988 suffered from severe wear, age, and combat damage problems.

—Seen from the viewpoint of an extremist revolutionary government – with a xenophobic if not paranoiac character – key Gulf states vastly exceeded Iran's post-Iran–Iraq war arms imports. Kuwait imported as many arms as Iran during 1990–93, while Saudi Arabia imported over five times as many.

—The data showing total expenditures by Gulf countries during 1990–93 (part A of Table 11.2) reinforce this point. They show that the GCC states imported more than seven times as many arms as Iran during 1990–93.

The most important trend data are revealed in the bottom section of Table 11.2, which show data for arms transfers in recent years. These data show that Iran took delivery during 1989 of massive orders it had

Table 11.2 Patterns in Iranian arms imports

a Key regional arms transfers (in millions of current dollars)

	US	Russia	China	Major European*	Other European	All others	Total
Iran							
1986–89	0	0	2,700	700	3,000	2,300	8,700
1990–93	0	3,700	1,100	100	100	700	5,700
Total	0	3,700	3,800	800	3,100	3,000	14,400
Iraq							
1986–89	0	6,100	2,200	2,600	3,800	1,600	16,300
1990–93	0	200	0	400	100	800	1,500
Total	0	6,300	2,200	3,000	3,900	2,400	17,800
Kuwait							
1986–89	2,200	200	0	200	500	700	3,800
1990–93	3,800	0	0	1,900	0	0	5,700
Total	6,000	200	0	2,100	500	700	9,500
Saudi Arabia							
1986–89	4,100	0	3,000	23,800	1,100	600	32,600
1990–93	30,400	200	300	2,700	1,300	200	35,100
Total	34,500	200	3,300	26,500	2,400	800	67,700

b Total Gulf: 1990–93 (transfers in millions of current dollars)

	US	Russia	China	Major European*	Other European	All others	Total
Iran	0	3,700	1,100	100	100	700	5,700
Iraq	0	200	0	400	100	800	1,500
Bahrain	300	0	0	0	0	0	300
Kuwait	3,800	0	0	1,900	0	0	5,700
Oman	100	0	0	900	0	0	1,000
Qatar	0	0	0	500	0	0	500
Saudi Arabia	30,400	200	300	2,700	1,300	200	35,100
UAE	600	400	0	100	0	400	1,500
Total GCC	5,200	600	300	6,100	1,300	600	44,100

Table 11.2 (cont.)

c Arms sales to Iran by year (in millions of current dollars)

	Deliveries		Agreements	
	Dollar value	Rank in Third World**	Dollar value	Rank in Third World**
1989	–	–	1,290	5
1990	2,860	3	1,400	4
1991	1,900	4	1,500	3
1992	300	10	–	–
1993	–	–	600	7

Note: * France, UK, Germany, and Italy.   ** Out of top 10 buyers. Not shown if rank is more than tenth.

Source: Data in sections A and B are adapted from Richard F. Grimmett, *Conventional Arms Transfers to the Third World, 1986–1993*, Congressional Research Service, 94-612F, p. 57. The annual data in section C are taken from various annual editions of Grimmett's work.

placed during the Iran–Iraq war, but that total deliveries tapered off sharply in 1990, and then fell to surprisingly low levels in 1992. The data also show that Iran's new arms orders – while substantial – were scarcely massive by Gulf standards during 1989–92, and that new orders had dropped sharply by 1993 – when Iran's economic crisis seems to have sharply reduced its level of imports.

These data put Iranian imports in a very different perspective from the kind of analyses that take individual Iranian orders out of context, or which focus on statements by Robert Gates, the former director of the CIA, that Iran's annual arms imports were worth as much as $2 billion a year in 1992.[25] While Gates was perfectly correct in what he said (there were an estimated $1,900 million in deliveries), Table 11.2 shows that this figure is not representative of the overall patterns of Iran's new arms imports as estimated by US intelligence.[26]

These data do not, however, mean that Iran is not a threat. Comparisons of data on Iranian arms transfers with data on the transfers of other Gulf countries can do as much to misinform as be useful. Such comparisons do not reflect the fact that 1) Iran pays very different prices for Soviet, PRC, and North Korean weapons from those that the Arab Gulf states pay for Western weapons; 2) the data on Arab Gulf states include major expenditures on services, support, parts, and munitions (30–40 percent) while those of Iran do not; and 3) Iran can meet more of its munitions and equipment needs through domestic military production.

Putting these trends in a broader context reveals the same kind of uncertainties in estimating Iran's capabilities. Continuing arms import problems between 1979 and 1988 played a major role in shaping Iran's defeat in the Iran–Iraq war, and long-standing shortages in Western arms, munitions, and spare parts crippled Iran's army, air force, and navy. Iran lacked the hard currency and access to the world market during the 1980s to compete with Iraq in expanding and modernizing its forces.

During 1979–83, Iran ordered only $5.4 billion worth of arms compared to Iraqi orders of $17.6 billion. During 1984–88, it ordered only $10.5 billion worth of arms compared to Iraqi orders of $29.7 billion. These figures indicate that Iraq was able to import more than three times as many arms as Iran during the war, and Iran normally could only buy relatively low-grade weapons from nations like the PRC and North Korea.[27]

The final battles of the Iran–Iraq war, then, cost Iran much of the land forces equipment it had been able to obtain from the PRC, North Korea, and Central Europe. According to most estimates, Iran lost over 40 percent of its major army equipment during its final battles before the August 1988 ceasefire. These wartime losses would still be crippling to Iran's military capabilities if it had had to continue to depend largely on countries like the PRC and North Korea, as it did during the Iran–Iraq war. The PRC and North Korea are at best capable of exporting third-rate tanks, second-rate artillery, and fifth-rate combat aircraft.

As Table 11.3 shows, however, the end of the Iran–Iraq war and the political impact of the Gulf war have helped to create a climate where Russia began major transfers of high-technology arms to Iran. Russian arms transfers to Iran began in 1989, and if sales for this year are added to the data for 1990–93, US intelligence values Russia's transfers at over $4.3 billion since the end of the Iran–Iraq war. Some of these transfers included advanced weapons systems like the T-72 tank, MiG-29 fighter, and Su-24 strike fighter. This access to Soviet arms helped cause Iran's conventional arms imports from China to drop from $3.6 billion in 1985–88 to $1.1 billion in 1989–92, although Iran's economic problems were also an important factor.[28]

As a result, Iran's arms purchases during the 1990s have reflected a mix of Iran's new access to arms from the Russian Republic and Central

Europe, and continuing dependence on the PRC and North Korea. While the details are anything but easy to document, Iran's access to spare parts, technical support, and dual-use items has also improved significantly. Iran's opposition to Iraq's invasion of Kuwait gave it new respectability and better access to the world's legal and black arms markets.[29] Beginning in 1991, Iran obtained easier access to equipment and supplies for its biological and chemical weapons efforts and got increased – if still limited – imports of high technology for its nuclear weapons program.

President Rafsanjani reached a $1.9 billion sales agreement with Russia during a June 1989 trip to Moscow that traded the delivery of Iranian gas through the IGAT II pipeline for a Soviet agreement to sell Iran 48 MiG-29 fighters, 100 T-72 tanks, and other equipment and services. What is far less clear is what happened after this sale. Iran may have made a $6 billion arms deal with Russia in July 1991. According to reports by the People's Mujahedin – a radical Marxist extremist group funded largely by Iraq – an agreement was signed in Moscow between Lt.-Gen. Yevgeny Shaposhnikov and the late General Mansur Sattari, then head of the Iranian air force, for Iran to buy a T-72 assembly plant, 122 mm and 130 mm guns, 100 MiG-21 fighters, a MiG-29 assembly plant, 48 MiG-31 air defense fighters, 24 Su-24 strike fighters, and 2 IL-76s equipped as airborne warning aircraft. Other reports during 1991, however, indicated Iran had ordered 200 T-72s and a T-72 production plant from the former Soviet Union, or had ordered 1,500 T-72s from Czechoslovakia.[30]

Other reports are even more speculative. For example, news sources reported in mid-1992 that Iran had a $10 billion arms plan to acquire new army, air defense, air, and naval equipment during 1990–94. Other sources indicated in the fall of 1992 that Iran had a plan that would increase its tank strength from 500 in 1990 to 1,400 in 1997, its combat aircraft strength from 275 to 350, its surface-to-air missile strength from 90 major launchers to 300, its surface-to-surface missile strength from 30 major launchers to 60, and its submarine strength from zero to three. Other sources reported orders of 400 more Soviet T-72s and 500 BMP-2s, and orders of 170 North Korean Scud B and Scud Cs, and People's Republic of China-made M-11 missiles in 1991.

Reports surfaced during 1993 that Iran had a $7 billion arms import plan and plans to order 1,500 T-54s/T-55s, and 300 T-72s, from Poland, and supersonic SS-N-22 "Sunburn" or "Sunburst" anti-ship missiles, SA-10 (S-300) surface-to-air missiles, three more Kilo submarines, 50 more MiG-29s, and 200 more T-72Ms from Russia and the Ukraine. One report indicated that Iran's arms import plan would cost up to $20 billion. Still other reports stated that Germany and other European countries were making massive transfers of dual-use technology, equipment, and manufacturing capabilities, and that Iran was seeking to buy Boeing and Airbus commercial aircraft for dual-use in military transport and refueling efforts.[31]

What is clear is that Iran sought additional combat aircraft, missiles, main battle tanks and other armored vehicles, and sometimes obtained them. Most experts agree that Iran did succeed in buying T-72s, Kilo submarines, MiG-29s, Su-24s, artillery, SA-5 surface-to-air missiles, and guided air weapons from Russia and other states of the former Soviet Union during 1991–93. It is clear that deliveries and orders from the People's Republic of China included versions of the SA-2 surface-to-air missile, F-7M fighters, and artillery. They agree that Iran obtained parts and supplies from Central Europe, electronics from Western Europe, and large numbers of parts and spares from Asia – including parts for US-made equipment from Vietnam.[32]

Experts also agree that Iran discussed buying other types of fighters from Russia, including the MiG-23/24 interceptor, MiG-25 interceptor and reconnaissance bomber, MiG-27 ground attack, MiG-31 long-range interceptor, Su-20 ground attack/reconnaissance, Su-22 ground attack, Su-25 close support, and Su-27 fighter/ground attack aircraft, the T-22M medium bomber and reconnaissance attack bomber, and the A-50 airborne early warning aircraft.[33]

Russia has not responded to these requests for more aircraft, tanks, and advanced weapons, and President Yeltsin agreed in October 1994 to prohibit further sales of high technology, although Russia stated it would fulfill existing Iranian orders. These Russian decisions are partly a result of Iran's failure to pay Russia for existing deliveries, but they also seem to be the result of Russian concern with Iran's role in Central Asia, and Russian sensitivity to US efforts to persuade the Russian government to limit its arms transfers. Russia has also shown growing caution in selling Iran the dual-use technologies it might use to obtain weapons of mass destruction, although this has not halted Russian sales of nuclear reactors.[34]

Iran has, however, obtained some advanced weapons from other sources. These weapons include deliveries of long-range missiles from North Korea, and missile production technology and some 200 CSS-8 short-range ballistic missiles from China.[35] It has also discussed buying the FH-8 fighter and Jian Hong 7 bomber and a new type of tank from China. Further, it has found a supply of parts for its M-113 armored personnel carriers, is buying F-5 parts on the black market, and is seeking to buy used F-5s from Indonesia.[36]

The practical question is whether this combination of new arms from different sources can offset the deterioration of Iran's existing inventory. Iran's successes must be weighed against 1) Iran's losses during the Iran—Iraq war; 2) the fact that most of its weapons are either low-grade PRC and North Korean exports or are Western-supplied systems that have seen hard service in combat, which are now 15–25 years old; and 3) Iran has had only limited access to the spare parts and technical support to maintain, repair, and modernize such systems.

The current state of the major Western-supplied systems in Iran are summarized in Table 11.3, and it is clear why Iran's former minister of defense and armed forces logistics, Akbar Torkan, described Iran's procurement priorities as follows:

> The first priority is spare parts, the second priority is spare parts, and the third priority is spare parts ... Only a very few countries, such as America, Russia, China, and France can produce all their requirements. The rest only produce a fraction. It might be possible for us to build tanks, submarines, missiles, aircraft, and the like. But, self-sufficiency is relative. We think of self-sufficiency in terms of those items which we use a lot, especially the sort of equipment we employed most during the Iran—Iraq war. And in any economic venture, the finished product is very important. For instance, if we followed a program of self-sufficiency and decided to produce something locally it might cost $5,000, whereas we might be able to buy the same thing abroad for $1,000. This would not make economic sense.[37]

Iran has shown that it can buy some Western spares, upgrades, weapons systems, and dual-use technologies on the black market. It continues to exploit the complex mix of overt and covert purchasing offices it established during the Iran—Iraq war. These offices include its State Procurement Organization, Aviation Technology Affairs (ATA), Foreign Procurement Management Center, Defense Support Organization (Saziman Poshtiban Defa), Ghoods Research Centre, Lavson Ltd., and the National Iranian Oil Company (NIOC). It also uses private companies, universities, ministries, and various foreign front companies and subsidiaries as important components of Iran's covert purchasing system.

Iran has utilized these organizations to buy older US equipment it can use to obtain spare parts to repair its holdings of US weapons. It has also used them to get high-technology components like radar-testing devices, navigation and avionics equipment, fiber optics, logic analyzers, high-speed computers, high-speed switches, precision machinery, jet engines, tank engines, and remote sensors. It has aggressively sought out chemical protection and detection gear, refueling technology, early-warning

Table 11.3 Iranian dependence on decaying Western-supplied major weapons

Military service	Weapon Type	Number	Comments
Land	Chieftain tank	100–150	Worn, underarmored, underarmed, and underpowered. Fire-control and sighting systems now obsolete. Cooling problems.
	M-47	100–150	Worn, underarmored, underarmed, and underpowered. Fire-control and sighting systems now obsolete.
	M-60	100–150	Worn, underarmored, underarmed, and underpowered. Fire-control and sighting systems now obsolete.
	Scorpion AFV	35–40	Worn, light armor, underarmed, and underpowered.
	M-109 155mm SP	95	Worn, fire-control system now obsolete. Growing reliability problems due to lack of parts.
	M-107 175mm SP	20	Worn, fire-control system now obsolete. Growing reliability problems due to lack of parts.
	M-110 203mm SP	10	Worn, fire-control system now obsolete. Growing reliability problems due to lack of updates and parts.
	TOW ATGM	?	Serious quality problems in remaining missiles.
	AH-1J Attack heli	100	Worn, avionics and weapons suite now obsolete. Growing reliability problems due to lack of updates and parts.
	CH-47 Trans heli	31	Worn, avionics now obsolete. Growing reliability problems due to lack of updates and parts.
	Bell helicopters	100–130	Worn, growing reliability problems due to lack of updates and parts.
Air	F-4D/E FGA	55–60	Worn, avionics now obsolete. Critical problems due to lack of updates and parts.
	60 F-5E/FII FGA	60	Worn, avionics now obsolete. Serious problems due to lack of updates and parts.

Table 11.3 (cont.)

Military service	Weapon Type	Number	Comments
Air	F-5A/B	10	Worn, avionics now obsolete. Serious problems due to lack of updates and parts.
	RF-4E	8	Worn, avionics now obsolete. Serious problems due to lack of updates and parts.
	RF-5E	5–10	Worn, avionics now obsolete. Serious problems due to lack of updates and parts.
	F-14 AWX	60	Worn, avionics now obsolete. Critical problems due to lack of updates and parts. Cannot operate some radars at long ranges. Phoenix missile capability cannot be used.
	P-3F MPA	5	Worn, avionics and sensors now obsolete. Many sensors and weapons cannot be used. Critical problems due to lack of updates and parts.
	Key PGMs	–	Remaining Mavericks, Aim-7s, Aim-9s, Aim-54s are all long past rated shelf life. Many or most are unreliable or inoperable.
	IHawk SAM	150–175	Worn, electronics, software, and some aspects of sensors now obsolete. Critical problems due to lack of updates and parts.
	Rapier SAM	30	Worn, electronics, software, and some aspects of sensors now obsolete. Critical problems due to lack of updates and parts.
Navy	Damavan DE	1	Worn, weapons and electronics suite obsolete, many systems inoperable or partly dysfunctional. Critical problems due to lack of updates and parts.
	Samavand DDG	5	Worn, weapons and electronics suite obsolete, many systems inoperable or partly dysfunctional. Critical problems due to lack of updates and parts.

Table 11.3 (cont.)

Military service	Weapon Type	Number	Comments
	Alvand FFG	3	Worn, weapons and electronics suite obsolete, many systems inoperable or partly dysfunctional. Critical problems due to lack of updates and parts.
Navy	Batander FF	2	Obsolete. Critical problems due to lack of updates and parts.
	Hengeman LST	4	Worn, needs full-scale refit.

Source: Estimate made by the author based on the equipment counts in IISS, *Military Balance, 1993–1994*, pp. 115–16. Note that different equipment estimates are used later in the text. The IISS figures are used throughout this chart to preserve statistical consistency.

radar technology, and avionics conversion equipment – although it is not clear whether it has been able to deploy such equipment in its forces.

Iran has also tried to deal with the problems summarized in Table 11.3 by "cannibalizing" some weapons to keep others operating. Often, however, it has still been unable to buy key major sub-assemblies or has had to buy parts that are worn or are of poor quality from Third World suppliers. It has not been able to upgrade or modernize most such systems to anything approaching Western standards for 10–20 years. Many key parts for Western-supplied equipment are no longer in supply because the original manufacturer has halted production, or has modified a given system so much since the 1960s and 1970s that the equipment can no longer be updated with new parts and sub-assemblies. While Iran has found some creative ways to work around these problems, the cumulative effect of the Iran–Iraq war, revolution, lack of adequate technical training, and the low technical standards of some elements of the Revolutionary Guards, has led to steady equipment losses through age and attrition.

The Bush and Clinton administrations have also had some success in persuading European states, Russia, and the PRC to limit arms transfers to Iran. The United States has put heavy pressure on Russia, Poland, Czechoslovakia, and Germany to limit their arms transfers of dual-use items, and has been joined in such efforts by Britain. The European Community strengthened its controls in June 1993, and began to examine additional sanctions.[38] These pressures force Iran to mix its aging Western-supplied equipment with a wide range of equipment that has been obtained from non-Western sources – most of which is inferior and not interoperable. This lack of standardization within Iranian forces creates additional training, battle management, and logistic support problems.

Iran's Military Industries

Iran is rebuilding and expanding its military industries.[39] It may be spending the equivalent of $200–$300 million a year to manufacture conventional arms in Iran, and as much or more on missiles and weapons of mass destruction.[40] According to Akbar Torkan, former minister of defense and armed forces logistics, it has merged its plants for the Iranian regular army and forces into one system to make them more efficient and has tripled its output of arms since 1979.

In 1993, Iran claimed to have at least 240 state-owned arms plants under the control of the Ministry of Defense and Armed Forces Logistics, Defense Industries Organization, IRGC, and Reconstruction Jihad Ministry, and some 12,000 privately owned workshops. The central direction of these organizations and their research and development (R&D) has improved steadily since 1989, when Akbar Torkan became minister of defense. These organizations employed about 45,000 people, and plan to expand their operations to a level that would employ 60,000 people within the coming five years.

These facilities include some relatively sophisticated plants, manufacturing equipment, and technology. Iran has had some recent Soviet, North Korean, People's Republic of China, Israeli, Pakistani, Argentine, Brazilian, Taiwanese, and German help in expanding its facilities, and is also nearly self-sustaining in many areas of less demanding military production. It can manufacture some aircraft and armored weapons parts, moderately sophisticated military electronics, wheeled armored vehicles, artillery weapons and parts, artillery and small arms ammunition, short- to long-range rockets, small arms, automatic weapons, and mortars.

Iranian officials, however, make exaggerated claims about the production capabilities of these facilities, and have claimed to be able to produce weapons like Scud missiles and tanks.[41] For example, Ali Akbar Nateq Nuri, speaker of the Iranian Majlis, claimed that Iran had reached "self-sufficiency" in defense industries on 1 January 1995, and stated that:

> Thanks to God, we stand today in such a position that we have reached self-sufficiency within the defense industries. This issue has caused fear and concern for the global powers, especially for the USA ... It is a great honor

for the armed forces that we do not depend on outside countries for military purchases.[42]

Iran cannot currently mass-produce a single sophisticated guided missile system or advanced conventional weapon unless it is given the major parts needed to assemble one. Yet these limitations may not be as severe in the future. It is giving the funding of long-range missile and weapons of mass destruction plants priority, and has obtained support from North Korea and China in developing missile and artillery production plants.[43] Iran may be able to slowly gain the ability to manufacture more sophisticated equipment in the future; it has sought T-72 assembly plants from Russia and Poland, and might well be able to operate such plants if it receives suitable outside technical assistance.

Iran's Demographics and Military Manpower

Iran's current military capabilities are heavily influenced by its demographics. It is by far the most heavily populated Gulf state, with a population of about 66 million and a high birthrate. This gives it a major potential advantage in building up its military forces.[44] Iran's total male manpower pool between ages 15 and 49 is about 14,382,000. The CIA estimates that 6,556,000 males are fit for military service and that 601,000 reach military age each year.[45] The IISS estimates that there are 3,487,000 males between the ages of 13 and 17, another 3,026,000 between the ages of 18 and 22, and a total of 4,861,000 between the ages of 23 and 32.[46]

At the same time, Iran's manpower base has deep ethnic divisions, and its ability to transform its manpower numbers into military power is severely limited by Iran's economic problems and access to arms imports. Its ethnic population is about 51 percent Persian, 24 percent Azerbaijani, 7 percent Kurd, 8 percent Gilaki and Mazandarani, 2 percent Lur, 2 percent Baloch, 3 percent Arab, 2 percent Turkoman, and 1 percent other. It has fewer significant religious divisions than Iraq. It is about 95 percent Shi'ite Muslim, with 4 percent Sunni Muslim, plus 1 percent Zoroastrian, Christian, Jewish, and Bahai.[47] It does, however, have a wide variety of linguistic groups. Only 58 percent of the population speaks Persian and Persian dialects, 26 percent speak some form of Turkic or Turkic dialect, 9 percent speak Kurdish, and five other linguistic groups total about 7 percent of the population.[48] This presents problems in military training and communications.

Estimates differ sharply regarding the size of Iran's current total military manpower. IISS estimates that Iran currently has about 513,000 full-time actives in its regular forces, plus 350,000 men in its reserves. It also estimates that it has 120,000 men in its Islamic Revolutionary Guards Corps (Pasdaran Inquilab), 90,000 in its Basijj (Mobilization of the Oppressed), 45,000 in its internal security forces, and around 12,000 men in an Iranian trained and funded Kurdish Democratic Party militia.[49] A combination of the regular and Revolutionary Guards forces would give Iran about 470,000 full-time actives – a small fraction of Iran's potential manpower strength. These Iranian totals compare with about 650,000 full-time actives for Iraq, 7,200 men for Bahrain, 14,000 for Kuwait, 36,700 for Oman, 9,500 for Qatar, 101,000 for Saudi Arabia, and 58,000 for the UAE;[50] thus, Iraq continues to pose a major challenge to Iran in terms of total manpower.

The Iranian Army

Iran's land forces have been in a constant state of change since the end of the Iran–Iraq war, and it is difficult to make accurate estimates of their strength.[51] Its army and Revolutionary Guard units have suffered from the combined impact of revolution, a Western embargo on arms transfers, and the Iran–Iraq war. Its ground forces also took far greater losses during the Iran–Iraq war than did the Iranian air force or navy, particularly during the final battles. Its defeats in land battles during 1988 were so severe that they led to the disintegration of some elements of the Pasdaran and even Iran's main regular army units. These defeats also caused massive losses of weapons and equipment.

While Iran's exact losses are in dispute, it is clear that it lost over half of its operational armor between February and July 1988. Iraq seems to be correct in claiming to have captured some 1,298 Iranian tanks and heavy armored fighting vehicles, 155 other armored fighting vehicles, 512 armored personnel carriers, large amounts of artillery, 6,196 mortars, 8,050 RPGs and recoilless rifles, 60,694 rifles, 322 pistols, 501 pieces of heavy engineering equipment, 6,156 pieces of communications gear, 16,863 items of chemical warfare defense equipment, and 24,257 caskets.[52] The degree of disintegration in Iran's land forces at the end of the Iran–Iraq war is reflected in the fact that much of this captured equipment showed no sign of combat damage or wear. Much was abandoned in the field, either out of panic or because of supply problems.

Iran has, however, rebuilt some of these capabilities. According to the IISS, the Iranian regular army had a strength of 12 division equivalents in 1995, and around 40 maneuver brigades. These formations included 4

armored divisions (2 with 3 brigades and 2 with 4 brigades), 7 infantry
divisions, and 1 special forces division with 4 brigades. Iran seems to
have at least 2, and probably 6, independent maneuver brigades. These
seem to include 1–2 airborne brigades and 4 special forces brigades, a
surface-to-surface missile brigade, and a logistic brigade.[53]

A few experts feel that Iran has a larger number of smaller formations
that include 25–28 divisions and over 100 "brigades" and "regiments".
According to these estimates, its divisions were estimated to include 5–
6 armored divisions, 3–6 mechanized divisions, 13–14 infantry divisions,
and one special forces division with four brigades. These estimates may
combine Iranian regular army and IRGC forces and confuse some brigade-
sized formations with divisions.

The Iranian army is currently deployed in three army-sized formations
north to south along the border with Iraq. Iran seems to have been able
to move some units away from the southern border since Iraq has
concentrated its forces to deal with the domestic threat posed by its
Shi'ites in the south and Kurds in the north, but tensions between the
Iranian government and the Kurds have forced Iran to maintain strong
forces in the northwest.

Many of the army's key deployment locations and billets are the same
as during the time of the Shah. They include Zahedan in the southeast;
Mashad and Gorgan in the northeast; Tehran, Qazvin, and Sarab in the
north-central region; Kharramabad, Isfahan, and Shiraz in central Iran;
Orimiyah, Maragheh, and Sanandaj in the northwest; Kermanshah in west-
central Iran; and Ahwaz and Shushter in the southeast. Army aviation is
headquartered at Tehran, Mashad, and Shiraz. Officer training takes place
at the Tehran Military Academy, infantry and armor training at Shiraz,
signal training at Tabriz, and missile and aviation training at Isfahan.[54]

Estimates of the current equipment holdings of Iran's land forces are
uncertain, and it is not possible to distinguish the holdings of the Iranian
regular army from those of the Islamic Revolutionary Guard Corps. Iran
does, however, seem to have had an inventory of around 1,245 tanks in
early 1994 – reflecting a rise of some 200 tanks over 1993 and 320–380
tanks over 1992. Iran's main battle tanks consisted of about 300 M-47s and
M-60s, 135 Chieftains, 150 T-62s and 150 T-72s, 175–200 T-54s and T-55s,
and 260 T-59s. Iran may have taken delivery on 150–200 additional T-72s,
and 100–200 T-59s during the rest of 1994, which would bring Iran's total
inventory up to over 1,500 tanks. Some experts, however, rate Iran's
sustainable *operational* tank strength at still only about 900–1,000 tanks.

Iran has claimed to have developed a world-class main battle tank. It announced in late December 1994 that it had spent a total of $10 billion on military forces in the preceding five years, and claimed to have begun production of a new main battle tank called the Zulfiqar, after two and one-half years of development. A prototype of this tank was shown in April 1994, and while some sources report it is based upon the T-72, the pictures of the prototype show a design closer to the M-48/M-60. There is as yet no evidence that Iran can manufacture the advanced armor, fire control, engines, suspensions, or guns for a first-line main battle tank.[55]

As a result, Iran is now dependent on its holdings of the export version of the Russian T-72M for anything approaching an advanced tank. The T-72M performed badly in Iraqi hands during the Gulf war, and lacks the thermal sights, night-vision systems, fire-control systems, and advanced armor to compete with first-line Western tanks like the M-1A1/2, Challenger, Le Clerc, or Leopard 2. Iran also only has about 250–350 T-72s, and a substantial number of its M-47s, M-60s, and Chieftains are probably not operational.

Iran seems to have about 1,000–1,250 operational armored personnel carriers and armored infantry fighting vehicles. These seem to include 40–50 operational British-supplied Scorpions, more than 200 BMPs, some 150–175 M-l 13s and other Western APCs, and 500 BTR-50s, BTR-60s, and BTR-152s. It has an unknown number of British Chieftain bridging tanks and may have another 100–150 BMPs in the process of delivery.[56] Iran's BMPs are its only modern AFVs. They total only about 20 percent of Iran's holdings of other armored vehicles. The BMPs have significant ergonomic problems in fighting from the vehicle, limited night-vision capabilities, and poor weapons-system ergonomics and performance.

Iran had 2,000–2,500 medium and heavy artillery weapons and multiple rocket launchers. This high total reflects a continuing Iranian effort to build up artillery strength that began during the Iran–Iraq war, when Iran used artillery to support its infantry and Islamic Revolutionary Guard Corps in their attacks on Iraq. Iran has had to use artillery as a substitute for armor and air power.

Iran's holdings of self-propelled weapons seem to include 8–10 M-110 203-mm howitzers, 20 M-107 175-mm guns, and 80–100 M-109 155-mm howitzers. These US-supplied weapons are badly worn, have not been modernized in over 15 years, lack modern fire-control systems and artillery radars, and total less than 10 percent of Iran's artillery strength. Iran is attempting to compensate for its lack of modern artillery and artillery mobility by replacing its US self-propelled weapons with Chinese and North Korean systems. It seems to have at least 50 Chinese 122-mm and

15 North Korean 146-mm self-propelled weapons, and may have significantly more. It may also have 20–30 Soviet 2S1 122-mm self-propelled howitzers.

Iran seems to have 20–25 M-115 towed 203-mm howitzers, 40–80 M-59 towed 155-mm howitzers, and 100–130 M-101 towed 105-mm howitzers surviving from the arms that Iran imported from the United States during the time of the Shah. It also seems to have 150–175 Austrian GHN-45 and French AMX towed 155-mm gun/howitzers. Its non-Western holdings of towed artillery weapons include 1,000–1,500 North Korean, Chinese, and Soviet M-46 and T-59 towed 130-mm guns; and Soviet, North Korean, Polish, and Czech D-30 122-mm gun-howitzers. They include Soviet M-1943 towed 152-mm howitzers, Czech-Type 83 towed 152-mm gun/howitzers, PRC 122-mm towed howitzers, and other former Soviet bloc, PRC, and North Korean towed weapons.[57]

Iran has over 200 multiple-rocket launchers, including some BM-24 240-mm multiple- rocket launchers, Chinese Type 63 107-mm multiple-rocket launchers, and Soviet BM-21 122-mm towed multiple-rocket launchers. It also has Oghab, Shahin, and Nazeat long-range unguided rockets.

Iran bought large numbers of mortars during the Iran–Iraq war, for the same reasons that it bought large numbers of towed tube artillery weapons. It had some 2,000 weapons in 1994, of which approximately 1,200 were medium and heavy mortars. It had at least several hundred of its heavy mortars mounted in armored vehicles – many of which were M-106 US-made mortar carriers sold to Iran during the time of the Shah.

These artillery weapons give Iran considerable ability to mass fires against relatively static area targets, but towed artillery is an anachronism in modern maneuver warfare operations, and Iran has only limited artillery fire-control and battle management systems, counter-battery radar capability, and long-range target acquisition capability (although it does have some remotely piloted vehicles (RPVs) to support its self-propelled weapons. Iran has actively sought more modem fire-control and targeting systems since the mid-1980s, but it is unclear how many it obtained or put into service, and most of its artillery units are only effective against slow-moving mass targets at ranges of under 10–15 kilometers or in harassment and interdiction.

There is no way to estimate the current size of Iran's holdings of anti-tank weapons. Iran does have TOW and Dragon weapons supplied by the United States, and seems to have introduced Soviet and Asian versions of the AT-2, AT-3, and AT-4 into its forces. It has large numbers of RPG-7 and Western 3.5" rocket launchers.

Iranian helicopter holdings are uncertain. According to the IISS, the Iranian army retains 100 AH-1J Sea Cobra attack helicopters, and 31 CH-47C, 100 Bell-214A, 20 AB205A, and 50 AB-206 transport and support helicopters out of the total supplied by the West. Some experts feel that these figures overestimate the number of attack helicopters and under-estimate the number of troop-carrying and utility helicopters. Most experts agree, however, that the operational readiness of Iranian helicopters is low, perhaps only about 25 percent of inventory, and that Iran has little sustained sortie capability. The IISS estimates that the army's fixed wing aircraft included 40 Cessna 185, 310, and O2A aircraft, 2 F-27s, 2 Falcon 20s, 15 PC-16s, and 5 Strike Commanders.

Islamic Revolutionary Guards Corps

There are significant uncertainties regarding the organization and role of the Islamic Revolutionary Guards Corps (IRGC).[58] Most sources agree that the IRGC was organized into eleven internal security regions in 1994. Some sources indicate that they were organized into 12–15 "divisions," although most such divisions had manning levels less than those of brigades in the Iranian regular army, and many had less firepower than Western combat battalions. It also had some 18–23 independent "brigades" – including armored, infantry, special forces, paratroops, air defense, artillery, missile, engineer, and border defense units. These brigades manning levels are equivalent to regiments and battalions in the regular forces.[59]

Most sources feel that these IRGC land forces are now organized, trained, and equipped largely as infantry, special forces, and internal security forces. The IISS reports that the IRGC has 2–4 armored "divisions", but it is unclear that it has any armored formations larger than brigade size, and these units seem to be far less heavily armored than Iranian regular army armored brigades.

There is some disagreement over the future role of the IRGC relative to the regular army. The armored elements of the IRGC are slowly expanding, and some IRGC units with T-54 tanks are reported to be upgrading their tanks with T-72 engines and laser-range finders. IRGC units have also conducted some recent combined arms exercises with Iranian land and sea forces.[60] As a result, a few experts feel that Iran may shift its T-72s and similar former communist-bloc armor to the IRGC to create heavy formations that will compete directly with the Iranian regular army in capability.

Most sources feel that the IRGC land forces will be kept as largely infantry forces, rather than be upgraded into full armored and mechanized forces, and that the Iranian regular army is getting most of Iran's new heavy weapons. Given the political power of the IRGC, it seems doubtful that it will be restricted to the role of an internal security force – and it seems likely that it will compete with the army for some heavy equipment – but it is far from clear that it will change its current focus on unconventional warfare and light forces.

Like the Iranian army, the IRGC possesses numerous anti-tank weapons, including Dragon, TOW, and AT-3 ATGMs, 3.5" rockets, and RPG-7s. It has about 1,500 air defense guns, large numbers of small and man-portable surface-to-air missiles, and increasing numbers of the HN-5 light surface-to-air missiles. Iran's holdings of such weapons are uncertain, but it seems to be importing both Chinese and Russian short-range air defense missiles.[61] The IRGC seems to be the principle operator of Iran's land-based surface-to-surface missile forces. Both the Iranian regular army and the IRGC have offensive and defensive chemical warfare capabilities.

The War-Fighting Capabilities of Iranian Land Forces

The split between the Iranian regular army and the IRGC helps prevent Iran from concentrating its total mix of land forces into standardized, well-manned and equipped, and well-trained land units that can conduct effective armored maneuvers or combined arms operations. While Iran's more recent exercises seem to be part of an effort to correct this situation, they seem to be making limited progress at best and usually seem designed more to intimidate the southern states of the Gulf and Iraq than to improve military effectiveness.

Yet, even if Iran's land forces were not divided, their overall mix of equipment has so many different types and generations that would be difficult to support and maintain. Iran had no way to standardize its equipment, and only limited ability to standardize its ammunition and missiles during the last fifteen years. Its land forces have nine types of tanks, seven types of anti-tank missiles, and a wide range of other equipment. Some of this equipment – particularly the Western armor and helicopters – has a limited life because of a lack of spares and maintenance skills. Iran's Chinese, North Korean, and former Soviet bloc equipment is usually more combat-ready, but is also usually less sophisticated and less effective.

Iran may have a well-structured plan to create modern standardized armored, mechanized, and artillery forces, but it still lacks a reliable supplier and/or the funds to make the massive integrated purchases it needs. Its purchases of the T-72 may be a step towards this end, but it would take deliveries of around 1,500–2,000 T-72s to meet Iran's needs.

Similarly, it needs to standardize the armored infantry fighting vehicles in its first-line units. This would require a total of 2,000 relatively modern armored vehicles. Iran also needs much larger inventories of self-propelled artillery, improved anti-tank weapons and short-range air defenses, and a much stronger support and logistic training system to sustain mobile armored warfare and fast moving offensive operations.

Iran faces other major challenges in improving its land forces. Most of its tanks lack modern fire-control systems, armor, night and thermal-vision devices, and guns and ammunition equal to those of the most advanced neighboring states. Sustainability and power projection capabilities are limited, as are battlefield recovery and repair capabilities. Overall night warfare capabilities and the ability to rapidly move artillery, mass and shift fires, and acquire beyond-visual-range targets are also limited. Communications, command, and control systems are obsolete and unreliable. Helicopter and combined operations training with fixed-wing aircraft is of very limited quality at best.

Improvements are needed in all these areas, not simply in a few selected areas like main battle tanks. In fact, all of Iran's land force equipment holdings must be modernized or reconditioned to recover from the combined impact of a cut-off of Western weapons and equipment, the wear of eight years of war, and the massive losses of 1988. It needs improved tank and artillery rounds, remotely piloted vehicles (RPVs) that are integrated into division or brigade level operations, improved mobile short-range air defense systems (SHORADS) and man-portable air-to-surface missiles, tank transporters, secure communications, night vision and improved sights, modern fire-control systems, and tracked support equipment. It would greatly benefit from advanced training and simulation technology.

The Iranian regular army almost certainly understands all of these requirements. It has learned from the Iran—Iraq war and the Gulf war that a reliance on mass, rather than quality, is ineffective. It has sought to give its existing unit strength more armor and artillery, to strengthen the firepower and mobility of selected specialized independent brigades, and to give its infantry divisions added artillery strength and armored infantry fighting vehicles. Even so, the preceding analysis has shown that it will be well beyond the year 2000 before Iran's land forces can acquire anything like the full mix of modern equipment they need.

It will be even longer before Iran can use such equipment effectively. The army is short of trained technicians, officers, and non-commissioned officers. Iran is only beginning to rebuild the level of training and discipline it had when the Shah fell. In spite of some recent large-scale exercises – like the Martyr Reysali Delvari, Val Fajr, Victory and Fatah series of exercises – it is only beginning to shift from a focus on defense in depth against an Iraqi invasion into a maneuver force, and to train a portion of its forces effectively for combined operations, high-tempo combined arms operations, and power projection and amphibious warfare missions.[62] The Victory 4 exercise in the spring of 1993 marked the first recent multi-service exercise involving amphibious and heliborne assaults of the kind that would give Iran the capability to project power across the Gulf, and this exercise was not particularly impressive. While there were follow-on exercises in 1994, they lacked the scale and content that would indicate that Iran has the capability to do much more than launch limited raids or attack small islands and oil facilities in the Gulf.

Conscript junior officer and non-commissioned officer training is poor to mediocre, and medium- to large-scale unit training is poor. Formations differ sharply in size, force mix, and equipment and are difficult to supply and support. Many units are badly under strength, and some combat and support units only have about 65–80 percent of the strength needed to man them fully.

Iran's high command remains divided, and its logistic system is compartmented and ineffective. Many combat units have low overall manpower strength, and some units lack the manpower and equipment to be employed in anything other than static defensive battles. Logistics, combat engineering, and support capabilities are limited and dependent on reinforcement from the civil sector for any sustained operations.

The land units of IRGC remain an ambivalent force that often seem to act as an independent force in Iranian politics. The training of the IRGC has improved, and it has conducted more realistic large-scale exercises with the army, navy, and air force – some involving missile, amphibious, and unconventional warfare exercises in the Gulf.[63] There are some elite IRGC units capable of performing demanding special forces, commando, infiltration, and unconventional warfare missions, and the IRGC has considerable capability for unconventional warfare and terrorism.

The IRGC land forces, however, have many defects. The IRGC is poorly organized and trained for conventional war fighting, it is relatively lightly equipped, and its ideology is a poor substitute for proper equipment, discipline, standardization, and coherent organization. Iran's land forces clearly lack the capability to sustain large-scale armored thrusts deep into the territory of a well-armed regional power like Iraq, and are not capable of significant amphibious operations in the face of opposition by a power like the United States. Iran is just beginning to acquire significant offensive and power projection capabilities, and could do little more than exploit an Iraqi civil war, or rush battalion-sized forces to support some coup attempt in an exposed country like Bahrain.

These problems do not, however, preclude Iran's land forces from defending the country against a weakened Iraq, and Iran would probably be much more capable of successful defensive operations than it was in 1988. Iran is also well deployed to fight Iraq, and could probably now conduct limited armored offensives in the Iran–Iraq border area. Given Iraq's diminished strength, it is unlikely that even an Iraqi attack into Iran led by the Republican Guard could achieve more than limited initial gains.

Iranian land forces could support the seizure of islands and off-shore oil facilities in the Gulf, defeat any Kurdish uprising, and play a significant role in low-intensity combat in Iran's northern and eastern border areas. Iranian army forces are also capable of intervening at the brigade and division level in a conflict like the war between Azerbaijan and Armenia, and could easily defeat the Iranian Kurds or any other internal opposition force. Iranian land forces, particularly the IRGC, can and do play a significant role in training, equipping, and supporting guerrilla and terrorist forces in countries like Lebanon and the Sudan – and possibly Bosnia. They can covertly project power in terms of supporting radical or extremist movements in other states.[64]

It is also impossible to rule out a sudden or surprise Iranian attack in support of an uprising against a southern Gulf regime that produced success out of all proportion to the size and effectiveness of the Iranian forces deployed. Iran has a number of land units that should perform well in unconventional warfare missions in support of any popular uprising. It could deploy brigade-sized forces relatively rapidly across the Gulf, if it were allowed to make an unopposed amphibious and air assault. It could intervene in a civil war in Bahrain, or another of the smaller Gulf states, under these conditions.

The Iranian Air Force

Iran's air force has gone through a decade and a half of revolution and war, and its current operational strength is as hard to estimate as the operational strength of Iran's ground forces.[65] While Iran had 85,000 men and 447 combat aircraft in its air force at the time the Shah fell from power, it steadily lost air strength from 1980 to 1988. The air force suffered combat losses in the Iran–Iraq war, and has long been cut off from its US suppliers. It has lacked effective foreign technical support for fifteen years, and has been purged of some of the pilots that served under the Shah, and of many other officers and technical personnel.

Iran's air strength has improved significantly, however, since 1988. By early 1995, the air force and air defense force built back to a total of around 15,000 men, not including 12,000 men in its land-based air defense forces, and a total inventory of around 260–300 combat aircraft. Recent IISS and other estimates indicate that the air force had a strength of about 18 combat squadrons. These forces included 9 fighter ground-attack squadrons, with 4/55-60 F-4D/Es, 4/60 F-5E/FIIs, and 1/27-30 Su-24s. They include 7 air defense squadrons, with 4/60-65 F-14s, 2/30-35 MiG-29s, and 1/25-30 F-7Ms. Iran had a reconnaissance squadron with 5–10 RF-5EIIs and 3–8 RF-4Es, and operates 5 P-3F maritime reconnaissance aircraft, RC-130s and other intelligence/reconnaissance aircraft, and large numbers of transports and helicopters. Iran also has 20–30 F-5Bs and F-5FIIs, 10 Tucanos, and some Chinese F-6s combat capable trainers.[66]

The Iranian air force is currently organized so that many squadrons can perform both air defense and attack missions – although this is not true of its F-14s and Su-24s. The IRGC also has some air elements; it operates some of Iran's PRC-made fighters and displayed some of the Iraqi fighters that Iran is absorbing into its forces at an air show in Tehran. It is also clear that the IRGC is expanding its air capabilities, although it is not clear what combat formations exist within the IRGC or whether it will become a direct competitor with the air force.

The Iranian air force is based principally at Bandar Abbas, Bushehr, Dezful, Doshan, Tehran (Tapeh, Ghaleh Morghi, Mehrabad), Hamadan, Isfahan, Shiraz, Tabriz, and Zahedan. Its fighter attack units are based at Bandar Abbas, Bushehr, Dezful, Mehrabad, Hamadan, and Tabriz. Its air defense units are based at Doshan, Tapeh, Mehrabad, and Shiraz. Shiraz also provides interceptor training and is the main base for transport aircraft.[67]

Force quality and readiness is, however, a major issue. Brigadier-General Mansour Sattari, the chief of staff of the Iranian air force, claimed in 1994 that the air force had:

> reached self sufficiency in all fields, including pilot training, missiles, radar, air defenses, maintenance and repair, manufacture of parts and basic repair of facilities ... We constantly patrol the international waters and have a watchful eye on the moves of foreign warships there ... If the foreigners pose any threat, we will meet them with all our might.[68]

Yet these statements lack credibility. Many of Iran's operational aircraft have only limited operational capability. As few as 50 percent of its US-supplied combat aircraft may be operational, and few of its operational US-equipped squadrons can long support sustained sortie rates higher than one per aircraft every three to four days. Some US-supplied aircraft may lack the operational avionics necessary to fire air-to-air and air-to-surface missiles properly.

Iran's success in obtaining parts and spares for its US-supplied aircraft has been mixed: it has had some successes, but has failed in such covert efforts as attempts to buy compressor blades for the F-5's engines in the UK, and to buy surplus F-5s.[69] These problems led Akbar Torkan to state that:

> Our equipment is mostly American: F-4, F-5, F-14 fighter jets. Our transport aircraft are also American: C-130s, Boeing 747s, and 707s. We have a very good fleet: 14 707s, 12 747s, and 53 C-130s. This should be enough to see us through the next 30 years ... we have 72 F-14s ... for close support we have F-5 fighters and for deep strikes we have F-4 fighters. This is a very good configuration. We have 750 helicopters. ... Unfortunately, because our fleet is mainly made up of American products, providing spares is very difficult.[70]

There is some debate over exactly how many new aircraft Iran is obtaining from the People's Republic of China, from the former Soviet Union, and from other sources. According to many experts, Iran had imported 30 F-7M fighters from the Chinese by mid-1993, out of a possible total order of 50–72, but did not take further deliveries. The PRC also sold Iran PL-2 and PL-2A air-to-air missiles (Chinese copies of the Sidewinder) and PL-7 air-to-air missiles (Chinese copies of the Matra Magic R-550) with these aircraft.

A few experts believe that Iran has made larger purchases of Chinese fighters, and that it had taken delivery of over 50 Chinese-made F-6 fighters between 1987 and mid-1992, and had nearly 70 Chinese-made F-7s in operation by mid-1994. Regardless of which estimate is correct, purchases of the F-7M will do little to affect the regional balance. It is a marginal copy of the MiG-21, has poor ground-attack performance and limited air-to-air combat capability against the first-line fighters of any potential opponent, and is difficult to upgrade and overhaul.[71] What could be more significant are reports that Iran is considering major imports of the much more advanced F-8 fighter and the Jian Hong 7 bomber.[72]

Iran's most important source of new aircraft has been Russia. Its new MiG-29s and Su-24s are far superior in quality to the aircraft it has obtained from the Chinese, and it may have signed agreements that would give it a total of 50 MiG-29s, 36 Su-24s, and the necessary support equipment.[73] These deliveries could greatly improve Iranian capabilities.

Iran's MiG-29s are late-model MiG-29As or MiG-29Bs. These aircraft are designed for the forward area air superiority and escort mission, including deep penetration air-to-air combat. Their flight performance and flying qualities are excellent, and are roughly equivalent to that of the best Western fighters.[74] They have relatively modern avionics and weapons, and an advanced coherent pulse-Doppler radar with look-down/shoot-down capabilities that can detect a fighter-sized (2 m²) target at a range of 130 km (70 nautical miles) and track at 70 km (38 nautical miles).

The MiG-29 also has a track-while-scan range of 80 km (44 nautical miles) against a 5 m² target and is designed to operate with the radar off or in the passive mode, while using ground-controlled intercept.[75] It has an infrared search and track system which includes a laser range finder and a helmet-mounted sight. It also contains an internal electronic countermeasure system, SPO-15 radar warning receiver, modern inertial navigation, and the modern Odds Rod IFF. The range of the infrared search and track system is 15 km (8.2 nautical miles) against an F-16-sized target. The maximum slant range of the laser is 14 km (7.7 nautical miles) and its normal operating range is 8 km (4.4 nautical miles).

The MiG-29 can carry up to six air-to-air missiles, a 30-mm gun, and a wide mix of bombs, and 57-mm, 84-mm, and 240-mm air-to-ground rockets. A typical air combat load would include 250 rounds of 30-mm gun ammunition, 335 gallons of external fuel, 4 AA-8 Aphid infrared-guided missiles, and 2 AA-10 Alamo radar-guided medium-range air-to-air missiles. Iran may have acquired AA-8, AA-10, and AA-11 Archer air-to-air missiles from Russia.

The MiG-29 does, however, have a number of ergonomic problems. The cockpit frame and high cockpit sills limit visibility. The cockpit display is fussy and uses outdated dials and indicators similar to those of the F-4. There is only a medium-angle heads-up display and only partial hands-on system control. The CRT (cathode ray tube) display is dated and the cockpit is cramped. The helmet-mounted sight allows the pilot to slave the radar, IRST, and HUM together for intercepts and covert attacks using off-boresight cueing, but the weapons computer and software supporting all combat operations are several generations behind those in fighters like the F-15C.[76] This makes it doubtful that even a well-trained MiG-29 pilot has the air-to-air combat capability of a well-trained pilot flying an F-16C/D, F-15C, F/A-18D, or Mirage 2000 in long-range missile or beyond-visual-range combat, or in any form of combat when only the other side has the support of an AWACS-type aircraft.

The Su-24 is a twin-seat, swing-wing strike-attack aircraft that is roughly equivalent in terms of weight to the F-111, although it has nearly twice the thrust loading, and about one-third more wing loading. The Su-24 can carry payloads of up to 25,000 pounds, and operate on missions with a 1,300-km radius when carrying 6,600 pounds of fuel. With a more typical 8,818 pound (4,000 kg) combat load, it has a mission radius of about 790 km in the LO-LO-LO profile, and 1,600 km in the LO-HI-LO profile. With extended range fuel tanks and airborne refueling by an aircraft like the F-14, the Su-24 can reach virtually any target in Iraq and the southern Gulf.[77]

Although it is not clear what variant of the Su-24 has gone to Iran, it seems likely to be the Su-24D, which includes a sophisticated radar-warning receiver, an improved electronic warfare suite, an improved terrain-avoidance radar, satellite communications and an aerial refueling probe, and which can deliver electro-optical, laser, and radar-guided bombs and missiles.[78]

The Su-24D is an excellent platform for delivering air-to-surface missiles and biological, chemical, and nuclear weapons. The air-to-ground missiles it can carry include up to three AS-7 Kerry radio command-guided missiles (5 km range), one AS-9 Kyle anti-radiation missile with passive radar guidance and an active radar fuse (90 km range), three AS-10 Karen passive laser-guided missiles with an active laser fuse (10 km range), three AS-11 Kilter anti-radiation missiles with passive radar guidance and an active radar fuse (50 km range), three AS-12 Kegler anti-radiation missiles with passive radar guidance and an active radar fuse (35 km range), three AS-13 Kingposts, and three AS-14 Kedge semi-active laser-guided missiles with an active laser fuse (12 km range). It also can carry demolition bombs, retarded bombs, cluster bombs, fuel air bombs, and chemical bombs. Some experts believe that Russia has supplied Iran with AS-10, AS-11, AS-12, and possibly AS-14/AS-16 air-to-surface missiles.

Iran's purchase of Soviet aircraft has the major additional benefit of enabling the Iranian air force to use some of the Iraqi aircraft that fled to Iran during the Gulf war. There is some question about the exact number of aircraft involved, and how many are flyable. Some sources report as few as 106 combat aircraft, but Iraq has officially claimed that they total 139 aircraft. The author's estimate, based on conversations with various experts, is 24 Mirage F-1s, 22 Su-24s, 40 Su-22s, 4 Su-17/20s, 7 Su-25s, 4 MiG-29s, 7 MiG-23Ls, 4 MiG-23BNs, 1 MiG-23UB, and 1 Adnan. This is a total of 112 combat aircraft – the total usually counted by the IISS. The transport and support aircraft include 2 B-747s, 1 B-707, 1 B-727, 2 B-737s, 14 IL-76s, 2 Dassault Falcon 20s, 3 Dassault Falcon 50s, 1 Lockheed Jetstar, 1 A-300, and 5 A-310s. This is a total of 31 aircraft, and would give a grand total of 143 aircraft.[79]

Iran has already begun to fly Iraqi MiG-29s and Su-24s, and is in the process of absorbing all of Iraq's flyable MiG-29s, Su-24s, and possibly its Su-20/Su-22s into Iran's force structure. This could give Iran up to 90 additional combat aircraft if it can obtain suitable support from Russia. Iran probably cannot operate Iraqi Mirage F-1s effectively without French technical assistance, which currently seems highly unlikely. The 8–12 Iraqi MiG-23s are sufficiently low in capability that Iran may be unwilling to pay for the training and logistic burden of adding this type to its inventory. The seven Su-25s are a more attractive option, since they are specially equipped for the close air support mission, but it would be very expensive for Iran to operate a force of only seven aircraft.

Iran is also reported to have discussed buying Tu-22M (Tu-26) bombers from Russia and other states of the former Soviet Union, as well as buying Su-25 close support aircraft, MiG-31 fighters, and Su-27 attack aircraft. Reports of efforts to buy the Tu-22M seem to be correct, and Iran evidently sought 10–15 such bombers – although the exact configuration it wanted is unclear. Unlike the obsolete Soviet Tu-16 and Tu-22 – or the even more obsolete Chinese H-5 and H-6 – the Tu-22M is a modern bomber with a maximum range near 2,500 miles, good-range payload, adequate avionics, and reasonable low-altitude flight performance. Any Russian sale of such aircraft would significantly improve Iranian offensive capability.

Iran has moderate airlift capabilities for a regional power. Its air transport assets include 1 tanker/transport squadron with 4 B-707s, and 5 transport squadrons with 9 747Fs, 11 B-707s, 1 B-727, 20 C-130E/Hs,

3 Commander 690s, 15 F-27s, and 5 Falcon 20As. Its helicopter strength included 2 AB-206As, 39 Bell 214Cs, and 5 CH-47 transport helicopters.

It is clear from Iran's imports that it is seeking to obtain first-line air defense and long-range strike fighters and to rebuild a high-technology air force that can provide both effective air defense and the ability to strike deep into Iraq, the southern Gulf states, and any other neighboring power. If Iran can obtain additional imports of 50–100 first-line combat aircraft, it may be able to achieve near parity with a decaying Iraqi air force by the year 2000, *if* Iraq continues to face an embargo on all shipments of aircraft, parts, and air munitions. However, Iran has only a limited current prospect of keeping its US-supplied aircraft operational much beyond the late 1990s, and may find it difficult to convert to Russian fighters quickly enough to offset its losses of US types.[80]

There is little evidence, however, that Iran can currently sustain high sortie rates for even its Russian-made fighters for more than one-third to one-half of its present combat aircraft for more than a matter of days. More generally, its air force is still organized to fight at the squadron level, and there is little sign that it is organized to fight effectively as a unified air force, using mass and technology effectively in air defense, close air support, or interdiction missions. Iran also lacks the training and sensors to compete with the West in beyond-visual-range combat, and the advanced training facilities to compete in beyond-visual-range and dog-fight combat.

There is a wide range of other areas where Iran needs to improve its training and technology – even if it obtains more MiG-29s and Su-24s and aircraft like the Su-27, Su-25, and MiG-31. These areas include acquiring some form of airborne warning and control system (AWACS), modern air-to-air missiles to replace its US inventory, modern RPVs, improved electronic countermeasures, and airborne refueling technology. Iran also needs support in repairing and reconditioning its captured Iraqi fighters, in rehabilitating and improving its F-4s, and in recovering the beyond-visual-range air combat capability of its F-14s. It must find ways of integrating its fighters into an effective air control and warning system that "nets" them with its ground-based air defense system, and which avoids the many war-fighting limitations caused by over dependence on ground-controlled intercepts.

Iran needs either to recondition and upgrade its RF-4Es and RC-130E/Hs or to acquire modern reconnaissance and intelligence aircraft. It also needs to work with the army to recondition and improve the sensors and weapons on its AB-206B and AH-1J attack helicopters and recondition its force of transport helicopters. It needs the spares, support organization, and training to improve its sortie rates and sustainability greatly, and some additional air bases for dispersal purposes to reduce its vulnerability.

At some point in the near future, Iran must also make a clear decision between trying to maintain a hybrid air force and standardizing on Russian aircraft. Continued reliance on aging US aircraft presents obvious risks, and there are no near-term prospects that the United States will relax its constraints on parts and new equipment. In contrast, an Iranian air force based on Russian attack aircraft like the Su-24 and Su-27, close support aircraft like the Su-25, Tu22M bombers, advanced Russian air-to-surface weapons like the AS-9, AS-10, and AS-14, air defense aircraft like the MiG-29 and MiG-31, and air-to-air missiles like the AA-8, AA-10, and AA-11 could be quite effective. Such an air force would take 5–8 years to create, however, and would be extremely costly. Iran also faces the risk of creating new supply problems with Russia, and Russia has so far failed to provide any Third World state with effective advanced air combat and air-to-ground training, and the associated equipment, training, and technical support to fight effectively as a coherent modern air force.

This mix of strengths and weaknesses is likely to leave the Iranian air force with limited to moderate war-fighting capability, but this capability can scarcely be disregarded. Iran has steadily improved its air combat and exercise training since the end of the Gulf war and has conducted combined operations exercises with the land forces, land-based air defense forces, and naval forces. It can now conduct limited air attacks against all of its neighbors, and can deliver precision-guided weapons, chemical weapons, and possibly biological weapons.

The Iranian air force can attack key military depots or bases, and attack hostile Kurdish camps and the bases of the People's Mujahedin. It can attack shipping in the Gulf, and could assist the naval forces in limited operations in the Gulf, unless it met US or Saudi resistance. It could assist the Iranian land forces in any new fighting with Iraq. It might not be able to win air superiority over the Iranian border area, but it could do a much better job of defending Iranian territory than during the Iran–Iraq war.

The Iranian air force is also strong enough to deter offensive strikes from any southern Gulf air force, except for the Saudi air force. Iran is capable of penetrating the air space of all southern Gulf countries except Saudi Arabia, at least to the extent of conducting selective slash and run attacks. It could probably execute at least one successful surprise attack on a Saudi target before the Saudi air force could fully organize its air defenses. The Iranian air force would not have this capability if the United States were actively supporting the southern Gulf states. Iran will continue to lag behind the rate of modernization in Saudi Arabia. Iran has no foreseeable near- to mid-term hope of challenging a combination of US, British, and Saudi air power.

The Iranian air force could also deploy quickly to a friendly air base in the southern Gulf – in the event of a coup or other change in the political posture of that state – although it would take several weeks for Iran to deploy enough support equipment and stocks to support more than limited squadron-sized operations from such a base. The Iranian air force could not compete with the Turkish or Pakistani air forces, but might be able to fly combat support and offensive missions over the territory of Azerbaijan or the other former Soviet republics near the Iranian border. Such operations would have to be squadron sized and involve low sortie rates, but Iran has at least some capability.

Iranian Ground-based Air Defenses

Iranian ground-based air defenses play a critical role in shaping Iranian willingness to take risks and use conventional military forces.[81] As long as Iran is vulnerable to the kind of air offensive that the UN coalition conducted against Iraq during Desert Storm, it is likely to be restrained in the risks it will take. Much depends, however, on how Iran perceives its vulnerability to air attack and the attrition levels it can inflict on attacking aircraft. This perception will be shaped in part by Iran's ability to modernize its fighter forces, but Iran has no near-term prospect of acquiring an airborne defense platform similar to the E-3 AWACS operated by the Saudi and US air forces, or matching the West in airborne electronic warfare capabilities. Its success in modernizing its ground-based air defenses will, therefore, probably be as important in influencing its willingness to take military risks as its acquisition of aircraft.

In early 1995, Iran seems to have assigned about 12,000 men to land-based air defense functions, including 4,000–6,000 regulars and 5,000–8,000 IRGC personnel. It is not possible to distinguish clearly between the major air defense weapons holdings of the regular air force and IRGC, but the air force seems to have operated most major surface-to-air missile systems and its total holdings seem to have included 30 Improved Hawk fire units (150+ launchers), 50–55 SA-2 and HQ-23 (CSA-1) launchers (Chinese-made equivalents of the SA-2), and 25 SA-6 launchers. The air force also had three Soviet-made long-range SA-5 units with a total of 10–15 launchers – enough for 6 sites.

Iran's holdings of lighter air defense weapons included 30 Rapier fire units in five squadrons, 5–10 Chinese FM-80 launchers, 10–15 Tigercat fire units, and a few RBS-70s. They also included large numbers of man-portable SA-7s, HN-5s, SA-14s, and possibly SA-16s, plus about 2,000 anti-aircraft guns – including some Vulcans and 50–60 radar-guided and self-propelled ZSU-23-4 weapons.[82] It is not clear which of these lighter air defense weapons were operated by the army, the IRGC, and the air force. The IRGC clearly had larger numbers of man-portable surface-to-air launchers, including some Stingers which it had obtained from Afghanistan. It almost certainly had a number of other light air defense guns.

During the Iran–Iraq war, Iran's major surface-to-air missiles were redeployed to cover the Iraqi border, its major cities, and its ports in the Gulf. There are no authoritative data on how Iran deployed these air defenses in early 1995, but it seems to have deployed its new SA-5s to cover its major ports, oil facilities, and Tehran. It seems to have concentrated its Improved Hawks and Soviet and Chinese-made SA-2s around Tehran, Isfahan, Shiraz, Bandar Abbas, Kharg Island, Bushehr, Bandar Khomeini, Ahwaz, Dezful, Kermanshah, Hamadan, and Tabriz.

These deployments gave Iran some point defense capability, plus long-range coverage of parts of the Gulf coast with SA-5s. At the same time, it lacked the missile strength, low-altitude coverage, and command and control assets, sensors, resistance to sophisticated jamming and electronic countermeasures, and systems-integration capability necessary to create an effective air defense net. Its missiles and sensors were most effective at high to medium altitudes against aircraft with limited penetrating and jamming capability.

Iran also faced serious problems in creating a modern air defense system, many of which dated back to the time of the Shah. Although it bought modern surface-to-air missiles at the time of the Shah, it never integrated these missiles into an effective land-based air defense system. It had made its air control and warning system fully operational, and had experienced serious problems in operating some of its largely British-supplied radars.

Once the Shah was deposed, Iran had no way of purchasing the equipment needed to improve or properly maintain its Western-supplied radars, communications system, and software. It also lost many of its Western-trained operators, technicians, and commanders during the purges following the revolution, and this reduced its ability to use its Western-supplied equipment effectively. In spite of limited deliveries as a result of the Iran–Contra deal, Iran has never been able to find a source of parts, equipment, and technical expertise that has allowed it to properly support its Western-supplied systems.[83] Many of the Western-supplied surface-to-air missiles in Iran's order of battle are not fully operational, and it is forced to rely on inadequate radars, data processing systems, and command and control links to support its missile units.[84]

Iran has responded by obtaining the SA-2, CSA-1, SA-6, and SA-S from the PRC, Russia, and Central Europe. It has acquired some Soviet warning and battle management radars, command, and communications equipment. It has deployed the SA-5 to several of its bases on the Gulf coast, including Bandar Abbas, and has obtained some new Soviet radars as part of the sale of SA-5 missiles. There are credible reports that Iran is seeking to import three more batteries of SA-5 missiles from the former Soviet Union, more CSA-1s, and further deliveries of Russian and Chinese radars. There are also reports that it may be buying North Korean assistance in creating a network of underground command centers in 18 sites – although such reports are uncertain.[85]

There have also been reports from Czechoslovakia that it might sell Iran an advanced mobile air surveillance system called Tamara. The manufacturer of this system, Tesla Pardubice, has claimed that it is capable of tracking stealth aircraft. Tamara, however, seems to be a signals intelligence system with some air defense applications, and its claims to special advantages in detecting "stealth" aircraft seem to be nothing more than sales propaganda.[86]

These transfers of surface-to-air missiles and sensors from Russia and the PRC have helped improve Iran's land-based capabilities, but they have not been adequate to meet its needs. They give Iran improved capability against regional air forces without sophisticated jammers and anti-radiation missiles, but they do not give it a modern integrated air defense system that can resist attack by a power like the United States. In fact, Iran needs substantial deliveries of added equipment to make its Western-supplied weapons fully operational, much more advanced heavy surface-to-air missiles, and a considerably more advanced C^4I/BM system. In the short term, it needs to find a reliable source of Hawk parts to make its current missiles functional. It also needs to rehabilitate and improve its radar-guided anti-aircraft guns and most of its short-range air defense systems. It needs either to modernize or to replace its Rapiers, Tigercats, and FM-80s, and to replace its obsolete mix of different systems of radars and command and control equipment.

However, improving the capabilities of its Western systems, and further purchases of SA-2 and SA-5 systems, cannot give Iran the capabilities it needs. The SA-2, CSA-1, SA-6, and SA-5 are highly vulnerable to active and passive countermeasures. Even the latest versions of the Improved Hawk do not approach the Patriot in performance capability, and the Improved Hawks in Iranian hands are nearly 17 years old. If Iran is to create the land-based elements of an air defense system capable of dealing with the retaliatory capabilities of US air forces, it needs a modern heavy surface-to-air missile system that is part of an integrated air defense system. Such a system may not be easy to obtain. No European or Asian power can currently sell Iran either an advanced ground-based air defense system, or an advanced heavy surface-to-air missile system. The United States and Russia are the only current suppliers of such systems, and the only surface-to-air missiles that can meet Iran's needs are the Patriot, SA-10, SA-12a, and SA-12b.

Iran has no hope of getting the Patriot systems from the United States, and this makes Russia the only potential source of the required land-based air defense technology. This explains why Iran has sought to buy from Russia the SA-10 heavy surface-to-air missile/anti-tactical ballistic missile systems, and a next generation warning, command, and control system. The SA-10 (variously named the Fakel 5300PMU or Grumble) has a range of 90 km or 50 nautical miles. It has a highly sophisticated warning radar, tracking radar, terminal guidance system and warhead, and has good electronic warfare capabilities. The SA-10 is a far more advanced and capable system than the SA-2, SA-3, SA-5, or SA-6.[87]

Accordingly, much depends on Russian willingness to make such sales – which would mean violating Russia's October 1994 agreement with the United States. If Russia did decide to make such sales, it could quickly provide the SA-10 or SA-12 in large numbers, a greatly improved early warning sensor system, and an advanced command and control system for both its fighters and land-based air defenses.

Such a Russian system would still have important limits. Russia has not fully completed integration of the SA-10 and SA-12 into its own air defenses, has significant limitations on its air defense computer technology, and relies heavily on redundant sensors and overlapping different surface-to-air missiles to compensate for a lack of overall system efficiency. A combination of advanced Russian missiles and an advanced sensor and battle management system would still be vulnerable to active and passive attack by the United States.

It would also take at least three to five years fully to deploy and integrate such a system once Russia agreed to the sale. Its effectiveness would also depend on the ability of Russia to provide suitable technical training and to adapt a Russian system to the specific topographical and operating conditions of Iran. A Russian system cannot simply be trans-ferred to Iran as an equipment package. It would take a major effort in terms of software, radar deployment, and technology – and considerable adaptation of Russian tactics and siting concepts – to make such a system fully combat effective.[88]

An advanced land-based Russian air defense system would, however, give Iran far more capability to defend against retaliatory raids from Iraq or any other Arab Gulf air force. It would allow Iran to allocate more fighter/attack aircraft to attack missions and use its interceptors to provide air cover for such attack missions. It would greatly complicate the problem of using offensive US air power against Iran, require substantially more US forces to conduct a successful air campaign, and probably greatly increase US losses.

The Iranian Navy and the Islamic Revolutionary Guards Corps

Most Gulf nations have treated seapower as an afterthought, but the Iranian navy and naval branch of the Islamic Revolutionary Guards Corps are likely to play a critical role in Iranian military action in the Gulf.[89] Any Iranian intervention in a Gulf state that does not involve the cooperation of an Arab Gulf government, and free access to ports and air fields, would require some kind of amphibious operation. Naval forces are equally essential to a wide spectrum of other possible conflicts that affect the islands in the Gulf, control of the Straits of Hormuz, unconventional warfare using naval forces, attacks on coastal targets in Iraq and the southern Gulf, and Western and Gulf Arab naval operations in the Gulf.

As a result, it is scarcely surprising that Iran has given the modern-ization of its naval forces a high priority since the end of the Iran–Iraq war. It has obtained missiles from the Chinese, some additional ships, midget submarines from North Korea, submarines from Russia, and significant logistic and technical support from Pakistan.[90] It has improved its naval training, acquired additional mine-warfare capability, and repaired some of its ships. It has stepped up training and exercise activity in exercises like the Lightning 3, Val Fajr 1 and 2, Fatah 3, and Naser series. It has bought new missiles and ships, purchased submarines from Russia, and improved its ports and strengthened their air defenses. It has conducted combined arms training exercises with the land forces and air force.[91]

These efforts have done more to improve Iran's capabilities to threaten Gulf shipping and off-shore oil facilities, and give it the capability to support unconventional warfare, than they have to allow it to act as an effective navy. Iranian naval forces still have many limitations, but their military capability should not be measured in terms of the ability to win a battle for sea control against southern Gulf and/or Western forces. Its forces are likely to lose any such battle if Western forces are involved for the foreseeable future. It is Iran's ability to conduct limited or unconventional warfare, or to threaten traffic through the Gulf, that gives it the ability to threaten or intimidate its neighbors.

In early 1995, Iran's regular navy, naval portion of the Islamic Revolutionary Guards Corps, and marines totaled around 38,000 men – with about 18,000 regulars and 20,000 Iranian Naval Revolutionary Guard forces. While some sources list Iran as having three Marine Brigades, it is not clear how the marine units are structured, trained, or equipped.[92]

While most Iranian major surface ships have limited operational capability, the combat strength of the Iranian navy was impressive by Gulf standards. According to various estimates, Iran's operational inventory included 2 destroyers, 3 frigates, 10 missile combatants, 33 light patrol and coastal combatants, 5 mine-warfare ships (less one training ship), 9 armed helicopters, 8 amphibious ships and craft. It had a small marine force and large numbers of naval revolutionary guards. It also had 5–7 Silkworm (HY-2) anti-ship missile sites to defend its ports and cover the Straits of Hormuz.

Most of the regular navy is based at Bandar Abbas, the only large Iranian port far enough away from Iraq to be relatively secure from Iraqi air attack during the Iran–Iraq war. This port is the home port of Iran's destroyers, frigates, and two Kilo-class submarines. Iran does not conduct extensive patrols in the Gulf of Oman, but it does hold occasional exercises there, and is expanding its base at Chah Bahar in the Gulf of Oman. It has another large naval base at Bushehr, where it deploys most of its guided missile patrol boats. It has operated hovercraft forces out of the oil port at Kharg Island since the time of the Shah, and has a moderate force at its western port of Bandar Khomeini, which covers the waters opposite Iraq and the entrance to the Shatt al-Arab. It has small bases at Bandar Anzali and Noshahr on the Caspian Sea. Noshahr is used for training Islamic Revolutionary Guard Corps forces in unconventional warfare.

Opinions differ as to how much of Iran's surface force is fully operational. Iran is clearly able to operate some of its British-made Saam-class
fast-attack craft. According to some reports, it can also operate most of
the weapons systems, at least 1 destroyer, 2 frigates, 6–10 fast attack craft
(FAC), 7 large patrol boats, 40 coastal patrol boats, a maximum of 14
Hovercraft, and 57 amphibious assault ships, logistic ships, and small
patrol boats. This would give Iran a total force of more than 80 vessels,
although it would lack adequate air defense and anti-ship missile capabilities for its major surface ships.[93]

All of Iran's major surface vessels are obsolescent or obsolete, although they could be updated in Western shipyards. They include two
Sumner-class (Babr-class) destroyers – the *Babr* and *Palang*. These ships
displace 3,200 tons fully and are capable of speeds of 31 knots. Each is
armed with four paired elevating Standard SM-1MR surface-to-surface
missile launchers, two twin 5-inch gun mounts, six Mark 32 torpedo
tubes, and an Agusta AB 204AS helicopter. The Standard is still a
potentially effective missile, with command guidance and semi-active
radar homing, and a maximum range of 46 km, but Iran's missile suites
have not been modernized in 20 years and all of its Standard missiles
have now aged beyond their normal shelf life. It is doubtful that these
ships have much effectiveness. They still patrol, but it is unclear that
they can use their anti-ship missiles and anti-submarine mortars effectively. They were originally laid down in 1943 and 1944 and have not
been refitted since 1971–72, and their weapons systems, sensors, and
equipment are over 20 years old.

Iran has one British-supplied 3,400 ton Battle-class ship called the
Damavand. The *Damavand* is a British guided-missile destroyer that displaces
3,360 tons fully loaded, has a speed of 31 knots, and is armed with four
paired elevating Standard SM-1MR surface-to-surface missile launchers,
two twin 5-inch gun mounts, a single Contraves RTN-1OX Sea Hunter
fire-control radar, and a quadruple Sea Cat ship-to-air missile launcher.
The *Damavand* had relatively modern air and sea search radars, and modern
commercial grade ESM and EW gear, when it was first transferred to
Iran. However, its main refitting took place in 1966, and its Standard
missiles were added in South Africa in 1974–75. Its Sea Cats no longer
seem to be operational, and it is unclear whether its Standards and
electronics are fully operational. The *Damavand* does not patrol regularly
and is not always counted as part of Iran's operational strength.

Iran has three British-supplied Vosper Mark S Samm-class frigates –
called the *Alvand, Alborz,* and *Sabalan*. These are 1,540-ton frigates with

maximum speeds of 39 knots. Each is armed with one five-missile Sea
Killer Mark II surface-to-surface missile launcher and one Mark 8 4.5-
inch gun mount. The Sea Killer has a relatively effective beam-riding
missile with radio command or optical guidance, a maximum range of 25
km, and a 70-kg warhead; but these Alvand-class ships were last refitted
in 1977, and have not been refitted or modernized since. The operational
readiness of their missiles and more sophisticated electronics is uncertain,
and there are some indications that Iran may have removed some of the
missile launchers and replaced them with a BM-21 multiple rocket launcher
to provide added fire support capability. Further, the *Sabalan* was
extensively damaged in combat with the US navy in 1988 during an
engagement where the United States sank its sister ship. It is not clear
that it is really operational.

Iran has two US PF-103 (Bayandor-class) corvettes called the *Bayandor*
and the *Naghdi*. These ships are 900-ton vessels, with two 76-mm guns
and a maximum speed of 18 knots. They were laid down in 1962 and
delivered in 1964. Neither has sophisticated weapons systems or sensors,
although one was re-engined and given 20-mm guns (in place of a 23-
mm gun) and depth-charge rack in 1988. The rest of Iran's surface navy
consists of 10 Combattante II (Kaman-class) fast-attack boats armed
with missiles and one 76-mm gun. These boats displace 275 tons, have
maximum speeds of 37.5 knots, and are Iran's most modern Western-
supplied combat ships. These ships were delivered during 1974–81 and
were originally equipped with four US Harpoon missiles. The combat
capability of the anti-ship missile systems on the surviving boats is
uncertain. Their Harpoons may not be operational, but some or all may
have been successfully converted to the C-801/C-802.

Iran has nine large patrol craft and fast-attack craft. Its operational
ships seem to include 1 captured Iraqi Bogomol (possible), 3 North
Korean Chaho-class fast-attack craft, 3 US Cape-class large patrol craft,
and 3 Improved PGM-71-class large patrol craft. These vessels are armed
with 23-mm to 40-mm guns, and the Chaho-class ships also had one
BM-21 40-barreled rocket launcher. Most of these craft are operational
and can be effective in patrol missions, but do not have sophisticated
weapons systems and have no air defenses other than machine guns and
SA-7s, SA-14s, and possibly SA-16s.

Iran ordered 10 68-ton Chinese fast-attack craft or missile patrol boats
in 1992, and at least five of these ships have been delivered. It is not yet
clear whether they are armed with the CS-801 or the more capable CS-
802 missile. There are some indications that such ships may be used for

the off-shore defense of islands like Abu Musa and oil facilities in the Gulf. They seem to have been transferred to the naval branch of the IRGC, and Iran seems to be "fortifying" Abu Musa.[94]

Iran's lack of modern long-range anti-ship missiles, suitable targeting capability, and competitive electronic warfare capability is a major weakness in its war-fighting capability. It seems to have expended virtually all of its Harpoon missiles during the Iran–Iraq war, and its Standards and the rest of its remaining US-supplied naval, air-to-air, and air-to-surface missiles have now aged well beyond their normal life cycle. It does not have a single reliable US-supplied missile in naval or air inventory, and some systems were almost certainly unreliable, which explains its reported interest in upgraded versions of the Chinese CS-802, the Russian SS-N-22, and Russian TU-22M bombers equipped with long-range anti-ship missiles. All of these purchases are ways of compensating for Iran's current lack of advanced sea-based anti-ship missile capability.[95]

Iran has obtained at least 60–100 C-801 or C-802 (YF-6) anti-ship missiles from the Chinese and may be using these to refit its surface fleet as well as to equip some shore-based facilities and the Naval Branch of the IRGC. The C-801 anti-ship missile (also called the Yinji (Hawk) or SY-2 missile) is a solid-fueled missile that began test flights in 1986. It is roughly equivalent to the French Exocet, and can be launched from land, ships, and aircraft. It has a range of approximately 74 kilometers in the surface-to-surface mode and uses J-Band active radar guidance. It has a 512-kg warhead and cruises at an altitude of 20–30 meters. The CS-802 is an upgraded C-801 that was first exhibited in 1988. It has many characteristics similar to the C-801, but uses a turbojet propulsion system with a rocket booster instead of the solid-fueled booster in the C-801.[96]

Iran has also sought to buy more advanced anti-ship missiles from Russia, North Korea, and China, and possibly Chinese-made missile frigates. There is no way to know how many Iranian ships will acquire effective new anti-ship and anti-air missiles, or when any new types of missiles and ships might be delivered. Iran will have to make an order by the late-1990s to keep up its present strength. However, major Western-supplied ships cannot be made fully modern and operational without a comprehensive refit, which can only be done in Western shipyards.[97]

Iran has 5 BH-7 and 7 SRN-6 Hovercraft. About half of these Hovercraft may be operational. They are capable of speeds of up to 60–70 knots, although normal cruising speed is about half that. The BH-7 can carry 53.8 tons of cargo, and the SRN-6 can carry 10 tons. They are lightly armed and vulnerable, but their high speed makes them useful for many reconnaissance and unconventional warfare missions, and they can rapidly land troops on suitable beaches.

Iran's mine-warfare vessels include 2–3 Shahrock-class MSC 292/268 coastal minesweepers (1 used for training in the Caspian Sea). The *Shahrock* and *Karkas* are known to be operational. They are 378-ton sweepers that can be used to lay mines as well as sweep, but their radars and sonars date back to the late 1950s, and are obsolete in sweeping and counter-measure activity against modern mines. Iran has 1–2 Cape-class (Riazzi-class) 239-ton in-shore minesweepers and seems to have converted two of its Iran Ajar-class LSTs for mine-warfare purposes. Many of its small boats and craft can lay mines.

Iran does have significant amphibious assets, including 4 Hengam-class (Larak-class) LST amphibious support ships (2,940 tons loaded), 3 Iran Hormuz-class (South Korean) LSTs (2,014 tons loaded), and 1 Iran Ajar-class LST (2,274 tons loaded). It also has 3 1,400 ton LCTs, 1 250 ton LSL, at least 6 and possibly more than 12 9-ton LCUs, and about 50 small patrol craft. Each Hengam-class ship could carry 227 troops, 9 tanks, and 1 helicopter; each Iran Hormuz-class could carry 140 troops and 8–9 tanks. The Ajar-class could carry 650 tons, but were converted to mine laying. These ships give Iran the capability to deploy 800 to 1,200 troops and 30–50 tanks in an amphibious assault, although it currently lacks the air and surface power to support a landing in a defended area or a movement across the Gulf in the face of significant air/sea defenses. It also would probably gain more from using commercial ferries and roll-on/roll-off ships to move Iranian forces across the Gulf to a friendly port.

Unlike Iraq, Iran has sufficient support ships to sustain "blue water" operations and support an amphibious task force. It has 1 Kharg-class 33,014-ton replenishment ship, 2 Bandar Abbas-class 4,673-ton fleet supply ships and oilers, 1 14,410-ton repair ship, 2 12,000-ton water tankers, 7 1,300-ton Delva-class support ships, 5–6 Hendijan-class support vessels, 2 floating dry-docks and 20 tugs, tenders, and utility craft to help support a large naval or amphibious operation.

The Iranian navy's air capability consists of two to three operational P-3F Orion maritime patrol aircraft out of an original inventory of five. According to reports from the Gulf, none of the surviving P-3Fs had fully operational radars and their crews often used binoculars. It also has up to 12 Sikorsky SH-3D ASW helicopters, 2 RH-53D mine-laying helicopters, and 7 Agusta-Bell AB-212 helicopters equipped with Italian-made Sea Killer missiles. It uses air force AH-1J attack helicopters, equipped with French AS-12 missiles, in naval missions, and adapted Hercules C-130 and Fokker Friendship aircraft for mine-laying and patrol missions.[98]

Iran has also attempted to offset the weakness of its major surface forces by emphasizing unconventional forms of naval warfare. It seems to have purchased or assembled one to three 27-ton midget submarines from North Korea in 1988. These submarines can dive to 300 feet, have a compartment for divers, and can carry 2 side-cargoes of 5 tons or 14 limpet mines. It is unclear, however, whether Iran has been able to operate them successfully.[99]

Iran has also obtained two submarines. It signed an agreement in early 1992 to buy 2–3 Russian Kilo-class submarines from the United Admiralty Sudomeh shipyard in St. Petersburg at a cost of $600 million each. It sent crews for training at a Russian-controlled naval base in Latvia. The first Kilo was transferred to Iran in November 1992, and was commissioned as the Tareq-901. The ship completed its work-up exercise in the Gulf of Oman in the winter of 1992/93. The United States reacted by sending the nuclear attack submarine *Topeka* into the Gulf as a show of strength. The *Topeka* was the first US nuclear submarine deployment into the Gulf, and demonstrated the seriousness with which the United States took Iran's acquisition of the Kilo.[100] The second Kilo was delivered to Iran in late July 1993.[101]

The Kilo is a relatively modern and quiet submarine which was first launched in 1980. The Iranian Kilos are Type 877EKM export versions that are about 10 meters longer than the original Kilos and are equipped with advanced command and control systems. Each Type 877EKM has a teardrop hull coated with anechoic tiles to reduce noise. It displaces approximately 3,076 tons when submerged and 2,325 tons when surfaced. It is 73.2 meters long, 10.0 meters in beam, has a draught of 6.6 meters, and is powered by 3 1,895-HP generator sets, 1 5,900-SHP electric motor and, 1 six-bladed propeller.

Each Kilo has 6 530-mm torpedo tubes in the box, and can carry 12 homing and wire-guided torpedoes or 30–40 mines. Some reports indicate that Iran bought over 1,000 modern Soviet mines with the Kilos, and that the mines were equipped with modern magnetic, acoustic, and pressure sensors. There is a remote anti-aircraft launcher with one preloaded missile in the sail, and Soviet versions have ten SA-16 man-portable surface-to-air missiles stored inside. It has a maximum surface speed of 10 knots, a maximum submerged speed of about 17 knots, a minimum submerged operating depth of about 30 meters, and a maximum diving depth of 300 meters. It has a crew of 45, a surface cruise range of

3,000–6,000 nautical miles and a submerged cruise range of 400 nautical miles – depending on speed and combat conditions.[102]

These submarines potentially give Iran a way of operating in the Gulf and in the Gulf of Oman that reduces its vulnerability to air and surface attack, and its mini-submarines give it the potential ability to hide in the shallow depths and currents near the Straits of Hormuz. Submarines can be used to fire torpedoes or launch mines near ports or against slow-moving tankers long before they can operate effectively against hostile combat ships. Iran has already shown that it can use its helicopters to communicate with its submarines using dipping sonars, and can improve its ability to target the submarines using its shore-based radars and patrol aircraft.[103]

At the same time, many Third World countries have found submarines difficult to operate, and Iran has evidently had to turn to India for help in developing batteries that are reliable in the warm waters of the Gulf. Some reports indicate that these problems may be severe enough to make Iran cancel its order for a third Kilo submarine, although others indicate that Iran has solved its problems and is delaying purchase because of a lack of hard currency.[104]

Iran also faces operational problems in using such submarines. Many areas of the Gulf do not favor submarine operations. The Gulf is about 241,000 km² in area and stretches 990 km from the Shatt al-Arab to the Straits of Hormuz. It is about 340 km wide at is maximum width, and about 225 km wide for most of its length. Its heat patterns disturb surface sonars, but they also disturb submarine sonars, and the advantage seems to be slightly in favor of sophisticated surface ships and maritime patrol aircraft.

The deeper parts of the Gulf are noisy enough to make anti-submarine work (ASW) operations difficult, but large parts of the Gulf – including much of the southern Gulf on a line from Al Jubail across the tip of Qatar to about halfway up the UAE – are under 20 meters deep. The water is deeper on the Iranian side, but the maximum depth is still only 88 meters, which is located about 30 km south of Qeys Island. This maximum depth is so shallow that there is no point in the Gulf deeper than the length of an SN-688 nuclear submarine, and even the keel to tower height of such a submarine is 16 meters. Even smaller coastal submarines have maneuver and bottom-suction problems and cannot hide in thermoclines or take advantage of diving for concealment or self-protection.

The Straits of Hormuz are about 180 km long, but have a minimum width of 39 km, and only the two deep-water channels are suitable for major surface ship or submarine operations. Each of these channels is only about 2 km wide. Further, a limited flow of fresh water and high evaporation make the Gulf extremely saline, and create complex under-water currents in the main channels at the Straits of Hormuz – complicating submarine operations but also complicating detection. There are some areas with considerable noise, but not of a type that masks submarine noise to sophisticated ASW detection systems of the kind operated by the US and the UK. Further, the minimum operating depth of the Kilo is 45 meters, and the limited depth of the area around the Straits can make submarine operations difficult.

Submarines are easier to operate in the Gulf of Oman, which is noisy enough to make ASW operations difficult, but such deployments expose the Kilos to operations by US and British nuclear attack submarines, and it is unlikely that they could survive for any length of time if hunted by a US or British navy air-surface-SSN hunter-killer team. On the other hand, no Arab Gulf navy now has advanced detection gear. Saudi Arabia is seeking to upgrade the limited ASW sensors on its Al Madinah-class frigates. Bahrain and the UAE are considering improved ASW assets, but Kuwait and Oman have so far concentrated on other force improvements.[105]

The effectiveness of the Iranian Kilos thus depends heavily on the degree of Western involvement in any ASW operation. If they did not face the US or the UK, the Iranian Kilos could operate in or near the Gulf with considerable impunity. If they did face US and British forces, they might be able to attack a few tankers or conduct some mining efforts, but are unlikely to survive extended combat. This makes the Kilos a weapon that may be more effective as a threat than in actual combat. Certainly, they have already convinced the Arab Gulf states that they must take Iran more seriously.

Anti-ship missiles, unconventional warfare, and mine warfare offer Iran other ways of compensating for the weakness of its conventional air and naval forces. The naval element of the Islamic Revolutionary Guard Corps in 1994 is sometimes estimated as 20,000 men, but the actual total could be as little as 12,000–15,000. It operated Iran's coastal defense artillery in three to five sites, each armed with artillery and CSS-N-2 (HY-2) Silkworm anti-ship missiles. The naval branch of the IRGC also had training facilities and five bases in the Gulf, including the islands of Sirri, Abu Musa, Al Farisyah, and Larak, and the Halul oil platform. Most of these facilities seem to be relatively small, although sources in the UAE claimed in early

1995 that the IRGC has fortified part of Abu Musa, has increased its troop presence from 150 to several thousand men, has deployed Silkworm anti-ship missiles, and has dug in tanks and artillery to support its fortifications.

While any such estimates are uncertain, and it is not possible to distinguish between the holdings of the navy and the IRGC, Iran had 47 barges and service craft, 2 floating docks, about 100 coastal patrol craft, 35–40 Boghammer 41-foot craft, 35 Boston Whaler 22-foot craft, and large numbers of river craft. The Naval Guards were definitely equipped with the Boghammer Swedish-built fast interceptor craft, as well as small launches equipped with anti-tank guided missiles and at least 30 Zodiak rubber dinghies to carry out rocket, small arms, and recoilless rifle attacks. They were also armed with machine-guns, recoilless rifles, and man and crew-portable anti-tank guided missiles.

The Guards have operated Iran's Chinese-supplied Silkworm surface-to-ship missiles since they were first delivered during the Iran–Iraq war. The Silkworm is designated the HY-2 or Sea Eagle 2 by the People's Republic of China. It is a copy of the Soviet CSS-N-2 "Styx" missile and is made by the China Precision Machinery Import and Export Corporation (CPMIEC). It has an 80–90 kilometer range, and a 450-kilogram warhead. It climbs to 145 meters (600 feet) after launch and then drops to a cruise profile at 30 meters (100 feet). There are two variants. One uses radar active homing at ranges from the target of 8 kilometers (4.5 nautical miles). The other is set to use passive infrared homing and a radar altimeter to keep it at a constant height over the water.[106] Iran fired at least eight Silkworms against targets in Kuwait during the Iran–Iraq war, three of which were hits.

In 1994, the naval branch of the IRGC had three to five operational land-based anti-ship missile units with three to six Silkworm launchers each, and a total of 50–60 missiles. At least some of these units were deployed near Iran's naval base at Chah Bahar, Bandar Abbas, and at Khuestak near the Straits of Hormuz to cover the entrance to the Gulf. These units may be operated with the support of the Iranian navy.

There are reports that Iran is working on a version of the Silkworm with a range of up to 400 kilometers, although it is unclear how it will target such a system without a remote surveillance and targeting platform, or whether it is attempting to build a longer-range anti-ship system or is using this development effort to build a land-attack system. It is also important to note that China is developing two follow-on supersonic missiles with cruise speeds of Mach 2.0 that could directly replace the

HY-2 with little or no warning. The missiles are the HY-3 and C-101 and use ramjet propulsion and active radar terminal homing.[107] The Guards have formed at least one new unit using Chinese-supplied C-801 anti-ship and ship-to-ship missiles, and there are reports that Iran is seeking to acquire much longer-range anti-ship cruise missiles from the People's Republic of China or former Soviet Union.

Some sources have claimed that Iran has already bought eight Soviet-made SS-N-22 "Sunburn" or "Sunburst" anti-ship missile launch units from the Ukraine or Russia, and has deployed them near the Straits of Hormuz, although many US experts doubt that it has any operational holdings of such systems. The "SS-N-22" is a title that actually applies to two different modern long-range supersonic sea-skimming systems — the P-270 Moskit (also called the Kh-15 or 3M80) and P80 or P-100 Zubi/Onika. Although the performance of these systems is not as advanced as some descriptions in the Western press might indicate, the deployed versions have a maximum range of up to 100–120 km. They have relatively sophisticated guidance systems and they are harder to intercept than the CS-801/802 or HY-2 and are more resistant to counter-measures.[108]

The naval branch of the Islamic Revolutionary Guard Corps provides one of the largest unconventional warfare capabilities of any maritime force in the world. It operates many of Iran's fast patrol boats as well as many of its CSS-2 Silkworm anti-ship missiles.[109] It currently operates 32–36 up-engined Boghammer craft (6.4 tons), 35 or more Boston Whaler craft (1.3 tons), and numerous River Roadsted patrol and hovercraft. The Boghammer fast interceptor craft is particularly important to IRGC exercises and operations. It is built by Boghammer Marine of Sweden. It can reach speeds of up to 69 knots, has a range of up to 926 km, and has a 1,000-pound equipment load. The Boghammers and other fast patrol boats are unarmed, but crews can be equipped with heavy machine guns, grenade launchers, and 106-mm recoilless rifles.

The Boghammers, the other smaller fast patrol boats, and light craft like Iran's Zodiacs are extremely difficult to detect by radar in anything but the calmest sea state. Iran bases them at a number of off-shore islands and oil platforms, and they can strike quickly and with limited warning. There are key concentrations at Al Farisyah, Halul Island (an oil platform), Sirri, Abu Musa, and Larak, with a main base at Bandar Abbas. The naval IRGC also has naval artillery divers, and mine-laying units. It had extensive stocks of Scuba equipment and an underwater combat center at Bandar Abbas.[110] Iran is also improving the defenses and port capabilities of its islands in the Gulf, adding covered moorings, more advanced sensors, and better air defenses.

The relative role of the IRGC and regular navy is unclear. While some experts had believed they would be merged with the regular navy when Admiral Ali Shamkhani was made commander of both forces in 1989, they were still an independent force in 1994 with their own island bases and a facility at Noshahr Naval Academy on the Caspian Sea. The naval branch of the IRGC may operate some of Iran's 11 US Mark III-class (41.6 ton) and 6–20 US Swift Mark II-class (22.9 ton), 20 operational PBI type (20.1 ton), 3 Sewart type (9.1 ton), and 12 Enforcer type (4.7 ton) coastal patrol craft.[111] The PBI-type has been sighted with crude installations of unguided Tigercats, which have a maximum range of 6 km, and the IRGC is operating some of the new missile patrol boats Iran has acquired from the PRC.

Both the Iranian navy and the naval branch of the IRGC are expanding their capabilities for mine warfare. While Iran has only a limited number of specialized mine vessels, it can also use small craft, LSTs, Boghammers, helicopters, and submarines to lay mines. It has a wide range of Soviet, Western, and Iranian-made moored and drifting contact mines. It is almost certainly seeking bottom-influence mines as well. If Iran does obtain modern mines, these could be placed in tanker routes, as was done during the Iran–Iraq war, placed near the Straits of Hormuz to deter commercial traffic, or used to threaten warships in narrow zones of operation, or placed in the Gulf of Oman – where sweeping and defensive coverage would be even more difficult than in the Gulf. While such activity would be more a harassment than a war-fighting capability, it could be combined with the use of land-based anti-ship missiles, commando raids, and submarine deployments. This would give Iran considerable leverage in terms of a cumulative threat to tanker and other shipping in the Gulf, and one that would be difficult to target, counter, and destroy.

Iran has significant stocks of US Mark 65 and Soviet AMD 500, AMAG-1, and KRAB anti-ship mines, and may have bought Chinese-made versions of the Soviet mines. It has claimed to be making its own non-magnetic acoustic free-floating and remote-controlled mines, and may have acquired significant stocks of non-magnetic mines, influence mines, and mines with sophisticated timing devices from other countries. Such mines are extremely difficult to detect and sweep, particularly when they are spaced at wide intervals in shipping lanes.

There also are reports that Iran has negotiated with China to buy the EM-52 rocket-propelled mine. The EM-52 rests on the bottom until it senses a ship passing over it, and then uses a rocket to hit the target. It can be set to fire only after it has sensed given numbers of ships passing over it, and some reports claim that it can operate to depths of 110 meters (363 feet). The maximum depth of the Straits of Hormuz is 80 meters (264 feet), although currents are strong enough to displace all but firmly moored mines.[112] Combined with modern submarine-laid mines and anti-ship missile systems like the CS-801/802, HY-2, and SS-N-22, the EM-52 would give Iran considerable capability to harass Gulf shipping and even the potential capability to close the Gulf until US naval and air power could clear the mines and destroy the missile launchers and submarines.

Mines can be used throughout the Gulf and in parts of the Gulf of Oman. The southern Gulf states may develop effective mine-sweeping capabilities to sweep concentrated fields in limited areas, but Iran could use such mines throughout the Gulf, and tanker companies and captains are unlikely to take their ships into harm's way in the face of even limited risks. It is also difficult for even the most advanced Western mine counter-measure systems to detect and sweep modern mines. The US ships damaged by mines during the Gulf war were all operating in waters that had supposedly been swept, and even the best trained and equipped minesweeping team has serious problems in sweeping non-magnetic mines, large areas with loose mines, and bottom mines or other mines which are timed to activate only after several ships have passed or at fixed intervals.

These new forms of sea power offer Iran the ability to threaten tacitly and actively the flow of oil through the Gulf and the economic life blood of Iran and its Gulf Arab neighbors. While its surface force cannot hope to challenge the power of the US Navy, it can use systems like anti-ship missiles, mines, and submarines to at least threaten US freedom of action and ability to deploy vulnerable high-value targets like carriers in Gulf waters. It can also take advantage of the long shipping routes through the Gulf and its ability to launch naval or air strikes from positions along the entire length of the Gulf or in the Gulf of Oman. While strategists sometimes focus on "closing the Straits," a bottle does not have to be broken at the neck, and low-level mine and unconventional warfare strikes on shipping that are designed to harass and intimidate may allow Iran to achieve its objectives much more safely than escalating to all-out attacks on the flow of oil.

As for power projection, Iran cannot project power by land without crossing Iraq, but amphibious operations again allow it to pose a tacit or active threat to the southern Gulf states, particularly small states like

Bahrain and Qatar. At present, the Iranian navy and IRGC are only able to conduct small operations at night or when they achieve total surprise. If Iran were to strike in forces across the Gulf, the Iranian navy and naval Guards would need effective air cover, a stronger surface fleet, and better night vision and targeting systems for their small craft, additional amphibious ships, and hovercraft. Large-scale assaults would also require Iran to use commercial ships with roll-on/roll-off capability. At the same time, Iran can already use small elements of its naval forces to covertly deploy unconventional warfare forces, to supply arms to radical movements in the Gulf, seize undefended islands, and threaten or attack offshore oil operations, ports, and desalinization facilities.

Much will depend on the extent to which Iran can rebuild the technical base for its navy and create an effective war-fighting capability. To do this, it will need adequate training, anti-ship missiles that are competitive with those of Arab Gulf nations, US and British naval forces, new torpedoes, advanced mines – like bottom and moored influence and smart mines – and better mine-laying capability. Iran will need to modernize and expand the coverage of its shore-based missiles, and deploy them in enough locations and in mobile enough form to make them more survivable. Iran badly needs improved C^3I/BM and electronic warfare systems, advanced land-based and surface ship-based sensor systems, the rebuilding and modernization of its P-3s or the purchase of a replacement, and new or modified air defense and anti-ship missiles and suitable electronics for its surface forces. It also needs better or modified naval helicopters and advanced exercise and training technology.

Iran's Paramilitary Forces

The current capabilities of Iran's paramilitary forces are difficult to determine. The Islamic Revolutionary Guards Corp has previously been discussed as a key component of Iran's regular combat forces, and it seems more accurate to discuss them in this way than to treat them as paramilitary forces. This leaves two main paramilitary forces: the Basijj and the national security forces.

The Basijj (Mobilization of the Oppressed) is a popular reserve force that is controlled by the Islamic Revolutionary Guard Corps and which consists largely of youths, men who have completed military service, and the elderly. During the Iran–Iraq war, the Basijj was organized into poorly trained and equipped infantry units which were often used in Iran's human wave assaults. Since the war, the Basijj has been restructured into a pool that can be called up in wartime, consisting of up to 500 battalions with about 300–350 men each, which are composed or three companies or four platoons plus support.

The primary peacetime mission of the Basijj now seems to be internal security, although it is used for civil projects or activities where the regime seeks to mobilize youth for a single task or for propaganda purposes. Organized Basijj units are equipped with small arms and can act as a force to secure rear areas or deal with ethnic forces or popular riots. They also, however, act as a potential way of expanding the IRGC in time of crisis and war. There is also a large home guard force which serves some of the purposes of the Basijj, but which is a static militia force tied to local defense missions.

Iran claimed to have integrated many of its other internal security forces in 1991. They are now said to be part of the Ministry of the Interior, and some sources indicate that they have a total of about 45,000 men – and include the former Gendarmerie, other police elements, and border guards. The border guards are organized as a paramilitary police force with wheeled armored vehicles, light patrol aircraft (Cessna 185/ 310 and AB-205 and AB-206s), coastal patrol craft, and harbor patrol craft. They keep order throughout the rural areas of Iran and deal with ethnic and tribal security problems, and they have a regional and regimental organization, but no real military training and equipment other than automatic weapons, mortars, and light anti-tank weapons. A new Tribal Guards force is being formed which may either be part of the Gendarmerie or the IRGC.[113]

These paramilitary forces seem unlikely to offer Iran much advantage in wars against its neighbors. Human wave attacks have failed in the past and can only be used in border areas. Iran lacks the equipment to waste on untrained and low quality forces in other combat roles. They can, however, provide rear-area security and a manpower pool to draw upon in an extended conflict. They offer Iran improved internal security and should be adequate to deal with most ethnic threats. The best trained forces of the Iraqi-backed People's Mujahedin are a possible exception.

Iran's intelligence forces pose a more serious threat. In addition to its main intelligence service – the Vevak – other elements operate with the Foreign Ministry, IRGC, and the Iranian armed forces. Iran supports other states and extremist movements in a number of unconventional warfare and terrorist roles, and there is considerable evidence that they have done so with the direct knowledge of Iran's foreign minister and senior leadership.[114]

Some of these activities, however, must be kept in careful perspective. The Iranian government has been involved in a murderous international war of assassination and counter-assassination with the Rajavi family and the People's Mujahedin since the early 1980s. This war, however, was started by the radical Marxist People's Mujahedin – which began a long series of assassination attempts when Khomeini rejected its ideology and attempts to change Iran's economic system. The People's Mujahedin has since continued this war from outside Iran and has become little more than an Iraqi front.[115] As a result, Iranian attacks on members of the People's Mujahedin, and Iran's air and Scud attacks on its camps in Iran, should be seen as part of a two-sided clandestine war and not as terrorism.[116]

Iran also continues ruthlessly to suppress legitimate political opposition, and increasingly arrests protesters and opposition spokesmen as drug sellers and users in an attempt to discredit them and defuse foreign charges of human rights abuses.[117] While the Iranian government reported in 1994 that 52,000 out of 100,000 people in Iranian prisons had been convicted on drugs charges, thousands of these prisoners had actually been arrested for political, religious, and ethnic reasons.[118] The Majlis also expanded the role of the Vevak in suppressing domestic political opposition in November 1994.[119] The supposed moderates in Iran's Foreign Ministry also recalled Iran's ambassador to Norway in January 1995 for taking a flexible stand on Iran's call for the execution of Salman Rushdie.[120]

Iran has strongly objected to both the PLO and Jordan's peace with Israel and the new contacts between moderate Arab states, like Morocco and Oman, with Israel. It has also supported acts of terrorism against Israel and the peace process, which may be a natural result of its ideology but poses a clear threat to regional peace and security. They also cannot be treated simply as "rogue" operations of the IRGC. While the full chain of events is not yet clear, senior officials in the Iranian Foreign Ministry seem to have directly supported acts of terrorism against Israelis, and various car bombings and attacks on Israeli embassies. There are also indicators that they have funded anti-peace elements within the PLO in an effort to divide them from Arafat.[121] While the Iranian government could not do so without Syrian tolerance and support, it plays an important role in supporting the Hizbollah and various armed extremist groups in Southern Lebanon. It has provided funds and other support to military elements of Hamas and may have helped train Hamas action teams in camps in Lebanon and/or the Sudan.

While Egypt and Algeria have exaggerated the role of Iran in backing the hardline Islamic extremist movements in these countries, Iran almost certainly does provide funds, training, and arms for such movements throughout the world. It also plays a role in influencing the civil war in Afghanistan and Kurdish affairs in Iraq, and it supports armed Shi'ite rebel groups in Iraq, unconventional warfare training in the Sudan, and the Kurdish and Islamic extremist movements in Turkey. The Iranian National Security Council seems to have directly approved and controlled at least some of these operations, and the Council includes the Ayatollah Ali Khamene'i and President Rafsanjani as well as Fallahian.[122]

These actions by the Vevak, IRGC, and other elements of Iran's security services and armed forces present a low-level threat to Iran's neighbors and to any power projecting armed forces into the region and can escalate at any time. The United States, for example, lost more men in the Marine barracks bombing in Lebanon than it lost in combat during the entire Gulf war, and these losses were a powerful factor in the precipitous US withdrawal from Lebanon. While such a withdrawal would never have taken place if the United States had the kind of clear strategic interests it does in the Gulf, there is no question that Iran played a role in this bombing and that similar acts of unconventional warfare or terrorism may occur in the future.

Iran and Weapons of Mass Destruction

Iran has long sought weapons of mass destruction and the means to deliver them, although its efforts cannot he compared in scale to those of Iraq. Iran has lacked the resources to finance a massive world-wide purchasing effort, and its revolutionary turmoil has limited its access to foreign technology and the efficiency of its industrial base. Iran has, however, sought long-range missiles, produced chemical weapons, developed biological weapons, and made efforts to acquire nuclear weapons.

Given the limitations of Iran's conventional forces, these efforts to acquire weapons of mass destruction are probably the most threatening aspect of Iran's present and future military capabilities. Once again, however, it is necessary to be cautious about the current threat. Although Iran already has a significant capability to wage chemical warfare, this capability is not large or lethal enough to pose a major threat to the southern Gulf if the southern Gulf states have the support of US forces.

Iran faces major problems in obtaining fissile material and in "weaponization" – loading a biological, chemical, or nuclear device into a bomb or warhead that will work safely, effectively, and reliably. Regardless of the theoretical significance of a device, the real threat is how well it can actually perform in combat. Delivery systems present additional difficulties. Making chemical warheads work is relatively easy at line-of-sight ranges. Artillery or multiple rocket launchers can fire enough of an agent to be effective even if the warhead design is poor.

Firing weapons at beyond-visual-range (BVR) targets, however, requires a sophisticated reconnaissance and intelligence system and effective warheads to produce highly lethal effects. Long-range attacks with aircraft and cruise missiles present challenges in terms of developing proven bomb and warhead designs that ensure safety, reliability, accurate targeting and navigation, and the proper dissemination of biological and chemical agents, and height of burst and weather conditions for the use of biological, chemical, and nuclear weapons. Ballistic missiles present more serious problems. Although they have the advantage that they are harder to defend against than aircraft, they also involve major challenges in terms of operational reliability, accuracy, and targeting. It is extremely difficult to disseminate biological and chemical agents effectively within the narrow time window allowed by the closing velocity of a ballistic missile, and the weapons package necessary to do so can use up much of the useful payload of such a missile.

In short, weaponization of sophisticated weapons of mass destruction like nuclear devices and biochemical devices involves major design and manufacturing difficulties. Nuclear weapons present challenges in weight reduction and in ensuring precisely the right height of burst to achieve the desired effect. The cost and scarcity of nuclear fissile material creates challenges in terms of the risk that a warhead package will fail to explode or a missile will not hit its intended target. Biological weapons require safe storage of dry or wet agents and high-technology fuses and agent dissemination systems. Safety is also a major issue, particularly with biological and nuclear devices.

The risk of accidents or misfires on friendly territory is very real. The technology to ensure safety and arming of a warhead only after a missile has performed properly on launch is complex and involves further weight penalties. No technology currently exists that can reliably disarm a missile warhead by remote command, or on a fail-safe basis, once a missile has completed its initial boost phase and apogee.

Another major uncertainty, which may be of critical importance to any estimate of the future war-fighting capability of Iran and Iraq, is the real-world operational lethality of advanced chemical weapons, toxins, and biological agents. Although experts have made the broad outlines of the debate public, it is impossible to discuss the details of these uncertainties within the limits posed by unclassified data.

It is clear, however, that the threat posed by Iran's weapons of mass destruction would be more important if Iran acquired more effective chemical weapons, and would be far more important if it acquired highly lethal biological agents, or even a few nuclear devices. Weapons of mass destruction produce unpredictable changes in the perceptions of both the attacker and defender in terms of political decisions and war fighting. While much of the discussion of such weapons focuses on casualty and physical damage effects, they have major psychological, political, and tactical effects that may prove to be more important than lethality in a given contingency. Relative willingness to take risks and deal with the real-world outcome of uncertainty becomes critical. So does the relative value assigned to human life, to the predictability of weapons effects and the nature of retaliation, and to the protection of troops, civilians, and potential target areas.

Weapons of mass destruction can also radically change crisis behavior, perceptions of the risks of escalation, acceptance of new levels of conflict, and acceptance of given kinds of conflict termination. They can do so in ways where decision-makers and military commanders at best have limited understanding of the technical capabilities and effectiveness of the weapons involved. They affect the transparency and predictability of war since neither Iran nor Iraq have anything approaching the intelligence assets to obtain near-real time data on the actual impact of such weapons, and there simply are too few empirical data to predict either short-term or long-term damage effects.

Iran's Long-Range Missile Programs

Iran has steadily improved its long-range missile forces since the beginning of the Iran–Iraq war.[123] It has succeeded in producing its own version of a Chinese Type-83 artillery rocket called the Oghab in a factory built with Chinese help and using Chinese tools, technology, and some Chinese parts.[124] The Oghab, however, has a range of only 40 km, may have a chemical warhead, and lacks the range and/or accuracy to hit anything smaller than large area targets like assembly areas and cities. It has a 70–300 kg warhead and an operational CEP that has proved to be in excess of 1,000 meters at maximum range.[125] Further, Iran has no way to accurately target the Oghab or any other long-range missile against mobile or point targets over long ranges other than a limited ability to use RPVs.[126]

Iran has also used Chinese help to produce a family of missiles called the "Nazeat," of which the longest range system is the Iran-130. The full details of this system remain unclear, but it seems to use commercially available components, a solid-fuel rocket, and a simple inertial guidance system to reach ranges of about 90–120 km. It is 355 mm in diameter, 5.9 meters long, weighs 950 kg, has a 150-kg warhead, and may also have a chemical warhead. It has poor reliability and accuracy.[127]

Since the end of the Iran–Iraq war, Iran has exhibited another large rocket called the Shahin 2. It has a 355-mm diameter, but is only 3.87 meters long and weighs only 580 kg. It evidently can be equipped with three types of warheads: a 180-kg high explosive warhead, a warhead using high explosive submunitions, and a warhead that uses chemical weapons. Both the Nazeat and Shahin are now in service with the regular Iranian armed forces in limited numbers, but such systems are little more than extended range artillery.

Iran's more capable missiles are now all imported. They consist of the Scud B, North Korean variants of the Scud, and the Chinese CSS-8. Iran's primary holdings consist of the Soviet-designed Scud B (17E) guided missile. Iran has had these missiles since the early 1980s, and their basic design is so old that it is derived from the German V-2. The Scud B has a maximum range of 180–190 miles (290–310 km) with its normal conventional payload and a maximum flight time of 325 seconds.[128] The missile is 11.25 meters long, is 85 cm in diameter, weighs 6,300 kg, and has a warhead weighing about 1,000 kg, of which 800 kg are high explosive and 200 are the warhead structure and fusing system.[129] It has a single-stage storable liquid rocket engine and is usually deployed on the MAZ-543 8-wheel transporter-erector-launcher (TEL). It has a strap-down inertial guidance using three gyros to correct its ballistic trajectory, and uses internal graphite jet vane steering. It has a warhead that detaches from the missile body during the final fall towards target. This provides added stability and allows the warhead to hit at a velocity above Mach 1.5.[130]

Iran seems to have bought an estimated 200–300 Scud Bs from North Korea between 1987 and 1992, and Israeli experts estimated that it had at least 250–300 Scud missiles and at least 8–15 launchers on hand in 1994, although some US experts believe the total is much smaller. All of these Scuds have been obtained from other countries, and Iranian claims of being able to actually manufacture Scuds are false. Iran can assemble missile systems manufactured by other countries, but it has failed to demonstrate any capability to produce whole missiles or major assemblies like the booster.[131]

Iran has made a major effort to obtain longer-range and more accurate missiles since the end of the Iran–Iraq war, almost certainly for the purpose of delivering WMDs. It has obtained some support from the PRC in supplying new missiles and in helping Iran to develop its own missile technology and production capabilities. Iran bought 150–200 CSS-8 missiles and 25–30 launchers from the PRC in 1989. The CSS-8 has a range of approximately 65 miles (150 km). While Iran has negotiated with the Chinese to buy "M-9" and "M-11" missiles – or related assembly and production technology – there is no evidence of such transfers. China also agreed on 4 October 1994 that it would observe the limits imposed by the Missile Technology Control Regime and would not transfer such missiles or technology to any other state.[132]

Iran has succeeded, however, in acquiring a more modern and longer-range North Korean missile system referred to as a "Scud C." A senior North Korean delegation traveled to Tehran to close the deal on 29 November 1990, and met with Mohsen Reza'i, the commander of the IRGC. Iran either bought the missile then or placed its order shortly thereafter. North Korea then exported the missile through its Lyongaksan Import Corporation. North Korea seems to have completed development of this missile in 1987, after obtaining technical support from the PRC. While the missile is sometimes called an improved Scud, it seems to differ substantially in detail from the original Soviet Scud B and seems to be based more on the Chinese-made DF-61 than to be a direct copy of Soviet technology. Iran now seems to have 5–10 launchers for this system with several missiles each. These missiles have a range of around 310 miles (500 km), a payload of at least 500 kg, and relatively good accuracy and reliability. This range would give Iran the ability to strike all the targets on the southern coast of the Gulf. It would allow it to cover all of the populated areas in Iraq. It could reach into part of eastern Syria, into the eastern third of Turkey, and cover targets in the border area of the former Soviet Union, western Afghanistan, and western Pakistan.

The sale of this missile could make a significant change in Iranian ability to deliver WMDs because North Korea normally deploys the missile with a chemical warhead and may have tested biological warheads as well. Neither Russia nor the PRC seem to have transferred the warhead technology for biological and chemical weapons to Iran or Iraq when they sold the Scud missile and CSS-8. North Korea may have sold Iran such technology. If it did so, Iran would be able to deploy far more effective warheads than Iraq had at the time of the Gulf war, and such a technology transfer would save Iran years of development and testing work in obtaining highly lethal biological and chemical warheads.

Iran imported some of these North Korean missile assemblies using its B-747s and seems to have used ships to import others. It probably had more than 60 of the longer-range North Korean missiles by 1995, although one source reports 170, and Iran seems to have set a goal of several hundred such missiles by the late 1990s.[133] Iran may also have begun to test its new North Korean missiles, firing from a mobile launcher at a test site near Qum about 310 miles (500 km) to a target area south of Shahroud. There are also reports that units equipped with such missiles have been deployed as part of Iranian exercises like the Saeqe-3 (Thunderbolt 3) exercise in late October 1993.[134]

Some experts feel that Iran, Syria, and possibly Pakistan are cooperating to acquire and produce a longer-range North Korean missile called the No-Dong 1. This missile is a single-stage liquid-fueled missile, with a range of up to 1,000 km (620 miles) and a 1,200 to 1,750-pound warhead. It is about 15 meters long – four meters longer than the Scud B. It has an estimated CEP of 700 meters at maximum range versus 900 meters for the Scud B. It seems to be transportable on a copy of the MAZ-543P TEL, although some experts question this. It has an estimated terminal velocity of Mach 3.5, versus 2.5 for the Scud B, which presents added problems for tactical missile defense.

The No-Dong missile now seems to be nearing final development in North Korea, possibly with substantial aid from military industries in the PRC. It underwent flight tests at ranges of 310 miles (500 km) on 29 May 1993. A number of experts believe that Syria and Iran will buy major assembly and production facilities for the No-Dong 1 as well as missiles or missile parts. Iran seems to be planning to acquire at least 150 such missiles, although some reports have surfaced that it is having financing problems in obtaining North Korean support.[135]

There are reports that Iran has at least two rocket and missile assembly plants, a missile test range and monitoring complex, and a wide range of smaller design and refit facilities.[136] The largest plant is said to be a North Korean-built plant near Isfahan. This is the center of much of Iran's advanced defense industry, including plants for munitions, tank overhaul, and helicopter and fixed-wing aircraft maintenance. Some reports say that the complex can produce liquid fuels and missile parts from a local steel mill. A second plant is said to be located 175 km east of Tehran, near Semnan. Some sources indicate this plant is Chinese-built and began rocket production as early as 1987. It is supposed to be able to build 600–1,000 Oghab rockets per year if Iran can import key ingredients for solid-fuel motors like ammonium perchlorate. It is also supposed to produce the Iran-130. Another plant may exist near Bandar Abbas for the assembly of the Silkworm. China is said to have built the plant in 1987, and to be helping the naval branch of the Guards modify the Silkworm to extend its range to 400 km.

It is far from clear whether Iran's plants have the ability to rapidly assemble large numbers of systems and whether Iran has the capability to build whole missiles, produce major components, or create and produce indigenous designs. The main Iranian test range is said to be further east, near Shahroud, along the Teheran–Mashhad railway. A telemetry station is supposed to be 350 km to the south at Taba, along the Mashhad–Isfahan road. All of these facilities are said to be under the control of the Islamic Revolutionary Guard Corps.

Iran may also be interested in a developmental North Korean IRBM called the Tapeo Dong 1 or Tapeo Dong 2, which was detected by US intelligence in early 1994. This missile has an estimated maximum range of 1,000–1,200 miles (2,000 km). It is a liquid-fueled missile, but seems to have two stages. Unlike the No-Dong, it must be carried to a site in stages and then assembled at a fixed site. The No-Dong transporter may be able to carry both stages of the Tapeo Dong, but some experts feel that a special transporter is needed for the first stage of the Tapeo Dong.[137]

It is also possible that Iran is developing a cruise missile with Chinese and other foreign assistance. While Iran has no capability to develop and deploy a missile as sophisticated as the Tomahawk (TLAM) missile, US studies have indicated that Third World nations like Iran and Iraq may be able to build a cruise missile about half the size of a small fighter aircraft and with a payload of about 500 kg by 2000 to 2005. The technology for fusing and CBW and cluster warheads would be within Iran's grasp. Navigation systems and jet engines would be a major potential problem.

Current inertial navigation systems (INS) would introduce errors of at least several kilometers at ranges of 1,000 km, and there would be a severe risk of total guidance failure – probably exceeding two-thirds of the missiles fired. A differential global positioning system (GPS) integrated with the inertial navigation system (INS) and a radar altimeter, however, might produce an accuracy as good as 15 meters. Some existing remotely piloted vehicles (RPVs), such as the South African Skua, claim such performance. Commercial technology is becoming available for differential GPS guidance with accuracies of 2 to 5 meters.

There are commercially available reciprocating and gas turbine engines that Iran could adapt for use in a cruise missile, although finding a reliable and efficient turbofan engine for a specific design application might be difficult. An extremely efficient engine would have to be matched to a specific airframe. It is doubtful that Iran could design and build such an engine, but over twenty other countries have most of the needed design and manufacturing skills. Airframe-engine-warhead integration and testing would be challenging and might be beyond Iran's manufacturing skills. However, it is inherently easier to integrate and test a cruise missile than a long-range ballistic missile. Further, such developments would be far less detectable than developing a ballistic system if the program used coded or low-altitude directional telemetry.[138]

Such cruise missile systems could reach a wide range of targets. A system deployed in Iran's border areas, with only a 500-km range, could cover most of Iraq, eastern Turkey, all of Kuwait, the Gulf coast of Saudi Arabia, Bahrain and most of Qatar, the northern UAE, and northern Oman. A system with a 1,200-km range could reach Israel, the eastern two-thirds of Turkey, most of Saudi Arabia, and all of the other southern Gulf states including Oman. Such a system could also be programmed to avoid major air defense concentrations at a sacrifice of about 20 percent of its range.

Even without new ballistic or cruise missile systems, Iran now has the capability to launch significant missile attacks against Iraq and to hit coastal area targets in much of the southern Gulf. It may well be able to use chemical warheads. The volume of such attacks is likely to be very similar to those Iraq launched during the Gulf war, or against Iran during the "war of the cities." The lethality would depend on the warhead, and much depends on the weaponization technology Iran has received from North Korea and/or the PRC. Iran does, however, lack sophisticated long-range targeting capability and missile systems with the accuracy to attack anything other than area targets. It can pose a major threat in terms of intimidation and popular fear using conventional warheads, but it can use missiles only to destroy military targets, paralyze war-fighting capabilities, or to destroy particular buildings and facilities, if it has effective chemical and biological warheads.

Iran's missiles would be vulnerable to point defense by the improved Patriot, and large-scale attacks could probably be broken up by offensive attacks against the launch facilities by US air power. The United States currently, however, has no way to prevent Iran from confronting it with the same "Scud hunt" problems it had during the Gulf war: It would be almost impossible to hunt out and destroy enough of Iran's missile capabilities to halt all attacks. The United States might well be forced into deterring Iranian missile strikes by escalating its attacks on other high-value Iranian targets.[139]

Iranian Chemical Weapons

Both Iran and Iraq have signed the Geneva Protocols of 1925, prohibiting the use of poison gas.[140] Both nations have also signed the Biological Warfare Convention of 1972, banning the development, production, and deployment or stockpiling of biological weapons.[141] Nevertheless, Iran began a crash effort to produce chemical weapons in the early 1980s in response to Iraq's use of chemical weapons against Iran. In fact, Rafsanjani once described chemical weapons as follows:

> Chemical and biological weapons are poor man's atomic bombs and can easily be produced. We should at least consider them for our defense. Although the use of such weapons is inhuman, the war taught us that international laws are only scraps of paper.[142]

The Islamic Revolutionary Guard Corps, with support from the Ministry of Defense, was put in charge of developing offensive chemical agents, and Iran has covertly obtained substantial outside support. It took several years to get this support and the necessary feedstocks to produce such weapons. While Iran did not make extensive use of chemical weapons during the Iran—Iraq war, it had moderate-scale chemical weapons plants in operation at Damghan and Parchin by March 1988, and may have begun to test-fire Scuds with chemical warheads. Iran produced sulfur mustard gas and blood agents like hydrogen cyanide, phosgene gas, and/or chlorine gas.[143] These gas agents have been loaded into bombs and artillery shells and were used sporadically against Iraq in 1987 and 1988.[144] Iran did not succeed in producing nerve gas during the Iran—Iraq war, but it may have started to produce nerve agents like Sarin and Tabun in the early 1990s.

The exact status of Iran's current chemical war-fighting capabilities is unknown, but it is clear that it has established a significant chemical weapons production capability of 25 to 100 tons per year, including mustard gas and dusty mustard gas, phosgene gas, and blood agents like cyanogen chloride or one of the cyanides.[145] While Iran's chemical warheads for its missiles are probably still of limited sophistication, it has had time to develop usable artillery, rocket warheads, and bombs. It probably has storable binary weapons, or will soon introduce them into inventory, and there are recent indicators it is seeking to buy equipment to support its forces in conducting nerve gas warfare.[146] This gives Iran a significant capability to conduct a chemical war near its borders, to launch limited long-range air raids using chemical bombs, and to use chemical weapons in unconventional warfare.

Iranian chemical warfare capabilities will grow steadily with time, and they will not be subject to the limitations Iraq faces because of UN inspection and sanctions. Iran may have little practical experience in large-scale chemical operations, but chemical weapons do give it new capabilities to intimidate its Gulf Arab neighbors and deter the West. Further, chemical weapons do not have to be delivered by missiles or aircraft. As is the case with biological weapons, devices can be smuggled into a target area and can be used as terrorist or unconventional warfare weapons. Agents can be dispersed by man-portable devices or even grenades and delivered into any building with central air-conditioning. A passenger airliner could be used to fly a line and disperse agents as an aerosol. Chemical devices could be smuggled in and detonated in commuter centers, stadiums, or other crowded areas.

Iran will, however, face serious problems in making any attributable offensive use of chemical weapons. If it uses chemical weapons, it could destabilize and/or escalate a conflict in ways in which it would face massive conventional retaliation. If Iran were to have any catastrophic success in attacking civilian targets or Western forces in the Gulf region, this raises the possibility of theater nuclear retaliation.

Iranian Biological Weapons

Iran seems to have begun developing biological weapons as early as 1982.[147] Reports surfaced that it was working on the production of mycotoxins – a relatively simple biological agent that requires only limited laboratory facilities.[148] US intelligence sources reported in August 1989 that Iran was trying to buy two new strains of fungus from Canada and the Netherlands that can be used to produce mycotoxins. German sources indicated that Iran had successfully purchased such cultures several years earlier.[149] The Imam Reza Medical Center at Mashhad Medical Sciences University and the Iranian Research Organization for Science and Technology were identified as the end users for this purchasing effort, but it is likely that the true end user was an Iranian government agency specializing in biological warfare.

Many experts now believe the Iranian biological weapons effort is under the control of the IRGC, who are known to have tried to purchase suitable production equipment for such weapons. It is clear that Iran conducted covert operations in Germany and Switzerland linked to biological weapons research and production in the 1990s. It has also conducted extensive research on more lethal active agents like anthrax, foot and mouth disease, and on biotoxins, and has repeatedly approached various European firms for the equipment and technology necessary to work with these diseases and toxins.

Little is known about the exact details of Iran's effort to weaponize and produce such weapons. Yet even the possibility that it has biological weapons gives it an enhanced capability to deter and intimidate the southern Gulf and the West. Iran could make overt use of biological weapons in much the same way it could use chemical weapons, but it also has incentives to make covert use of biological weapons since they are particularly well suited to unconventional warfare or "terrorism."[150] This makes it far harder to determine the actual nature of Iran's war-fighting capabilities than is the case with chemical and nuclear weapons. It does seem likely, however, that it will be able to create a significant production capability for storable encapsulated biological agents by the year 2000.

Iran may encounter continuing difficulties in developing effective ballistic missile warheads using biological agents, but it should be able to meet the technical challenges in improving its targeting and finding effective ways to disperse agents from cruise missile warheads and bombs. It may already have the technology to disperse agents like anthrax over a wide area by spreading them from a ship moving along a coast, or out of a large container smuggled into a city or industrial complex.

It is impossible to do more than guess at Iran's war-fighting doctrine for using biological weapons. Its leadership and military planners may well go on acquiring such weapons without making specific plans to use them. As for deterrence, Iran would be subject to the same threat of retaliation as with chemical weapons, and the level of conflict would be more intense and make such retaliation even more likely.

Highly effective biological weapons can also be as lethal as small nuclear weapons. The results of a recent study by the US Office of Technology Assessment that compared the impact of a 12.5-kiloton nuclear weapon dropped in the center of Washington with the minimum and maximum effect of using a single aircraft to deliver 300 kg of Sarin and 30 kg of anthrax spores indicates that the nuclear weapon would cover 7.8 km² and produce prompt kills of 23,000–80,000; the nerve gas would cover

0.22 km² and kill 60–200; and the anthrax spores would cover 10 km² and kill 3,000 to 10,000. Such calculations are dependent on scenario, time of day, and weather, and assume a sophisticated bomb or missile warhead. Such data are, however, a warning of the potential risks posed by biological weapons.[151]

Iranian Nuclear Weapons

During the Iran–Iraq war, the new government of Iran revitalized the nuclear weapons program that had originally begun under the Shah.[152] Since that time, it has engaged in many of the weapons design and fuel cycle activities necessary to build a nuclear weapon. However, Iran has never been able to fund the kind of massive program that Iraq established, and has found it difficult to obtain nuclear technology.

Iran's nuclear weapons efforts accelerated in the late 1980s. There are significant uranium deposits (at least 5,000 tons) in the Shagand region of Iran's Yazd Province.[153] Iran announced in 1987 that it had plans to set up a yellow cake (semi-refined uranium ore) plant in Yazd Province, and this facility was under construction by 1989.[154] It may have begun to build a uranium processing or enrichment facility at Pilcaniyeu. It may have opened a new uranium ore processing plant close to its Shagand uranium mine in March 1990, and it seems to have extended its search for uranium ore into three additional areas.[155]

Iran has also expanded its research efforts and has aggressively sought foreign technology and cooperation. On 7 February 1990, the speaker of the Majlis publicly toured the Iranian Atomic Energy Organization and opened the new Jabir Ibn al Hayyan laboratory to train Iranian nuclear technicians.[156] Reports surfaced later that Iran had at least 200 scientists and a workforce of about 2,000 working on nuclear research. Pakistan signed a nuclear cooperation agreement with Iran in 1987. Specialists from Iran's Atomic Energy Organization began to train in Pakistan, and Dr. Abdul Kadr Khan, who has directed much of Pakistan's effort to develop nuclear weapons material, visited Tehran and Bushehr in February 1986, and January 1987.[157]

Iran has strengthened its nuclear research ties to the PRC. The two countries signed a formal nuclear research cooperation agreement in 1990, but such cooperation actually began as early as 1985 – after Iran had suffered its first major chemical attacks from Iraq and began to give its nuclear effort high priority. Iranian nuclear engineers seem to have begun training in China, and China seems to have transferred nuclear research technology for reactor construction and other projects to an Iranian facility at Isfahan.[158]

Iran signed an agreement to build a small 27-kilowatt research reactor at Iran's nuclear weapons research facility at Isfahan with China's Commission on Science, Technology, and Industry for National Defense on 21 January 1991. This reactor was evidently to be plutonium-fueled, although its transfer was later blocked by US pressure on China.[159] On 4 November 1991, China stated that it had signed commercial cooperation agreements with Iran in 1989 and 1991, and that it would transfer an electromagnetic isotope separator (Calutron) and a smaller nuclear reactor for "peaceful" and commercial" purposes.[160]

Iran has sought much larger reactors from China. On 10 September 1992, Rafsanjani is reported to have finished negotiations to buy one or two 300–330 megawatt reactors from the People's Republic of China during his visit to Beijing. The sale of one such reactor was announced by Iran's minister of defense during the visit, and this led to immediate US protests to the PRC. The reactor sale seems to have been deferred as a result, but on 4 July 1994, Iran and the PRC announced they had signed an agreement for the PRC to build a 300-megawatt reactor near Tehran.[161]

Iran has conducted similar negotiations with Russia. It first sought nuclear reactors from Russia in the mid-1980s, and reports surfaced that Russia had signed a contract to sell two nuclear reactors to Iran in the late 1980s – although the existence of any such contracts was not made public. Iran formally announced on 20 November 1994, however, that Russia had agreed to an $800 million contract to fund the first stage of a program to complete the reactor at Bushehr that German companies had begun at the time of the Shah. Many US experts believe that Iran has aggressively sought to buy highly enriched and/or fissile material from the former Soviet Union as well as the services of Soviet nuclear weapons designers.[162]

The size and nature of Iran's nuclear weapons facilities is unclear. The People's Mujahedin, an anti-regime group, has claimed that Iran has succeeded in building a far more important mix of major nuclear weapons facilities. It has reported that these facilities include a weapons site called Ma'allem Kelayah, near Qazvin on the Caspian Sea. This is said to be an IRGC-run facility established in 1987, which has involved an Iranian investment of $300 million. This site was supposed to house the 10-megawatt reactor Iran tried to buy from India.

The People's Mujahedin has also claimed that the two Soviet reactors were to be installed at a large site at Gorgan on the Caspian Sea under the direction of Russian physicists. It has claimed that the PRC has provided uranium enrichment equipment and technicians for the site at Darkhouin, where Iran once planned to build a French reactor; that a nuclear reactor was being constructed at Karaj; and that another nuclear weapons facility exists in the south central part of Iran near the Iraqi border. It has claimed that the ammonia and urea plant that the British firm of M. W. Kellog was building at Borujerd, in Khorassan province near the border with Turkistan, might be adapted to produce heavy water. In addition, the People's Mujahedin has claimed that Amir Kabar Technical University, the Atomic Energy Organization of Iran, Dor Argham Ltd., the Education and Research Institute, GAM Iranian Communications, Ghoods Research Center, Iran Argham Co., Iran Electronic Industries, Iranian Research Organization, Ministry of Sepah, Research and Development Group, Sezemane Sanaye Defa, the Sharif University of Technology, Taradis Iran Computer Company, and Zakaria Al-Razi Chemical Company are all participants in the Iranian nuclear weapons effort.[163]

There is little direct evidence to confirm these People's Mujahedin claims. The IAEA conducted a limited pre-arranged visit to six of ten suspected sites in February 1992, and found no sign of weapons activity at any of these sites. It found that the uranium mining site at Saghand, which the IAEA visited, was at least five years away from production and had no uranium concentration plant. It found the facility at Ma'allem Kelayah, which was said to be a nuclear weapons research center, to be little more than a motel-sized training and conference center. It found that the PRC-supplied Calutron at Shiraz was so small it could only be used to produce isotopes for medical research.[164]

Some sources have since charged that the IAEA had only conducted a "familiarization tour," and that the IAEA may have been led to a decoy site when it thought it was investigating a facility called Ma'allem Kelayah. Nevertheless, the IAEA did not find any of the rumored facilities. Reports that the IAEA was led to the wrong site have also been vehemently denied by David Kidd, a spokesman for the IAEA.[165]

Further, Iran let a new team from the IAEA visit Iran in November 1993. This team had been given detailed briefings by the United States and other Western countries and was allowed to visit suspected buildings at three main nuclear research complexes near Tehran, Isfahan, and Karaj. Like the previous IAEA mission, it was a visit, not a full or special inspection mission, and was not equipped or organized to find covert Iranian activities or examine all of the activities in the research facilities it was allowed to visit. Moreover, the IAEA team did not have adequate access to soil and particle samples in the facilities it was allowed to visit.[166]

Although Deputy President Ayatollah Mohajerani stated in October 1991 that Iran should work with other Islamic states to create an "Islamic bomb," the Iranian government has never acknowledged that Iran is seeking nuclear weapons, and Iran has made proposals to create a nuclear-free zone in the Middle East.[167] Senior Iranian officials – such as Reza Amrollah, the head of the Iranian Atomic Energy Organization – have repeatedly denied that Iran was seeking a bomb and have claimed Iran is fully complying with all NPT and IAEA requirements. The Iranian official news agency stated on 8 January 1995 that "Iran simply does not have the ambition to become a nuclear weapons state. Iran does not, and will not, in light of its own interest, engage in a nuclear weapons program."[168]

Nevertheless, the IAEA visits and Iranian denials of the existence of a nuclear weapons program scarcely mean that Iran does not have a clandestine nuclear program and is not seeking weapons-grade material. In fact, most US experts believe that Iran has clandestinely sought the material needed for a nuclear weapons effort. It has repeatedly attempted to avoid Western controls on nuclear weapons technology since 1984, and new Iranian efforts to buy nuclear weapons-related components were uncovered in 1994. There are also some indicators that the Revolutionary Guard has been deeply involved in managing Iran's nuclear weapons efforts.[169]

Robert Gates, then director of the US Central Intelligence Agency (CIA), testified to Congress in February 1992, that Iran was "Building up its special weapons capability as part of a massive ... effort to develop its military and defense capability."[170] Press reports about the CIA's National Intelligence Estimate (NIE) on this subject for 1992 also indicated that the CIA estimated that Iran could have a nuclear weapon by the year 2000.[171]

US Secretary of Defense William Perry was somewhat more ambiguous when he stated on 9 January 1995 that, "We believe that Iran is trying to develop a nuclear program. We believe it will be many, many years until they achieve such a capability. There are some things they might be able to do to short-cut that time."[172] In referring to "short cuts," Perry was concerned with the risk that Iran could obtain fissile material and weapons technology from the former Soviet Union, and this risk creates a serious uncertainty about Iran's future nuclear capabilities. There is a growing black market in nuclear material. And while the radioactive material sold on the black market by CIS and Central European citizens to date has consisted largely of plutonium 240, low-grade enriched uranium, or isotopes of material which has little value in a nuclear weapons program, this is no guarantee for the future.

Reports during 1992 and 1993 that Iran had hired large numbers of Soviet nuclear scientists have proved to be unreliable.[173] So far, more dramatic reports deny that Iran had succeeded in buying weapons-grade material from the former Soviet Union and nuclear armed missiles from Khazakhstan. There is, however, a very real risk of sudden major technology transfers, and any working nuclear device Iran could develop could suddenly change the military balance in the region. Iran could destroy any hardened target, area target, or city in the Middle East.

As is the case with most of the Third World, Iran's neighbors are extremely vulnerable to attacks on a few cities. Even one successful nuclear attack might force a fundamental restructuring of their politics and/or economy. Given the most critical target, they are effectively "one-bomb" countries. Unlike anything Iran can do to improve its conventional forces, such Iranian nuclear capabilities raise major mid-term and long-term challenges in terms of deterrence, defense, retaliation, and arms control. Missile defense, while possible, seems unlikely to be either leak-proof, or the kind of "confidence builder" that will lead other powers to avoid preemption and attacks on Iranian facilities, or reduce reliance on retaliation. In practice, this raises the specter of either effective arms control based on full and reliable inspection, or the need for the United States to retain a superior capability for theater nuclear retaliation.

Deterrence, Dual Containment, and the Iranian Threat

There is no way to predict Iran's long-term behavior, but it is likely to remain sufficiently weak in the near to mid-term so that it will be deterred by the risks of initiating a major regional conflict, or escalating to one if a more limited struggle begins. It is impossible to dismiss the risk of such a war, but Iran seems far more likely to use force, or to threaten to use force in spite of its military weaknesses, in a wide range of lesser contingencies. These contingencies include:

—Intervention in a civil war or military upheaval in Iraq, involving religious issues or where Iraq appears vulnerable.

—A military response to Iraqi incursions into Iran, or attacks on People's Mujahedin forces and camps based in Iraq.

—Intervention in a Kurdish uprising in Iraq, suppression of a Kurdish uprising in Iran, or a military response to the spillover of the Kurdish conflicts in Turkey or Iraq.

—An Armenian military incursion into Iran, or an Armenian defeat of Azerbaijan which threatens its existence or takes on a religious character.

—Ethnic/religious conflicts with secular governments in the Islamic republics of the former Soviet Union, such as Tadjikistan.

—Covert or overt support of a coup in Bahrain, or Shi'ite uprising in Saudi Arabia or any other Gulf states.

—Military threats or action in the Gulf in response to a major crisis in oil prices, and/or a struggle over oil quotas – including possible escalation to the deployment of submarines and the use of anti-ship missiles and mines.

—Covert intervention or open use of IRGC forces in a major military encounter between Israel and the Shi'ites in Lebanon.

—Systematic expansion of military training, arms, and funding for Hamas in the West Bank and Gaza, and assassination and bombing attacks on Israeli embassies and citizens.

—Support of a religious coup in an accessible neighboring state, or conflict between an "Islamic" force and peace-keeping or secular forces.

—Response to a military challenge to Iranian control of the Tunbs and Abu Musa.

—An air or naval clash in the Gulf over oil rights or shipping lanes.

—Use of force to assert Iran's claims to off-shore gas fields claimed by Qatar, or an "energy grab" to attack other off-shore or on-shore oil and gas fields or facilities.

—A major clash between Israel and the Palestinians and/or Syria after the failure of the current peace settlement.

—Attacks on US citizens or forces to try to eliminate the US presence in the Gulf, or weaken US support of Israel.

—A military response to a crisis over the transfer of chemical, biological, or nuclear weapons material and technology to Iran, or the transfer of long-range missile systems.

It should be noted that many of these scenarios are not necessarily aggressive and could involve conflicts over what may be considered to be legitimate Iranian national interests. At the same time, they illustrate a wide range of potential risks, and every one of the above conflicts involves major uncertainties as to the exact mix of forces that Iran would threaten to commit or actually commit and the intensity of the conflict and escalation that might follow.

This range of contingencies would also change radically if Iran and Iraq should ever cooperate. While there is little present prospect that Iran and Iraq would join together in a "devil's bargain," regimes change and sometimes do so suddenly and with unpredictable motives. Any serious Iranian and Iraqi cooperation in using military force would rapidly alter the military balance in the Gulf, and a combination of Iranian and Iraqi military forces could put far more military pressure on any combination of Western and Allied Gulf forces. It would also be far harder for the Arab Gulf to resist a combination of Iranian and Iraqi intimidation short of war; in many cases, they would be likely to compromise or accommodate Iran and Iraq as long as this did not affect a major strategic interest.

Finally, no one should dismiss the risk that a limited Iranian and Iraqi political alliance could rapidly escalate into a very different and far more serious war. Miscalculation, miscommunication, misperceptions, and different values are more the norm in military history than the exception, and this has certainly been true of the recent actions of Iran and Iraq. Iran's failure to accept a favorable ceasefire in the Iran–Iraq war in 1985 is a good case in point.

Given these uncertainties, it is clear that the West and the Arab Gulf states must take every possible action to limit Iran and Iraq's present and future war-fighting options, and that such action must take place in four areas: arms control, limits on the transfer of technology and equipment, strengthening the deterrent and defensive capabilities of Arab Gulf forces, and building up Western power projection capabilities.

All of these measures need to be pursued in concert. Focusing on one type of measure – such as arms control or efforts to strengthen Arab Gulf forces – is almost certain to fail. The West must take every possible step to pressure Iran and Iraq to join international and regional arms control regimes that can bring stability to the Gulf. At the same time, the West must organize to develop tight controls on transfers of military and dual-use technology to Iran and Iraq, focusing on the risks posed by the transfer of both conventional technologies and those for weapons of mass destruction.

Such limits on trade and technology transfers may or may not be made part of arms control regimes and formal embargoes. One point, however, must be kept clearly in mind. Some arms control regimes stress equity to all signatories or tend to penalize moderate states that sign and honor such agreements while extremist states do not. "Fairness" is not the issue in dealing with Iran and Iraq. Security is the issue and it will best be achieved by understanding that weakening or limiting Gulf and moderate Arab states is scarcely a way of avoiding future conflicts in the Gulf region.

The worst possible path that outside nations could follow would be to treat Iran as an open market for arms, or to return to the Cold War struggle for influence in the northern Gulf. At the same time, military containment and limits on the transfers of arms and technology do not necessarily mean trying to isolate Iran and Iraq politically, culturally, and economically. Any effort to isolate Iran may well turn it into a more active threat, rather than moderate it.

A partnership between the West and the Gulf is the key to the continued deterrence of any Iranian adventures and to reacting to the buildup of Iran's conventional forces and the risks posed by proliferation. The West will be successful in achieving stability in the Gulf only if it understands that it must work in concert with the Gulf states. The West must continue to support selective arms transfers to buildup the defense capabilities of Bahrain, Kuwait, Oman, Qatar, Saudi Arabia, and the UAE. Such transfers of arms and technology are needed both to buildup the capability of the Gulf states to forge an effective deterrent to low and mid-intensity attacks and to permit rapid reinforcement from the West.

At the same time, the Gulf states need to understand that ultimate deterrent and defense against Iranian or Iraqi military action will depend on Western power projection capabilities. In practice, "the West" will also mean "the United States." Real world power projection capabilities in the Gulf are – and will remain – dependent on the American military commitment to Saudi Arabia and the other southern Gulf states. It will depend on support of this US commitment by the Gulf states, and to some extent on the willingness of outside powers to at least provide political support for the United States and Gulf states. It will also depend on the improvement of US power projection capabilities to provide for the rapid deployment of heavy armor. The forces and facilities of the Arab Gulf states will need to be structured to allow rapid deployment of US air power and heavy divisions. Providing the equivalent of forward air bases and prepositioned army equipment is the only way in which external reinforcements can offset the mid- and long-term threat of significant Iranian and Iraqi attacks on their neighbors in the Gulf.

CHAPTER 12

An Evaluation of Iran's First Development Plan and Challenges Facing the Second Plan

Hooshang Amirahmadi

Introduction

The 1979 revolution was a watershed in Iran's recent history. It was expected to inaugurate political and economic betterment, and to secure political sovereignty and economic development. The revolution, however, did not deliver what it had promised. In its first decade, the Islamic Republic faced the challenges of the Iran–Iraq war and a multitude of political and economic hardships, many of which were caused by exogenous factors. These challenges made for political ambivalence and precarious economic and social policies that precluded long-term planning and a focus on national development.

With the end of the Iran–Iraq war, as Iran entered the second decade of the revolution, the country had a chance to focus on political and economic development. Crucial items on the government's agenda included reconstruction of the war-ravaged areas and a general improvement of the quality of life of the population. Iran sought to concentrate on medium-term development programs, to balance the short-term needs of the populace against the nation's long-term interests. It was against this background that planners developed the first five-year plan, covering 1989 to 1993, for economic, social, and cultural development.[1] In practice, however, the implementation of the plan was delayed until early in 1990, primarily because of political and economic debates in the Parliament. Iranian statesmen envisioned the plan as the inauguration of a new era in prosperity and growth, previously inhibited by the protracted war with Iraq. In the analysis that follows, the first development plan receives mixed reviews; it is important to evaluate both its successes and failures to shed light upon the policy errors made by the Islamic Republic's leaders.

The goal of this chapter is to evaluate the performance of the first plan, including the underlying causal factors, and to suggest an outline of the major domestic and foreign challenges confronting the second plan. The chapter will conclude that political-economic and institutional reforms in Iran and regional economic cooperation and coordination are the two major preconditions for both economic well-being in Iran and stability in the Gulf region. The study is guided by an empirical methodology, enlisting field surveys, statistics, and an integrated, interdisciplinary study of economic, political, and social forces.

This chapter comprises seven sections. The first section looks at the defining characteristics and orientations of the first plan. The practical modifications of the first plan and the reasons these adjustments were undertaken are then discussed. The third section evaluates the plan's success rate, touching on the social implications of current economic policies. The weaknesses of the plan, focusing on political and economic factors that adversely affected the plan's implementation, are addressed in the fourth section. The fifth section compares and contrasts the two plans. The sixth part enumerates the multitude of domestic and international challenges facing the second plan. The final section focuses on policy implementation, relating the arguments of the chapter to Gulf security.

The First Plan

The first plan had to grapple with fundamental problems that had crippled the economy prior to 1989. Chief among these were:

—the economy's heavy dependence on fluctuating and falling oil revenues;
—sharp decreases in domestic production and per capita income;
—inefficient use of production capabilities, especially in the industrial sector;
—a rise in government spending and a bloated bureaucracy;
—huge budget deficits coupled with the high volume of liquidity in the private sector;
—negligible government revenue from taxation;
—sharp inequalities in income distribution and wealth;
—galloping inflation and price distortions;
—low levels of investment and low rates of return;
—rapid population growth and high level of unemployment;
—acute shortages in infrastructure, education, health care, and housing;
—inappropriate distribution of developmental activities over the national space.[2]

The first plan was conceived essentially to create structural improvements in the nation's economic condition. It intended to reverse the short-comings of the extant economic trends, and to achieve balanced growth in various sectors. The planners hoped to realize their goals through a combination of oil revenues, foreign aid, mobilization of domestic economic resources, removal of infrastructural obstacles, and support of the private sector. The eight-year-long Iran–Iraq war had severely damaged Iran's production capacity, and had fostered economic activity in trade and commerce and speculation in real estate and foreign currency exchange. To reverse these unproductive trends, the first plan adopted supply-side economics and focused on increasing production.

Alongside the main goal of accelerating economic growth, the first plan pursued other objectives: upgrading and expanding defense capabilities; reconstructing areas devastated by war; diversifying the economy; expanding infrastructure; developing the industrial, mining, petroleum, natural gas, agricultural, electricity, and telecommunications sectors; supporting higher education and research; improving medical care; pursuing an equitable distribution of resources; imposing the rule of law; reforming the administrative structure; and, finally, reorganizing distribution of the population and economic activity nationwide. The plan's preoccupation with economic growth, however, led to the neglect of other aspects of national development, even those originally within the plan's scope. Issues of social justice and rule of law, in particular, were neglected. Ultimately, the following areas prevailed as loci of emphasis.

Fostering economic growth   Economic growth was singled out as the most crucial objective of the first plan. Rapid population growth and weak economic performance had resulted in sharp declines in per capita income and a fall in living standards for the average Iranian household. To accomplish its main goals, the plan sought to exploit the petroleum sector and other underutilized resources, to alleviate structural deficiencies, and to introduce rational management. It also needed to increase the ratio of total investment to gross domestic production, which had experienced sharp declines in the pre-plan period, and to control domestic consumption in an attempt to increase savings and investment. The plan further sought to mobilize the private sector, whose financial resources were controlled by relatively few people and concentrated in non-productive activities. Along with increasing the role played by the private sector, the plan also intended to attract foreign investment and aid in the industrial, petroleum, natural gas, and infrastructural sectors.

Controlling population growth   Population control was vital, for growth had led to an increase in consumer demand and an unmanageable expansion of the labor force. By controlling population growth, the plan sought to reduce the gap between supply and demand in goods and resources, with direct bearing on living standards and expanding investments in productive activities.

Managing the budget deficit and inflation   The plan sought to strengthen the private sector's confidence in the government's economic policies and change the macro-budgetary structure by containing costs and expanding taxation as a source of government revenue. Controlling prices, restricting the money supply, and gathering idle private liquidity, especially by re-juvenating the banking system, were thought to be means to control inflation and alleviate hardships on the expanding indigent strata of the population.

Adopting import substitution and export promotion policies   Import substitution and non-oil export promotion were pursued simultaneously, both to diversify the economy and to reduce its dependence on foreign exchange earnings. Import substitution would reduce the demand for imported consumer goods, thus curtailing demand for foreign exchange and re-ducing the economy's dependence on volatile foreign exchange revenues. The lack of such policies in the past, coupled with falling oil revenues, had pushed a considerable portion of the country's economic capabilities into non-productive sectors; capital resources were employed in non-productive activities with quick returns, such as commerce and distribution, with a subsequent proliferation of middlemen.

Optimizing resource exploitation and completing unfinished projects   The plan's emphasis on utilizing existing economic resources to their fullest capacity was triggered by the low rate of return on public sector investments as well as by the realization that a shortage in revenue prevented capital injection into the productive sectors. Sheer numbers dictated the need for placing unfinished projects high on the agenda: stranded projects not only obstructed returns on previous investments, but meant unnecessary maintenance costs when the projects were idle. Thus, it was decided that new investments would be prohibited during the first plan, and that resources would instead be directed at completing projects that would either help reduce dependency on foreign exchange or generate foreign currency income through export promotion. In this regard, steel and petrochemical projects were singled out.

Revisions to the First Plan

While most plans are revised during their actual execution, in the case of Iran's first plan the modifications were fundamental. The Iranian government adopted the various revisions while the plan was being implemented. These are discussed below.

Although full utilization of current resources was one of the plan's main objectives, new investment projects were undertaken during the process of executing the first plan. Mas'ud Rowghani-Zanjani, head of Iran's Plan and Budget Organization, alluded to the number of hospital beds that had been added in the course of the first plan, but which had remained unutilized.[3] According to surveys, 11,000 new beds were added from 1989 to 1992; this amounts to an annual rate of increase of 4.5 percent. Conversely, occupancy rates of beds in this same period decreased from 248 days to 240 days per year.[4] In addition, private hospitals were currently creating 25,000 new beds. Not only did the utilization of current hospital beds remain unchanged, but in effect, additional unutilized hospital space was created. The point is that the old policy of quantitative – as opposed to qualitative – improvements in effect remained.

It is important to note that the number of projects envisaged during the course of the first plan far exceeded the government's financial capabilities, illustrating the lack of conviction on the part of administrators about maximizing the exploitation of present resources. One of the prerequisites for optimal utilization of resources is a hierarchical ranking of unfinished projects, so that investments toward their completion will follow the government's priorities and financial capabilities. In this way, top-priority projects would be the first to be completed. In fact, one of the deputies to the Iranian parliament has pointed out that "the government over-stretched itself much beyond its capability."[5] As a result, the completion time for many projects was long, and unnecessary costs were incurred. Some projects never saw the light of day, and thus did not contribute to the realization of the plan's objectives.

Another important revision affected non-oil export promotion. The plan primarily emphasized import substitution, with export promotion deemed desirable only as ancillary to the former. In fact, the plan sought first to contain the demand for foreign exchange and to realize the nation's economic potential. Such strategies entail the protection of domestic markets and government provision of foreign exchange for industries to enhance production of consumer goods and heavy machinery. In executing the plan, however, the government opted for export promotion over import substitution, and industries were expected to become self-sufficient in their demand for foreign exchange, mainly through exports. In addition, controls on imports were lifted, so the domestic market was flooded with foreign cars, household supplies, and other imported consumer goods. Instead, the government should have encouraged substitution by imposing stricter controls on imports, restricting imports to those products and heavy machinery vital for boosting domestic production.

Export promotion and government support for export-oriented industries are inherently positive developments. They encourage increased competitiveness and qualitative improvements in domestic production, and increase foreign exchange earnings, all of which contribute to economic diversification. But export promotion is not an alternative to import substitution. The former should have only been pursued alongside the latter, with long-term considerations in mind. Available studies on Iran generally show that foreign exchange earned from export goods is generally less than that used in their production, and that whatever small positive balance may remain is not returned to the domestic production process.[6]

Yet another modification to the original plan involved the setting of a single rate for foreign currencies and allowing their prices to float. Creating a single exchange rate has long been an important issue debated among the government policy-makers; its creation is regarded as one of the major accomplishments of the first plan.[7] But the original plan did not call for a single exchange rate for foreign currencies, and so far as economic growth was concerned, the plan sought to utilize present industrial capacities while maintaining several rates of exchange. Fixing a single rate of exchange by no means reduced the importance of having a precise foreign currency budget, including rational expenditure of such currencies. The first plan did not argue that the rates of exchange should be determined by supply and demand; instead, it required that the government adhere to a fixed currency budget.

Rapid privatization was still another modification to the plan. The first plan sought to encourage private investment in the productive sectors and public participation in decision-making regarding educational and cultural policies. The private sector was to assist in the tackling of economic hardships, and thus alleviate some of the government's burdens. The cooperative sector was to grow considerably. In practice, however, conservative thinking in government circles called for the rapid privatization of nationalized firms, whereby major public enterprises would be auctioned to the private sector. Despite government policy, public banks and quasi-public foundations also offered to purchase public enterprises. While the private sector was not yet prepared for full-scale participation in the economic process, the government prematurely offered it factories to buy and manage. The pragmatic attempt by President Hashemi Rafsanjani to sell the nationalized industrial units to their former owners and other capitalists was criticized by Ayatollah Khamene'i and the conservatives. In response, the government decided to offer the industries to those considered loyal to the regime – *bazaaris* (middle-class merchants) and those with ties to the government – at cheaper rates. Overall, privatization of government-owned services and industries did not follow a well-conceived plan; and rather than promoting development, it became an objective in itself. Consequently, privatization strengthened certain sections of the *bazaari* and those with strong government affiliations.

The Rationale for the Revisions

The revisions to the plan were molded for an array of factors, two of which were paramount. First, Iran's foreign exchange earnings increased in 1991. Iraq's occupation of Kuwait led to some $4 billion of extra oil revenue for Iran. This sudden boost created an illusion of prosperity, and Iranian policy-makers embarked on an ambitious plan for quick economic growth. Middlemen and representatives of foreign firms in Iran took advantage of corruption and the absence of long-term planning to encourage the implementation of consumerist policies.

The fifth development plan of Iran in the pre-revolutionary period shared a similar fate. Then, too, with rapid increases in the price of oil in 1973, revisions were made to the plan. In both instances, governments were unaware of the negative effect of radical changes in economic policy. Governments have simply lacked the means of sustaining projects initiated in boom periods. Opening domestic markets to imported consumer goods was indicative of inappropriate utilization of new economic potentials in the first plan. Import substitution was neglected, and new investments were undertaken without adequate financial backing. Economic free-zones, too, were adversely affected. Rather than promoting investment in non-oil export industries, they were being flooded by imported consumer goods.

Second, the revisions were implemented because of the government's perception of Iran's new position in the region and in the world. Iran's behavior during the Gulf war was a positive development and led to better relations with the West and with the Arab nations of the Gulf, Saudi Arabia in particular. That Iraq had attacked Kuwait and proved itself belligerent tended to corroborate Iran's claims that the Islamic Republic had fallen victim to Saddam Hussein's aggression and that Iran had been the innocent party in the Iran–Iraq war, merely defending itself against an "imposed war."

In the wake of Desert Storm, the Iranian government believed that the breakup of the Soviet Union had resulted in a less ideological global order, which is more than ever centered on economic issues and cooperation. With such considerations in mind and in the aftermath of the tragic earthquake of May 1990, Iran embarked on a mission to bring its economic policies in line with current trends in the international economy. Seeking loans and investments from abroad and approaching the IMF and the World Bank were initiatives taken in this light. As a prerequisite for IMF assistance, the government was compelled to accept the IMF's guidelines for economic liberalization, a typical requirement for this type of assistance. Privatization, floatation of exchange rates, and the elimination of price controls and subsidies were adopted to accommodate the international financial agencies and to integrate Iran into the world economy.

An Evaluation of the First Plan

Three points deserve particular emphasis in any assessment of the first plan. First, the plan cannot be held responsible for all of Iran's economic ills. Devastation wrought by the war with Iraq, domestic power struggles, natural disasters, and political pressures by the international community were among the culprits which fell outside the plan's purview. On the other hand, there were several positive developments in the country that likewise cannot be attributed to the plan. An example is the significant success of the efforts to control population growth.

Second, any evaluation is necessarily limited to the plan's short-term effects, which disregards the time lag between the inception of policies and their final outcome. The delay is especially significant for structural projects. For instance, major investments in heavy industries, petrochemicals, steel and aluminum, telecommunications networks, and utilities will bear fruit in the long run. By the same token, several projects that were successful during the first plan had in fact been initiated in previous eras. The Mubarakeh steel plant is an example.

Third, rather than solely analyzing the average growth rates of the economy in the period under discussion, annual growth rates should be emphasized. Thus, it becomes clear that the initial phases of the plan were marked by significant growth, culminating in 1991. The downward spiral followed as the plan was further diverted from its original premises. The fluctuating performance indicates the plan's failure in instituting stable, long-term trends in the economy. Moreover, the downward trend is likely to plague the economy in the years to come. Figures for the first half of 1994 denote an exacerbation of the problems. It can be argued that the economy's growth rate, however infinitesimal, was not caused by rational economic planning. Rather, it was caused by exogenous factors, such as the increase in oil revenue during the Gulf war and rapid injections of foreign aid into the economy. Indeed, the termination of the war-induced oil revenue, coupled with the first installments of loan repayments, completely reversed the growth cycle.

The evaluation that follows is based upon figures released by the Plan and Budget Organization, which at times contradict those released by other government agencies. Statistics gathered by the Central Bank, traditionally a more reliable source, are backlogged for two years. Moreover, official figures on the plan's performance in 1993 have not yet been released. Statistics cited here were based on a speech by Muhammad Hosain Adeli, the former governor of Iran's Central Bank. While the plan can claim some success in realizing its objectives, its blatant shortcomings hindered its effectiveness in spurring social and economic change.

Population growth rate Birth rates fell dramatically during the period of the plan. Prior to the plan, the annual population growth rate was 3.3 percent, which, when compared to the rate of 3.9 percent (including emigration) that marked the decade from 1978 to 1988, indicates a decline in the 1980s. The plan aimed at continuing the downward trend, reducing the growth rate to 2.9 percent per annum in 1993, with the view of reaching 2.3 percent by the year 2011. By the last year of the plan, however, the rate fell to 2.2 percent. In 1994, the Ministry of Health and Medical Education announced that the population growth rate had reached 1.8 percent per year.[8] The discrepancy between the last figure and the previously announced rate of 2.2 percent notwithstanding, excessive population growth in the country has been brought under control.[9]

Contrary to the government's claims, however, falling population growth rates are not fully attributable to successful family planning. The real explanations are dismal economic conditions and a general decline in living standards for the average Iranian household. This is not to deny that government policies such as providing clinical and health services to outlying areas and establishing family planning clinics, encouraging literacy among women, campaigning for birth control, and repatriating Afghani and Iraqi refugees have indeed contributed considerably to declining population growth. In other words, just as revolutionary euphoria and government espousal of larger families made for increasing growth rates in the early days of the revolution, gloomy economic forecasts, inflation, and falling government subsidies dissuaded population growth in the past decade.[10]

Economic growth and investment   Economic growth, too, was positive in comparison to the pre-plan years. The first decade of the revolution saw a negative growth rate when measured in constant prices. In 1974 prices, gross domestic product (GDP) in 1977 was IR 3,922 billion, whereas in 1988 it had fallen to IR 3,142 billion; and because the population growth rate was high in this period, per capita income, in real terms, fell by almost 50 percent.[11] This trend was reversed by the implementation of the first plan.

According to government reports, GDP rose by an average rate of 7.2 percent per year, in constant prices (see Table 12.1, a and b; Figure 12.1), slightly below the target rate of 8.1 percent.[12] With the fall in population growth rates, per capita production increased in this period. The increase did not lead to a rise in living standards, though, for it coincided with a sharp increase in the cost of living. In addition, by indulging in sudden privatization, the government passed on many of its socioeconomic expenses to individual households. The government's policy of increasing revenue from taxes and tariffs pushed the cost of living even higher.

An important indicator in assessing the plan is the ratio of investments to GDP. The plan had envisaged an average annual growth rate of 19.7 percent for this indicator, but its actual rate in the first four years of the plan was 10.6 percent – only 54 percent of the expected rate.[13] Thus, only a small portion of the GDP was invested in the economy. This portion grew infinitesimally during the plan years, from 12.1 percent in 1988 to 13.2 percent in 1992. Yet, to replace depreciated capital stock, the government needed to invest 10 to 12 percent of the GDP each year. Thus, the net increase in capital stock in the plan period was negligible, about 2 to 3 percent at best.

The figure for net investment becomes even less significant, considering the population growth of 2.2 percent per year. In contrast, in 1977, some 27.4 percent of the gross domestic product was invested, while in coun-

Table 12.1a GDP and its sectoral distribution during the first plan, 1989–93: planned and actual (billion rials, 1988 prices)*

	1989**		1990		1991		1992		1993		1989–93	
	Planned	Actual	Planned	Actual	Planned	Actual	Planned	Actual	Planned	Actual	Planned	Actual
Agriculture	5,430	5,404	5,678	5,842	6,026	6,139	6,454	6,594	7,001	6,957	6.1	5.9
Oil	2,500	2,218	2,741	2,659	2,834	2,954	3,156	3,016	3,250	3,125	9.5	8.7
Industry and mining	1,864	1,765	2,149	1,991	2,462	2,358	2,866	2,397	3,262	2,419	15.0	8.3
Industry	1,623	1,527	1,835	1,698	2,090	2,031	2,415	2,043	2,750	2,043	14.2	7.6
Mining	241	238	314	293	372	327	451	354	512	376	19.5	12.4
Water, electricity, and gas	490	512	526	611	587	706	618	766	714	840	9.1	12.7
Construction	1,593	1,214	1,844	1,249	2,073	1,449	2,282	1,563	2,429	1,591	14.5	5.2
Services	12,758	12,395	13,664	13,598	14,651	14,944	15,681	16,139	16,794	17,350	6.7	7.4
GDP***	24,290	25,272	26,533	25,914	28,346	28,608	30,747	30,354	33,315	31,871	8.1	7.2

Notes: * Whenever there was a difference in reported data, the latest figure was used. The 1993 data are derived mainly from the published interviews of the officials of the Islamic Republic. It should be noted that there are differences among data reported by the Central Bank, Plan and Budget Organization, and in interviews with officials of the Islamic Republic. **The Iranian year begins 21 March. *** Does not include the net factor earning (*Karmozd-e Ebtesabi*).

Sources: First Economic, Social, and Cultural Development Plan of the Islamic Republic of Iran (1989–93), Plan and Budget Organization, Tehran, 1990; *Economic Report[s]*, Plan and Budget Organization, Tehran, 1990, 1991, and 1992; "Economic Report of Mr. Mohammad Hosain Adeli (former director of the Central Bank) to the 34th annual meeting of the Central Bank," *Keyhan* daily, 14 August 1994, p. 2; various published interviews with government officials.

Table 12.1b GDP and its sectoral distribution during the first plan, 1989–93: planned and actual (growth rates, percent)

	1989 Planned	1989 Actual	1990 Planned	1990 Actual	1991 Planned	1991 Actual	1992 Planned	1992 Actual	1993 Planned	1993 Actual	1989–93 Planned	1989–93 Actual
Agriculture	4.2	3.7	4.6	8.1	6.1	5.1	7.4	7.4	8.5	5.5	6.1	5.9
Oil	21.4	7.7	9.6	19.9	3.4	11.1	11.3	2.1	3.0	3.6	9.5	8.7
Industry and mining	14.8	8.2	15.3	15.6	14.6	17.7	16.4	3.3	13.8	0.8	15.0	8.3
Industry	14.8	8.0	13.0	11.2	13.9	19.6	15.6	0.6	13.9	0.0	14.2	7.6
Mining	15.0	13.6	30.3	23.1	18.5	11.5	21.2	8.4	13.5	6.0	19.5	12.4
Water, electricity, and gas	6.4	11.0	7.2	19.4	11.7	15.5	5.3	8.5	15.4	9.7	9.1	12.7
Construction	29.0	-1.7	15.7	2.9	12.4	16.0	10.1	7.9	6.5	1.8	14.5	5.2
Services	5.1	2.1	7.2	9.7	7.4	9.9	7.1	8.0	7.1	7.5	6.7	7.4
GDP	7.9	3.0	9.2	11.8	6.8	10.4	8.5	6.1	8.4	5.0	8.1	7.2

Notes and sources: as Table 12.1a.

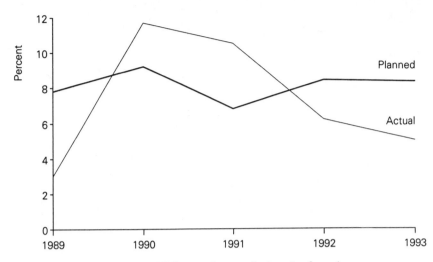

Figure 12.1 GDP growth rates during the first plan

tries with healthy, growing economies, the figure is above 30 percent. The adverse effects of this trend were exacerbated by the rapid increase in consumption. The first plan failed to contain consumption, in both the private and the public sectors. In 1991 and 1992, for example, the public sector's rate of consumption grew twice as much as had been projected.

Sectoral changes A sector-by-sector analysis of GDP shows positive growth as well, but not in line with the first plan's provisions. For this period, average annual growth rates in constant values were significant in the utilities sector (electricity, water, natural gas): about 12.7 percent compared to the plan's projection of 9.1 percent (Figure 12.2).

The petroleum sector grew at 8.7 percent, compared to the projected rate of 9.5 percent (Figure 12.3). The oil sector's positive performance was caused, in part, by the oil crisis following the Gulf war, and cannot be attributed to the plan. In addition, the oil sector grew only at the cost of non-conservationist extraction and a high waste ratio, both contrary to the plan's provisions.

Agriculture also experienced positive growth, although the growth was not evenly distributed among its sub-sectors. The sector's growth rate in this period (5.9 percent) approximated 90 percent of its projected targets of 6.1 percent (Figure 12.4). This partial success is particularly noteworthy considering that the agricultural sector employs about 22.5 percent of the country's labor force, produces about 22 percent of its GDP, and accounts for 32 percent of non-oil exports on a yearly basis.

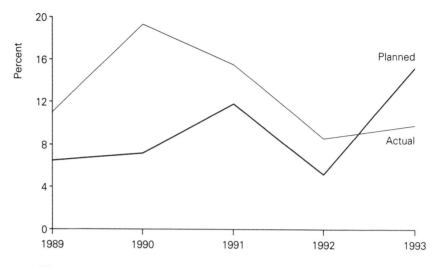

Figure 12.2 Growth rates of water, electricity, and gas sector during the first plan

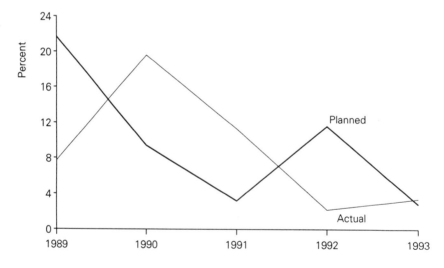

Figure 12.3 Growth rates of oil sector during the first plan

The plan failed in the industrial and mining sectors which *were* singled out for special performance, with a targeted expansion rate of 15 percent per year, the highest of all sectors. Average annual growth of the two sectors, however, did not exceed 8.2 percent (Figure 12.5).

The industrial sub-sector was largely responsible for this dismal record:

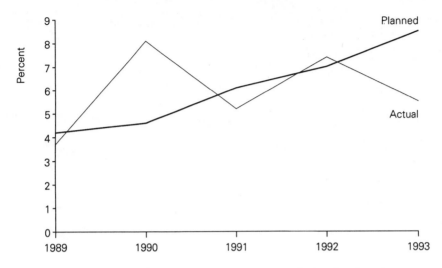

Figure 12.4 Growth rates of agricultural sector during the first plan

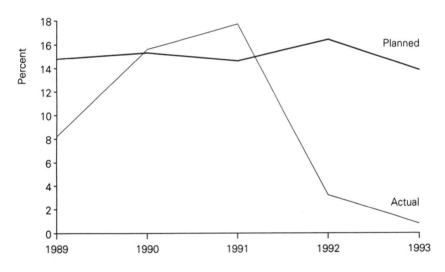

Figure 12.5 Growth rates of industry and mining sector during the first plan

it grew at less than 1 percent per year in 1992 and 1993. Over the first three years of the plan, the sub-sector grew at an average rate of 7.6 percent each year, achieving only 53 percent of its projected growth rate. The industrial sub-sector's growth fluctuated greatly, until it eventually stagnated in the plan's final years. Its track record shows that not only did

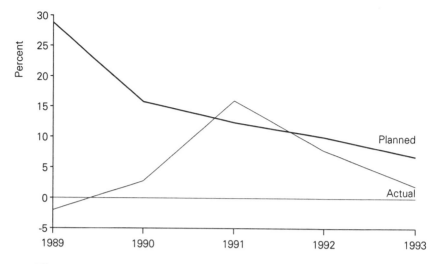

Figure 12.6 Growth rates of construction sector during the first plan

it suffer from intersectoral shortcomings, but that a clear strategy for national industrial development was also lacking. The sub-sector's performance was adversely affected by policies such as unbridled and sudden economic liberalization, floating exchange rates, and unplanned facilitation of imports in the mid-plan period. Small-sized and medium-sized industries, which had previously enjoyed considerable growth under protectionist government policy, were especially hard hit.

In the mining sub-sector, the average growth rate never exceeded 12.4 percent annually, although it was expected to reach 19.5 percent and be a major contributor to the nation's industrial development and to the diversification of its export base. The main culprit here was inadequate planning. Privatization schemes failed as well. Considering that this sub-sector accounted for 27 percent of jobs nationwide in 1992, its weak performance contributed considerably to the plan's overall failure to improve the social and economic situation in the country.

Construction was another ill-fated sector, failing to achieve even half of its projected growth rate of 14.5 percent annually. With an estimated growth rate of 5.2 percent, construction fared the worst among the various sectors (Figure 12.6). This failure will inevitably create an acute housing shortage in the near future. Construction has the highest intersectoral linkage within the economy, and its stagnation reflects a poor overall economic performance. In addition, this sector provides the largest number of jobs for the poorer classes, especially rural migrants, so its weakness

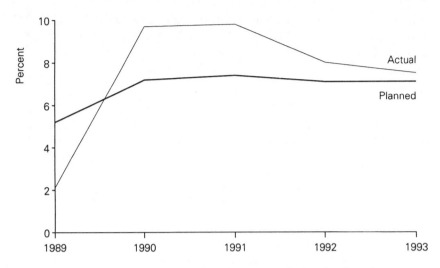

Figure 12.7 Growth rates of services sector during the first plan

also indicates high rates of unemployment, both seasonal and non-seasonal.

The first development plan was biased against the service sector, seeking to minimize its preponderant role in the country's economy. In actuality, however, the service sector outgrew its projection rates, except in 1989. It grew at an average annual rate of 7.4 percent for the plan period, exceeding the projected rate of 6.8 percent (Figure 12.7). Financial, monetary, and transportation sub-sectors grew the fastest. Their growth rates were not stable, however, declining in the plan's final years. Transportation, for instance, grew at 22.4 percent in 1990, while it was down to 7.8 percent in 1993.

Budget deficit and taxes Controlling the budget deficit was another of the plan's main objectives. The government succeeded in reducing it from 51 percent of the budget in 1988 to 6.7 percent in 1993. The ratio has been increasing again since 1993. As noted, the government passed on part of the burden of reducing the deficit to its banks and citizenry, and traces of the negative consequences are still felt in the Iranian economy. In order to reduce the deficit, the government entrusted the banking system with allocating funds to public enterprises.

Thus, much of the needed funds were not reflected in the national budget and were advanced as loans to enterprises and, in effect, to the populace. The net indebtedness of public enterprises to the Central Bank, for example, was estimated at IR 1,056 billion in 1991; it reached IR 3,657 billion in 1993. In the future, the banking system will be pressed to finance these forwarded credits. Also, the money handed over to these agencies was injected into the economy, adding inflationary pressures. Another option the government resorted to was concealing the real amount of the deficit by engaging in foreign exchange dealings on the black (free) market. Selling dollars on the black market proved profitable: the profits (difference between official and free-market rates) of selling foreign currencies in the black market accounted for 41 percent of government revenues in 1992.[14]

In addition to balancing government expenditures with revenues, structural changes in the budget composition were also to be affected under the plan, specifically through raising the share of taxation. The plan aspired to raise 44.8 percent of total government revenues from taxes. In practice, from 1989 to 1993, taxes accounted for 37.3 percent, 30.1 percent, 39.5 percent, and 38.1 percent of total government revenues, respectively. Not only did the ratio of taxes to government revenues never reach the projections, it actually declined after 1992. On the average, the plan's performance was between 10 percent and 20 percent behind expectations. In 1992, only 6.2 percent of GDP returned to government coffers as taxes, while the projection was for 7.3 percent. In addition, because the nation's tax structure is not progressive, it did not provide for a more equitable distribution of income. The plan did succeed, however, in diverting budget allocations to development funds. Such funds accounted for 19.2 percent of the annual budget in 1988, while in 1992 they accounted for 34 percent.

Inflation, unemployment, and poverty   Galloping inflation, especially in the final years of the plan, was another indicator of failure. The plan intended to reduce inflation from an annual rate of 28.5 percent in 1988 to 8.9 percent in 1993. Thus certain monetary, financial, and commercial guidelines were central; paramount among them was reducing the economy's liquidity. Liquidity grew at an annual rate of 23.8 percent in 1988, and the plan proposed to reduce this growth to a modest 3.5 percent per year by 1993, mainly by reducing the budget deficit and containing liquidity. The government would have to terminate cash injections into the economy.

In actuality, however, the economy's liquidity grew at an annual rate of 25 percent in the plan's period. It was projected to reach IR 23,000 billion in 1993, but it was actually double that amount, at IR 47,000 billion. In fact, the inflationary trend of recent years can be best explained by comparing the 25 percent average annual rate of increase in liquidity with the 7.2 percent average annual rate of increase in GDP. This explains why the inflation rate, which was supposed to be tamed at 8.9 percent in 1993, reached 30.7 percent in 1992. In 1993, the actual rate of inflation was approximately 20 percent, but instabilities in foreign exchange and monetary policies resulted in an inflation rate of about 60 percent for 1994.[15]

Floating exchange rates and the elimination of subsidies were instrumental in driving inflationary pressures in the plan's final years. There is more to the story, however. In the pre-plan period, the budget deficit – indebtedness to the country's banking system – was the chief reason for the high rates of liquidity. During the plan years, however, liquidity grew because of increases in private indebtedness. In 1993, IR 7,237.9 billion was added to the economy's liquidity of which IR 5,292.5 billion (73.1 percent) was attributed to a net increase in private indebtedness over the course of that one year.

The plan gets a mixed review regarding employment. In its initial years, it exceeded its own projections on job creation, which was set at 394,000 new jobs a year. But in the final years it fell short of its goal. Overall, the plan succeeded in decreasing the unemployment rate from 15.9 percent in 1988 to 11.4 percent in 1992. The target was to lower it to 13.4 percent. It should be noted that the unemployment figures include official as well as unofficial jobs, full-time and part-time jobs, and real as well as under-employment. In addition, most new jobs were created in the public sector, while the private sector showed little growth, and only in the low-paying service sector.

The plan was also unable to effect changes in the nation's employment structure. Planners wanted to reduce employment in the service sector from 47.2 percent in 1988 to 45.5 percent in 1993. The opposite happened: employment in the service sector soared to 50.4 percent in 1993. Over the same period, employment in the agricultural sector fell from 28.4 percent in 1988 to 22.2 percent in 1993. The share of the industry and mining sector increased slightly, from 24.4 percent to 27.4 percent. The majority of new jobs were created in the service sector. Each new job in the agricultural, petroleum, industry and mining, construction, and service sectors requires an initial investment of (in 1982 prices), IR 1.66 million, IR 10.55 million, IR 2.00 million, IR 0.21 million, and IR 6.74 million, respectively.[16]

Inflation, unemployment, the elimination of subsidies, and extremely inequitable distribution of income have taken their toll on lower- and middle-income families. It is true that social justice was not high on the agenda of the first plan, but there are more families in Iran today whose living standards fall below the poverty line, and income distribution has deteriorated sharply. An estimated 60 percent of the Iranian population currently live below the poverty line.[17] This will undoubtedly have negative social ramifications. There is a widespread bribe culture and corruption is prevalent, while addiction, theft, and other types of social delinquency have proliferated.

Foreign debts and export promotion   Foreign debts accumulated at an unprecedented rate. Forecasts estimated total government revenues, from oil as well as non-oil exports sales, at $99.2 billion for the entire plan period. Parliament also approved $27 billion in foreign loans.[18] Actual government foreign exchange revenues amounted to only 86 percent of the forecasts. Under the government's policy, the domestic market was flooded with imports. The total value of goods imported was $9 billion in 1988, $27.8 billion in 1991, and $29 billion in 1992.[19] Additional foreign exchange was obtained from loans and "usance" credits. Foreign debts accumulated, and, at the end of the plan in 1993, surpassed $30 billion.[20]

The distribution of interest payments on these loans also shows a lack of foresight. Some 60 percent of accumulated foreign debts were two-year usance, with short pay-back periods.[21] Thus, not only did the Central Bank, and ultimately Iran, lose face in the international community for missing interest payments, but foreign loan financing also put further strains on the economy. After successful renegotiation of payment plans, the government decided to allocate 15 percent to 20 percent of foreign exchange earnings, over the course of the second plan, to servicing its foreign debts. The loan payment schedule is demonstrated in Table 12.2.

The government's export promotion policy was also unsuccessful. Non-oil exports performed well in these years and more than doubled their share of total exports, although they never achieved targeted goals. From 1989 to 1993, non-oil exports rose from $1.1 billion to $1.3 billion, $2.5 billion, $2.9 billion, and $3.7 billion. The total of $11.7 billion over the plan period was, however, substantially below the $17.8 billion projected by the plan. In the first trimester of 1994, non-oil exports produced $1.1 billion in foreign currency earnings. Falling domestic purchasing power, coupled with high rates for the dollar, will inevitably make for a lucrative export sector, especially since the export levels still lag behind the country's productive capacities.

However, the non-oil sector is still not well integrated into domestic

Table 12.2 Schedule for the repayment of foreign debts (negotiated as of August 1994)

Year	$ Million
1994	3,400
1995	4,400
1996	4,500
1997	4,100
1998	3,850
1999	3,570
Total	23,820

Source: Bahman Komaili-Zadeh and Behnam Nateghi, "Finances Look Up, for Now," *Iran Business Monitor*, September 1994, p. 4.

production resources and is dependent on imported goods for the production process. A large proportion of the export earnings generated by this sector is, therefore, absorbed by its own production process, so that the positive balance – i.e., value added – at the end of the day is negligible. Also, the products in this sector were not what the plan had in mind, and domestic industries played a minor role in their production. Over the plan period, industrial exports were supposed to earn the highest amount of foreign exchange of all non-oil exports – $9 billion, compared to $4 billion for carpets, Iran's traditional main non-oil export. In reality, however, export earnings from carpets were double those from industrial exports. From 1989 to 1993, carpet exports totaled $3,194 million, while industrial exports lagged behind at $1,416 million. This shows the vulnerabilities of the export sector and the need for government support for expanding the nation's industrial base.

Causes of the Plan's Weak Performance

Factors that led to the plan's weak performance can be divided into two categories: First, structural and institutional obstacles, to which we shall return in our discussion of challenges facing the second plan, and second, administrative and policy shortcomings. The latter category is discussed below.

Erroneous assessment of international opportunities The Islamic Republic's miscalculation of the political opportunity caused by Iraq's invasion of

Kuwait was instrumental in the failure of the first plan. The government believed that appropriate economic policies would inevitably result in a stronger political and economic standing in the global community. These higher expectations were crafted into the plan's targeted objectives. What was lacking was a concomitant policy of political normalization, both domestically and *vis-à-vis* the world. To begin with, the Islamic Republic's hostilities with the United States endured, and the US continued to exert economic pressure on Tehran, more or less in concert with other Western states. The Islamic Republic's support for Islamic movements throughout the region and its opposition to the Arab–Israeli peace plan made enemies of Israel and several Arab countries, including Egypt. As a result, Iran failed to attract the political and economic cooperation it had anticipated.

Officials of the Islamic Republic point to defectors in the Western camps, countries that supposedly did not follow the United States in excluding Iran from the global economy. These countries, however, did not help Iran achieve its targeted objectives in the first plan. Japan and Germany, for example, traded extensively with Iran, but only to gain access to Iran's domestic markets. Neither country invested in Iran and both ran large positive trade balances with the Islamic Republic. Oil exports to Germany in the third trimester of 1994 were 22 percent lower than in the same period in 1993.[22] In fact, Iran supplies only 2 percent of Germany's demand for oil. The IMF and the World Bank were also lukewarm to Iran, and the Islamic Republic failed in attracting significant investment from abroad. Surely, these facts cannot be divorced from Iran's political image. Iran should have first adopted a reasonable political framework within which it could conduct its international relations, and then exploited that framework to its benefit.

Managerial shortcomings   Managers in Iran are selected on the basis of their ideological affiliations, a fact which proved detrimental to the implementation of the first plan. The Islamic Republic has not invested in its human resources. Iranian managers are not familiar with the modern techniques and strategies in the field; moreover, the limited experience they have gathered in the post-revolutionary period has been insufficient. Effective managerial skills cannot be mastered solely on the basis of on-the-job training. Chosen on the basis of their ideological commitment rather than qualifications, managers inevitably lack the requisite experience and expertise. Thus, organizational and managerial space is politicized, riddled with ideological and partisan confrontations. Managers promote political creed rather than increase efficiency and production. The first plan suffered a major setback as a result of its unqualified managerial staff.

Inefficient administrative structure   The plan also lacked the necessary executive system to oversee its smooth implementation. The plan was conceived in a sector-intensive framework, and a stable and vertical power structure was crucial for its success. However, the Islamic Republic is characterized by plural and parallel power centers, similar to the distribution of power among various religious clusters in the country. Moreover, these centers are not just linked horizontally, but have numerous vertical ties. The semi-feudal structure of power has a debilitating effect on the country's administrative structure. It creates discord and strife in the upper echelons of government, reduces effectiveness, and works against efficient utilization of resources.

Hasty revisions to the plan   The plan was handicapped by the many revisions and modifications made to it. The revisions disrupted the plan's internal cohesion, replacing it with a series of disjointed and at times incompatible policies. Thus, the plan also lost its long-term vision and was modified according to day-to-day economic considerations. Hasty revisions precluded an appropriate scrutiny of prerequisites and consequences. Poor public relations also inhibited adequate utilization of economic wisdom, and the government failed to attract Iranian expatriates with expertise in economics and management.

Unstable and incoherent policies   Perhaps the principal factor contributing to the failure of the first plan was the government's inability to produce definitive, rational, and cohesive policies in the financial, monetary, foreign exchange, and industrial sectors. The policy of creating a single exchange rate perhaps illustrates this weakness.

Foreign exchange, like all other commodities, is bound to have a single price, determined by the laws of supply and demand. But economic theory accommodates circumstantial differences, and does not prescribe unified exchange rates in all places. In Iran, the imposition of a single exchange rate was a problem not just because of its consequences, but also because of the way in which it was implemented. The provision was sought to alleviate the problems resulting from several exchange rates.

In a multi-tiered exchange rate system, especially when the official and market rates diverge widely, government subsidies to production and service units, provided at a rate lower than the market rate, are camouflaged and never accounted for. Consequently, the managerial efficiency of these units cannot be assessed. Managers and directors whose firms enjoy favorable foreign exchange rates lack the incentive to cut costs, increase production, or improve services.

Throughout the 1980s, firms with government affiliations tended to sell, on the free market, raw materials they had imported at the lower official exchange rate. They were, therefore, profitable and unproductive at the same time. This system clearly fails to encourage efficiency, discipline, productivity, and innovation. Units of production are transformed into non-productive, trading enterprises.

Multi-tiered exchange rate systems also play a negative role by fostering demand for imported goods. Imports, or any transactions involving foreign exchange, become more profitable. Lucrative dealings in foreign exchange lead to increased corruption as eligible units seek to expand their access to the government agencies in charge of allocating foreign exchange at the official rate.

Creating a single exchange rate, however, does not necessarily put an end to such abuses. Once the single exchange rate mechanism was in place, it failed to prevent capital flight and to induce investment in productive sectors. Instead, it created a balance of payments crisis, led to an expansion of the black market for foreign exchange, and encouraged bribery and other forms of corruption.

The imposition of a single exchange rate – or the devaluation of the country's official currency – should have entailed a decrease in imports and an increase in exports. In Iran, however, this policy failed in raising the country's foreign exchange earnings significantly. Most of Iran's foreign exchange revenue comes from exporting oil, which operates independently from domestic fluctuations in foreign exchange rates. The single exchange rate produced mixed results in the case of non-oil exports. While devaluation helped make these goods more competitive in the international market, it also increased their cost, in line with the increased cost of imports used to manufacture them. The fall in the price of the Iranian rial also failed to reduce domestic demand for foreign goods. The accumulation of wealth and income in a relatively small sector of society had increased that group's purchasing power to the extent that it was entirely unresponsive to fluctuations in exchange rates.

Meanwhile, the productive sectors of the Iranian economy suffered negative effects from the imposition of a single exchange rate mechanism. In the short term, their liquidity was adversely affected, so many were forced to stop production or close shop. Since domestic production relied heavily on the availability of raw and semi-manufactured goods and foreign technology, the cost of production soared with an increase in foreign exchange rates. Some units were driven out of business, and some, on the advice of the government, turned to banks and accumulated huge debts. The single exchange rate also put upward pressure on inflation, another negative effect on production units. Increased costs reduced demand. In some cases, higher-priced domestically produced goods were unable to compete with imports.

Another reason the single exchange rate failed in Iran was that the government concentrated on foreign currencies and neglected the rial. To be successful, a currency policy must deal with both. To help the single rate mechanism succeed, the government should have implemented reforms in the country's financial, monetary, and commercial sectors. For example, the inflationary pressures of a single exchange rate mechanism should be counterbalanced by appropriate fiscal management and measures to control private liquidity. In 1991 and 1992, private liquidity grew at about 25 percent a year; the figure was about 36 percent for 1993. Clearly, an appropriate monetary policy was lacking. Also, since the government earned a large portion of its revenue by dealing in the foreign currency black market – 41 percent in 1992 – it did not respond adequately to price increases in foreign currencies. Moreover, the implementation of a single exchange rate mechanism has been transformed into an end in itself rather than a means to a higher end. For Iran, economic policy should be based on industrialization; and any measures, including a single exchange rate, should be adopted only if they contribute to that objective.

Another factor contributing to the failure of the single exchange rate mechanism is weak policy-making practices. As a rule, policy-makers in Iran concentrate on the pros and cons of policies, rather than on assessing policies in terms of the government's ability or inability to implement them. An example is the performance of the country's banking system in extending foreign exchange credits without proper guarantees, negotiating loans with simultaneous due dates, and adopting passive, short-term policies to regulate the chaotic foreign exchange market. The banking system is plagued by its multi-layered connections with the government. Without an independent central bank, economic policies are bound to be undermined by political pressures.

Finally, policy-makers in Iran concentrated on the supply side of the foreign exchange issue, neglecting the demand side. They were concerned with the volume of foreign exchange earnings and not with the expenditure of foreign exchange. Thus, fluctuations in oil revenues become primary, and a foreign exchange budget is considered unnecessary. In 1991, Iran earned $16 billion in foreign currency and spent $27.8 billion on imports; the figures for the following year were $18 billion and $29 billion, respectively. Had demand for foreign exchange figured more prominently in policy-making, then expenditure would have been prioritized and planned. Another problem is that projections of foreign currency earnings tend to be inflated. The first plan assumed revenues of $81.5 billion from petroleum exports, and $17.8 billion from non-oil exports for the entire plan period. Petroleum earnings were 90 percent and non-oil export earnings were only 65 percent of their projected rates. A plan based on incorrect assumptions of the supply of foreign exchange is bound to run into problems.

Comparing the First and Second Plans

The first plan ended in 1993, but 1994 did not mark the beginning of the second one. Policy-makers devoted 1994 to evaluating the first plan, understanding its full ramifications, and considering their alternatives. The Parliament, too, decided to spend 1994 on gathering data, increasing legislative input in drawing up the second plan, and overseeing the executive branch. The second plan, therefore, covers the five-year period from 1995 to 1999.[23] In essence, the second plan is not much different from the first; it is a centralized, sectoral plan, that includes social and cultural policies. As Mas'ud Rowghani Zanjani, director of Iran's Plan and Budget Organization has pointed out, the second plan is a continuation of the first. But experiences gained in implementing the first plan have led to some modifications in the second plan. The following are among the major features of the second development plan.

Securing sustained economic growth   The second development plan, like its predecessor, gives top priority to economic growth. Unlike the first plan, however, it puts the emphasis on stable and sustainable growth. Lessons drawn from Iran's economic performance from 1989 to 1993 have been incorporated into the new plan. Unstable growth bred chaos, waste, opportunism, short-term planning, and speculation, leading to a loss of confidence in the government. The first plan also demonstrated that economic growth is impossible without structural changes in the economic, social, political, and cultural spheres of the country. The rate of economic growth will reflect the effectiveness of these changes. In the current situation, high growth rates are not feasible without injections of

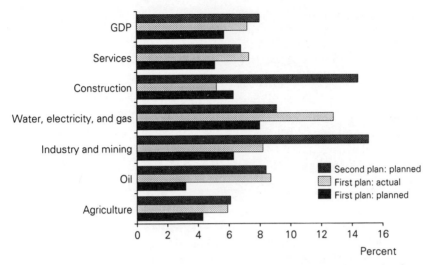

Figure 12.8 GDP growth rates and their sectoral distribution during the first and second plans (average annual, percent)

money, a recipe that has proved to be problematic. Thus, the second plan envisages a moderate growth rate. In the first plan, the average annual GDP growth rate was projected at 8.1 percent. In the second plan, the target is lowered to 5.8 percent (see Table 12.3; Figure 12.8).

How this modified rate of growth is to be maintained is not specified in the second plan, although more realistic targets are surely more likely to be achieved. But this is no guarantee for stable growth. The first plan had selected the oil, petrochemical, and heavy industries (especially steel) sectors to provide rapid economic growth. The assumption was that these sectors could, on the one hand, provide foreign exchange earnings, and on the other hand, support the agricultural and industrial sectors, and ultimately serve as engines of growth for the national economy. The second plan envisages a slower growth rate for the petroleum sector (average annual rate of 3.2 percent), and an average annual growth rate of 6.2 percent for the industrial sector and 6.3 percent for the construction sector. For the industrial sector, the projected growth rate is slightly higher than the actual rate achieved under the first plan, and for the construction sector it is slightly higher than the actual rate in the first plan. The assumption in the second plan is that with more conservative projections for the petroleum sector, and realistic ones for construction, industry, and mining, it will be possible to pursue quantitative goals that are both feasible and sustainable.

Table 12.3 GDP growth rate and its sectoral distribution during the first and second plans (average annual percentage rate)

	Second plan* (1995–99)**	First plan (1989–93)	
	Planned	Planned	Actual
Agriculture	4.3	6.1	5.9
Oil	3.3	9.5	8.7
Industry and mining	6.2	15.0	8.3
Water, electricity, and gas	8.0	9.1	12.7
Construction	6.3	14.5	5.2
Services	5.0	6.7	7.4
GDP	5.8	8.1	7.2

Notes: * Proposed Plan Bill by the government. Although the Plan Bill has 1994–98 as the plan period, in reality, the plan will cover the 1995–99 period. ** Iranian year begins 21 March.

Sources: As Tables 12.1a and 12.1b.

Emphasizing social justice Issues of social justice were at best peripheral to the first plan, restricted to government support for families of martyrs and war veterans. The underlying premise of the first plan was that the first step toward development was economic growth. Thus, the government gave priority to economic growth over improving living standards of lower-income families. Increased national wealth, it was assumed, would then be redistributed equitably through taxation. The government was proven wrong. Economic liberalization policies, along with the single, floating exchange rate mechanism, fueled inflation and disparity in incomes. Most severely affected were lower-income and middle-class or fixed-income households. Dissatisfaction with the government's economic policies were widespread. Its commercial policies, stemming from a non-productive orientation and inadequate protectionism for small industries, exacerbated the hardships. Demonstrations ensued in major cities in the summer of 1992. Thus, the government was obliged to accommodate the grievances, and in drawing up the second plan, it devoted special attention to strengthening social security, reinstating subsidies on basic goods, and expanding infrastructure in peripheral areas.

Reducing demand for foreign exchange and foreign debts The performance of the first plan revealed a high margin of error in the area of foreign exchange strategies. Revenues from oil exports, the main source of foreign exchange, fluctuated greatly and amounted to only 90 percent of the plan's projections. Similarly, non-oil exports succeeded in generating only 65 percent of projected earnings. In addition, the foreign exchange accrued from these sources did not circulate in the economy, hence the need for policy-makers to curtail demand for foreign exchange. Projections for oil revenues are lowered in the second plan. Specifically, the oil sector is projected to generate $73 billion over the second plan period, and the non-oil sector is to bring in an additional $27 billion (a rather high expectation). Consequently, demand for foreign exchange has to fall, and imports need to be restricted. From 1995 to 1999, imports are projected to grow at 7.3 percent a year from actual 1994 levels, which means $91 billion in imports during the plan years. It is worth remembering here that in 1994 imports fell dramatically compared to 1992, reaching $16.1 billion, a 45 percent decrease from 1992.

In the second plan, foreign investment is listed among potential sources for foreign exchange and technological know-how. Foreign loans and investments are not prioritized, however, primarily for two reasons. First, the Islamic Republic was not successful in attracting foreign investment in the first plan period. Moreover, since prospects for structural changes in the country's judicial, political, social, and organizational systems are not favorable, at least in the short run, it is unlikely to have any more success in the second plan. Second, high volumes of foreign debt accumulated in the first plan period have adversely affected the economy; and the banking system has not handled the situation with great foresight. Nevertheless, the plan allows the government to raise some $10 billion in foreign loans in buy-back and other forms to finance projects in the oil and gas sectors and in infrastructure. On the whole, however, the second plan focuses on repaying foreign debts, a factor which will undoubtedly diminish its economic potential. In fact, the plan aims to reduce the actual volume of foreign debts by its final years (See Table 12.2).[24]

Emphasizing domestic sources of investment and reducing the government's financial obligations One of the main lessons of the first plan was to restrain overreliance on oil revenues and overoptimism regarding the future price of oil. Although fluctuations in oil prices occurred in the 1980s, they were usually attributed to the war effort and thus thought to be temporary. But the fluctuations persisted in the plan period, and policy-makers came to realize that oil prices are really determined by demand in the international market. Thus, in the second plan, policy-makers have opted instead for domestic capital as a source of revenue.

This policy choice is further strengthened because of pessimistic forecasts for attracting foreign capital and the conviction that the country is in fact rich in human and material capital, and that these resources have remained untapped in previous plans.[25] The second plan seeks to invigorate these resources and expand their contribution to national economic growth. Factors that in the past have impeded the participation of these resources in the economic process include: slow return on investment in both the private and public sectors, low levels of professional training and industrial research, inclination toward imports rather than domestic production, weak intersectoral linkages in economic activities, inefficient mobilization and generation of investment, non-productive consumption patterns, wasteful usage of vital resources, high depreciation value of investment, and large numbers of unfinished projects and incremental costs of their eventual completion.

Expanding educational and employment opportunities   The first half of the 1980s was marked by high birth rates. This young population (42 percent of whom are under 15 years of age) will enter the labor force during the period of the second plan.[26] In addition, 16 million women will reach child-bearing age by the end of the second plan. Although population growth rates have declined, the growing demand for jobs and services, as well as changes in the age composition of the population, have pushed policy-makers to focus on employment and education in the second plan. The plan's goal is to create two million new jobs during its five-year span. Primary and secondary education are to be expanded, as are higher education, professional training, and physical education programs. The total budget devoted to education will grow 115 percent, from IR 4,789.3 in 1993 to IR 10,302.7 in 1998. The expansion of educational services is another example of the plan's emphasis on the development of domestic resources, rather than on foreign investment and revenues. A central aim of the second plan is to create a competitive labor force, in line with international trends of giving high priority to human resources. In this respect, it would be appropriate for the Islamic Republic to take advantage of the highly trained Iranian expatriates living abroad.

Thus, three determinants distinguish the second plan from the first plan. First, the second plan is more conservative. Unrealistic assessments in the first plan show that the government should approach economic growth with more caution. The second plan is drawn with two high-end and low-end scenarios for resources and quantitative goals. The Iranian government is now aware that it has a limited impact on economic trends.

The Parliament's approach to the 1994–95 budget, too, reflects a similar realization in the legislative branch: the budget is drawn on the premise of $10 billion in guaranteed oil sales, whereas the actual volume is estimated at $14 billion.

Second, the new plan is also more balanced than its predecessor. An attempt is being made to balance economic dimensions of social change with its societal ramifications. Economic growth is accompanied with social justice, and the latter is to extend to all low-income sectors of the population, not just a select few.

Third, the plan is more inward-looking. It focuses on utilizing domestic resources, reducing the role for petroleum earnings, developing human resources, and confronting social problems. The first plan, in contrast, focused on linking the economy to the international scene, rapidly expanding the oil sector, promoting exports, reducing import controls, and attracting foreign investment.

Principal Challenges Confronting the Second Plan

The Parliament has placed two key demands on the second plan: first, it must be realistic in terms of costs and revenues, and it must economize on costs; and second, its macro-structure must be in line with Ayatollah Khamene'i's guidelines. Generally, the guidelines call for improving social justice, prioritizing revolutionary values in the provision of resources for the expansion of domestic production, reducing imports, reforming the bureaucratic and judicial structures, supporting development of social sectors, orienting administrative activities toward ethics and values, prioritizing structural investments, attending to public participation in building the nation, strengthening national defense, harmonizing financial and banking policies with the Islamic Republic's principles in the conduct of foreign relations, and preserving the nation's integrity and interests.[27]

An assessment of the second plan's chances for success in actualizing its objectives will have to wait until the final version of the plan is released. Like the first plan, the second plan, too, might be subjected to major revisions. Nonetheless, the challenges confronting the second plan and the prospects for national development need to be scrutinized before it is put into practice. These challenges are, in effect, the same ones that handicapped the first plan. The plan's inadequate preparation for those challenges, which are enumerated below, paints a gloomy outlook for national development.

Regulating relations between government and civil society   One of the challenges
the second plan faces is the establishment of dynamic and democratic
relations between the government and civil society. Both parties need to
foster pro-development orientations. The environment necessary for
development can be defined by such basic characteristics as scientific
thinking, production ethos, inner discipline, and mutual accountability on
the part of the government and civil society. These values must originate
with the government and then spread to the society at large. Governments
are instrumental in facilitating the early stages of a country's development
(i.e., economic growth); this indicates that the future of sustainable growth
is dependent upon structural changes at the governmental level. This has
been confirmed by the experiences of developed countries such as the
UK and the US, as well as newly developed ones such as South Korea
and Taiwan.

In Iran, relations between government and civil society leave much to
be desired. The Iranian state has traditionally lacked the prerequisite
qualities noted above, chief among them accountability *vis-à-vis* its citizenry.
The state's alienation from civil society is rooted in the country's long
history of totalitarian rule. In recent years, oil revenue has fostered the
state's economic autonomy, increasing its alienation from the populace.
As a rentier state, the Iranian government has not been pressured to
respond to social and political demands from below. This situation has
directly influenced the spread of a counterproductive and cynical political
culture in Iran. Civil society has followed suit, mirroring the state's defining
characteristics. They have mutually ignored and neglected one another.

The state needs to be reformed before any structural changes can be
instituted in civil society. It will not be sufficient simply to reduce the
role played by government and to delegate power to civil society and the
private sector. This is the case, first, because counterproductive traits are
also prevalent in the civil society of Iran; and second, this approach
underestimates the positive role that a strong, pro-growth government
can play in national development, especially in the early stages of economic growth. Resources need to be diverted from the petroleum sector;
the state has to rely less on oil revenues and focus more on revenues
derived from domestic production in the non-oil sectors. This will foster
interdependence between the state and civil society, which in turn will
encourage greater public participation and more accountability on the
part of the government. Increased accountability will encourage discipline
and efficiency in government, qualities that will in turn spread to the rest
of the society.

Creating Institutions Necessary for Development

Overall, the second plan, like the first, is not committed to initiating the structural changes in social, economic, political, and cultural institutions necessary for development. Like other underdeveloped countries, Iran lacks the required institutions for increasing material and human potentials. A development plan must address the absence of well-integrated institutional and organizational infrastructure. For example, independent political and social institutions with a clear division of responsibilities and the capablility of assisting the government are either non-existent or only marginally present. Such institutions could enhance popular participation in governance. Moreover, in the absence of such independent institutions the economic sector has been politicized, resulting in inefficient utilization of resources, reduced productivity, and managerial ineffectiveness.

Examples of these institutions include provincial or city councils, capable of playing an important role in local, regional, and national development. Local councils have a long history in developed and developing countries. Political parties and social organizations are also important for development as they play a central role in raising public awareness and fostering educated political and social decision-making. Scientific and research organizations are another prerequisite for development. They must take root and grow in the educational, professional, and productive units, as well as in recreational and residential spaces. Professional organizations, guilds, and labor unions are also necessary, as they improve efficiency and capability. Obviously, a single plan cannot encompass the entire scope of such changes, which require time, investment, conviction, and persistence. But policy-makers could have committed the second plan to initiating structural and institutional change. Unfortunately, like the first plan, the new plan does not focus on institution building or structural change, and it is likely to fail in initiating large-scale development.

Adopting strategic forecasting Both the first and the second development plans can be characterized as short-term in vision. Although the plans are concerned with the future, they are engulfed in the problems of the day. The documents of the second plan do not reveal a cohesive concept of development. There is no future-oriented guiding principle to protect the plan from short-term pressures and to prevent it from straying from its proposed track.

Part of the problem lies with the nation's planning system. Planning in Iran is not the function of independent, dynamic, think-tank types of organizations steering the nation on its path to economic growth. Instead, planning decisions are over-responsive to pressures from the executive branch and sector-specific needs. There is no mechanism for strategic thinking, for positioning the country to attain balanced growth in the future. Of course, current problems cannot be underestimated, but it is necessary to stress the importance of forward-looking strategic planning, committed to effecting far-reaching structural change.

A development plan instead of an economic plan   The present plan, like its predecessor, is first and foremost an economic plan, and a sectoral one at that. Planners charged with implementing a development program cannot rely solely on a framework based primarily on economic considerations. An economic plan, by definition, approaches development primarily from an economic angle, focusing on increasing GDP, balancing the budget, promoting exports, etc. Development, however, encompasses a much larger agenda that includes political, social, cultural, as well as economic domains. While economic plans provide the means for achieving development, they are not in themselves sufficient.

Again, the focus has to be on structural and organizational weaknesses in the political, social, cultural, and economic realms. Economic growth alone will not foster development. If progress is limited to economic growth, it will be short-lived and unstable – the first plan being a case in point. The political, social, cultural, and economic lives of a nation are interconnected; however, development in one sector does not necessarily lead to development in the other areas. For example, supporting popular participation in economic activities will bear fruit only if accompanied by increased participation in the political affairs of the nation. The second plan does include categories on culture and society, but allocates budget lines only to creating educational, medical, recreational, etc. facilities. There is no indication of long-term strategic planning for social and cultural growth. Political development is not mentioned and receives no budgetary allotment, despite the fact that the country has been suffering from a reactionary, pre-modern political culture for a long time.[28]

The second plan is also heavily sectoral, addressing sectoral performance rather than the spatial and social distribution of performance. While the plan is concerned with social justice, it is primarily devoted to economic growth. The assumption is that growth will eventually spread from the strong economic sector to other sectors, and that development will be equally distributed among regions and social classes. This assumption led the first plan to ignore the social and spatial ramifications of sectoral performance. For instance, it is unclear as to how the new plan proposes to raise the living standards of the 60 percent of Iranians who today live below the poverty line. Moreover, the issue of equitable distribution of wealth has not been satisfactorily addressed. While increased attention to welfare and social equity is necessary, the government's efforts need to be sustained for long periods before they can have an impact.

The second plan also lacks adequate spatial guidelines in the industrial sector. It assumes, often erroneously, that the country faces a shortage of capital and therefore emphasizes industrial growth in areas with an adequate infrastructural base. This will inevitably lead to increased spatial concentration of economic activities. It is also unclear how the plan can implement balanced and harmonious growth among the various sectors of the economy. The plan is sectoral in essence and does not pay enough attention to regional, social, and intersectoral equilibria. Thus, although the plan does mention spatial planning, spatial awareness is not germane to its provisions. Such oversights and their negative consequences once again justify the creation of an independent agency for strategic national planning.

Need for industrial development   The hegemonic preponderance of oil in the national economy and its vulnerability to price fluctuations underscore the nation's need to diversify its economic base. Per capita income in foreign currency, approximately $260 annually ($200 from oil exports and $60 from non-oil exports) is insufficient for a young and rapidly growing population. Thus, developing the country's industrial sector assumes paramount importance. The industrial sector is the medium through which Iran can realize new economic resources, increase ties with the international economy, create new opportunities in employment and production, and sustain economic growth. Unfortunately, however, the second plan follows in the footsteps of the first in neglecting the industrial sector. This is likely to prove disastrous for the Iranian economy.

To spur industrial growth, industrial planning must become a priority. First, there must be educational and retraining programs for both managers and skilled labor. A highly trained labor force is a prerequisite for industrial growth. In today's global economy education, creativity, and proper exploitation of a country's human resources have emerged as central factors in economic development.[29] Second, more attention needs to be devoted to research. In Iran private institutions of research are practically non-existent, and government-supported facilities are underfunded and ineffective. Research appropriates only 0.3 percent of GDP; whereas in South Korea, for example, the corresponding figure is about 4 percent. Research facilities in universities and institutes need to be supported, and the link between industries and research facilities needs to be strengthened.[30]

Emphasis must be put on output. Managers and policy-makers need to pay more attention to efficiency, both in the utilization of human resources as well as in technology. Technological know-how has to be updated. An open, democratic workplace fosters cooperation and enhances productivity, both of which are discouraged by ideologically motivated decision-making at the managerial level. Industrial management should rely more on the latest findings in operations research and information technology. Finally, marketing strategies need to be invigorated; not only is a clear-cut strategy crucial, but a conducive political climate needs to be cultivated.

Foreign relations and economic growth   In the Islamic Republic's world view, there are three types of nations: friends, foes, and the undecided. Needless to say, this world view has marginalized Iran in the Western world. In the realm of economics, however, friendly relations with the rest of the world are necessary for access to foreign markets, technology, and investments.[31] In this regard, Western countries and Iran's neighbors in the region are of paramount importance. In the past, OECD member countries, particularly Germany, Japan, France, England, and Italy, were Iran's major trading partners. This arrangement also prevails at present because of these nations' dependence on oil-producing countries and Iran's dependence on OECD markets for both its imports and exports. But Iran also needs friendly relations with its neighbors if it wants to export its industrial goods. While recent developments in post-Soviet Central Asia have opened many economic opportunities, the countries of the Gulf remain Iran's significant trading partners in the region, and shall remain so in the foreseeable future.

The Islamic Republic is seeking to improve its diplomatic and commercial ties with countries in the region. Economic cooperation treaties have been signed with Central Asian states, and diplomatic ties with Jordan, Kuwait, Saudi Arabia, Iraq, and the UAE have been resumed or strengthened. Efforts are being made to improve relations with Morocco, Egypt, and Tunisia. Cooperation with Arab states fosters regional security and strengthens OPEC. Iran's relations with the UAE have recently been ruffled by ownership claims over the three islands of Abu Musa, the Lesser Tunb and the Greater Tunb in the Gulf. Other Arab states have supported the UAE's claim, including Egypt, Saudi Arabia, and Iraq. Also, Iran's refusal to recognize the state of Israel, its denunciation of the Arab–Israeli peace process, and its support for Islamic movements in the region (Hamas and Hizbollah in particular) have undermined its efforts to cultivate a better standing in the region.

Iran's plans for economic reconstruction also face challenges from the West. Iran needs to reestablish relations with Western nations, reclaim its position in the community of nations, and gain access to technological know-how, foreign investment, and advanced techniques of production in order to sustain stable economic growth. Improved relations with the West will also lead to a more advantageous positioning in the region. Iran has an ancient history, marked by centuries of interaction with other nations and peoples. Prolonged isolation and marginalization will not serve the country's long-term interests. Although relations with most Western nations have improved since the early days of the revolution, they remain marked by mutual distrust and instability. Iran needs to reformulate its relations with key Western countries, the United States in particular. Only then can it beneficially pursue economic and political relations with the outside world. The experience of the first plan reinforces this contention.

Implications for Gulf Security

The Clinton administration's policy of dual containment seeks to weaken Iran by crippling its economy. The proponents of the policy assume that a weaker Iran will be less adventurous and incapable of aggression against its neighbors, and thus better for regional stability. Yet the historical record indicates that in times of economic malaise, Iranian leaders have tended to deflect public attention from domestic problems by adventurism abroad. Besides, a weaker Iran has often encouraged ambitious neighbors to act on their aggressive motives. The upheavals of the 1980s corroborate this hypothesis. For example, if Iraq had not perceived Iran to be weak and disorganized in 1980, it would have been less likely to invade Iran; and in the absence of the Iran–Iraq war, Iraq would not have descended into the economic ruin that caused Saddam Hussein to invade Kuwait in 1990. Conversely, an economically vibrant Iran has often contributed to the Gulf's stability. Indeed, encouraging a strong and capable Iran was the cornerstone of the Gulf policies of the Nixon and Carter administrations, where Iranian might was the bedrock of the Gulf's stability. Twentieth-century Iran has not initiated any regionally significant hostility against its neighbors; and when the country's central government and its economy have been strong, Iran's neighbors have acted more responsibly as well.

To ensure Gulf security, therefore, it is critical that Iran's economy is placed on the road to sustainable development. Conversely, unless the Gulf is a stable region, the Iranian economy may not experience substantial growth for any significant length of time. Iran depends on the Gulf to export its oil, the source of over 90 percent of its foreign currency earnings. The Iranian province of Khuzestan, the site of most of the country's oil production, abuts the Gulf and remains vulnerable to instability and skirmishes in the region. The Gulf is also the main transport route of Iran's trade with the world and neighboring states; trade with the UAE is already valued at $1 billion a year and growing. Iran has a stake in Gulf security, and if its Arab neighbors also seek regional stability, they should foster economic well-being in Iran. From this perspective, the poor performance of the Iranian economy, as explained above, may translate into instability in the Gulf.

To reverse these destabilizing trends, domestic reforms and international cooperation, particularly from Iran's Arab neighbors, must come together to build the Iranian economy. The necessary domestic political-economic reforms have been outlined above; on the international front, dual containment must be replaced by a policy of reconciliation. Instead of zero-sum thinking, the major producers in OPEC must concentrate on mutual gain through enhanced coordination. The arms race in the Gulf is exacting a heavy toll on all the regional economies. Incorporating Iran in the GCC's security arrangements can go a long way in curbing the spiralling arms race. Finally, to encourage stability in the Gulf, regional and international trade with and investment in Iran must increase; the liberal economic policies of President Hashemi Rafsanjani should be viewed as a window of opportunity.

PART FOUR

Iran and Gulf Security

CHAPTER 13

The Gulf Security Dilemma: The Arab Gulf States, The United States, and Iran

Jamal S. al-Suwaidi

Introduction

The quest for enduring peace and stability in the Gulf has captured the interest of scholars and occupied the minds of policy-makers for some time. The scholars are expected to illuminate as thoroughly and dispassionately as possible the issues that define the discourse, but the role of the policy-makers values political acceptance more than judicious evaluation of the arguments. While recognizing that this gap between theory and practice bedevils the implementation of reasonable policy prescriptions, this chapter offers some insights into the key issues and recent developments affecting the future of Gulf security and Iran's role in them.

As the world prepares for the twenty-first century, nations grapple to comprehend the challenges of a newly unfolding global order. Brimming with hopes and aspirations for a better world, today's leaders may seize the opportunity of a new beginning to lay the foundation for a post-Cold War era that avoids the tension and conflict of recent centuries. The search for peace and tranquillity in and around the Gulf region may serve as a litmus test to gauge the chances for a more stable world order. Here, the nexus of political, economic, and social factors has created a complex set of interactions among regional and extraregional states that poses a range of formidable obstacles on the road to lasting stability. Typically, contentious issues of a specific nature are difficult to disentangle from the multifarious maelstrom of conflict that has enveloped the area in recent times.

In 1996, it is difficult to assess whether the Gulf region's security environment is more or less worrisome than in earlier years. Nevertheless, the political actions and foreign policies of the Islamic Republic of Iran are a major concern for the stability and security in the Gulf region. Arab nations of the Gulf, in particular, are threatened by Iranian-encouraged activists who attempt to aggravate domestic tension that might otherwise have been successfully addressed by these states.[1] Other equally distressing activities and policies contributing to this concern include: 1) Iran's continued occupation of the UAE islands of Abu Musa and the greater and the lesser Tunbs; 2) ongoing Iranian programs to develop a conventional military arsenal and to acquire weapons of mass destruction, including the continuing ambition to acquire nuclear weapons; 3) Iranian sponsorship of extremist groups and covert operations around the world; 4) Iran's active role in attempting to destabilize Arab Gulf governments; 5) Iranian public opposition to the peace process between Israel and the Arab states; and 6) Iran's nationalist quest to expand Persian influence and its attempt to dominate the Gulf region as the sole hegemonic power. All of these factors have played a major role in shaping the Iranian image in the world and have kept Iran at the center of international attention.[2]

The maintenance of Gulf security has become increasingly detached from the regional system of the Arab world. The contribution to regional security provided by the presence of Western military forces is an important component of the Gulf regional security debate and is a significant area of disagreement between Iran and the Arab governments of the Gulf Cooperation Council. Moreover, the United States, in expressing its concerns over Iraq and Iran as the two major threats to an unimpeded flow of Gulf oil and as primary detractors from Gulf stability in the long term, has adopted a policy of dual containment. This policy has created a power vacuum in the area that has to be filled by major world powers external to the region, including the United States. The potential consequences of isolating Iran may adversely affect the security and stability of the region; this necessitates due reflection by the parties involved, especially by the neighboring Arab states of the Gulf.

Although attempts to resolve the Gulf security dilemma abound, these descriptions and analyses commonly focus on the regional powers of Iraq and Iran and the relations between these countries and between the United States and its Western allies. Rarely mentioned are the roles played by the six actors of the Gulf Cooperation Council, especially their complex patterns of interaction and the manner in which they view their national security needs, and regional security requirements in general. Policy analysts and strategists have essentially ignored the GCC's role in fostering Gulf stability and have attributed the absence of security in the region to the GCC states' inability to identify the elements required for regional security, and, at times – which is even more problematic – for their own individual national security.

In undertaking an examination of Gulf security, consideration should be given to the following themes. First is the collapse of the Arab regional system in the aftermath of the Iraqi invasion of Kuwait and the inability of the Arab league and other regional organizations to cope with the 1990 crisis. Second is the US policy of dual containment – its foundations and potential ramifications – along with the continuing international sanctions against Iraq and the ongoing conflict between the United States and Iran. Third is the collapse of the Soviet Union and the end of the Cold War, both watersheds having two important implications for Gulf security: a) a strengthened US commitment to ensuring security in the Gulf, which includes the frequent docking of US ships in Gulf ports, the pre-positioning of military equipment, and the periodic deployment of military personnel; and b) continuing Russian military sales to Iran, including the transfer of advanced technology and military hardware.

A fourth theme is Arab–Israeli peace, which, while having generally reduced tensions between Arab nations and the Jewish state, has increased the probability of hostilities in the Gulf, especially in light of the vehement Iranian opposition to the peace process and harsh criticism by Iranian leaders of the Arab partners at peace with Israel. Even more worrisome is the Islamic Republic's quest to acquire weapons of mass destruction – most notably its development of a nuclear program, which puts Iran at the top of the list of Israel's security concerns. Fifth is the declining state of the Iranian economy, due in part to fiscal mismanagement, a lack of skilled administrators, and high rates of population growth. Economic prosperity is inextricably dependent upon political stability. In reaction to continual economic deterioration, domestic discontent may spill over into the process of foreign policy formulation and become manifest in the adoption of more radical foreign policy options.

The proposition that the Islamic Republic of Iran is generally viewed today by the international community as a major threat to the stability of the Gulf region is the focus of this chapter. Incorporating the themes outlined above, the chapter begins by focusing on the domestic factors that contribute to Iranian foreign policy. The post-Cold War relationship between the United States and Iran is examined in the second part. The third and fourth sections discuss the relationship between the GCC states and Iran and examine the security dynamics that attend that strained relationship, including the economic factors that influence Gulf security.

Iran and Gulf Stability

In view of the merits in taking a different point of departure in examining questions over the security and stability of the Gulf region, prospects for amicable relations among the Gulf states can scarcely be addressed without a thorough examination of Iran's domestic policy, its economic agenda, and the social forces that will shape its society in the future.[3] The sources of instability in the Gulf are many, and their regional impact rarely follows a concentric pattern. Challenges are often precipitated by a composite of domestic and regional factors encompassing ideological, economic, and social grievances that both evoke and respond to the involvement of extraregional actors. While alliances have shifted and issues have changed, the concept of Gulf security is immutably tied to the stability of Iran. Still reeling from the effects of a costly eight-year war with Iraq and the aftershocks of a revolution whose consequences continue to unfold, the Islamic Republic will in important ways determine the path the region will embark on as the twentieth century comes to a close.

While the ascendancy of the clerics in the wake of the revolution changed Iranian politics in both process and outcome, members of the clergy are neither monolithic nor are their methods and goals invariably contrary to those of the late Shah. Hence, even at the height of clerical rule during the reign of Ayatollah Khomeini, Tehran's policies adhered to the precepts of Islamic revivalism punctuated by Iranian nationalism.[4] The revolution expanded public expectations beyond the government's ability to deliver, however, and the influence of the clerics has been waning steadily since.[5] This process is exacerbated by a seeming institutional decadence whereby politicized clerics – responsible for much of the corruption, greed, and managerial ineptitude that attends Iran's economic malaise – are sapping the country's moral fiber and exhausting the people's patience.[6] Revolutionary puritanism has run its course, and ideological zealotry is tempered by the exigencies of responsible governance.

Furthermore, as revolutionary ideals recede into the background, the question over Iran's spiritual leadership of the Shi'a community and the associated debate over the extent to which the clergy should participate in government and by whom it should be led – Ayatollah Khamene'i's aspirations to assume the mantle of religious authority have been rejected due to insufficient religious credentials – are all increasingly subsumed under the pressing need to steer the country clear of economic and social problems. There is an acute sense that combining the spiritual and temporal leadership in one person, signifying the ultimate merging of religion and politics, has outgrown its usefulness in the absence of revolutionary momentum sustained by the charisma of the late Ayatollah Khomeini. Mounting indifference and cynicism among average Iranians about the niceties of religious hierarchy and the philosophical merits of revolutionary ideals have been amply documented.[7] The clerical challenge has been slowly eroded by the consequences of a devastating eight-year war, the bid for independence from global economic forces, pervasive government mismanagement, and the corrosive influence of foreign ideas.

However ambiguous, incoherent, cumbersome, and even irrational Iranian politics may appear, the confluence of dramatic events following the death of Khomeini – including the collapse of Soviet communism, the swift allied victory over Iraq in the second Gulf war, and the progressive worsening of the Iranian economy – has shifted Tehran's foreign policy from one of non-alignment to one of guarded engagement. Revolutionary romanticism is giving way to greater economic pragmatism, while fierce radicalism is increasingly eschewed in favor of political moderation.

Although the Tehran leadership can no longer ignore lingering economic stagnation and simmering social discontent at home, its foreign policy will likely continue to be informed by strident nationalism, which principally seeks to stem extraregional influences (particularly from the United States) that challenge Iranian ambitions in the Gulf, rather than by the propagation of political Islam. Pursuing its bid for regional preponderance without encouraging political isolation *vis-à-vis* its neighbors, Tehran's Gulf policy of combining assertive, if not confrontational, positions with accommodative gestures will likely persist.

Keenly aware of how its national ambitions were thwarted by Britain and Russia in the nineteenth and early twentieth centuries, Tehran is sensitized to outside interference and regards bilateral security ties between Arab Gulf states and Western powers as a concerted attempt to deny Iran its rightful place in the region. Yet there is a recognition that in order to obviate further tensions across the Gulf, Iran must reassure its neighbors of its intentions. Obscured by ubiquitous intrigues and enigmatic personalities, the Iranian stance is not easily deciphered. Worse, as one observer aptly points out, "Iranians' stunning propensity for deception, issuing from a profound historical belief that Shi'ites are safer in a larger Sunni world if they speak disingenuously, can easily drive an outsider to frustration, exhaustion, and an assumption of Iranian guilt before innocence."[8]

In judging whether Iran engages in undue militarization, one must be mindful of Tehran's sense of beleaguerment. Internally, the leadership presides over a multi-ethnic society where Persians make up no more than 50 percent of the population, with sizable minority communities (e.g., Kurds, Armenians, Azeris, Baluchis) challenging the social cohesion in geostrategic border areas, and where linguistic differences (e.g., Turkish, Arabic) test the people's national identity. Enter the turmoil and civil unrest along Iran's northern and eastern periphery, and the specter of serious spillover associated with the unraveling of neighboring states, especially the nascent republics of the former Soviet Union, poses an incalculable threat to the stability of Iran. Moreover, the Tehran regime must cope with armed attacks against oil and military installations in Khuzestan by the Mojahedin-e Khalq, an opposition group operating out of Iraq. The regime also needs to replenish depleted hardware stocks after the war with Iraq, a country which could invade again should Iran neglect its defenses.

Iran was attacked by its neighbor to the West, and subjected to a drawn-out war of attrition including chemical weapons, with only scant reaction from the West and only a belated condemnation of Iraq by the United Nations. Consequently, Iran is under the distinct impression – enhanced by a sense of historical injustice – that the world is "out to get it." From the vantage point of leaders in Tehran, the supply of arms to Baghdad, the UN-engineered secession of Iranian territory to Iraq after the ceasefire, and the selective reasoning on the question of nuclear weapons possession – a signatory to the Nuclear Non-Proliferation Treaty (NPT), Iran faces constant pressures, while nuclear-capable Israel goes virtually unattended – together demonstrate that the Islamic Republic is denied equitable treatment. All these factors and perceptions, along with a military buildup that drains Iran's national resources, make up the domestic environment for an aggressive Iranian foreign policy towards its Arab neighbors and increase the probability of another regional conflict in the Gulf.

US Policy and the Islamic Republic of Iran

The United States has developed defense and security arrangements with the GCC states along with aggressive programs for the procurement of US military equipment by Arab Gulf states. In addition, the US military presence, pre-positioning of equipment, and the development of the Fifth Fleet all are measures to demonstrate US commitment to Gulf security and to contain the Iran and Iraq threats to regional security. Nevertheless, American–Iranian relations involve more than the security of Western access to oil. Each government today enjoys a great and apparently durable domestic consensus which holds that the others' government represents a real threat to its national interests. The origins of this enmity are several: they include, from the Iranian perspective,[9] the role of the United States in elevating the Shah Muhammad Reza Pahlavi to the throne of Imperial Iran in 1953, the undisguised intention of the United States militarily to ensure its access to Gulf oil, and the role of the United States government in the military defeat of Iran by Iraq, including the hostilities that occurred during Operation Earnest Will.[10] Adding to the strain from the US perspective are: the violent actions against and incarceration of the US diplomats then in Iran which followed the Iranian revolution; the post-revolutionary Iranian government's inflammatory rhetoric questioning the legitimacy of both the US military presence in the Gulf and of the US-sponsored Middle East peace process; the attempts of the post-revolutionary Iranian government to subvert Arab Gulf regimes with whom the United States enjoys cordial and economically important relations; and the undisguised intentions of Iran to complicate and perhaps at times to interfere with US access to Gulf oil.[11]

While control of access to Gulf oil plays an important role in the enduring dispute between the United States and Iran, other components of that dispute are attributable to events that are not specifically related to this issue. Much of the history of US–Iranian relations stems from the perceptions held during the Cold War era.[12] The willingness of the Pahlavi government to permit the United States to monitor Soviet activities electronically from Iranian soil was particularly important in the days preceding satellite surveillance capabilities. The Soviet invasion of Afghanistan in 1979 was viewed by the United States as a Soviet attempt to increase its presence in the Gulf region, and perhaps to gain military access to an Iranian Gulf seaport. Reactions of the Carter administration to Soviet activity in Afghanistan included the activation of the US military Rapid Deployment Joint Task Force, a predecessor to the United States Central Command. Cold War bipolarity inspired numerous such competitive assessments and reactions throughout the world, many having little to do with critical natural resources such as Gulf oil. Given the political demise of the Soviet Union, and the near-unanimous international consensus that the United States, at least in military terms, is the dominant global power, how might the existing enmity that characterizes the US–Iranian relationship be affected in the years ahead?

The Clinton administration has labeled the Iranian government as a "backlash" state, and includes Iran, Iraq, and Libya as nations governed by individuals and political regimes that are irreconcilable with the US conception of the ideals of the international community.[13] This portrayal should be viewed in part as an obligatory nod to a domestic consensus concerning Iran within the United States. As a policy statement, it responds both to US domestic political imperatives and to international political demands. A US Democratic administration cannot permit itself to be successfully characterized by its opposition as "soft" on Iran,[14] and it is quite likely that any near-term future Republican administration in the United States would be less approachable to a normalization of relations with the Islamic Republic. Recently, the Clinton administration extended and strengthened its unilateral economic sanctions against Iran, and, albeit with limited success, lobbied the Russian and Chinese governments to restrict the transfer of nuclear technology to the Islamic Republic.[15]

Reacting to public opinion and government rhetoric, political success in Iran will continue to demand the frequent and vehement condemnation of the United States for the foreseeable future. In turn, this rhetoric of condemnation will fuel and excite public opinion in and government policies of the United States to punish Iran. The closely associated Iranian rhetoric frequently and vociferously condemning the Middle East peace process produces a related and complementary effect.

Like pre-revolutionary Iran, Israel was an important Cold War ally of the United States. Because of the large and influential domestic constituency supportive of Israel within the United States, Israel has received very large monetary transfers to support its security and economy. In the post-Cold War era, and in response to a favorable Middle East peace process, a deficit-conscious and increasingly isolationist United States might have supported reductions in these transfers to Israel. However, through Iran's unrelenting condemnations of the Middle East peace process, and its visible support of Lebanon-based para-military forces opposed to any negotiation with Israel, the Iranian government has assisted in creating in the United States a perception of an ideologically fervent radical Islamic threat to the West. This has provoked a vigorous debate, and prominent journals have published numerous influential articles by noted scholars on Islamic fundamentalism and terrorism.[16] The debate has produced a false perception of an enduring ideological contest between the West and Islam and has provided an ideological foundation for the dual containment policy toward Iran and Iraq.

Iranian policy toward Israel and the Middle East peace process, and the often extreme rhetoric that articulates that policy, has assisted the pro-Israeli lobby groups within the US policy community in creating a "regional Cold War" between the United States and Iran. This regional Cold War protects Israel's strategic alignment as an important ally of the United States, despite the near-term possibility of an enduring peace in the Middle East. It also ensures that the issue of normalization with Iran will remain as unlikely and as politically perilous within the United States as was the subject of normalization of relations with the then USSR during the height of the Cold War.

The Iranian revolution did not originally define itself by its opposition to a bilateral relationship with the United States. Neither the politics of Iranian nationalism nor the politics of Islamic activism insisted that the United States become the enemy. Indeed, the political position of the early leaders of post-revolutionary Iran were by and large compatible with a constructive bilateral relationship between the two nations.

In the several months following the triumph of the Khomeini-led government, as the clergy in Iran assumed control of all important Iranian national institutions and the foreign policy process, the definition began to change. The increasingly influential Iranian Shi'a clergy generally applauded the actions of the students who wrested control of the US embassy, and the "hostage crisis" of 1979 ensued. It was not only politically impossible for the new revolutionary Khomeini government to reject or moderate the actions of its students in the streets; the litmus test of loyalty to the revolution during its first year became the expression of active opposition to the United States, as well as the continued rejection of the governmental policies instituted by the Pahlavi administration.

A few years after the revolution, however, informal consultations between the governments of Iran and the United States occurred and produced agreements. Remarkably, these private discussions transpired during the administrations of Ayatollah Ruholla Khomeini and Ronald Reagan and have not taken place during the more moderate administrations that followed. This historical inversion deserves some thoughtful analysis[17] – bilateral private consultations were undertaken during comparatively "hardline" administrations, while the more "pragmatic", post-Cold War administrations of today consider private consultations impossible.

In the late 1980s, a devastating period for the Islamic Republic, hostilities developed with renewed intensity. Iran found itself militarily defeated, economically restrained, and diplomatically isolated, and, in the eyes of the Iranian leadership, the government of the United States had a strong and visible hand in all three dimensions. A long war with Iraq ended on unfavorable terms, and the costs of that war were enormous. An aging revolutionary leader finally succumbed to a death of natural causes, and the revolution lost a charismatic figure. The Iranian claim to ideological and political leadership throughout the Muslim world – although never as strong as Khomeini had believed – lessened, and the revolutionary consensus even within Iran lost momentum. Factionalism grew. In the dispute between groups who sought bureaucratic prominence and control of the national Iranian agenda, the goals of the revolution remained the test of legitimacy. Even as some pragmatic policies were pursued (e.g., socioeconomic programs), and as certain hegemonic policies of the Khomeini government were quietly reversed (e.g., export of the revolution and domination of the Islamic world), the rhetoric against the United States was retained as evidence that the revolution continued to guide the actions of senior officials within the government. Because political legitimacy in the Islamic Republic of Iran requires opposition to the United States, Iran, in one sense, volunteered to replace the former Soviet Union as the regional Cold War opponent of the United States.

For the United States, the late 1980s was an important and celebrated period in its history: The Cold War was over and won, as witnessed by the 1989 destruction of the Berlin wall. Influential US national security analysts began to articulate a "selective engagement" policy, a national security policy that responded to the absence of bipolar restraint on the pursuit of US interests abroad.[18] As a national security policy, selective engagement suggested that the United States possessed greater freedom in the post-Cold War era to influence significantly the outcomes of issues it deemed important, such as Middle East peace or Gulf security.[19] Consequently, the military forces of the United States were preparing for, and would retain budgetary priority for, selective engagement against governments who remained hostile to America's vital interests and its concept of governance.

Iran, as its rhetoric became stronger and more directed toward the United States and its allies in the post-Cold War era, became a perfect candidate for attention. The Islamic Republic qualified on both counts – it interfered with the pursuit of US vital interests, and espoused political and societal systems incompatible with the Western concept of free markets and democratic governance. Iraq's invasion of Kuwait provided a more urgent need and opportunity "selectively" to engage the military forces of the United States. General Schwarzkopf's central military planning effort had always focused on the military defeat of Iran, and the deployment of US forces that occurred during Operation Desert Shield followed the guidelines of the standing US operations plan for the invasion of Iran.[20]

The US policy of isolating Iran politically and controlling its military buildup created a victimization complex in the Iranian political consciousness. The ongoing debate over Iranian plans to acquire a nuclear capability illustrates this point: Tehran argues that under the NPT it is not only allowed access to nuclear technology for peaceful purposes, but such technology must be made available under advantageous conditions by the declared nuclear powers. Having been cleared by the IAEA inspectors of any contravention, Tehran stresses that its plan to complete the Bushehr nuclear power plant, started in the 1970s with the help of Germany, is part of an effort to free up more oil for export to secure much-needed hard currency. The proposed purchase of two Russian light-water nuclear reactors as well as the construction of hydroelectric power stations are intended to meet the mounting energy consumption of its burgeoning population. Without the establishment of alternative energy sources, Iran argues, its oil exports may dry up by the year 2000.[21] Hence, US and Israeli pressure to stop the transfer of Russian nuclear technology and to arrest Japanese funding of a hydroelectric dam are seen as attempts to strangle Iran economically. The feeling of being singled out is further reinforced by US willingness to furnish light-water reactors at no cost to North Korea, a country that has consistently refused international inspection of its nuclear facilities.

Yet there are signs that cast suspicion on Iran's nuclear program. Members of the Majlis have criticized it as an inefficient allocation of limited funds; Iranian analysts are afraid it will taint the country's reputation at the expense of desperately needed foreign investment; and international observers worry that the level of spending on nuclear hardware is well beyond what is needed for peaceful energy production.[22] Reports of Iranian delegations visiting Kazakhstan to explore the possibility of acquiring enriched uranium sufficient to fuel 20 nuclear bombs prompted the secret US purchase of the material to prevent its transfer to Iran. Also, Russian military attachés are believed to be assisting Iran to augment the power of a Chinese-built gas centrifuge capable of producing weapons-grade uranium. There are similar reports regarding the delivery of Chinese rocket components, possibly in violation of the Missile Technology Control Regime, to improve the accuracy, payload, and range of Iran's No-Dong missile.[23]

Although the details of Iran's nuclear program remain shrouded in obscurity, one may reasonably conjecture about the effects of a nuclear Iran on regional Gulf stability. Since Iran is at least five to ten years away from attaining a militarily significant nuclear capability, could it readily extract diplomatic and, if need be, military concessions from its Gulf neighbors? Indications are that the leverage Iran could exercise with a nascent nuclear force (no more than a few deliverable bombs) over GCC members would be minimal.[24] However, in judging the minimal effect of a small Iranian nuclear capability, many appear to be assuming an offensive use. It may be that it would be used mainly as a deterrent, to prevent the retaking of territory seized in a successful conventional attack. Using nuclear weapons for intimidation to drive a wedge between the GCC and the United States would risk inciting the latter to confront Iran in ways, including military ones, that the international community would not support otherwise. It may also invite a preemptive strike by Israel or Iraq. Both are eminently more important to Tehran's possible nuclear strategy: Deterring Israel, albeit only from direct attacks on Iranian territory, may give it heightened standing in the Muslim world; and considering Iraq's past use of chemical weapons and its potential to re-emerge militarily, a nuclear option may offer Tehran the type of insurance policy needed to cope with future threats. Although a nuclear Iran may in limited ways be more confident *vis-à-vis* GCC states, a more tangible benefit is likely to be greater reassurance regarding Iraq. At the same time, possession of nuclear arms may discipline Tehran's foreign policy, if only to demonstrate the regime's ability to exercise power responsibly. In the near term, however, Tehran's ability to conduct a rational process of foreign policy formulation appears tenuous, given the nature of its present leadership.

This perhaps unduly benign speculation about Iran's nuclear intentions must not obscure Tehran's concerted effort to sustain and expand conventional military capabilities in areas that could directly threaten the security of Arab states on the other side of the Gulf. In particular, Iran has the requisite force to stage long-range air attacks against point targets across the Gulf; its mine warfare capability, long-range anti-ship missiles, and fast-attack boats could seriously impede maritime traffic to and from the Gulf; and its production of chemical toxins in conjunction with medium-range missiles superior to those fielded by Iraq, as well as its acquisition of several submarines, indicate a troubling expansion of Iran's operational spectrum. Though Iran lacks an air- and sea-lift capability and the logistics to support large-scale integrated attacks far from its borders, the size of its total full-time active manpower – roughly twice that of the GCC – and the mounting intensity of military exercises by combined-force complements scarcely justify a relaxed attitude by Arab neighbors.[25] Also, Iranian efforts to establish military industrial links with the outside – more recently in an unlikely agreement with India[26] – to hone its indigenous skills for weapons production could be a further source of apprehension.

The GCC and the Islamic Republic of Iran

Following the Iranian revolution, the new government of Iran conducted itself as an Islamic critic of the Arab states of the Gulf. Iran has pursued an active policy to destabilize the Gulf states, particularly the state of Bahrain.[27] It also has frequently questioned the Islamic legitimacy of the Gulf states, specifically targeting the ruling family of the Kingdom of Saudi Arabia. At the outset of the revolution, Iran's attempts to "export" the revolution to the Arab Gulf states not only ended in failure, but helped produce a higher level of political integration between the states of the Arab Gulf. Nevertheless, it remains an imperative of domestic Iranian politics to continue to critique the policies and practices of GCC leaders. The present-day Iranian government continues to assert its leadership authority throughout the Islamic world generally, and within the Gulf region specifically, while GCC leaders continue to reject Iran's claim to transnational Islamic credentials.

Many security studies analysts have noted Iranian military resurgence with alarm, and scholars list in substantial detail specific Iranian military acquisitions of recent years.[28] These verifiable purchases of conventional military hardware and the equally undeniable yet infinitely more troubling Iranian effort to acquire unconventional weaponry are, at minimum, questionable policy choices for a country experiencing economic crises. Despite its financial constraints, Iran is determined to invest significant and scarce national assets in increasing its military capability.

A reasonable explanation for the weapons resurgence is that the present Iranian leadership is preparing to assert military superiority over one or several of the GCC states. It is the Iranian perception that the acquisition of unconventional weapons will not only facilitate such assertions, but also will enable the Islamic Republic to: 1) secure its position as the regional superpower of the Gulf; 2) gain leverage over the United States – believing that it can follow the North Korean example – by trading nuclear capability for economic support; and 3) use its power to blackmail neighboring Arab Gulf states into increasing oil quotas and participating in foreign investment opportunities in Iran. While it is necessary and

prudent to train and equip GCC forces for conventional and unconventional defense in light of the increased military capabilities of the
Islamic Republic, present-day Iran is unlikely to attack GCC states with
overt and attributable military force. As a principal combatant of the
lengthy, costly, and inconclusive first Gulf war, and as a close and greatly
interested observer of the second, the Iranian military establishment would
without doubt counsel their national leadership to refrain from taking
any action which could generate a response against Iran from a GCC–
Western coalition. However, if circumstances change (e.g., a weakening in
Western commitment to Gulf security), Iran might advance, or it could
attempt to destabilize neighboring Gulf states from within.

Indeed, the Iranian leadership should have confidence that the states
of the GCC, in conjunction with their security partners, would systematically and thoroughly destroy the Iranian military establishment, and
perhaps the Iranian state, should Iran engage in a serious conventional
attack against GCC targets. An attributable Iranian unconventional attack
against GCC targets would in all probability provoke a reciprocal unconventional attack by the Western Gulf allies. For these reasons an
overt attack by Iranian military forces against the GCC is for the
immediate future effectively deterred.[29]

The leadership in Iran seeks to project its national power (military,
demographic, geographic, etc.) in ways which increase its international
leverage over the Arab states of the Gulf, and which provide a meaningful
and visible economic dividend to important groups who remain supportive
of the revolutionary ideology. Without question, the economic and political platform of President Rafsanjani is strong evidence that the Iranian
government must deliver more than revolutionary ideology to its domestic
petitioners. Younger Iranians are increasingly articulating a demand to
reverse Iranian economic decline. As mentioned, Iran's economy has
deteriorated steadily, some would argue precipitously, since the revolution.
It is domestically essential that Iran's second five-year plan, which covers
the years 1995–2000, produces a revitalized national economy. Yet, subjected to sanctions by the United States externally, and bedeviled by a
plethora of economic crises internally, the regime in Iran may experience
great difficulty in achieving the necessary economic success.

Thus it is reasonable to conclude that an important objective of the
Iranian leadership is substantially to increase net foreign investment within
the Iranian economy, and specifically to attract investment from the
comparatively prosperous neighboring states of the Gulf. An infusion of
financial capital from Gulf Arab treasuries, as well as a more accom-

modating approach to Iranian oil production quotas within OPEC, would provide Iranian leadership with the means to develop the economy and overcome the deterorating standard of living among the Iranian populace. These contradictory foreign policy objectives – the need to challenge rhetorically the legitimacy of GCC leaders, and the desire to attract GCC financial capital – can be reconciled only when viewed from an Iranian perspective as an attempt to use Iranian national power, including expanding Iranian military power, to intimidate the Arab Gulf states.[30] It is reasonable to argue that the purpose of Iran's effort to intimidate is to gain economic leverage through military means, and to use this leverage in a way which enables or accelerates Iran's economic development.

Intimidation is most efficient, and economic appeasement the most likely response, when the relative disparity of military power is greatest. When standing alone, each of the GCC states is at greatest disadvantage in comparison to Iran. It is for this reason that the political and security relationship between GCC states, a relationship which continues specifically to exclude Iran, is viewed with distaste by the Iranian leadership. Yet it is the first tenet of Iranian foreign policy – initially to sponsor subversion and dissidence and to continue to sponsor intrigues against the governments of the independent and sovereign GCC states – which causes these nations to enter and sustain this political relationship. As such, the foreign policy practices and particularly the rhetoric of Iran have helped produce the collective security relationship between the GCC states. Because of the GCC alliance, the Gulf's military balance is less favorable to Iran, even without the direct participation of the United States and its Western allies. The foreign and security policy relationship of the GCC states, both collectively and individually, with the United States and Western allies directly reduces the ability of Iran to exert intimidative leverage in the Gulf region and is resultingly viewed with great concern by the Iranian leadership. The strengthened security relationship between the United States and GCC states in turn reduces the probability that GCC governments will increase their economic investment within Iran in any significant sense. Once again, Iranian intimidative weight is reduced, and important economic goals of the Iranian foreign policy agenda are not served.

Some outcomes of Iranian foreign policy necessitated by the revolution, namely the rhetorical attacks against the legitimacy of GCC leaders, have worked against the Iranian objective of establishing greater influence in the Gulf region. Bilateral relationships between GCC states and Iran have generally remained problematic since the revolution, but at times have been confrontational (e.g., the dispute over Iran's occupation of the UAE islands in the Gulf). Continuing Iranian military acquisitions are viewed as threatening by GCC states in part because the respective interstate relationships are less than cordial. The Iranian military buildup well exceeds the capability needed to defend itself against present-day Iraq – the only state that has attacked Iran in recent history, and the only state in the Gulf region (including Iran) that has overtly attacked a neighbor with military force in the twentieth century. The acquisition of submarines, ballistic missiles, and weapons of mass destruction can be explained only as an attempt by Iran to gain political influence in the Gulf. Should Iran ever use these weapons against a GCC neighbor, it must be aware that it would bring about its own devastation by a military coalition of the GCC states and their Western allies. Regional intimidation is the only outcome of the buildup that, if successfully attained and exercised, could permit Iran successfully to bridge the contradictory foreign policy objectives of ideological condemnation of and financial investment from the GCC. Yet economically useful intimidation may be a more difficult objective to achieve than the Iranian leadership realizes. At least in the near term, Iranian military resurgence has helped produce a tighter GCC and a closer relationship between GCC states and the West. In short, GCC states will always experience difficulty with Iranian ambitions and military strategies, whether they be articulated by the current regime of the Islamic Republic or by any other nationalist regime. Iran, regardless of its regime, will continue to attempt to dominate the Gulf region.

The GCC and Iran: The Economic Challenge

Arab Gulf economies, while confronting far fewer economic and demographic challenges than Iran, have witnessed significant budget deficits and the deterioration of financial reserves due to the revenue squeeze associated with low oil prices, expensive military operations and procurements, and the undiminished expectation of per capita prosperity from their growing populations. Iran, however, for a variety of reasons, has fared least well of all petroleum-based Gulf economies save Iraq in recent years. Prominent among these reasons is the necessity for Iran to offer oil at a discount price to compensate buyers for the uncertainty of dealing with an unstable producer.[31] Additional factors contributing to the economic crisis include: the revolutionary imperative to emphasize ideological acceptability over competence when placing personnel in economic leadership positions; a significant population increase within Iran since the revolution; the absence of innovation within the country, which maintains one of the most centrally controlled decision-making processes in the world; and the absence of confidence among traditional Iranian merchants and businessmen in the ability of the government to sustain economic growth. The crisis has also been exacerbated by the political decisions of Iranian leaders to pursue significant and expensive military modernization and expansion within Iran, and to continue economically to sponsor paramilitary activity in Lebanon and other countries.

To be sure, Iran's need for economic development and for the foreign direct investment that would make development possible has become increasingly dire. In response, President Rafsanjani's election platform and mandate was to improve Iran's economic condition. Because of the intimate relationship between Iran's economic crisis and Gulf security, however, this objective was never realized. An examination of the security dynamics of Iran's economic challenge reveals that Iran's economic objective of developing reliable international trade and investment relationships will be thoroughly ill served by Iranian threats to "freedom of navigation" within the Gulf. The petroleum segment of the Iranian economy is more dependent upon safe and reliable maritime transit of the Gulf than is the petroleum segment of the economy of any other Gulf state. Iran has invested enormous sums of capital in Gulf-situated oil terminals, of which the massive and recently refurbished facility at Kharg Island is only the most notable example. Much of Iran's oil and gas resources is within the Iranian coastal region, or offshore under the waters of the Gulf. Iran's enormous and recently reinvigorated investment in nuclear energy is also located adjacent to its Gulf port of Bushehr. Successful diversification of the Iranian economy will, without question, require access to safe and reliable Gulf-based transit for both import and export functions and processes that will be integral to successful diversification. With respect to a secure, peaceful, and internationally navigable Gulf, no nation-state has more at stake economically than Iran.

Iran also has a greater and more immediate need to increase the competitiveness and diversification of its economy and obtain external investment than do its Gulf neighbors. Iran's oil reserves are dwindling, although its gas reserves remain impressive. However, the global oil and gas market has experienced fundamental transformations in recent years, and the changes do not generally favor Gulf producers. Iran's extensive gas reserves are neither as developed nor as internationally marketable as petroleum. Other Iranian exports, notably carpets, are unlikely to produce a significant economic exchange between Iran and its trading partners. Iran's future prosperity can be achieved only through the establishment of a non-oil, export-based market. Iranian industrial development, which would serve this market, can be established only with an infusion of Western technology and foreign financial capital. Despite a significant raw material base, a large population, and geographic proximity to the import-dependent Arab Gulf, Iran has been unable or unwilling to achieve significant foreign participation in its economy, with the exception of petroleum and armaments. The palpable aura of instability that attends post-revolutionary Iran repels potential foreign investors. Identical export products, almost exclusively petroleum based, are available from any of several more stable international exporters at essentially the same price. Gulf instability has reduced the status of all Gulf exporters to residual suppliers of oil; Iranian oil exports have become the residual of the residual.

As the OPEC leverage of previous years has essentially vanished, Arab Gulf oil producers, such as Saudi Arabia, the United Arab Emirates, and Kuwait, compete with Iran in the current oil market. Moreover, Arab oil exporters also compete with the Islamic Republic for foreign investment and joint-venture partners in non-oil sectors. With the realization among all Gulf oil producers, including producers with very large proven oil reserves such as the UAE, that oil "rents" will not ensure prosperity in the twenty-first century, the drive for diversification has intensified.

Within the Arab Gulf, these factors combine to produce the "offset" program. The offset program requires foreign firms that export armaments to several Arab Gulf countries, and many non-Gulf, non-Arab countries as well, to invest directly as joint minority partners in non-oil sector, export-related enterprise within the country concerned. Offsets will increasingly enable participating Arab Gulf economies to acquire foreign direct investment, which, in turn, will create, or at least accelerate, the development of non-petroleum, export-based industries while the participating country modernizes its respective military equipment account. An important outcome of the offset program is that the government of the minority partner acquires an additional stake in the security of the Arab Gulf partner, as well as in the stability of the Gulf region as a whole, as a result of its participation. Moreover, as ties between the GCC governments and their security partners in the West are further strengthened, without the presence of a large, visible, land-based Western military establishment in the participating country, Western commitment to the security of the region is less clearly communicated to adversaries. Offset programs will, therefore, contribute to regional stability and national military modernization, as well as national economic diversification.

In stark contrast, on the other side of the Gulf lies Iran. A recent report on inflation within the Islamic Republic revealed that consumer prices have increased by more than thirty percent in the past year, one of the highest rates in the Middle East region.[32] The world's second largest producer of oil, Iran is presently able to generate a gross domestic product per capita slightly greater than Egypt's, slightly lower than Syria's.[33] The future market for oil, and even the future market for gas, in which Iran should be quite prominent, are nonetheless very unlikely to significantly alter Iran's economic marginalization. Moreover, high-technology ventures, such as nuclear power stations and missile manufacturing, do not offer an "appropriate technology" for Iran's growth and development in the mid and longer terms. As suggested by the Soviet experience, such ventures cannot serve as building blocks for economic development. Given Iran's demographics, emphasis must be placed on labor-intensive industry. Thus, Iran's need to pursue a policy stressing increased competitiveness and diversification is much more urgent than that of the Arab Gulf states. A successful formula for gaining and sustaining joint-venture economic partnerships, however, is not apparent at this time. While Iran may succeed in increasing "rental" income through additional oil and gas exploration ventures, there is little evidence of any non-oil/non-gas joint venture activity in Iran's economy at present, nor is significant direct foreign investment or joint venture activity likely. In short, the perception of risk is too great: Revolutionary Iran is one of the poorest prospects for foreign investment and joint venture in the oil-producing world.

Political stability in the Gulf is invariably tied to economic prosperity. While the correlation between economic misery and the emergence of political radicalism in the Middle East is neither established nor easily understood – Turkey, Jordan, Tunisia, and Morocco experienced a rise in Islamic radicalism in spite of economic progress[34] – there is a consensus that the fate of the Islamic Republic, the relevance of revolutionary ideals, and public support for the regime largely hinge on the government's ability to turn around a moribund economy. Despite the fact that neighboring Iraq has learned that the military intimidation of GCC states to achieve economic objectives is a failed strategy, Iran appears to be pursuing this tactic. It is certainly not in the interests of the GCC states to accelerate or aggravate the economic crisis within Iran. On the contrary, the interests of the GCC states would be well served if Iranian economic pragmatism succeeded. Attaining the goal of Gulf regional stability is dependent upon a domestically stable Iran, and Iran can only achieve domestic stability if it can attain economic balance, including increased competitiveness in and diversification of its economy. The risk of a popular backlash led by Iran's *bazaari* community (the middle-class merchants), which is bearing the brunt of a revolution strong on platitudes and devoid of economic realism, may introduce a level of domestic instability that could motivate leaders to pursue a more rash foreign policy.

The quest for revolutionary puritanism led to the amputation of Iran from the international economy. The ensuing material deprivation of its people gradually worsened under growing global interdependence. Lacking any realistic vision of economic development, post-revolutionary Iran is subjected to the ineptitude, greed, and corruption that plague market reforms in the former Soviet Union. Saddled with a mounting foreign debt (over $30 billion), rampant inflation (45–50 percent per annum), severe devaluation of the rial, and massive inefficiencies and waste due to inadequate infrastructure and exorbitant government subsidies, the Iranian economy may teeter on the brink of collapse. For example, fueled by uncontrolled imports and a precipitous slide in the value of the dollar, Iran's average annual debt-servicing burden has grown to one-fourth of oil export revenues; rising consumer prices have led to widespread discontent, including riots across several cities; and problems in storage, transportation, and distribution account for an annual loss of 30 percent of the country's agricultural production.[35]

Today, Iran is in the throes of transition away from a centralized hydrocarbon-based economy to a diversified free-market system, a process that may slow down to a crawl should the 1996 successor for the presidency cave in to the conservative mullahs who seek to derail economic reforms. Gradual lifting of government subsidies and ensuing price-driven inflation is likely to engender further civil unrest, which imperils steps toward deregulation and private-sector growth. Progress in these areas is crucial in order to attract desperately needed foreign investment and technology. Outside assistance is imperative to expand exploration and production of oil and gas and to stimulate both the upstream and downstream end of the industry. However, to spur foreign participation, restrictions limiting joint ventures must be relaxed, corporate taxes must be reduced, foreign exchange retention rules must be liberalized, and unclear, contradictory investment rules must be abolished. Rafsanjani's proposal for liberal investment law in free-trade zones (e.g., Qeshm, Kish, and Chah Bahar) may not be ratified by the conservative Majlis, which would be an ominous signal to potential outside investors already deterred by constitutional interpretations that forbid foreign holdings in Iran's major industries.[36]

The road to economic recovery is further obstructed by US stiffening of trade sanctions and a containment policy to isolate Iran politically. These measures almost certainly play into the hands of the radically minded mullahs, who eagerly blame the nefarious West for the country's self-inflicted economic woes. Though the US ban on all trade with Iran may enhance Washington's credibility in urging Europe and Japan to fall in line, on a practical level it will scarcely harm the Iranian economy, as commercial competitors readily pick up the slack and as non-American traders of US goods are unwilling to shoulder the cost. If anything, the US squeeze on Iran may disturb Washington's relations with some states in the Gulf that benefit from trade in American-made goods.[37] Apart from generating tensions among friends, encouraging a siege mentality among Iranians, and ostracizing their leadership as the *bête noire* in the region, sanctions jeopardize efforts to promote moderate policies in Tehran. Faced with bullying tactics, Iran may become more intransigent concerning issues that otherwise may be open for discussion.

Conclusion

The security policy of GCC states must be structured to accommodate the contradictions in Iranian security policy. Specifically, GCC security policy toward Iran should emphasize: reducing the revolutionary rhetoric of the Iranian leadership; increasing the per capita GDP of Iran; privatizing the Iranian economic apparatus; developing labor-intensive, non-oil export industries within Iran, particularly those industries which will meet a reliable forecast for demand within the Arab Gulf; reducing Iran's military capability, particularly in unconventional and power projection capabilities; reducing Iran's military presence within the Gulf; and, ultimately, implementing a phased reduction of military assets within the Gulf, first those of Iraq and Iran and secondly those of the Western powers, most notably the United States. Such a security policy will not be easy to construct.

The Iranian people have experienced significant economic and social deprivation since the revolution, and many analysts believe that current Iranian leaders are increasingly seeking economic rather than religious solutions to their everyday problems and challenges. The technological imperative to improve Iranian industrial output, and to increase the international export of oil and non-oil products to the global market, requires the Iranian government to import Western technical assistance. This pragmatic approach by the Iranian leadership to economic policy, in combination with the imperative of the revolution to despise the West, occasionally requires Iranian newspapers to condemn Western society while simultaneously welcoming the corporate members of that society with open arms.[38] GCC leaders generally support the moderating influence of Iranian economic pragmatism, believing that it will, over time, reorient Iranian priorities in ways that encourage mutual respect and the constructive resolution of disputes. It is certainly not in the interests of the GCC to participate in a more aggressive effort to bring about the economic strangulation of Iran. There is good reason to believe that a more economically desperate Iran would also be a more internationally radical Iran – an unwelcome outcome for Iran's closest neighbors. Yet the process of Iranian military modernization and rearmament which is occurring contemporaneously with the process of economic pragmatism engenders great concern. It would be a very poor security policy for GCC states to assist the Iranian economy financially while Iranian financial capital were diverted into strategic armaments which threatened the existence of the members of the GCC. As in the case of the Cold War, the party seeking external economic investment must first remove the devastating military threat.[39] And the threat must be removed in a verifiable manner.

The contradictions in Iranian foreign and security policy, and the apparent strategy of intimidation those contradictions make possible, will continue to prove dysfunctional for Iran. The GCC states will retain cohesiveness and will remain aligned with the United States and other Western powers. The combination of GCC and Western forces will continue to deter Iran militarily and marginalize Iran economically. Ultimately, the only policy option available to Iran which will provide an economic future is a policy of demilitarization. Adoption of this policy will reduce the reliance of the GCC on Western forces, decrease the tendency within GCC governments to modernize their militaries, free up additional financial investment capital from within Iran, and increase the willingness of (at least) non-US investors to join with Iranian entrepreneurs in joint ventures. Iran should replace its military modernization program with an economic development program and join with its present oil and gas trading partners, particularly Germany and Japan, in cooperative non-military programs. As a future labor-intensive economy, the Islamic Republic may offer capital-intensive trading partners such as

Germany and Japan significant wage-rate advantage for joint-venture manufacturing activity in labor-intensive industries.

The quest for Gulf security is unlikely to succeed without a concerted attempt to harmonize relations among all Gulf states. While the GCC grouping has been a step in the right direction, the outlines of a comprehensive regional security regime will take shape only once tensions between Iran and its Arab neighbors give way to a progressive rapprochement that builds on mutual interests. Economic issues will increasingly move center-stage as regional trading blocks define the unfolding global order. The Gulf, with its abundant hydrocarbon resources and its nascent markets, constitutes a fertile region for economic expansion. Industry diversification away from the energy sector – a national priority of all Gulf states – offers a splendid opportunity for transnational trade and investment within the region. Building up cross-border commercial stakes between Iran and the Arab Gulf states may pave the way for further confidence-building measures without which security arrangements amenable to all sides are scarcely possible.

The formation of an effective regional security arrangement is fraught with disagreements over the source of instability and how best to guard against it. Tehran is suspicious of a US-sponsored arrangement, fearing that Washington would merely use its presence as an open-ended challenge to contain Iran at will. Similarly, Iran would find little interest in an arrangement that elevated Saudi Arabia into a position of regional hegemon, a situation that would conflict with its own view of itself as the *primus inter pares* in the Gulf. For the same reason Tehran is receptive to participation of non-Gulf Arab states in a regional pact in order to counterbalance the Saudi influence. However, given the failure of Egyptian and Syrian participation in the "GCC plus two" trial, Tehran may normalize its relationship with Iraq and wager its future on an unlikely alliance driven by shared animosity toward Washington and Riyadh. Striking this Faustian bargain would further diminish chances for a comprehensive security regime and heighten Iran's sense of isolation, having entered a precarious alliance that would likely prompt closer cooperation among GCC member states and invigorate calls for greater US and Western presence in the area.

The search for a *modus vivendi* governing an acceptable Gulf security framework will bear no fruits unless misperceptions on all sides start to subside. Iran may indeed harbor a desire to stem, and eventually eliminate, the influence of outside powers in the Gulf region, and it may continue to propagate political Islam in the Muslim world in accordance with its self-appointed leadership role. However, as some scholars argue, post-Khomeini Iran appears to have dropped its messianic goal of supporting government change in Muslim countries in favor of a defensively motivated policy that seeks to minimize US influence in the Gulf region. Subjected to interacting domestic and international events – most prominently the economic transformation at home, the 1991 Gulf war, and the collapse of the Soviet Union – Iran is forced to realign its priorities. For example, the swift victory by the coalition over the Iraqi army and Moscow's almost concurrent disappearance as a countervailing pole in the international system had an indelible effect on Tehran's capacity to mitigate forces working toward its political isolation. Because of the propensity for mutual misperception, Tehran may readily conclude that Washington has set out to exclude Iran from regional security arrangements, to polarize the country's secular and religious factions, to counter at every step its influence in Central Asia, to strangle its economy by orchestrating international embargoes, and to portray Iran as an unrepentant fanatical terrorist state bent on wrecking the Middle East peace process.

Tehran may have unwittingly added tensions by calibrating its position on key issues, such as Gulf security and Arab–Israeli peace, based on the ostensibly incorrect assumption that US policy in the Gulf would be hamstrung by calls for overseas retrenchment in the face of mounting domestic problems (e.g., the staggering national debt, persistent unemployment, dwindling economic competitiveness, etc.). Whatever the leadership's foreign policy predilections and perceptions, Tehran is keenly aware that in the wake of a disappointing first five-year economic plan, the regime's waning political fortunes are scarcely reversed with turgid talk of unflagging external threats; only pragmatically inspired policy directed at rational economic development at home and constructive dialogue abroad will improve the country's future.

Yet, as a seasoned observer remarked, "Iran's economic and political future is inescapably tied to access to the Gulf and, by extension, to the seven Arab states which line its shore."[40] It is incumbent upon these states to work towards normalization in relations with the Islamic Republic and to address the need to cultivate mutual trust and confidence. On the basis of the prevailing discussion in this chapter, the process of tension reduction and reassurance must follow from a realization of several, largely immutable, factors: First, Gulf stability hinges primarily on the triangular relationship between Iran, Iraq, and the GCC member states. This constellation is under constant challenges, such as Iraq's eventual re-entry into the global community after a UN go-ahead which will (re)introduce political as well as economic pressures.

Second, although Western powers are unlikely to disengage from the area any time soon, the Gulf states must work towards *regional* solutions that are sustained through the commitment and effort of their leaders to work and cooperate harmoniously with one another. Given the demographic and territorial differences between Iran and its Arab Gulf neighbors, Tehran naturally prefers a bilateral approach to this process. Conversely, the neighboring states to the south have good reasons to operate within the multilateral GCC forum. It is important, however, that they reasssure Tehran about GCC links to outside powers. US assistance, in particular, is not an open invitation to Washington to exercise regional hegemony, but a policy of furnishing selected services to member states to enhance their capacity for autonomous defense.

Third, the Iranian revolution has run its course, which forces the Tehran government to address the spate of economic problems that is weighing down the Islamic Republic. Revolutionary romanticism is giving way to nationalism tempered with the exigency of diplomatic normalization abroad and economic pragmatism at home. Iran is not, for example, intractably opposed to the Middle East peace process, but fears that accommodation might exact political concessions that may threaten the survival of the current regime. Similarly, confronted with mounting global interdependence, commercial considerations begin to override ideological objectives in Iran's formulation of economic policy. These are welcome trends, for they offer new opportunities for cooperation across the Gulf.

Contributors

Jamal S. al-Suwaidi is director of the Emirates Center for Strategic Studies and Research (ECSSR) in Abu Dhabi, and teaches at the UAE University in Al Ain. Dr. al-Suwaidi has taught courses in political methodology, political culture, comparative governments, and international relations at the UAE University and at the University of Wisconsin-Milwaukee. He is the author of numerous scholarly articles on a variety of subjects, including perceptions of democracy in Arab and Western societies, women and development, women and religion, and UAE public opinion on the Gulf Crisis. Dr. al-Suwaidi is a contributing author to the book *Democracy, War, and Peace in the Middle East*, and the editor of *The Yemeni War: Causes and Consequences.*

Hooshang Amirahmadi holds a Ph.D. in regional economic planning and international development from Cornell University. He is a professor in the Department of Urban Planning and Policy Development at Rutgers, The State University of New Jersey, where he is chair and graduate director of the department and director of the university's Middle Eastern Studies program. He also serves as a consultant on Iranian economic, oil, and regional policies for many international organizations, including the UNDP, the Aga Khan Foundation, and the World Bank. Professor Amirahmadi is the author of *Revolution and Economic Transition: The Iranian Experience*, and is editor and first co-editor of numerous books including: *The United States and the Middle East: A Search for New Perspectives*; *Post-Revolutionary Iran*; and *U.S.–Iran Relations: Areas of Tension and Mutual Interest.*

Bahman Baktiari received his Ph.D. in government from the University of Virginia, and is presently associate professor of political science at the University of Maine. Dr. Baktiari is a frequent contributor to numerous periodicals, including the *Journal of Church and State, Journal of South Asian and Middle Eastern Studies*, and *Comparative Strategy*, and is the author of *Parliamentary Politics in Revolutionary Iran.*

James A. Bill is professor of government and director of the Reves Center for International Studies at The College of William and Mary. A Princeton

Ph.D., Dr. Bill is the author or co-author of six books, including the award-winning *The Eagle and the Lion: The Tragedy of American-Iranian Relations*. His co-authored *Politics in the Middle East*, is in its 4th edition. Professor Bill has undertaken research in all eight Gulf states and in 20 Middle Eastern countries; and in December 1990, he testified on the Gulf crisis before the US House of Representatives Committee on Armed Services.

Anthony H. Cordesman is a professor of national security studies at Georgetown University, a military analyst for ABC News, and national security assistant to Senator John McCain of the Senate Armed Services Committee. He has served in senior positions in the State Department, Office of the Secretary of Defense, and NATO and in several posts in the Middle East, including Tehran. Professor Cordesman is the author of numerous books and articles on military forces in the Middle East, including *Iran and Iraq: The Threat from the Northern Gulf*, and *After the Storm: The Changing Military Balance in the Middle East*.

Anwar M. Gargash received his Ph.D. from Kings College, University of Cambridge in 1990, and has served as assistant professor of political science at the UAE University in Al Ain. Dr. Gargash teaches Gulf and comparative politics and is a frequent participant in conferences related to Gulf security. Born in Dubai, United Arab Emirates, Dr. Gargash received his BA and MA in political science from George Washington University.

W. Nathaniel Howell is director of the Arabian Peninsula and Gulf Program at the University of Virginia and a member of the senior faculty of the Center for the Study of Mind and Human Interaction, an interdisciplinary center focusing on large-group political psychology. During twenty-six years in the United States Foreign Service, he held diplomatic posts in Cairo, Paris, Brussels, Beirut, Abu Dhabi, and Algiers before being named in 1987 Ambassador to the State of Kuwait, a position he held until February 1991. Retiring from the Department of State in 1992, he returned to the faculty of the University of Virginia, from which he received his Ph.D. in 1965. The recipient of numerous honors and awards, including the Kuwait Decoration with Sash of the First Class, Ambassador Howell has lectured extensively in the United States, France, Bulgaria, Cyprus, Italy, and Austria. His publications include several journal articles, contributions to volumes on the Middle East, and two books.

Kenneth Katzman received his Ph.D. in political science from New York

University. He has worked as a Gulf intelligence analyst at the CIA and within the private sector, and currently analyzes US policy-making in the Middle East for the Congressional Research Service (CRS), in Washington, DC. Dr. Katzman is the author *Warriors of Islam: Iran's Revolutionary Guards*, as well as numerous articles written at the CRS and many classified publications for previous employers.

Geoffrey Kemp is director of the Carnegie Endowment's Middle East Arms Control Project. He received his Ph.D. in political science at MIT and his MA and BA degrees from Oxford University. He served in the White House during the first Reagan administration and was special assistant to the president for National Security Affairs and senior director for Near East and South Asian Affairs on the National Security Council Staff. Dr. Kemp is the author of *The Control of the Middle East Arms Race*; co-editor of *Arms Control and Weapons Proliferation in the Middle East and South Asia*; co-author of *India and America after the Cold War*; and author of *Forever Enemies?: American Policy and the Islamic Republic of Iran*.

Saleh A. al-Mani' received his Ph.D. in international relations from the University of Southern California in 1981, after which he accepted a faculty position and subsequently an appointment as an assistant dean with King Saud University (KSU), Riyadh, Kingdom of Saudi Arabia. He remains a faculty member at KSU, but during his tenure he also served as a consultant to the Saudi Arabian Ministry of Finance and National Economy, as a visiting scholar of the School of Advanced International Studies, Washington, DC, and as a consultant to the United Nations Institute for Disarmament Research (UNIDIR), Geneva, on the Middle East Arms Control Project.

Mohsen M. Milani earned his Ph.D. from the University of Southern California in 1981, and is an associate professor of politics at the University of South Florida in the Department of Government and International Affairs. Dr. Milani's research has focused on comparative revolutionary movements, Iran's Islamic revolution, and the Gulf, and in 1990 he was a research fellow at the Center for Middle East Studies, Harvard University. His book, *The Making of Iran's Islamic Revolution*, has been used as a required text in many universities.

Roy P. Mottahedeh is professor of Islamic History in the Harvard History Department, and from 1987 to 1990 was director of Harvard's Center for Middle Eastern Studies. He has participated in a variety of academic programs, including the Shaw Traveling Scholar program, Harvard Society of Fellows, and has received numerous awards, including a Guggenheim Fellowship. Dr. Mottahedeh is the author of two books: *Loyalty and Leadership in an Early Islamic Society*, and *The Mantle of the Prophet: Religion and Politics in Iran*.

Mehdi Noorbaksh is director of the Institute for Research and Islamic Studies in Houston. His areas of specialty are international relations, comparative politics, and international political economy, focusing predominately on the Middle East. Dr. Noorbaksh's publications include numerous articles and two edited books: *Mutual Contributions of Islam and Iran*, and *Islam, Nationalism and the Question of Identity*.

Notes

1. Religion, Politics, and Ideological Trends in Contemporary Iran

1. Mehdi Bazargan, *Mudafi'at dar Dadgah Gheir Salih-i Tajdid-e Nazar-e Nizami* (Bellville, IL: Liberation Movement of Iran, 1977), pp. 214–305.

2. Hamid Algar (trans.), *Islam and Revolution: Writings and Declarations of Imam Khomeini* (Berkeley, CA: Mizan Press, 1981), p. 242.

3. Ibid., p. 230.

4. Fada'yan-e Islam, *Hukumat-e Islami, Barnameh-e Enqelabi-e Fada'yan-e Islam* (Tehran: Fada'yan-e Islam, 1980).

5. For Mulla Ahmad Naraqi, consult Seyyed Hossein Nasr, Hamid Dabashi, and Seyyed Vali Reza Nasr (eds), *Expectations of the Millennium: Shi'ism in History* (Albany, NY: State University of New York Press, 1989), pp. 287–300; and Vanessa Martin, "Religion and State in Khomeini's Kashf-e Asrar," *Bulletin of the School of Oriental and African Studies*, LVI, I (London: University of London (SOAS), 1993), pp. 34–45.

6. I personally posed this question to Ibrahim Yazdi, Iran's foreign minister in the Provisional Government of Mehdi Bazargan, in an interview in 1986.

7. Speech by Ayatollah Khomeini in Behesht-e Zahra in February 1979 (12 Bahman 57).

8. Ayatollah Khomeini's declaration for the establishment of the Provisional Government in February 1979 (17 Bahman 1957).

9. For Ayatollah Beheshti's role in the Majlis Khobregan [Assembly of Experts] consult *Surat-e Mashruh-e Mozakerat-e Majlis-e Barresi-e Naha'i-e Qanun-e Asasi-e Iran*, 3 vols (Tehran, 1985). See also Said Saffari, "The Legitimation of the Clergy's Right to Rule in the Constitution of 1979," *British Journal of Middle Eastern Studies*, 20, no. 1 (spring 1993).

10. Ibid., 73.

11. See, for example, Sharough Akhavi, who argues that "In it [*Kashr-e Asrar*] Khumayni undertook a mild defense of the monarchcical system." Sharough Akhavi, *Religion and Politics in Contemporary Iran* (Albany, NY: State University of New York Press, 1980), p. 163. See also Michael M. J. Fisher, *Iran: From Religious Dispute to Revolution* (Cambridge, MA: Harvard University Press, 1980), p. 152.

12. This view is shared by Shaul B. Bakhash in his *The Reign of the Ayatollahs: Iran and the Islamic Revolution* (New York: Basic Books, 1984), p. 23.

13. Ayatollah Khomeini, *Kashf-e Asrar*, pp. 186–7.

14. Ibid., pp. 187–8.

15. Ibid., p. 189.

16. Ibid.

17. Algar, *Islam and Revolution*, p. 31.

18. Ibid., p. 38.

19. Ibid., p. 40.

20. Ibid., p. 41.

21. Ibid., p. 59.

22. Ibid., p. 62.

23. Hamid Algar (trans.), *The Constitution of the Islamic Republic of Iran* (Berkeley, CA: Mizan Press, 1980), p. 29.

24. Ibid., pp. 67–8.

25. For these frictions consult Mehdi Bazargan, *Masa'il va Mushgelat-e Avvalin Sal-e Enqelab as Zaban-e Muhanddis Mehdi-e Bazargan*, 2nd edn (Tehran: Nehzat-e Azadi-e Iran, 1981).

26. *Ettela'te*, "Yadwareh Ustad Shahid Murtada Mutahhari," 1984. (12 Orbidehesht-e 1362), p. 9.

27. *Jumhuri-e Islami*, 1987 (17 Azar 1366).

28. Ibid. (21 Azar 1366).

29. Ibid. (12 Dey 1366).

30. *Keyhan International*, 1987 (14 Dey 1366).

31. *Ettela'te*, 1987 (11 Dey 1366).

32. *Keyhan International*, 1987 (16 Dey 1366).

33. Ibid. (25 Dey 1366).

34. *Resalat*, 1987 (28 Dey 1366).

35. *Keyhan International*, 1987 (3 Bahman 1366).

36. Ibid. (1 Bahman 1366).

37. Ibid. (2 Bahman 1366).

38. *Resalat*, 1989 (19 Tir 1368).

39. *Keyhan International*, 1987 (28 Dey 1366).

40. Muhammad Javad Larijani, *Hukumat va Marz-e Mashru'iyyat, Majmu'ih Maqalat-e Avvalin Seminar-e Tahavvul-e Mafahim*, p. 33.

41. Ibid., pp. 329–41.

42. Ayatollah Mesbah Yazdi, *Jame'eh va Tarikh az Didgah-e Qur'an* (Tehran: Sazman-e Tabliqat-e Islami, 1989), p. 372.

43. Ayatollah Mesbah Yazdi, *Hukumat-e Islami va Velayat-e Faqih* (Tehran: Sazman-e Tabliqat-e Islami, 1990), pp. 158–9.

44. A similar line of argument has been followed in the public speeches and writings of individuals like Azari Qumi, Ali Meshkini, Jannati, and others from the Guardian Council. For a more detailed discussion of the theory of *Valayat-e Faqih* in the same line, consult Ja'far Subhani, *Mabani-e Hukumat-e Islami*, 2 vols (Qum: Entesharat-e Towhid, 1983).

45. For this orientation, consult Hamid Paydar, "Paradox-e Islam va Democracy," *Kiyan*, 19 (June 1994); and Bizhan Hekmat, "Mardom Salari va Din Salari," *Kiyan*, 21 (September–October 1994).

46. Ayatollah Muhammad Hussein Na'ini, *Tanbih al-Ummah va Tanzih al-Millah*, 8th edn (Tehran: Sherkat-e Enteshar, 1982), p. 61.

47. Ayatollah Mahmud Taliqani, *The Friday Prayer Speech in Behesht-e Zahra*, 1979. For other arguments of Taliqani in this regard, consult Mahmud Taliqani, *Tabyin Resalat Baray-e Qiam beh Qest* (Tehran: Sherkat-e Enteshar, 1981).

48. Ezzatullah Radmenesh, *Enqelab va Ebtedal va Shuwra Rukni az Arkan-e Nezam-e Towhidi* (Tehran: Mu'asseseh Khadamat-e Farhangi-e Rasa, 1980), p. 103.

49. Reza Ustadi, *Shuwra dar Qur'an va Hadith* (Tehran: Entesharat-e Buniad Farhangi-e Imam Reza, 1981). For further argument about shura consult, Reza Feiz, *Hakemiyyat-e Kudha va Hukumat-e Mardum* (paper presented at the Center for the Study of Management, Tehran, 1979); Su'ar Ja'far, *Sanad Hay-e Shuwra dar Qur'an va Hadith* (Tehran: Sazman-e Pazhuhesh, 1981); Muhammad Maleki, *Shuwra dar Islam* (Tehran: Entesharat-e Zanan-e Musalman, 1980); Ayatollah Mahmud Taliqani, *Shuwra az Didgah-e Taliqani* (Tehran: Mu'asseseh Khadamat-e Farhangi-e Rasa, 1981).

50. Islamic Republic Party (IRP), *Shi'ite va Shuwra* (Tehran: IRP, 1981), pp. 24–7.

51. Abdul Ali Bazargan, *Shuwra va Bey'at: Hakemiyyat-e Khuda va Hukumat-e Mardum* (Tehran: Sherkat-e Enteshar, 1982), p. 5.

52. Mehdi Bazargan, "Din va Azadi," *Bazyabiy-e Arzeshha* (Tehran: Liberation Movement of Iran, 1983), p. 74.

53. Ibid., p. 5.

54. Ibid., pp. 11–13.

55. Ezatullah Radmanesh, *Enqelab va Ebtedal*, p. 102.

56. Ayatollah Murtada Mutahhari, *Piramun-e Jomhuri-e Islami* (Qom: Entesharat-e Sadra, 1979), pp. 153–4.

57. Salehi Najaf Abadi, *Velayat-e Faqih, Hukumat-e Salehan* (Tehran: Mu'asseseh Khadamat-e Farhangi-e Rasa, 1984), p. 51.

58. Ibid., p. 130.

59. Ayatollah Hossein Muntazeri, *Mabani-e Fiqhi-e Hukumat-e Islami* (Qom: Nashr-e Tafak-kur, 1984), p. 321.

60. Ibid., p. 202.

61. Ayatollah Muhammad Hussein Muntazeri, *Fi Velah al-Faqih va Fiqh al-Dowlah al-Islamiyyah* (Qom: Al-Markaz al-Alami lidderasat al-Islamiyyah, 1987), p. 538.

62. Mehdi Bazargan, "Din va Azadi," p. 85.

63. Liberation Movement of Iran (LMI), *Azadi va Entekhabat, Peik-e Nehzat*, no. 21 (Tehran: LMI, 1983), p. 19.

64. Ibid., p. 22.

65. For the views of the LMI on war and its emphasis on people's participation in the process of this policy issue consult Liberation Movement of Iran, *Hushdar: Piramun-e Tadavum-e Jang-e Khanemansuz* (Tehran: LMI, 1988); *Tahlili Piramun-e Jang va Sulh* (Tehran: LMI, 1984); *Tuwzihati Piramun-e Muzakereh, Atash Bas va Sulh* (Tehran: LMI, 1985); and *Jang-e bi Payan* (Tehran: LMI, 1985).

66. Mehdi Bazargan, *Din va Azadi*, p. 74.

67. Ibid., p. 75. For Bazargan's positions on these issues, consult Mehdi Bazargan, *Enqelab-e Iran dar Du Harekat* (Tehran: LMI, 1984); and Mehdi Bazargan, *Masa'il va Mushgelat-e Avvalin Sal-e Enqelab* (Tehran: LMI, 1981).

68. Ibid., pp. 76–7. For LMI and Bazargan arguments in defense of freedom, consult LMI, *Azadi az Du Didgah* (Tehran: LMI, 1983), and LMI, *Sargozasht-e Seminar-e Ta'min-e Azadi-e Entekhabat, Peik-e Nehzat*, no. 23 (Tehran: LMI, 1983).

69. Abdul Ali Bazargan, *Muqadameh iy dar Zamineh Azadi dar Qur'an* (Tehran: Entesharat-e Qalam, 1984); and *Azadi dar Nahjulbalaqa* (unpublished manuscript).

70. Liberation Movement of Iran, *Tafsil va Tahlil-e Velayat-e Mutlaqeh-e Faqih* (Tehran: LMI, 1988), pp. 136–7.

71. Abdul Karim Soroush, *Qabz va Bast-e Theorik-e Shari'at* (Tehran: Mu'asseseh Farhangi-e Serat, 1991). Soroush's argument is in line with that of Thomas S. Kuhn in Thomas S. Kuhn, *The Structure of Scientific Revolutions* (Chicago: University of Chicago Press, 1970).

72. Abdul Karim Soroush, "Hukumat-e Democratic-e Dini," *Kiyan*, 11 (Tehran: 1993), p. 15.

73. Ibid., p. 13.

74. Ibid.

75. Mehdi Bazargan, *Din va Azadi*, p. 64.

76. Ayatollah Muhammad Hossein Na'ini, *Tanbih al-Ummah va Tanzih al Millah*.

77. Soroush, "Hukumat-e Democratic-e Dini," p. 14.

78. Ayatollah Murtada Mutahhari, *Piramun-e Jumhuri-e Islami*, pp. 118–19.

79. Soroush, "Hukumat-e Democratic-e Dini," p. 14.

80. For the critical views of Bazargan and Mutahhari on this topic, consult *Bahthi dar Mowred-e Marja'iyyat va Ruhaniyyat* (Tehran: Sherkat-e Enteshar, 1964).

81. Abdul Karim Soroush, "Mudara va Mudiriyyat-e Mu'menan: Sukhani dar Nesbat-e Din va Democracy," *Kiyan*, 21 (Tehran) (September–October 1994), p. 8.

82. Ibid., p. 9.

83. Ibid., p. 11.

84. Ibid., p. 14.

85. Algar, *The Constitution of the Islamic Republic of Iran*, p. 31.

86. Liberation Movement of Iran, *Azadi va Entekhabat, Peyk-e Nehzat*, no. 21, p. 18.

87. Ettela'te, *Yadvareh Ustad Shahid Murtada Mutahhari*, p. 8.

88. Ayatollah Khomeini, *Velayat-e Faqih* (Tehran: Entesharat-e Nas, 1981), p. 41.

89. Ibid., 43. For further discussion of this issue, consult Akbar Ganji, "Mashruiyyat, Velayat va Vekalat," *Kiyan*, 13 (Tehran: 1993).

90. For al-Farabi's views on government consult, for example, Ralph Lerner and Muhsin Mahdi, *Medieval Political Philosophy* (New York: Cornell University Press, 1978).

91. Interview with Muhammad Kazim Anvar Luhi by Radio Seday-e Iran, 9 December 1994.

92. Interview by author with Dr. Ibrahim Yazdi, December 1994.

93. Mehdi Bazargan, "Azadi dar Iran Darakht-e bi Risheh Boud," *Adineh*, pp. 84–5 (1993–Mehr va Aban 1372).

2. The Governing Institutions of the Islamic Republic of Iran

1. Theda Skocpol, *States and Social Revolutions: A Comparative Analysis of France, Russia, and China* (Cambridge: Cambridge University Press, 1979).

2. Shaul B. Bakhash, *The Reign of the Ayatollahs: Iran and the Islamic Revolution* (New York: Basic Books, 1984), pp. 82–3.

3. Hamid Algar (trans.), *Islam and Revolution: Writings and Declarations of Imam Khomeini* (Berkeley, CA: Mizan Press, 1981); Hamid Enayat, "Iran: Khumayni's Concept of the Guardianship of the Jurisconsult," in *Islam in the Political Process*, ed. James P. Piscatori (Cambridge: Cambridge University Press, 1983), pp. 160–80.

4. Mohsen M. Milani, *The Making of Iran's Islamic Revolution: From Monarchy to Islamic Republic*, 2nd edn (Boulder, CO: Westview Press, 1994), p. 262.

5. *Surat-e Mashru'e Mozakerat-e Majles Barese'i Qanun-e Asasi* [Proceedings of the Assembly of Experts], vols 1 and 2 (Islamic Consultative Assembly Press, 1993), pp. 1115–16.

6. Ibid., vol. 1, p. 300.

7. A. Hashemi Rafsanjani, *Enqlelab ya Be'sat-e Jadid* [Revolution or a New Mission] (Tehran: Yaser Publications, n.d.), p. 18.

8. FBIS-South Asia, 4 October 1988.

9. *Economist*, 30 November 1985.

10. *Keyhan International*, 3 November 1988.

11. *Tehran Times*, 24 January 1989.

12. *Keyhan International*, 23 February 1989.

13. *New York Times*, 9 March 1989.

14. *Guardian*, 11 June 1989.

15. *Keyhan*, 12 June 1989.

16. *Iran Times*, 23 June 1989.

17. *Ettela'ate*, 16 June 1989.

18. Mohsen M. Milani, "Iranian Active Neutrality during the Kuwaiti Crisis," *New Political Science*, no. 21 (spring 1992) and no. 22 (summer 1992), pp. 41–60.

19. *Resalat*, 6 December 1994.

20. *Iran Times*, 13 September 1993.

21. From 1979 to 1989 the Islamic Republic had one president impeached (Bani-Sadr), one assassinated (Raja'i), and one who served from 1981 to 1989 (Ali Khamene'i).

22. *Keyhan International*, 17 August 1985. What Khamene'i's defenders had in mind was whether the revolutionary fervor had made it politically unwise to create a strong presidency when the central message of the revolution was to overthrow the Shah's dictatorship.

23. FBIS-South Asia, 3 September 1985.

24. *Ettela'ate*, 4 September 1985.

25. *Keyhan International*, 29 September 1985.

26. *Iran Times*, 27 April 1989.

27. Mohsen M. Milani, "The Evolution of the Iranian Presidency: From Bani-Sadr to Rafsanjani," *British Journal of Middle Eastern Studies* 20, no. 1 (1993), p. 94.

28. Ibid., p. 95.

29. *Keyhan International*, 4 August 1989.

30. Ibid.

31. *Karnameh Majles Shuray-e Eslami* [Annual Reports of the Majlis], Third Majlis, second year (Islamic Consultative Assembly Press), 1990, p. 239.

32. Other models of presidential management are called competitive, or formalistic. In the competitive model, the president purposely seeks to promote conflict and competition among his advisers, thus forcing problems to be brought to the president's attention for resolution and decision. In a formalistic model, the president seeks to establish clear lines of authority and to minimize the need for presidential involvement in the politicking among cabinet heads. A chief of staff is often used as a buffer between the president and the cabinet heads. See Alexander George, "Presidential Management Styles and Models," in *The Domestic Sources of American Foreign Policy: Insights and Evidence*, ed. Charles W. Kegley and Eugene R. Wittkopf (New York: St. Martin's Press, 1988), pp. 107–26.

33. *U.S.–Iran Review* 2, no. 5 (June–July) 1994.

34. David Barber, *The Presidential Character*, 3rd edn (Englewood Cliffs, NJ: Prentice-Hall, 1985), p. 32.

35. *Ettela'ate*, 27 May 1984.

36. The Council of Guardians' role is analogous to that of the Supreme Court in the United States. In theory, the latter has the power to review congressional legislation and see to it that they are in conformity with the constitution, and to declare them void if they are held not to be.

37. S. J. Madani, *Huquq-e Asasi dar Jumhuri Eslami Iran* [Constitutional Laws of the Islamic Republic of Iran], vol. 3, "The Majles" (Tehran: Suroush Publications, 1986), pp. 66–71.

38. *Resalat*, 12 March 1992.

39. Ibid., 16 March 1992.

40. All data are from *Resalat*, 20 May 1992; 26 May 1992; and *Iran Times*, 29 May 1992.

41. *Resalat*, 6 April 1992.

42. *Salam*, 4 June 1992.

43. *Iran Times*, 24 July 1992.

44. *Salam*, 2 September 1992; 3 September 1992.

45. Ibid., 16 February 1994.

3. Shi'ite Political Thought and the Destiny
of the Iranian Revolution

1. The author's article, "Wilayah al-Faqih," in the *Oxford Encyclopedia of the Modern Islamic World* (New York: Oxford University Press, 1995), pp. 320–2, offers a survey of some of this literature.

2. See the highly important review by Professor Hossein Modarressi of A. A. Sachedina, *The Just Ruler or the Guardian Jurist: An Attempt to Link Two Different Shi'ite Concepts*, 1988, published in the *Journal of the American Oriental Society*, no. 3 (July–September 1991), pp. 549–62.

3. Al Ghazali, *al-Mankhul* (Beirut: Dar al Fikr, 1980), p. 483; al Khatib al-Baghdadi, *Kitab al-faqih wa '-mutaffaqih*, II (Beirut: Yutlabu min Dar al-Kurub al-Ilmiyah, 1980), p. 179; al-Sha'rani, *al-Tabaqat al-Sughra* (Cairo: Maktabat al-Qahirah, 1970), p. 122. All these citations are taken from the brilliant essay by Devin J. Stewart, "Islamic Juridical Hierarchies and the Office of Marji' al-Taqlid" (unpublished paper presented at a conference on Shi'ism in Philadelphia, PA, September 1993). This study by Stewart has influenced much of the thinking in the present chapter.

4. Hamid Algar (trans.), *Islam and Revolution: Writings and Declarations of Imam Khomeini* (Berkeley, CA: Mizan Press, 1981), p. 62.

5. Husain-Ali Montazeri, *Kitab al-Khums* (Qum, n.d.), pp. 369–91.

6. FBIS, 11 February 1989.

7. Ibid., 2 February 1989.

8. Text of the letter in *Iran Times*, 31 March 1989.

9. The rebuttal is entitled: *Tafsil va-Tahlil-e Velayat-e Motlaqeh-ye Faqih*, and, although it is anonymous, it is generally considered to be by Mehdi Bazargan.

10. The author has described the career of Khamene'i and his opponents from a somewhat different perspective in Roy P. Mottahedeh, "The Islamic Movement: The Case for Democratic Inclusion," *Contention*, 4, no. 3 (spring 1995), pp. 107–27.

11. On the funeral of Golpaygani, see *Iran Times*, 17 December 1993.

12. Ibid. The wording in the report in *Iran Times* has "*muhraz*," but an actual copy of the statement has "*muta'ayyan*".

13. The politics of the clerics in this period are discussed with characteristic thoroughness and depth of insight by Shaul B. Bakhash in his unpublished essay: "Iran: The Crisis of Legitimacy," in *Middle East Lectures: I*, ed. Martin Kramer (Syracuse, NY: Syracuse University Press, 1995) Professor Bakhash makes clear the social and, above all, economic agenda that Iranians have sought to support by their various stands on *marja'iyah* and "the guardianship of the jurist."

14. *Iran Times*, 2 December 1994.

15. *Iran Times*, 9 December 1994; 16 December 1994.

16. Husain-Ali Montazeri, *Dirasat fi Wilayah al-Fiqh*, vol. 1 (Qum: 1408 AH), pp. 495–6.

17. For Jannati on the need for "papacy," see *Iran Times*, 9 December 1994.

18. Stewart, "Islamic Juridical Hierarchies," discusses the changes in the office of *mujtahid* in the nineteenth century.

19. Eskandar Monshi, *The History of Shah 'Abbas the Great*, trans. Roger Savoy, 2 vols (Boulder, CO: Westview Press, 1978), p. 205. Sayyid Husayn ibn Hasan al-Karaki is called simply "the *mujtahid*," citation from Stewart, "Islamic Juridical Hierarchies."

4. Iran's Gulf Policy

I would like to express my gratitude to the Emirates Center for Strategic Studies and Research for their hospitality during my stay in Abu Dhabi.

1. See, for example, Judith Miller, "The Challenge of Radical Islam," *Foreign Affairs*, 72, no. 2 (1993), pp. 43–56. For a different view, see Leon Hadar, "What Green Peril?" *Foreign Affairs*, 72, no. 2 (1993), pp. 27–43.

2. Samuel P. Huntington, "The Clash of Civilizations," *Foreign Affairs*, 72, no. 3 (May–June 1993), pp. 22–49.

3. For a critical assessment of Iran's foreign policy, see Anthony H. Cordesman, *Iran and Iraq: The Threat from the Northern Gulf* (Boulder, CO: Westview Press, 1994); James A. Phillips, "The Saddomization of Iran," *Policy Review*, no. 69 (summer 1994), pp. 6–13; and Daniel Pipes and Patrick Clawson, "Ambitious Iran, Troubled Neighbors," *Foreign Affairs*, 72, no. 1 (January–February 1993), pp. 124–41. For a more favorable analysis, see R. K. Ramazani, "Iran's Foreign Policy: Both North and South," *Middle East Journal*, 46, no. 3 (summer 1992), pp. 392–411; James A. Bill, *The New Iran: Relations with its Neighbors and the United States* (Washington, DC: Asia Society Contemporary Affairs Dept., 1991); Shireen T. Hunter, *Iran and the World: Continuity in a Revolutionary Decade* (Bloomington, IN: Indiana University Press, 1990); Bahman Bakhtiari, "Revolutionary Iran's Persian Gulf Policy: The Quest for Hegemony," in Hooshang Amirahmadi, and Nader Entessar (eds), *Iran and the Arab World* (New York: St. Martin's Press, 1992), pp. 69–93; K.L. Afrasiabi, *After Khomeini: New Directions in Iran's Foreign Policy* (Boulder, CO: Westview Press, 1994); Nikola B. Schahgaldian, *Iran and the Postwar Security in the Persian Gulf* (Santa Monica, CA: Rand Corporation, 1994); and Mohsen M. Milani, "Iran's Post-Cold War Policy in the Persian Gulf," *International Affairs* XLIX, no. 2 (spring 1994), pp. 328–54.

4. For an informed discussion of these issues see Lynn Hunt, *Politics, Culture, and Class in the French Revolution* (Berkeley, CA: University of California Press, 1984).

5. Crane Brinton, *The Anatomy of Revolution* (London: Peter Smith Publishers, 1953).

6. Hamid Algar (trans.), *Constitution of the Islamic Republic of Iran* (Berkeley, CA: Mizan Press, 1980), pp. 3–14. Specifically see Article 10.

7. V. S. Naipaul, *Among the Believers: An Islamic Journey* (New York: Random House, 1981), p. 1682.

8. *Mardom*, 15 and 19 Khordad 1358 (7 August 1979). For more details, see Mohsen M. Milani, "Harvest of Shame: The Policy of the Tudeh Party and the Bazargan Government," *Middle Eastern Studies*, 29, no. 2 (April 1993), pp. 307–20.

9. For details, see Mohsen M. Milani, *The Making of Iran's Islamic Revolution: From Monarchy to Islamic Republic*, 2nd edn (Boulder, CO: Westview Press, 1994), pp. 141–70.

10. See Nikki R. Keddie, and Mark J. Gasiorowski (eds), *Neither East Nor West: Iran, the Soviet Union, and the United States* (New Haven, CT: Yale University Press, 1980).

11. On the start of the war, see R. K. Ramazani, "Who Started the Iran–Iraq War? A Commentary," *Virginia Journal of International Law* 33, no. 1 (spring 1993), pp. 69–89. For the Iraqi version of the war, see Phebe Marr, "The Iran–Iraq War: The View from Iraq," in *The Persian Gulf War: Lessons for Strategy, Law, and Diplomacy* (Westport, CT: Greenwood Press, 1990), pp. 59–67; for the Iranian version, see Farhang Rejaee (ed.), *The Iraq–Iran War* (Gainseville, FL: University Press of Florida, 1993); and, for a general discussion of the war, see Shahram Chubin, and Charles Tripp, *Iran and Iraq at War* (Boulder, CO: Westview Press, 1988); and Gary Sick, "Trial by Error: Reflections on the Iraq–Iran War," *Middle East Journal*, 43 (spring 1989), pp. 230–47.

12. Piscatori offers a perceptive discussion of the dilemma the Islamic leaders face when

they have to choose between what is good for Islam and what serves the national interest of the countries they rule. James P. Piscatori, *Islam in the World of Nation-States* (Cambridge: Cambridge University Press, 1986).

13. For details of how the fundamentalists consolidated their power, see Mohsen M. Milani, *The Making of Iran's Islamic Revolution*, pp. 16–167, 172–89. For a more general discussion, see Shaul B. Bakhash, *The Reign of the Ayatollahs: Iran and the Islamic Revolution* (New York: Basic Books, 1984; and, David Menashiri, *Iran: A Decade of War and Revolution* (New York: Holmes & Meier Publishers, 1990).

14. Workman has a very interesting discussion of the benefits of the war for the Ba'ath Party in Iraq and for the Islamic fundamentalists in Iran. Thom Workman, *The Social Origins of the Iran–Iraq War* (Boulder, CO: Lynne Rienner, 1994).

15. For the role of the GCC, see Gerd Nonneman, *Iraq, the Gulf States, and the War: A Changing Relationship, 1980–1986 and Beyond* (London: Atlantic Highland, 1986), pp. 31–134. For a more general discussion of the GCC, see J. Sandwick (ed.), *The Gulf Cooperation Council: Moderation and Stability in an Interdependent World* (Boulder, CO: Westview Press, 1987).

16. R. K. Ramazani, *Revolutionary Iran: Challenge and Response in the Middle East* (Baltimore, MD: Johns Hopkins University Press, 1986), p. 76. This is a figure for the first five years of the war. James Aiken, US Ambassador to Saudi Arabia, believes that Kuwait and Saudi Arabia contributed about $60 billion to Iraq. See *Frontline* (Transcript), 16 February 1993, p. 5.

17. For example, Iran was accused of plotting to assassinate government officials in Bahrain. See Fred Lawson, *Bahrain: The Modernization of Autocracy* (Boulder, CO: Westview Press, 1989), p. 125.

18. House Joint Resolution 216, 100th Congress, *Overview of the Situation in the Persian Gulf: Hearings Before the Committee on Foreign Affairs* (Washington, DC: GPO, 1987), p. 302. Also see: *War in the Persian Gulf: The U.S. Takes Sides*, Staff Report to the Committee on Foreign Relations, United States Senate, Washington, DC, November 1987.

19. For the UN role in the war, see Cameron Hume, *The United Nations, Iran, and Iraq: How Peacemaking Changed* (Bloomington, IN: Indiana University Press, 1994).

20. Kerman Mofid, *The Economic Consequences of the Gulf War* (New York: Routledge, 1990), p. 147. He claims that the cost of the Iran–Iraq war was about $1,097 billion.

21. Hooshang Amirahmadi, *Revolution and Economic Transition: The Iranian Experience* (New York: State University of New York Press, 1990), p. 292. For a more critical assessment of the Iranian economy, see Jahangir Amuzegar, "The Iranian Economy before and after the Revolution," *Middle East Journal*, 46, no. 3 (summer 1992), pp. 413–25.

22. The constitutional changes in the *velayat-e faqih* are discussed by the author in Mohsen M. Milani, "The Transformation of the *Velayat-e Faqih* Institution: From Khomeini to Khamenei," *The Muslim World*, LXXXII, no. 3 (July 1992) and no. 4 (October 1992), pp. 175–90.

23. On the constitutional changes related to the presidency, see Mohsen M. Milani, "The Evolution of the Iranian Presidency: From Bani Sadr to Rafsanjani," *British Journal of Middle Eastern Studies*, 20, no. 1 (1993), pp. 83–97.

24. See Sohrab Shahabi, "A Review of Iran's Five-Year Development Plan," *Iranian Journal of International Affairs*, 4, no. 4 (1992), pp. 421–9.

25. Ali Akbar Hashemi Rafsanjani, *Amir Kabir* (Tehran: Farahani Press, 1982). Rafsanjani's other writings before the Islamic Revolution in 1979 include an unpublished novel, a series of articles about the Qur'an which was recently published as a book, the translation of a book about Palestine written by a former Jordanian ambassador to Iran, and a co-authored book with Hojatolislam Muhammad Javad Bahonar, who was killed in the early days of the revolution. The latter book is about the socioeconomic and political conditions of the major world powers before the rise of Islam in the seventh century.

26. Correspondence with President Rafsanjani, Tehran, August 1991. For a brief account of his life and activities, see Mohsen M. Milani, *The Making of Iran's Islamic Revolution*, pp. 225–7.

27. Richard Barnet, "Reflections: The Disorder of Peace," *New Yorker*, 20 January 1992, p. 74.

28. An example of this thinking can be found in Mohammad Masjed Jame, *Iran Va Khaleeje-e Fars* [Iran and the Persian Gulf] (Tehran: Zendegi Press, 1989).

29. On the role of the United States in the region, see Zbigniew Brezezinski, *Out of Control: Global Turmoil on the Eve of the 21st Century* (New York: Maxwell Macmillan International, 1993). For a more specific discussion, see Michael A. Palmer, *Guardians of the Gulf: A History of America's Expanding Role in the Persian Gulf* (New York: The Free Press, 1992). For a critical assessment, see Amin Saikal, "U.S. Strategy in the Persian Gulf: A Recipe for Insecurity," *World Policy Journal*, 9, no. 3 (1992), pp. 515–33.

30. On the GCC formation and its role, see R. K. Ramazani, *The Gulf Cooperation Council: Record and Analysis* (Charlottesville, VA: University Press of Virginia, 1988). Also see Joseph A. Kechichian, "The Gulf Cooperation Council: Containing the Iranian Revolution," *Journal of South Asian and Middle Eastern Studies*, 8, no. 1 (fall 1992) and no. 2 (winter 1992), pp. 146–65.

31. *Washington Post*, 18 August 1989.

32. Paul Stevens, *Oil and Politics: The Post-War Gulf* (London: Royal Institute of International Affairs, 1992).

33. Elaine Sciolino, *The Outlaw State: Saddam Hussein's Quest for Power and the Gulf Crisis* (New York: John Wiley and Sons, 1991), p. 188.

34. For details, see Mohsen M. Milani, "Iran's Active Neutrality During the Kuwaiti Crisis," *New Political Science*, no. 21 (spring 1992) and no. 22 (summer 1992), pp. 41–60.

35. President Saddam Hussein's letter to President Rafsanjani, 3 August 1990, translated by the Islamic Republic of Iran, p. 3.

36. Some of the issues related to the Iraqi civil war are discussed in Kanan Makiya, *Cruelty and Silence: War, Tyranny, and Uprising and the Arab World* (New York: Norton Press, 1993).

37. See Mohiaddin S. Mesbahi, *Russia and the Third World* (Gainesville, FL: University Press of Florida, 1994).

38. Asadollah Alam, *The Shah and I: The Confidential Diary of Iran's Royal Court 1969–1977* (London: I.B.Tauris, 1991) translated into the Persian language *Gofteguhaye- Man Ba Shah* [My Conversations with the Shah], vol. 1, by Abdolreza Hoshang Mahdavi (Tehran: Tarhe Nou, 1993), p. 65.

39. Anthony Lake, "Confronting the Backlash States," *Foreign Affairs*, 73, no. 2 (March–April 1994), pp. 45–55. For a rebuttal of the policy, see F. Gregory Gause, "The Illogic of Dual Containment," *Foreign Affairs*, 73, no. 2 (March–April 1994), pp. 56–66.

40. For details, see Yahya Sadowski, *Scuds or Butter? The Political Economy of Arms Control in the Middle East* (Washington, DC: Brookings Institution, 1993); James Adams, *Engines of War: Merchants of Death and the New Arms Race* (New York: Atlantic Monthly Press, 1990); and Simon Henderson, *Instant Empire: Saddam Hussein's Ambition for Iraq* (San Francisco, CA: Mercury House, 1991).

41. The data were collected from various issues of Stockholm International Peace Research Institute (SIPRI), *SIPRI Yearbook 1992: World Armaments and Disarmament*; International Institute for Strategic Studies (IISS), *The Military Balance* and *National Trade Data Banks Market Report*. For more details, see Mohsen M. Milani, "Iran's Post-Cold War Policy in the Persian Gulf," pp. 328–54.

42. Sadowski, *Scuds or Butter*, pp. 51–4.

43. On the Memorandum, see R. K. Ramazani, "Sheikh of Sharjah's Announcement of the Abu Musa Agreement," *The Persian Gulf: Iran's Role* (Charlottesville, VA: University Press of Virginia, 1972), Appendix C. Also see Pirouz Mojtahedzadeh, "Iran's Maritime Boundaries and the Persian Gulf: The Case of Abu Musa Islands," in *The Boundaries of Modern Iran*, ed. Keith McLachlan (New York: St. Martin's Press, 1994), pp. 101–27.

44. On the historical background on the three islands, see Pirouz Mojtahedzadeh, "Tarikh Va Joghrafeya-ye Seyasi-ye Jazayer-e Tunb Va Abu Musa" [The Political and Geographic History of the Tunb and Abu Musa Islands], *Rahavard*, no. 31 (summer 1992), pp. 130–45, and no. 32 (winter 1992), pp. 66–78.

45. On the UAE, see Rosemarie Zahlan, *The Origins of the United Arab Emirates* (New York: St. Martin's Press, 1978).

46. Hooshang Moghtader, "The Settlement of the Bahrain Question: A Study in Anglo-Iranian-United Nations Diplomacy," *Pakistan Horizon*, 6, no. 2 (1973).

47 Ramazani, *The Persian Gulf: Iran's Role*, p. 59.

5. The Geometry of Instability in the Gulf

1. This taxonomy has been developed as a result of nine different research trips to the Gulf states in the 1980s and 1990s. Egyptian scholar and long resident in Qatar, Yusif al-Karadawi, has referred to populist Islam as "genuine" Islam and establishment Islam as "bridled," "crippled," "twisted," and "stunted" Islam. Interview by author, University of Qatar, 10 October 1983. I first discussed the dialectic between populist and establishment Islam in James A. Bill, "Resurgent Islam in the Persian Gulf," *Foreign Affairs*, 63, no. 1 (January–February 1984), pp. 109–27.

2. For an excellent discussion of the theory of civil society as applied to the Middle East, see A. Richard Norton, *Civil Society in the Middle East*, 2 vols (Leiden, The Netherlands: E.J. Brill, 1994, 1995).

3. Abdel R. Omran and Farzaneh Roudi, "The Middle East Population Puzzle," *Population Bulletin*, 48 (July 1993), p. 4.

4. *Economist*, "A Survey of Islam," 6 August 1994, p. 12.

5. Ibid.

6. In this chapter, the important concept of "hegemon" is defined in terms of relative national power. The bases of power are demographic, geographic, economic, educational, military, and political. Although Saudi Arabia may possess more economic resources due to its rich oil reserves and Iraq may possibly have a military edge, Iran remains a serious competitor for influence. Its huge population base, geographic situation with long borders both along the Gulf and along Central Asia, and its institutionalized political system are among the reasons for identifying Iran as the hegemon of the Gulf. For a narrower definition of the concept of "hegemon," see Robert O. Keohane, *After Hegemony: Cooperation and Discord in the World Political Economy* (Princeton, NJ: Princeton University Press, 1984). Emphasizing economic considerations, Keohane defines a hegemonic power as one that has "control over raw materials, control over sources of capital, control over markets, and competitive advantages in the production of highly valued goods" (see p. 32).

7. Ibid.

8. Bahrain's minister of information, Tariq Mo'ayyad, argues effectively that the very looseness of the organization of the GCC countries has been a major reason for its continuing survival. In his judgment, the GCC was never intended to be a political unit or union. Interview by author, Manama, Bahrain, 19 August 1982.

9. John Duke Anthony, *Arab States of the Lower Gulf* (Washington, DC: The Middle

East Institute, 1975), p. 25. This book, now somewhat dated, remains an indispensable source on Gulf history, society, and politics.

10. Ibid.

11. Joseph J. Malone, *The Arab Lands of Western Asia* (Englewood Cliffs, NJ: Prentice-Hall, 1973), p. 228.

12. US Department of Commerce, International Trade Administration, *U.S. Foreign Trade Highlights, 1993* (Washington, DC: Office of Trade and Economic Analysis, 1994), pp. 29, 73.

13. *Washington Post*, 28 October 1994, p. 1. Each brigade is equipped with 108 Bradley Fighting Vehicles and 58 M1-A1 Abrams tanks.

14. See Congressional Quarterly, *The Middle East*, 7th edn (Washington, DC: Congressional Quarterly, 1991), p. 87.

15. This surprising number was provided as the result of research by William F. Hickman, a former naval captain and student. An information official at Cinqlantfleet at the Norfolk Naval Station indicated that the number $150 million was "in the ball park."

16. The writer estimates that in 2025, the combined population of Iran and Iraq will near 210 million people, while the other six Gulf states will have a combined headcount of approximately 40 million. This estimate is based upon a number of demographic sources, including especially Omran and Roudi, "The Middle East Population Puzzle," referred to in note 3 above.

17. For a revealing account of this incident, see David Evans, "Vincennes: A Case Study," *Proceedings of the U.S. Naval Institute* (USNI) (Annapolis, MD: Naval Institute Press, August 1993), pp. 49–56.

18. Although Cuba and Nicaragua are not regional hegemons, they have consistently pursued foreign policies antithetical to US interests. China, because of its size and economic potential, presents a special problem for the United States. When these independent units have shown a willingness to modify their policy more in accord with American demands, e.g., North Vietnam and Syria, the United States has shown a willingness to release some of its pressure. On basic issues, the Islamic Republic of Iran has shown little willingness to accede to American wishes.

19. In September 1994, seven Western oil companies signed an $8 billion agreement with Azerbaijan to drill for oil in the Caspian Sea. The American companies involved include Amoco, Pennzoil, Unocal, and McDermott International. See *Washington Post*, 20 September 1994, p. C1.

20. The effectiveness of the Mujahedin's propaganda is seen in the fact that the *New York Times* all but endorsed the Mujahedin in a 25 September 1994 editorial. The US Department of State, however, more knowledgeable about Middle East realities and embarrassed by the growing trend in the American press to present a radical cult as a force for democracy, has prepared a report documenting the violent history of the Mujahedin and listing its acts of terrorism. For a balanced history of the Mujahedin, see Ervand Abrahamian, *The Iranian Mojahedin* (New Haven, CT: Yale University Press, 1989).

21. *Los Angeles Times*, 2 January 1993.

22. These comments by Khamene'i and Rafsanjani were made during major speeches delivered on 27 October 1994 and 4 November 1994, respectively. Texts of the speeches are in the possession of the author.

6. The Impact of Iranian Foreign Policy on Regional Security

1. The material on Iran draws upon a recent book by the author: *Forever Enemies: American Policy and the Islamic Republic of Iran* (Washington, DC: Carnegie Endowment for International Peace, 1994).

2. Islamic Republic of Iran Permanent Mission to the United Nations, "Defence Minister: Iran Will Not Be Dragged into Mid East Arms Race" (release no. 075, 15 April 1993).

3. For more on Iran's military programs, see Shahram Chubin, *Iran's National Security Policy: Capabilities, Intentions, and Impact* (Washington, DC: Carnegie Endowment for International Peace, 1994).

4. Mark Hibbs, "Iran May Withdraw from NPT over Western Trade Barriers," *Nucleonics Week*, 35, no. 38, 22 September 1994, p. 1.

5. "Iran May Turn Down Third 'Kilo' Delivery," *Jane's Defence Weekly*, 22, no. 14, 8 October 1994.

6. Youssef Ibrahim, "Arabs Raise a Nervous Cry over Iranian Militancy," *New York Times*, 21 December 1992, pp. A1, A10; and *Al-Sharq Al-Awsat*, 19 November, 1992, p. 1, in FBIS-NES, 23 November 1992, p. 52.

7. "Algeria Breaks Diplomatic Ties with Iran," Reuters, 27 March 1993; an abbreviated version of the Reuters report appeared in "Algeria Breaks Ties with Iran," *New York Times*, 28 March 1993, p. 14.

8. "U.S. Sees Iranian Role in Buenos Aires Blast," *New York Times*, 9 May 1992, p. 3. The US statement explained that "information has been gathered that indicates Iranian involvement in the attack, but there is not conclusive evidence at this time."

9. According to Peoples' Mujahedin press releases, Ghorbani was kidnapped in June 1992, tortured, and murdered with direction from Tehran. See also "Turkey Asserts Islamic Ring That Killed Three Has Iran Links," *New York Times*, 5 February 1993, p. A6; and, "Widow of Iranian Dissident Blames Tehran in His Death," *New York Times*, 10 February 1993, p. A14.

10. Voice of the Islamic Republic of Iran, 27 October 1994, in FBIS-NES, 27 October 1994, pp. 42–4.

11. For an interesting review of Russian arms sales by a young Russian scholar, see Andrei Volpin, "Russian Arms Sales Policy Toward the Middle East," Research Memorandum no. 2B (Washington, DC: Washington Institute for Near East Policy, 1993).

12. "Comfort Blanket for the Gulf," *Economist*, 5 December 1992, pp. 39–40.

13. "Buying Security from the West," *Jane's Defence Weekly*, 28 March 1992, p. 534.

14. Michael Gordon, "Kuwait is Allowing US to Station a Squadron of Warplanes," *New York Times*, 28 October 1994, p. A3.

7. Iran, the GCC States, and the UAE

1. *Tehran Times*, 30 December 1993.

2. Shahram Chubin and Charles Tripp, "Domestic Politics and Territorial Disputes in the Persian Gulf and the Arabian Peninsula," *Survival* (winter 1993), p. 8.

3. Mahmood Sariolghalam, "Conceptual Sources of Post-Revolutionary Iranian Behavior toward the Arab World," in *Iran and the Arab World*, Hooshang Amirahmadi and Nader Entessar (eds) (New York: St. Martin's Press, 1992), p. 21.

4. J. B. Kelly, *Arabia, the Gulf and the West: A Critical View of the Arabs and Their Oil Policy* (New York: Basic Books, 1980), p. 313.

5. Graham E. Fuller, *The Center of the Universe: The Geopolitics of Iran* (Boulder, CO: Westview Press, 1991), p. 68.

6. Assodollah Alam, *The Shah and I: The Confidential Diary of Iran's Royal Court, 1969–1977* (London: I.B.Tauris, 1991), pp. 205, 252.

7. Chubin and Tripp, "Domestic Politics and Territorial Disputes," pp. 8–9.

8. *Tehran Times*, 6 May 1993.

9. Saeed Badeeb, *Saudi–Iranian Relations 1932–1982* (London: Centre for Arab and Iranian Studies, 1993), p. 57.

10. *Tehran Times*, 7 April 1994.

11. Anoushiravan Ehteshami, "Wheels within Wheels: Iran's Foreign Policy towards the Arab World," in *Reconstruction and Regional Diplomacy in the Persian Gulf*, Hooshang Amirahmadi and Nader Entessar (eds) (London: Routledge, 1992), p. 164.

12. Shahram Chubin, "Iran's National Security Policy: Capabilities, Intentions and Impact" (Washington, DC: Carnegie Endowment for International Peace, 1994), p. 60.

13. W. W. Maggs, "Armenia and Azerbaijan: Looking toward the Middle East," *Current History* (January 1993), p. 7.

14. Ibid., pp. 8–9.

15. Abdulaziz Bashir and Stephen Wright, "Saudi Arabia: Foreign Policy after the Gulf War," *Middle East Policy*, no. 1 (1992), p. 110.

16. M. E. Ahrari, "Iran, the GCC, and the Security Dimension in the Persian Gulf," in Amirahmadi and Entessar, *Reconstruction and Regional Diplomacy in the Persian Gulf*, p. 198.

17. See discussion by Charles Tripp of the Declaration in Charles Tripp, "The Gulf States and Iraq," *Survival* (fall 1992), pp. 44–7.

18. *Al-Khalij*, 22 January 1993.

19. *Al-Hayat*, 6 July 1993.

20. Bashir and Wright, "Saudi Arabia," p. 110.

21. "Iran: New Force of Stability," *The Middle East* (March 1991), p. 8.

22. "Whose Gulf is it Anyway?" *The Middle East* (July 1991), p. 6.

23. *Al-Khalij*, 25 April 1993.

24. *Al-Hayat*, 2 April 1993.

25. *Al-Sharq Al-Awsat*, 18 May 1993.

26. Fuller, *The Center of the Universe*, p. 101.

27. Ibid., p. 70.

28. *Tehran Times*, 13 January 1994.

29. R. K. Ramazani, "Iran's Foreign Policy: Both North and South," *Middle East Journal* 46, no. 3 (summer 1992), p. 402.

30. *Keyhan International*, 30 June 1994.

31. Ibid., 4 February 1993.

32. *Al-Hayat*, 31 March 1993.

33. For an example of such opinion see Daniel Pipes and Patrick Clawson, "Ambitious Iran, Troubled Neighbors," *Foreign Affairs*, 72, no. 1 (January–February 1993), pp. 126–7.

34. "Now What's the Problem?" *The Middle East* (June 1991), p. 12.

35. R. K. Ramazani, "Iran's Foreign Policy: Contending Orientations," *Middle East Journal*, 43, no. 2 (spring 1989), p. 206.

36. For a discussion of the Iranian position on the second Gulf war see the Fundamentalism Project Report by Said Amir Arjomand, "A Victory for the Pragmatists: The Islamic Fundamentalist Reaction in Iran," in *Islamic Fundamentalism and the Gulf Crisis*, James P. Piscatori (ed.) (Chicago: Fundamentalism Project, 1991), pp. 52–66.

37. Ramazani, "Iran's Foreign Policy: Both North and South," p. 395.

38. "Iran: Rafsanjani's Shock Therapy," *Middle East Economic Digest (MEED)*, 30 April 1993.

39. *Keyhan International*, 26 May 1994.

40. Dilip Hero, "The Revolution Stumbles," *The Middle East* (July 1993), pp. 13–14.

41. *Guardian Weekly*, 9 May 1993.

42. Shahram Chubin, "Iran and Regional Security in the Persian Gulf," *Survival* (fall 1993), p. 69.

43. Jerrold D. Green, "Iran's Foreign Policy: Between Enmity and Conciliation," *Current History* (January 1993), p. 12.

44. "Dubai (Non-Oil) Foreign Trade with Iran during the Years 1989–1993 and the First Half of 1994," Dubai Chamber of Commerce and Industry, Research and Studies Department (Dubai, 1994).

45. Hassan Al-Alkim, *The Foreign Policy of the United Arab Emirates* (London: Saqi Books, 1989), p. 145.

46. Ibid., p. 148.

47. *Keyhan International*, 17 September 1992.

48. Ibid., 7 April 1994.

49. See the discussion of the Memorandum in Husain M. Albaharna, *The Arabian Gulf States: Their Legal and Political Status and Their International Problems*, 2nd edn (Beirut: Khayats, 1975), p. 345.

50. Ibid., p. 341.

51. *Keyhan International*, 17 September 1992.

52. *Tehran Times*, 31 March 1994.

53. *Nashrat Al-Ittihad*, 26 August 1992.

54. *Al-Watan*, 25 August 1992.

55. Various interviews by author with residents of Abu Musa in Sharjah, UAE, November–December 1994.

56. *Al-Hayat*, 19 September 1992.

57. *Nashrat Al-Ittihad*, 21 April 1992.

58. Ibid., 13 September 1992.

59. "Statement by H.E. Mr. Rashid Abdullah Al-Nuaimi, Minister of Foreign Affairs in the General Debate of the Forty-Seventh Session of the General Assembly of the United Nations," Wednesday 30 September 1992.

60. *Keyhan International*, 1 October 1992.

61. Ibid., 8 October 1992.

62. *Nashrat Al-Ittihad*, 25 September 1992.

63. *Al-Safir*, 16 September 1992.

64. *Al-Siyasah*, 16 September 1992.

65. *Tehran Times*, 30 June 1994.

66. *Al-Watan*, 16 September 1992.

67. *Tehran Times*, 3 June 1993.

68. *Al-Anba*, 6 September 1992. Iranian Foreign Minister Velayati, attending the non-aligned conference in Jakarta, insisted that there were problems with the UAE.

69. *Al-Hayat*, 22 November 1994.

70. Ibid., 19 September 1994.

71. *Al-Sharq Al-Awsat*, 2 October 1994.

72. Interview by author with residents of Abu Musa in Sharjah, UAE, November–December 1994.

73. Ibid.

74. Ahrari, "Iran, the GCC, and the Security Dimension," p. 209.

75. Ramazani, "Iran's Foreign Policy: Contending Orientations," p. 211.

76. See *Keyhan International*, 27 May 1993; 7 October 1993.

77. Shaul B. Bakhash, "Prisoners of the Ayatollah," *New York Review of Books*, 11 August 1994, p. 45.

8. The Ideological Dimension in Saudi–Iranian Relations

1. See, for example, Fred Halliday, "Iranian Foreign Policy since 1979: Internationalism and Nationalism in the Islamic Revolution," in *Shi'ism and Social Protest*, ed. Juan Cole and Nikki R. Keddie (New Haven, CT: Yale University Press, 1986), pp. 88–107. For further analysis of Saudi–Iranian Relations, see James P. Piscatori, "Islamic Values and National Interest: The Foreign Policy of Saudi Arabia," and R. K. Ramazani, "Khumayni's Islam in Foreign Policy," both of which can be found in *Islam in Foreign Policy*, ed. Adeed Dawisha (Cambridge: Cambridge University Press, 1985). See also R. K. Ramazani, *Revolutionary Iran: Challenge and Response in the Middle East* (Baltimore, MD: Johns Hopkins University Press, 1986); R. K. Ramazani, "Iran's Foreign Policy: Contending Orientations," *Middle East Journal*, 43, no. 2 (spring 1989), pp. 202–17; and R. K. Ramazani, "Iran's Foreign Policy: Both North and South," *Middle East Journal*, 46, no. 3 (summer 1992), pp. 393–412. For a study of the role of religion in this relationship, see Jacob Goldberg, "Saudi Arabia and the Iranian Revolution: The Religious Dimension," in *The Iranian Revolution and the Muslim World*, ed. David Menashiri (Boulder, CO: Westview Press, 1990), pp. 155–70. For the role of nationalism, see Hooshang Amirahmadi, "Iranian–Saudi Arabian Relations since the Revolution," in *Iran and the Arab World*, ed. Hooshang Amirahmadi and Nader Entessar (New York: St. Martin's Press, 1993), pp. 139–60. For a historical review of the relations during the Shah period, see Saeed Badeeb, *Saudi–Iranian Relations 1932–1982* (London: Centre for Arab and Iranian Studies, 1993).

2. Nasser Al-Braik, "Al-Ibadhiyyah in the Islamic Political Thought and its Role in State Building," *Al-Ijtihad* (Beirut, fall 1991), p. 129 (in Arabic).

3. See Said Amir Arjomand, "History and Revolution in the Shi'ite Tradition in Contemporary Iran," *International Political Science Review*, 10, no. 2 (1989), pp. 111–19; and Nikki R. Keddie, "The Roots of the Ulama Power in Modern Iran," in *Scholars, Saints and Sufis: Muslim Religious Institutions in the Middle East since 1500*, ed. Nikki R. Keddie (Berkeley, CA: University of California Press), pp. 211–30.

4. Arjomand, "History and Revolution," p. 113.

5. This estimate by the author is based on calculations of the number of Saudi graduates from Saudi universities and students studying abroad in the last ten years. See Saudi Arabian Ministry of Finance, *Annual Yearbook 1985* and *Annual Yearbook 1990* (Riyadh: General Directorate of Statistics).

6. For the role of *ulama* in education in post-revolutionary Iran, see Shahrazad Mojahed, "Iranian Women in Higher Education", paper presented at the 6th annual meeting of the American Council for the Study of Islamic Societies, Villanova, PA, 19–20 May 1989. For the role of *ulama* in Iranian foreign policy and diplomacy, see Halliday, "Iranian Foreign Policy since 1979," pp. 105, 107.

7. See Abdullah Al-Ahsan, *OIC: The Organization of the Islamic Conference* (Herndon, VA: International Institute of Islamic Thought, 1988), p. 80.

8. Over one-half of the Iranian Muslims follow the Jaafari school (Al-Madhhab Al-

Jaafari), which is associated with the name of the Versed Imam, Jaafar Al-Sadiq (d. AD 765 /148 AH). This school compromises the Shi'ite Twelvers' jurisprudence.

9. Ayatollah Khomeini, *Al-Hukomah Al-Islamiah* [The Islamic Government], Arabic edn, ed. Hassan Hanafi, (n.p., September, 1979), p. 52.

10. Khomeini referred in his book to the Prophet's *hadith* 88 times, cited Caliph Ali in 57 instances and the Imams in 42 instances, and referred to Fatimah and to *fadk* (a symbolic land-tenure dispute between Ali and Al-Abbas) three times. See Khomeini, *Al-Hukomah Al-Islamiah*, ed. Hassan Hanafi.

11. See, for example, the following sources (all in Arabic), Ibrahim Al-Jabhan, *Tabdid Al-Dhalam wa Tanbih Al-Niam* [Clearing of Darkness and Raising the Conscious of the Passive] (Riyadh: Maktabat Al-Harmain, 1979); Ihsan Ilahi Zahir, *Al-Shiah wa Ahl Albeit* [Shi'ism and the House of the Prophet] (Lahore, Pakistan: Idarat Tarjuman Al-Sunnah, 1980); Ihsan Ilahi Zahir, *Al-Shiah Wal-Quran* [Shi'ism and Quran] (Lahore, Pakistan: Idarat Turjaman Al-Sunnah, 1981); Muhib Al-Din Al-Khatib, *Al-Khutut Al-Ariedhah* [Bold Lines] 2nd printing, (n.p., 1981); and Muhammad Malullah, *Mawaqif Al-Shiah Min Ahl Al-Sunnah* [The Stand of Shia from the Sunnah] (n.p., n.d.).

12. See Chibli Mallet, "Religious Militancy in Contemporary Iraq: Muhammad Baqir al-Sadr and the Sunni–Shi'a Paradigm," *Third World Quarterly*, 10, no. 2 (1988), p. 702.

13. Muhib Al-Din Al-Khatib, *Al-Khutut Al-Ariedhah*, p. 9.

14. See Ihsan Ilahi Zahir, *Al-Radd Al-Kafi Ala Magalat Ali Abdul Wahid Wafi Fi Kitabih Bein Al-Sheiah Wal-Sunnah* [The full response to Wafi's book, *Bein Al-Shiah Wal Sunnah*] (Lahore, Pakistan: Idarat Turjaman Al-Sunnah, 1986).

15. See Chibli Mallet "Religious Militancy in Contemporary Iraq," p. 717.

16. See Musa Al-Mawsawi, *Al-Shiah Wal-Tashieh: Al-Siraa Bein Al-Shiah Wal-Tashieua* [Shi'a and Rectification: The Conflict between Shi'a and Political Shi'ism] (Los Angeles, CA: The High Islamic Council, 1988) (in Arabic).

17. Henry Kissinger, *The Necessity for Choice* (New York: Harber and Brothers, 1961), p. 170.

18. Quoted by R. K. Ramazani in, *Revolutionary Iran*, p. 94.

19. See *Crescent International*, 16 January 1988, pp. 1, 11.

20. FBIS, 31 May 1994.

21. Saudi Arabian Ministry of Interior, Directorate-General of Passports, *Pilgrims Statistics 1970* (Riyadh: Directorate-General of Passports, 1987), Tables 7, 9.

22. Ihsan Hijazi, "Pro-Iranian Terror Group Targeting Saudi Envoys," *New York Times*, 8 January 1989, p. 15.

23. See Shahram Chubin, *Iran's National Security Policy: Capabilities, Intentions, and Impact* (Washington, DC: Carnegie Endowment for International Peace, 1994); and Ian Alexander, "Troubled Oil," *National Review*, 9 August 1993, pp. 45–7.

24. See interview of Ahmad Baqir Al-Hakim with the Saudi Arabian daily, *Al-Sharq Al-Awsat*, 28 February 1992; and *New York Times*, 25 February 1992.

25. See Saeed Badeeb, *Saudi Iranian Relations*, for a review of the relationship during the Shah period.

26. *Middle East International*, no. 449, 30 April 1993, pp. 9–10.

27. FBIS, 28 September 1993.

28. Ibid., 5 October 1993.

29. Ibid., 15 October 1993.

30. Ibid., 26 May 1993.

31. Public opinion in Iran may have also been negatively affected by the incident on 4 September 1993, in which the United States and Saudi Arabia inspected the *Yin He*, the

Chinese vessel bound for Iran, at the Saudi port of Dammam with suspicion that it was carrying banned chemicals.

32. FBIS, 16 March 1994.

33. *Middle East International* no. 464, 3 December 1993, p. 9.

34. FBIS, 2 May 1994.

35. Ibid., 1 April 1994.

36. See the full text of Khamene'i's sermon in FBIS, 14 March 1994.

37. FBIS, 20 May 1994.

38. See FBIS, 11 April 1994, for excerpts of the article in *Keyhan International*.

39. FBIS-AFP, 7 October 1993.

40. See Joseph A. Kechichian, "The Role of the Ulama in the Politics of an Islamic State: The Case of Saudi Arabia," *International Journal of Middle East Studies*, 18, no. 1 (February 1988), pp. 53–71.

9. Iran's Policy in Northwest Asia

1. This usage follows Professor R. K. Ramazani, who used the term "Northwest Asia" in 1992 to comprehend both the territories of Central Asia and the Transcaucasia region west of the Caspian Sea. See R. K. Ramazani, "Iran's Foreign Policy: Both North and South," *Middle East Journal*, 46, no. 3 (summer 1992), p. 404. Professor Ramazani's article is a seminal contribution to a holistic analysis of contemporary Iranian policy.

2. While the peoples of Central Asia and Transcaucasia were, of course, under the domination of the Tsarist Empire before the Soviet era, it was only after the consolidation of Soviet power that effective cultural isolation of indigenous populations was imposed. Thus, at the beginning of the twentieth century, some 40,000 Muslim clerics served almost 8,000 mosques and madrassahs in the Emirate of Bukhara alone.

3. Developments originating in the dissolution of the Ottoman Empire following the First World War, for example, continue to find expression in contemporary international politics, influencing crises from the brutal conflict in Bosnia to the Iraqi "justification" for its aggression against Kuwait.

4. See, for example, Graham E. Fuller, "Central Asia: The Quest for Identity," *Current History*, 93, no. 582 (April 1994), pp. 145–54, for a discussion of the challenges of nation-building and "establishing a track record as independent states."

5. Richard K. Herrmann, "The Role of Iran in Soviet Perceptions and Policy, 1946–1988," in *Neither East Nor West: Iran, the Soviet Union, and the United States*, ed. Nikki R. Keddie and Mark J. Gasiorowski (New Haven, CT: Yale University Press, 1990), p. 81, suggests that Soviet refusal to permit Iranian consulates in Central Asia was a factor that cooled relations between Tehran and Moscow.

6. See, for example, Firuz Kazemzadeh, "Iranian Relations with Russia and the Soviet Union, to 1921," in *The Cambridge History of Iran*, vol. 7 (Cambridge: Cambridge University Press, 1992), pp. 314–49, for a brief review of the relationship.

7. Quoted in Gary Sick, "U.S. Interests in Iran and U.S. Iran Policy," in *U.S.–Iran Relations: Areas of Tension and Mutual Interest*, ed. Hooshang Amirahmadi and Eric Hooglund (Washington, DC: Middle East Institute, 1994), p. 14.

8. Islamic Republic News Agency (IRNA), 6 September 1991.

9. See, for example, Daniel Pipes and Patrick Clawson, "Ambitious Iran, Troubled Neighbors," *Foreign Affairs*, 72, no. 1 (January–February 1993), p. 126. "Looking at the world through the combined filters of fundamentalist Islam and a resurgent Persian nationalism,

they [Iranians] aspire to a sphere of influence that includes Iraq, the Transcaucasus, Central Asia, Afghanistan, and the Persian Gulf."

10. The author wishes to acknowledge the contribution of Mr. Scott W. Harrop of the University of Virginia to the research for this portion of the chapter. His unpublished study, "Iran's Objectives in Northwest Asia: With a Focus on Tajikistan," presented at the 35th annual convention of the International Studies Association, Washington, DC, 29 March 1994, has been a useful source of factual material for this survey.

11. Foreign Broadcast Information Service / SOV (FBIS/SOV), 21 October 1994, p. 50.

12. Professor R. K. Ramazani identifies two contending trends or orientations within the governing elite of Iran: "revolutionary idealists" who "want to establish an Islamic world order *now*" and "revolutionary realists" who "are willing to come to terms with the realities of the existing international system." The latter accord greater importance to "Iranianness" and, concomitantly, the interests of the Iranian state. See R. K. Ramazani, "Iran's Foreign Policy: Contending Orientations," *Middle East Journal*, 43, no. 2 (spring 1989), p. 211.

13. Deputy Foreign Minister Mahmoud Va'ezi, IRNA, 19 May 1992, cited by Harrop, "Iran's Objectives in Northwest Asia," p. 3.

14. See, for example, Voice of the Islamic Republic, 25 January 1990.

15. Ibid., 8 December 1991.

16. Iranian efforts have apparently concentrated on bringing about an end to fighting without addressing the underlying issues. Evidence of Iranian views about a resolution of the Nagorno-Karabakh dispute specifically is sketchy, but Tehran's insistence on avoiding territorial adjustments would appear to incline it toward the Azerbaijani position that the Armenian enclave, ceded to Baku as part of Stalin's strategy for maintaining Soviet dominance, should remain part of the Azerbaijani Republic. Voice of the Islamic Republic radio, 17 May 1992, characterized "any change in geographic borders in the region as aggression" immediately following the breakdown of the Tehran ceasefire agreement.

17. Personal chronology, 8 May 1992.

18. Ibid., 19 May 1992.

19. Interfax, 7 June 1992.

20. Following the intervention of Russian and Uzbek forces to support the neo-communist regime, for example, IRNA, on 19 November 1992, cited "informed sources" as characterizing the conflict as a "war between Islam and blasphemy." Harrop, "Iran's Objectives in Northwest Asia," p. 19.

21. In April 1992, the Iranian ambassador in Dushanbe highlighted his country's close kinship with Tadjiks, pointing out that "We have blood ties; we share a common culture, language, religion, and history; we share historical figures, customs, and traditions; and we have similar feelings." Quoted in Harrop, "Iran's Objectives in Northwest Asia," p. 16.

22. For a discussion of the twists and turns of the struggle in Tadjikistan, see Shahrbanou Tadjbakhsh, "Tadjikistan: From Freedom to War," *Current History*, 93, no. 582 (April 1994), pp. 173–7.

23. Harrop, "Iran's Objectives in Northwest Asia," pp. 19–20.

24. Tadjbakhsh, "Tajikistan: From Freedom to War," p. 176, argues that "Iran does not want to risk the commercial potential of maintaining good relations with Central Asia for the sake of backing a Persian-speaking minority deeply engulfed in war."

25. *Ettela'at*, 8 September 1993, in Harrop, "Iran's Objectives in Northwest Asia," p. 21.

26. A further advantage of Iranian restraint is acceptability as a potential mediator in area disputes. Beginning in 1994, Iran emerged as a "peacemaker" in efforts to defuse the

Tadjik conflict. Deputy Foreign Minister Abbas Maleki announced on 14 January that Iran was undertaking a mediatory initiative that has subsequently involved meetings with various parties to the civil war. Harrop, "Iran's Objectives in Northwest Asia," p. 21. Iran has reportedly also engaged in efforts, encouraged by the United Nations, to mobilize its influence and that of the governments of Pakistan, Afghanistan, and Uzbekistan in the effort to restore peace in Tadjikistan. See Tadjbakhsh, "Tajikistan: From Freedom to War," p. 174.

27. Turkey, the other major neighbor of the new republics, suffered similar disabilities in framing its response to developments in Northwest Asia. Philip Robins, "Between Sentiment and Self-Interest: Turkey's Policy toward Azerbaijan and the Central Asian States," *Middle East Journal*, 47, no. 4 (fall 1993), pp. 593–610, provides an excellent analysis of the evolution of Turkish policy, including useful insights on difficulties encountered by outside powers in coming to grips with the unfamiliar and unprecedented constellation of new entities.

28. FBIS/NES, 17 August 1994, p. 53.

29. Rail traffic from Turkmenistan to Bandar Abbas must currently travel by a round-about route; Iran is reportedly considering a new, more direct route from Mashad to Bafq, but this major project remains on the drawing boards. In addition to links with Turk-menistan, Iran plans a 150-kilometer route through its territory to link Baku with the Azerbaijani Republic's Nakhichvan enclave. This highway would also benefit Turkey's access to the main part of Azerbaijan and the Caspian Sea, although obviously Iran would retain control of its use.

30. Iran is also reportedly improving its existing rail network to facilitate connections from the railhead at Mashad to Iranian ports on the Gulf.

31. *Turkmenskaya Iskra*, 8 August 1994, from FBIS/NES, 17 August 1994, p. 54.

32. Ibid., p. 54. Turkey has been lobbying hard with Turkmenistan for a route that debouches on Turkey's Mediterranean coast and, in 1992, initialed an agreement for con-struction with Ashgabat. Selection of this route over alternatives has the advantage of permitting Turkmenistan to please both Tehran and Ankara. Robins, "Between Sentiment and Self-Interest," p. 605.

33. Observers in the region speculate that the pipeline may be delayed by financial difficulties in Iran and Turkmenistan. See Reuters (Tashkent), 12 August 1994.

34. The Islamic Republic Shipping Company, for example, has announced that it is initiating shipments from Central Asia through Bandar Abbas with 500,000 tons of cotton from Turkmenistan destined for Italy and China. Reuters, 21 August 1994.

35. Reuters (Kazakhstan), 13 September 1994. According to the deputy minister for foreign economic relations, "The rail link through Iran is of great importance to us for diversifying our trade relations." Although Central Asian officials deny that their interest in diversification is spurred by difficulties in their relationships with the Russian Republic, it is worth noting that Kazakh oil exports have been limited by Moscow, which has also apparently cut exports of raw materials and fuel to Kazakhstan. Tashkent is also improving rail connections with China.

36. Established in the early 1980s, the ECO initially grouped Iran, Turkey, and Pakistan.

37. Harrop, "Iran's Objectives in Northwest Asia," p. 5.

38. CASCO was established with a mandate including ecological, fishing, and shipping issues.

39. Analyzing the Turkish experience in the region, Robins, "Between Sentiment and Self-Interest," p. 595, concludes that "[G]iven the complete absence of interaction between the modern state of Turkey and these former Soviet republics until their independence, Turkish and Western expectations appear to have been born of ignorance."

40. Significantly, Iran made extensive efforts in the period immediately after the Soviet collapse to improve its understanding of the peoples and societies within the new republics. One such endeavor was an international conference, hosted by the Institute for Political and International Studies (IPIS) in Tehran in March 1992. See Mohiaddin S. Mesbahi, ed., *Central Asia and the Caucasus after the Soviet Union: Domestic and International Dynamics* (Gainesville, FL: University Press of Florida, 1994).

41. During 1992, Iran established a Persian-language cultural organization with Tadjikistan and Afghanistan, but the initiative has had little result, in part at least because of the strife in both countries. Iranian cultural programs in Tadjikistan during the period in 1992 when democratic/Islamist elements were included in the government appear to have been unusually supportive. See Reuters (Tehran), 19 February 1992.

42. Harrop, "Iran's Objectives in Northwest Asia," p. 13.

43. See Richard K. Herrmann, "Russian Policy in the Middle East: Strategic Change and Tactical Contradictions," *Middle East Journal*, 48, no. 3 (summer 1994), p. 456, for a brief summary of Russian press commentary about the Islamic "threat" in Central Asia.

44. See, for example, the comment by Ayatollah Ebrahim Amini-Najafbadi on Tehran television, 11 May 1992, quoted in Harrop, "Iran's Objectives in Northwest Asia," p. 12, or remarks by the former minister of Islamic guidance and culture, Muhammad Khatami, on the occasion of the signing of two cultural memoranda with Kyrgyzstan: "In our belief, cultural ties are the basis for any kind of relations between states. Iran inspired movements in Muslim states following the victory of the Islamic revolution (1979), drawing their attention and emerging as a focal point for the struggles against the common foes of Islam." Middle East News Network, 17 May 1992.

45. FBIS/NES, 12 August 1994. The paper went on to accuse the Uzbek regime of "advising other regional countries to sever their ties with the Islamic Republic," and working to eradicate "Islamic Thinking" in the region. The *Tehran Times* no longer reflects the thinking of the Foreign Ministry as a consequence of personnel changes.

46. IRNA, 1 February 1993. Harrop, "Iran's Objectives in Northwest Asia," p. 28, observes that "Iran has essentially ignored the fact that all the Central Asian republics have positive relations with Israel, and several have employed significant contingents of Israeli agricultural specialists."

47. Voice of the Islamic Republic, 22 June 1993, characterized the series of agreements as "highly positive."

48. Martha Brill Olcott, "Central Asia's Islamic Awakening," *Current History*, 93, no. 582 (April 1994), p. 151.

49. Conversations with mosque officials in Baku, Azerbaijan SSR, April 1983.

50. Olcott, "Central Asia's Islamic Awakening," p. 152. While Iran has made important investments in Northwest Asia to underwrite its influence there, it is constrained in the competition by its financial difficulties and, in the case of scholarships, by the strains of accommodating the domestic demand for higher education.

51. The foreign policy choices of any state may be understood as the outcome of the complex interaction of several critical factors: the geopolitical situation it faces (what are the perceived threats and opportunities?); its internal dynamics, including competing visions of its identity (how does it define itself? What does it regard as the desired future?); and its assessment of its needs and capabilities (what are its strengths and vulnerabilities? Which desired goals are achievable and in what time-frame? How can inconsistencies between maximal objectives and realistic achievements be rationalized within the foreign policy elite? ... for public opinion? ... to allies and adversaries?). It is seldom given to outside observers to "know" the specific calculations that determine foreign policy, and the task is complicated in cases of "revisionist" regimes, like Iran's, where considerations of ideology contend

with "reasons of state" in official rhetoric and in practice. The informed observer, consequently, has little choice but to work backward from the state's behavior to reasoned assessments of its policy judgments, motivations, and objectives. It is beyond the scope of this chapter to evaluate domestic conditions within Iran, but it may be presumed that judgments of political stability, economic necessity, and sociocultural consensus figure prominently in the foreign policy mix.

52. Ramazani, "Iran's Foreign Policy: Contending Orientations," p. 211.

53. The Iranian strike on the Ashraf base of the Iranian Mujahedin in late 1994 illustrates Tehran's continuing vigilance regarding potential threats to its interests along its border with Iraq. See Reuters (Baghdad), 7 November 1994.

54. Ramazani, "Iran's Foreign Policy: Both North and South," p. 404, also points out the Iranian interest in preserving workable relations with the Russian Federation and other "Slavic" successor states "to ensure that the members of the Commonwealth of Independent States (CIS) honor its predecessors' commitments to sell Iran arms and provide military training, buy Iran's natural gas, and continue to help with some 19 economic reconstruction projects."

55. Iran has in recent years hosted up to 4 million refugees from Iraq and Afghanistan. Beginning in early 1994, the flow into the country resumed as a consequence of fighting in Afghanistan, Baghdad's offensive operations against the inhabitants of southern Iran, and the Armenian military successes in the Azerbaijani Republic. Harrop, "Iran's Objectives in Northwest Asia," p. 4.

56. Mark N. Katz, "Nationalism and the Legacy of Empire," *Current History*, 93, no. 585 (October 1994), p. 330.

57. Martin Klatt, "Russians in the 'Near Abroad,'" *RFE/RL Research Report* 3, no. 32 (19 August 1994), p. 42.

58. It is still too soon to predict how Russia's misadventure in Chechnya will impact on Russia's political behavior. To be sure, Chechnya's status as a part of the Russian state places it in a category different from the independent states of Northwest Asia. Nevertheless, the problematic military performance, the Islamic character of the Chechens, and a number of other factors have the potential to influence the way in which many Russians regard developments in the periphery of the former Soviet state.

59. One particularly crucial aspect of the process of self-definition under way in Russia today is the debate over appropriate boundaries. Identity is, in the final analysis, quintessentially a function of boundaries, psychological as much as geographic. Some elements within Russia have argued or implied that Russia's natural frontiers coincide with those of the CIS (i.e., the former Soviet Union). In late 1994, for example, the Commander of Russian Border Troops argued that Russia can best protect itself by "guarding the CIS outer borders." Noting that Russian troops are already performing this function in Armenia, Georgia, Tadjikistan, and Kyrgyzstan "at these states' request," Colonel General Nikolaev implied that Russia is actively seeking similar "requests" from Azerbaijan, Uzbekistan, and Turkmenistan. *Rossiiskaya Gazeta*, in *RFE/RL Daily Report* no. 217, 15 November 1994.

60. Personal conversations with Russian officials and intellectuals, April and October 1994.

61. Turkey, the other major Muslim state on the periphery of Northwest Asia, faces similar dilemmas *vis-à-vis* a Russian Federation as sensitive to Pan-Turkism as it is to Islamic solidarity. Robins, "Between Sentiment and Self-Interest," p. 596, argues that similar concerns have conditioned Turkish policies: "Short of the disaggregation of Russia, it is likely that in the future Turkey once more will have to deal with a strong state that has major interests to the south. Turkey, therefore, is wary of antagonizing Russia even at a time of weakness, an important factor informing its policy toward Central Asia."

62. This analysis was originally previewed in abbreviated form in an unpublished paper presented in September 1994. See W. Nathaniel Howell, "Arabian Peninsula and Gulf Security after Desert Storm," unpublished paper presented at conference, "The Middle East and New World Order," University of Virginia, Charlottesville, Virginia, 9–10 September 1994, pp. 25–6.

63. Even should Iran's efforts in Northwest Asia inadvertently excite a vigorous Russian counter-offensive to monopolize resources and influence there, the resulting confrontation would create a dangerous and fluid situation that would absorb Iranian energy and attention, once again providing Tehran with incentives to keep the Gulf stable.

64. Tehran IRIB Television First Program Network (in Persian), 23 August 1994, cited in FBIS/NES, 26 August 1994, pp. 94–166.

10. The Politico-Military Threat from Iran

1. For further discussion of the dual containment policy, see Kenneth Katzman, *Iran: U.S. Containment Policy* (Washington, DC: US Library of Congress, Congressional Research Service, CRS Report 94-652-F, 11 August 1994); and two articles in *Foreign Affairs*, 73, no. 2 (March–April 1994) by Anthony Lake, "Confronting the Backlash States," and F. Gregory Gause, "The Illogic of Dual Containment."

2. Nabila Megalli, "Admiral Seeks Gulf Stability," *Washington Times*, 8 September 1994, p. 11.

3. For a further discussion of the Revolutionary Guard's relationship to the overall military structure, see Kenneth Katzman, *Warriors of Islam: Iran's Revolutionary Guard* (Boulder, CO: Westview Press, 1993).

4. US officials report that President Clinton, during his September 1994 summit with Russian President Boris Yeltsin, made some progress in persuading Russia to end arms sales to Iran. See Robert Greenberger, "Clinton Gains on Iran Arms with Yeltsin," *Wall Street Journal*, 28 September 1994, p. A20.

5. For details on Iraq's military inventory, see International Institute for Strategic Studies (IISS), *The Military Balance 1993–1994* (London: Brassey's, for IISS, 1995).

6. Woolsey's comments are excerpted in *Peacewatch*, no. 33, 26 September 1994, by the Washington Institute for Near East Policy.

7. Philip Finnegan, Robert Holzer, and Neil Munro, "Iran Pursues Chinese Mine to Bolster Gulf Clout," *Defense News*, 17–23 January 1994, pp. 1–29; Fouad Ashraf, "Iran Mines, Not Submarines, Pose Threat in the Gulf," Reuters, 13 October 1993.

8. Ashraf, "Iran Mines, Not Submarines."

9. "Submarines: Iran Sparks Off a Boat Race," *Middle East Economic Digest* (*MEED*), 29 April 1994, p. 15.

10. "U.S. Commander Says Iran Keeping the Peace," Reuters, 7 September 1994.

11. "China Delivers Five FACs to Iran," *Jane's Defence Weekly*, 1 October 1994, p. 6.

12. Ibid.

13. "Clinton to Press Yeltsin on Iran Arms Sales," Reuters, 27 September 1994.

14. Michael Eisenstadt, "Déjà Vu All Over Again: An Assessment of Iran's Military Buildup," in *Iran's Strategic Intentions and Capabilities*, ed. Patrick Clawson (Washington, DC: National Defense University, Institute of National Strategic Studies, McNair Paper 29, April 1994), p. 128.

15. "Iranian Air Force Sukhoi, MiG Pilots Graduate," Reuters, 11 August 1994. The report, which quoted the Tehran newspaper *Jomhuri Elsami*, did not say how many pilots graduated.

16. *Jane's Defence Weekly*, 20 July 1991, p. 89; 1 February 1992, pp. 158–9; *Flight International*, 15–21 July 1992, p. 13; 18–24 August 1993, p. 12; *New York Times*, 8 August 1992, p. A3.

17. Anoushiravan Ehteshami, "The Armed Forces of the Islamic Republic of Iran," *Jane's Intelligence Review*, February 1993, pp. 76–80.

18. Stockholm International Peace Research Institute (SIPRI), SIPRI Yearbook, 1991, *World Armaments and Disarmaments* (London and New York: Oxford University Press, 1991), 287.

19. Comments by DCI Woolsey, 23 September 1994, in *Peacewatch*, no. 33, Washington Institute for Near East Policy.

20. "Armed Forces, IRGC Participate in Exercise," Voice of the Islamic Republic of Iran First Program Network, 26 January 1994.

21. Douglas Jehl, "Iran is Reported Acquiring Missiles," *New York Times*, 8 April 1993, p. 9A; Knut Royce, "Iran Buying 150 'Terror' Missiles," *Long Island Newsday*, 14 April 1992, p. 6.

22. Comments by DCI Woolsey, 23 September 1994, in *Peacewatch*, no. 33, Washington Institute for Near East Policy.

23. Joseph Bermudez, *Proliferation for Profit: North Korea in the Middle East* (Washington, DC: Washington Institute for Near East Policy, July 1994), p. 21.

24. "Guard Corps Commander on Struggle in Mideast," *Resalat* (Tehran), 25 September 1994, pp. 1–2.

25. "IRGC Defence Industries Manufacture First Helicopter," Islamic Republic News Agency (IRNA) (in English), 15 January 1994.

26. James Bruce, "Iran Claims to Have Built Its Own MBT," *Jane's Defence Weekly*, 23 April 1994, p. 5.

27. The contract came amid a claim by Iran that it has converted 45 percent of its military industries to civilian uses. "Iran Gives Dam Project to Revolutionary Guards," Reuters, 26 September 1994; "Iranian Conversion Claims Mystify," *Jane's Defence Weekly*, 10 September 1994, p. 11.

28. "Syria and Iran Hold Military Cooperation Talks," Reuters, 14 November 1993; "IRGC Commander Receives Delegation," IRNA, 26 June 1992; "Pakistani Ground Forces Commander Arrives 2 November," Voice of the Islamic Republic of Iran, 2 November 1991.

29. "IRNA Carries New Minister's Biographies," Islamic Republic News Agency, in FBIS, 20 September 1988.

30. "Bakhtaran Mopping Up Operations Successful," *Paris Daily News*, 29 August 1984.

31. "History and Present Status of IRGC," *Iran Press Digest* (Tehran), 7 August 1984.

32. "China Delivers FACs to Iran," *Jane's Defence Weekly*, 13 October 1994, p. 6.

33. "The JDW Interview," *Jane's Defence Weekly*, 16 November 1991, p. 980.

34. See Katzman, *Warriors of Islam.*

35. "Opposition Leader on Reform, Ties with Iran," *Keyhan International* (Tehran), 6 October 1992, p. 16.

36. "Iran Admits Smuggling Explosives," Riyadh Domestic Service, 17 May 1989.

37. "Pro-Iranian to Head Algerian Islamist Group-Paper," Reuters, 18 April 1994.

38. US Department of State, Office of the Coordinator for Counterterrorism, *Patterns of Global Terrorism: 1993*, released April 1994, p. 4.

39. "Iran Hostage Takers Now Hold Key Posts," *Newsday*, 8 September 1994, p. A11.

11. Threats and Non-Threats from Iran

1. The military manpower, force strength, and equipment estimates in this chapter are made by the author using a wide range of sources, including computerized databases, interviews, and press clipping services. Some are impossible to reference in ways of use to the reader. The force strength statistics are generally adapted from informal estimates by US, Israeli, and British experts and from the figures in various editions of the International Institute for Strategic Studies, *Military Balance* (London: IISS), and the Jaffee Center for Strategic Studies *The Military Balance in the Middle East* (JCSS: Tel Aviv). Material has also been drawn from computer printouts from NEXIS, the United States Naval Institute database, and from the DMS/FI Market Intelligence Reports database. Other sources include the *Military Technology* "World Defense Almanac for 1993–1994," published in early 1994; Foreign Affairs Division, "Middle East Arms Control and Related Issues," Washington, Congressional Research Service, 91–384F, 1 May 1991; *Middle East Economic Digest*, "MEED Special Report: Defense," vol. 35, 13 December 1991; Peter Lewis Young, "American Perceptions of Iran," *Asian Defense*, February 1993, pp. 25–8; Anoushiravan Ehteshami, "The Armed Forces of the Islamic Republic of Iran," *Jane's Intelligence Review* February 1993, pp. 76–9; Gordon Jacobs and Tim McCarthy, "China Missile Sales – Few Changes for the Future," *Jane's Intelligence Review*, December 1992, pp. 559–63; Alan George, "Tehran Asserts its Independence," *The Middle East*, April 1993, pp. 36–7; Claude van England, "Iran on Military Renewal," *Christian Science Monitor*, 4 March 1993, p. 7; Shireen T. Hunter, "Iran: Renewed Threat in the Persian Gulf?" *The World and I*, April 1993, pp. 80–7; James Wyllie, "Iran – Quest for Security and Influence," *Jane's Intelligence Review*, July 1993, pp. 311–12; and material in Patrick Clawson, *Iran's Challenge to the West: How, When, and Why* (Washington, DC: Washington Institute Policy Papers, no. 33, 1993).

Weapons data are taken from many sources, including computerized material available in NEXIS, and various editions of *Jane's Fighting Ships* (Jane's Publishing), *Jane's Naval Weapons Systems* (Jane's Publishing), *Jane's Armor and Artillery* (Jane's Publishing), *Jane's Infantry Weapons* (Jane's Publishing), *Jane's Military Vehicles and Logistics* (Jane's Publishing), *Jane's Land-Based Air Defence* (Jane's Publishing), *Jane's All the World's Aircraft* (Jane's Publishing), *Jane's C³I Systems* (Jane's Publishing), *Jane's Air-Launched Weapons Systems* (Jane's Publishing), *Jane's Defense Appointments and Procurement Handbook (Middle East Edition)* (Jane's Publishing), *Tanks of the World* (Bernard and Grafe), *Weyer's Warships* (Bernard and Grafe), and *Warplanes of the World* (Bernard and Grafe).

Other military background, effectiveness, strength, organizational, and history data are taken from Anthony H. Cordesman, *The Gulf and the Search for Strategic Stability* (Boulder, CO: Westview Press, 1984); *The Gulf and the West* (Boulder, CO: Westview Press, 1988); *Weapons of Mass Destruction in the Middle East* (London: Brassey's/RUSI, 1991); *After the Storm* (Boulder, CO: Westview Press, 1992); and *Iran and Iraq: The Threat from the Northern Gulf* (Boulder, CO: Westview Press, 1994); Anthony H. Cordesman and Abraham Wagner, *The Lessons of Modern War*, vol. II (Boulder, CO: Westview Press, 1989); Anoushiravan Ehteshami, "Iran's National Strategy," *International Defense Review* 4 / 1994, pp. 29–37; Department of Defense, *Conduct of the Persian Gulf War: Final Report* (Department of Defense, April 1992), pp. 10–12; the relevant country or war sections of Herbert K. Tillema, *International Conflict since 1945* (Boulder, CO: Westview Press, 1991); Department of Defense and Department of State, *Congressional Presentation for Security Assistance Programs, Fiscal Year 1993* (Washington, DC: Department of State, 1992); various annual editions of John Laffin's *The World in Conflict* or *War Annual* (London: Brassey's); and John Keegan, *World Armies* (London: Macmillan, 1983).

2. Reuters, 26 December 1994; *Los Angeles Times*, 13 December 1994, pp. C1, C5; *Wall Street Journal*, 7 December 1994, p. A10; *Washington Times*, 1 December 1994, p. A21; *New York Times*, 2 February 1994, p. A2; *Economist*, 12 February 1994, p. 40.

3. *Philadelphia Inquirer*, 8 January 1994, p. C8.

4. This analysis is based on the *Wall Street Journal*, 7 December 1994; Xinhua News Agency, 28 December 1994; *Los Angeles Times*, 2 December 1994, pp. A1, A3, 12 December 1994, pp. C1, C5; *The Middle East*, December 1994, pp. 28–9; *Washington Times*, 1 February 1994, p. A11; *New York Times*, 15 January 1994, p. A3, 2 February 1994, p. A2; *Economist*, 12 February 1994, pp. 40–1; *Washington Post*, 8 February 1994, p. A16, 30 June 1994, p. A22; *Christian Science Monitor*, 28 June 1994, p. A1.

5. *Los Angeles Times*, 7 December 1994, pp. A1, A3, electronic edition, 4 January 1995; *The Middle East*, December 1994, pp. 28–9; *New York Times*, 20 November 1994, p. A18.

6. Petroleum Economist, Petroleum Finance Company, and Congressional Quarterly, *The Middle East*, 7th edn (Washington, DC: Congressional Quarterly, 1990), p. 195.

7. CIA, *World Fact Book, 1994* (Washington, DC: Government Printing Office (GPO), 1994), 190; *New York Times*, 18 January 1994, p. D7.

8. *Oil and Gas Journal*, 23 September 1991, p. 62.

9. Some estimates put Iran's 1991 oil revenues at about $15 billion and its domestic spending needs at $15 billion. Economist Intelligence Unit, *Country Report on Iran, 1993*; *New York Times*, 11 February 1992, p. A11; *Defense News*, 2 March 1992, pp. 3 and 29; *Washington Post*, 10 September 1991, p. A21, 2 February 1992, p. A1; *Wall Street Journal* 16 September 1991, p. A1; *Washington Times* 29 April 1989, p. A9; *Jane's Defense Weekly*, 17 June 1989, pp. 1254–5; *Los Angeles Times*, 13 January 1992, p. A9.

10. *Wall Street Journal*, 7 June 1993, p. A10, 28 June 1994, p. A1; *Christian Science Monitor* 12 August 1993, p. 9; *Philadelphia Inquirer*, 3 February 1994, p. A18; *New York Times*, 5 July 1994, p. A1; *Los Angeles Times*, 7 February 1994, p. A1; *The Middle East*, April 1993, pp. 36–47; Xinhua News Agency, 28 December 1994.

11. Estimates based on the data in the Iran sections of various editions of the CIA *World Factbook*; work by Jim Placek, and the IISS, *The Military Balance, 1993–1994* (London: IISS, 1994), and *The Military Balance, 1994–1995* (London: IISS, 1995); and Anthony H. Cordesman, *Iran and Iraq: The Threat from the Northern Gulf* (Boulder, CO: Westview, 1994).

12. This, however, only amounts to about 1,362 cubic meters per person, less than half the total for a citizen of the United States. *Los Angeles Times*, 28 January 1992, p. C1.

13. IISS, *The Military Balance, 1993–1994*, and *The Military Balance, 1994–1995*, pp. 127–9; and CIA, *World Factbook, 1994* (Washington, DC: GPO, 1994), pp. 189–91.

14. Author's guestimate. Iran claimed in February 1992, that it was spending only 1.3 percent of its GNP on defense. *Washington Times*, 20 February 1992, p. A9.

15. US Arms Control and Disarmament Agency (ACDA), *World Military Expenditures and Arms Transfers, 1991–1992* (Washington, DC: GPO, 1994), p. 67.

16. Iran claimed in February 1992, that it was spending only 1.3 percent of its GNP on defense. *Washington Times*, 20 February 1992, p. A9.

17. British sources quoted in *Jane's Defense Weekly*, 1 February 1992, p. 158. The *Egyptian Gazette* projected expenditures of $5 billion per year in 1992, 1993, and 1994 in its 29 January 1992 issue. The Jaffee Center estimated expenditures of $8.5 billion in 1989 and $8.6 billion in 1990. Andrew Duncan of the IISS estimated expenditures of $10 billion annually in 1992, 1993, 1994 in *Defense News*, 27 January 1992. The CIA estimates are taken from the relevant editions of the CIA *World Factbook*. It is extremely difficult to relate any Iranian statistics to dollar figures because Iran uses multiple exchange rates, and often reports inaccurate statistics. See Patrick Clawson, *Iran's Challenge to the West*, p. 58.

18. IISS, *The Military Balance*, 1990–91, 1991–92, 1993–94, 1994–95 editions. The IISS also quotes Iranian official government statistics.

19. Defense expenditure data taken from IISS, *The Military Balance, 1993–1994.*

20. *New York Times*, 2 November 1992, p. A4, 18 June 1994, p. D7, 18 January 1995, p. D7; Reuters, Manama, 17 January 1995.

21. CIA, *World Factbook 1994*, 189; *Los Angeles Times*, 2 December 1994, pp. A1, A3; *The Middle East*, December 1994, pp. 28–9; *Wall Street Journal*, 7 December 1994.

22. *Los Angeles Times,* 2 December 1994, pp. A1, A3.

23. Based on US Department of Commerce estimates, data in relevant editions of the CIA *World Factbook* (especially the 1994 edition, p. 190), and the trend data shown in the ACDA *World Military Expenditures and Arms Transfers, 1991–1992*, p. 109.

24. For typical reporting, see Xinhua News Agency, 1228187, 28 December 1994; *Los Angeles Times*, 2 December 1994, pp. A1, A3; *The Middle East, December 1994*, pp. 28–9; *Wall Street Journal*, 7 December 1994.

25. Robert Gates, "Statement of the Director of Central Intelligence Before the U.S. House of Representatives Armed Services Committee Defense Policy Panel," 27 March 1992.

26. Richard F. Grimmett, *Conventional Arms Transfers to the Third World, 1985–1992* (Washington, DC: Congressional Research Service, CRS-93-656F, 19 July 1993), pp. 56–8, 67–70.

27. ACDA, *World Military Expenditures and Arms Transfers, 1989* (Washington, DC: GPO, 1990), p. 117.

28. Richard F. Grimmett, *Iran: Conventional Arms Acquisitions*, (Washington, DC: Congressional Research Service, 94-138F, 22 February 1994), p. 2; and *Conventional Arms Transfers to the Third World, 1985–1992* (CRS-93-656F, 19 July 1993), pp. 56, 57.

29. See *Washington Times*, 8 June 1994, p. A8, for typical reporting on Iranian smuggling efforts. For a broader discussion, see "Insight," *Washington Times*, 4 April 1994, pp. 12–15.

30. For more reliable reports on arms sales to Iran during this period, see *Defense News*, 1 February 1992, p. 159, 2 March 1993, p. 93, 4 October 1993, p. 26, 17 January 1994, pp. 1, 29; *Flight International*, 15 July 1993, p. 13, 24 November 1993, p. 59; *Jane's Defense Weekly*, 6 October 1990, p. 619, 27 April 1991, p. 684, 20 July 1991, p. 89, 27 July 1991, p. 138, 1 February 1992, pp. 158–9, 17 October 1992, p. 19, 24 August 1993, p. 12; *Jane's Intelligence Review*, July 1992, pp. 313–14; *Military Technology*, November 1993, p. 18; *New York Times,* 8 April 1992, p. A9, 8 August 1992, p. A3; *Washington Post*, 13 June 1993, pp. H1, H5, H6.

31. *Inside the Navy*, 10 January 1994, p. 1; *Navy News and Undersea Technology*, 11 April 1994, p. 4; *The Estimate*, 5 May 1994, p. 4; *Defense News*, 17 January 1994, p. 1.

32. Grimmett, *Iran: Conventional Arms Acquisitions* (CRS 94-138F, 22 February 1994), p. 7; *Defense News*

33. Grimmett, *Iran: Conventional Arms Acquisitions* (CRS 94-138F, 22 February 1994), p. 7.

34. *Jane's Defense Weekly*, 8 October 1994, p. 2; *Washington Post*, 10 June 1993, p. A27; *New York Times*, 10 June 1993, p. A5.

35. The data on Iran's recent purchases are based on discussions with various US, British, and Israeli experts. Also see Robert Gates, "Statement of the Director of Central Intelligence Before the U.S. House of Representatives Armed Services Committee Defense Policy Panel," 27 March 1992; Statement of Robert Gates on McNeil-Leher News Hour, 6 January 1993; *Defense News*, 17 February 1992, pp. 1, 52, 17 January 1994, p. 29, 28 March 1994, p. 38; Posture Statement of Rear Admiral Edward D. Sheafer, director of naval intelligence, 3 May 1993; Ashraf Fouad, "Iran Mines, Not Submarines Pose Threat in Gulf," *Armed Forces Journal International*, November 1993; *Washington Times*, 4 June 1992, p. G3; *New York Times*, 8 August 1992, p. 2; *Sunday Times* (London), 31 May 1992, pp. 22–3; Joseph S.

Bermudez, "Proliferation for Profit: North Korea in the Middle East," (Washington, DC: Washington Institute, July 1994), pp. 8–9.

36. Reports differ sharply. One indicated that the Soviet Republic was selling T-72s for as little as $50,000 each while another indicated that it was selling Iran a T-72 production plant for $9 billion. On the other hand, Marshal Yevgeny Shaposhnikov, the senior military officer in the CIS, stated that it had curbed all sales to Iran on 1 February 1992. *Washington Post*, 1 February 1992, p. A1, 2 February 1992, p. A19, 16 June 1992; *Keyhan*, 18 April 1990; *Los Angeles Times*, 7 January 1992, p. A7; Clawson, *Iran's Challenge to the West*, 50–8; *Le Monde*, 25 July 1992; *New York Times*, 8 August 1992; *Financial Times*, 30 January 1992, 22 March 1992, and 30 April 1992; *Washington Times*, 22 April 1992, 14 October, 1992, p. A8, 11 May 1993, p. A7; *MEED*, 8 February 1991; *Sunday Telegraph*, 31 May 1992.

37. Northrop helped Iran set up Iran Aircraft Industries in 1970, but this operation virtually ceased in 1979. See *Jane's Defense Weekly*, 4 February 1989, pp. 163, 167, 11 February 1989, p. 219, 19 November 1988, pp. 1252–3, 30 June 1989, pp. 1299–301, 11 February 1992, p. 159; *London Financial Times*, 8 February 1993, p. 4; *Time*, 7 December 1992, p. 26; *Washington Post*, 6 December 1992, p. A33; *St. Louis Post-Dispatch*, 25 November 1992, p. 6; *New York Times*, 8 August 1992, p. A3; *The Middle East*, December 1992, pp. 39–40; *Defense and Foreign Affairs*, October–November 1992.

38. *Washington Post*, 10 November 1992, pp. A1, A30, 23 May 1992, p. A26, 10 June 1993, p. A27; *New York Times*, 18 November 1992, p. A5; *Defense News*, 8 March 1993, p. 4; *Business Week*, 14 June 1993, p. 31; *Los Angeles Times*, 10 June 1993, p. A3; *Washington Times*, 10 June 1993, p. A1; *Philadelphia Inquirer*, 21 November 1993, p. A2.

39. Iran has long been making light arms and ammunition. The Shah set up the Import Substitute Industrialization (ISI) program in 1970 with the goal of making Iran self-sufficient in arms.

40. *Jane's Defense Weekly*, 30 June 1989, pp. 1299–301.

41. *Jane's Defense Weekly*, 7 January 1995, p. 4.

42. BBC Summary of World Broadcasts, 3 January 1995, ME/219/MED.

43. See *Middle East Defense News*, 1 March 1993, and *JINSA Security Affairs*, June–July 1993, p. 7; Anoushiravan Ehteshami, "Iran Boosts Domestic Arms Industry," *International Defense Review*, 4/1994, pp. 72–3.

44. CIA, *World Factbook, 1994*, pp. 189–91.

45. *Washington Post*, 8 May 1992, p. A17; CIA, *World Factbook, 1992*, pp. 160–3.

46. IISS, *The Military Balance, 1994–1995*. While Iran occasionally shows women in military roles for propaganda purposes, it does not employ them in any meaningful military roles.

47. Based on CIA estimates in CIA, *World Factbook, 1994*, pp. 189–91. Sources disagree sharply on the exact percentages involved.

48. Ibid.

49. IISS, *The Military Balance, 1994–1995*. Some estimates show totals for the Gendarmerie alone. This is incorrect. They have been merged with the national police and some elements of the internal security forces.

50. IISS, *The Military Balance, 1993–1994*.

51. In addition to the general sources on Iranian force strength referenced at the beginning of this section, this analysis draws on the *Washington Times*, 2 May 1989, p. A9, 23 June 1989, p. A9, 1 March 1992, p. B3, 22 March 1989, p. A8, 17 January 1992, p. A1, 20 February 1992, p. A9; *Armed Forces Journal*, March 1992, pp. 26–7; *Defense Electronics*, March 1992, p. 16; *Inside the Air Force*, 28 February 1992, p. 1; *Jane's Defense Weekly*, 19 November 1988, pp. 1252–3, 3 June 1988, p. 1057, 11 February 1989, p. 219, 30 June 1990, pp. 1299–302, 11 February 1992, pp. 158–9; Andrew Rathmell, "Iran's Rearmament: How Great a Threat?" *Jane's Intelligence Review*, July 1994, p. 317–22; *Armed Forces (UK)*, May 1989, pp.

206–9; *Washington Post*, 23 June 1989, p. A1, 18 August 1989, p. A25, 20 August 1989, p. A1, 3 September 1989, p. A25, 1 February 1992, p. A1, 2 February 1992, p. A1, 5 February 1992, p. A19; *New York Times*, 3 September 1989, p. A4; *The Estimate*, 13–26 October 1989, p. 1; *Christian Science Monitor*, 6 February 1992, p. 19; *Philadelphia Inquirer*, 6 February 1992, p. A6; *Los Angeles Times*, 7 January 1992, p. A1; *Baltimore Sun*, 25 January 1992, p. 4A; *Defense News*, 27 January 1992, p. 45, 17 February 1992, p. 1; *Chicago Tribune*, 19 January 1992, p. 1.

52. The author visited this display in August after a substantial amount of the equipment had been moved to Jordan and to other areas. Even then, there were immense stocks of heavy weapons, almost all of which had been abandoned without any combat damage. It should be noted, however, that Iraq made claims about capturing tanks that seem to have included all light tanks and BMP-1s.

53. The identification of unit size and title is a major problem for all Middle Eastern armies. Most do not have standard tables of organization and equipment, and unit titles may have little to do with the actual total manpower and equipment mix.

54. Anoushravan Ehteshami, "The Armed Forces of the Islamic Republic of Iran, *Jane's Intelligence Review*, February 1993, pp. 76–9.

55. *Jane's Defense Weekly*, 7 January 1995, p. 4.

56. Based on estimates by Israeli and US civilian experts, and the IISS, *The Military Balance, 1993–1994*, pp. 115–17, and *The Military Balance, 1994–1995*, pp. 127–9.

57. These counts are very uncertain and mix interview and IISS data.

58. In addition to the general sources on Iranian force strength referenced at the beginning of this section, this analysis draws on the *Washington Times*, 2 May 1989, p. A9, 23 June 1989, p. A9, 1 March 1992, p. B3, 22 March 1989, p. A8, 17 January 1992, p. A1, 20 February 1992, p. A9; *Armed Forces Journal*, March 1993, pp. 26–7; *Defense Electronics*, March 1992, p. 16; *Inside the Air Force*, 28 February 1992, p. 1; *Jane's Defense Weekly*, 19 November 1988, pp. 1252–3, 3 June 1988, p. 1057, 11 February 1989, p. 219, 30 June 1989, pp. 1299–302, 11 February 1992, pp. 158–9; Rathmell, *Iran's Rearmament*, pp. 317–22; *Armed Forces (UK)*, May 1989, pp. 206–9; *Washington Post*, 23 June 1989, p. A1, 18 August 1989, p. A25, 20 August 1989, p. A1, 3 September 1989, p. A25, 1 February 1992, p. A1, 2 February 1992, p. A1, 5 February 1992, p. A19; *New York Times*, 3 September 1989, p. A4; *The Estimate*, 13–26 October 1989, p. 1; *Christian Science Monitor*, 6 February 1992, p. 19; *Philadelphia Inquirer*, 6 February 1992, p. A6; *Los Angeles Times*, 7 January 1992, p. A1; *Baltimore Sun*, 25 January 1992, p. 4A; *Defense News*, 27 January 1992, p. 45, 17 February 1992, p. 1; *Chicago Tribune*, 19 January 1992, p. 1.

59. Division, brigade, regiment, and battalion are Western terms applied to Iranian and Iraqi formations. Actual unit strengths and organization often have nothing to do with the titles applied in Western reporting.

60. Rathmell, "Iran's Reamament," pp. 317–22; *Defense and Foreign Affairs*, 1 (1994), pp. 4–7.

61. Adapted from interviews with US, British, and Israeli experts, Iranian exiles, Anthony H. Cordesman, *Iran and Iraq: The Threat from the Northern Gulf*; John W. R. Taylor and Kenneth Munson, "Gallery of Middle East Air Power," *Air Force* (October 1994), pp. 59–70; IISS, *The Military Balance 1993–1994*, pp. 115–17; and *The Military Balance, 1994–1995*, pp. 127–9; USNI Database; Military Technology, *World Defense Almanac: The Balance of Military Power*, 17, no. 1 (1993), ISSN 0722-3226, pp. 139–42; Anoushiravan Ehteshami, "Iran's National Strategy," *International Defense Review*, 4/1994, pp. 29–37; and working data from the Jaffee Center for Strategic Studies (JCSS) and the *Washington Times*, 16 January 1992, p. G4; *Washington Post*, 1 February 1992, p. A1, 2 February 1992, pp. A1, A25, 5 February 1992, p. A19; *Financial Times*, 6 February 1992, p. 4; *Christian Science Monitor*, 6 February 1992, p. 19; *Defense News*, 17 February 1992, p. 1.

62. *Defense and Foreign Affairs*, 1 (1994), pp. 4–7.

63. Ibid.

64. See James P. Wootten, "Terrorism: U.S. Policy Options" (Washington, DC: Congressional Research Service, IB92074, 6 October 1994), pp. 6–7; Kenneth Katzman, "Iran: Current Developments and US Policy" (Washington, DC: Congressional Research Service, IB93033, 9 September 1994), pp. 5–7; *Christian Science Monitor*, 22 March 1994, p. 6, 28 June, 1994, p. A1; *Time*, 21 March 1994, pp. 50–4; *Washington Times*, 19 December 1993, p. A3, 19 February 1994, p. A8, 9 March 1994, 22 June 1994, p. A14, 24 June 1994, p. A1, 27 June 1994, p. A22; *Washington Post*, 1 January 1994, p. A15, 4 February 1994, p. A14.

65. In addition to the general sources on Iranian force strength referenced in this section, this analysis draws on *Washington Times*, 1 March 1992, p. B3, 22 March 1989, p. A8, 17 January 1992, p. A1, 20 February 1992, p. A9; *Armed Forces Journal*, March 1992, pp. 26–7; *Defense Electronics*, March 1992, p. 16; *Inside the Air Force*, 28 February 1992, p. 1; Rathmell, "Iran's Rearmament," pp. 317–22; *Jane's Defense Weekly*, 11 February 1992, pp. 158–9; *Armed Forces (UK)*, May 1989, pp. 206–9; *Washington Post*, 1 February 1992, p. A1, 2 February 1992, p. A1, 5 February 1992, p. A19; *Christian Science Monitor*, 6 February 1992, p. 19; *Philadelphia Inquirer*, 6 February 1992, p. A6; *Los Angeles Times*, 7 January 1992, p. A1; *Baltimore Sun*, 25 January 1992, p. 4A; *Defense News*, 27 January 1992, p. 45, 17 February 1992, p. 1; *Chicago Tribune*, 19 January 1992, p. 1.

66. Based on interviews with British, Israeli, and US experts, and Anthony H. Cordesman, *Iran and Iraq: The Threat from the Northern Gulf*, IISS, *The Military Balance 1993–1994*, pp. 115–17, and *The Military Balance 1994–1995*, pp. 127–9; USNI Database; Military Technology, *World Defense Almanac*, pp. 139–42; Ehteshami, "Iran's National Strategy," pp. 29–37; and working data from the JCSS. US and Israeli experts do not confirm reports that Iran has ordered and taken delivery of 12 TU-22M Backfire bombers. There are some indications that it may have discussed such orders with the then USSR.

67. Anoushiravan Ehteshami, "The Armed Forces of the Islamic Republic of Iran," *Jane's Intelligence Review*, February 1993, pp. 76–9.

68. *Philadelphia Inquirer*, 5 February 1994, p. A18.

69. Based on interviews with British, Israeli, and US experts. *Washington Times*, 16 January 1992, p. G4; *Washington Post*, 1 February 1992, p. A1, 2 February 1992, pp. A1, A25, 5 February 1992, p. A19; *Financial Times*, 6 February 1992, p. 4; *Christian Science Monitor*, 6 February 1992, p. 19; *Defense News*, 17 February 1992, p. 1; *Flight International*, 17–23 February 1992.

70. See *London Financial Times*, 8 February 1993, p. 4. Northrop helped Iran set up Iran Aircraft Industries in 1970, but this operation virtually ceased operation in 1979.

71. One source indicates that Iran is modifying its F-7M fighters to use Western avionics at old Iranian Aircraft Industries facility, but such modification efforts have had little value in other countries.

72. *Defense News*, 28 March 1994, p. 38.

73. *Washington Times*, 16 January 1992, p. G4; *Washington Post*, 1 February 1992, p. A1, 2 February 1992, pp. A1, A25, 5 February 1992, p. A19; *Financial Times*, 6 February 1992, p. 4; *Christian Science Monitor*, 6 February 1992, p. 19; *Defense News*, 17 February 1992, p. 1; *Jane's Defense Weekly*, 1 February 1992, p. 159.

74. Dick Pawloski, *Changes in Threat Air Combat Doctrine and Force Structure*, 24th edn (Fort Worth, TX: General Dynamics DWIC-91, Fort Worth Division, February 1992), pp. I-85–I-117.

75. Rostislav Belyakov and Nikolai Buntin, "The MiG 29M Light Multirole Fighter," *Military Technology*, August, 1994, pp. 41–4; Pawloski, *Changes in Threat Air Combat*, pp. I-85–I-117.

76. Pawloski, *Changes in Threat Air Combat*, pp. I-85–I-117.

77. *Aviation Week and Space Technology*, 10 April 1989, pp. 19–20; *New York Times*, 5 April 1989, 7 September 1989; *Washington Times*, 16 January 1989; *FBIS/NES*, 10 April 1989.

78. The Su-24 has a wing area of 575 square feet, an empty weight of 41,845 pounds, carries 3,385 gallons or 22,000 pounds of external fuel, has a combat thrust-to-weight ratio of 1.02, a combat wing loading of 96 pounds per square foot, and a maximum load factor of 7.5 G. *Jane's Soviet Intelligence Review*, July 1990, pp. 298–300; *Jane's Defense Weekly*, 25 June 1985, pp. 1226–7; and Pawloski, *Changes in Threat Air Combat*, pp. I-65, and I-110–I-117.

79. Based on interviews with British, Israeli, and US experts, and Cordesman, *Iran and Iraq: The Threat from the Northern Gulf*, IISS, *The Military Balance, 1993–1994*, pp. 115–17, and *The Military Balance, 1994–1995*, pp. 127–9; USNI Database; Military Technology, *World Defense Almanac: The Balance of Military Power*, pp. 139–42; and working data from the JCSS.

80. Source: USAF briefing, September 1981. One B-727 and 2 B-767ERs are unaccounted for.

81. In addition to general sources on Iranian force strength referenced at the beginning of this section, this analysis draws on *Washington Times*, 2 May 1989, p. A9, 23 June 1989, p. A9, 1 March 1992, p. B3, 22 March 1989, p. A8, 17 January 1992, p. A1, 20 February 1992, p. 9; *Armed Forces Journal*, March 1992, pp. 26–7; *Defense Electronics*, March 1992, p. 16; Rathmell, "Iran's Rearmament, pp. 317–22; *Inside the Air Force*, 28 February 1992, p. 1; *Jane's Defense Weekly*, 19 November 1988, pp. 1252–3, 3 June 1988, p. 1057, 11 February 1989, p. 219, 30 June 1989, pp. 1299–302, 11 February 1992, pp. 158–9; *Armed Forces (UK)*, May 1989, pp. 206–9; *Washington Post*, 23 June 1989, p. A1, 18 August 1989, p. A25, 20 August 1989, p. A1, 3 September 1989, p. A25, 1 February 1992, p. A1, 2 February 1992, p. A1, 5 February 1992, p. A19; *New York Times*, 3 September 1989, p. A4; *The Estimate*, 13–26 October 1989; *Christian Science Monitor*, 6 February 1992, p. 19; *Philadelphia Inquirer*, 6 February 1992, p. A6; *Los Angeles Times*, 7 January 1992, p. A1; *Baltimore Sun*, 25 January 1992, p. 4A; *Defense News*, 27 January 1992, p. 45, 17 February 1992, p. 1; *Chicago Tribune*, 19 January 1992, p. 1.

82. Based on interviews with British, Israeli, and US experts, and Cordesman, *Iran and Iraq: The Threat from the Northern Gulf*, IISS, *The Military Balance, 1993–1994*, pp. 115–17, and *The Military Balance, 1994–1995*, pp. 127–9; USNI Database; Ehteshami, "Iran's National Strategy," pp. 29–37; Military Technology, *World Defense Almanac: The Balance of Military Power*, pp. 139–42; working data from the JCSS; Rathmell, "Iran's Rearmament," pp. 317–22.

83. Based on interviews with British, Israeli, and US experts. Reports of MiG-31s do not seem to be correct. Adapted from the IISS, Annapolis, and JCSS databases, and the *Washington Times*, 16 January 1992, p. G4; *Washington Post*, 1 February 1992, p. A1, 2 February 1992, pp. A1, A25, 5 February 1992, p. A19; *Financial Times*, 6 February 1992, p. 4; *Christian Science Monitor*, 6 February 1992, p. 19; *Defense News*, 17 February 1992, p. 1.

84. Adapted from the IISS, Annapolis, and JCSS databases, and the *Washington Times*, 16 January 1992, p. G4; *Washington Post*, 1 February 1992, p. A1, 2 February 1992, pp. A1, A25, 5 February 1992, p. A19; *Financial Times*, 6 February 1992, p. 4; *Christian Science Monitor*, 6 February 1992, p. 19; *Defense News*, 17 February 1992, p. 1.

85. *Defense and Foreign Affairs*, 1 (1994), pp. 4–7.

86. *Defense News*, 12 July 1993, p. 1; *New York Times*, 27 December 1993, p. A17.

87. *Flight International*, 24 August 1993, p. 12.

88. Based on interviews with British, Israeli, and US experts. *Washington Times*, 16 January 1992, p. G4; *Washington Post*, 1 February 1992, p. A1, 2 February 1992, pp. A1, A25, 5 February 1992, p. A19; *Financial Times*, 6 February 1992, p. 4; *Christian Science Monitor*, 6 February 1992, p. 19; *Defense News*, 17 February 1992, p. 1.

89. In addition to the general sources on Iranian force strength referenced at the beginning of Chapter 3, this analysis draws on Cordesman, *Iran and Iraq: The Threat from the Northern Gulf*; Rathmell, "Iran's Rearmament," pp. 317–22; US Naval Institute (USNI), *The Naval Institute Guide to the Combat Fleets of the World, 1993: Their Ships, Aircraft, and Armaments* (Annapolis, MD: Naval Institute, 1993); John Hordan, "The Iranian Navy," *Jane's Intelligence Review*, May 1992, pp. 213–16; Ehteshami, "Iran's National Strategy," pp. 29–37; *Washington Times*, 2 May 1989, p. A9, 23 June 1989, p. A9, 1 March 1992, p. B3, 22 March 1989, p. A8, 17 January 1992, p. A1, 20 February 1992, p. A9; *Armed Forces Journal*, March 1992, pp. 26–7; *Defense Electronics*, March 1992, p. 16; *Inside the Air Force*, 28 February 1992, p. 1; *Jane's Defense Weekly*, 19 November 1988, pp. 1252–3, 3 June 1988, p. 1057, 11 February 1989, p. 219, 30 June 1989, pp. 1299–302, 11 February 1992, pp. 158–9; *Armed Forces (UK)*, May 1989, pp. 206–9; *Washington Post*, 23 June 1989, p. A1, 18 August 1989, p. A25, 20 August 1989, p. A1, 3 September 1989, p. A25, 1 February 1992, p. A1, 2 February 1992, p. A1, 5 February 1992, p. A19; *New York Times*, 3 September 1989, p. A4; *The Estimate*, 13–26 October 1989; *Christian Science Monitor*, 6 February 1992, p. 19; *Philadelphia Inquirer*, 6 February 1992, p. A6; *Los Angeles Times*, 7 January 1992, p. A1; *Baltimore Sun*, 25 January 1992, p. 4A; *Defense News*, 27 January 1992, p. 45, 17 February 1992, p. 1; *Chicago Tribune*, 19 January 1992, p. 1.

90. *FBIS-NES*, 89-144, 28 July 1989, p. 51; *FBIS-NES*, 89-191, 4 October 1989, p. 66; *FBIS-NES*, 89-206, 26 October 1989, p. 66; *FBIS-NES*, 89-214, 7 November 1989, p. 73; *International Defense Review*, June 1990, pp. 51–2.

91. *Defense and Foreign Affairs*, 1 (1994), pp. 4–7; *Navy News and Undersea Technology*, 11 April 1994, p. 4; *Defense News*, 17 January 1994, p. 1.

92. This analysis draws heavily on USNI, *The Naval Institute Guide to the Combat Fleets of the World, 1993: Their Ships, Aircraft, and Armaments*; Cordesman, *Iran and Iraq: The Threat from the Northern Gulf*; Ehteshami, "Iran's National Strategy," pp. 29–37; *Jane's Fighting Ships, 1992–1993*; IISS, *The Military Balance, 1993–1994*, pp. 115–17, and *The Military Balance, 1994–1995*, pp. 127–9; USNI Database; Military Technology, *World Defense Almanac: The Balance of Military Power*, pp. 139–42; *Washington Times*, 16 January 1992, p. G4; *Washington Post*, 1 February 1992, p. A1, 2 February 1992, pp. A1, A25, 5 February 1992, p. A19; *Financial Times*, 6 February 1992, p. 4; *Christian Science Monitor*, 6 February 1992, p. 19; *Defense News*, 17 February 1992, p. 1; and working data from the JCSS.

93. Adapted from the IISS, Annapolis, and JCSS databases, and the *Washington Times*, 16 January 1992, p. G4; *Washington Post*, 1 February 1992, p. A1, 2 February 1992, pp. A1, A25, 5 February 1992, p. A19; *Financial Times*, 6 February 1992, p. 4; *Christian Science Monitor*, 6 February 1992, p. 19; *Defense News*, 17 February 1992, p. 1.

94. *Jane's Defense Weekly*, 1 October 1994, p. 6; *Sea Power*, November 1994, p. 21.

95. *Inside the Navy*, 8 January 1994, p. 1; *Defense and Foreign Affairs*, 1 (1994), pp. 4–7; *Navy News and Undersea Technology*, 11 April 1994, p. 4; *Defense News*, 17 January 1994, p. 1.

96. Teal Group Corporation, *World Missiles Briefing*.

97. Ehteshami, "The Armed Forces of the Islamic Republic of Iran, pp. 76–9; Gordon Jacobs and Tim McCarthy, "China Missile Sales – Few Changes for the Future," *Jane's Intelligence Review*, December 1992, pp. 559–63.

98. Cordesman, *Iran and Iraq: The Threat from the Northern Gulf*; IISS, *The Military Balance, 1993–1994*, pp. 115–17, and *The Military Balance, 1994–1995*, pp. 127–9; USNI Database; Military Technology, *World Defense Almanac: The Balance of Military Power*, pp. 139–42; and working data from the JCSS.

99. The submarines are based on Second World War designs. They can lay mines and have a five-man crew, a maximum range of 1,200 miles, and a speed of 6 knots. Iran

claims to have made one of the submarines. The first underwent trials in 1987; the second was delivered in 1988. These ships are difficult to use in mine-laying and often require frogmen to place the mines. It is not surprising if Iran abandoned them as lacking effectiveness once the Iran–Iraq war was over. *Jane's Fighting Ships, 1992–1993* (London, Jane's Publishing); USNI database.

100. *Washington Times*, 16 January 1992, p. G4; *Washington Post*, 1 February 1992, p. A1, 2 February 1992, pp. A1, A25, 5 February 1992, p. A19, 26 September 1992, p. A15, 2 October 1992, p. A40, 30 October 1992, p. A1, 5 November 1992, p. A3; *Financial Times*, 6 February 1992, p. 4; *Christian Science Monitor*, 6 February 1992, p. 19; *Defense News*, 17 February 1992, p. 1, 1 March 1993, p. 1; *Time*, 7 December 1992, p. 26; *Wall Street Journal*, 16 November 1992, p. A4; *Jane's Defense Weekly*, 3 October 1992, p. 12, 21 November 1992, p. 9, 27 February 1992, p. 9; *London Times*, 5 October 1992, p. 9.

101. *Washington Post*, 4 August 1993, p. A12; *Washington Times*, 12 June 1993, p. A2.

102. Only two torpedo tubes can fire wire-guided torpedoes. *Defense News*, 17 January 1994, pp. 1, 29.

103. *Defense News*, 6 December 1993, p. 1.

104. *Jane's Defense Weekly*, 8 October 1994, p. 4; *The Estimate*, 5 May 1994, p. 4; *International Defense Review*, December 1994, p. 9; *Washington Times*, 17 January 1995, p. A11.

105. See David Miller, "Submarines in the Gulf," *Military Technology*, June 1993, pp. 42–5.

106. *Jane's Defense Weekly*, 6 June 1987, p. 1113; Palowski, *Changes in Threat Air Combat Doctrine and Force Structure*, p. II-275.

107. *Jane's Intelligence Review*, November 1992, pp. 512–13; *Time*, 25 April 1994, p. 39.

108. *Naval Forces*, 15, no. 3 (1994), p. 62; Teal Group Corporation, *World Missiles Briefing; Defence and Foreign Affairs*, 1 (1994), pp. 4–7; *Defense News*, 17 January 1994, pp. 1, 29; *Inside the Navy*, 8 January 1994, p. 1, 10 January 1994, p. 1; *Navy News and Undersea Technology*, 1 April 1994, p. 4, 11 April 1994, p. 4; *Washington Times*, 9 March 1989, p. A1, 11 May 1993, p. A7; *Los Angeles Times*, 14 February 1989, p. 5.

109. There have been unconfirmed reports that Iran is seeking to modify the Silkworm to extend its range and use it to deliver weapons of mass destruction.

110. In addition to the sources listed at the start of this section, these assessments are based on various interviews, prior editions of the IISS, *The Military Balance*; the JCSS, *The Jaffee Center Middle East Military Balance*; and *Jane's Defense Weekly*, 11 July 1987, p. 15.

111. Counts of these vessels differ sharply. Some estimates of the number of operational PBI types exceed 60. There are some reports that Iran is building its own version of the Boghammer.

112. *Defense News*, 17 January 1994, pp. 1, 29.

113. Based on various interviews. Strength data are taken from IISS, *The Military Balance, 1993–1994*, pp. 115–17, and *The Military Balance, 1994–1995*, pp. 127–9; USNI Database; Military Technology, *World Defense Almanac: The Balance of Military Power*, pp. 139–42; and working data from the JCSS.

114. The details of this involvement are uncertain, and a great deal of the literature involved adds charges that cannot be confirmed. For a good press summary of the evidence, see *Time*, 21 March 1994, pp. 50–4. Also see *Washington Post*, 22 August 1994, p. A17, 28 October 1994, p. A17, 27 November 1994, p. A30; *Los Angeles Times*, 3 November 1994, pp. A1, A12.

115. *New York Times*, 7 November 1994, p. A6; *Washington Times*, 1 November 1994, p. A13; U.S. State Department Report, 31 October 1994; *Wall Street Journal*, 14 October 1994, p. 1.

116. For typical recent reporting on such events see Reuters, 31 December 1994, BC cycle.

117. *Wall Street Journal*, 7 December 1994, p. 10; *Los Angeles Times*, 13 December 1994, pp. C1, C5; *New York Times*, 28 November 1994, p. A5.

118. *New York Times*, 11 December 1994.

119. *Wall Street Journal*, 7 December 1994, p. A10.

120. *Philadelphia Inquirer*, 11 January 1995, p. A6.

121. Reuters, 29 December 1994, BC cycle; *New York Times*, 5 July 1994, p. A1, 2 September 1994, p. A6; *Washington Post*, 22 August 1994, p. A17, 27 August 1994, p. A15; *Washington Times*, 24 August 1994, p. A11.

122. The author has questioned the amount of direct involvement by the Iranian leadership in such incidents and actions in the past. Extensive interviews indicate, however, that many US experts now feel there is no apparent split between the Iranian leadership in supporting many of these actions and that they do receive the direction and support of the Iranian leadership. For recent press reporting, see Wooten, "Terrorism: U.S. Policy Options," pp. 6–7; Katzman, "Iran: Current Developments in U.S. Policy," pp. 5–7; *Christian Science Monitor*, 22 March 1994, p. 6; 28 June 1994, p. A1; *Time*, 21 March 1994, pp. 50–4; *Washington Times*, 19 December 1993, p. A3, 19 February 1994, p. A8, 9 March 1994, 22 June 1994, p. A14, 24 June 1994, p. A1, 27 June 1994, p. A22; *Washington Post*, 1 January 1994, p. A15, 4 February 1994, p. A14; *New York Times*, 24 December 1994, p. A5. For fuller details, see the author's *Iran and Iraq: The Threat from the Northern Gulf*.

123. For additional details, see Cordesman, *Iran and Iraq: The Threat from the Northern Gulf*, and Roger C. Herdman, *Technologies Underlying Weapons of Mass Destruction* (Washington, DC: GPO, Office of Technology Assessment, US Congress, OTA-BP-ISC-115, December 1993), pp. 197–255.

124. W. Seth Carus and Joseph S. Bermudez, "Iran's Growing Missile Forces," *Jane's Defense Weekly*, 23 July 1988, pp. 126–31.

125. Iran publicly displayed the Oghab at a military show in Libreville in 1989. It is 230 mm in diameter, 4,820 mm long, and weighs 320 kg, with a 70-kg warhead. Iran also displayed another rocket called the Nazeat, which is 355 mm in diameter, 5,900 mm long, weighs 950 kg, and has a 180-kg warhead. *Jane's Defense Weekly*, 11 February 1989, p. 219; Lora Lumpe, Lisbeth Gronlund, and David C. Wright, "Third World Missiles Fall Short," *The Bulletin of the Atomic Scientists* (March 1992), pp. 30–6.

126. *Jane's Defense Weekly*, 20 June 1987, p. 1289; Lumpe, Gronlund, and Wright, "Third World Missiles Fall Short," pp. 30–6.

127. Some estimates indicate a range of up to 200 kilometers. For background on the system, see *Financial Times*, 8 June 1988, p. 20, and *The Middle East*, April 1988, pp. 1, 18.

128. *Christian Science Monitor*, 27 December 1993, p. 4; *Washington Times*, 25 February 1994, p. A15, 16 June 1994, p. A13. The reader should be aware that all such performance data are nominal, and that various sources report significant differences in given performance characteristics.

129. CRS Report for Congress, *Missile Proliferation: Survey of Emerging Missile Forces* (Washington, DC: Congressional Research Service, Report 88-642F, 9 February 1989) pp. 52–3.

130. Edward L. Korb, *The World's Missile Systems*, 7th edn. General dynamics, Pomona Division (April 1982), pp. 223–6.

131. The following details of the Iranian missile program are taken from Carus and Bermudez, "Iran's Growing Missile Forces," pp. 126–31; Ehteshami, "The Armed Forces of the Islamic Republic of Iran," pp. 76–9; Jacobs and McCarthy, "China Missile Sales," pp. 559–63; *Jane's Intelligence Review*, 4, no. 5 (1994), pp. 218–22; *Jane's Intelligence Review*, 4, no. 4 (1994), p. 149.

132. US State Department press release, "Joint U.S.–P.R.C. Statement on Missile Proliferation," Washington, DC, 4 October 1994; Robert Shuey and Shirley Kan, *Chinese Nuclear*

and Missile Proliferation (Washington, DC: Congressional Research Service, IB92056, 4 October 1994).

133. Robert A. Nagler, *Ballistic Missile Proliferation: An Emerging Threat* (Arlington, VA: Systems Planning Corporation, 1992).

134. *Defense and Foreign Affairs*, no. 1 (1994), pp. 4–7; *Baltimore Sun*, 9 March 1989; *New York Times*, 12 March 1992, p. A12, 18 March 1992, p. A12; *Washington Post*, 2 February 1992, p. A1; Lumbe, Gronlund, and Wright, "Third World Missiles Fall Short," pp. 30–6; "North Korea Corners ME Missile Market," *Mednews* 5, no. 16 (18 May 1992), pp. 1–5; *Newsweek*, 22 June 1992, pp. 42–4; Jacobs and McCarthy, "China Missile Sales," pp. 559–63; *Jerusalem Post*, 6 November 1993, p. 24.

135. Iran allowed a North Korean freighter, the Dae Hung Ho, to dock at Bandar Abbas and transshipped to missiles by air. Syria is reported to have allowed Iran to deliver arms to the Hizbollah and Party of God in Lebanon in return. *Defense News*, 16 October 1989, p. 60, 17 January 1994, p. A1; Lumpe, Gronlund, and Wright, "Third World Missiles Fall Short," pp. 30–6; *Mednews* 5, no. 16 (18 May 1992), pp. 1–5; *Newsweek*, 22 June 1992, pp. 42–4; *Washington Times*, 18 June 1990, p. A1, 24 May 1991, p. 5, 10 March 1992, p. A3, 23 October 1993, p. A6, 24 February 1994, p. A15, 16 June 1994, p. A13; Jacobs and McCarthy, "China Missile Sales," pp. 559–63; *Wall Street Journal*, 19 July 1993, p. A6; *New York Times*, 8 April 1993, p. A9; *Jane's Defense Weekly*, 24 July 1993, p. 7, 15 January 1994, p. 4, 7 May 1994, p. 1; *Aviation Week*, 5 July 1993, p. 17; *Agence France Press*, 4 January 1995; *Christian Science Monitor*, 27 December 1993, p. 4.

136. See "Iran's Ballistic Missile Program," *Middle East Defence News*, *Mednews* 6, no. 6 (21 December 1992); Jacobs and McCarthy, "China Missile Sales," pp. 559–63; James Wyllie, "Iran: Quest for Security and Influence," *Jane's Intelligence Review*, July 1993, pp. 311–12; and material in Clawson, *Iran's Challenge to the West*; and Ehteshmi, "The Armed Forces of the Islamic Republic of Iran," pp. 76–80.

137. *Jane's Defense Weekly*, 19 March 1994, p. 1, 15 January 1994, p. 4; *Washington Times*, 25 February 1994, p. A15.

138. *Jane's Defense Weekly*, 30 January 1993, pp. 20–1; *Defense Electronics and Computing*, IDR Press, September 1992, pp. 115–20; *International Defense Review*, May 1992, pp. 413–15; *Jane's Remotely Piloted Vehicles, 1991–1992*; Keith Munson, *World Unmanned Aircraft* (London: Jane's, 1988); *Air Force Magazine*, March 1992, pp. 94–9, May 1992, p. 155; Alan George, "Iran: Cut-Price Cruise Missiles," March 1993, pp. 15–16.

139. The technical content of this discussion is adapted in part from the author's discussion of the technical aspects of such weapons in *After the Storm: The Changing Military Balance in the Middle East*, and *Iran and Iraq: The Threat from the Northern Gulf*, working material on biological weapons prepared for the United Nations, and from the Office of Technology Assessment, *Proliferation of Weapons of Mass Destruction: Assessing the Risks* (Washington, DC: United States Congress OTA-ISC-559 (GPO), August 1993); Kenneth R. Timmerman, *Weapons of Mass Destruction: The Cases of Iran, Syria, and Libya* (Los Angeles: Simon Wiesenthal Center, August 1992); Robert A. Nagler, *Ballistic Missile Proliferation* (1992); and translations of unclassified documents on proliferation by the Russian Foreign Intelligence Bureau provided to the author by the staff of the Government Operations Committee of the US Senate.

140. For additional details, see Cordesman, *Iran and Iraq: The Threat from the Northern Gulf*, Herdman, *Technologies Underlying Weapons of Mass Destruction*, pp. 15–70.

141. General references for this section include "Chemical and Biological Warfare," Hearing Before the Committee on Foreign Relations (US Senate, 91st Congress, 30 April 1989); Department of Political and Security Council Affairs, *Chemical and Bacteriological (Biological) Weapons and the Effects of Their Possible Use* (Report of the Secretary General,

United Nations, New York, 1989); unpublished testimony of W. Seth Carus before the Committee on Governmental Affairs (US Senate, 9 February 1989); W. Seth Carus, "Chemical Weapons in the Middle East," *Policy Focus*, no. 9 (Washington, DC: Washington Institute for Near East Policy, December 1988); unpublished testimony of David Goldberg, of the Foreign Science and Technology Center, US Army Intelligence Agency, before the Committee on Governmental Affairs (US Senate, 9 February 1989); unpublished testimony of Barry J. Erlick, Senior Biological Warfare Analyst of the US Army, before the Committee on Governmental Affairs (US Senate, 9 February 1989); unpublished testimony of Robert Mullen Cook-Deegan of Physicians for Human Rights, before the Committee on Governmental Affairs (US Senate, 9 February 1989); Elisa D. Harris, "Chemical Weapons Proliferation in the Developing World, *RUSI and Brassey's Defense Yearbook, 1989* (London: RUSI/Brassey's, 1988), pp. 67–88; and "Winds of Death: Iraq's Use of Poison Gas against its Kurdish Population" (Report of a medical mission to Turkish Kurdistan by Physicians for Human Rights, February 1989).

142. IRNA (English version) 19 October 1988, as reported in *FBIS-Near East and South Asia*, 19 October 1988, pp. 55–66.

143. Unpublished statement of the Honorable William H. Webster, director of the Central Intelligence Agency, before the Committee on Governmental Affairs, Hearing on Global Spread of Chemical and Biological Weapons (US Senate, 9 February 1989).

144. Ibid.

145. *Journal of Commerce*, 6 January 1993, p. 5A; *Washington Post*, 6 January 1992, p. A22, 3 September 1993, p. A33; *Washington Times*, 14 August 1993, p. A2; *New York Times*, 9 August 1993, p. A6; *Defense News*, 27 September 1993, p. 23.

146. Based on discussions with various experts the sources listed earlier, and working papers by Leonard Spector; *Observer*, 12 June 1988; *U.S. News and World Report*, 12 February 1990; *FBIS-NES*, 23 March 1990, p. 57; *Defense and Foreign Affairs*, 20 November 1989, p. 2; *New York Times*, 1 July 1989, 9 May 1989, 27 June 1989; *Financial Times*, 6 February 1992, p. 3; *Washington Times*, 8 January 1995, p. A9.

147. For additional details, see Cordesman, *Iran and Iraq: The Threat from the Northern Gulf*; Herdman, *Technologies Underlying Weapons of Mass Destruction*, pp. 71–118.

148. Such reports begin in the SIPRI Yearbooks in 1982, and occur sporadically through the 1988 edition.

149. *New York Times*, 13 August 1989, p. 11.

150. The technical content of this discussion is adapted in part from the author's discussion of the technical aspects of such weapons in *After the Storm: The Changing Military Balance in the Middle East*, and *Iran and Iraq: The Threat from the Northern Gulf*; working material on biological weapons prepared for the United Nations, and from the US Office of Technology Assessment, *Proliferation of Weapons of Mass Destruction*; Timmerman, *Weapons of Mass Destruction*; Nagler, *Ballistic Missile Proliferation*; and translations of unclassified documents on proliferation by the Russian Foreign Intelligence Bureau provided to the author by the staff of the Government Operations Committee of the US Senate.

151. US Office of Technology Assessment, *Proliferation of Weapons of Mass Destruction* (Washington, DC: GPO August 1993), especially p. 53.

152. For additional details, see Cordesman, *Iran and Iraq: The Threat from the Northern Gulf*, and Herdman, *Technologies Underlying Weapons of Mass Destruction*, pp. 119–96.

153. The agreement made under the Shah was to have given Iran about 250–300 metric tons of uranium enriched to 3 percent. During 1980–90, Iran refused to accept the material or to pay for it. When Iran did ask for the material in 1991, France used the fact that Iran's option to obtain enriched material for its investment had expired in order to deny Iran shipment of the material guaranteed under the original terms of the Iranian investment.

Washington Times, 15 November 1991, p. F4; Albright and Hibbs, "Spotlight Shifts to Iran," pp. 9–12.

154. *Washington Post*, 12 April 1987, p. D1; James Bruce, "Iraq and Iran: Running the Nuclear Technology Race," *Jane's Defense Weekly*, 5 December 1988, p. 1307; working papers by Leonard Spector; JPRS-TND, 6 October 1989, p. 19.

155. *El Independente*, Madrid, 5 February 1990, 6 February 1990; *FBIS-Middle East*, 1 December 1988.

156. Ibid.

157. Working papers by Leonard Spector; *Observer*, 12 June 1988; *U.S. News and World Report*, 12 February 1990; *FBIS-NES*, 23 March 1990, p. 57; *FBIS-EAS*, 9 December 1989, 11 December 1989; *Defense and Foreign Affairs*, 20 November 1989, p. 2; *New York Times*, 8 May 1989, 27 June, 1989.

158. *Nucleonics Week*, 2 May 1991; Shuey and Kan, *Chinese Missile and Nuclear Proliferation*, pp. 6–7.

159. Shuey and Kan, *Chinese Nuclear and Missile Proliferation*; *Washington Times*, 16 October 1991, p. 6 November 1991, p. F4, 1 November 1991, p. 7; *Los Angeles Times*, 31 October 1991, p. B4, 17 March 1992, p. 1, 18 January 1993, p. A1; Albright and Hibbs, "Spotlight Shifts to Iran," pp. 9–12; *Washington Post*, 31 October 1991, p. 1, 12 January 1992, p. C7, 2 February 1992, p. A1, 12 September 1992, p. A13, 26 June 1991, 30 October 1991; "Iran's Nuclear Weapons Program," *Mednews*, 5, nos. 17 and 18 (8 June 1992), pp. 1–7; *New York Times*, 11 September 1992, p. A6, 27 May 1993; *Nucleonics Week*, 2 May 1991, 24 September 1992, 1 October 1992.

160. Shuey and Kan, *Chinese Missile and Nuclear Proliferation*, pp. 6–7.

161. *Washington Post*, 17 November 1992, p. A1; *Wall Street Journal*, 11 May 1993, p. 14; *Shuey and Kan,* Chinese Missile and Nuclear Proliferation, pp. 6–7; *Nucleonics Week,* 24 September 1992, 1 October 1992; *New York Times*, 27 May 1993; *The Middle East* (July–August, 1994), pp. 9–10.

162. *Khaleej Times*, 11 January 1995, p. 1; *New York Times*, 5 January 1995, p. A10.

163. *Washington Times*, 15 November 1991, p. F4; *Washington Post*, 7 February 1992, p. A18, 15 February 1992, p. A29, Associated Press (PM Cycle), 6 February 1992; "Iran's Nuclear Weapons Program," *Mednews*, 5, nos. 17 and 18 (8 June 1992), pp. 1–7.

164. Shuey and Kan, *Chinese Missile and Nuclear Proliferation*, pp. 6–7.

165. Clawson, *Iran's Challenge to the West*, pp. 60–1; *Financial Times*, 6 February 1992, p. 4; *Washington Post*, 15 February 1992, pp. A29–A30, 17 November 1992, p. A30; *Los Angeles Times*, 17 March 1992, p. A1, Associated Press (AM Cycle), 12 February 1992; *Agence France Presse*, 12 February 1992; *Christian Science Monitor*, 18 February 1993, p. 7; *Wall Street Journal*, 11 May 1993, p. A14.

166. The major uncertainty in such matters is whether Iran has a significant centrifuge effort in a secret or underground location. A few experts feel there is some risk that Iran might also have a secret reactor to produce plutonium, but this seems unlikely. *Washington Post*, 20 November 1993, p. A13.

167. Congressional Research Service (CRS) Issue Briefs 92076, 92056, and 93033; *Washington Times*, 19 December 1994, p. A18.

168. *Khaleej Times*, 9 January 1995, p. 6; *New York Times*, 5 January 1995, p. A10, 8 January 1995, p. A8, 10 January 1995, p. A3; *Washington Times*, 6 January 1995, p. A15; *Washington Post*, 7 January 1995, p. A17.

169. For more background, see the author's *Weapons of Mass Destruction in the Middle East*, and *Iran and Iraq: The Threat from the Northern Gulf*. For recent reporting, see *U.S. News and World Report*, 14 November 1994, pp. 87–8, and *New York Times*, 27 December 1994, p. A17.

170. *Los Angeles Times*, 17 March 1992, p. A1.

171. *New York Times*, 30 November 1992, pp. A1, A6.

172. *Khaleej Times*, 10 January 1995, p. 31; *Washington Times*, 19 January 1995, p. A18.

173. Although the possibility is a real one. *Financial Times*, 30 January 1992, p. 4; *Agence France Presse*, 26 January 1992; *Sunday Times* (London), 26 January 1992; *Der Spiegel*, 20 July 1992, p. 117; Clawson, *Iran's Challenge to the West*, pp. 63–5; and *U.S. News and World Report*, 14 November 1994, p. 88.

12. An Evaluation of Iran's First Development Plan and Challenges Facing the Second Plan

1. The Iranian solar calendar year, which starts on 21 March has been converted to the Gregorian calendar by adding 621 to the solar year. Thus, the Iranian year 1969, which corresponds to the period 21 March 1990 through 20 March 1991, is equated with 1990, and so on for other solar years. Another factor to consider is the exchange rate between the Iranian rial and the US dollar. In 1994, the rate was some IR 2,650 to the dollar. The rate, however, fluctuates and sometimes very wildly.

2. For a comprehensive examination of the Iranian economy at the beginning of the first plan period, see Hooshang Amirahmadi, *Revolution and Economic Transition: The Iranian Experience* (Albany, New York: State University of New York Press, 1990); Hooshang Amirahmadi, "Economic Destruction and Imbalances in Post-Revolutionary Iran," and "Iranian Economic Reconstruction Plan and Prospects for Its Success," both in *Reconstruction and Regional Diplomacy in the Persian Gulf*, ed. Hooshang Amirahmadi and Nader Entessar (London: Routledge, 1992); and Jahangir Amuzegar, *Iran's Economy under the Islamic Republic* (New York: I.B.Tauris, 1993).

3. "Gozaresh-e Rais-e Sazman-e Barnameh [va Boudgeh] az Etlaf-e Manabe'a Mali" [The Report of the Director of Plan [and Budget] Organization about the wasteful use of Financial Resources], *Hamshahri* daily, 1 Mordad 1373 (1994), p. 4.

4. Ibid.

5. See the statements by Morteza Nabavi, Tehran's representative to the Parliament, in *Keyhan International* daily, 11 Mordad 1373 (1994), p. 7.

6. For example, see Sa'id Lailaz, "Saderat-e Ghair-e Nafti dar Negahi Digar" [Non-Oil Exports in a Different Perspective], *Ettela'at-e Siasi va Eqtesadi*, nos 53–54, Bahman and Esfand 1370 (1991), pp. 80–2.

7. See Alinaqi Mashayekhi, "Barnameh-e Avval-e Touse'ah: Dastavardha va Kastiha" [The First Development Plan: Achievements and Shortcomings], *Hamshahri* daily, 30 Shahrivar 1372 (1993), p. 10.

8. See "Ta'mmoli dar Bare-he Seminar-e Jam'iyat va Touse'ah" [A Retrospective View of the Seminar on Population and Development], *Ettela'at* daily, 6 Mordad 1372 (1993), p. 2.

9. See *Gozaresh-e Eqtesadi-ye Sal-e 1371* [The Economic Report of the Year 1992] [Tehran: Plan and Budget Organization, 1373 (1994)].

10. On the government's population policy in the years preceding the first plan, see Hooshang Amirahmadi and Fereydoun Nikpour, "Roshd-e Jam'iyat va Touse'ah-e Eqtesadi va Ejtema'i" [Population Growth and Economic and Social Development], *Ettela'at-e Siasi va Eqtesadi*, no. 40, Day 1369 (1990), pp. 47–57.

11. Hooshang Amirahmadi, *Revolution and Economic Transition*.

12. See Muhammad Hosain Adeli, Former Director of the Central Bank, "Gozaresh-e Seey-o Chaharomin Ejlas-e Salaneh-e Bank-e Markazi-ye Jomhouri-ye Eslami-ye Iran" [The

Report of the 34th Annual Meeting of the Central Bank of the Islamic Republic of Iran],
Keyhan International daily, 23 Mordad 1373 (1994), p. 2.

13. See Alinaqi Mashayekhi, "Barnameh-e Avval-e Touse'ah".

14. Muhammad Mehdi Rezaii, "Tahavoulat-e Arz az Didgah-e Kalan-e Eqtesadi"
[Changes in Foreign Exchange from a Macroeconomic Perspective], *Rouznameh-e Ettela'at,
Vizeh-e Kharej az Keshvar*, 6 Mordad 1373 (1994), p. 7.

15. This figure for inflation is based on the author's research in Iran. Various sources
give different figures for inflation. For example, in its June 1994 issue (p. 3), *Iran Business
Monitor* (quoting an official of the Central Bank), puts the average annual inflation rate for
the first plan period (1989–93) at 40 percent to 60 percent; and The *Economist Intelligence
Unit*, 1994–95 (p. 21), reports the average annual inflation rate for 1993–94 period at 30
percent to 70 percent, depending on specific economic sectors.

16. *Gozaresh-e Eqtesadi-ye Sal-e 1370* [The Economic Report of the Year 1991] [Tehran:
Plan and Budget Organization, 1372 (1993)], p. 81.

17. Various sources have reported different figures for the Iranians living below the
poverty line. In two sources, in addition to the author's, where the subject has received
some careful treatment, the figure 60 percent has been confirmed. These sources are:
Hooshang Amirahmadi, *Revolution and Economic Transition*; Hosain Azimi, "Boudgeh va
Touse'ah-e Eqtesadi dar Iran [Budget and Economic Development in Iran], *Ettela'at-e Siasi
va Eqtesadi*, no. 5, Bahman 1366 (1987), p. 32; and an interview with Gholamhosain Naadi,
a deputy of the Parliament, in *Resalat* daily, 14 Esfand 1366 (1987). For more recent statistics
on the subject, see *Iran Times*, 24, no. 48 (10 February 1995), pp. 5, 12.

18. The First Plan Bill did not outline a time schedule for the government to receive
foreign loans.

19. *Gozaresh-e Eqtesadi-ye Sal-e 1371*.

20. See *Iran Business Monitor*, January 1994, p. 5.

21. Ahmad Mir Motahari, "Barnameh-e Avval: Pendarha, Entezarat, Vaqeiytha" [The
First Plan: Beliefs, Expectations, Realities], *Ettela'at-e Siasi va Eqtesadi*, nos 83–84, p. 89.

22. See the article "German Oil imports from Iran Drop," *Rouznameh Ettla'at, Vizeh-e
Kharej az Keshvar*, 26 Aban 1373 (1994).

23. See *Payvast-e Layhe-ye Barnameh-e Dovvum-e Touse'ah Eqtesadi, Ejtema'i va Farhangi-ye
Jomhouri-ye Eslami-ye Iran 1373–1377* [Appendage to the Bill of the Second Economic, Social,
and Cultural Development Plan of the Islamic Republic of Iran] [Tehran: Plan and Budget
Organization, 1372 (1993)].

24. Ibid., p. 4.

25. See the article "Afsaneh-e Kamboud-e Sarmayeh dar Iran" [The Legend of Capital
Shortage in Iran] *Hamshahri* daily, 1–2 Mordad 1373 (1994), p. 1.

26. See the article "Khososiat-e Ejtema'i-Eqtesadi-ye Khanavar" [Social-Economic
Characteristics of Households], *Rouznameh Ettla'at, Vizeh-e Kharej az Keshvar*, 11 Aban 1373
(1994), p. 3.

27. Interview with Mr. M. Shahriari, member of the Parliament's Integration Committee,
in *Keyhan International* daily, 11 Mordad 1373 (1994), p. 11.

28. See Hooshang Amirahmadi, *Revolution and Economic Transition*, pp. 283–8.

29. See Hooshang Amirahmadi and Chris Wallace, "Information Technology, the Organization of Production, and Regional Development," *Environment and Planning A*, vol. 26
(1994).

30. See Hooshang Amirahmadi and Grant Saff, "Science Parks: A Critical Assessment,"
Journal of Planning Literature, 8, no. 2 (1993), pp. 107–23.

31. See Hooshang Amirahmadi and Weiping Wu, "Foreign Direct Investment in
Developing Countries," *Journal of Developing Areas*, 28 (January 1994), pp. 167–90.

13. The Gulf Security Dilemma

1. Stephen C. Pelletiere, *The Iran–Iraq War: Chaos in a Vacuum* (New York: Praeger, 1992) provides a detailed account of Iranian political activism and adventurism within several Arab Gulf states, including specifically Bahrain, the Kingdom of Saudi Arabia, and Kuwait in the years immediately after the 1979 Iranian revolution, and continuing throughout the 1980s. It should be noted that the 1996 civil unrest in Bahrain was linked to Shi'ite activists supported by Iran.

2. As James Piscatori explains, "Rarely has there been a day in the past decade when Iran has escaped the attention of the world's foreign offices, press, and academic experts on the Middle East and Islam. Turbulent shifts of power within the revolutionary regime; the headstrong anathematizing of the great powers; the presence of Revolutionary Guards in Lebanon, and, in general, the export of the revolution; seemingly interminable war with Iraq; secret arms deals with Israel and the US; shadowy relations with Middle Eastern groups that hold Westerners hostage, and unambiguous threats of death against a British novelist – these have been the issues which have kept Iran at the centre of international attention and concern." Anoushiravan Ehteshami and Manshour Varasteh (eds), *Iran and the International Community* (London: Routledge, 1991), p. ix.

3. See, for instance, Mahmood Sariolghalam, "Conceptual Sources of Post-Revolutionary Iranian Behavior toward the Arab World," in *Iran and the Arab World*, ed. Hooshang Amirahmadi and Nader Entessar (London: Macmillan, 1993), pp. 19–41; and Shireen T. Hunter, *Iran after Khomeini* (New York: Praeger, 1992), pp. 101ff.

4. For further details on the role of nationalism in Iranian culture, see Mehrdad Mashayekhi, "The Politics of Nationalism and Political Culture," in *Iran: Political Culture in the Islamic Republic*, ed. Samih K. Farsoun and Mehrdad Mashayekhi (London: Routledge, 1992), pp. 82–115.

5. See Mohammad Borghei, "Iran's Religious Establishment: The Dialectics of Politicization," in Farsoun and Mashayekhi, *Iran: Political Culture*, pp. 57–81.

6. Edward G. Shirley, "The Iran Policy Trap," *Foreign Policy*, 96 (fall 1994), pp. 80–7; Edward G. Shirley, "Is Iran's Present Algeria's Future?" *Foreign Affairs*, 74 (May–June 1995), p. 39.

7. Kambiz Foroohar and Tahsin Akti, "Khamenei Didn't Make It," *The Middle East* (February 1995), pp. 12–13; Colin Barraclough, "The Marja' and the Man on the Street," *Middle East Insight*, 11 (March–April 1995), p. 20; Geraldine Brooks, "Teen-Age Infidels Hanging Out," *The New York Times Magazine*, 30 April 1995; Lara Marlowe, "Revolutionary Disintegration," *Time*, 26 June 1995, pp. 50–1.

8. Shirley, "The Iran Policy Trap," p. 82.

9. The Iranian perspective was ably articulated by Bahman Fouzoni at the first annual conference of the ECSSR held in Abu Dhabi, UAE, 8–12 January 1995. Fouzoni noted: "The end of the Cold War has laid bare the imperialist intentions of the great powers: their primary foreign policy motivation for militarily supporting the status quo regimes and promoting stability is, as always, economic imperialism."

10. The occasional hostilities between the US Navy and Iranian forces that occurred during the re-flagging of Kuwaiti oil tankers as US vessels during the latter stage of the Iran–Iraq war, and most importantly the shooting down of an Iranian civil aircraft by the Gulf-based US Navy Warship *Vincennes* in mid-1986.

11. Lecture by Ambassador Richard Murphy, "U.S. policy towards the Gulf Region," delivered at the Emirates Center for Strategic Studies and Research (ECSSR), Abu Dhabi, UAE, on 4 November 1995. Ambassador Murphy acknowledged the ideological component

of the hostile relationship between Washington and Tehran. Murphy argued, however, that Washington's chief complaints with Tehran were objective not ideological, and specifically addressed three "problem areas": 1) Iran is seeking a capability to produce nuclear weapons; 2) As part of its policy in support of international terrorism, Iran works to undermine moderate Arab governments; and 3) Iran is working to destroy the Arab–Israeli peace process. It is doubtful that every analyst would agree that these "problem areas" are objective complaints.

12. For a brief history of US–Iran relations, see Thomas Ricks, "Power Politics and Political Culture: U.S.–Iran Relations," in Farsoun and Mashayekhi, *Iran: Political Culture*, pp. 234–61.

13. Anthony Lake, "Confronting Backlash States," *Foreign Affairs*, 73, no. 2 (March–April 1994) p. 54.

14. This characterization of the Iranian government (and others) as incorrigible plays well to the domestic audience within the United States. President Clinton chose to announce the institution of a new and more stringent trade embargo against Iran during remarks at a dinner for the World Jewish Congress at the Waldorf-Astoria Hotel in New York City, 30 April 1995.

15. The United States has received international cooperation on the issue of arms technology transfers to Iran, specifically cooperation from Russia. The United States has received substantially less cooperation in the enforcement of a non-weapons related embargo. Germany, Japan, and France all pursue the policy of constructive engagement with Iran. The issue of how to deal with the Islamic Republic of Iran is extensively discussed in a number of policy-oriented institutions. For example, it was addressed recently at the Washington Institute for Near East Policy. Significantly, perhaps, the discussion was sponsored by the American Jewish Committee and entitled "Business as Usual? Western Policy Options towards Iran." With the exception of the United States and Israel, there are virtually no other members of the international community that accept the argument that isolation and containment will moderate Iranian international behavior. A principle spokesman at the discussion was Patrick Clawson, an analyst well known for his hardline stance concerning Iran. Clawson stated that the best option was to treat Iran as George Kennan proposed the West treat the then Soviet Union, i.e., protect against any external aggression while awaiting the inevitable downfall of a bankrupt system that cannot meet its peoples' needs.

16. Samuel P. Huntington, "The Clash of Civilizations?" *Foreign Affairs*, 72, no. 3 (July–August 1993), has been widely discussed. The May-June 1995 issue of *Foreign Affairs* featured an entire section on "The Islamic Cauldron." Anthony Parsons, "Prospects for Peace and Stability in the Middle East," *Conflict Studies*, 262 (London: Research Institute for the Study of Conflict and Terrorism, 1993). Bernard Lewis, "Muslim Rage," *Atlantic Monthly* (June 1992) was very alarmist in nature.

17. See, for instance, Robert G. Darius, John W. Amos, and Ralf H. Magnus (eds), *Gulf Security into the 1980s* (Stanford: Hoover Institution Press, 1984); Shireen T. Hunter, *Iran and the World: Continuity in a Revolutionary Decade* (Bloomington, IN: Indiana University Press, 1990), pp. 46 ff.; and Pelletiere, *The Iran–Iraq War*, p. 111. Since the Iranian revolution, all dialogue between the United States and Iran, whether at official or unofficial levels, has been inconclusive.

18. See, for example, Zbigniew Brzezinski, "Selective Global Commitment," *Foreign Affairs*, 70 (fall 1991).

19. See *A National Security Strategy of Engagement and Enlargement* (Washington, DC: The White House, January 1994). The national security policy of selective engagement is one of the theoretical underpinnings of the Clinton administration's national security strategy.

Engagement is a common thread in most, if not all, national security policy literature of the US government. This term is used to caution against isolationism. Selective engagement suggests that the post-Cold War US national security policy should tend to those locations and crises in the world where vital interests are at stake with focused attention, and ignore those locations and crises in the world where US interests are not vital, or less so. The debate ensues concerning the criteria for inclusion, although the principle is accepted by prominent defense and security policy analysts of both major political parties.

20. US Central Command (CENTCOM) had not fully prepared an operations plan for the assumption of hostilities with Iraq, although CENTCOM had begun the practice known as "crisis planning." The "deliberate planning" model adapted and modified for Operation Desert Shield/Desert Storm was CENTCOM Operations Plan 1008, a document which outlined necessary military actions for a sustained engagement between US and Soviet forces on Iranian soil.

21. "Iran Oil Exports Could Stop by 2000, Says Officials," Reuters, 3 July 1995, 19:19 GMT; William Dawkins, "Japan under Pressure on Iranian Dam," *Financial Times* (London), 19 October 1994.

22. Business Monitor International, *Iran 1995–1997*, June 1995, p. 24; Sohrab Shahabi and Farideh Farhi, "Security Considerations and Iranian Foreign Policy," *Iranian Journal of International Affairs*, 7 (spring 1995), p. 95; Stephen J. Hedges and Peter Cary, "The Other Problem in the Persian Gulf," *U.S. News and World Report*, 14 November 1995, p. 87.

23. Bill Gertz, "U.S. Defuses Efforts by Iran to Get Nukes," *Washington Times*, 24 November 1994; Elaine Sciolino, "CIA Report Says Chinese Sent Iran Arms Components," *New York Times*, 22 June 1995; Hedges and Cary, "The Other Problem," p. 88.

24. See Shahram Chubin's incisively argued article, "Does Iran Want Nuclear Weapons?", *Survival*, 37 (spring 1995), pp. 86–104.

25. International Institute for Strategic Studies (IISS), *The Military Balance 1993–1994* (London: Brassey's, 1993), pp. 111–32; *Military Technology: World Defense Almanac 1994–1995*, pp. 207–12, 222, 227–30, 234. Many in the series of military exercises are held in and around the Gulf states, including the Strait of Hormuz, underlining the importance of maritime warfare. See Yossef Bodansky, "Iran's Persian Gulf Strategy Emerges through its Recent Military Exercises," *Defense and Foreign Affairs Strategic Policy*, 31 January 1994, pp. 4–5.

26. India is slated to assist Iran in maintaining its Russian-made submarines, in upgrading its T-72 main battle tanks, and in furnishing spare parts for MiG aircraft. "Iran Cultivates Ties with India in Military Business Ventures," *Washington Times*, 21 June 1995.

27. Pelletiere, *The Iran–Iraq War*.

28. See two important works by Anthony H. Cordesman: *After the Storm: The Changing Military Balance in the Middle East* (Boulder, CO: Westview Press, 1993) and *Iran and Iraq: The Threat from the Northern Gulf* (Boulder, CO: Westview Press, 1994). Also see M. H. Ahrari in *The Persian Gulf After the Cold War*, ed. M. H. Ahrari and James H. Noye (Westport, CT: Praeger Publishers, 1993), p. 93. For a detailed account of Iran's chemical weapons capability, to include associated delivery systems present and future, and organizational alignment of these systems to Pasdaran within the Iranian defense structure, see Shahram Chubin, *Iran's National Security Policy* (Washington, DC: Carnegie Endowment for International Peace, 1994).

29. There is a very wide range of opinion on the topic of Iranian pragmatism, i.e., whether the modern-day Iranian government is capable of responding to a rational concept of deterrence. The dual containment policy of the United States seems to regard Iran as incapable of assessments of this sort. One analyst recently suggested that Iranian military resurgence could well result in the practice of military adventurism in the Gulf to "keep

the (Iranian) populace politically mobilized and unfocused on socioeconomic decay, while validating the revolutionary government." See Philip L. Ritcheson, "Iranian Military Resurgence: Scope, Motivations, and Implications for Regional Security," *Armed Forces and Society*, 21, no. 4 (summer 1995), pp. 573–92. The arguments of Gary Sick may be more persuasive. Sick believes that the current Iranian leadership is quite capable of understanding the folly of provoking a high-scale conflict with the United States and GCC partners. See Gary Sick, "Iran: The Adolescent Revolution," *Journal of International Affairs*, 49, no. 1 (summer 1995), pp. 145–66, particularly p. 165.

30. A member of the international community does not normally attract foreign investment from another member through hegemonic behavior, particularly when the hegemony specifically includes military threat. However, foreign investment, or at least foreign transfers of capital, have often been exacted as an informal tax or tribute from hegemonic powers. For an interesting account which establishes that many influential Iranians accept the concept of Iranian hegemony in the Gulf as a historical imperative, see Pirouz Mojtahedzadeh, *The Changing World Order and Geopolitical Regions of Caspian-Central Asia and the Persian Gulf* (London: Urosevic Foundation Monographs, 1992).

31. Iran is the ultimate Gulf residual oil producer and deals extensively on the spot market.

32. Data provided by Economist Intelligence Unit, *Country Report*, Fourth Quarter, 1995.

33. Ibid.

34. Correlating Islamic fundamentalism with economics speak of a "materialist bias" in Western analysis. See "It's Not the Economy, Stupid," *Washington Post*, 2 July 1995.

35. *Business Monitor International*, pp. 52–3, 63; *APS Diplomat: News Service*, 24–31 October 1994, p. 2.

36. *Business Monitor International*, p. 70; Chris Kutschera, "Iran's Peeling Veneer," *The Middle East* (September 1994), p. 21.

37. For example, the 500,000 barrels of oil previously destined for US clients have been quickly absorbed by other customers, while the French oil firm Total SA clinched the contract originally awarded to the US company Conoco for the extraction of Iranian oil and residual gas. See Youssef M. Ibrahim, "Iran Shrugs Off Sanctions," *International Herald Tribune*, 22 June 1995, p. 15; "Total Takes the Bait," *Middle East Monitor*, 5 (August 1995) p. 9; John Lancaster, "Despite Trade Ban, U.S. Goods Still Find Their Way to Iran," *Washington Post*, 26 June 1995.

38. Much has been written about the role of the Clinton administration in canceling the $1 billion agreement reached by the Conoco Company and the Iranian Government with respect to the development of oil reserves within Iran. Little has been written which discusses the inconsistency of the government of Iran by, on the one hand entering into agreements with a US firm, and on the other, by engaging in continuous and official foreign policy rhetoric which condemns the Western, particularly the US, role in the production and delivery of oil in other Gulf states.

39. The Nunn-Lugar Amendment to the US Defense Authorization Act of 1993 specifically "conditions" the provision of US economic assistance to Russia and other former Soviet Union states to the dismantlement of nuclear systems, a process that is proceeding apace.

40. John Calabrese, *Revolutionary Horizons: Regional Foreign Policy in Post-Khomeini Iran* (New York: St. Martin's Press, 1994), p. 73.

Bibliography

Abadi, Salehi Najaf. *Velayat-e Faqih. Hukumat-e Salehan.* Tehran: Mu'asseseh Khadamat-e Farhangi-e Rasa, 1984.

Abrahamian, Ervand. *The Iranian Mojahedin.* New Haven, CT: Yale University Press, 1989.

Adams, James. *Engines of War: Merchants of Death and the New Arms Race.* New York: Atlantic Monthly Press, 1990.

Adeli, Mohammad Hosain. "Gozaresh-e Seey-o Chaharomin Ejlas-e Salaneh-e Bank-e Markazi-ye Jomhouri-ye Eslami-ye Iran" [The Report of the 34th Annual Meeting of the Central Bank of the Islamic Republic of Iran]. *Keyhan* daily, 23 Mordad 1373 [1994]. (In Persian).

Afrasiabi, K. L. *After Khomeini: New Directions in Iran's Foreign Policy.* Boulder, CO: Westview Press, 1994.

Ahrari, M. E. "Iran, the GCC, and the Security Dimension in the Persian Gulf." In *Reconstruction and Regional Diplomacy in the Persian Gulf,* ed. Hooshang Amirahmadi and Nader Entessar. London: Routledge, 1992.

— and James H. Noye (eds.) *The Persian Gulf after the Cold War.* Westport, CT: Praeger, 1993.

Al-Ahsan, Abdullah. *OIC: The Organization of the Islamic Conference.* Herndon, VA: International Institute of Islamic Thought, 1988.

Aiken, James. Interview on *Frontline.* (Transcript). 16 February 1993.

Akhavi, Sharough. *Religion and Politics in Contemporary Iran.* Albany, NY: State University of New York Press, 1980.

Alam, Assodollah. *The Shah and I: The Confidential Diary of Iran's Royal Court, 1969–1977.* London: I.B.Tauris, 1991. Translated by Abdolreza Hoshang Mahdavi into Persian, *Gofteguhaye-Man Ba Shah* [My conversations with the Shah], vol. 1. Tehran: Tarhe Nou, 1993.

Albaharna, Husain M. *The Arabian Gulf States: Their Legal and Political Status and Their International Problems* (2nd ed.) Beirut: Khayats, 1975.

Albright, David and Mark Hibbs. "Spotlight Shifts to Iran." *Bulletin of the Atomic Scientists,* March 1992.

Alexander, Ian. "Troubled Oil." *National Review,* 9 August 1993.

Algar, Hamid (trans.) *Islam and Revolution: Writings and Declarations of Imam Khomeini.* Berkeley, CA: Mizan Press, 1981.

— (trans.) *The Constitution of the Islamic Republic of Iran.* Berkeley, CA: Mizan Press, 1980.

Amirahmadi, Hooshang. *Revolution and Economic Transition: The Iranian Experience.* Albany, NY: State University of New York Press, 1990.

— "Iranian–Saudi Arabian Relations since the Revolution." In *Iran and the Arab World,* ed. Hooshang Amirahmadi and Nader Entessar. New York: St. Martin's Press, 1993.

— "Economic Destruction and Imbalances in Post-Revolutionary Iran." In *Reconstruction and Regional Diplomacy in the Persian Gulf*, ed. Hooshang Amirahmadi and Nader Entessar. London: Routledge, 1992.

— "Iranian Economic Reconstruction Plan and Prospects for Its Success." In *Reconstruction and Regional Diplomacy in the Persian Gulf*, ed. Hooshang Amirahmadi and Nader Entessar. London: Routledge, 1992.

Amirahmadi, Hooshang and Fereydoun Nikpour. "Roshd-e Jam'iyat va Touse'ah-e Eqtesadi va Ejtema'i" [Population growth and economic and social development]. *Ettela'at-e Siasi va Eqtesadi* 5, no. 40, Day 1369 [1990]. (In Persian).

Amirahmadi, Hooshang and Grant Staff. "'Science Parks': A Critical Assessment." *Journal of Planning Literature* 8, no. 2 (1993).

Amirahmadi, Hooshang and Chris Wallace. "Information Technology, the Organization of Production, and Regional Development." *Environment and Planning* A 26 (1994).

Amirahmadi, Hooshang and Weiping Wu. "Foreign Direct Investment in Developing Countries." *Journal of Developing Areas* 28 (January 1994).

Amuzegar, Jahangir. *Iran's Economy under the Islamic Republic*. New York: I.B.Tauris, 1993.

— "The Iranian Economy before and after the Revolution." *Middle East Journal* 46, no. 3 (summer 1992).

Anthony, John Duke. *Arab States of the Lower Gulf*. Washington, DC: The Middle East Institute, 1975.

Arjomand, Said Amir. "History and Revolution in the Shi'ite Tradition in Contemporary Iran." *International Political Science Review* 10, no. 2 (1989).

— "A Victory for the Pragmatists: The Islamic Fundamentalist Reaction in Iran." In *Islamic Fundamentalism and the Gulf Crisis*, ed. James P. Piscatori. Chicago: Fundamentalism Project, 1991.

Ashraf, Fouad. "Iran Mines, Not Submarines Pose Threat in the Gulf." Reuters, 13 October 1993.

— "Iran Mines, Not Submarines Pose Threat in the Gulf." *Armed Forces Journal International*, November 1993.

Azimi, Hosain. "Boudgeh va Touse'ah-e Eqtesadi dar Iran [Budget and Economic Development in Iran], *Ettela'at-e Siasi va Eqtesadi* no. 5, Bahman 1366 [1987]. (In Persian).

Badeeb, Saeed. *Saudi–Iranian Relations, 1932–1982*. London: Centre for Arab and Iranian Studies, 1993.

Bakhash, Shaul B. "Iran: The Crisis of Legitimacy." In *Middle East Lectures: I*, ed. Martin Kramer. Syracuse, NY: Syracuse University Press, 1995.

— "Prisoners of the Ayatollah." *New York Review of Books*, 11 August 1994.

— *The Reign of the Ayatollahs: Iran and the Islamic Revolution*. New York: Basic Books, 1984.

Baktiari, Bahman. "Revolutionary Iran's Persian Gulf Policy: The Quest for Hegemony." In *Iran and the Arab World*, ed. Hooshang Amirahmadi and Nader Entessar. New York: St. Martin's Press, 1992.

Barber, David. *The Presidential Character*, 3rd ed. Englewood Cliffs, NJ: Prentice-Hall, 1985.

Barnet, Richard. "Reflections: The Disorder of Peace." *New Yorker*, 20 January 1992.

Barraclough, Colin. "The Marja' and the Man on the Street." *Middle East Insight* 11 (March–April 1995).

Bashir, Abdulaziz and Stephen Wright. "Saudi Arabia: Foreign Policy after the Gulf War." *Middle East Policy* no. 1 (1992).

Bazargan, Abdul Ali. *Muqadameh iy dar Zamineh Azadi dar Qur'an.* Tehran: Entesharat-e Qalam, 1984. (In Persian).

— *Shuwra va Bey'at: Hakemiyyat-e Khuda va Hukumat-e Mardum.* Tehran: Entesharat-e Enteshar, 1982. (In Persian).

— *Azadi dar Nahjulbalaqa.* Unpublished book. (In Persian).

Bazargan, Mehdi. *Enqelab-e Iran dar Du Harekat.* Tehran: Liberation Movement of Iran (LMI), 1984. (In Persian).

Bazargan, Mehdi. "Azadi dar Iran Darakht-e bi Risheh Boud." *Adineh.* 1993-Mehr va Aban 1372.

— "Din va Azadi." *Bazyabiy-e Arzeshha.* Tehran: LMI, 1983. (In Persian).

— *Masa'il va Mushgelat-e Avvalin Sal-e Enqelab as Zaban-e Muhanddis Mehdi-e Bazargan.* 2nd ed. Tehran: Nehzat-e Azadi-e Iran, 1981. (In Persian).

— *Masa'il va Mushgelat-e Avvalin Sal-e Enqelab.* Tehran: LMI, 1981. (In Persian).

— *Mudafi'at dar Dadgah Gheir Salih-i Tajdid-e Nazar-e Nizami.* Bellville, IL: LMI, 1977. (In Persian).

Belyakov, Rostislav and Nikolai Buntin. "The MiG 29 M Light Multirole Fighter." *Military Technology,* August 1994.

Bermudez, Joseph S. *Proliferation for Profit: North Korea in the Middle East.* Washington, DC: The Washington Institute for Near East Policy, July 1994.

Bernard & Grafe. *Tanks of the World.* London: Bernard & Grafe. Various editions.

— *Warplanes of the World.* London: Bernard & Grafe. Various editions.

— *Weyer's Warships.* London: Bernard & Grafe. Various editions.

Bill, James A. *The New Iran: Relations with its Neighbors and the United States.* Washington, DC: Asia Society Contemporary Affairs Dept., 1991.

— "Resurgent Islam in the Persian Gulf." *Foreign Affairs* 63, no. 1 (January–February 1984).

Bodansky, Yosseff. "Iran's Persian Gulf Strategy Emerges through its Recent Military Exercises." *Defense and Foreign Affairs Strategic Policy,* 31 January 1994.

Borghei, Mohammad. "Iran's Religious Establishment: The Dialectics of Politicization." In *Iran: Political Culture in the Islamic Republic,* ed. Samih K. Farsoun and Mehrdad Mashayekhi. London: Routledge, 1992.

Al-Braik, Nasser. "Al-Ibadhiyyah in Islamic Political Thought and its Role in State Building." *Al-Ijtihad.* Beirut. (Fall 1991). (In Arabic).

Brzezinski, Zbigniew. *Out of Control: Global Turmoil on the Eve of the 21st Century.* New York: Maxwell Macmillan International, 1993.

— "Selective Global Commitment." *Foreign Affairs* 70 (1991).

Brinton, Crane. *The Anatomy of Revolution.* London: Peter Smith Publishers, 1953.

Brooks, Geraldine. "Teen-Age Infidels Hanging Out." *New York Times Magazine,* 30 April 1995.

Bruce, James. "Iran Claims to Have Built Its Own MBT." *Jane's Defence Weekly,* 23 April 1994.

— Bruce, James. "Iraq and Iran: Running the Nuclear Technology Race." *Jane's Defence Weekly,* 5 December 1988.

Business Monitor International. *Iran 1995–1997,* June 1995.

Calabrese, John. *Revolutionary Horizons: Regional Foreign Policy in Post-Khomeini Iran.* New York: St. Martin's Press, 1994.

Carus, W. Seth. "Chemical Weapons in the Middle East." *Policy Focus* no. 9. Washington, DC: Washington Institute for Near East Policy, December 1988.

Carus, W. Seth and Joseph S. Bermudez. "Iran's Growing Missile Forces." *Jane's Defense Weekly*, 23 July 1988.

Central Intelligence Agency (CIA). *World Factbook*. Washington, DC: Government Printing Office (GPO), 1994.

Chubin, Shahram. "Does Iran Want Nuclear Weapons?" *Survival* 37 (spring 1995).

— *Iran's National Security Policy: Capabilities, Intentions, and Impact*. Washington, DC: The Carnegie Endowment for International Peace, 1994.

— "Iran and Regional Security in the Persian Gulf." *Survival* (fall 1993).

Chubin, Shahram and Charles Tripp. *Iran and Iraq at War*. Boulder, CO: Westview Press, 1988.

— "Domestic Politics and Territorial Disputes in the Persian Gulf and the Arabian Peninsula." *Survival* (winter 1993).

Clawson, Patrick. *Iran's Challenge to the West: How, When, and Why*. Washington, DC: Washington Institute Policy Papers, no. 33, 1993.

Congressional Quarterly. *The Middle East*, 7th ed. Washington, DC: Congressional Quarterly, 1991.

Congressional Research Service (CRS). Foreign Affairs Division. "Middle East Arms Control and Related Issues." Washington, DC: Congressional Research Service. CRS Report 91-384F, 1 May 1991.

— Report for Congress. *Missile Proliferation: Survey of Emerging Missile Forces*. Washington, DC: Congressional Research Service. CRS Report 88-642F, 9 February 1989.

Cordesman, Anthony H. *Iran and Iraq: The Threat from the Northern Gulf*. Boulder, CO: Westview Press, 1994.

— *After the Storm: The Changing Military Balance in the Middle East*. Boulder, CO: Westview Press, 1993.

— *The Gulf and the Search for Strategic Stability*. Boulder, CO: Westview Press, 1984.

— *The Gulf and the West*. Boulder, CO: Westview Press, 1988.

— *Weapons of Mass Destruction in the Middle East*. London: Brassey's RUSI, 1991.

Cordesman, Anthony H. and Abraham R. Wagner. *The Lessons of Modern War: Volume Two: The Iran–Iraq Conflict*. Boulder, CO: Westview Press, 1990.

DMS/FI. Market Intelligence Reports. Computerized military database.

Darius, Robert G., John W. Amos, and Ralf H. Magnus (eds.). *Gulf Security into the 1980s*. Stanford, CA: Hoover Institution Press, 1984.

Dawkins, William. "Japan under Pressure on Iranian Dam." *Financial Times* (London), 19 October 1994.

Dubai Chamber of Commerce and Industry. Research Studies Department. "Dubai (Non-Oil) Foreign Trade with Iran during the Years 1989–1993 and the First Half of 1994." Dubai: Dubai Chamber of Commerce and Industry, 1994.

Economist. "A Survey of Islam." 6 August 1994.

— "Comfort Blanket for the Gulf." 5 December 1992.

Economist Intelligence Unit (EIU). *Country Report*. Fourth Quarter, 1995.

— *Country Report on Iran, 1993*. London: Economist Publications, 1994.

Ehteshami, Anoushiravan. "The Armed Forces of the Islamic Republic of Iran. *Jane's Intelligence Review*, February 1993.

— "Wheels within Wheels: Iran's Foreign Policy towards the Arab World." In *Reconstruction and Regional Diplomacy in the Persian Gulf*, ed. Hooshang Amirahmadi and Nader Entessar. London: Routledge, 1992.

— "Iran's National Strategy." *International Defense Review*. April 1994.

— "Iran Boosts Domestic Arms Industry." *International Defense Review*. April 1994.

Ehteshami, Anoushiravan and Manshour Varasteh (eds.). *Iran and the International Community*. London: Routledge, 1991.

Eisenstadt, Michael. "Déjà Vu All Over Again: An Assessment of Iran's Military Buildup." In *Iran's Strategic Intentions and Capabilities*, ed. Patrick Clawson. Washington, DC: Institute of National Strategic Studies, National Defense University. McNair Paper no. 29. April 1994.

Enayat, Hamid. "Iran: Khumayni's Concept of the Guardianship of the Jurisconsult." In *Islam in the Political Process*, ed. James P. Piscatori. Cambridge: Cambridge University Press, 1983.

Ettela'at daily. "Ta'mmoli dar Bare-h Seminar-e Jam'iyat va Touse'ah" [A Retrospective View of the Seminar on Population and Development]. 6 Mordad 1372 [1993]. (In Persian).

Evans, David. "Vincennes: A Case Study." *Proceedings of the U.S. Naval Institute* (USNI). Annapolis, MD: Naval Institute Press, August 1993.

Fada'yan-e Islam. *Hukumat-e Islami, Barnameh-e Enqelabi-e Fada'yan-e Islam*. Tehran: Fada'yan-e Islam, 1980. (In Persian).

Feiz, Reza. *Hakemiyyat-e Kukha va Hukumat-e Mardum*. Paper presented at the Center for the Study of Management. Tehran, 1979. (In Persian).

Finnegan, Philip, Robert Holzer, and Neil Munro. "Iran Pursues Chinese Mine to Bolster Gulf Clout." *Defense News*, 17–23 January 1994.

Fischer, Michael M. J. *Iran: From Religious Dispute to Revolution*. Cambridge, MA: Harvard University Press, 1980.

Foroohar, Kambiz and Tahsin Akti. "Khamenei Didn't Make It." *The Middle East* (February 1995).

Fuller, Graham E. *The Center of the Universe: The Geopolitics of Iran*. Boulder, CO: Westview Press, 1991.

Ganji, Akbar. "Mashruiyyat, Velayat va Vekalat." *Kiyan* 13 (Tehran, 1993).

— "Central Asia: The Quest for Identity." *Current History* 93, no. 582 (April 1994).

Gates, Robert. Statement on McNeil-Leher News Hour. 6 January 1993.

Gause, F. Gregory. "The Illogic of Dual Containment. *Foreign Affairs* 73, no. 2 (March–April 1994).

George, Alan. "Tehran Asserts its Independence." *The Middle East*. April 1993.

— "Iran: Cut-Price Cruise Missiles." March 1993.

George, Alexander. "Presidential Management Styles and Models." In *The Domestic Sources of American Foreign Policy: Insights and Evidence*, ed. Charles W. Kegley and Eugene R. Wittkopf. New York: St. Martin's Press, 1988.

Gertz, Bill. "U.S. Defuses Efforts by Iran to Get Nukes." *Washington Times*, 24 November 1994.

Al-Ghazali, Abu Hamed. *Al-Mankhul*. Beirut: Dar al-Fikr, 1980.

Goldberg, Jacob. "Saudi Arabia and the Iranian Revolution: The Religious Dimension." In *The Iranian Revolution and the Muslim World*, ed. David Menashiri. Boulder, CO: Westview Press, 1990.

Gordon, Michael. "Kuwait is Allowing U.S. to Station a Squadron of Warplanes." *New York Times*, 28 October 1994.

Green, Jerrold D. "Iran's Foreign Policy: Between Enmity and Conciliation." *Current History* (January 1993).

Greenberger, Robert. "Clinton Gains on Iran Arms with Yeltsin." *Wall Street Journal*, 28 September 1994.

Grimmett, Richard F. *Conventional Arms Transfers to the Third World: 1985–1992*. Washington, DC: Congressional Research Service, CRS Report 93-656F, 19 July 1993.

— *Conventional Arms Acquisitions*. Washington, DC: Congressional Research Service, CRS Report 94-138F, 22 February 1994.

Hader, Leon. "What Green Peril?" *Foreign Affairs* 72, no. 2 (March–April 1993).

Halliday, Fred. "Iranian Foreign Policy since 1979: Internationalism and Nationalism in the Islamic Revolution." In *Shi'ism and Social Protest*, ed. Juan Cole and Nikki R. Keddie. New Haven, CT: Yale University Press, 1986.

Hamshahri daily. "Gozaresh-e Rais-e Sazman-e Barnameh [va Boudgeh] az Etlaf-e Manabe'a Mali" [The Report of the Director of Plan [and Budget] Organization about the Wasteful Use of Financial Resources]. 1 Mordad, 1373 [1994]. (In Persian).

— "Khososiat-e Kamboud-e Sarmayeh dar Iran" [The Legend of Capital Shortage in Iran]. 1–2 Mordad [1994]. (In Persian).

— "Afsaneh-e Kamboud-e Sarmayeh dar Iran." [The Legend of Capital Shortage in Iran]. 1–2 Mordad 1373 [1994]. (In Persian).

Harris, Elisa D. "Chemical Weapons Proliferation in the Developing World. *RUSI and Brassey's Defense Yearbook*, 1989. London: RUSI/Brassey's, 1988.

Harrop, Scott W. "Iran's Objectives in Northwest Asia: With a Focus on Tajikistan." Unpublished paper presented at the 35th annual convention of the International Studies Association. Washington, DC, 29 March 1994.

Hedges, Stephen J. and Peter Cary. "The Other Problem in the Persian Gulf." *U.S. News and World Report*, 14 November 1995.

Hekmat, Bizhan. "Mardom Salari va Din Salari." *Kiyan* 21 (September–October 1994).

Henderson, Simon. *Instant Empire: Saddam Hussein's Ambition for Iraq*. San Francisco, CA: Mercury House, 1991.

Herdman, Roger C. *Technologies Underlying Weapons of Mass Destruction*. Washington, DC: GPO, Office of Technology Assessment, U.S. Congress, OTA-BP-ISC-115, December 1993.

Herrmann, Richard K. "The Role of Iran in Soviet Perceptions and Policy, 1946–1988." In *Neither East Nor West: Iran, the Soviet Union, and the United States*, ed. Nikki R. Keddie and Mark J. Gasiorowski. New Haven, CT: Yale University Press, 1990.

— "Russian Policy in the Middle East: Strategic Change and Tactical Contradictions." *Middle East Journal* 48, no. 3 (summer 1994).

Hibbs, Mark. "Iran May Withdraw from NPT over Western Trade Barriers." *Nucleonics Week* 35, no. 38 (22 September 1994).

Hijazi, Ihsan. "Pro-Iranian Terror Group Targeting Saudi Envoys." *New York Times*, 8 January 1989.

Hiro, Dilip. "The Revolution Stumbles." *The Middle East*, July 1993.

Hordan, John. "The Iranian Navy." *Jane's Intelligence Review*, May 1992.

Howell, W. Nathaniel. "Arabian Peninsula and Gulf Security after Desert Storm." Unpublished paper presented at the conference *The Middle East and the New World Order*. University of Virginia, Charlottesville, VA, 9–10 September 1994.

Hume, Cameron. *The United Nations, Iran, and Iraq: How Peacemaking Changed*. Bloomington, IN: Indiana University Press, 1994.

Hunt, Lynn. *Politics, Culture, and Class in the French Revolution*. Berkeley, CA: University of California Press, 1984.

Hunter, Shireen T. *Iran and the World: Continuity in a Revolutionary Decade*. Bloomington, IN: Indiana University Press, 1990.

— *Iran after Khomeini*. New York: Praeger 1992.

— "Iran: Renewed Threat in the Persian Gulf?" *The World & I*, April 1993.

Huntington, Samuel P. "The Clash of Civilizations?" *Foreign Affairs* 72, no. 3 (May–June 1993).

Ibrahim, Youssef. "Arabs Raise a Nervous Cry over Iranian Militancy." *New York Times*, 21 December 1992.

— "Iran Shrugs Off Sanctions." *International Herald Tribune*, 22 June 1995.

International Institute for Strategic Studies (IISS). *The Military Balance*. London: Brassey's for IISS. Various Editions.

— *Military Technology: World Defense Almanac 1994–1995*. London: Brassey's for IISS.

— *National Trade Data Banks Market Report*. London: IISS. Various editions.

Iran Plan and Budget Organization. *Gozaresh-e Eqtesadi-ye Sal-e 1371* [The Economic Report of the Year 1992]. Tehran: Plan and Budget Organization, 1373 [1994]. (In Persian).

— *Gozaresh-e Eqtesadi-ye Sal-e 1370* [The Economic Report of the Year 1991]. Tehran: Plan and Budget Organization, 1372 [1993]. (In Persian).

— *Payvast-e Layhe-ye Barnameh-e Dovvum-e Touse'ah Eqtesadi, Ejtema'i va Farhangi-ye Jomhouri-ye Eslami-ye Iran 1373–1377* [Appendage to the Bill of the Second Economic, Social, and Cultural Development Plan of the Islamic Republic of Iran]. Tehran: Plan and Budget Organization, 1372 [1993]. (In Persian).

Iran Press Digest (Tehran). "History and Present Status of IRGC." 7 August 1984.

Islamic Republic News Agency (IRNA). "IRGC Defence Industries Manufacture First Helicopter." 15 January 1994. (In English).

— "IRGC Commander Receives Delegation." 26 June 1992.

Islamic Republic of Iran Permanent Mission to the United Nations. "Defence Minister: Iran Will Not Be Dragged into Mid East Arms Race." Release no. 075, 15 April 1993.

Islamic Republic Party (IRP). *Shi'ite va Shuwra*. Tehran: IRP, 1981. (In Persian).

Al Jabhan, Ibrahim. *Tabdid Al-Dhalam wa Tanbih Al-Niam* [Clearing of Darkness and Raising the Conscious of the Passive] Riyadh: Maktabat Al-Harmain, 1979. (In Arabic).

Jacobs, Gordon and Tim McCarthy. "China Missile Sales – Few Changes for the Future." *Jane's Intelligence Review*, December 1992.

Ja'far, Su'ar. *Sanad Hay-e Shuwra dar Qur'an va Hadith*. Tehran: Sazman-e Pazhuhesh, 1981. (In Persian).

Jaffee Center for Strategic Studies (JCSS). *The Military Balance in the Middle East*. Tel Aviv: JCSS. Various editions.

Jame, Mohammad Masjed. *Iran Va Khaleeje-e Fars* [Iran and the Persian Gulf]. Tehran: Zendegi Press, 1989. (In Persian).

Jane's. *All the World's Aircraft*. London: Jane's Publishing. Various editions.

— *Armour and Artillery*. London: Jane's Publishing. Various editions.

— *Aviation Annual*. London: Jane's Publishing. Various editions.

— *Battlefield Surveillance Systems*. London: Jane's Publishing. Various editions.

— *C³I Systems*. London: Jane's Publishing. Various editions.

— *Combat Support Equipment*. London: Jane's Publishing. Various editions.

— *Defence Appointments & Procurement Handbook (Middle East Edition)* London: Jane's Publishing. Various editions.

— *Defence Review*. London: Jane's Publishing. Various editions.

— *Defence Weekly*. London: Jane's Publishing. Various editions.

— *Fighting Ships*. London: Jane's Publishing. Various editions.

— *Infantry Weapons*. London: Jane's Publishing. Various editions.

— *Intelligence Review*. London: Jane's Publishing. Various editions.

— *Land-Based Air Defence*. London: Jane's Publishing. Various editions.

— *Military Annual*. London: Jane's Publishing. Various editions.

— *Military Communications*. London: Jane's Publishing. Various editions.

— *Military Vehicles and Logistics*. London: Jane's Publishing. Various editions.

— *Naval Annual*. London: Jane's Publishing. Various editions.

— *Naval Review*. London: Jane's Publishing. Various editions.

— *Naval Weapons Systems*. London: Jane's Publishing. Various editions.

— *Radar and Electronic Warfare Systems*. London: Jane's Publishing. Various editions.

— *Remotely Piloted Vehicles*. London: Jane's Publishing. Various editions.

— *Soviet Intelligence Review*. London: Jane's Publishing. Various editions.

Jane's Defence Weekly. "Iran May Turn Down Third 'Kilo' Delivery," 22, no. 14, 8 October 1994.

— "Buying Security from the West," 28 March 1992.

— "China Delivers Five FACs to Iran," 1 October 1994.

— "Iranian Conversion Claims Mystify," 10 September 1994.

— "China Delivers FACs to Iran," 13 October 1994.

— "The JDW Interview," 16 November 1991.

Jehl, Douglas. "Iran is Reported Acquiring Missiles," *New York Times*, 8 April 1993.

Katz, Mark N. "Nationalism and the Legacy of Empire," *Current History* 93, no. 585 (October 1994).

Katzman, Kenneth. *Warriors of Islam: Iran's Revolutionary Guards*. Boulder, CO: Westview Press, 1993.

— *Iran: U.S. Containment Policy*. Washington, DC: Congressional Research Service. CRS Report 94-652-F, 11 August 1994.

— "Iran: Current Developments and U.S. Policy." Washington, DC: Congressional Research Service, CRS Issue Brief IB 93033, 9 September 1994.

Kazemzadeh, Firuz. "Iranian Relations with Russia and the Soviet Union, to 1921." In *The Cambridge History of Islam*, vol. 7. Cambridge: Cambridge University Press, 1992.

Kechichian, Joseph A. "The Gulf Cooperation Council: Containing the Iranian Revolution." *Journal of South Asian and Middle Eastern Studies* 8, no. 1 (fall 1992), no. 2 (winter 1992).

— "The Role of the Ulama in the Politics of an Islamic State: The Case of Saudi Arabia." *International Journal of Middle East Studies* 18, no. 1 (February 1988).

Keddie, Nikki R. "The Roots of the Ulama Power in Modern Iran." In *Scholars, Saints, and Sufis: Muslim Religious Institutions in the Middle East since 1500*, ed. Nikki R. Keddie. Berkeley, CA: University of California Press, 1972.

Keddie, Nikki R. and Mark J. Gasiorowski (eds.). *Neither East Nor West: Iran, the Soviet Union, and the United States*. New Haven, CT: Yale University Press, 1980.

Keegan, John. *World Armies*, 2nd ed. London: Macmillan, 1983.

Kelly, J. B. *Arabia, the Gulf and the West: A Critical View of the Arabs and Their Oil Policy*. New York: Basic Books, 1980.

Kemp, Geoffrey. *Forever Enemies: American Policy and the Islamic Republic of Iran*. Washington, DC: The Carnegie Endowment for International Peace, 1994.

Keohane, Robert O. *After Hegemony: Cooperation and Discord in the World Political Economy*. Princeton, NJ: Princeton University Press, 1984.

Keyhan International. (Tehran). "Opposition Leader on Reform, Ties with Iran," 6 October 1992.

Keyhan daily. Statements made by Morteza Nabavi, Tehran's Representative to the Parliament. 11 Mordad 1373 [1994]. (In Persian).

— Interview with Mr. M. Shahriari, member of the Parliament's Integration Committee. 11 Mordad 1373 [1994]. (In Persian).

Al-Khatib, Al-Baghdadi, Abu Bakr Ahmad ibn Ali. *Kitab al faqih wa 'l-mutaffaqih*. Vol. 2.

Al-Khatib, Muhib Al-Din. *Al Khtut Al-Ariedhah* [Bold Lines] 2nd printing. n.p.: 1981. (In Arabic).

Khomeini, Ayatollah. *Valayat-e Faqih*. Tehran: Entesharat-e Nas, 1981. (In Persian).

— *Kashf-e Asrar.*

— Speech in Behesht-e Zahra. February 1979 (12 Bahman 57).

— Declaration for the Establishment of the Provisional Government. February 1979 (17 Bahman 1957).

— Al Hukomah Al-Islamiah [The Islamic Government] Arabic edn. Ed. Hassan Hanafi. n.p.: September 1979.

— Sermon. FBIS, 14 March 1994.

Kissinger, Henry. *The Necessity for Choice*. New York: Harber and Brothers, 1961.

Klatt, Martin. "Russians in the 'Near Abroad'." *RFE/RL Research Report* 3, no. 32, (19 August 1994).

Korb, Edward L. *The World's Missile Systems*, 7th ed. General Dynamics, Pomona Division. April 1992.

Kuhn, Thomas S. *The Structure of Scientific Revolutions*. Chicago: University of Chicago Press, 1970.

Kutschera, Chris. "Iran's Peeling Veneer." *The Middle East*. September 1994.

Lafflin, John L. *The War Annual*. London: Brassey's. Various editions.

Lailaz, Sa'id. "Saderat-e Ghair-e Nafti dar Neghi Digar" [Non-Oil Exports in a Different Perspective], *Ettela'at-e Siasi va Eqtesadi*, nos. 53–54. Bahman and Esfand 1370 [1991]. (In Persian).

Lake, Anthony. "Confronting Backlash States." *Foreign Affairs* 73, no. 2 (March–April 1994).

Lancaster, John. "Despite Trade Ban, U.S. Goods Still Find Their Way to Iran." *Washington Post.* 26 June 1995.

Larijani, Muhammad Javad. *Hukumat va Marz-e Mashru'iyyat, Majmu'ih Maqalat-e Awwalin Seminar-e Tahavvul-e Mafahim,* p. 33.

Lawson, Fred. *Bahrain: The Modernization of Autocracy.* Boulder, CO: Westview Press, 1989.

Lerner, Ralph and Muhsin Mahdi. *Medieval Political Philosophy.* New York: Cornell University Press, 1978.

Lewis, Bernard. "Muslim Rage." *Atlantic Monthly* (June 1992).

Liberation Movement of Iran (LMI). *Hushdar: Piramun-e Tadavum-e Jang-e Khanemansuz.* Tehran: LMI, 1988. (In Persian).

— *Tafsil va Tahli-e Velayat-e Mutlaqeh-e Faqih.* Tehran: LMI, 1988. (In Persian).

— *Jang-e bi Payan.* Tehran: LMI, 1985. (In Persian).

— *Tuwzihati Piramun-e Muzakereh, Atash Bas va Sulh.* Tehran: LMI, 1985. (In Persian).

— *Tahlili Piramun-e Jang va Sulh.* Tehran: LMI, 1984. (In Persian).

— *Azadi va Entekhabat, Peik-e Nehzat.* No. 21. Tehran: LMI, 1983. (In Persian).

— *Azadi az Du Didgah.* Tehran: LMI, 1983. (In Persian).

— *Sargozasht-e Seminar-e Ta'min-e Azadi-e Entekhabat, Peik-e Nehzat.* No. 23. Tehran: LMI, 1983. (In Persian).

Lumpe, Lora, Lisbeth Gronlund, and David C. Wright. "Third World Missiles Fall Short." *Bulletin of the Atomic Scientists,* March 1992.

Madani, S. J. *Hugug-e Asasi dar Jumhuri Eslami Iran* [Constitutional Laws of the Islamic Republic of Iran], vol. 3, "The Majles." Tehran, Soroush Publications, 1985. (In Persian).

Maggs, W. W. "Armenia and Azerbaijan: Looking toward the Middle East." *Current History* (January 1993).

Makiya, Kanan. *Cruelty and Silence: War, Tyranny, and Uprising in the Arab World.* New York: Norton Press, 1993.

Mallet, Chibli. "Religious Militancy in Contemporary Iraq: Mohammed Baqir al-Sadr and the Sunni–Shi'a Paradigm." *Third World Quarterly* 10, no. 2 (1988).

Malone, Joseph. *The Arab Lands of Western Asia.* Englewood Cliffs, NJ: Prentice-Hall, 1973.

Malullah, Mohamed. *Mawaqif Al-shiah Min Ahl Al-Sunnah* [The Stand of Shiah from Sunnah]. n.p.: n.d. (In Arabic).

Marlowe, Lara. "Revolutionary Disintegration." *Time,* 26 June 1995.

Marr, Phebe. "The Iran–Iraq War: The View From Iraq." In *The Persian Gulf War: Lessons for Strategy, Law, and Diplomacy.* Westport, CT: Greenwood Press, 1990.

Martin, Vanessa. "Religion and State in Khoemeini's *Kashr-e Asrar.*" *Bulletin of the School of Oriental and African Studies* LVI, no. 1. London: University of London (SOAS), 1993.

Maleki, Muhammad. *Shuwra dar Islam.* Tehran: Entesharat-e Zanan-e Musalman, 1980. (In Persian).

Mashayekhi, Alinaqi. "Barnameh-e Avval-e Touse'ah: Dastavardha va Kastiha." [The First Development Plan: Achievements and Shortcomings], *Hamshahri* daily, 30 Shahrivar 1372 [1993]. (In Persian).

Mashayekhi, Mehrdad. "The Politics of Nationalism and Political Culture." In *Iran: Political Culture in the Islamic Republic,* ed. Samih K. Farsoun and Mehrdad Mashayekhi. London: Routledge, 1992.

Al Mawsawi, Musa. *Al Shiah Wal-Tashieh: Al Siraa Bein Al-Shiah Wal-Tashieua* [Shi'a and Rectification: The Conflict between Shi'is and Political Shi'ism]. Los Angeles, CA: The High Islamic Council, 1988. (In Arabic).

Megalli, Nabila. "Admiral Seeks Gulf Stability." *Washington Times*, 8 September 1994.

Menashiri, David. *A Decade of War and Revolution*. New York: Holmes & Meier Publishers, 1990.

Mesbahi, Mohiaddin S. *Russia and the Third World*. Gainesville, FL: University Press of Florida, 1994.

— (ed.). *Central Asia and the Caucasus after the Soviet Union: Domestic and International Dynamics*. Gainesville, FL: University Press of Florida, 1994.

Middle East, The. "Whose Gulf is it Anyway?" July 1991.

— "Now What's the Problem?" June 1991.

— "Iran: New Force of Stability." March 1991.

Middle East Defense News (Mednews). "North Korea Corners ME Missile Market." *Mednews* 5, no. 16 (18 May 1992).

— "Iran's Nuclear Weapons Program." *Mednews* 5, nos. 17 and 18 (8 June 1992).

— "Iran's Ballistic Missile Program." *Mednews* 6, no. 6 (21 December 1992).

Middle East Economic Digest (MEED). "MEED Special Report: Defense." *MEED* 35, 13 December 1991.

— "Iran: Rafsanjani's Shock Therapy." 30 April 1993.

— "Submarines: Iran Sparks Off a Boat Race." 29 April 1994.

Middle East International, no. 464, 3 December 1993.

— no. 449, 30 April 1993.

Middle East Monitor. "Total Takes the Bait," 5 (August 1995).

Milani, Mohsen M. *The Making of Iran's Islamic Revolution: From Monarchy to Islamic Republic* (2nd ed.) Boulder, CO: Westview Press, 1994.

— "Iran's Post-Cold War Policy in the Persian Gulf." *International Affairs* XLIX, no. 2 (spring 1994).

— "The Evolution of the Iranian Presidency: From Bani Sadr to Rafsanjani." *British Journal of Middle Eastern Studies* 20, no. 1 (1993).

— "Harvest of Shame: The Policy of the Tudeh Party and the Bazargan Government." *Middle East Studies* 29, no. 2 (April 1993).

— "The Transformation of the *Velayat-e Faqih* Institution: From Khomeini to Khamenei." *The Muslim World* LXXXII, no. 3 (July 1992), no. 4 (October 1992).

— "Iran's Active Neutrality during the Kuwaiti Crisis: Reasons and Ramifications." *New Political Science* no. 21 (spring 1992), no. 22 (summer 1992).

Military Technology. *World Defense Almanac*. Special issue of the magazine *Military Technology*. Various editions.

— *World Defense Almanac: The Balance of Military Power* 17, no. 1 (1993). ISSN 0722-3226.

Miller, David. "Submarines in the Gulf." *Military Technology*, June 1993.

Miller, Judith. "The Challenge of Radical Islam." *Foreign Affairs* 72, no. 2 (March–April 1993).

Modarressi, Hossein. "The Just Ruler or the Guardian Jurist: An Attempt to Link Two Different Shi'ite Concepts." *Journal of the American Oriental Society*. III, no. 3 (July–September 1991).

Mofid, Kerman. *The Economic Consequences of the Gulf War*. New York: Routledge, 1990.

Moghtader, Hooshang. "The Settlement of the Bahrain Question: A Study in Anglo-Iranian-United Nations Diplomacy." *Pakistan Horizon* 6, no. 2 (1973).

Mojahed, Shahrazad. "Iranian Women in Higher Education." Paper presented at the 6th annual meeting of the American Council for the Study of Islamic Societies, Villanova, PA, 19–20 May 1989.

Mojtahedzadeh, Pirouz. "Tarikh Va Joghrafeya-ye Seyasi-ye Jazayer-e Tunb Va Abu Musa" [The Political and Geographic History of the Tunb and Abu Musa Islands]. *Rahavard*, no. 31 (summer 1992) and no. 32 (winter 1992).

— "The Political Geography and History of the Island of Abu Musa." *Iranian Journal of International Affairs* 4 (1992).

— *The Changing World Order and Geopolitical Regions of Caspian-Central Asia and the Persian Gulf*. London: Urosevic Foundation Monographs, 1992.

— "Iran's Maritime Boundaries and the Persian Gulf: The Case of Abu Musa Island." In *The Boundaries of Modern Iran*, ed. Keith McLachlan. New York: St. Martin's Press, 1994.

Monshi, Eskandar. *The History of Shah 'Abbas the Great*. Trans. Roger Savoy. 2 vols. Boulder, CO: Westview Press, 1978.

Montazari, Husain-Ali. *Kitab al-Khums*. Qom: n.d. (In Persian).

— *Dirasat fi Wilayah al-Fiqh*. Qom: 1408 A.H., 1988/9.

Motahari, Ahmad Mir. "Barnameh-e Avval: Pendarha, Entezarat, Vaqeiytha" [The First Plan: Beliefs, Expectations, Realities], *Ettela'at-e Siasi va Eqtesadi*, nos. 83–84. (In Persian).

Mottahedeh, Roy P. "Wilayah al-Faqih." *The Oxford Encyclopedia of the Modern Islamic World*. New York: Oxford University Press, 1995.

— "The Islamic Movement: The Case for Democratic Inclusion." *Contention* 4, no. 3 (spring 1995).

Munson, Keith. *World Unmanned Aircraft*. London: Jane's Publishing, 1988.

Muntazeri, Ayatollah Muhammad Hossein. *Mabani-e Fiqhi-e Hukamat-e Islami*. Qom: Nashr-e Tafakkur, 1984.

— *Fi Velah al-Faqih va Fiqh al-Dowlah al-Islamiyyah*. Qom: Al Markaz al-Alami lidderasat al-Islamiyyah, 1987.

Mutahhari, Ayatollah Murtada. *Piramun-e Jomhuri-e Islami*. Qom: Entesharat-e Sadra, 1979. (In Persian).

Nagler, Robert A. *Ballistic Missile Proliferation: An Emerging Threat*. Arlington, VA: Systems Planning Corporation, 1992.

Na'ini, Ayatollah Muhammad Hussein. *Tanbih al-Ummah va Tanzih al-Millah*. 8th ed. Tehran: Sherkat-e Enteshar, 1982. (In Persian).

Naipaul, V. S. *Among Believers: An Islamic Journey*. New York: Random House, 1981.

Nasr, Seyyed Hossein, Hamid Dabashi, and Seyyed Vali Reza Nasr (eds.) *Expectations of the Millennium: Shi'ism in History*. Albany, NY: State University of New York Press, 1989.

Newsday. "Iran Hostage Takers Now Hold Key Posts." 8 September 1994.

New York Times. "Widow of Iranian Dissident Blames Tehran in His Death." 10 February 1993.

— "Turkey Asserts Islamic Ring that Killed Three Has Iran Links." 5 February 1993.

— "U.S. Sees Iranian Role in Buenos Aires Blast." 9 May 1992.

— Interview of Ahmad Baqir Al-Hakim. 25 February 1992.

Nonneman, Gerd. *Iraq, the Gulf States, and the War: A Changing Relationship, 1980–1986 and Beyond.* London: Atlantic Highland, 1986.

Norton, Richard A. *Civil Society in the Middle East.* 2 vols. Leiden, The Netherlands E.J. Brill, 1994, 1995).

Olcott, Martha Brill. "Central Asia's Islamic Awakening." *Current History* 93, no. 582 (April 1994).

Omran, Abdel R. and Farzaneh Roudi. "The Middle East Population Puzzle." *Population Bulletin* 48, (July 1993).

Palmer, Michel A. *Guardians of the Gulf: A History of America's Expanding Role in the Persian Gulf.* New York: The Free Press, 1992.

Paris Daily News. "Bakhtaran Mopping Up Operations Successful." 29 August 1984.

Parsons, Anthony. "Prospects for Peace and Stability in the Middle East." *Conflict Studies* 262 (London: Research Institute for the Study of Conflict and Terrorism, 1993.)

Paydar, Hamid. "Paradox-e Islam va Democracy." *Kiyan* 19 (June 1994).

Pawloski, Dick. *Changes in Threat Air Combat Doctrine and Force Structure.* 24th ed. Fort Worth, TX: General Dynamics, DWIC-01, Fort Worth Division, February 1992.

Pelletiere, Stephen C. *The Iran–Iraq War: Chaos in a Vacuum.* New York: Praeger, 1992.

Phillips, James A. "The Saddomization of Iran. *Policy Review* 2, no. 69 (summer 1994).

Physicians for Human Rights. "Winds of Death: Iraq's Use of Poison Gas against its Kurdish Population. February 1989.

Pipes, Daniel and Patrick Clawson. "Ambitious Iran, Troubled Neighbors." *Foreign Affairs* 72, no. 1 (January-February 1993).

Piscatori, James P. *Islam in the World of Nations.* Cambridge: Cambridge University Press, 1986.

— "Islamic Values and National Interest: The Foreign Policy of Saudi Arabia." In *Islam and Foreign Policy*, ed. Adeed Dawisha. Cambridge: Cambridge University Press, 1985.

Radmenesh, Ezzatullah. *Enqilab va Ebtedal va Shuwra Rukni as Arkan-e Nezam-e Towhidi.* Tehran: Mu'asseseh Khadamat-e Farhangi-e Rasa, 1980. (In Persian).

Rafsanjani, Hashemi A. *Enqelab ya Be'sat-e Jadid* [Revolution or a New Mission] Tehran: Yaser Publications, n.d. (In Persian).

Rafsanjani, Ali Akbar Hashemi. *Amir Kabir.* Tehran: Farahani Press, 1982.

Rajaee, Farhang, (ed.) *The Iraq–Iran War.* Gainesville, FL: University Press of Florida, 1993.

Ramazani, R. K. *The Gulf Cooperation Council: Record and Analysis.* Charlottesville, VA: University Press of Virginia, 1988.

— *Revolutionary Iran: Challenge and Response in the Middle East.* Baltimore, MD: Johns Hopkins University Press, 1986.

— *Revolutionary Iran: Challenge and Response in the Middle East.* 2nd ed. Baltimore, MD: Johns Hopkins University Press, 1988.

— *The Persian Gulf: Iran's Role.* Charlottesville, VA: University Press of Virginia, 1972.

— "Who Started the Iran–Iraq War?: A Commentary." *Virginia Journal of International Law* 33, no. 1 (spring 1993).

— "Iran's Foreign Policy: Both North and South." *Middle East Journal* 46, no. 3 (summer 1992).

— "Iran's Foreign Policy: Contending Orientations." *Middle East Journal* 43, no. 2. (spring 1989).

— "Khumayni's Islam in Foreign Policy." In *Islam in Foreign Policy*, ed. Adeed Dawisha. Cambridge: Cambridge University Press, 1985.

Rathmell, Andrew. "Iran's Rearmament: How Great a Threat?" *Jane's Intelligence Review*. July 1994.

Resalat. (Tehran). "Guard Corps Commander on Struggle in Mideast." 25 September 1994.

Resalat daily. Interview with Gholamhosian Naadi, deputy of the Parliament. 14 Esfand 1366 [1987]. (In Persian).

Reuters. "Algeria Breaks Diplomatic Ties with Iran." 27 March 1993.

— "U.S. Commander Says Iran Keeping the Peace." 7 September 1994.

— "Clinton to Press Yeltsin on Iran Arms Sales." 27 September 1994.

— "Iranian Air Force Sukhoi, MiG Pilots Graduate." 11 August 1994.

— "Iran Gives Dam Project to Revolutionary Guards." 14 November 1993.

— "Pro-Iranian to Head Algerian Islamist Group-Paper." 18 April 1994.

Rezaii, Mohammad Mehdi. "Tahavoulat-e Arz az Didgah-e Kalan-e Eqtesadi" [Changes in Foreign Exchange from a Macroeconomic Perspective], *Rouznameh-e Ettela'at, Vizeh-e Kharej az Keshvar*, 6 Mordad 1373 [1994]. (In Persian).

Ricks, Thomas. "Power Politics and Political Culture: U.S.–Iran Relations." In *Iran: Political Culture in the Islamic Republic*, ed. Samih K. Farsoun and Mehrdad Mashayekhi. London: Routledge, 1992.

Ritcheson, Philip L. "Iranian Military Resurgence: Scope, Motivations, and Implications for Regional Security." *Armed Forces and Society* 21, no. 4 (summer 1995).

Riyadh Domestic Service. "Iran Admits Smuggling Explosives." 17 May 1989.

Robins, Philip. "Between Sentiment and Self-Interest: Turkey's Policy toward Azerbaijan and the Central Asian States." *Middle East Journal* 47, no. 4 (fall 1993).

Royce, Knut. "Iran Buying 150 'Terror' Missiles." *Long Island Newsday*, 14 April 1992.

Sadowski, Yahya. *Scuds or Butter? The Political Economy of Arms Control in the Middle East.* Washington, DC: Brookings Institute Institution, 1993.

Saffari, Said. "The Legitimation of the Clergy's Right to Rule in the Constitution of 1979." *British Journal of Middle Eastern Studies* 20, no. 1 (spring 1993).

Saikal, Amin. "U.S. Strategy in the Persian Gulf: A Recipe for Insecurity." *World Policy Journal* 9, no. 3 (1992).

Sandwick, John A, (ed.). *The Gulf Cooperation Council, Moderation and Stability in an Interdependent World.* Boulder, CO: Westview Press, 1987.

Sariolghalam, Mahmood. "Conceptual Sources of Post-Revolutionary Iranian Behavior toward the Arab World." In *Iran and the Arab World*, ed. Hooshang Amirahmadi and Nader Entessar. New York: St. Martin's Press, 1992., London: Macmillan Press, 1993.

Saudi Arabia Ministry of Finance. *Annual Yearbook.* Riyadh: General Directorate of Statistics, 1985, 1990, 1991.

Saudi Arabia Ministry of Interior. Directorate-General of Passports. *Pilgrims Statistics.* Riyadh: Directorate-General of Passports, 1987.

Schahgaldian, Nikola B. *Iran and the Post War Security in the Persian Gulf.* Santa Monica, CA: Rand Corporation, 1994.

Sciolino, Elaine. *The Outlaw State: Saddam Hussein's Quest for Power and the Gulf Crisis.* New York: John Wiley and Sons, 1991.

— "CIA Report Says Chinese Sent Iran Arms Components." *New York Times*, 22 June 1995.

Shahabi, Sohrab. "A Review of Iran's Five-Year Development Plan." *Iranian Journal of International Affairs* 4, no. 4 (1992).

Shahabi, Sohrab and Farideh Farhi. "Security Considerations and Iranian Foreign Policy." *Iranian Journal of International Affairs* 7 (spring 1995).

Al-Sha'rani, Abd al-Wahhab ibn Ahmad. *Al-Tabaqat al-Sughra*. Cairo: Maktabat al-Qahirah, 1970.

Al-Sharq Al-Awsat, 19 November 1992. In FBIS-NES, 23 November 1992.

— Interview of Ahmad Baqir Al-Hakim. 28 February 1992.

Shirley, Edward G. "Is Iran's Present Algeria's Future?" *Foreign Affairs* 74, no. 3 (May–June 1995).

— "The Iran Policy Trap." *Foreign Policy* 96 (fall 1994).

Shuey, Robert, and Shirley Kan. *Chinese Nuclear and Missile Proliferation*. Washington, DC: Congressional Research Service, CRS Issue Brief IB 92056, 4 October 1994.

Sick, Gary. "U.S. Interests in Iran and U.S. Iran Policy." In *U.S.–Iran Relations: Areas of Tension and Mutual Interest*, ed. Hooshang Amirahmadi and Eric Hooglund. Washington, DC: Middle East Institute, 1994.

— "Iran: The Adolescent Revolution." *Journal of International Affairs* 49, no. 1 (summer 1995).

— "Trial by Error: Reflections on the Iraq–Iran War." *Middle East Journal* 43 (spring 1989).

Skocpol, Theda. *States and Social Revolutions: A Comparative Analysis of France, Russia, and China*. Cambridge: Cambridge University Press, 1979.

Soroush, Abdul Karim. *Qabz va Bast-e Theorik-e Sari'at*. Tehran: Mu'asseseh Farhangi-e Serat, 1991. (In Persian).

Soroush, Abdul Karim. "Mudara va Mudiriyyat-e Mu'menan: Sukhani dar Nesbat-e Din va Democracy." *Kiyan* 21. (Tehran, September–October 1994).

Soroush, Abdul Karim. "Hukumat-e Democratic-e Dini." *Kiyan* 11 (Tehran, 1993).

Stevens, Paul. *Oil and Politics: The Post-War Gulf*. London: Royal Institute of International Affairs, 1992.

Stewart, Devin J. "Islamic Juridical Hierarchies and the Office of *Marji' al-Taqlid*." Unpublished paper presented at a conference on Shi'ism. Philadelphia, PA, September 1993.

Stockholm International Peace Research Institute (SIPRI). *SIPRI Yearbook: World Armaments and Disarmaments*. London and New York: Oxford University Press, London: Taylor & Francis. Various editions.

Subhani, Ja'far. *Mabani-e Hukumat-e Islami*. 2 vols. Qom: Entesharat-e Towhid, 1983. (In Persian).

Tadjbakhsh, Shahrbanou. "Tajikistan: From Freedom to War." *Current History* 93, no. 582 (April 1994).

Taliqani, Ayatollah Mahmud. *Tabyin Resalat Baray-e Qiam beh Qest*. Tehran: Sherkat-e Enteshar, 1981. (In Persian).

— *Shuwra az Didgah-e Taliqani*. Tehran: Mu'asseseh Khadamat-e Farhangi-e Rasa, 1981. (In Persian).

Taylor, John W.R. and Kenneth Munson. "Gallery of Middle East Air Power." *Air Force*, October 1994, pp. 59–70.

Teal Group Corporation. *World Missiles Briefing*.

Tillema, Herbert K. *International Armed Conflict since 1945: A Bibliographic Handbook of Wars and Military Interventions*. Boulder, CO: Westview Press, 1991.

Timmerman, Kenneth R. *Weapons of Mass Destruction: The Cases of Iran, Syria, and Libya.* Los Angeles: Simon Wiesenthal Center, August 1992.

Tripp, Charles. "The Gulf States and Iraq." *Survival* (fall 1992).

U.S.–Iran Review 2, no. 5 (June–July 1994).

United Nations. *Chemical and Bacteriological (Biological) Weapons and the Effects of Their Possible Use.* Report of the Secretary General of the United Nations. New York: United Nations, 1989

United Nations General Assembly. "Statement by H.E. Mr. Rashid Abdullah Al-Nuaimi, Minister of Foreign Affairs in the General Debate of the Forty-Seventh Session of the General Assembly of the United Nations." New York: United Nations: 30 December 1992.

United States Arms Control and Disarmament Agency (ACDA). *World Military Expenditures and Arms Transfers: 1991–1992.* Washington, DC: GPO, 1994.

— *World Military Expenditures and Arms Transfers: 1989.* Washington, DC: GPO, 1990.

United States Congress. Office of Technology Assessment. *Proliferation of Weapons of Mass Destruction: Assessing the Risks.* Washington, DC: United States Congress OTA-ISC-559, GPO, August 1993.

United States Department of Commerce. International Trade Administration. *U.S. Foreign Trade Highlights, 1993.* Washington, DC: U.S. Office of Trade and Economic Analysis, 1994.

United States Department of Defense. *Conduct of the Persian Gulf War: Final Report to Congress.* Washington, DC: Department of Defense. April, 1992.

United States Department of Defense and Department of State. *Congressional Presentation for Security Assistance Programs: Fiscal Year 1993.* Washington, DC: Department of State, 1992.

United States Department of State. Press Release. "Joint U.S.–P.R.C. Statement on Missile Proliferation." Washington, DC: Department of State, 4 October 1994.

— State Department Report. Washington, DC: Department of State, 31 October 1994.

— Office of the Coordinator for Counterterrorism. *Patterns of Global Terrorism: 1993.* Washington, DC, released April 1994.

United States House of Representatives. "Statement of Robert Gates, the Director of Central Intelligence Before the U.S. House of Representatives Armed Services Committee Defense Policy Panel." 27 March 1992.

— House Joint Resolution 216,100th Congress. *Overview of the Situation in the Persian Gulf: Hearings Before the Committee on Foreign Affairs.* Washington, DC: GPO, 1987.

United States Naval Institute (USNI). *Military Database.* Computerized military database.

— *The Naval Institute Guide to the Combat Fleets of the World, 1993: Their Ships, Aircraft, and Armaments.* Annapolis, MD: USNI, 1993.

United States Senate. "Chemical and Biological Warfare." Hearing Before the Committee on Foreign Relations, US Senate, 91st Congress, 30 April 1989.

— Staff Report to the Committee on Foreign Relations. *War in the Persian Gulf: The U.S. Takes Sides.* Washington, DC: GPO, November 1987.

— Unpublished testimony of W. Seth Carus before the Committee on Governmental Affairs. Washington, DC: US Senate. 9 February 1989.

— Unpublished testimony of David Goldberg of the Foreign Science and Technology

Center, US Army Intelligence Agency, before the Committee on Governmental Affairs. Washington, DC: US Senate. 9 February 1989.

— Unpublished testimony of Barry J. Erlick, Senior Biological Warfare Analyst of the U.S. Army, before the Committee on Governmental Affairs. Washington, DC: US Senate. 9 February 1989.

— Unpublished testimony of Robert Mullen Cood-Deegan, of Physicians for Human Rights, before the Committee on Governmental Affairs. Washington, DC: US Senate. 9 February 1989.

— Unpublished testimony of the Honorable William H. Webster, Director (frmr.) of the Central Intelligence Agency, before the Committee on Governmental Affairs. Hearing on Global Spread of Chemical and Biological Weapons. Washington, DC: US Senate. 9 February 1989.

Ustadi, Reza. *Shuwra dar Qur'an va Hadith*. Tehran: Entesharat-e Buniad Farhangi-e Imam Reza, 1981. (In Persian).

van England, Claude. "Iran on Military Renewal." *Christian Science Monitor*, 4 March 1993.

Voice of the Islamic Republic of Iran. 27 October 1994. In FBIS-NES, 27 October 1994.

Voice of the Islamic Republic of Iran First Program Network. "IRGC Armed Forces Participate in Exercise." 26 January 1994.

— "Pakistani Ground Forces Commander Arrives 2 November." 2 November 1991.

Volpin, Andre. *Russian Arms Sales Policy toward the Middle East*. Research Memorandum no. 2B. Washington, DC: The Washington Institute for Near East Policy, 1993.

Washington Institute for Near East Policy, The. *Peacewatch* no. 33, 26 September 1994.

Wooten, James P. "Terrorism: U.S. Policy Options." Washington, DC: Congressional Research Service, CRS Issue Brief IB 92074, 6 October 1994.

Workman, Thom. *The Social Origins of the Iran–Iraq War*. Boulder, CO: Lynne Rienner, 1994.

Wylie, James. "Iran – Quest for Security and Influence." *Jane's Intelligence Review*. July 1993.

Yazdi, Ayatollah Mesbah. *Hukumat-e Islami va Velayat-e Faqih*. Tehran: Sazman-e Tabliqat-e Islami, 1990. (In Persian).

— *Jame'eh va Tarikh as Didgah-e Qur'an*. Tehran: Sazman-e Tabliqat-e Islami, 1989. (In Persian).

Young, Peter Lewis. "American Perceptions of Iran." *Asian Defense*. February 1993.

Zahir, Ihsan Ilahi. *Al Radd AlKafi AlMagalat Ali Abdul Wahid Wafi Fi Kitabih Bein Al- Sheiah Wal-Sunnah* [The full response to Wafi's book, *Bein Al-Shiah Wal Sunnah*]. Lahore, Pakistan: Idarat Turjaman Al-Sunnah, 1986.

— *Al-Shiah Wal-Quran* [Shi'ism and Quran]. Lahore, Pakistan: Idarat Turjaman Al-Sunnah, 1981. (In Arabic).

— *Al-Shiah wa Ahl Albeit* [Shi'ism and the House of the Prophet]. Lahore, Pakistan: Idarat Tarjuman Al-Sunnah, 1980. (In Arabic).

Zahlan, Rosemarie. *The Origins of the United Arab Emirates*. New York: St. Martin's Press, 1978.

Index

142, 157, 169, 195, 196, 217, 223, 234,
238, 275, 295, 331
Gulf war, second *see* Iran–Iraq war

hadith, 34
hajj, 7, 162, 166, 173; boycott of, 168;
problems arising, 115, 143, 167 (with
Iranian pilgrims, 140, 145); question of
explosives, 209
Al-Hakim, Sheikh Muhammad Baqr, 170
Hamas, 113, 127, 128, 267, 323
Hanbali school, 139, 172
Hashemi, Mehdi, 51
Hashemi, Muhammad, 54, 55, 68
Hassan, King, 128
health services, 288, 296
Hegel, G. W. F., 70
helicopters, 123, 206, 236, 237, 241, 246,
254, 257
Helli, Allemeh, 21
Hizb Al-Dawah, 163
Hizbollah, 7, 113, 126, 127, 128, 163, 200,
204, 208, 209, 210, 267, 323
hospitals, 291
housing, 288
hovercraft, 256–7
human rights in Iran, 102, 113, 120, 267
Hussein, King, 128
Hussein, Saddam, 86, 88, 92, 93, 104, 105,
107, 111, 112, 114, 130, 131, 132, 133,
134, 294, 323

Ibn Abdul-Wahhab, Muhammad, 159
Ibn Saud, Muhammad, 159
ideological trends in Iran, 15–46
ijtihad, 37, 79, 174
Imam Reza Medical Center, 277
Imam-line group, Kuwait, 163
import substitution, 290, 292, 293
imports: controls on, 292; facilitation of,
302, 346; of arms, to Iran, 219, 220,
221, 223
India, 259; weapons agreement with, 339
Indonesia, arms supply, 226
industrial development, 321–2
inflation, 11, 120, 214, 288, 290, 304–6, 311,
345, 346
institutions, creation of, 319–23
intellectuals, Muslim, 16, 19; role of, 15
International Atomic Energy Agency
(IAEA), 123, 124, 202, 281, 282, 337
International Court of Justice (ICJ), 130,
153, 154, 155

International Institute for Strategic Studies
(IISS), 215, 217, 229, 231, 232, 236
International Monetary Fund (IMF), 294,
308 investment, 288, 296–9; domestic,
315; foreign, 337, 339, 340, 343, 344,
346
Iran–Contra affair, 52, 250
Iran–Iraq war, 4, 10, 36, 37, 45, 47, 50, 54,
57, 83, 86, 87, 91, 92, 95, 98, 104, 106,
111, 112, 121, 130, 139, 140, 142, 147,
151, 152, 158, 163, 168, 195, 198, 199,
200, 201, 204, 205, 208, 211, 214, 216,
217, 218, 219, 220, 222, 223, 226, 229,
235, 238, 241, 247, 249, 252, 253, 261,
265, 271, 272, 276, 287, 289, 294, 323,
331, 333, 336, 340; ending of, 115;
Iranian losses, 226
Iran–Sharjah Memorandum, 97
Iranian Atomic Energy Organization, 282
Iranian Naval Revolutionary Guard, 253
Iranian Research Organization for Science
and Technology, 277
Iranian revolution, 16, 17, 20, 47, 111, 287,
339, 351
Irankhah, Reza, 203
Iraq, 4, 5, 48, 92, 93, 98, 99, 101, 110, 112,
114, 115, 123, 124, 125, 130, 139, 143,
152, 162, 163, 200, 202, 211, 212, 216,
232, 237, 240, 246, 248, 252, 253, 264,
268, 270, 273, 277, 279, 283, 284, 285,
322, 323, 328, 329, 332, 333, 334, 338,
342, 349, 350; as aggressor, 104–5;
containment of, 94; military in, 105;
military spending of, 217; Iranian
relations with, 5, 91, 131–3, 199, 350
Islam, 15, 21, 22, 26, 40, 42, 49, 50, 54, 74,
83, 84, 100, 120, 130, 134, 144, 162, 164,
173, 181, 211; and democracy, 30,
31–46; establishment, 100;
fundamentalist, 114, 334; modernist, 17,
18; political, 349; populist, 17, 18, 100,
116; puritanical, 2, 17, 18, 34; radical,
129, 345; reformist, 2, 17, 18, 30, 31–46;
revolutionary, promotion of, 184–6; role
in government, 2
Islam-e fiqahati, 17
Islam-e Nab-e Muhammadi, 17
Islamic Action, 127
Islamic Development Bank (IDB), 169
Islamic Front for the Liberation of Bahrain
(IFLB), 208
Islamic government, definition of, 16

Machiavelli, Niccolo, 80

Madinah, 172

Al-Madinah al-Fadilah, 45

majlis, 28, 37, 47–69, 101, 347; electoral process, 64–9; structure of, 63–4; system, 100

Majlis Khobregan *see* Assembly of Experts

Mal-Ullah, Muhammad, 165

Maliki Baluchis, 164

Al-Malki, Saleh, 168

Mallat, Chibli, 165

Mar'ashi-Najafi, Ayatollah, 53, 75

marja', 3, 4, 37, 45, 46, 50, 53, 55, 70, 71, 72, 74, 75, 76, 77, 78, 79, 212

marja' mujtahid, 28

marja'e taqlid, ('source of emulation'), 3, 17

Martyr Reysali Delvari exercise, 239

Marxism, 18, 87

Mecca, 162, 172; bombs exploded, 167; custody of mosques, 7; deaths from disturbances, 167, 168; demonstrations by pilgrims, 169; sovereignty over, 166

Meshkini-Ardabili, Ayatollah, 53, 73

migrant workers, expelled from Iran, 97

militarization in Iran, 332

military ambitions of Iran, 2

military capability of Iran, 5, 213, 341, 347

military forces of Iran, 120–6

military industries in Iran, 230–1

military manpower of Iran, 231–2

military modernization of Iran, 197–202, 343, 348

military spending of Iran, 10, 122, 213–19, 220

military stocks of Iran depleted by war, 223, 232, 332

military threat of Iran, 10

mine sweeping, 264

mine warfare, 260, 263, 302, 338; vessels, 257, 258

mines, 263, 264, 265

Ministry of Construction Jihad, 203, 230

minorities, 63, 332; religious, treatment of, 118

Mishkini, Ayatollah, 27

missiles, 103, 125, 201, 211, 224, 225, 226, 231, 238, 242, 243, 244, 247, 249, 250, 251, 252, 254, 255, 256, 257, 258, 260, 265, 268, 269, 338, 342; assembly plants, 273, 274, 345; cruise, 274, 275; CSS-8, 271; long-range, 270–6; Nazeat, 271; No-Dong, 273, 337; Oghab, 270, 274;

Scud, 201, 205, 224, 230, 267, 271, 272, 276 (hunting for, 275); Shahin, 271; Silkworm, 122, 201, 253, 261, 262, 274; SS-N- 22, 262; surface-to-air, 200; Tapeo Dong, 274

Mohajerani, Ayatollah, 282

Mohtaj, Abbas, 205

Mohtashemi, Ali Akbar, 66, 147

Mojahedin-e Khalq Organization (MEK), 207, 332

monarchy, 21, 22, 46, 47; incompatibility with Islam, 86

Montazeri, Ayatollah Hossein Ali, 50, 51, 52, 73, 74, 76, 78, 146

Morocco, 267, 322, 345

mosques, as economic force, 87

Mottaki, Manuchechr, 178

Mubarak, Hosni, 143–4, 155

Mubarakeh steel plant, 294

Mudarassi, Abd al-Hadi, 208

Muhammad, prophet, 32, 33, 34, 37

Muhammad Reza Shah, 94

Mujahedin, 7, 162, 163, 209

Mujahedin-e Khalq, 18, 87, 114, 148

mujtahid, 21, 71, 72, 74, 75, 78

Mumcu, Ugur, 127

Muntazeri, Ayatollah, 35, 36

Al-Murtada, Al-Seid, 165

Musaddiq, Muhammad, 15, 31

Musavi, Mir Hossein, 26, 50, 51, 56, 57, 73, 147

Muscat, 159

Muslim Congress, 162

Mutahhari, Ayatollah, 18, 25, 35, 42, 44; assassination of, 67

Nadir Shah, 137, 159, 164

Nagorno-Karabakh, 141, 180

Al-Nahda organization, 126

Na'ini, Ayatollah, 31, 34, 41, 43

Naipaul, V. S., 85

Najaf Abadi, Salehi, 35

Najaf, Khomeini's presence in, 17, 18, 22, 23, 72

Naraqi, Mullah Ahmad, 19, 38, 72

Nasser, Gamal Abdul, 150

Nateq Nuri, Ali Akbar, 54, 67, 76, 173, 212, 230

National Iranian Oil Company (NIOC), 218, 226

nationalism: Iranian, 4, 85, 90, 116, 138, 139, 170, 171, 328, 330, 335, 351; Arab, 150